Cat

ℓ

ᒻ

C000078548

Optimality Theory, Phonological Acquisition and Disorders

Advances in Optimality Theory

Editors: Ellen Woolford, University of Massachusetts, Amherst, and Armin Mester, University of California, Santa Cruz

Optimality Theory is an exciting new approach to linguistic analysis that originated in phonology but was soon taken up in syntax, morphology, and other fields of linguistics. Optimality Theory presents a clear vision of the universal properties underlying the vast surface typological variety in the world's languages. Cross-linguistic differences once relegated to idiosyncratic language-specific rules can now be understood as the result of different priority rankings among universal, but violable constraints on grammar.

Advances in Optimality Theory is designed to stimulate and promote research in this provocative new framework. It provides a central outlet for the best new work by both established and younger scholars in this rapidly moving field. The series includes studies with a broad typological focus, studies dedicated to the detailed analysis of individual languages, and studies on the nature of Optimality Theory itself. The series publishes theoretical work in the form of monographs and coherent edited collections as well as pedagogical texts and reference texts that promote the dissemination of Optimality Theory.

Consultant Board
Judith Aissen, University of California, Santa Cruz
Daniel Büring, University of California, Los Angeles
Gisbert Fanselow, University of Potsdam
Jane Grimshaw, Rutgers University
Géraldine Legendre, Johns Hopkins University
John J. McCarthy, University of Massachusetts, Amherst
Alan Prince, Rutgers University
Paul Smolensky, Johns Hopkins University
Donca Steriade, MIT, Cambridge, MA
Moira Yip, University College London

Published:
Hidden Generalizations: Phonological Opacity in Optimality Theory
John J. McCarthy

Forthcoming:
Modeling Ungrammaticality in Optimality Theory
Edited by Curt Rice

Phonological Argumentation: Essays in Evidence and Motivation
Edited by Steve Parker

Understanding Allomorphy: Perspectives from Optimality Theory
Edited by Bernard Tranel

Optimality Theory, Phonological Acquisition and Disorders

Edited by Daniel A. Dinnsen and Judith A. Gierut

LONDON   OAKVILLE

Published by
UK: Equinox Publishing Ltd., Unit 6, The Village, 101 Amies St.,
London SW11 2JW
USA: DBBC, 28 Main Street, Oakville, CT 06779
www.equinoxpub.com

First published 2008

© Daniel A. Dinnsen, Judith A. Gierut and contributors 2008

All rights reserved. No part of this publication may be reproduced or transmitted
in any form or by any means, electronic or mechanical, including photocopying,
recording or any information storage or retrieval system, without prior
permission in writing from the publishers.

British Library Cataloguing-in-Publication Data
A catalogue record for this book is available from the British Library.

ISBN-13   978 1 84553 120 1   (hardback)
            978 1 84553 121 8   (paperback)

Library of Congress Cataloging-in-Publication Data

Optimality theory, phonological acquisition and disorders / edited by
Daniel A. Dinnsen and Judith A. Gierut.
    p. cm. -- (Advances in optimality theory)
 Includes bibliographical references and indexes.
 ISBN-13: 978-1-84553-120-1 (hbk.)
 ISBN-13: 978-1-84553-121-8 (pbk.)
 1. Optimality theory (Linguistics) 2. Language acquisition. 3.
Language disorders in children. 4. Grammar, Comparative and
general--Phonology. I. Dinnsen, Daniel A. II. Gierut, Judith A., 1955-
 P158.42.O6838 2007
 415--dc22
                              2006039459

Typeset by Catchline, Milton Keynes (www.catchline.com)
Printed and bound in Great Britain and the USA

Contents

List of Contributors

Jessica A. Barlow, Ph.D., Professor, School of Speech, Language, and Hearing Sciences at San Diego State University

Steven B. Chin, Ph.D., Associate Professor of Otolaryngology-Head and Neck Surgery at the Indiana University School of Medicine, Indianapolis

Daniel A. Dinnsen, Ph.D., Chancellor's Professor of Linguistics and Cognitive Science and Adjunct Professor of Speech and Hearing Sciences at Indiana University, Bloomington

Ashley W. Farris-Trimble, National Institutes of Health Pre-doctoral Fellow, Department of Linguistics, Indiana University, Bloomington

Judith A. Gierut, Ph.D., CCC-SLP, Professor of Speech and Hearing Sciences and Cognitive Science and Adjunct Professor of Linguistics at Indiana University, Bloomington

Michele L. Morrisette, Ph.D., CCC-SLP, Assistant Scientist, Department of Speech and Hearing Sciences at Indiana University, Bloomington

Holly L. Storkel, Ph.D., CCC-SLP, Associate Professor of Speech-Language-Hearing: Sciences and Disorders at the University of Kansas, Lawrence

Preface

This volume addresses phonological acquisition and disorders from the perspective of optimality theory. It is intended for linguists, psychologists, clinicians, second-language researchers/instructors, and students interested in the latest developments in phonological theory, with special attention given to the ways that theory and application benefit one another. The focus is on the approach and empirical findings of the research team of the Learnability Project at Indiana University and affiliated sites (http://www.indiana.edu/~sndlrng/). The team has had a long and productive history of working together, bringing a rare integration of expertise from linguistics, speech pathology, and cognitive psychology. We have used our disciplinary differences to our advantage by adopting some relatively unique approaches to the ways in which phonological theory, language acquisition and clinical treatment inform one another.

Our studies have focused primarily on the phonologies and learning patterns of young children between the ages of 3 and 7, who present with functional (non-organic) phonological disorders. This population has been of special interest to us because of the window they offer to phonology, the acquisition process and change in grammar. Children with functional phonological disorders generally follow a typical path of development, with exception of their acquisition of the sound system. In this respect, they display reduced consonantal inventories and simplification errors that are not unlike those that might be seen in a younger cohort of children. Yet, because of their age, children with phonological disorders afford at least two distinct research advantages for the investigation of phonological development. One is that the children are able to complete more complex linguistic tasks than their younger peers. This allows for data collection of the type that is conventionally used to motivate and support descriptive linguistic claims and test linguistic theory. Another is that the study of phonological disorders provides an experimental testing ground for the manipulation of linguistic variables. Because children with phonological disorders warrant clinical remediation of the sound system, it is possible to design that treatment as a carefully controlled experiment. The phonological property being treated serves as the independent variable and the resulting gains, the dependent variable. The phonological changes that take place over the duration of treatment provide snapshots of learning, thereby allowing us to trace the emergence of successive grammars for insight into the longitudinal course of language development. Based on the results of such experiments, the validity of phonological claims and theoretical proposals can be assessed by evaluating longitudinal data from a given child, in conjunction with the cross-sectional results obtained across children, to form a typological convergence of evidence. This is particularly relevant in disambiguating competing linguistic accounts of the data. While it may be the case that multiple accounts are equally compatible with data obtained at a single point in time, it is likely that only one of those is compatible with successive samples, thereby pinpointing the one accurate interpretation. The theoretical orientation of our research has further practical significance, in that the results contribute directly to the assessment and differential diagnosis of phonological disorders in children, the design of treatment programs to remediate such disorders, and the predictions of phonological learning that derive from the application of those treatment programs. In all, these efforts have advanced the efficacy of clinical treatments for this disorder. In this volume, our aim is to highlight this bridge between linguistic and developmental theory and clinical application. While few linguists would doubt that theory contributes to applied research, there might be greater surprise about the contributions that applied research has for linguistic theory. Likewise, clinicians and educators may be skeptical about the formal details of models of language structure, but they too may come away with a new appreciation about how linguistic theory critically informs clinical practice. The success of our research team has been built on repeated demonstrations of this two-way street with mutual benefits, where theory feeds application and vice versa.

The volume is unique in other ways given its intent to capture the inherent synergies envisioned by a single research team, which provides for a coherent and unified perspective on optimality theory, phonological acquisition, and disorders. To achieve this, we draw from a considerable amount of data that has amassed from complementary descriptive and experimental studies of the Learnability Project. To date, nearly 300 children have participated in our research, and we are especially grateful for their cooperation and for the investments of their families in this endeavor. The children have contributed extensive and structured speech samples that have been phonetically transcribed and coded, along with complementary test data from norm referenced and supplementary batteries that assess their related language, auditory, motor, and processing skills. The speech samples are sufficiently rich to allow for independent and relational analyses of the structure of the sound system, and include potential minimal pairs to establish the phonemic status of sounds and related pairs of words to test for morphophonemic alternations. All of the data have been archived to facilitate electronic searches and analyses, resulting in a database of over 700,000 utterances. Members of the team at affiliated sites have established similar databases of their own, adding further evidence for the study of phonological disorders, while also expanding the scope of study to include children with cochlear implants and children who are acquiring Spanish or Korean as the first language.

Two earlier books on phonological disorders resulted from the research of the team (Elbert, Dinnsen, & Weismer, 1984; Elbert & Gierut, 1986), representing the early phases of the project and embracing the rule-based framework of standard generative phonology. In the current volume, we build upon and extend the early efforts by reporting our most recent research findings as set within the context of optimality theory. In doing so, it becomes apparent how our research has evolved in step with advancements in phonological and also psycholinguistic theories. Part I of the volume is comprised of three introductory chapters for readers who may be less familiar with the tenets of optimality theory, the population of children with phonological disorders, and the Developmental Phonology Archive that we established, or the experimental design of treatment studies. These are intended as background to the fundamental questions and methods of study outlined in the volume. Parts II through IV report current research findings that bear on three sets of phenomena: phonological opacity effects (i.e., regularities that are either not surface-true or not surface-apparent), developmental shifts and learning, and acquisition of consonant clusters. Some of the reports are descriptive, others are experimental, and still others incorporate perceptual evidence with production and compare atypical with typically developing phonological systems. There are common themes that crosscut and unify the chapters in these sections: What is the proper characterization of children's error patterns? What evidence from the input do children need to suppress their errors? How do children's developing phonologies (albeit typical or disordered) compare with fully developed phonologies? What role do implicational laws play in acquisition or treatment? How well does optimality theory account for phonological phenomena associated with acquisition and disorders? What do these phenomena contribute to optimality theory? What are the clinical implications of the findings from optimality theory? What experimental paradigms are available to explore questions about phonological acquisition, and what new paradigms are needed to fully address the issues? The volume closes with an epilogue in Part V that connects the various research reports and identifies some future research directions. Author and subject indices, a comprehensive list of constraints with definitions, and a consolidated list of references are provided at the end of the volume.

We recognize that the research we have reported could not have been accomplished without the contributions of a host of individuals. These include undergraduate honors students, graduate clinicians, doctoral students, postdoctoral fellows, research associates, graphic illustrators, and technical support staff. We offer our sincere thanks to past and present members of the lab: Elizabeth Anttonen, Karen Baertsch, Jessica Barlow, Lori Bass, Elizabeth Becker, William Bowers, Aaron Brown, Diane Bultemeyer, Toby Calandra, Nancy Caplow, Steven Chin, Mi-Hui Cho, Sarah Clifton, Rachel Dale, Amanda Edmonds, Nancy Etson, Leanne Ewald, Brian Farnsley, Ashley Farris-Trimble, Barbara Fox, Tatia Friet, Susan Giger, Christopher Green, Jane Hardy, Bob Harrison, Jerin Harvey, Nick Henriksen, Derek Houston, Amy Howard, Mary Hughes, Jennifer Huljak, Lauren Hulse, Annette Hust Champion, Lisa Kasch, Marc Kerr, Melissa Knoll, Ricci Kohlmeyer, Jill Kraft Scott, Amy Lee, David Long, Katharine Mader, Michael Marlo, Suzanne Martin, Wayne Martin, Kelly McAllister, Laura McGarrity, Robert Meyerson, Erik Miller, Nikole Miller, Kelly Morgan, David Montgomery, Michele Morrisette, Traci Nagle, Heidi Neumann, Kathleen O'Connor, Maureen Orawiec, Michelle Parks, Brechin Polley, Thomas Powell, Heather Rice, Susan Rowland, Susan Roy, Faith Salesin, Abigail Scott, Kristen Selfridge, Paul and Alice Sharp of Sharp Designs, Christina Simmerman, Naemi So, Nola Stephens, Holly Storkel, Kimberly Swanson, Jennifer Taps, and Kemp Williams. Special thanks go to Amanda Edmonds, Ashley Farris-Trimble, Christopher Green, Nick Henriksen, Nikole Miller, Michele Morrisette, and Traci Nagle for their editorial assistance in the preparation of the manuscript for this volume. We are especially indebted to Michele Morrisette, for her commitment and loyalty to the project starting as an undergraduate, and continuing on with us through her doctoral training and now in her current position as Assistant Research Scientist. It is unusual to find a working partnership of this type that has lasted for this duration and with such positive outcomes.

Several of our colleagues at Indiana University have made valuable contributions on various fronts. We are especially grateful to David Pisoni for his friendship, collegiality, and generosity over the years. As Director of the Training Program in Speech, Hearing and Sensory Communication funded by the National Institutes of Health (NIDCD 00012), David has endorsed the type of interdisciplinary research we have undertaken by providing some of the essential infrastructure and funding for several of the pre- and postdoctoral fellows, all of which has benefited the lab. We would also like to thank Phil Connell, Stuart Davis, Mary Elbert, and Karen Forrest for their willingness to share their expertise with us on a broad range of issues. The clinical faculty of the Department of Speech and Hearing Sciences deserve mention for their support in recruitment of children to the project, as does the Monroe County Community School Corporation for their cooperation and referrals to our clinical program.

We have been fortunate to benefit from discussions with distinguished colleagues from other institutions in their visits to our lab. These include Arto Anttila, John Archibald, Martin Ball, Catherine Balthazar, Jan Charles-Luce, Andries Coetzee, Katherine Demuth, Jill deVilliers, Fred Eckman, LouAnn Gerken, Lila and Henry Gleitman, Susan Goldin-Meadow, Heather Goad, Tiffany Hogan, George Hollich, David Ingram, Gregory Iverson, Junko Itô, Peter Jusczyk, Larry Leonard, Conxita Lleó, Paul Luce, John McCarthy, Steve Parker, Joe Pater, Richard Schwartz, Lisa Selkirk, Amanda Seidl, Bruce Tomblin, Isao Ueda, Michael Vitevitch, Ehud Yairi, and Tania Zamuner. John McCarthy and Paul Smolensky have obviously influenced our thinking about phonology and acquisition through their seminal work on optimality theory, but we have also benefited from their discussions with us about many of the issues presented in this volume. Likewise, Leija McReynolds can be credited with stimulating our interest in single-subject experimental designs, which we have found to be so valuable in testing many claims.

Finally, our research has been made possible through support from the American Speech-Language-Hearing Foundation and the National Institutes of Health. The National Institutes of Health in particular has provided continuous funding for our research since 1985 through various mechanisms and titles: NIDCD R01 DC00260 Phonological knowledge and learning patterns (1985–1998), NIDCD 00433 Learnability of sound systems (1988–1994), RR7031K Clinical linguistic treatment models for speech disordered children (1988–1989), NIDCD 00076 Clinical change in phonological categories (1992–1997), and NIDCD 001694 Development of phonological categories (1992–2008). We are especially grateful to Judith Cooper, Deputy Director of the National Institute on Deafness and Other Communication Disorders, for the significant role she has played in educating us about the grant process.

Dedicated to Grace, Eliot, and Jack.

dad & jag

October, 2007

Part I

Background to the Study

1 Fundamentals of optimality theory*

Daniel A. Dinnsen
Indiana University

This chapter is intended as a tutorial introduction to optimality theory with an emphasis on those aspects most relevant to acquisition and disorders. The principles and workings of the theory are illustrated by considering some fundamental phenomena in the developing sound systems of young children with phonological delays. Issues of learnability and the nature of children's underlying representations are considered along with phonological conspiracies and their clinical implications.

1   Introduction

Phonological theory has undergone something of a revolution in recent years with important implications for acquisition. Over the better part of the last 40 years, phonological research has been dominated by the rule-based derivational framework of generative phonology (e.g., Chomsky & Halle, 1968; Kenstowicz, 1994). More recently, there has been a dramatic shift toward the very different constraint-based framework of optimality theory (e.g., Prince & Smolensky, 1993/2004; McCarthy & Prince, 1995). This chapter attempts to illustrate some of the principles and workings of this newer framework with special attention to phonological acquisition and disorders.

We begin with a brief discussion of some of the factors that motivated the move away from a rule-based approach, followed by an initial sketch of the essentials of optimality theory. The fundamentals of the theory are spelled out in more detail in §2 by considering how three basic developmental phenomena would be accounted for. §3 takes up learnability issues related to these basic phenomena. In §4, we consider a characteristic set of phenomena known as 'conspiracies'. Such phenomena in fully developed languages have been pivotal in the theoretical revolution that has taken place. Conspiracies also occur in developing phonologies and have important clinical implications. The issue of children's underlying representations is touched upon throughout the chapter but is returned to in more detail in §5. The chapter concludes with a brief summary.

By way of background, standard generative phonology has provided various means for characterizing differences across languages. The most central of these is the rules that mediate between underlying and phonetic levels of representation. One of the ways in which languages are presumed to differ is by the presence, absence, substantive formulation or order of rules. Additionally, the underlying representations of a language are presumed to be language-specific. Languages can thus also differ by the phonemes and phoneme combinations that are permitted to occur within a morpheme at the underlying level of representation. Research on phonological acquisition and disorders has found these aspects of generative phonology to be especially useful in the characterization of individual differences in young children's phonologies. Despite the theory's many successes and insights, it became clear as the theory evolved that it suffered from several fundamental shortcomings. One of the earliest and most serious problems was the discovery that a language might require several rules that were structurally quite different but that all functioned together to achieve the same end (e.g., Kisseberth, 1970; Kiparsky, 1976). This was described as a 'conspiracy' and posed a problem for the theory because there was no straightforward way to express the phonotactic generalization or relate the rules that participated in the conspiracy. We will see in §4 how optimality theory accounts for conspiracies, which also occur in developing phonologies. A different and persistent problem that has its basis in acquisition is the fact that young children's phonologies often include rules that the children could not have learned from the primary linguistic data to which they are exposed (e.g., Stampe, 1969; Donegan & Stampe, 1979). A similar observation has also been made for second-language acquisition (Eckman, 1981; Broselow, Chen & Wang, 1998). This problem extends to fully developed languages as well in that certain rules recur across unrelated languages. The dilemma in this instance is that some rules seemed to emerge naturally and spontaneously, suggesting that they may instead be innate or universal. We will see again that optimality theory has a straightforward means for accounting for these observations.

In addition to generative phonology's reliance on language-specific rules, the theory has also made essential reference to a variety of universal principles and constraints to explain certain phenomena. The problem is that these principles, while generally well supported, do not follow from anything in the theory per se, and they suggest that rules alone are not sufficient. Universal markedness relations represent one instance of a principle that has played a central role, especially in accounting for why rules have the effect they do. For example,

Houlihan and Iverson (1979) argued that non-assimilatory neutralization rules are constrained to merge contrasts in favor of unmarked properties. Conversely, allophonic rules are constrained to produce marked properties. Markedness is also relevant to the explanation of observed implicational universals regarding phonetic inventories, phonotactic sequences, and the order of acquisition of sounds and sound sequences (e.g., Jakobson, 1941/68; Dinnsen, Chin, Elbert & Powell, 1990; Bernhardt & Stoel-Gammon, 1996). Other principles such as the Obligatory Contour Principle (Leben, 1973) and the Alternation Condition (e.g., Kiparsky, 1976) have been invoked to constrain underlying representations or to explain why a rule does or does not apply. The necessity of constraints coupled with the insufficiency of rules in these instances raises the larger question of whether rules are indeed necessary.

Optimality theory has been advanced as a constraint-based alternative that avoids the pitfalls of standard generative phonology. Optimality theory differs from derivational theories in several important respects. The central hypothesis of optimality theory is that language is a system of conflicting constraints. There are no rules and thus no rule-ordering relationships, no serial derivations, no intermediate levels of representation, and no language-specific restrictions on the set of available input representations (underlying representations). For any given input representation, a ranked set of universal constraints evaluates in parallel a potentially infinite set of competing phonetic output candidates and selects one as optimal. The optimal candidate is the one that best satisfies the constraint hierarchy. Languages are presumed to differ solely by the ranking of constraints. The ranking of constraints can thus vary across languages. Constraints are of two fundamental and often antagonistic types, namely markedness constraints and faithfulness constraints. Markedness constraints are sometimes also referred to as well-formedness constraints or structural constraints. They are formulated exclusively in terms of output properties and militate against marked segment types, sequences and structures. While markedness constraints are similar to rules in that they disfavor certain properties, they differ from rules by not specifying how the output is to be repaired. The repair instead follows from the interaction of the constraints. Faithfulness constraints demand identity between corresponding elements in input and output representations. These constraints assign violation marks to output candidates that differ from the associated input representation. Faithfulness constraints are the antithesis of rules in that they disfavor change. Another important difference between constraints and rules is that the constraints are presumed to be universal (whereas rules are language-specific). The constraints are thus the same across languages and are present in all grammars. The conflict between constraints is resolved by constraint ranking. Some constraints will dominate or outrank other constraints.

The many production errors that occur in children's early speech have been characterized by an initial state or default ranking of the markedness constraints over the faithfulness constraints (Demuth, 1995; Smolensky, 1996a; Gnanadesikan, 2004). By ranking markedness constraints over faithfulness constraints, target contrasts will be sacrificed in favor of simplified, unmarked outputs. The process of acquisition leading to target-appropriate realizations is presumed to proceed by the reranking of constraints, specifically by the minimal demotion of markedness constraints (Tesar & Smolensky, 1998; Hayes, 2004; Prince & Tesar, 2004).

The following section builds on these concepts by considering how three basic developmental phenomena are accounted for. For a more in-depth textbook introduction to optimality theory, see Kager (1999) and McCarthy (2002b). For tutorial introductions to the theory with special attention to acquisition concerns, see Barlow and Gierut (1999), Gierut and Morrisette (2005), and Dinnsen and Gierut (2008).

2   Characterization of basic phenomena

This section illustrates some of the principles and workings of optimality theory by considering how three basic phenomena in young children's developing phonologies are accounted for. The focus will be on error patterns affecting place of articulation, but the same points hold for other error patterns involving voice and manner features.

2.1   Restrictions on phonetic inventories

A fundamental property of any language is its phonetic inventory. All languages exhibit restrictions on the sounds that are permitted to occur in the phonetic inventory. For example, languages such as English are characterized by the systematic exclusion of uvulars, pharyngeals, and retroflex segments, among others. Children's early phonologies are typified by a phonetic inventory that is usually even more restricted than that of the target language. For example, in the course of acquiring English, it is commonly observed in both typical and atypical development that young children exclude velar consonants from their inventories and replace them with alveolar stops (e.g., Smit, 1993a; Bernhardt & Stoel-Gammon, 1996; cf. Morrisette, Dinnsen & Gierut, 2003). This error pattern has been referred to as 'Velar Fronting'. The data in (1) illustrate this error pattern for a child with a phonological delay.

(1) Child 179 (age 4 years;7 months)

 a) Velars replaced by alveolar stops (Velar Fronting)
   [toʊm] 'comb'   [doʊ]   'girl'
   [tʌp] 'cup'   [dʌm]   'gum'
   [wɑt] 'rock'   [bæd]   'bag'
   [bʊt] 'book'   [hʌd]   'hug'
   [pɔtɪt˺] 'pocket'   [fwɑdi] 'froggie'
   [dʌti] 'duckie'   [wædɪn] 'wagon'

 b) Alveolar stops produced correctly
   [toʊz] 'toes'   [doʊ]   'door'
   [baɪt] 'bite'   [mʌd]   'mud'
   [budi] 'bootie'   [mʌdi]   'muddy'

The forms in (1a) exemplify the error pattern whereby the more marked target velars are replaced by less marked alveolar stops in all contexts, effectively excluding velars from the inventory. The forms in (1b) show that target alveolar stops are produced with the appropriate place of articulation. This error pattern thus results in a merger of the lingual contrast between velars and alveolars.[1]

Standard generative phonology would account for these facts in one of two ways. One possible account would claim that the child's grammar includes a phonological rule that operates on underlying velars, converting them into alveolars in all contexts. The question that always arises with such an account is: How do we know that the child represents any words with velars at the underlying level, especially given that velars do not occur phonetically? One piece of evidence that is often adduced in support of the more abstract claim is that children seem to comprehend the intended distinction between words—even if they do not produce the distinction. Children's learning patterns have also been brought to bear in support of the postulation of target-appropriate underlying representations. The evidence is the strongest when a new sound comes into the child's phonetic inventory and occurs in just the right words with little or no overgeneralization.[2] The other possibility is to adopt a somewhat different account that limits the child's underlying representations to just those sounds that also occur in the child's speech. Under this approach, then, Child 179's Velar Fronting error pattern would come about, not from a phonological rule, but rather from a language-specific restriction that excludes velars from his underlying representations. Accounts of this latter sort must either limit their focus to the production side of grammar (e.g., Dinnsen, 1984) or adopt something along the lines of a two-lexicon model (e.g., Menn, 1978) that can connect with the receptive side of grammar.

An optimality theoretic account of this error pattern must appeal to the two conflicting constraints in (2).

(2) Constraints

   a) Markedness
       *k: Dorsal consonants are banned

   b) Faithfulness
       ID[place]:   Corresponding segments must have identical place features[3]

While the markedness constraint *k bans velar consonants, the faithfulness constraint ID[place] demands that corresponding input and output segments be identical in terms of place features. The conflict between these two constraints is resolved by ranking one over the other. The facts of this particular case require that the markedness constraint outrank the faithfulness constraint. This ranking is expressed as: *k >> ID[place]. This ranking represents what has been assumed to be the default ranking of constraints (e.g., Smolensky, 1996a). The necessity of this ranking can be demonstrated by comparing the different results from the two rankings shown in the tableaux in (3). The input in these two tableaux is the same and is given in the upper left corner. Competing output candidates are listed in the first column below the input. The constraints are listed across the top in accord with their ranking. A candidate's violation of a constraint is indicated by '*' in the intersecting cell. Violations that result in the elimination of a candidate from the competition are termed 'fatal violations' and are indicated by '!'. The winning or optimal candidate is identified by the manual indicator '☞'. The first of these two tableaux yields the attested error (i.e., the actual output for that input); the second tableau with the opposite ranking makes the wrong prediction for this child (but the right one for adult English).

(3) Ranking argument

/koʊm/ 'comb'	*k	ID[place]
a. koʊm	*!	
b. ☞ toʊm		*

/koʊm/ 'comb'	ID[place]	*k
a. ☞ koʊm		*
b. toʊm	*!	

For ease of exposition, we have limited the output candidates in these tableaux to the two most likely competitors. Other candidates would be ruled out by other high ranked constraints not directly relevant to the issues of this case.

Notice that the faithful candidate (a) in the first tableau incurs a fatal violation of the markedness constraint *k and is thus eliminated from the competition. Candidate (b) with the substitution error is correctly selected as optimal even though it violates the faithfulness constraint. The lower ranking of that constraint makes the violation less serious. On the other hand, if these constraints were ranked as in the second tableau, candidate (b) would incorrectly be ruled out due to its fatal violation of the faithfulness constraint. The winning output in that tableau would thus be predicted to be the faithful candidate (a).

The tableau in (4) shows that target alveolars are guaranteed to be realized as alveolars even though the faithfulness constraint must be ranked below the markedness constraint. Candidate (b) with a velar substitute is especially bad given that it violates both the markedness constraint and the faithfulness constraint.

(4) Target-appropriate realization of alveolars

/touz/ 'toes'	*k	ID[place]
a. ☞ touz		
b. kouz	*!	*

Our optimality theoretic account of this case assumed that Child 179 represented some words underlyingly with velars and others with alveolars. This highlights an important principle of optimality theory that distinguishes it from earlier approaches. The principle is 'richness of the base' (e.g., Prince & Smolensky, 1993/2004) and maintains that there are no language-specific (or by extension, no child-specific) restrictions on underlying representations. This means that optimality theory does not have available one of the derivational accounts that we considered earlier, namely the one where it was assumed that the child's underlying representations might have excluded velars. Optimality theory requires that we allow for the possibility that some words are represented underlyingly with velars (and even other marked sounds that are not in English). The fact that velars or other sounds do not occur phonetically must be handled by the constraint hierarchy. The default ranking of markedness over faithfulness has the desired effect in this instance of excluding many underlying sounds from the phonetic inventory. This should not be taken to mean that children's underlying representations must be target-appropriate. It is still possible for individual lexical items to be represented incorrectly at the underlying level due to misperception or failure to assign significance to certain properties of the signal. Nevertheless, in the remainder of this chapter and throughout the volume we will assume target-appropriate underlying representations because those input representations reflect a relatively rich base with more distinctions than might actually occur in the child's speech.

2.2   Complementary distribution

A common distributional fact of fully developed languages is that certain sounds occur in complementary contexts, being judged as allophones of the same phoneme. Children's phonologies also include error patterns that result in the complementary distribution of sounds. An interesting example is illustrated by a child with a phonological delay, Child NE (age 4;6). The relevant data are given in (5). A similar pattern is reported for other children (e.g., Davis & MacNeilage, 1995; Chen & Kent, 2005) and for fully developed languages (e.g., Clements, 1990).

(5)   Child NE (age 4;6)

  a)   Velars produced correctly
       [ko]   'comb'   [goʔ]   'goat'

  b)   Velars replaced by alveolar stops (Velar Fronting)
       [te]   'cage'   [deʔ]   'gate'

  c)   Alveolars produced correctly
       [dɪʊ]   'deer'   [dɛ]   'dress'

  d)   Alveolars replaced by velars (Coronal Backing)
       [ka]   'Tom'   [ga]   'dog'

The facts of this case differ from those of the prior case in several important ways. First, this child's phonetic inventory includes velar consonants, some of which are produced with the target-appropriate place of articulation as shown in (5a). Velars are, however, also produced incorrectly in certain other words, being replaced by alveolar stops as shown in (5b). The Velar Fronting error pattern observed in Child 179's phonology appears to be operative to some extent in this case as well.

The factor that distinguishes correct from incorrect production of velars is revealed when we consider how target alveolars were produced. Note first the forms in (5c), which show that alveolars were produced with the target-appropriate place of articulation in some words, specifically when followed by a front vowel. Interestingly, that context is exactly the same one where velars were produced in error. The words in (5d) are suggestive of a different and seemingly contradictory error pattern that replaces alveolars with more marked velars (Coronal Backing). The fact is, however, that this error pattern affects alveolars only when followed by a back vowel. That context also happens to be exactly the same one where velars were produced correctly.

While the two error patterns (Velar Fronting and Coronal Backing) might appear to be contradictory processes, the fact is that they operate in complementary contexts. Stated differently, alveolars and velars occur in complementary distribution. Velars only occur before back vowels, and coronals occur elsewhere.

A rule-based account of these production facts would claim that alveolars and velars are simply allophones of an alveolar phoneme (e.g., Williams & Dinnsen, 1987). An allophonic rule would change alveolar stops into velars before a back vowel. This would further entail a language-specific restriction that excluded velar phonemes from the child's underlying representations.

An optimality theoretic account of these facts reveals one additional constraint to be active beyond what was needed for Child 179. The fuller set of constraints is given in (6). The addition to this set is the contextually conditioned markedness constraint *t/[back]. While coronals are generally considered to be unmarked, they have a more marked distribution when followed by a back vowel.

(6) Constraints

    a) Markedness
        *k: Dorsal consonants are banned
        *t/[back]:   Coronal consonants are banned before back vowels

    b) Faithfulness
        ID[place]:   Corresponding segments must have identical place features

Allophonic phenomena of this sort require that the two markedness constraints be ranked relative to one another with both also ranked above the faithfulness constraint. The specific ranking needed in this instance is: *t/[back] >> *k >> ID[place].

The tableaux in (7) consider two English words that begin with different consonantal place features and are followed by a back vowel.

(7) Velars before back vowels

/tam/ 'Tom'	*t/[back]	*k	ID[place]
a. ta	*!		
b. ☞ ka		*	*

/koum/ 'comb'	*t/[back]	*k	ID[place]
a. ☞ ko		*	
b. to	*!		*

The first of these tableaux shows that the faithful candidate (a) with an alveolar before a back vowel incurs a fatal violation of *t/[back] and is eliminated in favor of the errored candidate (b) with a velar. If the ranking had been reversed, candidate (b) could not have been selected as optimal. The second of these tableaux shows that input velars are permitted to surface without error if followed by a back vowel.

While velars were the preferred output in the prior tableaux, the next set of tableaux show that alveolars are preferred when a front vowel follows.

(8)   Alveolars before front vowels

/get/ 'gate'	*t/[back]	*k	ID[place]
a. geʔ		*!	
b. ☞ deʔ			*

/dir/ 'deer'	*t/[back]	*k	ID[place]
a. ☞ dɪʊ			
b. kɪʊ		*!	*

The first of these tableaux considers an input with a velar before a front vowel. The faithful candidate (a) only violates *k. That violation is, however, fatal due to the greater demand to comply with markedness over faithfulness. The errored candidate (b) thus wins, even though it violates the faithfulness constraint.

The second tableau considers an input with an alveolar before a front vowel. The faithful candidate (a) violates none of these constraints and is correctly selected as optimal.

Notice across the last four tableaux that we did not have to restrict this child's input representations (as we had to do in the rule-based account). We complied with richness of the base by allowing alveolar and velar phonemes to occur before different vowels in this child's input representations. The constraint hierarchy did all of the work in guaranteeing the attested outputs.

Optimality theory distinguishes between the two cases considered thus far by employing different rankings of the same constraints. As just established, Child NE's allophonic phenomenon requires the ranking: *t/[back] >> *k >> ID[place]. The more restricted phonetic inventory of Child 179 who excluded velars altogether requires the ranking: *k >> *t/[back] >> ID[place].

2.3   Contrast and contextual neutralization

The phonological phenomena we have considered thus far involved the complete absence of a lingual place contrast in any context. We now turn to a consideration of another common phenomenon in developing and fully developed languages, namely the maintenance of a contrast in one context along with the merger of that contrast in other contexts. The data in (9) exemplify both situations with regard to a lingual place distinction in the speech of a child with a phonological delay, Child 171 (age 3;9).

(9) Child 171 (age 3;9)

   a) Alveolars produced correctly word-initially
      [toʊd] 'toes'   [dʌn] 'done'

   b) Velars produced correctly word-initially
      [koʊt] 'coat'   [gʌn] 'gun'

   c) Velars realized as alveolars postvocalically (Velar Fronting)
      [bʊt] 'book'   [bæt] 'back'
      [bæd] 'bag'   [hʌd] 'hug'

   d) Alveolars realized correctly in postvocalic position
      [but] 'boot'   [bait] 'bite'
      [bɛd] 'bed'   [mʌd] 'mud'

The forms in (9a) and (9b) show that alveolars and velars contrast in word-initial position. The contrast appears to be limited to that context given the forms in (9c) and (9d). That is, the target distinction between velars and alveolars is merged in favor of alveolars in postvocalic position. The Velar Fronting error pattern that we saw in the phonologies of the other two children appears to be operative to some extent in this child's phonology as well. These facts should not be surprising from the perspective of fully developed languages. Word-initial position has long been recognized to be a prominent context for the preservation of contrasts. It is thus not unexpected that this child might have acquired the lingual place contrast first in that presumably salient context. Conversely, it is well known that contrasts tend to be neutralized in other weaker contexts such as codas or word-medial position. Extending this trend to developing phonologies, we might expect children to acquire contrasts later, if at all, in these weaker contexts. For a fuller discussion and different perspective on this issue, see Chapter 9 in this volume.

A rule-based account of these facts would allow for the inclusion of alveolar and velar phonemes in the child's underlying representations. The distinction between those phonemes would be permitted to surface phonetically in word-initial position due to the fact that no phonological rule operated in that context. The absence of the lingual place contrast in postvocalic position would be accounted for in one of two ways—either by a phonological rule that changed velars into alveolars in that context or by a morpheme-structure condition that excluded velars from postvocalic position at the underlying level of representation.

The facts of this case reveal an element of optimality theory that we did not see in the other two cases, namely the active role of faithfulness. When faithfulness constraints outrank markedness constraints, underlying distinctions will be realized phonetically. The fact, then, that alveolars and velars contrast in this child's phonology requires the faithfulness constraint that preserves place to take precedence over the markedness constraint that bans velars. However, because the contrast is limited to word-initial position and is merged elsewhere, markedness also plays a role. To resolve what might appear to be a ranking paradox, context must also be taken into account in the substantive formulation of constraints. One approach to this problem has been to explode individual faithfulness constraints into a positionally restricted version of the constraint along with a context-free version of the constraint (e.g., Beckman, 1998; Lombardi, 1999; Smith, 2002). By ranking the positional faithfulness constraint above the markedness constraints, a contrast will be preserved in a specified context. By further ranking the markedness constraints over the context-free version of the faithfulness constraint, the contrast will be merged elsewhere. We adopt this approach in our account of Child 171 with the fuller set of constraints in (10).

(10) Constraints

a) Markedness
    *k: Dorsal consonants are banned
    *t/[back]:   Coronal consonants are banned before back vowels

b) Faithfulness
    ID-INITIAL[place]: Corresponding segments in word-initial position must
                       have identical place features
    ID[place]:   Corresponding segments must have identical place
                       features
    Ranking: ID-INITIAL[place] >> *k, *t/[back] >> ID[place]

Note in the above ranking statement that the two markedness constraints are separated by a comma, indicating that the two constraints are unranked relative to one another. This situation is depicted in a tableau by separating the constraint columns by a dotted line. The tableaux in (11) show how the lingual place contrast is preserved in word-initial position. The unfaithful candidate (b) in both tableaux is ruled out due to its violation of the top-ranked positional faithfulness constraint. That candidate also incurs a gratuitous violation of the lower ranked faithfulness constraint.

(11) Contrast preserved word-initially

/touz/ 'toes'	ID-Initial[place]	*k	*t/[back]	ID[place]
a. ☞ toʊd			*	
b. koʊd	*!	*		*

/koʊt/ 'coat'	ID-Initial[place]	*k	*t/[back]	ID[place]
a. ☞ koʊt		*		
b. toʊt	*!		*	*

The next tableaux consider two words that differ by place postvocalically at the underlying level of representation. All of these candidates fare equally well in terms of the positional faithfulness constraint. However, the merger of place is attributed to the next higher ranked constraint *k, which assigns fatal violation marks to those candidates with a velar consonant. Alveolars thus survive as optimal whether they are faithful or not.

(12) Contrast merged postvocalically

/but/ 'boot'	ID-Initial[place]	*k	*t/[back]	ID[place]
a. ☞ but				
b. buk		*!		*

/buk/ 'book'	ID-Initial[place]	*k	*t/[back]	ID[place]
a. buk		*!		
b. ☞ but				*

3   Learning and the constraint demotion algorithm

We have shown above how optimality theory accounts for certain basic phonological phenomena in acquisition. We now turn to a consideration of the principles by which children come to rank and rerank their constraints during the learning process. It is hypothesized that all of the markedness constraints outrank the faithfulness constraints in the initial state (e.g., Smolensky, 1996a). This is intended to address the subset problem (e.g., Baker, 1979; Angluin, 1980) by ensuring that the child begins with the most restrictive (subset) grammar and arrives at the superset grammar on the basis of positive evidence.

While markedness constraints outrank faithfulness constraints in the initial state, we saw in the case of Child NE that some markedness constraints still need to be ranked relative to one another to account for the complementary distribution of coronal and dorsal consonants. So, how might that ranking have arisen from the initial state? Let us assume that NE might have begun with an even more restrictive grammar that excluded dorsals altogether from the phonetic inventory. This would assume little or no prior learning and would be similar to what we observed for Child 179 in (1) above where *k was undominated. Now imagine that Child NE discovered that dorsals do in fact occur in English. This discovery could have been made if, for example, he had been exposed to a word like 'comb' and took note of the fact that that word did not begin with a coronal, as he had been producing it, but rather that it began with a dorsal, at least when followed by a back vowel. This represents positive evidence and is certainly a correct observation about words like 'comb'. However, this observation alone may not go far enough to eliminate the original error pattern unless it is also observed that dorsals can occur before front vowels in words such as 'key'. It is also the case that the observation about 'comb' could go too far. That is, unless the child also explicitly observed that coronals can occur before back vowels (e.g., 'toes'), those coronal consonants that had been produced correctly by default in the hypothesized prior stage would be replaced by dorsals. An examination of the phonotactic probabilities of English[4] suggests that this scenario is in fact quite likely. More specifically, a velar is approximately two times more likely than a coronal to occur before a back vowel in English, and a coronal is almost two times more likely than a velar to occur before a front vowel. Assuming, then, the influence of phonotactic probabilities, the constraint demotion algorithm (e.g., Tesar & Smolensky, 1998) would claim that the constraint that had been responsible for the exclusion of dorsals (*k) would be demoted minimally in the hierarchy to a point just below the highest ranked constraint that the previous winning candidate violated, namely just below the markedness constraint *t/[back]. The ranking of *k over the faithfulness constraint ID[place] would follow from the persistent need for faithfulness constraints to be ranked as low as possible. The lower ranking of the faithfulness constraints is consistent with the default ranking of constraints and the limited observations made by the child.

A display known as a comparative tableau can be used to support the ranking arguments and to illustrate the principles by which constraints are ranked. In such a tableau, the intended winning candidate is opposed to different losing candidates in a pair-wise fashion, and each pair is evaluated by each constraint. The candidate pairs are listed down the left side of the tableau. The optimal candidate is the first member of each pair. The constraints are given along the top and can at this point be arranged in any order. The purpose of the comparative tableau is to arrive at the required ranking. A constraint's evaluation of a candidate pair can have one of three results. One result is that the constraint can be violated by the losing candidate, thus favoring the winner. In such a case, a 'W' is assigned to the intersecting cell to designate that the violation is a winner-favoring mark. Another possible result is that the constraint can be violated by the winning candidate, thus favoring the loser. In that instance, an 'L' is assigned to the cell to designate that the violation is a loser-favoring mark. Finally, a constraint might violate both the winner and the loser or neither, in which case the cell is left blank. After all violation marks are assigned, we can use that information to rank the constraints in accord with general principles.

To see how this works in the case of Child NE's complementary distribution of coronals and dorsals, consider the comparative tableau in (13) for several different types of words. The winner-favoring and loser-favoring designations reflect the child's judgments of the facts and have been filled in accordingly.

(13) Comparative tableau for Child NE (unranked constraints)

	*k	*t/[back]	ID-Initial[place]	ID[place]
a. ka ~ ta	L	W	L	L
b. ko ~ to	L	W	W	W
c. deʔ ~ geʔ	W		L	L
d. dɪʊ ~ kɪʊ	W		W	W

The first step is to identify all constraints that favor only winners. Such constraints include one or more W's and no L's in their respective columns. These winner-favoring constraints (or 'free W's', as they are sometimes termed) are installed in the highest stratum of the hierarchy, and all remaining constraints are demoted below those constraints. This means that for Child NE *t/[back] will be undominated, and all remaining constraints are demoted below that. Once a constraint has been installed in the hierarchy, the column for that constraint is shaded out and is not considered further. Additionally, the row for a candidate pair with a free W is also shaded out, and any other marks in that row are ignored. This yields the intermediate comparative tableau in (14).

(14) Intermediate comparative tableau after the first demotion

	*t/[back]	*k	ID-Initial[place]	ID[place]
a. ka ~ ta	W	L	L	L
b. ko ~ to	W	L	W	W
c. deʔ ~ geʔ		W	L	L
d. dɪʊ ~ kɪʊ		W	W	W

The demotion of constraints can sometimes reveal additional free W's, in which case, the above process is repeated. Notice from the intermediate comparative tableau in (14) that this is exactly what happened with *k, which favors only winners. As a result, *k is installed in the next stratum (below *t/[back]) with all of the remaining constraints being demoted below that. The comparative tableau in (15) reflects the result of having repeated this process. Notice that all columns and rows are now shaded. This leaves the two faithfulness constraints, ID[place] and ID-INITIAL[place] unranked relative to one another. There is no further information available that would bear on the ranking of these constraints, and none is needed. The ranking that is arrived at from this algorithm is: *t/[back] >> *k >> ID-INITIAL[place], ID[place].

(15) Final comparative tableau

		*t/[back]	*k	ID-INITIAL[place]	ID[place]
a.	ka ~ ta	W	L	L	L
b.	ko ~ to	W	L	W	W
c.	deʔ ~ geʔ		W	L	L
d.	dɪʊ ~ kɪʊ		W	W	W

We now turn to a demonstration of how a child might arrive at the ranking of constraints needed to account for contrasts and contextual neutralization phenomena. Recall, for example, the case of Child 171 in (9) above. That child maintained the target place contrast among lingual consonants in word-initial position, but merged the contrast in favor of a coronal in all other contexts. Let us assume that this child might also have begun with a highly restrictive grammar that excluded dorsal consonants from the phonetic inventory. In order to arrive at the required ranking for this contextual neutralization, he would have had to take note of the fact that different words can and do begin with coronals or dorsals independent of the following vowel. Words such as 'comb' and 'toe' and 'keep' and 'teeth' would provide the child with the relevant information about the occurrence of dorsal consonants and the existence of a word-initial place contrast between coronals and dorsals. In the absence of any similar discovery by the child about the occurrence of dorsals in postvocalic contexts, the error pattern from the prior stage of development would persist in that context. The comparative tableau in (16) gives an unranked set of constraints with the appropriate winner/loser marks filled in in accord with the child's observations at that point in time.

(16) Comparative tableau for contrast and contextual neutralization (unranked constraints)

	*k	*t/[back]	ID-INITIAL[place]	ID[place]
a. toʊd ~ koʊd	W	L	W	W
b. koʊt ~ toʊt	L	W	W	W
c. but ~ buk	W			W
d. bʊt ~ bʊk	W			L

The first step of the algorithm identifies ID-INITIAL[place] as a free W. Accordingly, it is installed in the highest stratum of the hierarchy, and all other constraints are demoted below that. The column for ID-INITIAL[place] is thus shaded out along with the two intersecting rows with free W's. This results in the intermediate comparative tableau given in (17).

(17) Intermediate comparative tableau after first demotion

	ID-INITIAL[place]	*k	*t/[back]	ID[place]
a. toʊd ~ koʊd	W	W	L	W
b. koʊt ~ toʊt	W	L	W	W
c. but ~ buk		W		W
d. bʊt ~ bʊk		W		L

Notice that, as a result of this first round of demotion, one additional constraint with a free W is revealed, namely *k. Additionally, the column for *t/[back] has no marks. Both situations require that these two constraints be installed in the same stratum immediately below ID-INITIAL[place]; the remaining constraint ID[place] is demoted further yet. The result of this second step is shown in (18) and yields the ranking ID-INITIAL[place] >> *k, *t/[back] >> ID[place].

(18) Final comparative tableau

	ID-INITIAL[place]	*k	*t/[back]	ID[place]
a. toʊd ~ koʊd	W	W	L	W
b. koʊt ~ toʊt	W	L	W	W
c. but ~ buk		W		W
d. bʊt ~ bʊk		W		L

A proper ranking of constraints is characterized by a comparative tableau with at least one W to the left of all L's in each row. Additionally, there should be no row with only L's because that would mean that no ranking of the constraints could ever yield the intended winner. If either of these conditions fails to be complied with, something is wrong with the analysis. However, we can see from the cases presented here that our accounts of these phenomena accord with the general principles for learning and the constraint demotion algorithm.

4   Conspiracies in acquisition

Recall from the introduction that the existence of conspiracies among phonological rules in fully developed languages posed a significant problem for standard generative phonology. Conspiracies have, however, been taken as strong support for optimality theory because a straightforward account becomes available. A conspiracy typically involves three (or more) constraints that are crucially ranked relative to one another. The top-ranked of these constraints is a markedness constraint that prohibits a particular class or combination of sounds (e.g., a ban on fricatives, clusters, etc.). The next two constraints are different faithfulness constraints that are also ranked relative to one another. Each of the faithfulness constraints results in a different repair for the banned structure. Conspiracies also occur in developing phonologies and represent an additional source of support for the theory. We touch on two cases with the intent of illustrating how optimality theory accounts for conspiracies. We conclude this section by considering some of the clinical implications of conspiracies.

Łukaszewicz (2007) described a typically developing child (age 4;0–4;4) who was acquiring Polish as her first language and had four different strategies for reducing onset clusters: deletion and coalescence (both found in word-initial clusters), and metathesis and gemination (found in word-medial clusters). Łukaszewicz argued that each of these strategies was a way to satisfy a highly ranked markedness constraint against onset clusters (*COMPLEXONSET). The interaction between this constraint and other constraints determined which strategy the child employed. The ranking of *COMPLEXONSET over the faithfulness constraint that militated against deletion (MAX) allowed the more sonorous of two consonants to be deleted. In clusters consisting of a coronal stop and a coronal fricative (in any order), the segments coalesced to an affricate. It was argued that the coalescence of these particular clusters was due to the ranking of two identity constraints above MAX, which in turn was ranked above another faithfulness constraint that disallowed coalescence. In medial clusters, on the other hand, neither segment was deleted, but the cluster was altered such that it was syllabified as a coda plus an onset, rather than an onset cluster. One strategy that achieved this result was metathesis. For instance, a medial [dn] cluster became [nd], with the [n] syllabified as a coda. Łukaszewicz achieved this by ranking *COMPLEXONSET and other markedness constraints above the faithfulness constraint that preserved the linear order of segments. This ranking allowed metathesis as a repair for medial complex clusters, without resorting to deletion. Finally, word-medial fricative+sonorant clusters were realized as geminate fricatives. A high-ranked markedness constraint induced gemination in these cases, as opposed to metathesis.

A different type of conspiracy was described by Pater and Barlow (2003) for a child with a phonological delay (Child LP65, age 3;8). The conspiracy involved different repairs to produce outputs that satisfied a highly ranked markedness constraint that banned fricatives (*FRICATIVE). Singleton fricatives were produced as stops, and fricatives in clusters were deleted. The stopping error pattern for singleton fricatives was achieved by ranking *FRICATIVE over the faithfulness constraint against deletion (MAX), which in turn was ranked over the faithfulness constraint that demanded identity in manner features (ID[continuant]). In fricative+sonorant clusters, LP65 deleted the fricative. Deletion was compelled by a highly ranked markedness constraint that banned clusters (*COMPLEXONSET). The important point is that it was the fricative that was deleted rather than the sonorant. This was achieved by ranking *FRICATIVE over the hierarchy of markedness constraints that govern onsets in terms of sonority. Thus even a glide was a better onset than a fricative. The ranking of ID[continuant] over the sonority hierarchy also explained why the fricative in a cluster did not become a stop.

The identification of conspiracies in delayed phonologies and their characterization within optimality theory have important clinical implications. Conspiracies pose special opportunities and special challenges for treatment. Most importantly, conspiracies reveal that, while error patterns may differ, some of those error patterns are in fact related and have the same source. To fully eradicate the different error patterns associated with the conspiracy, it would be necessary to first target for treatment those structures that the highly ranked markedness constraint prohibits. It is that constraint that is at the heart of the various error patterns participating in the conspiracy. Second, because a conspiracy involves two or more dominated, but crucially ranked faithfulness constraints, it would be important to demote that highly ranked markedness constraint below the lowest ranked of these faithfulness constraints.

To see how this might work, let us reconsider the case of LP65 described above. There are several different options for structuring treatment, and each option makes different predictions. The goal of any plan in this case is to demote the highly ranked markedness constraint that banned fricatives (*FRICATIVE) below the lowest ranked faithfulness constraint (ID[continuant]). One option would be to simultaneously focus treatment on both the stopping and deletion error patterns. This might be done by, for example, contrasting a fricative cluster with a stop cluster (e.g., 'swim' versus 'twin'). The presentation of clusters should highlight the occurrence of clusters and motivate the demotion of *COMPLEXONSET below MAX. The deletion error pattern would thus be eradicated. Additionally, cluster pairs of this sort would emphasize the contrast between stops and fricatives, motivating the demotion of *FRICATIVE below ID[continuant]. Consequently, the stopping error pattern would also be suppressed. The tableaux in (19) show the results of demoting *COMPLEXONSET and *FRICATIVE below the respective faithfulness constraints for words beginning with a fricative cluster and a singleton fricative.

(19) Stopping and deletion suppressed

/swɪm/ 'swim'	MAX	ID[continuant]	*COMPLEXONSET	*FRICATIVE
a. ☞ swɪm			*	*
b. twɪm		*!	*	
c. wɪm	*!			
d. sɪm	*!			*
e. tɪm	*!		*	

/sʌn/ 'sun'	MAX	ID[continuant]	*COMPLEXONSET	*FRICATIVE
a. ☞ sʌn				*
b. tʌn		*!		
c. ʌn	*!			

An alternative treatment option that should also result in the demotion of *FRICATIVE below ID[continuant] would instead focus on the stop/fricative contrast in singletons. This treatment might involve, for example, the presentation of pairs of words such as 'sun' versus 'ton'. The prediction in this instance would be different. That is, stopping would be expected to be suppressed as an error pattern, allowing fricatives to occur in singletons, but fricatives in clusters would likely continue to be deleted. The reason for the persistence of the deletion error pattern is that there is nothing about the structure of the treatment words that would have compelled the demotion of *COMPLEXONSET below MAX. The tableaux in (20) show the different results that would obtain for singleton fricatives and fricative clusters if only *FRICATIVE were demoted.

(20) Stopping suppressed in singletons but deletion persists in clusters

/sʌn/ 'sun'	*ComplexOnset	Max	ID[continuant]	*Fricative
a. ☞ sʌn				*
b. tʌn			*!	
c. ʌn		*!		

/swɪm/ 'swim'	*ComplexOnset	Max	ID[continuant]	*Fricative
a. swɪm	*!			*
b. twɪm	*!		*	
c. ☞ wɪm		*		
d. sɪm		*		*!
e. tɪm		*	*!	

The first of these tableaux considers an input singleton fricative. The deletion candidate (c) is eliminated from the competition by its violation of Max. The stopping candidate (b) is ruled out by its violation of ID[continuant]. The faithful candidate (a) thus survives as optimal, even though it violates *Fricative. The second of these tableaux with an input fricative cluster is more interesting. Candidates (a) and (b) with clusters both fatally violate *ComplexOnset. The remaining reduction candidates all violate Max; so the decision is passed down to lower ranked constraints. Candidate (e) with a stop violates ID[continuant] and is thus eliminated. This leaves candidates (c) and (d) still in the running. While *Fricative is low ranked, it is still active and assesses a fatal violation to candidate (d) with a fricative. Candidate (c) with an initial glide would thus win when an input fricative cluster is involved.

Under this second treatment option, then, an additional round of treatment would still be called for. This time, treatment would need to be aimed specifically at the suppression of the deletion error pattern affecting fricative clusters (e.g., 'swing' versus 'wing'). This would presumably lead to the demotion of *ComplexOnset below Max.

We have seen here that optimality theory makes the very interesting and clinically valuable prediction that some treatment designs will be more efficacious than others in eradicating the error patterns associated with conspiracies. The most efficacious treatment of a conspiracy would target those structures banned by the top-ranked markedness constraint in a context where the different repairs could coincide (i.e., where the various faithfulness constraints were violated). This meant in the case of LP65 that fricatives should be targeted for treatment in clusters rather than in singletons. The reason is that clusters provided the context for deletion, and the occurrence of fricatives in clusters would entail a manner contrast in contradiction to the stopping error pattern. This option has the advantage of avoiding an additional round of treatment that would have been required under the other treatment option. These predictions take on added interest because they run counter to standard clinical practice, which would likely have chosen to work on fricatives in singletons rather than in clusters because of developmental considerations relating to order of acquisition. However, the predictions of optimality theory in this instance accord well with a hallmark of our project, which is to treat the more complex or marked structures to maximize learning. This point is illustrated and expanded upon in several of the chapters in this volume (especially Chapters 3 and 11). The significance of these predictions and general findings is that optimality theory offers a principled explanation for the effects.

Developmental conspiracies of the sort considered in this section also contribute to optimality theory by providing an additional venue for support and testing. Conspiracies represent just one class of error patterns that can benefit from an optimality theoretic characterization. The characterization that optimality theory provides for other types of error patterns has many other clinical implications that are explored in more detail in Chapter 8 in this volume.

5   Children's underlying representations revisited

We have been assuming throughout this chapter that children's input representations are target-appropriate. This assumption accords with optimality theory's fundamental principle of richness of the base in that no language-specific or child-specific restrictions are being imposed on underlying representations. Most other acquisition researchers have also assumed that children's underlying representations are target-appropriate. This assumption is, however, not uncontroversial. It may thus be worthwhile to revisit some of the considerations that are typically brought to bear on this issue to see how optimality theory deals with those issues.

5.1   The comprehension/production dilemma

One piece of evidence that is often cited in support of the claim that a child's underlying representations are target-appropriate, even if the production facts do not support this, is that the child comprehends the target distinctions. This evidence can come from various sources, including perception experiments (e.g., Jusczyk, 1997; Stager & Werker, 1997; Werker & Stager, 2000), clinical diagnostic tests (e.g., Locke, 1980a; 1980b), or more commonly from informal anecdotal observations (e.g., Smith, 1973). The problem is that none of these sources provides results that are as reliable or interpretable as those from adult studies. Children do, after all, pose a number of methodological challenges not encountered in adult studies. Nevertheless, it does seem that children's comprehension is generally better than their production. This has long been referred to as the comprehension/production dilemma. So, how does optimality theory account for the comprehension/production dilemma?

One approach to the problem has been spelled out by Smolensky (1996b). Under his proposal, the child's production facts would be accounted for in the standard way as we have described above. Given a target-appropriate input representation and highly ranked markedness constraints, the optimal phonetic output will be rather different from the input and will be in error relative to the target language. Comprehension is also assumed to follow from the same grammar, but what serves as the input and outputs is very different. That is, the input for comprehension purposes is the perceived form that the child actually hears. The competition is then between forms that could serve as the underlying representation for that perceived form. The highly ranked markedness constraints are not relevant because the perceived form already violates those constraints. The decision is thus passed down to the faithfulness constraints. The form that is selected as the underlying representation will be the one that incurs no serious faithfulness violations. The perceived form and the underlying form should be identical (or nearly so). This approach has, however, met with a number of criticisms (e.g., Hale & Reiss, 1998). One problem is that the accurate perception of a distinction would be expected to result in the instantaneous reranking of the constraints that yielded the production error pattern. There thus could not be a mismatch between comprehension and production.

Another general approach for resolving the comprehension/production dilemma has been to expand the constraint set to include faithfulness constraints that are perception-based (e.g., Boersma, 1998; Pater, 2004). A generic perception-based faithfulness constraint would involve a mapping from a perceived surface form to a lexical representation and would be defined as in (21).

(21) Generic perception-based faithfulness constraint

    P-FAITH: The perceived surface form and the lexical representation must be identical

The P-FAITH constraints would be in addition to and ranked above standard faithfulness constraints (FAITH). A mismatch between comprehension and production would then follow from the ranking of P-FAITH over some markedness constraint, which in turn would be ranked above FAITH. This would yield accurate comprehension but an error in production.

This approach also allows for the possibility that children might at an earlier stage of development both misperceive and mispronounce words due to the default ranking of markedness over the two types of faithfulness constraints. Finally, accurate perception and accurate production would follow from the dominance of faithfulness over markedness. While this approach seems promising, it fails to account for those cases where production appears to be better than perception (e.g., Gierut, 2004).

5.2   Overgeneralization errors

Independent of how the comprehension/production dilemma might be resolved theoretically, the phenomenon is taken as support for the claim that children have target-appropriate underlying representations. This phenomenon constitutes synchronic evidence, discernable at a single point along the developmental continuum. Longitudinal evidence of a different sort is sometimes also brought to bear on the issue of children's underlying representations. For example, when a child acquires a new sound in all of the right words and in all of the right contexts, this is taken as good evidence that the child had fully intact underlying representations because he/she would not otherwise have known where to produce the new sound. Across-the-board change of this sort is, however, relatively rare. Even more serious is the fact that some children's productions change over time from correct to incorrect. This phenomenon occurs in both typical and atypical development and has been described as overgeneralization or recidivism (e.g., Smith, 1973; Macken, 1980; Leonard & Brown, 1984; Bernhardt & Stemberger, 1998; Gierut, 1998b). It has been argued within rule-based frameworks that overgeneralization errors are indicative of incorrectly internalized underlying representations that are more restricted than in the target language (e.g., Macken, 1980). If the characterization of overgeneralization errors does indeed require restricting children's underlying representations, this would constitute a significant challenge for optimality theory and the principle of richness of the base. We have, however, shown elsewhere that optimality theory can account for overgeneralization errors in a straightforward fashion without violating richness of the base (Dinnsen, O'Connor & Gierut, 2001; Dinnsen & Gierut, 2008; Chapters 5 and 8 in this volume).

The problem that overgeneralization errors pose and the solution that optimality theory offers can be illustrated by briefly considering a representative case, Child 78 (age 4;2–4;5), as described in Dinnsen and Gierut (2008). Child 78 presented (age 4;2) with correct productions of the interdental fricative /θ/. All other fricatives were replaced by [θ]. More specifically, the alveolar fricative [s] and the labial fricative [f] did not occur in the child's inventory and were replaced by [θ], as shown in (22a) and (22b), respectively. Target /θ/ was, however, produced correctly, as shown in (22c).

(22) Stage 1 for Child 78 (age 4;2)

a) Target /s/ replaced by [θ]
   [θoʊp]   'soap'   [maʊθ]   'mouse'
   [θoʊ]   'sew'   [trihaʊθ] 'treehouse'

b) Target /f/ replaced by [θ]
   [θætʼ]   'fat'   [naɪθ]   'knife'
   [θɪθ]   'fish'   [kɔθ]   'cough'

c) Target /θ/ realized as [θ]
   [θʌm]   'thumb'   [bæθ]   'bath'
   [θʌndʊ:]   'thunder' [tiθ]   'teeth'

At a second point in time (three months later and after having been taught a word-initial s-cluster), the situation was just the reverse. Note that target /s/ came to be produced correctly, as shown in (23a). In addition, the substitute for target /f/ changed from [θ] at Stage 1 to [s] at Stage 2 (compare (22b) to (23b)), revealing the emergence of a new error pattern. More importantly, /θ/, which had been produced correctly, was lost from this child's phonetic inventory. At Stage 2, /θ/ was now produced in error, being realized as [s], as in (23c). While Child 78 introduced correct realizations of [s] into the inventory, she overgeneralized its use for other target fricatives, creating two new error patterns.

(23) Stage 2 for Child 78 (age 4;5)

a) Target /s/ realized as [s]
   [soʊp]   'soap'   [maʊs]   'mouse'
   [soʊ]   'sew'   [twihaʊs] 'treehouse'

b) Target /f/ replaced by [s]
   [sæt]   'fat'   [naɪs]   'knife'
   [sɪs]   'fish'   [kɔs]   'cough'

c) Target /θ/ replaced by [s]
   [sʌm]   'thumb'   [bæs]   'bath'
   [sʌndʊ]   'thunder' [tis]   'teeth'

A rule-based account of these facts would have claimed that Child 78 at the first stage had incorrectly internalized all fricatives as /s/, and that a rule converted all of those fricatives to [θ]. The loss of the rule at the second stage would reveal those incorrectly internalized underlying representations and result in the observed overgeneralization errors.

Optimality theory can account for the facts of this case with the constraints in (24).

(24) Constraints

a) Markedness

*s:	Grooved coronal fricatives are banned
*θ:	Interdental fricatives are banned
*f:	Labial fricatives are banned

b) Faithfulness

ID[continuant]:	Corresponding segments must have identical [continuant] features
FAITH:	Inputs and outputs must be identical

The markedness constraints in (24a) all belong to the family of constraints disfavoring fricatives generally (*FRICATIVE). Each individual constraint militates against a different class of fricatives and each is independently necessary to account for observed individual differences in the occurrence and non-occurrence of particular fricatives across children (Ingram, Christensen, Veach & Webster, 1980). The fact is that some children exclude all fricatives from their inventories, others exclude only one class or some combination of those classes, and yet others exclude none. While many different fricatives were banned from Child 78's inventory, it is noteworthy that the substitute for all target fricatives was a fricative, specifically an interdental fricative at Stage 1. This is suggestive of a highly ranked faithfulness constraint, ID[continuant], which demands that the input manner feature [continuant] be preserved in the corresponding output segment. The dominance of this constraint would ensure that a target stop is realized as a stop and a target fricative as a fricative. Furthermore, Child 78's exclusion of labial and alveolar fricatives is indicative of the highly ranked markedness constraints *f and *s. These two markedness constraints are ranked over another generalized family of faithfulness constraints, which we will abbreviate as FAITH. FAITH demands that all properties of corresponding input and output segments be the same. By this analysis, it is more important to avoid labial and alveolar fricatives than it is to preserve their various input features. The consequence of these constraints and rankings is that labial and alveolar fricatives would be excluded from the inventory and replaced by the only remaining class of English fricatives, namely interdental fricatives. It is, however, also well known that many children exclude interdental fricatives from their inventories (Smit, 1993a), suggesting the need for the additional independent markedness constraint, *θ, which disfavors interdental fricatives. Given that Child 78 produced interdental fricatives target-appropriately at Stage 1 and, in fact, preferred interdentals as the substitute for all other fricatives, *θ must be ranked just low enough that its violation can be tolerated. We will see that *θ must be ranked above FAITH but below the other markedness constraints during the early stage.

The ranking of constraints needed for Stage 1 is schematized in (25). The notation uses solid lines to connect those constraints that are crucially ranked with the higher ranked constraints positioned above the lower ranked constraints. Constraints that cannot be ranked relative to one another are given on the same horizontal plane and are not connected by a line.

(25) Constraint ranking for Stage 1

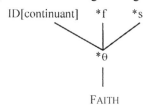

(26) Target /s/ realized as [θ] for Stage 1

/soʊp/ 'soap'	*f	*s	*θ	FAITH
a. foʊp	*!			*
b. ☞ θoʊp			*	*
c. soʊp		*!		

The tableau in (26) considers how different output candidates would fare given this ranking of constraints for Child 78. We use as an example an input representation that begins with /s/ as in 'soap'. For expository purposes, we have limited the candidates to be considered to those that begin with a fricative. The faithfulness constraint ID[continuant] has, thus, been left out of the tableau. Candidate (a) with an initial [f] fatally violates the highly ranked markedness constraint *f and is eliminated from the competition. The faithful candidate (c) violates the other highly ranked markedness constraint *s and is also eliminated. Candidate (b) with the interdental is all that remains and is thus selected as optimal in accord with the child's error pattern even though it violates both *θ and FAITH. The lower ranking of those two constraints makes their violations less serious. This illustrates another important point, namely that the constraints are violable, and any winning output candidate will likely violate some constraint.

This same ranking of constraints ensures the target-appropriate realization of /θ/ as shown in the tableau in (27) for an input such as 'thumb'. Candidates (a) and (c) are again eliminated because each violates one of the undominated markedness constraints. The only remaining candidate (b) complies with FAITH and is selected as optimal even though it violates the markedness constraint *θ.

(27) Target /θ/ realized as [θ] for Stage 1

/θʌm/ 'thumb'	*f	*s	*θ	FAITH
a. fʌm	*!			*
b. ☞ θʌm			*	
c. sʌm		*!		*

By ranking the markedness constraints relative to one another, specifically both *f and *s above *θ, all but the interdental fricative candidates (26b, 27b) are effectively eliminated. Thus, even though *θ is ranked above FAITH, which would seem to disallow interdentals, interdental fricatives are permitted to survive as optimal. This is because of the greater demand to preserve the manner of the input segment in the corresponding output segment, i.e., as a result of undominated ID[continuant]. The novel claim of optimality theory is that interdental fricatives are produced not because they are faithful to the input, but because the hierarchy claims that interdentals are better fricatives than [f] or [s]. Thus, interdentals are the fricative of last resort in this instance. No matter which fricative the child might have internalized for the underlying representation of a fricative, [θ] would have been the realization. It is also striking that correct realizations of /θ/ resulted from a constraint ranking that does not conform to the target ranking of constraints; in adult English, FAITH dominates *θ. From a clinical perspective, then, a child's correct production cannot necessarily be taken as evidence that the child has arrived at a target-appropriate grammar. This is in keeping with other reports that children may arrive at the 'right' output for the 'wrong' reason (Dinnsen, 1999). Importantly, there was no need to restrict any of this child's underlying representations to incorrectly internalized forms. This is in complete accord with richness of the base.

Let us now turn to the characterization of Stage 2 and its transition from Stage 1. Given the ranking of constraints for Stage 1 (repeated in (28a)), a coherent account becomes available for the transition to Stage 2 with its target-appropriate realizations of /s/ and the overgeneralization errors associated with the other fricatives. Specifically, the grammar change that took place involves a minimal demotion of *s below *θ, resulting in the new ranking for Stage 2 as shown in (28b). This reranking follows from the constraint demotion algorithm

(Tesar & Smolensky, 1998). That is, upon the child's discovery that [s] could occur, she demoted the constraint responsible for the exclusion of [s], namely *s. This is shown in (28b) where *s is demoted just below *θ, which was the highest ranked constraint that the previous winner violated. This has the effect of bringing *s into the stratum with FAITH. In terms of continuity considerations, the grammars for the two stages otherwise remain the same.

(28) Constraint demotion for Stage 2

a) Stage 1:

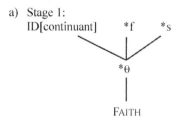

b) Stage 2:

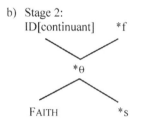

Note that the ranking of *θ over FAITH is retained in the transition from Stage 1 to Stage 2, accounting for the new error pattern where [θ] was no longer in use, with [s] being produced instead. Also common to both stages was the continued dominance of *f, which accounted for the persistent exclusion of labiodental fricatives from the child's inventory.

The effect of the new Stage 2 ranking can be illustrated by considering Child 78's production of target /s/ words. The tableau in (29) provides an example using the word 'soap' to capture the child's accurate productions of /s/ at Stage 2. The faithful candidate (c) only violates the lowest ranked markedness constraint *s with all of the competitors being eliminated by their violations of the higher ranked markedness constraints.

(29) Target /s/ realized as [s] for Stage 2

/soʊp/ 'soap'	*f	*θ	FAITH	*s
a. foʊp	*!		*	
b. θoʊp		*!	*	
c. ☞ soʊp				*

Recall however that at Stage 2, Child 78 also exhibited overgeneralization errors. Whereas /θ/ had been produced correctly in Stage 1, it now was replaced by [s] in Stage 2. The tableau in (30) shows the overgeneralization effects from the Stage 2 reranking. Given a target word such as 'thumb', candidates (a) and (b) are both eliminated by their fatal violations of the more highly ranked markedness constraints. Candidate (c) with the substitute [s] is selected as optimal in accord with the child's new error pattern even though that candidate violates the two lower ranked constraints. This also explains why the substitute for /f/ would have changed from [θ] to [s] at the same time. That is, the higher ranking of *f and *θ precludes the occurrence of candidates (a) and (b) independent of the particular fricative that might have been internalized by the child.

(30) Target /θ/ realized as [s] for Stage 2

/θʌm/ 'thumb'	*f	*θ	FAITH	*s
a. fʌm	*!		*	
b. θʌm		*!		
c. ☞ sʌm			*	*

The case of Child 78 illustrates the way in which optimality theory accounts for overgeneralization errors. Perhaps the most significant distinguishing characteristic of an optimality theoretic account of overgeneralization is that the substance of a child's underlying representations plays a much smaller role and is less decisive than might have been thought under earlier approaches. We saw, for example, that the underlying specification of target place features did not matter for Child 78, although target manner features did, as captured by the dominance of ID[continuant]. Importantly, these overgeneralization errors do not require us to abandon the widely held assumption that children's underlying representations are correct relative to the target system. The fact that overgeneralization errors involve correct and incorrect productions during the first two stages of development apparently has less to do with the substance of underlying representations and more to do with the nature of the constraints and the constraint hierarchy. In these circumstances, optimality theory views overgeneralization errors as an expected and unavoidable intermediate step in the right direction, but one that may require multiple rounds of treatment to induce a series of constraint rerankings before conformity with the target language can be achieved.

5.3 Lexical diffusion

As mentioned earlier in this section, a new sound usually does not come into a child's phonology on an across-the-board basis. Instead, the new sound begins to appear in some words, but not others. This fact has been taken as evidence that the child may have had a more restricted set of underlying representations prior to the introduction of the new sound, making it difficult for the child to know which words warrant change (e.g., Dinnsen & Barlow, 1998). Individual lexical items would then need to restructure to allow the new sound to occur in those specific underlying forms. Such an account poses two problems for optimality theory. One problem relates to the assumption that the underlying representations in the early stage might have been restricted to exclude the new sound—in violation of richness of the base. The other problem relates to the variable occurrence of the new sound.[5] Why does the new sound occur in some words, but not others? This would seem to involve a ranking paradox. On the one hand, the dominance of markedness over faithfulness would prevent the sound from occurring in words. On the other hand, the dominance of faithfulness over markedness would ensure the sound's realization in words. A possible solution to these problems has been put forward by Gierut, Morrisette and Champion (1999). One part of the solution draws on the observation that sounds tend to be produced more accurately in high frequency words (e.g., Leonard & Ritterman, 1971; Luce & Pisoni, 1998; Morrisette, 1999; Beckman & Edwards, 2000). This suggests that faithfulness constraints may be sensitive to lexical properties such as a word's frequency of occurrence. This is in line with other positional faithfulness constraints that are sensitive to prosodic and morphosyntactic categories (e.g., Beckman, 1998; Lombardi, 1999; Smith, 2002). Consequently, in addition to conventional faithfulness constraints, there would be constraints formulated as in (31).

(31) Generic word frequency faithfulness constraint

> FAITH[HighFreq]: Corresponding segments in high frequency words must be
> identical

With a faithfulness constraint of this sort, we can formally explain why, for example, velars might begin to emerge first in high frequency words but continue to be produced in error in other words. That is, the markedness constraint that bans velars (*k) would be demoted just below FAITH[HighFreq], but above the general faithfulness constraint (FAITH). The rationale behind this proposal is that high frequency words afford greater exposure to the new sound, increasing the likelihood that the child would take note of the relevant fact and demote the conflicting markedness constraint. Both high and low frequency words can be represented underlyingly with target-appropriate velars, but this ranking would permit velars to surface only in high frequency words. Such an account complies with richness of the base in that the newly emergent sound would never have needed to be excluded from the child's underlying representations at any stage of development. The fact that velars might not have occurred phonetically in any word at an earlier stage would be achieved not by restricting the phonemic inventory but rather by appealing to the default ranking of markedness over both types of faithfulness constraints (cf., Child 179 in §2.1).

A word's frequency of occurrence is clearly a language-specific property. This might seem at odds with the assumption that constraints are universal. FAITH[HighFreq] is, however, assumed to belong to the universal constraint set, but it must interface with a language-specific lexical property. This ultimately may not be very different from other faithfulness constraints that are relativized to, for example, nouns or morphological categories (e.g., Smith, 2002). More specifically, the dominance of noun faithfulness would result in the preservation of phonological distinctions in words that happen to be nouns in that particular language. The novel proposal here is simply that word frequency is one more factor that is relevant to the systematic behavior of sounds.

Summing up this entire section, the principle of richness of the base has had a major impact on what has been a fundamental issue in phonological acquisition, namely the nature of children's underlying representations. Evidence that had been taken as support one way or the other for claims about underlying representations is now not as compelling as might have been thought. The evidence and phenomena are certainly real, but optimality theory forces us to look to a variety of other grammatical factors for the account, including the ranking of constraints and the nature of the constraints in the universal constraint set. It is, of course, still possible within optimality theory for children to misrepresent words underlyingly. This could, for example, result from misperception. This shifts the burden to diagnostic tests that can distinguish between errors that are the result of highly ranked markedness constraints and/or the misrepresentation of lexical items.

6   Conclusion

The developmental phenomena presented in this chapter represent relatively simple and basic aspects of phonology. All theories of phonology must account for the fact that only certain sounds occur in the phonetic inventory, that there are restrictions on the distribution of sounds, and that only certain sounds function to distinguish meaning. Optimality theory accounts for each of these phenomena in a characteristic way. For example, restrictions on inventories are achieved by ranking context-free markedness constraints over faithfulness constraints (§2.1). The complementary distribution of sounds is achieved by ranking a contextually conditioned markedness constraint over a context-free markedness constraint, which in turn is ranked above a faithfulness constraint (§2.2). Contrasts are achieved by ranking faithfulness constraints over markedness constraints. The more limited realization of a contrast in some contexts, but not others, is achieved by ranking a positional faithfulness constraint over a markedness constraint, which in turn is ranked above a context-free faithfulness constraint (§2.3). Optimality theory also provides an algorithm for learning these phonotactic generalizations by constraint demotion and an assumed initial-state of relative unmarkedness (§3). The discovery of phonological conspiracies in fully developed languages has proven especially problematic for rule-based theories, but these phenomena have a straightforward account within optimality theory. Conspiracies are characterized by a highly ranked markedness constraint that dominates multiple crucially ranked faithfulness constraints. The occurrence of conspiracies in developing phonologies provides additional support for optimality theory with novel clinical implications (§4). Finally, while the issue of children's underlying representations was touched upon throughout the chapter, we saw that optimality theory forces a reconsideration of the evidence that has been adduced in support of claims about underlying representations (§5).

This is by no means the whole story of children's developing phonologies, nor is it necessarily representative of the broader range of phenomena that can be observed in acquisition. These phenomena were selected because they serve to illustrate some of the fundamentals of optimality theory, and they involve issues that come up over and over again in analyses of more complex phenomena. The following chapters in this volume will present some of the more complex phenomena and will build more intricate analyses on this foundation.

Notes

*   I am especially grateful to Judith Gierut, Ashley Farris-Trimble and Nick Henriksen for their comments on earlier versions of this chapter. This work was supported in part by a grant to Indiana University from the National Institutes of Health (DC001694).

1   Claims about the merger of an underlying distinction are usually based on impressionistic phonetic transcription. Some instrumental acoustic studies have, however, found that some children do in fact maintain subtle, but systematic distinctions that may not be perceptually salient (e.g., Kornfeld & Goehl, 1974; Maxwell & Weismer, 1982; Hoffman, Stager & Daniloff, 1983; Weismer, 1984; Forrest, Weismer, Milenkovic & Dougall, 1988; Hoffman & Damico, 1988; Forrest, Weismer, Hodge, Dinnsen & Elbert, 1990; Forrest, Weismer, Elbert & Dinnsen, 1994; Scobbie, 1998; Cohn & Kishel, 2002; 2003). Such findings can certainly be taken as evidence that the child represents the distinction at the underlying level. However, from a communicative point of view, it remains that the distinction is effectively neutralized at the phonetic level.

2   We will see in §5 of this chapter that change does not always occur in an across-the-board fashion.

3   This constraint abbreviates a family of constraints preserving individual place features in accord with universal hierarchies that give preference to labials and dorsals over coronals (e.g., de Lacy, 2002).

4   See Michael Vitevitch's website: http://www.people.ku.edu/~mvitevit/ and associated links for computing these probabilities.

5   Richness of the base would not be challenged by the stage of development where the new sound has already begun to diffuse through the lexicon because the presumed restriction on underlying representations would have been lifted at that point. The seemingly exceptional behavior of those words that continue to exhibit the error pattern is the problem here.

2 Phonological disorders and the Developmental Phonology Archive

Judith A. Gierut
Indiana University

The study of children's developing phonological systems has the potential to provide new insights to fundamental questions about the structure of sound systems, and how those systems may change over time. Yet, children present unique challenges to the research process, which can make it difficult to obtain the kinds of data that are necessary to evaluate linguistic claims. In this chapter, we describe a descriptive protocol that addresses limitations associated with the study of phonological development by shifting the focus from typically developing toddlers to preschoolers with functional phonological disorders. This population affords an opportunity for the use of sophisticated elicitation materials, procedures, and data analyses, as employed on the Learnability Project. The population, coupled with methodological advantages, has facilitated the establishment of the Developmental Phonology Archive, which has broad based utility in descriptive linguistic, developmental, and clinical research on phonological acquisition.

1 Introduction

The study of phonological acquisition offers a unique and rich opportunity to explore basic questions in theoretical linguistics, but it also poses a number of challenges, both theoretical and methodological. Some have expressed concerns about acquisition as primary evidence (Kenstowicz & Kisseberth, 1979; Anderson, 1981; de Lacy, 2002), and others have gone so far as to claim that acquisition has no bearing on the study of phonology since children's language patterns are merely a reflection of performance limitations due to their immature motor systems (Hale & Reiss, 1998). Others have reservations about the elicitation of data and whether samples obtained from children provide adequate kinds of data to advance linguistic claims (Ferguson & Farwell, 1975). Further questions arise with respect to the recording of children's utterances, and the analyzability and interpretability of their data (Weismer, 1984). The misgivings notwithstanding, the advantages that obtain from the study of phonological acquisition far outweigh the challenges. In this vein, two main approaches have guided acquisition research in phonology. One line of study goes about detailing the utterances of a given child longitudinally, with the assumption that the observed patterns are representative of development generally. The contributions of Smith (1973), Menn (1976), and Vihman (1996) are key examples of this kind of work. Another approach is to aggregate cross-sectional patterns, with the intent of plotting a pseudo-longitudinal course of learning. Data of this type have been reported primarily for English, as exemplified by the work of Templin (1957), Sander (1972), or Smit and colleagues (Smit, Hand, Freilinger, Bernthal & Bird, 1990). There are constantly new normative data being reported for other languages including, for example, Arabic (Amayreh & Dyson, 1998), Cantonese (So & Dodd, 1995), Putonghua (Hua & Dodd, 2000), and Spanish (Jimenez, 1987). In all, the complementarity of these lines of investigation has served the research community well by providing a wealth of descriptive data for linguistic comparisons and analyses.

There is yet a third research approach that is less commonly pursued, but follows the path of examining atypical populations. The view is that anomalies in language development actually help to delineate the basic principles and properties of linguistic systems (Applegate, 1961; Haas, 1963; Lorentz, 1976; Thomas & Karmiloff-Smith, 2005). Groundbreaking contributions have come, for example, from studies of the deaf (Brentari, 1998; Emmory, 2002; Goldin-Meadow, 2003), with interest also in children who are blind (Landau & Gleitman, 1985), feral (Curtiss, 1977), presenting with Williams Syndrome (Bellugi & St. George, 2001) or savant conditions (Smith & Tsimpli, 1995), to name a few. Studies of atypical language learning take on an added dimension because they are often experimental in nature. This thereby affords for the carefully controlled manipulation of linguistic variables, which in turn provides for a convergence of evidence by bridging description with experimentation, and linguistic with psycholinguistic demonstrations of effects. It is this approach that has guided the research program of the Learnability Project. The aim of the project is to describe the phonologies of children with functional phonological disorders, in keeping with the intent of formal linguistic theory. From the linguistic hypotheses that obtain, children are then enrolled in clinical treatment, which is designed as a single-subject experiment, in keeping with the goals of speech-language pathology. Thus, our approach consists of a two-step process with theoretical and applied missions. In this chapter, we take up the descriptive methodologies that are used on the Learnability Project; the experimental component is presented in Chapter 3 in this volume. By way of background, we begin with a general overview of the population of children with functional phonological disorders and then outline the inclusionary criteria that are used to determine eligibility for participation in the Learnability Project. The protocols used in data elicitation and analyses are described, along with methodologies for ensuring the reliability of data. A description of the Developmental Phonology Archive that has resulted from this line of investigation is provided as an example of how to structure and use databases in the study of language acquisition.

2   Characteristics of functional phonological disorders

Phonological disorders are among the most prevalent linguistic disorders of childhood. Population estimates of the prevalence of phonological disorder ranges from 3 to 13% for children in the United States (National Institute on Deafness and Other Communication Disorders, 1994). In 80% of these cases, the disorder is sufficiently severe as to require direct clinical intervention to affect change in the sound system.

The general definition of a phonological disorder is a breakdown in the production, perception, or processing of sounds of the ambient language in the absence of any other overt symptoms (Gierut, 1998c). Production errors are the primary characteristic that is used to diagnose the disorder, but children may have related perceptual and/or processing difficulties. It is estimated that 27 to 39% of the contrasts children produce in error may be misperceived, but this varies by the nature of the phonemic distinction and the merger (Locke, 1980a). To our knowledge, there are no estimates of the occurrence of processing difficulties in this population. There is also no known cause of a phonological disorder, but it appears that, in some families, there may be a genetic predisposition. In this regard, the incidence of the disorder is greater in males than in females on the order of 1.5 to 1 (Shriberg & Kwiatkowski, 1994).

On linguistic grounds, children with phonological disorders typically present with a severely limited repertoire of sounds in the inventory, and these may include nonambient sounds or sounds that are considered 'late acquired' based on normative scales (Leonard, 1992). Consonants and/or vowels (Stoel-Gammon & Herrington, 1990) may be affected, but studies have emphasized the consonantal inventory for reasons associated with intelligibility. Children's errors may be associated with limited syllable structure (Levelt, Schiller & Levelt, 1999/2000; Barlow, 2001b), prosody (Kehoe & Stoel-Gammon, 1997;

2001), or systematic rule-governed sound changes that have neutralizing and/or allophonic effects (Lorentz, 1976; Elbert, Dinnsen & Powell, 1984; Ingram, 1989). Aside from their phonological system, the population as a whole appears to be typically developing in other respects. Children perform within the expected range on measures such as hearing acuity, oral-motor structure and function, intelligence, receptive and expressive vocabulary, and receptive and expressive language. They are also typically functioning in terms of emotional and social development and achieve developmental milestones at appropriate rates. Thus, children with phonological disorders experience a path of development that falls within normal limits, except in the area of phonology.

To be expected, there may be variability among children in terms of the presenting conditions for the disorder. For example, children may have an organic (as opposed to functional) disorder, as in cases of cleft palate, hearing impairment, or cognitive deficits. There is also a debated category, termed as 'developmental apraxia of speech', where the planning and execution of motor gestures in production of speech sounds is affected (Shriberg, Aram & Kwiatkowski, 1997a; 1997b; 1997c). Children may present with co-occurring disorders such as Specific Language Impairment (Leonard, 1998) or stuttering (Nippold, 2001). Others may face academic challenges in math, reading, or spelling (Shriberg, Kwiatkowski, Best, Hengst & Terselic-Weber, 1986). Still others may have a history of otitis media (Shriberg & Kwiatkowski, 1982). It is significant though that none of these patterns is predictive of a phonological disorder. Moreover, it is not possible to predict which children will eventually master the phonology on their own, and which will require direct treatment; yet there is potential for the disorder to have long lasting effects. Shriberg and colleagues (Shriberg, Gruber & Kwiatkowski, 1994) report 'critical periods' for phonological learning between 4 and 6 years of age, and again between 7 and 8.5 years of age, when a child's potential for phonological learning is accelerated. They also report that after 8.5 years of age, expansion of the sound system appears to plateau. In addition to these observations, there are retrospective studies of adults who were diagnosed with a phonological disorder in childhood which point to lingering effects on language processing and use (Felsenfeld, Broen & McGue, 1992; 1994; Lewis & Freebairn, 1992; Felsenfeld, McGue & Broen, 1995). Adults with a history of the disorder appear to perform more slowly and less accurately on standardized measures of language and language-related skills. They also tend not to achieve the same educational level as unaffected age-matched controls, nor do they realize the same employment potential. Childhood phonological disorders thus constitute a significant health problem given their incidence, unknown cause, predictability of recovery, and possibility of lifelong consequences. The potentially handicapping nature of the disorder, coupled with a critical period for sound learning motivates an aggressive approach, warranting early diagnosis and treatment particularly during the preschool period of development. This overview of the population has only skimmed the surface of available work describing the characteristics of children with functional phonological disorders. The interested reader may explore the general topic of functional phonological disorders in representative texts such as Grunwell (1981), Nettelbladt (1983), Stoel-Gammon and Dunn (1985), Ingram (1989), Dodd (1995), Yavaş (1998), Bauman-Waengler (2000), Bernthal and Bankson (2004), and Kamhi and Pollock (2005).

2.1   The population of study

In light of the population demographics and needs, the Learnability Project has focused its attention on identifying preschool children, ages 3 to 7 years, with functional phonological disorders who are acquiring English as their first (and only) language. Children are recruited through the community and surrounding regions, where the preschool population is estimated at 21,000 (United States Census Bureau, 2000). Brochures and advertisements are disseminated to families, day cares, schools, clinics, pediatricians, hospitals, and public outreach services; referrals also come from special service providers. In all, we reach approximately 15,000 families annually through Learnability Project recruitment efforts. In keeping with federal guidelines, children are not solicited to the research; rather the family must initiate contact with the Learnability Project. Participation is entirely voluntary, and families may withdraw from participation at any time without consequence. There is no monetary compensation for participation in the research, but families receive complete diagnostic and clinical services for their child, along with service reports, referrals, and extended care at no cost. Children also receive a small token of appreciation (Learnability Project t-shirt) upon completion of the treatment program. In account of the benefits, there is understandably little attrition.

To determine eligibility for participation, all children complete an initial screening followed by an in-depth diagnostic evaluation. The screening establishes that the child may be at risk for phonological learning as evidenced by errors in sound production. The diagnostic evaluation confirms the phonological lag, establishes that the lag is significant to warrant intervention, and rules out other contributing factors to the disorder. A uniform battery of tests is administered to all children and has remained constant over the lifetime of the project to preserve the integrity of the database for comparison purposes. The tests and measures are listed in Table 1. Testing involves a minimum of five 60-minute sessions.

Table 1. Diagnostic battery of the Learnability Project.

Norm Referenced Measures	Behavioral Objective
Audiometric screening (ASHA, 1997)	Evaluates hearing of 1000, 2000, and 4000 Hz tones at 20 dB
Clinical Assessment of Oropharyngeal Motor Development in Young Children (Robbins & Klee, 1987)	Evaluates oral mechanism structure & function (ages 2;6 to 6;11)
Clinical Evaluation of Language Fundamentals-Preschool/Revised (Wiig, Secord & Semel, 1992; 1995)	Evaluates receptive & expressive language (ages 3;0 to 6;11/5;0 to 16;11)
Expressive Vocabulary Test (Williams, 1997)	Evaluates expressive vocabulary (ages 2;6 to 90+)
Goldman-Fristoe Test of Articulation–2 (Goldman & Fristoe, 2000)	Evaluates articulation of target English sounds (ages 2;0 to 21;11)
Illinois Test of Psycholinguistic Abilities-Revised (Kirk, McCarthy & Kirk, 1968)	Evaluates digit span recall as a reflection of lexical storage and retrieval (ages 4;0 to 8;11)
Leiter International Performance Scale-Revised (Roid & Miller, 1997)	Evaluates nonverbal intelligence (ages 2;0 to 20;11)
Peabody Picture Vocabulary Test-III (Dunn & Dunn, 1997)	Evaluates receptive vocabulary (ages 2;6 to 90+)
Rice/Wexler Test of Early Grammatical Impairment (Rice & Wexler, 2001)	Evaluates receptive & expressive language (ages 3;0 to 8;11)
Test of Early Language Development-Third Edition (Hresko, Reid & Hammill, 1999)	Evaluates receptive & expressive language (ages 2;0 to 7;11)
Test of Language Development-Primary Third Edition (Newcomer & Hammill, 1997)	Evaluates receptive & expressive language (ages 4;0 to 8;11)
Supplementary Measures	
Children's Test of Nonword Repetition (Gathercole & Baddeley, 1996)	Evaluates phonological representations in working memory
Percentage Consonant Correct-Revised (Shriberg, Austin, Lewis, McSweeny & Wilson, 1997)	Estimates severity of involvement
Perception-Production Task (Locke, 1980b)	Estimates misperception of speech sounds
Stimulability testing (Powell, Elbert & Dinnsen, 1991)	Samples child's ability to imitate speech sounds

To be eligible for participation, children must be between the ages of 3 and 7 years, and generally in good health, with the primary distinguishing characteristic being errors in production of the sound system of English, which thereby results in unintelligible speech. A predetermined set of inclusionary and exclusionary criteria must be further met. Inclusionary criteria are (1) normal hearing, (2) no evidence of cognitive delay, (3) no known history of organic or motor disorders, (4) normal oral-motor structure and function, (5) performance of at least 1 standard deviation below the mean relative to age- and gender-matched peers on the *Goldman-Fristoe Test of Articulation–2* (Goldman & Fristoe, 2000), and (6) a reduced phonemic inventory with a minimum of six target English consonants excluded from the pretreatment repertoire across all word positions. Assuming these criteria are met, a child is eligible for participation, barring three exclusionary criteria: (1) concurrent enrollment in a phonological treatment program other than the Learnability Project, (2) acquisition of a first language other than English, and (3) a home environment that is not monolingual. Children who meet the minimum inclusionary and exclusionary criteria may participate, regardless of gender, racial or ethnic background.

Those children who qualify for participation are then evaluated further upon their admission to the program. Diagnostic testing helps to establish, for example, severity of the disorder, stimulability (i.e., the child's ability to accurately imitate a sound when given an instructional model), expressive and receptive vocabulary, expressive and receptive language, and language processing as based on digit span recall and nonword repetitions. In some instances, it is necessary to supplement the test battery if a child's performance warrants further evaluation of, for example, perceptual skills (e.g., Gierut, 1998c) or acoustic analyses of phonological neutralizations (Weismer, Dinnsen & Elbert, 1981; Weismer, 1984).

To date, the Learnability Project has enrolled 279 children; 188 have been boys and 91, girls. The average age of participants is 4 years, 5 months, and the average number of target English phonemes excluded from the pretreatment repertoires of the children is 8.23 consonants.

3 Descriptive protocol of the Learnability Project

3.1 Phonological samples

The primary measure that is used to assess a child's phonological system for linguistic purposes is the Phonological Knowledge Protocol (PKP, Gierut, 1985). The PKP is a set of 293 common and picturable words that are likely to be in the vocabularies of preschool children; a list of PKP items is shown in Table 2. As can be seen, the PKP samples each target English consonant in a minimum of five different exemplars in each of three relevant positions. In addition, the PKP provides an opportunity to sample minimal pairs in establishing phonemic contrasts. It also elicits morphophonemically related forms by adding present progressive and diminutive suffixes to base forms so as to probe for the occurrence of systematic alternations. PKP items include a variety of syllable types, both mono- and multisyllabic, that have varying canonical shapes. Syntactic class is also varied, with about 70% of the sample targeting nouns, 17% verbs, and 13% other categories. This is consistent with the distribution of syntactic categories generally in English (Hudson, 1994; Aitchison, 2000).

Table 2. Phonological Knowledge Protocol (PKP).

Target Sound	Probe Words		
	Initial	Medial	Final
/m/	mud	gum-i	gum
	mouth	comb-i	comb
	mother	thumb-i	thumb
	mouse	game-i	game
	moon	swimming	swim
		camera	
		hammer	
/n/	knife	raining	rain
	nose	running	run
	noise	moon-i	moon
	nail	van-i	van
	nothing	sunny	sun
		piano	
		money	
/ŋ/		finger	tongue
			ring
			nothing
/p/	pig	soupy	soup
	pie	chip-i	chip
	pants	soapy	soap
	peach	cup-i	cup
	paint	sleeping	sleep
		happy	
		open	

Target Sound	Probe Words		
	Initial	Medial	Final
/b/	big	tub-i	tub
	bite	rubbing	rub
	back	cob-i	cob
	bus	robe-i	robe
	boot	web-i	web
		rabbit	
		bubble	
/t/	tub	eating	eat
	tear	foot-i	foot
	toes	cutting	cut
	tail	bootie	boot
	tooth	biting	bite
		button	
		potato	
/d/	duck	bed-i	bed
	deer	reading	read
	done	muddy	mud
	door	riding	ride
	dog	hiding	hide
		ladder	
		lady	
/k/	cup	book-i	book
	cob	duckie	duck
	cut	sock-i	sock
	coat	rocky	rock
	comb	back-i	back
		pocket	
		cracker	
/g/	gum	doggie	dog
	gate	frog-i	frog
	girl	piggie	pig
	gun	baggy	bag
	goat	hugging	hug
		wagon	
		tiger	

Target Sound	Probe Words		
	Initial	Medial	Final
/f/	foot	laughing	laugh
	face	coughing	cough
	fire	knife-i	knife
	five	leafy	leaf
	fish	roof-i	roof
		Goofy	
		elephant	
/v/	van	waving	wave
	vegetable	shaving	shave
	vanilla	glove-i	glove
	vacuum	driving	drive
	valentine	stove-i	stove
		seven	
		over	
/θ/	thumb	toothy	tooth
	thank (you)	bath-i	bath
	thunder	mouth-i	mouth
	thief	teeth-i	teeth
	thirsty	wreath-i	wreath
/ð/	them	feather	
	these	mother	
	there	brother	
	theirs	father	
	that	other	
/s/	soup	juicy	juice
	soap	mouse-i	mouse
	sock	icy	ice
	sun	bus-i	bus
	santa	dressy	dress
		eraser	
		baseball	
/z/	zebra	cheezy	cheese
	zipper	nosy	nose
	zoo	noisy	noise
	zipping	rosy	rose
	zero	buzzing	buzz
		raisin	
		scissors	

Target Sound	Probe Words		
	Initial	Medial	Final
/ʃ/	shave	fishing	fish
	shoe	washing	wash
	shirt	brushing	brush
	shovel	crashing	crash
	shampoo	pushing	push
		marshmallow	
		lotion	
/tʃ/	chip	peach-i	peach
	cheese	catching	catch
	chalk	pinching	pinch
	chair	punching	punch
	chicken	watch-i	watch
		picture	
		kitchen	
/dʒ/	juice	orange-i	orange
	jail	bridge-i	bridge
	jeep	badge-i	badge
	jump	cage-i	cage
	jelly	page-i	page
		angel	
		vegetable	
/l/	laugh	tail-i	tail
	leaf	nail-i	nail
	light	shovel-i	shovel
	ladder	calling	call
	leg	hilly	hill
		color	
		yellow	
/r/	read	starry	star
	rock	deer-i	deer
	rain	door-i	door
	run	fire-i	fire
	ride	chair-i	chair
		carrot	
		giraffe	
/w/	water	growing	grow
	watch	sewing	sew
	wash	throwing	throw
	wave	blowing	blow
	window	snowing	snow
		flower	
		towel	

Target Sound	Probe Words		
	Initial	Medial	Final
/j/	yes yellow you yawn yard	crayon onion	
/h/	hide hug hill hat house	treehouse grasshopper behind forehead bluehouse	

While the PKP was originally developed to test the claims and predictions of standard generative theory, the data that are collected are readily interpretable within newer frameworks. The PKP has been used, for example, to test models of feature geometry and underspecification (Chin & Dinnsen, 1991; Gierut, Cho & Dinnsen, 1993; Dinnsen, 1996; Dinnsen, Barlow & Morrisette, 1997; Dinnsen, 1998), and now more recently, Optimality Theory (e.g., Barlow & Gierut, 1999; Morrisette, Dinnsen & Gierut, 2003; Gierut & Morrisette, 2005). Besides remaining in sync with linguistic advances, the PKP is amenable to the examination of psycholinguistic variables relative to children's productions. The lexical factors of word frequency, neighborhood density, and phonotactic probability have been computed for the PKP items using public on-line sources http://neighborhoodsearch.wustl.edu/ (Nusbaum, Pisoni & Davis, 1984) and http://www.people.ku.edu/~mvitevit/ (Vitevitch & Luce, 2004). In addition, the PKP has been coded for word familiarity (cf. Nusbaum et al., 1984) and age of word acquisition (Gilhooly & Logie, 1980a; 1980b; Bird, Franklin & Howard, 2001). A full set of descriptive characteristics of the PKP is provided in the appendix as a resource.

In complement to the PKP, we have also developed two measures that sample target English clusters, the 146-item Onset Cluster Probe (OCP, Gierut, 1998c) and the 105-item Coda Cluster Probe (CCP). These are shown in Tables 3 and 4, respectively. The structure of the OCP is similar to the PKP in that each target cluster is elicited in a minimum of five different exemplars; the CCP samples three exemplars per target cluster. The items are again picturable and familiar, and can be described in terms of their lexical properties. Relevant data on the OCP and CCP are also included in the appendix.

Table 3. Onset Cluster Probe (OCP).

Sonority Difference	Target Cluster	Probe Words
6	/tw–/	Twinkie, twins, Tweety, twist, twelve
	/kw–/	quack, quiet, queen, quilt, quick
	/pj– kj–/	pu, cute
5	/pl–/	plate, play, plane, plug, plant
	/kl–/	clean, clothes, clown, cloud, clock
	/pr–/	pretzel, prize, princess, present, pretty
	/tr–/	tree, trick-or-treat, truck, triangle, train
	/kr–/	crayon, crack, cry, cream, crawl
	/bj–/	beauty
4	/bl–/	black, blanket, blocks, blue, blow
	/gl–/	glasses, globe, glove, glow, glue
	/br–/	bread, bridge, brush, brown, broom
	/dr–/	dress, draw, drum, drink, drive
	/gr–/	grass, grapes, green, grandma, grow
	/sw–/	swing, sweater, swim, sweet, sweep
	/fj–/	few
3	/fl–/	fly, flute, flower, floor, flag
	/sl–/	sleep, slipper, sled, sleeve, slide
	/fr–/	fruit, french fries, frog, friend, front
	/θr–/	three, throne, throw, throat, thread
	/ʃr–/	shrink, shrug, shred, shrimp, shrub
	/vj–/	viewmaster
2	/sm–/	smell, smoke, smile, smooth, small
	/sn–/	sneeze, snail, snowman, snack, snake
	/mj–/	music
Adjuncts	/sp–/	spill, spoon, spider, space, spaghetti
	/st–/	stop, store, stove, stamp, star
	/sk–/	skunk, skate, skirt, scarf, school
3-element clusters	/spl–/	splash, splitting, splinter, splashing, split
	/spr–/	spread, spray, sprite, sprinkle, spring
	/str–/	stripe, straight, street, strong, straw
	/skr–/	scream, scribble, scratch, screw, scrub
	/skw–/	squeak, squeeze, square, squirt, squirrel

Table 4. Coda Cluster Probe (CCP).

Target Cluster	Probe Words
/–mp/	lamp, jump, stamp
/–nt/	tent, paint, point
/–nd/	blonde, hand, stand
/–nθ/	ninth, tenth, month
/–nts/	fence, bounce, dance
/–ntʃ/	lunch, branch, punch
/–ndʒ/	orange, sponge, change
/–ŋk/	pink, sink, trunk
/–ks/	box, six, fix
/–ft/	lift, soft, raft
/–sp/	wasp, gasp, grasp
/–st/	nest, toast, vest
/–sk/	mask, desk, ask
/–lp/	help, scalp, gulp
/–lt/	belt, salt, melt
/–ld/	old, gold, cold
/–lk/	milk, sulk, silk
/–lf/	wolf, golf, shelf
/–lθ/	health, wealth, filth
/–rm/	arm, worm, farm
/–rn/	barn, corn, horn
/–rp/	burp, sharp, chirp
/–rb/	curb, verb, barb
/–rt/	shirt, heart, cart
/–rd/	bird, card, yard
/–rk/	fork, bark, park
/–rg/	iceberg, burglar, hamburger
/–rf/	scarf, surf, Nerf
/–rv/	curve, carve, starve
/–rθ/	hearth, Earth, birth
/–rs/	horse, purse, nurse
/–rz/	ours, Mars, cars
/–rtʃ/	church, torch, porch
/–rdʒ/	large, George, sarge
/–rl/	girl, curl, squirrel

Together, the PKP, OCP, and CCP contribute the essential phonological data that are gathered on the Learnability Project. These probe measures also serve an experimental purpose in establishing baseline performance, stability of baseline, and generalization learning based on production accuracy (see Chapter 3 in this volume for details). Probe data are gathered longitudinally from each child at a minimum of five points in time: prior to enrollment in a treatment experiment, at a midpoint of treatment, immediately posttreatment, two weeks following the completion of treatment, and again two months following treatment. In all, each child contributes a minimum of 544 productions at any given sampling point, yielding at least 2,520 productions per individual. Because the same items are elicited at each sampling, it is possible to evaluate a given child's use of target sounds and sound sequences at multiple points in time, to monitor changes in the nature and use of error patterns, and to track a given word's trajectory of development. Further, because all children are administered the same probes, it is possible to evaluate the same kinds of data cross-sectionally to explore commonalities in phonological acquisition. Across the 279 children who have participated thus far, we have amassed a database of more than 700,000 utterances for use in descriptive phonological analyses.

3.2 Materials and elicitation procedures

The probe materials have been developed in both paper and digital format. The paper copy consists of mounted pictures assembled in a book and randomized by sound; the digital version also consists of pictures but presented on a computer screen. We have assembled five different sets of materials for each of the PKP and OCP, which is relevant to issues of learning. Specifically, a given child never sees the same probe pictures more than once. This eliminates concerns about lexically- or stimulus-bound responding. It also minimizes the practice effects that are associated with repeated presentation of the same stimuli.

The probe materials are presented as a spontaneous picture-naming task. A child is shown a picture and asked to name it, using cues like 'What's this?' or 'Who is this?' When needed, a child's attention may be drawn to a particular aspect of the picture using a question like 'What color is the girl's dress?' or 'What's she sitting on?' Alternatively, cloze sentences may be used, as in 'The girl's dress is (red) or 'The girl is sitting on a (chair).' Following such cues, a child is afforded a chance to name the word independently. If spontaneous naming does not occur, then the elicitation switches to delayed imitation. Here, the examiner states the word in the context of a longer utterance, and after the intervening delay, the intended form is expected from the child. Following from above, delayed imitation might take the form of 'Oh look, the girl's shoes are black, her dress is *red*, her socks are brown, and her balloon is pink! What color is her dress?' for the child's response 'red.' If the child still does not respond, then the examiner uses direct imitation. This takes the form of 'Say red', with the child's response to follow. For every probe item, a child's output is coded as a spontaneous production, delayed, or direct imitation. The cueing hierarchy may then be interpreted differentially in data analysis depending on the stringency of the criteria that are used in a given study. The occurrence of non-response is rare due to the extensive diagnostic testing that had already been obtained in identifying children with a single-faceted phonological disorder.

The same sampling procedures are followed in administration of the different types of probes, but it is necessary to clarify the elicitation of present progressive and diminutive forms on the PKP. First, morphophonemically-related forms are not sampled back-to-back, as in 'run' followed immediately by 'running' or vice versa. Rather, all base forms of the PKP are sampled, and then in a subsequent testing session, the subset of related forms is elicited. To obtain present progressive suffixing, the examiner cues in the form of appropriate questions such as 'What's the dog doing?' or 'What's the frog doing?' For diminutives, the examiner instructs the child in a 'silly' game of adding [i] to the ends of words. The examiner demonstrates using nonPKP items such as 'horse+i' or 'pen+i', and then the child has an opportunity to say these same items to show an understanding of the task. Typically, 3 to 5 trials are needed in demonstration before a child advances to the diminutive probe.

Besides the present progressive and diminutive forms, the PKP items can be prefixed if these data are needed to verify a particular error pattern. For example, Gierut (1989b) described a child who omitted consonants in word-initial position, but not postvocalically. On the surface, the pattern could have either been associated with a constraint on the distribution of segments, or alternatively, a systematic positionally-specific process of deletion. To disambiguate between the two in establishing a child's knowledge, relevant PKP items were sampled with the prefix 're-,' as in 'reread' or 'rerun.' The procedural format was the same as in the elicitation of diminutives. In the case of this particular child, the data showed that the error was attributable to distributional restrictions and not rules. Examples of the child's productions included 'comb' [oʊm], 'recomb' [wʳioʊm], and 'chip' [ɪp], 'rechip' [wʳiɪp]. For a complementary scenario, where a child's errors were due to rules as opposed to distributional restrictions, see Rockman, Dinnsen and Rowland (1983) and the related discussion in Chapter 9 in this volume.

3.3   Transcriptions and reliability

A child's probe responses are audio recorded and phonetically transcribed. With respect to audio recording, tabletop microphones are used in combination with a digital recorder. In some studies of early acquisition, children wear a vest mike during sampling (Vihman, Ferguson & Elbert, 1986), but given the ages of the children participating in the Learnability Project, this is unnecessary. In terms of transcription, standard notation of the IPA is used with diacritic markings. Each word of the probes is transcribed by trained assistants, who are recruited from the graduate programs in Linguistics and in Speech and Hearing Sciences. Before an assistant is given the responsibility of transcription, she or he must first pass an audiometric screening and must demonstrate 90% baseline agreement with a master transcription. The assistant transcribes a set of data that has been selected specifically for the purpose of establishing baseline transcription reliability. The data set was selected as representative of the degree of severity of the cases seen by the Learnability Project, along with the range of errored outputs. A master transcription of these data had been developed in advance by the Principal Investigators of the Learnability Project. The assistant's transcription is compared to the master, point-to-point for consonant agreement. If agreement is 90% or greater, then the assistant is given transcription responsibilities. If agreement is poorer, the assistant receives further instruction by reviewing the points of discrepancy. Then, another set of data is transcribed for comparison to the master. If agreement is not adequate after this, the assistant is assigned other duties.

Reliability of transcriptions is then established for 10% of the descriptive data that are obtained from each child. Two assistants, who have met the aforementioned baseline level of reliability, transcribe the data independent of each other. Then, their transcriptions are compared, consonant-by-consonant. For any given child, approximately 400 consonant productions are submitted for transcription agreement. The overall mean interjudge reliability of consonant transcriptions on the Learnability Project is 92%. This falls above the standard of 85% agreement that has been set in the clinical literature (Shriberg & Lof, 1991). While some may view articulatory phonetic data as generally suspect, it should be recognized that these data are the backbone of every published grammar that is used in phonological analyses and in support of linguistic theory. Without such data, the field of phonology would be lost. Consequently, if there are indeterminacies in the transcription of children's data, these are exactly the same limitations that are associated with every grammar of a language. However, an advantage of the child data is that the degree of discrepancy in transcriptions can be assessed given that reliability is documented. This exceeds published grammars of fully developed languages, where reliability of transcriptions is rarely, if ever, reported.

3.4   The Developmental Phonology Archive

Once the data have been collected, transcribed, and deemed reliable, they are entered into the Developmental Phonology Archive. The archive is a compendium of the children's data collected to date, which is used in the formulation of descriptive phonological analyses and in the evaluation of generalization learning following from experimental treatment. This is the cornerstone of the descriptive side of the Learnability Project.

Standard database software is used to enter each child's phonetic transcriptions of probe data. As with the transcriptions, data entry is also subject to interjudge reliability, with 24% of all data checked for accuracy of entry in the database. A given child's data are organized into fields that correspond with the words on the probe measures and the sampling points in time. This allows for database searches based on target phoneme, child output, word, and/or point in time. From the search, it is possible to cull qualitative and quantitative information from the archive.

Qualitatively, a child's error patterns may be examined from relational and independent perspectives. In a relational search, a child's productions are compared to the adult target. Figure 1 illustrates a relational search for target /s/ in a portion of the data obtained from Child 216. Notice in the columns labeled 'Target Snd' and 'Target Word,' the PKP items that sample /s/ are shown. Notice also the discrepancy between the intended adult target /s/ and the child's output at longitudinal sampling points from pre- to 2 months posttreatment. These data are shown in the columns labeled 'PKP pre,' 'PKP phase shift,' 'PKP post,' and so on. In particular, at posttreatment, Child 216 produced [s] in only one lexical item 'sun.' By comparison, in an independent search, it is possible to discover where a child might have produced [s], irrespective of the intended target. Figure 2 shows the use of [s] by Child 216 following an independent search of a portion of the data. Here, it is noteworthy that Child 216 did produce [s] but its occurrence extended to words like 'face', 'thief,' and 'fish', target words which obviously do not contain /s/.

The qualitative information that derives from relational and independent analyses of children's data may not always correspond, and therefore a dual approach to the evaluation of data has been recommended in the literature (Stoel-Gammon & Dunn, 1985). On the quantitative side, the relational and independent searches are again relevant. From the different types of searches, it is possible to compute percentages of accuracy using a relational search or percentages of decline in the application of an error pattern using an independent search (e.g., Gierut & Champion, 2000). Quantitative interpretations are crucial to the experimental side of the Learnability Project as discussed in Chapter 3 in this volume.

S# 216

Target Snd	no.	Target Word	PKP pre	PKP phase shift	PKP post	PKP 2wk	PKP 2mo
s	47	eraser	jeɪtʊ	ijeɪtʊ	ijeɪtʊ	əjeɪtʊ	ijeɪtʊ
s	51	baseball	beɪbɔd []	beɪʔbɑ	beɪʔbɔ	beɪʔbɔ	beɪbɔ
s	73	santa	jæ°	dʲæte	tæte	sæte	sæte
bs	108	bus	bʌt	bʌʔ	bʌt	bʌt	bʌt
s	108a	busi	bʌti []	bʌti	bʌti	bʌtʃi	bʌti
sk	125	sock	wɑt	fwɑt	hwɑt	sɑt	fɑt
sp	136	soap	woup	foup	foup	foup	foup˺
s	142	ice	aɪtʃ	aɪt []	aɪt	aɪt	aɪts
s	142a	icy	aɪti	aɪti	aɪti	aɪti	aɪti
sn	147	sun	wʌn	fwʌn	sʌn	sʌn	sʌn
sp	151	soup	wup	fup	fup	sup	sup

s	152	dress	dɛt	dɛt	dɛt	dɛt	dɛt
s	152a	dressy	dɛti	dɛti	dɛdi	dɛti	dɛti
m s	160	mouse	maut	maut []	maut	maut	mautʔ
s	160a	mouse i	maudi	mauti	mauti	mauti	mauti
dʒ s	163	juice	dʒutʃ	dʒut	dʒutʃ	dʒut	dʒut
s	163a	juicy	dʒuti	dʒuti	dʒuti	dʒuti	dʒuti

Figure 1. Example of a relational search of the Developmental Phonology Archive.
A portion of the search results for target /s/ are shown for Child 216. Columns identify the target sound, PKP item number, target word sampled on the PKP, and child's output at pretreatment, phase shift between imitation and spontaneous steps of treatment, posttreatment, 2 weeks and 2 months posttreatment. Transcriptions include diacritic markings and responses cued using delayed imitation [ ].

S# 216

Target Snd	no.	Target Word	PKP pre	PKP phase shift	PKP post	PKP 2wk	PKP 2mo
f	8	face	j e ɪ t	s e ɪ t	s e ɪ t	s e ɪ t	s e ɪ t
w	13	flower	j a u ə	sʲ a u hʲ a u	h j a u wᵊ	tʃ a u	s a u
v	15	seven	j ɛ ʒ ɪ n	hʲ ɛ ɹ j ɛ n	j ɛ ʒ ɛ n	s ɛ ʒ ɛ n	s ɛ ʒ ɛ n
f	39	five	j a ɪ	j a ɪ	j a ɪ	j a ɪ	s a ɪ f a ɪ
z	48	scissors	j i d u	h i d o u	s i z o u	t i d u	s ɪ d u
θ	53	thief	d i t [ ]	h i t	s i t	θ i t	s i t
s	73	santa	j æᵊ	dʲ æ t e	t æ t e	s æ t e	s æ t e
ð	96	feather	j ɛ d ᵊ	j ɛ d ɛ	d j ɛ d ɛ	d ɛ d ɛ s	d ɛ d ɛ s
p	136a	soapy	v w o u p i	f o u p i	ʃ o u p i	t w o u p i	s o u p i
k	144	book	b u d	b u ᵊ t	b u t	b u t	b u tˢ
s n	147	sun	w ʌ n	f w ʌ n	s ʌ n s	s ʌ n	s ʌ n

n	147a	sunny	vʌni	hʌni	sʌni	sʌni	sʌni
sp	151	soup	wup	fup	fup	sup	sup
p	151a	soupy	vupi	hupi	tupi	fupi	ˢupi
p	167	sleep	sip	hip	sip	sip	sip
p	167a	sleeping	jipin	sipin	tʃipin	sipin	slipin
w	183a	sewing	vwouwin	fouwin	fouwin	fouwin	souwin
fʃ	185	fish	djɪtʃ	sɪtʃ	sɪt	ʃɪt	ˢfɪt fɪtʃ
m	198	swim	jɪm	sɪm	sɪm	tsɪm	sɪm
m	198a	swimming	jɪmi	simin	simin	simĩ	simin

Figure 2. Example of an independent search of the Developmental Phonology Archive.
A portion of the search results for [s] as produced by Child 216 are shown. Columns identify the target sound, PKP item number, target word sampled on the PKP, and child's output at pretreatment, phase shift between imitation and spontaneous steps of treatment, posttreatment, 2 weeks and 2 months posttreatment. Transcriptions include diacritic markings and responses cued using delayed imitation [].

In complement to these kinds of searches, the Developmental Phonology Archive has also been structured to facilitate examinations of data across children. An error pattern template (Figure 3) is used to enter each child's phonetic and phonemic inventory, the occurrence and distribution of these sounds, and common error patterns; information about clusters is also recorded, including allowable sonority differences. With this information entered, it is possible to search for all children of a given age who might display a particular set of sounds in the repertoire or a particular pattern of error. An illustration of a pattern search of the Archive is shown in Figure 4. This shows a portion

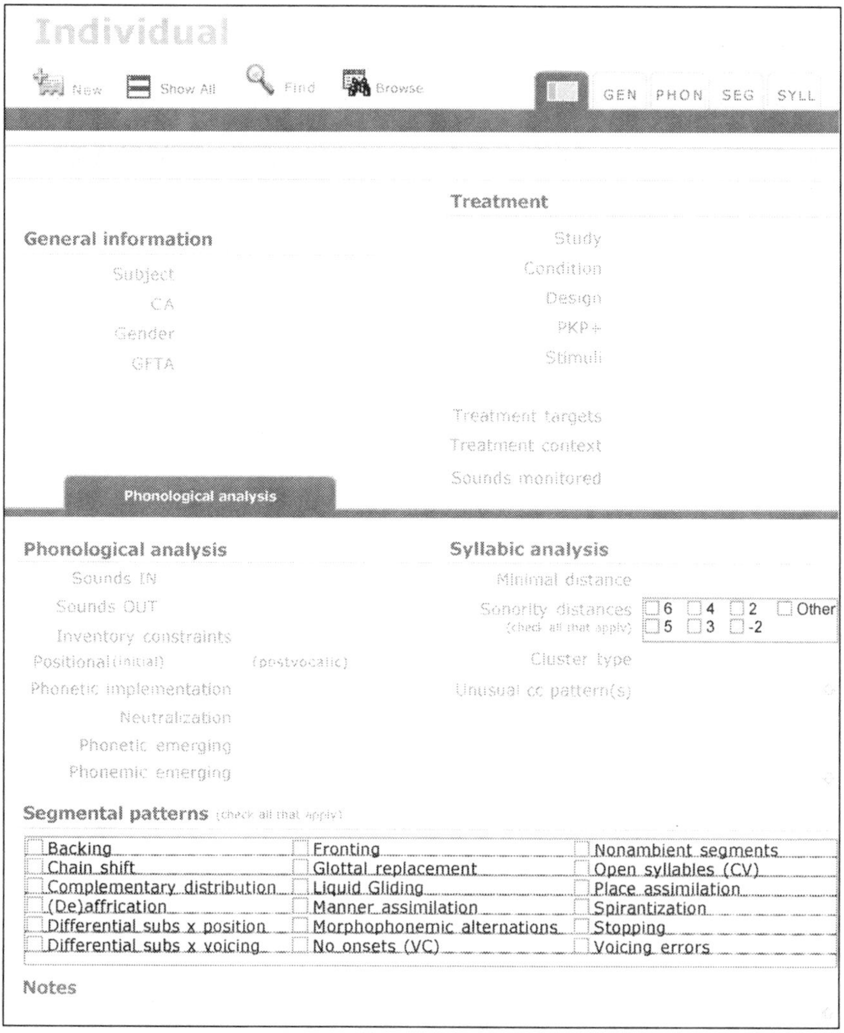

Figure 3. Example of the error pattern template of the Developmental Phonology Archive.

Patterns

New | Show All | Find | Browse

GEN PHON SEG SYLL

Subject	CA	Segmental patterns		
141	4;0	☒ Backing ☐ Chain shift ☐ Complementary distribution ☒ (De)affrication ☒ Differential subs x position	☒ Differential subs x voicing ☒ Fronting ☒ Glottal replacement ☒ Liquid Gliding ☒ Manner assimilation	☐ Morphophonemic alternations ☒ No onsets (VC) ☐ Nonambient segments ☐ Open syllables (CV) ☐ Place assimilation	☐ Spirantization ☒ Stopping ☐ Voicing errors
81	5;4	☒ Backing ☐ Chain shift ☒ Complementary distribution ☐ (De)affrication ☐ Differential subs x position	☐ Differential subs x voicing ☒ Fronting ☒ Glottal replacement ☒ Liquid Gliding ☒ Manner assimilation	☒ Morphophonemic alternations ☒ No onsets (VC) ☒ Nonambient segments ☒ Open syllables (CV) ☒ Place assimilation	☒ Spirantization ☐ Stopping ☒ Voicing errors
99	3;10	☒ Backing ☐ Chain shift ☒ Complementary distribution ☒ (De)affrication ☒ Differential	☒ Differential subs x voicing ☒ Fronting ☒ Glottal replacement ☒ Liquid Gliding ☒ Manner assimilation	☒ Morphophonemic alternations ☒ No onsets (VC) ☒ Nonambient segments ☒ Open syllables (CV) ☒ Place assimilation	☐ Spirantization ☒ Stopping ☐ Voicing errors
152	5;8	☒ Backing ☐ Chain shift ☐ Complementary distribution ☒ (De)affrication ☒ Differential subs x position	☒ Differential subs x voicing ☒ Fronting ☐ Glottal replacement ☒ Liquid Gliding ☒ Manner assimilation	☐ Morphophonemic alternations ☒ No onsets (VC) ☒ Nonambient segments ☒ Open syllables (CV) ☐ Place assimilation	☐ Spirantization ☐ Stopping ☐ Voicing errors
66	3;2	☐ Backing ☐ Chain shift ☒ Complementary distribution ☒ (De)affrication ☒ Differential subs x position	☒ Differential subs x voicing ☒ Fronting ☒ Glottal replacement ☒ Liquid Gliding ☒ Manner assimilation	☒ Morphophonemic alternations ☒ No onsets (VC) ☒ Nonambient segments ☒ Open syllables (CV) ☐ Place assimilation	☐ Spirantization ☐ Stopping ☒ Voicing errors
200	4;1	☒ Backing ☐ Chain shift ☐ Complementary distribution ☒ (De)affrication ☒ Differential subs x position	☒ Differential subs x voicing ☒ Fronting ☒ Glottal replacement ☐ Liquid Gliding ☒ Manner assimilation	☐ Morphophonemic alternations ☒ No onsets (VC) ☒ Nonambient segments ☐ Open syllables (CV) ☐ Place assimilation	☒ Spirantization ☐ Stopping ☒ Voicing errors

Figure 4. Example of a portion of the data returned following a pattern search for manner assimilation.
The search identifies the participants and ages of those exhibiting the relevant pattern. Other error patterns evidenced by the children are also marked.

of the results of children who exhibited manner assimilation. This type of search is useful in establishing co-occurring patterns, as in this example where manner assimilation coincides with deaffrication, fronting, and stopping across children (e.g., Dinnsen & O'Connor, 2001a). A pattern search is also relevant in establishing the typicality of error patterns in children's productions as, for example, the occurrence of velar fronting relative to velar backing in evaluations of stringent relationships within OT (e.g., Morrisette et al., 2003).

3.5 Phonological analyses

Archival searches of the type described are central to the formulation of a phonological analysis of each child's sound system over time. In terms of the analysis, there is a predetermined set of procedures that is followed on the Learnability Project. A sample analysis format is shown in Figure 5 for target fricatives. For each child, information is extracted from the Archive in establishing the phonetic inventory, as based on a two-time occurrence of sounds following from Stoel-Gammon (1985), among others. Also determined is the phonemic inventory, following criteria outlined in Gierut, Simmerman and Neumann (1994). This is based on the occurrence of two unique sets of minimal pairs as extracted from an independent search. If two pairs cannot be identified (as is often the case, for example, with /ŋ/), then relational information is considered in conjunction. Specifically, in the absence of minimal pairs, a sound is deemed phonemic if it is produced with 65% accuracy. Archival data are further used to identify gaps in the segmental repertoire, as well as the distribution of phones and phonemes by context. Morphophonemically-related alternations are noted, as well as variability in production within and across word positions.

Besides singletons, cluster data are examined to determine minimal sonority distance. To be credited with a particular sonority difference, a child must demonstrate two instantiations of that distance, albeit from relational or independent perspectives (Gierut & O'Connor, 2002). For instance, if /tw/ occurs twice in a sample, albeit accurately in 'twelve' and 'twist' or inaccurately as a substitute in 'sled' [twɛd] and 'throw' [twoʊ], then a child is credited with a sonority difference of 6 (cf. Selkirk, 1982).

From this collection of facts, an initial summary (Figure 6) of a child's grammar is developed showing sounds in and out of the phonemic inventory, along with corresponding descriptions about the source of errors. These data have obvious applications for linguistics, but they are also used to establish the phonological properties that warrant treatment in the experimental studies that follow from the description. This is outlined in Chapter 3 in this volume.

Subj. No./Initials: _____

Phono. Anal.: _____

Phoneme	Summary	Min. prs.	Accuracy	Subs. pattern	Morph. alt.	Free var.	
f	inventory positional phonetic impl. neutralization emerging	d.i.? alternation?	# % d.i.? alternation?				
v	inventory positional phonetic impl. neutralization emerging	d.i.? alternation?	# % d.i.? alternation?				
θ	inventory positional phonetic impl. neutralization emerging	d.i.? alternation?	# % d.i.? alternation?				
ð	inventory positional phonetic impl. neutralization emerging	d.i.? alternation?	# % d.i.? alternation?				
s	inventory positional phonetic impl. neutralization emerging	d.i.? alternation?	# % d.i.? alternation?				
z	inventory positional phonetic impl. neutralization emerging	d.i.? alternation?	# % d.i.? alternation?				
ʃ	inventory positional phonetic impl. neutralization emerging	d.i.? alternation?	# % d.i.? alternation?				

Figure 5. Sample phonological analysis sheet for target fricatives.

Data to be evaluated in the analysis includes the characterization of the source of the error, occurrence of minimal pairs, accuracy of productions, substitution patterns by context, and evidence of morphophonemic alternations, free variation, or other unusual production patterns. Also noted is the level of cueing (d.i. as delayed imitation), occurrence of alternations, raw number of occurrences, and percentages of accuracy.

Phonological Analysis _____
Cover Page Summary

Subj. No.: _____ CA: _____ GFTA: _____
Probe: _____ Date administered: _____
R.A.: _____ Date completed: _____

IN

OUT

O
*
☐

O
*
☐

Syllabic analysis
Minimal distance: _____

Sonority distances (check all that apply):
_____ 6   _____ 3
_____ 5   _____ 2
_____ 4   _____ -2

Cluster type:
_____ no cc
_____ ambient cc only
_____ nonambient cc only
_____ ambient and nonambient cc

Unusual cc patterns: ☐ yes   ☐ no

Treatment summary
Treatment target: _____

Study/condition: _____

BL: PKP+ _____

Sounds monitored:
_____

Segmental Patterns

☐ Backing	☐ Fronting	☐ Nonambient segments
☐ Chain shift	☐ Glottal replacement	☐ Open syllables (CV)
☐ Complementary dist	☐ Liquid Gliding	☐ Place assimilation
☐ (De)affrication	☐ Manner assimilation	☐ Spirantization
☐ Differential subs X posit	☐ Morphophonemic alt	☐ Stopping
☐ Differential subs X voice	☐ No onsets (VC)	☐ Voicing errors

Notes

Figure 6. Phonological analysis summary of the phonetic, phonemic, and syllabic properties of a child's grammar and corresponding error patterns.

3.6   Complementary phonological data

A few other features of the Learnability Project descriptive protocol warrant mention. In particular, we have developed two measures that are specific to the evaluation of manner and place assimilation in children; these are shown in Tables 5 and 6, respectively. The Manner (MAP) and Place (PAP) Assimilation Probes were designed to elicit supplementary data from children who exhibit consonant harmony because the PKP falls short in this regard. Note that the assimilatory probes elicit two kinds of data: baseline items demonstrate that the relevant consonants occur in nonassimilatory contexts, and mono- and multisyllabic items establish that these same consonants fall prey to assimilation in other triggering contexts. A demonstration of the differential occurrence of sounds that is crucial to establishing assimilation is typically lacking in the acquisition literature (Cruttenden, 1978; Vihman, 1978) .

Table 5. Manner Assimilation Probe (MAP).

Target	Probe Words
Baseline items	
CV	mow, zoo, pie, shoe, key, chew, see, row, sew, you
VC	in, ear, ape, eat, off, ice, edge
CVC	man, cat, moon, cut, pig, coat, boot, goat, bite, face, bed, fish, back, five, book, vase, bag, thief, big, these, duck, shave, dog, judge, cob, roll
Monosyllabic Assimilation	
Nasal-Stop	map, nap, mop, nut, mud
Nasal-Fricative	mouse, nose, mouth, noise, knife
Nasal-Affricate	match, much
Nasal-Liquid	mail, nail, mall, near, more
Stop-Nasal	open, done, pan, comb, pinecone, game, bone, gum, tongue
Stop-Fricative	push, toes, bath, dish, bus, cough, buzz, kiss, teeth, give, tooth
Stop-Affricate	peach, catch, page, cage, badge
Stop-Liquid	pool, towel, ball, deer, bear, door, tail, call, tear
Fricative-Nasal	fan, same, van, sun, them, song, thumb
Fricative-Stop	fat, soup, feet, shot, that, sick, soap, sock
Fricative-Affricate	fetch, fudge
Fricative-Liquid	fall, seal, full, other, four, over, there
Affricate-Nasal	chime, chin, chain
Affricate-Stop	chip, chick, chalk, jeep, cheek, jet
Affricate-Fricative	chief, juice, chase, jaws, cheese
Affricate-Liquid	chair, Jill, cheer, jar, jail, jelly
Liquid-Nasal	lime, rain, limb, run, room, ring
Liquid-Stop	lake, rub, lick, read, leg, rake, robe, rock
Liquid-Fricative	laugh, roof, leaf, wreath, lash, rose
Liquid-Affricate	latch, rich, ledge
Glide-Nasal	win, yawn, wing
Glide-Stop	web, wick, wet
Glide-Fricative	wave, wish, wash, yes
Glide-Affricate	watch, witch
Glide-Liquid	wear, yell, yellow, your

Table 6. Place Assimilation Probe (PAP).

Target	Probe Words
Baseline items	
Labial-V	pie, boy
Coronal-V	knee, tie
Dorsal-V	cow, go
V-Labial	ape, up
V-Coronal	on, eat
V-Dorsal	egg, ache
Labial-Labial	bib
Labial-Dorsal	pig, bug, back, wing, book
Coronal-Coronal	done
Dorsal-Labial	comb, game, cap, gum, cup
Dorsal-Dorsal	cake
Dorsal-Labial-Dorsal	comic
Monosyllabic Assimiliation	
Labial-Coronal	moon, boot, mouse, fish, pin
Coronal-Labial	tape, knife, top, soup, tub
Coronal-Dorsal	neck, sick, duck, cheek, dog
Dorsal-Coronal	can, gun, cat, goat, kiss
Multisyllabic Assimilation	
Labial-Labial-Coronal	muppet, pepper, muffin, woman, puppet
Labial-Coronal-Labial	bottom
Labial-Coronal-Coronal	mitten, button, mother, feather, police
Labial-Coronal-Dorsal	magic, biting, music, fishing, pushing
Labial-Dorsal-Coronal	pocket, bucket, package, wagon, bacon
Coronal-Labial-Coronal	towel, shovel, seven, rabbit, zipper
Coronal-Labial-Dorsal	napping, shaving, dipping, laughing, zipping
Coronal-Coronal-Labial	tulip, syrup, giraffe
Coronal-Coronal-Dorsal	nothing, reading, tooting, riding, raining
Coronal-Dorsal-Coronal	naked, chicken, ticket, jacket, tiger
Coronal-Dorsal-Dorsal	knocking, sucking, ticking, joking, digging
Dorsal-Labial-Coronal	comet, cabin, camel, cover
Dorsal-Coronal-Labial	ketchup, gallop
Dorsal-Coronal-Coronal	kitten, carrot, kitchen, color
Dorsal-Coronal-Dorsal	cutting, catching, kissing, calling
Dorsal-Dorsal-Coronal	cocoon

In terms of cross-linguistic evidence, we have developed a probe for Korean that is mirrored after the PKP, which is shown in Table 7. The K-PKP was designed specifically to examine the emergence of contrasts in typical development, with a focus on the 3-way laryngeal distinction relative to place and manner. With respect to typical phonological development, we have supplemented the Developmental Phonology Archive with a smaller set of corpora from toddlers learning Korean and also English. These include facilitating electronic searches of the data from Amahl (Smith, 1973). As relevant, the supplementary descriptive elements that we have added follow the protocols outlined for elicitation, recording, transcription and reliability, data entry and reliability, archival entry, and phonological analysis.

Table 7. Korean Phonological Knowledge Protocol (K-PKP).

Target			Gloss
/p/	/pam/	[pam]	night
	/pap/	[pap]	cooked rice
	/pæ/	[pæ]	ship, pear
/pʼ/	/pʼaŋ/	[pʼaŋ]	bread
	/pʼalkaŋ/	[pʼalgaŋ]	red
	/pʼuŋpʼuŋ/	[pʼuŋpʼuŋ]	sound of car
/pʰ/	/pʰoto/	[pʰodo]	grape
	/pʰatʰ/	[pʰat]	red bean
	/pʰal/	[pʰal]	arm
	/pʰuŋsən/	[pʰuŋsən]	balloon
/t/	/tantʃʰu/	[tantʃʰu]	button
	/talamtʃwi/	[taramdʒwi]	squirrel
	/taŋkiŋ/	[taŋgɨn]	carrot
/tʼ/	/tʼək/	[tʼək]	rice cake
	/tʼalki/	[tʼalgi]	strawberry
	/tʼallaɲtʼallaŋ/	[tʼallaɲtʼallaŋ]	sound of bell

Target			Gloss
/tʰ/	/tʰokˀi/	[tʰokˀi]	rabbit
	/tʰal/	[tʰal]	mask
	/tʰəl/	[tʰəl]	hair
/k/	/kækuli/	[kæguri]	frog
	/kapaŋ/	[kabaŋ]	bag
	/kuk/	[kuk]	soup
/kˀ/	/kˀamaŋ/	[kˀamaŋ]	black
	/kˀotʃʰ/	[kˀot]	flower
	/kˀəm/	[kˀəm]	chewing gum
/kʰ/	/kʰo/	[kʰo]	nose
	/kʰal/	[kʰal]	knife
	/kʰokˀili/	[kʰokˀiri]	elephant
/tʃ/	/tʃənhwa/	[tʃənhwa]	telephone
	/tʃam/	[tʃam]	sleep
	/tʃəntiŋ/	[tʃəndiŋ]	electric light
/tʃˀ/	/tʃˀatʃaŋmyən/	[tʃˀadʒaŋmyən]	Chinese noodle
	/tʃˀata/	[tʃˀada]	salty
	/tʃˀikæ/	[tʃˀigæ]	Korean soup
/tʃʰ/	/tʃʰimtæ/	[tʃʰimdæ]	bed
	/tʃʰæk/	[tʃʰæk]	book
	/tʃʰaŋmun/	[tʃʰaŋmun]	window

Target			Gloss
/s/	/sakwa/	[sagwa]	apple
	/sæ/	[sæ]	bird
	/satʃin/	[sadʒin]	picture
	/satɑli/	[sadɑri]	ladder
/ʃ/	/sikye/	[ʃigye]	watch
	/sikɨmtʃʰi/	[ʃigimtʃʰi]	spinach
	/sinpal/	[ʃinbɑl]	shoes
/sˀ/	/sˀəlmæ/	[sˀəlmæ]	sled
	/sˀista/	[sˀittˀa]	V. wash
	/sˀal/	[sˀal]	raw rice
/h/	/hanil/	[hanil]	sky
	/holaŋi/	[horaŋi]	tiger
	/hæ/	[hæ]	sun
/m/	/motʃa/	[modʒa]	hat
	/mul/	[mul]	water
	/mal/	[mal]	horse
/n/	/namu/	[namu]	tree
	/napi/	[nabi]	butterfly
	/nalta/	[nalda]	V. fly
	/naktʰa/	[naktʰa]	camel

4   Closing remarks

In summary, the descriptive data that have amassed on the Learnability Project have aided in delineating the characteristics of children with functional phonological disorders. Importantly, the data hold clinical, theoretical, and experimental utility in advancing research on language acquisition. On the clinical side, the demographic data used in identification of participants to the Learnability Project help in delineating the general traits of the population. The data also pinpoint common patterns of production within the group, along with any anomalies for use in differential diagnosis of the disorder. Theoretically, the sheer amount of data, coupled with the ability to conduct online searches, has allowed for tests of linguistic hypotheses within the context of language acquisition. In this way, acquisition data may be used to validate, refute, and refine current linguistic models. Experimentally, the descriptive protocol of the Learnability Project (as described in Chapter 3 in this volume) sets the stage for our manipulation of linguistic variables in clinical treatment. This is yet another venue for the validation of linguistic theory, but it has applied consequences in establishing the efficacy of clinical treatment. While the study of language acquisition in an atypical population may not be a mainstream research approach, it is a mutually beneficial paradigm for advancing theoretical and applied sciences that aim for a better understanding of the structure, emergence, and change in grammar.

Appendix

This supplement provides a full listing of the Learnability Project probe words that are used in sampling children's sound systems. It includes words from the Phonological Knowledge Protocol, Onset Cluster Probe, Coda Cluster Probe, Manner Assimilation Probe, and Place Assimilation Probe. Each word is coded in terms of dimensions of structure that may be of value to scientists, clinicians, and students in the design of research and/or clinical programs. The codings include the canonical shape of a word, its raw frequency, neighborhood density, phonotactic probability, lexical familiarity, and estimated age of word acquisition. The codings are, for the most part, based on published analyses of phonological and lexical structure, and are consistent with general research use and application in the published literature. Where there is departure, this is noted. Also, some of the probe items are not included in published corpora, and consequently, corresponding structural data are unavailable. In these instances, the relevant cell is left blank. The operational definitions and source of the codings is outlined below.

Canonical shape[a] is the consonant-vowel composition of the intended target output. Each sound of a word is given full segmental status, which departs from some codings (e.g., Hoosier Mental Lexicon) that weight sonorants as vocalic in nature. In alternate codings, the canonical structure of a word like 'bear' would be CV, whereas in our usage, this same word is coded as CVC on our probes.

Raw frequency[b] is the number of times a given word occurs in printed form in target English. The counts are taken from Kučera and Francis (1967) and based on a sample size of 1,000,000 words. A raw frequency value of 4, as for example for the word 'ache,' means that this particular word occurred 4 times out of the pool of 1,000,000 words studied.

Neighborhood density[c] defines the degree of phonetic similarity of a given word based on one-phoneme substitutions, additions, and deletions (Luce, 1986). For example, for the probe word 'ache,' some possible neighbors include 'ate' (substitution), 'bake' (addition), or 'A' (deletion). The density counts are drawn from the Hoosier Mental Lexicon, which is based on the 20,000 word Merriam-Webster Pocket Dictionary (Nusbaum et al., 1984).

Phonotactic probability[d] refers to the statistical likelihood of a given segment in English. The likelihood of occurrence has been defined in terms of biphone frequency and positional segment frequency. Biphone frequency refers to the likelihood of a given pair of phonemes occurring in sequence relative to all other possible sequences that could occur in the language. For example, in the word 'ache,' biphone frequency establishes the likelihood of [e] being followed by [k] relative to all other cooccurrences, such as [et], [ep], or [sk] as examples. The biphone values reflect the sum of individual biphone frequencies within a word. Positional segment frequency refers to the likelihood of a given sound occurring in a given position in a form. In our example, positional segment frequency establishes that probability that [e] occurs in the first position of a form relative to [s] or [u] or [h] as examples. The positional segment values reflect the sum of individual segment frequencies within a word. An on-line phonotactic probability calculator was used to compute the values we report (http://www.people.ku.edu/~mvitevit/).

Familiarity[e] is based on subjective ratings of the familiarity of words, as reported for the Hoosier Mental Lexicon (Nusbaum et al., 1984). Adult judges rated words of the Merriam-Webster Pocket Dictionary on a 7-point scale, with 7 being most familiar.

Age-of-word acquisition[f] (AoA) is a learner's estimate of when a given word was acquired. Like familiarity, it too is based on a subjective rating. The AoA ratings we report are based on Bird, Franklin, and Howard (2001), as the most current and comprehensive set of estimates available. It is based on a 7-point rating scale, where the rating of 1 equals an estimated age of word learning between 0 and 2 years; 2, between 3 and 4 years; 3, between 5 and 6 years, and so on to the rating of 7, which corresponds to an estimated age of word learning of 13 years and older. In cases where our probe words were not included in the Bird et al. corpus, we supplemented the AoA ratings with comparable data from Gilhooly and Logie[g] (1980a; 1980b).

Probe word	Canonical Shape[a]	Raw Frequency[b]	Neighborhood Density[c]	Phonotactic Probability[d] Biphone Frequency	Phonotactic Probability[d] Positional Segment Frequency	Familiarity[e]	Age-of-Word Acquisition[f]
ache	VC	4	24	0.0004	0.0313	7	
angel	VCCVC	18	1	0.0016	0.0958	7	2.42[g]
ape	VC	3	17	0.0003	0.0243	7	3.24
arm	VCC	94	9	0.006	0.1528	7	1.92[g]
ask	VCC	128	8	0.0027	0.0937	7	1.95
back	CVC	967	32	0.0113	0.1841	7	3.13
back-i	CVCV			0.0127	0.2273		
bacon	CVCVC	10	5	0.021	0.2514	7	
badge	CVC	5	13	0.0067	0.1414	6.9167	
badge-i	CVCV			0.0071	0.1846		
bag	CVC	42	28	0.0087	0.1485	7	2.17[g]

Probe word	Canonical Shape[a]	Raw Frequency[b]	Neighborhood Density[c]	Phonotactic Probability[d] Biphone Frequency	Positional Segment Frequency	Familiarity[e]	Age-of-Word Acquisition[f]
baggy	CVCV	4	3	0.0092	0.1917	6.9167	
ball	CVC	110	24	0.0043	0.1414	7	1.5[g]
barb	CVCC	1	10	0.0221	0.208	5.8333	5.28[g]
bark	CVCC	14	15	0.0228	0.2323	7	
barn	CVCC	29	11	0.0227	0.2368	7	2.98[g]
baseball	CVCCVC	57	0	0.0062	0.2192	7	
bath	CVC	26	17	0.0069	0.138	7	1.91
bath-i	CVCV			0.0072	0.1812		
bear	CVC	57		0.0107	0.2025		2.2
beauty	CCVCV	71	3	0.0123	0.2036	7	3.44[g]
bed	CVC	127	25	0.0069	0.1621	7	1.69[g]
bed-i	CVCV			0.0106	0.2053		
behind	CVCVCC	258		0.0104	0.2201		2.27
belt	CVCC	29	17	0.0158	0.2872	7	
bib	CVC	2	13	0.0064	0.1734	6.8333	
big	CVC	360	20	0.0076	0.1653	6.9167	1.55
bird	CVCC	31	22	0.0031	0.1139	7	2.06[g]
birth	CVCC	66		0.0022	0.0833		3.17
bite	CVC	10		0.0057	0.1515		2.14[g]
biting	CVCVC	6	2	0.0193	0.2125	6.8333	
black	CCVC	203	10	0.0156	0.1664	7	2.08
blanket	CCVCCVC	30	0	0.0316	0.3305	7	2.11[g]
blocks	CCVCC	37		0.0115	0.2134		
blonde	CCVCC	20	5	0.0151	0.1959	7	
blow	CCV(C)	33	15	0.0079	0.1145	7	
blowing	CCV(C)VC	19		0.0160	0.1754		
blue	CCV	143		0.0075	0.1106		2.06
bluehouse	CCVCVC			0.0081	0.172		
bone	CVC	33	30	0.0045	0.1966	7	
book	CVC	193	18	0.0022	0.1149	6.9091	1.74
book-i	CVCV			0.0036	0.1581		

Probe word	Canonical Shape[a]	Raw Frequency[b]	Neighborhood Density[c]	Phonotactic Probability[d] Biphone Frequency	Positional Segment Frequency	Familiarity[e]	Age-of-Word Acquisition[f]
boot	CVC	13	32	0.0039	0.1393	7	2.51[g]
bootie	CVCV	1	7	0.0069	0.1825	6.8333	
bottom	CVCVC	88	2	0.0068	0.1793	6.9167	1.85
bounce	CVCC	8	4	0.0147	0.2071	6.9167	
box	CVCC	70	5	0.0122	0.2153	7	3.4
boy	CV	242	13	0.0003	0.0546	7	1.5
branch	CCVCC	33	5	0.0265	0.2237	6.75	3.03[g]
bread	CCVC	42	15	0.0166	0.2083	7	
bridge	CCVC	98	6	0.0218	0.1887	6.9167	2.84
bridge-i	CCVCV			0.0226	0.2291		
broom	CCVC	2	10	0.0135	0.1867	6.9167	
brother	CCVCVC	73	0	0.0121	0.1986	7	2.19[g]
brown	CCVC	176	10	0.0107	0.1931	7	2.43
brush	CCVC	44	5	0.0114	0.1631	7	2.36
brushing	CCVCVC	6		0.0176	0.2172		
bubble	CVCVC	12	10	0.0096	0.1392	7	2.72[g]
bucket	CVCVC	7	1	0.0202	0.2658	7	
bug	CVC	4	26	0.0047	0.1083	7	3.83
burglar	CVCCCVC	1		0.0044	0.1725		
burp	CVCC	1	8	0.0026	0.113	6.3333	
bus	CVC	35	20	0.0073	0.1692	7	
bus-i	CVCV			0.0094	0.2124		
button	CVCVC	10	6	0.0082	0.1665	7	1.92[g]
buzz	CVC	13	15	0.0044	0.1105	7	
buzzing	CVCVC	6		0.0139	0.1715		
cabin	CVCVC	23	1	0.0287	0.3156	6.9167	
cage	CVC	9	17	0.0027	0.1327	7	3[g]
cage-i	CVCV			0.0031	0.1759		
cake	CVC	13	26	0.004	0.1754	7	2.14[g]
call	CVC	188	26	0.006	0.1829	7	2.54
calling	CVCVC	45	3	0.0199	0.2439	7	

Probe word	Canonical Shape[a]	Raw Frequency[b]	Neighborhood Density[c]	Phonotactic Probability[d]		Familiarity[e]	Age-of-Word Acquisition[f]
				Biphone Frequency	Positional Segment Frequency		
camel	CVCVC	1	8	0.0177	0.2443	7	3.03
camera	CVCCV	36	0	0.0225	0.3539	7	
can	CVC	1772	35	0.0266	0.2682	7	1.97
cap	CVC	27	30	0.017	0.2092	7	
card	CVCC	26	15	0.0362	0.2719	6.5	
carrot	CVCVC	1		0.0373	0.4098		
cars	CVCC	112		0.033	0.2437		
cart	CVCC	5	14	0.0392	0.321	7	2.58[g]
carve	CVCC	3	4	0.033	0.2463	6.9167	3.62
cat	CVC	23	35	0.0181	0.2381	7	
catch	CVC	43	20	0.0137	0.1801	7	
catching	CVCVC	9		0.0216	0.2411		
chain	CVC	50	19	0.0036	0.1342	7	3.11[g]
chair	CVC	66	20	0.0085	0.1602	7	
chair-i	CVCV			0.0155	0.2034		
chalk	CVC	3	13	0.0011	0.0789	7	
change	CVCC	240	3	0.0062	0.1454	6.5	3.32
chase	CVC	18	17	0.0036	0.1169	7	2.82
cheek	CVC	20	21	0.0028	0.0942	7	2.67[g]
cheer	CVC	8	27	0.0065	0.1835	7	3.08
cheese	CVC	9	13	0.0021	0.0608	7	2.11[g]
cheezy	CVCV			0.0036	0.104		
chew	CV	2	19	0.0002	0.031	7	2.23
chick	CVC	3	23	0.0099	0.1586	7	
chicken	CVCVC	37		0.0273	0.2762		2.5[g]
chief	CVC	119	12	0.0015	0.0604	7	
chime	CVC	1	8	0.0018	0.0926	7	
chin	CVC	27	21	0.0108	0.2012	7	
chip	CVC	17	24	0.0062	0.1422	6.9167	
chip-i	CVCV			0.0075	0.1854		
chirp	CVCC	1	9	0.0011	0.0707	7	

Probe word	Canonical Shape[a]	Raw Frequency[b]	Neighborhood Density[c]	Phonotactic Probability[d]		Familiarity[e]	Age-of-Word Acquisition[f]
				Biphone Frequency	Positional Segment Frequency		
church	CVCC	348	8	0.0013	0.0416	7	2.78[g]
clean	CCVC	70	11	0.0103	0.2029	7	2.13
clock	CCVC	20	15	0.0106	0.2	7	
clothes	CCVC	89	7	0.0101	0.1681	6.4167	1.94[g]
cloud	CCVC	28	7	0.0079	0.1816	7	
clown	CCVC	3	5	0.0089	0.188	7	
coat	CVC	43	31	0.0105	0.208	7	1.97[g]
cob	CVC	1	22	0.0185	0.1792	6.5	
cob-i	CVCV			0.0201	0.2224		
cocoon	CVCVC	3	0	0.0188	0.2748	7	
cold	CVCC	171	15	0.0159	0.256	7	1.8
color	CVCVC	141	8	0.0114	0.2564	7	
comb	CVC	6	24	0.0086	0.1914	7	2.17
comb-i	CVCV			0.0103	0.2346		
comet	CVCVC	2	4	0.0397	0.3619	6.9167	
comic	CVCVC	9	3	0.0341	0.2891	6.6667	
corn	CVCC	34	20	0.0268	0.2671	6.5	
cough	CVC	7	11	0.0031	0.1289	7	2.26
coughing	CVCVC	3		0.0123	0.1899		
cover	CVCVC	88	4	0.0084	0.2063	7	2.89[g]
cow	CV	29	19	0.0018	0.1024	7	1.74
crack	CCVC	21	18	0.0233	0.2545	6.9091	3.05
cracker	CCVCVC	1	2	0.0244	0.2977	6.8333	
crash	CCVC	20	13	0.0205	0.2214	7	
crashing	CCVCVC	7		0.0267	0.2755		
crawl	CCVC	11	9	0.0119	0.2242	7	
crayon	CCVCVC	1	2	0.0175	0.2908	7	
cream	CCVC	20	12	0.0185	0.2323	6.9167	2.45
cry	CCV	48	10	0.015	0.196	7	1.59
cup	CVC	45	18	0.0055	0.169	7	
cup-i	CVCV			0.0068	0.2122		

Probe word	Canonical Shape[a]	Raw Frequency[b]	Neighborhood Density[c]	Phonotactic Probability[d]		Familiarity[e]	Age-of-Word Acquisition[f]
				Biphone Frequency	Positional Segment Frequency		
curb	CVCC	13	12	0.0029	0.1434	6.5	
curl	CVCC	2	23	0.0026	0.1911	7	3.2
curve	CVCC	45	13	0.0028	0.141	7	3.64[g]
cut	CVC	192	25	0.0067	0.1979	7	
cute	CCVC	5	6	0.0085	0.2047	7	
cutting	CVCVC	66	2	0.0203	0.2589	7	
dance	CVCC	90	6	0.0264	0.2774	6.75	2.69
deer	CVC	13		0.0204	0.2264		2.81[g]
deer-i	CVCV			0.0274	0.2696		
desk	CVCC	65	3	0.0198	0.2457	6.9167	
digging	CVCVC	7		0.0269	0.2269		
dipping	CVCVC	1		0.0291	0.2461		
dish	CVC	16	12	0.0164	0.1557	7	
dog	CVC	75	8	0.0016	0.0862	7	1.69[g]
doggie	CVCV			0.0021	0.1294		
done	CVC	321	30	0.0081	0.1871	7	
door	CVC	312	13	0.0018	0.1108	7	2.14[g]
door-i	CVCV			0.002	0.154		
draw	CCV	56	6	0.0066	0.1478	7	2.22
dress	CCVC	67	9	0.0145	0.2187	6.8333	2.31
dressy	CCVCV	2		0.0175	0.2591		
drink	CCVCC	82	6	0.0229	0.2215	7	1.66
drive	CCVC	105	9	0.0115	0.1698	7	3.3
driving	CCVCVC	53	3	0.0185	0.2239	6.8333	
drum	CCVC	11	10	0.0103	0.1841	7	3.19
duck	CVC	9	25	0.0043	0.1445	6.75	1.64[g]
duckie	CVCV			0.0057	0.1877		
ear	VC	29	31	0.0026	0.1536	7	
Earth	VCC	150	12	0.0003	0.0032	7	3.17[g]
eat	VC	61	24	0.0002	0.0308	7	1.67
eating	VCVC	32		0.0041	0.0714		

Probe word	Canonical Shape[a]	Raw Frequency[b]	Neighborhood Density[c]	Phonotactic Probability[d]		Familiarity[e]	Age-of-Word Acquisition[f]
				Biphone Frequency	Positional Segment Frequency		
edge	VC	78	15	0.0003	0.0195	7	3.08[g]
egg	VC	12		0.0003	0.0227		1.86[g]
elephant	VCVCVCC	7	1	0.0345	0.3764	7	2.22[g]
eraser	VCVCVC	2		0.0102	0.2612		
face	CVC	371	21	0.0049	0.1546	7	1.78
fall	CVC	147	26	0.005	0.1368	7	2.1
fan	CVC	18	21	0.0178	0.2221	7	
farm	CVCC	125	6	0.0214	0.215	7	2.56
fat	CVC	60	28	0.0093	0.192	7	2.36[g]
father	CVCVC	183	6	0.0039	0.161	7	1.85
feather	CVCVC	6	8	0.0051	0.1734	7	
feet	CVC	283		0.0042	0.1444		
fence	CVCC	30	10	0.0278	0.2657	7	4.67
fetch	CVC	6	9	0.0031	0.1275	7	2.84
few	CCV	601	12	0.007	0.0692	6.9167	2.92
filth	CVCC	2	9	0.014	0.2211	7	
finger	CVCCVC	40	1	0.0122	0.2114	7	
fire	CV(CV)C	187	22	0.0036	0.1593	7	1.89
fire-i	CV(CV)CV			0.0106	0.2025		
fish	CVC	35	13	0.0059	0.1505	7	2.75
fishing	CVCVC	32		0.0139	0.2115		
five	CVC	286	12	0.0032	0.1045	7	2.08
fix	CVCC	14	10	0.0182	0.2464	7	
flag	CCVC	16	8	0.0147	0.1333	7	2.58[g]
floor	CCVC	158	6	0.0093	0.1607	7	2.04
flower	CCVCVC	23	5	0.0072	0.146	7	1.83
flute	CCVC	1	12	0.0107	0.1954	7	
fly	CCV	33	13	0.0085	0.1033	7	2
foot	CVC	70	10	0.0014	0.1228	7	1.63
foot-i	CVCV			0.0044	0.166		
forehead	CVCCVC	16	0	0.0258	0.2427	6.5	

Probe word	Canonical Shape[a]	Raw Frequency[b]	Neighborhood Density[c]	Phonotactic Probability[d] Biphone Frequency	Phonotactic Probability[d] Positional Segment Frequency	Familiarity[e]	Age-of-Word Acquisition[f]
fork	CVCC	14	13	0.0267	0.2165	7	2.25[g]
four	CVC	359		0.0239	0.1743		1.89
french (fries)	CCVCC	139	4	0.0198	0.2163	7	
friend	CCVCC	133	5	0.0242	0.243	7	2.36
(french) fries	CCVC			0.0115	0.162		
frog	CCVC	1	4	0.0076	0.1563	7	2.58[g]
frog-i	CCVCV			0.0077	0.1967		
front	CCVCC	221	5	0.016	0.2756	7	2.44
fruit	CCVC	35	7	0.0113	0.242	6.9167	2.19[g]
fudge	CVC	1	6	0.0015	0.0966	7	2.78[g]
full	CVC	230	15	0.0026	0.1305	7	
gallop	CVCVC	4	2	0.0234	0.2784	6.8333	
game	CVC	123	20	0.0028	0.1046	6.9167	2.42[g]
game-i	CVCV			0.0045	0.1478		
gasp	CVCC	3	6	0.0185	0.2204	7	4.35
gate	CVC	37		0.0042	0.1212		
George	CVCC	129		0.0190	0.1527		
giraffe	CVCVC	1	1	0.0023	0.067	7	3.42
girl	CVCC	220	16	0.0014	0.1244	7	1.83[g]
give	CVC	391	7	0.0043	0.1458	7	2.43
glasses	CCVCVC	29		0.0169	0.2073		
globe	CCVC	13	8	0.0068	0.1072	6.8333	3.64[g]
glove	CCVC	9	3	0.0067	0.0969	7	2.28[g]
glove-i	CCVCV			0.0077	0.1373		
glow	CCV	16	13	0.006	0.0893	7	
glue	CCV	8	11	0.0056	0.0854	7	3.04
go	CV	626	26	0.0015	0.0753	6.8333	2.21
goat	CVC	6	26	0.0056	0.1413	7	2.82
gold	CVCC	52	15	0.011	0.1893	7	3.05
golf	CVCC	56	4	0.0079	0.1548	7	4.63
Goofy	CVCV			0.0014	0.111		

Probe word	Canonical Shape[a]	Raw Frequency[b]	Neighborhood Density[c]	Phonotactic Probability[d]		Familiarity[e]	Age-of-Word Acquisition[f]
				Biphone Frequency	Positional Segment Frequency		
grandma	CCV(CC)CV	13		0.0208	0.1892		
grapes	CCVCC	7		0.0145	0.2227		
grasp	CCVCC	17	3	0.0225	0.2152	7	
grass	CCVC	53	13	0.021	0.1957	7	
grasshopper	CCVCCVCVC			0.0228	0.2515		
green	CCVC	116	13	0.0171	0.1828	7	2.25[g]
grow	CCV(C)	63	18	0.0146	0.1359	7	
growing	CCV(C)VC	108		0.0212	0.1966		
gulp	CVCC	2	5	0.0073	0.1751	7	
gum	CVC	14	16	0.0067	0.1146	7	
gummy	CVCV	2		0.0084	0.1578		
gun	CVC	118	20	0.0073	0.1613	7	2.28[g]
hamburger	CVCCVCCVC	6	0	0.0149	0.2308	7	
hammer	CVCVC	9	6	0.0124	0.219	7	2.97
hand	CVCC	431	13	0.0327	0.2552	7	
happy	CVCV	98	3	0.0113	0.1991	7	2.58
hat	CVC	56	34	0.0111	0.1848	7	
health	CVCC	105	7	0.0131	0.1906	7	4[g]
heart	CVCC	173		0.0262	0.2677		2.81[g]
hearth	CVCC	4	6	0.0205	0.1829	5.8333	
help	CVCC	311	11	0.0139	0.2222	7	2.62
hide	CVC	22	21	0.0056	0.1117	7	2.56[g]
hiding	CVCVC	17	3	0.0172	0.1725	6.9167	3.72
hill	CVC	72	33	0.013	0.2093	7	2.56[g]
hilly	CVCV			0.0189	0.2525		
horn	CVCC	31	13	0.0232	0.2138	7	3.08[g]
horse	CVCC	117		0.0229	0.2171		2.08
house	CVC	591	7	0.0019	0.1279	7	1.89
hug	CVC	3	21	0.0037	0.0965	7	2.45
hugging	CVCVC	7		0.0119	0.1575		
ice	VC	45	16	0.0008	0.0142	7	2.53

Probe word	Canonical Shape[a]	Raw Frequency[b]	Neighborhood Density[c]	Phonotactic Probability[d]		Familiarity[e]	Age-of-Word Acquisition[f]
				Biphone Frequency	Positional Segment Frequency		
iceberg	VCCVCC			0.0014	0.0591		
icy	VCV	12	4	0.0009	0.033	6.8333	
in	VC	21350	26	0.0359	0.1206	7	2.05
jacket	CVCVC	33		0.0088	0.2749		
jail	CVC	21		0.0033	0.1167		
jar	CVC	16	16	0.0172	0.1527	7	2.42[g]
jaws	CVC	10		0.0008	0.0504		
jeep	CVC	16		0.0026	0.0827		
jelly	CVCV	3	5	0.0176	0.2036	7	
jet	CVC	29	20	0.0079	0.1527	7	
Jill	CVC			0.0105	0.1837		
joking	CVCVC	5		0.0113	0.1776		
judge	CVC	77	6	0.0019	0.0638	7	4.48
juice	CVC	11	13	0.0027	0.1147	7	2.5[g]
juicy	CVCV	6	1	0.0048	0.1579	7	
jump	CVCC	24	8	0.0156	0.1386	7	2.22[g]
ketchup	CVCVC	1		0.0143	0.207		
key	CV	88		0.006	0.1245		
kiss	CVC	17	13	0.0188	0.2677	7	
kissing	CVCVC	6		0.0304	0.3287		
kitchen	CVCVC	90	0	0.0172	0.3144	7	2.34
kitten	CVCVC	5	7	0.0103	0.265	7	2.13
knee	CV	35	31	0.0017	0.0556	7	2.31[g]
knife	CVC	76	8	0.0027	0.0778	6.75	
knife-i	CVCV			0.0033	0.121		
knocking	CVCVC	5		0.0154	0.1987		
ladder	CVCVC	19	10	0.0115	0.2023	6.75	
lady	CVCV	80	6	0.0079	0.1445	7	2.31[g]
lake	CVC	54	32	0.0039	0.1168	7	
lamp	CVCC	18	11	0.0185	0.1991	7	2.83[g]
large	CVCC	361	7	0.0189	0.1842	7	2.84

Probe word	Canonical Shape[a]	Raw Frequency[b]	Neighborhood Density[c]	Phonotactic Probability[d]		Familiarity[e]	Age-of-Word Acquisition[f]
				Biphone Frequency	Positional Segment Frequency		
lash	CVC	6	26	0.0065	0.1212	6.1667	
latch	CVC	5	18	0.006	0.1215	7	3.86g
laugh	CVC	28	19	0.0058	0.1332	7	2.3
laughing	CVCVC	27		0.015	0.1942		
leaf	CVC	12	25	0.0033	0.0856	7	
leafy	CVCV	1		0.0039	0.1288		
ledge	CVC	6	18	0.0056	0.1178	6.8333	
leg	CVC	58	15	0.0056	0.1249	7	1.65
lick	CVC	3	32	0.0148	0.1838	6.75	
lift	CVCC	23	11	0.0115	0.2394	7	2.77
light	CVC	333	35	0.007	0.1344	7	2.95
limb	CVC	5	20	0.013	0.1797	7	
lime	CVC	13	23	0.0047	0.1178	6.9167	3.78g
lotion	CVCVC	8	5	0.0187	0.2086	7	
lunch	CVCC	33	7	0.0102	0.1795	7	2.75g
magic	CVCVC	37	0	0.0202	0.2339	7	3.08
mail	CVC	84	35	0.0057	0.1601	7	
mall	CVC	3	24	0.0044	0.1474	7	5.89g
man	CVC	1207	26	0.0245	0.2327	7	1.76
map	CVC	13	20	0.0149	0.1737	7	3.61
Mars	CVCC	21	8	0.0228	0.2082	6.9167	
marshmallow	CVCCCVCV(C)	1	0	0.0263	0.2997	6.9167	3.14g
mask	CVCC	10	8	0.023	0.2576	7	
match	CVC	41	14	0.0116	0.1446	7	4.26
melt	CVCC	4	15	0.0185	0.2932	7	3.03
milk	CVCC	49		0.0189	0.2693		
mitten	CVCVC	1	8	0.0166	0.2295	6.8333	
money	CVCV	265	10	0.0134	0.2357	6.9167	2.47g
month	CVCC	130	2	0.0101	0.1971	7	2.97
moon	CVC	60	21	0.0033	0.1754	7	
moon-i	CVCV			0.0071	0.2186		

| Probe word | Canonical Shape[a] | Raw Frequency[b] | Neighborhood Density[c] | Phonotactic Probability[d] | | Familiarity[e] | Age-of-Word Acquisition[f] |
				Biphone Frequency	Positional Segment Frequency		
mop	CVC	3	16	0.0089	0.1548	7	3.31
more	CVC	2216		0.0219	0.1849		2.28
mother	CVCVC	216	4	0.006	0.1503	7	1.44[g]
mouse	CVC	10	14	0.0017	0.1457	7	2.42[g]
mouse-i	CVCV			0.0038	0.1889		
mouth	CVC	103	7	0.0014	0.0743	7	
mouth-i	CVCV			0.0017	0.1175		
mow	CV(C)	1	20	0.0009	0.0669	6.8333	
much	CVC	937	17	0.0046	0.1044	7	2.95
mud	CVC	32	20	0.0049	0.1344	7	2.39[g]
muddy	CVCV	10		0.0086	0.1776		
muffin	CVCVC	1	2	0.0241	0.271	6.9167	
muppet	CVCVC			0.0168	0.2928		
music	CCVCVC	216	0	0.021	0.1805	6.9167	2.72[g]
nail	CVC	6	26	0.0046	0.1267	7	2.72[g]
nail-i	CVCV			0.0105	0.1699		
naked	CVCVC	32	0	0.011	0.1818	7	
nap	CVC	4	20	0.0067	0.1403	7	
napping	CVCVC	1		0.0157	0.2013		
near	CVC	198	25	0.0071	0.1984	7	2.6
neck	CVC	81	13	0.0094	0.1502	7	
Nerf	CVCC			0.001	0.0682		
nest	CVCC	20	15	0.0324	0.2649	6.5	
ninth	CVCC	20	1	0.0068	0.1588	6.5	
noise	CVC	37	4	0.0005	0.0473	7	2.17
noisy	CVCV	6	3	0.002	0.0905	7	
nose	CVC	60	18	0.0047	0.0932	7	2.06[g]
nosy	CVCV	1	7	0.0062	0.1364	6.75	
nothing	CVCVC	412	0	0.0096	0.1314	7	2.73
nurse	CVCC	17	10	0.0035	0.1273	7	3.03
nut	CVC	15	25	0.0038	0.129	7	

Probe word	Canonical Shape[a]	Raw Frequency[b]	Neighborhood Density[c]	Phonotactic Probability[d] Biphone Frequency	Positional Segment Frequency	Familiarity[e]	Age-of-Word Acquisition[f]
off	VC	639	12	0.0011	0.0127	6.9167	2.19
old	VCC	660	11	0.0008	0.0922	7	2.6
on	VC	6745		0.0005	0.0658		1.93
onion	VCCVC	15	1	0.0249	0.2285	7	2.86[g]
open	VCVC	319	4	0.0058	0.1009	7	
orange	VCVCC	23	2	0.019	0.191	7	2.03[g]
orange-i	VCVCCV			0.0197	0.2386		
other	VCVC	1702	5	0.0004	0.0223	7	3.25
ours	VCC	27	1	0.0006	0.1152	7	2.64
over	VCVC	1236	10	0.0057	0.0265	7	2.84
package	CVCVC	20	1	0.0189	0.2765	7	3.64[g]
page	CVC	66	16	0.0033	0.1244	7	2.58
page-i	CVCV			0.0037	0.1676		
paint	CVCC	37	12	0.0214	0.2991	7	2.38
pan	CVC	16	31	0.0231	0.2599	7	
pants	CVCC	9	11	0.0332	0.31	7	
park	CVCC	94	18	0.0267	0.2655	7	2.51
peach	CVC	3	22	0.0029	0.1242	7	2.92[g]
peach-i	CVCV			0.003	0.1674		
pepper	CVCVC	13	5	0.0109	0.2452	7	2.69[g]
piano	CVCVCV	38	0	0.0108	0.2111	7	2.53[g]
picture	CVCCVC	162	2	0.0162	0.2874	6.8333	2.32
pie	CV	14		0.0017	0.1187		
pig	CVC	8	19	0.0083	0.1985	7	2.33[g]
piggie	CVCV			0.0088	0.2417		
pin	CVC	16	31	0.0143	0.2767	7	2.61[g]
pinch	CVCC	6	10	0.017	0.2868	6.75	2.88
pinching	CVCCVC	2		0.0228	0.3409		
pinecone	CVCCVC			0.0108	0.3601		
pink	CVCC	48	16	0.0131	0.2345	7	2.77
plane	CCVC	114		0.0105	0.1901		5.22

Probe word	Canonical Shape[a]	Raw Frequency[b]	Neighborhood Density[c]	Phonotactic Probability[d]		Familiarity[e]	Age-of-Word Acquisition[f]
				Biphone Frequency	Positional Segment Frequency		
plant	CCVCC	125	8	0.0259	0.2836	7	3.08
plate	CCVC	22		0.0103	0.2328		
play	CCV	200	16	0.0087	0.1434	7	1.92[g]
plug	CCVC	23	8	0.0098	0.1543	7	2.42[g]
pocket	CVCVC	46	7	0.0261	0.3203	7	2.28[g]
point	CVCC	395	8	0.017	0.2733	6.9167	2.79
police	CVCVC	155	1	0.018	0.2984	7	2.92
pool	CVC	111	18	0.0018	0.1802	7	2.39[g]
porch	CVCC	43	7	0.0232	0.2222	7	3.19[g]
potato	CVCVCV	15	0	0.0124	0.3072	7	2.33[g]
present	CCVCVCC	377	3	0.0341	0.3205	7	2.21
pretty	CCVCV	107	4	0.044	0.3405	6.9167	2.73
pretzel	CCVCVC	1	0	0.0337	0.3677	7	
princess	CCVCCVC	10	0	0.0595	0.4234	7	2.95
prize	CCVC	28		0.0298	0.1998	0	
pu	CCV			0.0068	0.107	0	
punch	CVCC	5	8	0.0108	0.2298	7	3.01
punching	CVCCVC	2		0.0166	0.2839		
puppet	CVCVC	6	0	0.0152	0.32	7	
purse	CVCC	14	19	0.0066	0.1879	7	
push	CVC	37	5	0.0012	0.1023	6.9167	2.39
pushing	CVCVC	17		0.0092	0.1633		
quack	CCVC	9	8	0.0087	0.1785	6.75	
queen	CCVC	41		0.0069	0.1735		2.47[g]
quick	CCVC	68	14	0.0122	0.1852	7	2.69
quiet	CCV(C)VC	76	1	0.0175	0.2419	7	2.21
quilt	CCVCC	1	4	0.0119	0.258	6.75	5.42
rabbit	CVCVC	11		0.0106	0.2837		2.06[g]
raft	CVCC	4	14	0.0081	0.2386	7	
rain	CVC	80	38	0.0061	0.1754	7	2.11[g]
raining	CVCVC	7		0.0179	0.2364		

Probe word	Canonical Shape[a]	Raw Frequency[b]	Neighborhood Density[c]	Phonotactic Probability[d]		Familiarity[e]	Age-of-Word Acquisition[f]
				Biphone Frequency	Positional Segment Frequency		
raisin	CVCVC	1	7	0.0057	0.1095	7	
rake	CVC	11	30	0.0051	0.1328	7	3.36[g]
read	CVC	178	28	0.0066	0.1199	6.8333	
reading	CVCVC	140	1	0.0182	0.1809	7	
rich	CVC	74	21	0.0184	0.1543	7	
ride	CVC	49	30	0.0045	0.1224	7	2.43
riding	CVCVC	45	7	0.0161	0.1834	7	
ring	CVC	49	23	0.0203	0.158	7	3.31
robe	CVC	6	18	0.0039	0.1254	7	
robe-i	CVCV			0.0055	0.1686		
rock	CVC	75	23	0.0045	0.1641	6.6667	
rocky	CVCV	10		0.0059	0.2073		
roll	CVC	35		0.0081	0.1731		
roof	CVC	59	13	0.0024	0.0919	7	5.19
roof-i	CVCV			0.003	0.1351		
room	CVC	383		0.0041	0.1216		2.44[g]
rose	CVC	86	26	0.0039	0.1195	6.8333	3.01
rosy	CVCV	9	7	0.0054	0.1627	7	
row	CV(C)	35		0.0026	0.0994		3.89
rub	CVC	6	23	0.0062	0.1153	6.9167	
rubbing	CVCVC	11		0.0154	0.1763		
run	CVC	212	26	0.0083	0.1854	7	
running	CVCVC	123	1	0.0201	0.2464	7	
salt	CVCC	46	11	0.0086	0.282	7	2.33[g]
same	CVC	686	21	0.0034	0.181	7	
santa	CVCCV	28		0.0405	0.4489		
sarge	CVCC			0.0193	0.2525		
scalp	CCVCC	4	2	0.0101	0.2131	6.8333	
scarf	CCVCC	4	2	0.0113	0.2063	7	
school	CCVC	492	8	0.0087	0.18	7	2.28[g]
scissors	CVCVCC	1	0	0.0154	0.281	7	

Probe word	Canonical Shape[a]	Raw Frequency[b]	Neighborhood Density[c]	Phonotactic Probability[d]		Familiarity[e]	Age-of-Word Acquisition[f]
				Biphone Frequency	Positional Segment Frequency		
scratch	CCCVC	9	2	0.0119	0.2313	7	2.69[g]
scream	CCCVC	13	6	0.0181	0.2796	7	2.88
screw	CCCV	21	4	0.0108	0.2195	6.9167	
scribble	CCCVCVC	1	1	0.0184	0.2963	7	
scrub	CCCVC	9	2	0.0112	0.2329	7	3.18
seal	CVC	17	31	0.0055	0.2079	7	3.76
see	CV	772		0.0028	0.1342		2.39
seven	CVCVC	113	2	0.0322	0.3538	7	2.39
sew	CV	1990	29	0.0027	0.1517	7	2.82
sewing	CVCVC	10	5	0.0052	0.1923	7	
shampoo	CVCCV	2	0	0.0156	0.1896	7	
sharp	CVCC	72	5	0.0182	0.1848	7	
shave	CVC	6	16	0.0022	0.0625	7	
shaving	CVCVC	6		0.012	0.1235		
shelf	CVCC	12	6	0.0113	0.1722	6.9167	
shirt	CVCC	27	15	0.0026	0.1004	7	2.69[g]
shoe	CV	14	24	0.0002	0.0318	6.9167	
shot	CVC	112	23	0.0033	0.1362	7	3.4
shovel	CVCVC	5	4	0.0033	0.0953	7	
shovel-i	CVCVCV			0.0039	0.1357		
shred	CCVC	3	8	0.0101	0.1668	6.75	
shrimp	CCVCC	2	2	0.0189	0.185	7	
shrink	CCVCC	5	6	0.0191	0.1794	6.5	4.04
shrub	CCVC	1	4	0.0052	0.1304	7	3.83[g]
shrug	CCVC	2	3	0.005	0.1262	7	4.08[g]
sick	CVC	51	29	0.0182	0.2521	7	
silk	CVCC	12	10	0.0202	0.3145	7	
sink	CVCC	23	17	0.0179	0.2525	7	2.36
six	CVCC	220	8	0.0231	0.3022	7	2.32
skate	CCVC	1	11	0.01	0.2335	6.5	3.57
skirt	CCVCC	21	10	0.009	0.2232	7	2.58[g]

Probe word	Canonical Shape[a]	Raw Frequency[b]	Neighborhood Density[c]	Phonotactic Probability[d]		Familiarity[e]	Age-of-Word Acquisition[f]
				Biphone Frequency	Positional Segment Frequency		
skunk	CCVCC	1	5	0.0124	0.1847	6.5	5.01
sled	CCVC	1	10	0.0099	0.2129	7	
sleep	CCVC	65	13	0.0073	0.2021	7	1.93
sleeping	CCVCVC	39		0.0145	0.2562		
sleeve	CCVC	11	7	0.0076	0.1806	7	2.72[g]
slide	CCVC	20	10	0.0074	0.1994	7	2.47
slipper	CCVCVC	3	7	0.0144	0.2615	7	2.51
small	CCVC	542	5	0.0027	0.1619	7	2.17
smell	CCVC	34	7	0.0043	0.1827	7	2.41
smile	CCVC	58	5	0.0026	0.1692	6.75	2.15
smoke	CCVC	41	7	0.0041	0.1825	7	3.48
smooth	CCVC	42	1	0.002	0.1378	6.9167	3.92
snack	CCVC	6	10	0.0061	0.2312	7	
snail	CCVC	1	5	0.0031	0.2105	6.75	
snake	CCVC	44	6	0.003	0.2172	7	2.89[g]
sneeze	CCVC	1	3	0.003	0.1916	7	
snow	CCV(C)	59		0.002	0.1793		2.3
snowing	CCV(C)VC	4		0.0086	0.24		
snowman	CCV(C)CVC			0.007	0.3088		
soap	CVC	22	21	0.0037	0.1888	7	2.22[g]
soapy	CVCV	2		0.005	0.232		
sock	CVC	4	26	0.0056	0.2164	7	1.72[g]
sock-i	CVCV			0.007	0.2596		
soft	CVCC	61	5	0.0036	0.228	7	2.39
song	CVC	70	11	0.0021	0.1306	7	2.42[g]
soup	CVC	16	22	0.0041	0.1616	7	2.32
soupy	CVCV			0.0054	0.2048		
space	CCVC	184	6	0.0106	0.1872	7	3.87
spaghetti	CCVCVCV	1	0	0.0232	0.3419	7	
spider	CCVCVC	2	1	0.0137	0.2183	7	2.54
spill	CCVC	1	13	0.0133	0.1933	7	2.49

Probe word	Canonical Shape[a]	Raw Frequency[b]	Neighborhood Density[c]	Phonotactic Probability[d]		Familiarity[e]	Age-of-Word Acquisition[f]
				Biphone Frequency	Positional Segment Frequency		
splash	CCCVC	3	2	0.0128	0.2283	7	2.39
splashing	CCCVCVC	3		0.0170	0.2811		
splinter	CCCVCCVC	4	1	0.0369	0.4511	6.5833	
split	CCCVC	30	3	0.0185	0.3247	7	3.55
splitting	CCCVCVC	3		0.0304	0.3775		
sponge	CCVCC	7	1	0.0121	0.1915	7	
spoon	CCVC	6	11	0.01	0.1842	7	1.86[g]
spray	CCCV	16	7	0.014	0.2156	7	3.83
spread	CCCVC	83	1	0.0141	0.2607	7	
spring	CCCVC	127	5	0.0239	0.2622	7	
sprinkle	CCCVCCVC	7	0	0.0281	0.3356	7	
sprite	CCCVC	1	5	0.015	0.293	6.5	
square	CCCVC	143	3	0.0135	0.2102	7	2.5[g]
squeak	CCCVC	1	3	0.0125	0.2159	6.9167	
squeeze	CCCVC	11	2	0.0126	0.1896	7	
squirrel	CCCVC(V)C	1	2	0.0116	0.1696	7	3.53
squirt	CCCVCC	1	5	0.0124	0.2225	7	
stamp	CCVCC	8	4	0.0237	0.2071	7	2.69
stand	CCVCC	148	3	0.0329	0.2377	7	
star	CCVC	25	12	0.0213	0.193	7	
starry	CCVCV			0.0267	0.2334		
starve	CCVCC	1	4	0.0216	0.2045	7	
stop	CCVC	120	11	0.0214	0.1864	7	2.43
store	CCVC	74	18	0.0238	0.1912	7	3.94
stove	CCVC	15	8	0.0197	0.1631	6.5	2.97[g]
stove-i	CCVCV			0.0207	0.2035		
straight	CCCVC	119	8	0.0283	0.3021	7	3.01
straw	CCCV	15	3	0.0245	0.2125	7	2.89[g]
street	CCCVC	244	6	0.0316	0.3309	7	2.47
stripe	CCCVC	4	8	0.0249	0.24	7	3.08[g]
strong	CCCVC	202	3	0.0251	0.2248	7	2.8

Probe word	Canonical Shape[a]	Raw Frequency[b]	Neighborhood Density[c]	Phonotactic Probability[d]		Familiarity[e]	Age-of-Word Acquisition[f]
				Biphone Frequency	Positional Segment Frequency		
sucking	CVCVC	8		0.0163	0.2560		
sulk	CVCC	1	7	0.0121	0.2575	7	3.33
sun	CVC	112		0.0116	0.2377		1.81[g]
sunny	CVCV	13		0.0154	0.2809		
surf	CVCC	1		0.0041	0.1468		
sweater	CCVCVC	14	3	0.0149	0.2758	7	
sweep	CCVC	15	9	0.005	0.1727	6.9167	2.88
sweet	CCVC	70		0.0056	0.2259		1.72
swim	CCVC	15	11	0.0099	0.1822	7	2.75
swimming	CCVCVC	37		0.0175	0.2363		2.91
swing	CCVC	24	12	0.0093	0.1583	7	2.37
syrup	CVCVC	4	1	0.0051	0.1876	7	
tail	CVC	45	30	0.0041	0.1474	7	
tail-i	CVCV			0.01	0.1906		
tape	CVC	35	16	0.0029	0.1108	7	4.06[g]
tear	CVC	11		0.0077	0.2191		2.38
teeth	CVC	103	12	0.0016	0.0837	7	
teeth-i	CVCV			0.0019	0.1269		
tent	CVCC	20	19	0.0371	0.3029	7	2.83[g]
tenth	CVCC	7		0.0218	0.2181		
thank (you)	CVCC	36	11	0.009	0.1401	7	2.91
that	CVC	10595	14	0.0063	0.1483	6.4167	2.48
theirs	CVCC	21	1	0.009	0.1663	6.75	3.02
them	CVC	1789	5	0.0059	0.1252	7	2.66
there	CVC	2724		0.0087	0.1542		2.45
these	CVC	1573	9	0.0017	0.0548	6.25	2.6
thief	CVC	8	8	0.0018	0.0583	7	3.22[g]
thirsty	CVCCCV	5		0.0315	0.2401		
thread	CCVC	15	6	0.0109	0.1639	7	2.67[g]
three	CCV	610	9	0.0098	0.1169	6.5	1.78
throat	CCVC	51	6	0.0099	0.2061	6.75	

Probe word	Canonical Shape[a]	Raw Frequency[b]	Neighborhood Density[c]	Phonotactic Probability[d]		Familiarity[e]	Age-of-Word Acquisition[f]
				Biphone Frequency	Positional Segment Frequency		
throne	CCVC	45	8	0.0097	0.1634	7	
throw	CCV(C)	42		0.0083	0.1167		2.64[g]
throwing	CCV(C)VC	17		0.0164	0.1776		
thumb	CVC	10	15	0.0055	0.0954	7	1.83[g]
thumb-i	CVCV			0.0072	0.1386		
thunder	CVCCVC	14	3	0.0221	0.2256	7	3.14
ticket	CVCVC	16	4	0.026	0.3161	7	2.94[g]
ticking	CVCVC	1	0	0.0195	0.2552	7	
tie	CV	23		0.0021	0.0788		
tiger	CVCVC	7	0	0.0038	0.1475	7	3.31
toast	CVCC	19	11	0.0281	0.262	7	3.64
toes	CVC	19		0.0038	0.1139		
tongue	CVC	35	16	0.0041	0.0954	6.8333	
tooth	CVC	20	14	0.0027	0.074	7	
toothy	CVCV			0.003	0.1172		
tooting	CVCVC			0.0184	0.1936		
top	CVC	204	21	0.0047	0.1421	7	2.28
torch	CVCC	2	8	0.0209	0.1823	7	
towel	CV(CV)C	6	9	0.0007	0.0568	7	
train	CCVC	82	15	0.0195	0.1968	7	4.43
(trick or) treat	CCVC	26	10	0.0216	0.244	7	3.74
tree	CCV	59	16	0.0204	0.1546	7	2.13
treehouse	CCVCVC			0.0212	0.216		
triangle	CCV(C)VCCVC	4	0	0.0205	0.2154	6.9167	
trick (or treat)	CCVC	15	13	0.0291	0.0213	7	3.2
truck	CCVC	57	9	0.0167	0.1895	7	
trunk	CCVCC	8	3	0.0198	0.1907	7	3.28[g]
tub	CVC	13	17	0.005	0.1097	6.5	
tub-i	CVCV			0.0066	0.1529		
tulip	CVCVC	4	1	0.0152	0.2396	7	
Tweety	CCVCV			0.0079	0.2084		

Probe word	Canonical Shape[a]	Raw Frequency[b]	Neighborhood Density[c]	Phonotactic Probability[d]		Familiarity[e]	Age-of-Word Acquisition[f]
				Biphone Frequency	Positional Segment Frequency		
twelve	CCVCC	48	0	0.0057	0.1323	7	3.01
Twinkie	CCVCCV			0.0106	0.1858		
twins	CCVCC	12		0.0089	0.153		
twist	CCVCC	18	3	0.0198	0.2244	7	3.38
up	VC	1895	7	0.0022	0.0327	6.5	1.89
vacuum	CVCCVC	20	0	0.0155	0.2133	7	4.39
valentine	CVCVCCVC	2	0	0.0441	0.5182	7	
van	CVC	32	12	0.0169	0.1979	7	2.67[g]
van-i	CVCV			0.0207	0.2411		
vanilla	CVCVCV	1	0	0.0239	0.323	7	
vase	CVC	4	16	0.0042	0.1304	7	2.97[g]
vegetable	CVCCVCVC	10	0	0.0226	0.3208	7	2.69[g]
verb	CVCC	4	6	0.0037	0.0731	7	4.36[g]
vest	CVCC	4	19	0.0336	0.2635	6.9167	
Viewmaster	CCVCVCCVC			0.0281	0.2828		
wagon	CVCVC	55	0	0.0179	0.2351	6.8333	
wash	CVC	37	7	0.0026	0.0445	7	1.95
washing	CVCVC	44		0.0106	0.1055		
wasp	CVCC	2	2	0.0113	0.1958	7	2.79
watch	CVC	81	5	0.0022	0.0448	7	
watch-i	CVCV			0.0023	0.088		
water	CVCVC	442	3	0.0139	0.1536	7	1.8
wave	CVC	46		0.0029	0.0731		2.13
waving	CVCVC	13		0.0127	0.1341		
wealth	CVCC	22	6	0.0114	0.1715	7	4.37
wear	CVC	36		0.0099	0.1716		2.6
web	CVC	6	10	0.0031	0.1192	7	
web-i	CVCV			0.0047	0.1624		
wet	CVC	53	29	0.0073	0.1592	7	
wick	CVC	4	26	0.0132	0.17	6.6667	3.53[g]
win	CVC	55	31	0.0141	0.2126	7	2.69[g]

Probe word	Canonical Shape[a]	Raw Frequency[b]	Neighborhood Density[c]	Phonotactic Probability[d]		Familiarity[e]	Age-of-Word Acquisition[f]
				Biphone Frequency	Positional Segment Frequency		
window	CVCCV(C)	119	5	0.0277	0.2728	7	2.31[g]
wing	CVC	18	18	0.0078	0.1282	6.9167	
wish	CVC	110	13	0.0058	0.1242	6.9167	2.6
witch	CVC	5	20	0.0059	0.1245	7	2.58[g]
wolf	CVCC	6	3	0.0048	0.1201	7	3.16
woman	CVCVC	224	2	0.0269	0.2348	7	2.58[g]
worm	CVCC	4	10	0.0043	0.0944	7	2.49
wreath	CVC	8	17	0.0048	0.0893	7	
wreath-i	CVCV			0.0051	0.1325		
yard	CVCC	35	10	0.0201	0.1871	7	3.08[g]
yawn	CVC	2	12	0.0015	0.1205	7	2.84
yell	CVC	9	19	0.0093	0.1545	7	
yellow	CVCV(C)	55	7	0.0119	0.1755	7	2.56
yes	CVC	144	9	0.0075	0.1596	7	1.69
you	CV	3293		0.0033	0.03		2.13
your	CVC	924		0.0182	0.1356		2.56
zebra	CVCCV	1	1	0.0123	0.1848	6.8333	3.7
zero	CVCV	24	1	0.0082	0.1982	7	
zipper	CVCVC	1	6	0.0089	0.1867	7	
zipping	CVCVC			0.0144	0.1969		
zoo	CV	9		0.0001	0.0247		

3 Fundamentals of experimental design and treatment

Judith A. Gierut
Indiana University

Single-subject experimental designs offer a unique framework from which to test the basic premises and predictions of linguistic theory. As applied to phonological development, this set of designs capitalizes on the heterogeneity that is characteristic of development, while aiming to extract patterns of learning that are common across children. The designs have particular utility in the study of children with phonological disorders because they may be executed in the context of clinical treatment to promote learning. In this chapter, the assumptions of single-subject design are outlined, with illustrations of their application to cases involving phonological acquisition. Extensions to clinical populations are highlighted in descriptions of treatment protocols that follow from single-subject design. The experimental protocols are specific to research conducted on the Learnability Project, but are meant to serve as a springboard from which other studies, involving other populations, in tests of other theories may be initiated. The experimental findings that have emerged from these protocols are also discussed, supporting linguistic complexity as the trigger of phonological learning in children. The implications of these results for optimality theory are considered.

1 Introduction

The validity of linguistic theory is conventionally confirmed by reference to cross-linguistic descriptive data. The robustness of a hypothesis is gauged against the consistency of its application across languages and the lack of counterexamples. Complementary data may be used to further bolster the arguments, taking the form, for example, of acoustic phonetic descriptions, instances of slips of the tongue, or errors in first or second language acquisition. Perhaps one of the most powerful demonstrations of the validity of linguistic claims comes from experimental studies. The behavioral effects that result from a systematic experimental manipulation of language variables attest to the psychological reality of the phenomenon (e.g., Greenberg & Jenkins, 1964; Žagar & Locke, 1986; Lahiri & Marslen-Wilson, 1991; Marslen-Wilson & Warren, 1994). Experimental studies of language have tended to follow the mainstream of large N (group) designs. Single-subject designs are less well understood, but they may actually be better suited to research on language acquisition in general and children with phonological disorders in particular. The goal of this chapter is to provide an overview of the single-subject model, its assumptions, and characteristic applications, with design protocols of the Learnability Project included as a reference for those interested in theoretically driven experimental studies of language. The protocols may also be used by speech-language pathologists and second language instructors in their development of instructional programs. The chapter is organized beginning with an overview of the underlying premises of single-subject design. Two key designs, the ABA and multiple baseline (MBL), are described, with corresponding protocols for their implementation. Single-subject applications drawn from the clinical literature are also presented as further illustrations of design applications, particularly in the identification of higher order principles that govern learning. In this respect, phonological complexity is highlighted as a facilitating factor in motivating gains in learning.

2   Single-subject design

2.1   Assumptions

Single-subject design is a research approach that was initiated in the 1960's as part of the behaviorist movement, but has gone well beyond the narrow scope of its founding. It has been shown to be relevant to the evaluation of learning through instruction and applicable to a wide range of populations (e.g., Hersen & Barlow, 1976; Kratochwill, 1978; McReynolds & Kearns, 1983; Kratochwill & Levin, 1992). It is well suited to the study of development because an understanding of the trajectory of change is one of its outcomes. It is also a good match to the study of phonological disorders because these children require treatment to bring their sound systems in line with the target phonology. Like group design, single-subject design has all of the makings of an experimental paradigm including (1) operationally defined independent and dependent variables, (2) control of extraneous variables, (3) data that are reliable and valid, and (4) generalizability to the population at-large. However, the way it meets these criteria differs as best understood by its underlying assumptions.

By its name, single-subject design obviously emphasizes the individual. There are few participants in any given study. Contrary to the assumption of homogeneity in group design, single-subject design assumes heterogeneity of the population. This fits with the study of phonology, acquisition, and disorders given the range of variation that occurs within and across languages. For children with phonological disorders, heterogeneity is the norm rather than the exception. Children may present with the same inventory, but how sounds of the system pattern are often very different (Compton, 1970; Dinnsen & Chin, 1993; Dinnsen, 1999). Moreover, when it comes to children's learning (albeit language related or not), the general consensus is that it follows a heterochronic multidimensional trajectory (Thelen & Smith, 1994). This raises an important question because, if we assume heterogeneity, then how can we be sure that the results from one or two children will be indicative of how all children will perform? There is a set of related assumptions of single-subject design that bear on this question.

We begin first with a brief review of the definition of independent and dependent variables. The independent variable is the property that is manipulated in an experiment, and it is determined a priori by the hypothesis being tested. For example, in phonology, the independent variable of a study might differentially test the effects of markedness to establish whether marked or unmarked structure is more facilitating of learning (Dinnsen & Elbert, 1984). As another example, a psycholinguistic manipulation might involve an evaluation of word frequency by presenting high versus low frequency forms to establish their differential effects on children's learning (Morrisette & Gierut, 2002). A clinical example might involve method of treatment in comparison of the learning that takes place following a minimal pair versus a cycles model (Tyler, Edwards & Saxman, 1987).

The dependent variable is the property that is measured in an experiment, and it too is dictated by the hypothesis. In single-subject design, the dependent variable is typically a measure of generalization learning. Generalization is the transfer of a newly acquired property in treatment to other untreated and previously unknown properties. Generalization is thus an extension of learning that benefits or promotes gains in behavior following a minimum of instruction. Three types of generalization are often cited as dependent variables in studies of phonology (Gierut, 1998c).

Generalization to the treated class is transfer of the treated sound to untreated words and contexts. For example, if /s/ is taught in word-initial position, generalization would be measured in word-initial, intervocalic, and final contexts using novel stimuli. Within-class generalization is the transfer of learning to untreated properties that are related to the treated property. In our example of word-initial /s/ as the treated sound, within-class generalization would be monitored for other untreated fricatives in error. Across-class generalization refers to the transfer of learning to untreated properties that are not related to the treated property. For the case of /s/, across-class generalization might be sampled in liquids or affricates if these classes were in error. It is important to note that the notion of a generalization 'class' or category is defined a priori by the variables of study. In the example of /s/, treated, within- and across-class generalization were defined along the dimension of manner. However, it is equally possible to define the generalization class along any number of linguistic, psycholinguistic, or clinical variables, e.g., distinctive features, syntactic category, word frequency, normative age of sound mastery. The point to keep in mind is that category membership is delineated by the goal of treatment (i.e., the independent variable). If the goal is to teach a distinctive feature contrast, then features become the generalization class. Similarly, if teaching is aimed at verbs, then syntactic category is the relevant generalization variable. If teaching emphasizes early acquired sounds, then normative age defines the generalization sample.

The measure of generalization learning is planned in advance, but there is an important post hoc consequence of examining change in terms of treated, within- and across-class gains. In particular, children's generalization may be revealing of their own conceptualizations of the sounds that are introduced in treatment (Gierut, 1989b). By identifying which phonological properties improve with treatment, it is possible to gain insight to the internal organization of a child's grammar. In this way, generalization learning may be used to establish or confirm a child's linguistic competence as a complement to descriptive evidence (Dinnsen & Elbert, 1984; Gierut, Elbert & Dinnsen, 1987). The operational definition of the independent and dependent variables is thus a critical first step in single-subject design, as is the case in large N studies.

Inherent to the set up of a single-subject experiment is the premise that every child serves as his or her own demonstration of experimental control. The demonstration of control means that there is a causal relationship established between the variables of study, which cannot be attributed to other extraneous factors. In most applications of single-subject design, the cause-effect involves treatment and learning, such that treatment is responsible for the change in learning. In demonstrating experimental control then, single-subject design relies on the ups and downs of a given child's performance. Presumably, the level of 'noise' that is associated with extraneous influences in an individual's daily routine (e.g., fatigue, hunger, irritability, illness, emotion) is relatively stable, fluctuating within a narrow band. To measure the noise, a repeated baseline of a subject's performance is obtained prior to the instatement of treatment. This then is factored out of the treatment results; hence, experimental control in establishing causal effects is achieved for a given child. This contrasts with large N designs, which utilize control groups or conditions that involve withholding the experimental manipulation for a set of subjects. The practice of withholding treatment for children with phonological disorders (in addition to a number of other populations) would not be desirable, ethical or timely, so a demonstration of control within subject is a more viable option.

Single-subject design addresses data collection from a similar vantage. Even though only a handful of subjects participate in any given experiment, each contributes multiple points of data. Because the delivery of treatment takes place over time, there is the potential for a micro view of development through trial-by-trial, day-by-day, or step-by-step learning. The quantity of data obtained in a single-subject study often exceeds that collected in large N studies. Many points of data obtained from one child in single-subject design is thus on par with a single point of data from many subjects in group design. As in group design, statistical analyses can be completed using nonparametric time series analyses (Siegel, 1956; Kazdin, 1976; Marascuilo & Busk, 1988; Marascuilo & Serlin, 1988; Busk & Marascuilo, 1992). However, the more conventional approach to data analysis is through visual inspection of a child's learning curve, with attention to level, slope or magnitude of change as examples.

Single-subject design also stands apart in its handling of the validity of findings. Conventionally, the validity of an experimental finding is confirmed by its generalizability to the population at-large. With few participants in a single-subject design, there is a risk that the findings to emerge will have limited relevance, such that the effects are child-specific. To address this, single-subject design employs direct and systematic replications. A direct replication occurs when different children with similar profiles are exposed to the same experimental condition and show exactly the same pattern of learning. In this case, the effect of treatment is explicitly repeated for different subjects enrolled in the same study. A majority of single-subject studies involve the direct replication of effects, but a more powerful demonstration is a systematic replication. A systematic replication takes place when different children with different profiles are exposed to different experimental conditions and still show the same degree of learning. Here, the learning effects are one step removed from a given experimental manipulation, but the effect is consistently repeated. Theoretically, systematic replications are especially valuable because they have the potential to identify higher order principles that govern learning and development. In subsequent sections of this chapter, we will show an example of how systematic replications in treatment of children with phonological disorders have pinpointed complexity of the input as an inherent property of change in grammar.

In all, the properties of single-subject design meet the requisites of an experimental study in the systematic manipulation and measurement of behavior under carefully controlled conditions, with the outcome being replicable, reliable and valid to the extent that it is applicable to a standard normative distribution. The key difference between the single-subject and large N models is the emphases on hetero- versus homogeneity respectively. The different vantage points thus drive the subsequent ways in which each model approaches an experimental question. It should be noted too that the single-subject design is different from case studies because it employs experimental methodologies. A case study is a descriptive report of an individual's behavior, without also a manipulation of that behavior (e.g., Leopold, 1947; Smith, 1973). In the progression of science, case studies are thought to be the entry level to an experimental question, tackled first using single-subject design and subsequently, with large N studies. Having established the underlying premises of the single-subject model, we turn now to a description of two commonly used designs within the acquisition literature.

2.2   Basics

The ABA design is the fundamental protocol of single-subject research because all other design variants stem from this framework. The ABA consists of three sequential phases, as depicted in Figure 1. The first A phase is the baseline period, where the dependent variable is measured prior to the application of the independent variable. During baseline, a child's performance is monitored but not manipulated. In phonology, a child's production of sounds might be measured during baseline. The baseline phase has three requirements. One is that the behavior is sampled repeatedly over time; another is that the behavior remains stable over the sampling period; and a third is that the same measurement tool is used over the extended period. Repeated and stable baselines demonstrate that a subject's performance is not in a state of fluctuation or process of change. Baseline stability helps to delineate a child's entry levels of performance from later performance that follows from the application of the independent variable. To achieve baseline stability, the same measurement tool or probe should be used over time. This ensures that the same skills are being tapped from baseline to baseline. If the tool were to change with each probe administration, and if a child's performance were to fluctuate accordingly, it would not be possible to disambiguate whether this was a true change in behavior or an artifact of the probe itself. It is typically recommended that two to three baselines be obtained with an intervening interval of time in between. Likewise, an accepted level of fluctuation in baseline performance is ±10% variation. This could be gauged by comparing performance from sample to sample (Powell, Elbert & Dinnsen, 1991) or it could be based around the mean of all samples (Jamieson

& Rvachew, 1992), depending on the stringency of the operational definition. For example, if a child's production accuracy of a particular sound were 5%, 0%, and 10% across three successive baseline administrations, this would be considered stable sample-to-sample performance. The reason is that production accuracy never vacillates more than 10% per sample. Using the same example, the mean baseline of the three samples is 5%; therefore an acceptable range of stability based on the mean would be 0 to 15% accuracy in this case. As another illustration, if baseline accuracy were 10%, 15%, and 25%, this would satisfy sample-to-sample stability. When evaluated from the mean of 17% baseline accuracy, the acceptable range of performance is 7 to 27%.

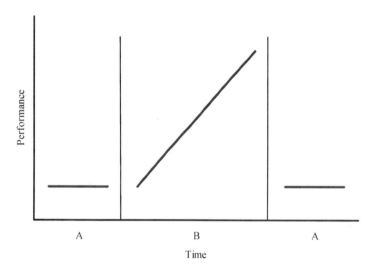

Figure 1. Schematic of the ABA design.

While ±10% may be the typical standard for stability of a baseline, it is also important to examine the trajectory of the baseline, particularly if the trend in performance is rising. A rising baseline is one indicator that the dependent variable is undergoing change in advance of any application of the independent variable. A rising baseline may cloud the interpretation of the effects of the experimental manipulation (e.g., Powell & Elbert, 1984; Jamieson & Rvachew, 1992). In the event of a rising baseline, there are at least two options on how to proceed. One is to continue to track performance with added baselines to determine if there is a leveling effect prior to the instatement of treatment. A second option is to avoid any treatment of that particular behavior in lieu of another treatment goal. Thus, an investigator should define and track baseline stability and trajectory before advancing to the experimental phase.

Following the A phase of stable baseline performance, the B phase of the design is instated. During the B phase, the independent variable is applied, namely, treatment is administered to affect phonological change. A treatment protocol is developed in advance and may involve a series of graded steps. In phonological treatment, the B phase usually involves production training beginning with imitative, and then advancing to spontaneous responding. The steps of training continue to pre-established levels, which may be defined by time and/or performance. Time-based criteria for teaching can be set, for example, by number of sessions or trials completed. Performance-based criteria depend on the child achieving a certain level of response accuracy. Time- and performance-based criteria are not mutually exclusive and may be used in conjunction with each other, such that treatment continues for a fixed period of time or until a child reaches a particular level of performance, whichever occurs first. Throughout the B phase, trial-by-trial learning is documented, such that each response is judged as correct or incorrect with appropriate feedback provided to the learner. This is necessary to demonstrate that learning has occurred during treatment and supports that the independent variable has had an observable effect on behavior. The structure of the ABA design assumes that there will be a measurable change in performance with treatment.

There is a second A phase following treatment, which is a repetition of the baseline. The assumption is that there will be a return to baseline levels of performance following the removal of the independent variable. This presumably shows that treatment is the factor controlling behavior. When treatment is removed, the behavior returns to pretreatment levels; hence, there is a causal relationship between the independent and dependent variables. The return to baseline in the ABA design is crucial to the demonstration of experimental control; however, it is a point of contention for ecological validity. A return to baseline may be viewed as unethical, particularly where children with phonological disorders are concerned. It is also artificial in the context of language: if treatment induces change in a learner's underlying grammar, then why would there be a reversion back to an earlier state? This is one case where the behavioristic origins of single-subject design are most apparent because there is no distinction made between a change in behavior and a change in knowledge (Johnston, 1988).

In step with theoretical advances of this kind, applications of the ABA design have undergone modification. Investigators may report pseudo-experimental AB effects, where the outcomes of treatment may be demonstrated, but not experimentally controlled (Tyler & Figurski, 1994). In these cases, there is no claim of causality between independent and dependent variables and consequently, the presentation of data is on par with descriptive case studies. Another alternative is to use the AB design with control behavior. The AB is instated as has been described, but another behavior is also identified as the control (e.g., Powell, 1991). The control is monitored but not treated as an extended baseline over the course of the entire study. For experimental control to be demonstrated, the behavior that is untreated must also be unchanging over time. This then shows that treatment has a direct impact on the targeted behavior alone; hence a causal relationship is established. A third alternative is to use the MBL design in lieu of the ABA. This is by far the design that is used most often in treatment studies of phonological acquisition.

The MBL design involves stacking several ABs in a time-lagged sequence. Multiple ABs provide direct replications of the effects of treatment and serve as a demonstration of experimental control. Each AB replication is called a leg, and the recommendation is that there be at least three AB legs in any given MBL application. Consistent with the AB protocol, the MBL involves a baseline followed by treatment. During the A phase, all legs of the design are measured. As the number of legs increases, so do the number of baselines. The number of baselines to be administered for successive legs of the design is determined by the time-lagged administration of treatment. Nonetheless, the assumption of baseline stability still holds.

Figure 2 illustrates the AB implementation across three legs of an MBL. First, baseline stability is demonstrated for the first leg of the MBL, and then the B phase is initiated for this leg of the design. All other legs remain in an extended baseline that continues until treatment of the first leg is completed. Then the experimental manipulation shifts to the second leg of the MBL. This leg has been in an extended baseline period, but now treatment is instated. Meanwhile, the remaining third leg of the MBL continues in baseline and remains there until treatment of the second leg is complete. Then the manipulation shifts again, with treatment delivered to the final leg. Thus, the AB sequence of extended baseline followed by treatment is applied sequentially for each leg of the MBL design.

With the MBL, a key assumption is that change will not occur in successive legs of the design until treatment is instated. With each baseline–treatment replication, it is further assumed that there will be a direct replication of effects to demonstrate causality between the delivery of treatment and change. Finally, because baselines are time-lagged, there is a further assumption that the effects of treatment are not due to extraneous variables. The logic is that, if extraneous factors were influencing learning, then they would apply uniformly across all legs of the design. In other words, 'noise' associated with interference presumably impacts an entire system. In the study of acquisition, this levels countering claims that maturation is responsible for behavioral change in such studies. Specifically, if change were due to maturational development in lieu of treatment, then all legs of the MBL would be expected to mature accordingly.

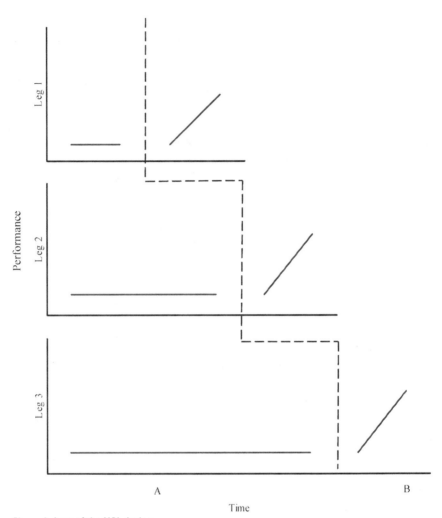

Figure 2. Legs of the MBL design.

However, if the only behavior that advances is the one being treated, then maturation cannot be responsible for the gains. The distinguishing properties of the MBL are thus its demonstration of control through a time-lagged sequence of no change and the direct replication of experimental effects.

There are three common MBL applications, where generalization learning is explored across behavior, subject, or setting. As applied to language, the MBL across behavior manipulates legs of the design to induce changes in the phonological system, e.g., successive treatment of three sounds. An across-behavior application has unique potential for optimality theory in that the successive legs of the design might parallel the rank ordering of constraints. The MBL across subjects applies each leg of the design to a different child, e.g., three children with similar presenting phonologies are enrolled sequentially in treatment. An across-subjects application holds the possibility for systematic replications of effects particularly if different children have an individualized goal of treatment that is matched to the unique properties of his or her own grammar. The MBL across settings application varies the situation of treatment across legs of the design. This might be useful in sociolinguistic studies where production differences by social context are explored. Examples that come to mind include evaluations of variables that control code switching or in acquisition, the use of motherese.

2.3   Protocols

For both the ABA and MBL designs, the discussion has emphasized learning during the experimental phase of treatment. However, of greater importance is the demonstration of generalization, as it is typically the dependent variable. Generalization is monitored during treatment using a subset of the baseline items as the probe measure. Items that are probed are reserved specifically as a measure of transfer; they are never taught or presented during the teaching sessions. In the development of an experiment then, an investigator must detail two protocols, one that guides the delivery of treatment and another that determines how change is measured. These constitute the treatment and generalization packages respectively.

Table 1 shows a standard treatment and generalization protocol that is the foundation of Learnability Project research. With respect to the treatment package, there are two phases of instruction. These are delivered in hour long individualized sessions, three times weekly. Imitation is the first phase, during which a child repeats a clinician's model of the treated items. There are typically 8 to 10 treated items, but this varies depending on the experimental question. Items are arranged in blocks, so that a child produces each of the items as a discrete trial, before a second block of imitation begins. The accuracy of each trial is scored as a measure of trial-by-trial learning. On average, children produce 100 trials per treatment session. During treatment, feedback is provided about the accuracy of sound production and corrective models are provided. This continues until the child achieves 75% accuracy of imitation over two consecutive sessions, or until 7 total sessions are completed whichever occurs first. (Notice that this is a time- and/or performance-based criterion). Treatment then advances to the second phase of spontaneous production of the same treatment stimuli. During this phase, the child produces each item independently, without a model. The procedures for blocking items, recording trial-by-trial accuracies, and delivering feedback are the same as in the imitation phase. The only difference is that the criterion for completion of spontaneous treatment is set at 90% accuracy of spontaneous production over three consecutive sessions or until 12 total sessions are completed whichever occurs first. The experimental phase of treatment is thus completed in a maximum of 19 sessions (hours). Treatment of sounds in connected speech is not a component of treatment because research has shown that single word productions alone motivate transfer to conversational speech (Elbert, Dinnsen, Swartzlander & Chin, 1990).

Table 1. Treatment and generalization protocol.

Pretreatment phonological analysis
     Administer entire PKP, OCP, CCP
     Establish interjudge transcription reliability

Multiple baselines as determined by experimental assignment
     Administer subset of PKP, OCP, CCP
     Establish interjudge transcription reliability

Treatment phase 1: Train independent variable in imitation
     75% accuracy x 2 consecutive sessions OR 7 sessions
     Treatment probes administered on VR2 schedule
     Establish procedural reliability of treatment administration

Phase shift generalization probe
     Administer entire PKP, OCP, CCP
     Establish interjudge transcription reliability

Treatment phase 2: Train independent variable spontaneously
     90% accuracy x 3 consecutive sessions OR 12 sessions
     Treatment probes administered on VR2 schedule
     Establish procedural reliability of treatment administration

Immediate posttreatment generalization probe
     Administer entire PKP, OCP, CCP
     Establish interjudge transcription reliability

Two-week posttreatment generalization probe
     Administer entire PKP, OCP, CCP
     Establish interjudge transcription reliability

Two-month posttreatment generalization probe
     Administer entire PKP, OCP, CCP
     Establish interjudge transcription reliability

In the course of treatment, data are obtained to ensure fidelity in the administration of the protocol, both within and across clinicians. On average, 10% of each child's sessions are monitored by an independent observer. A checklist is used to verify that the elicitation and feedback procedures are delivered as prescribed, that scoring is immediate and appropriate to a child's response, and that a child is directed to the treatment materials accordingly. Data are also taken to ensure that the design is accurate, with particular attention given to number of trials and administration of probe measures. Procedural reliability thus establishes consistency in treatment within and across experiments of the Learnability Project.

The specific methods of teaching that are used vary with the experimental question. Some questions necessitate the use of a minimal pair format of teaching, whereas others motivate the use of traditional instructional methods directed at single sounds. Likewise, the items that are treated may be real or nonwords, presented as picture stimuli or computer graphics. Treatment of nonwords is a hallmark of our work, dating back to 1990 (Gierut, 1990). The nonwords used in treatment are phonotactically permissible forms that are balanced for canonical structure, vowel context, stress, and syntactic category. The segmental composition of nonwords is tailored to an individual child's phonological needs. The nonwords are introduced in children's stories to provide lexical support for learning. Nonwords correspond to character names or unusual objects or actions that take place in the stories. At the start of each treatment week, the nonword story is presented to the child prior to production practice, but the imitation and spontaneous phases of treatment involve only single nonword productions. Table 2 provides examples of nonwords used in treatment of the targets /r/, /br/, and contrast of /r/-/l/.

Table 2. Sample nonword sets for treatment of /r/, /br/, and contrast of /r/ – /l/.

/r/	/br/	/r/ – /l/
[ron]	[brɪb]	[rɪb] – [lɪb]
[rɛb]	[brɪd]	[rʌd] – [lʌd]
[ræd]	[bræm]	[rɑm] – [lɑm]
[rɪn]	[brʌn]	[reɪb] – [leɪb]
[rimi]	[brɛmoʊ]	[rɪdu] – [lɪdu]
[reɪmoʊ]	[breɪdɑ]	[rɛmoʊ] – [lɛmoʊ]
[rumən]	[brunəd]	[runəd] – [lunəd]
[rʌbəd]	[broʊbəm]	[rænəm] – [lænəm]

Initially, we developed this paradigm as a means of controlling the treatment experience across children. Because nonwords are unique, none of the children would have had prior exposure to, or practice in saying the nonword sequences. Moreover, the same visual stimuli are used for all children, varying only in their phonological content as based on a child's own phonology. Clinically, there is a precedent for the use of nonwords in treatment, dating to one of the original models of treatment used in speech-language pathology. Van Riper's (1963) traditional method of teaching had children perceive and produce a treated sound in Consonant-Vowel, then Vowel-Consonant and then Consonant-Vowel-Consonant sequences. For example, in one report, children were taught target /s/ in the discrete syllables [si], [sa], [su], [isi], [asa], [usu] (Elbert & McReynolds, 1979). In terms of acquisition, the use of nonwords accords with Slobin's (1973) operating principle 'Teach new information rather than adapting old knowledge.' With recent advances in cognitive psychology, treatment of nonwords takes on added significance. Specifically, one hypothesis is that spoken word recognition takes place dually at lexical and sublexical levels (Vitevitch & Luce, 1998; 1999; Vitevitch, 2003). In lexical processing, details about the word as a whole are extracted as, for example, its frequency of use in the language (word frequency) or its number of phonetically similar counterparts (neighborhood density). In sublexical processing, the details about phonological structure are the focus, most notably, the phonotactic probabilities of sounds and sound sequences. Because nonwords do not have lexical status, the emphasis of nonword treatment is at the sublexical level of processing. Moreover, because children with phonological disorders have difficulty learning the specifics of the target sound system, the use of nonwords may be especially beneficial. In fact, one hypothesis is that the locus of the problem for these children may lie at a level of sublexical processing (Beckman & Edwards, 2000; Storkel & Morrisette, 2002; Munson, Edwards & Beckman, 2005; Munson, Swenson & Manthei, 2005). Indeed, our research on phonological disorders has shown that treatment of nonwords facilitates generalization within- and across-classes to a greater extent than does treatment of real words (Martin & Gierut, 2004). The range of benefits that accrue from children's exposure to nonwords is still being explored, but there may be differential effects by populations—typical learners versus children with specific language impairment versus those with phonological disorders, or by domain of learning—lexical versus phonological (Storkel, 2002; 2003; 2004a; 2004b).

In summary, the treatment package outlines the details of day-to-day instruction, with decisions about the stimulus materials, number of trials and teaching steps, and methods of presentation, feedback and advancement. The data to emerge from application of the treatment package serve an important purpose in that they document whether a child has learned from the instruction.

This is crucial as it bears on the interpretation of generalization learning as the dependent measure. Consider that if learning takes place in day-to-day treatment and if generalization also occurs, then it can be claimed that the treatment affected the change. Likewise, if learning occurs in treatment but if no generalization follows, then it can be argued that treatment affected no change. However, if learning does not occur in treatment, then any generalization to follow (albeit positive or negative) must be due to some other extraneous factors. If generalization takes place in the absence of learning, then it cannot be due to the treatment itself, thereby violating causality in the experiment. Alternatively, if there is no learning and no generalization, this is an uninterpretable null result. For these reasons then, the treatment package is essential to the generalization package.

In the generalization package, decisions must be made about how to measure change, and to some extent, when to measure change although this is largely dictated by the experimental design. The generalization probe must be rich enough to cull information about change in treated and untreated properties. Probes must also be easy to administer and score, and should be ecologically valid. They should resemble the treatment in part, but must also stand alone as a reflection of change to address the potential of teaching to the test. Because probes are administered frequently, it is necessary that the learner's responses do not become stimulus or lexically bound. In these cases, the learner's response to a given picture or word respectively is atypical relative to other items on the probe in that it is consistently better than general performance. When an item is bound, this inflates the results giving a false impression that the learner knows more than they actually do. To address this, the probe should include multiple exemplars and contexts in sampling behavior. On the Learnability Project, the primary measures of generalization include the PKP, OCP, CCP as was described in Chapter 2. Multiple renditions of each relevant sound and cluster are elicited to prevent lexical binding, and multiple copies of the probes are used longitudinally to prevent stimulus binding. In the latter case, the same words are administered each time, but the way in which they are pictured varies (e.g., <u>red</u> truck, <u>red</u> apple, <u>red</u> dress, etc).

The generalization probe is always presented during the A phase of the single-subject design as the baseline measure. The number of probe administrations is determined by the nature of the design. During treatment, the same probe is again administered to monitor change. This may involve the entire probe measure or a smaller subset of items. On the Learnability Project, for example, because the PKP is a measure of the overall phonology, only those items related to the experimental manipulation are repeated as the probes of treatment. Probe administration may follow a fixed or variable schedule. To differentiate these, a fixed schedule of probing might take place, for example, during sessions 3, 6, and 9, with probes set for every third session of treatment; whereas a variable probe schedule might occur in sessions 1, 2, and 6, where sampling occurs on average every third session. The advantage of a variable schedule is that it is less predictable in time as a potential cue to testing. Probes may also be delivered based on a learner's performance, such that a particular level of accuracy is required in treatment before generalization is measured (e.g., Powell & Elbert, 1984; Powell, 1991). Regardless of the probe schedule, feedback is never provided about a learner's responses. On the Learnability Project, a variable schedule of 2 is used in probing during treatment, as in Table 1.

Perhaps the most important probe administration occurs at posttreatment because these data confirm the causal effects of treatment. In some studies, probes may continue to be administered after treatment has stopped, however any observed generalization cannot be attributed to the treatment itself. The reason is that treatment as the independent variable is no longer the only influence on behavior, leaving open the possibility that some other factors may contribute to learning. Nonetheless, continued probing for generalization is often used to plot trajectories of longitudinal change. This can be useful in determining which treatments set the foundation for continued learning and which do not. The Learnability Project protocol elicits probe data at baseline, phase shift from imitation to spontaneous production, immediately posttreatment, and at two weeks and two months after treatment is completed (Table 1). The PKP is utilized on these longitudinal probes as a benchmark of change in the phonological system, in complement to the aforementioned generalization data that are obtained in treatment. Collectively, the generalization package provides the evidence that is needed to document change in the treated sound and untreated sounds within and across contexts, as the primary dependent variables of single-subject design.

2.4   Applications

It is helpful to see the use of single-subject design in context to understand some of its nuances. In this section, we illustrate the AB design with control behavior and the staggered MBL across subjects, drawing from published work on the treatment of phonological disorders.

Gierut and Champion (2000) used the AB design with control behavior to treat a child (age 4 years;5 months) who substituted ingressive fricatives for target English sibilants /s z ʃ tʃ dʒ/. The ingressives further patterned in complementary distribution with egressives: ingressives occurred postvocalically, but egressives elsewhere. (Notably, the elsewhere condition did not extend to target sibilants; in prevocalic contexts, these were either omitted or realized as stops.) This case presented a particularly unique situation for experimental study because the documentation of ingressives in the acquisition literature is rare (Ingram & Terselic, 1983; Bedore, Leonard & Gandour, 1994), and the occurrence of complementary distribution is particularly resistant to change with treatment (Camarata & Gandour, 1984; Gierut, 1986; Dinnsen & Barlow, 1998).

The AB manipulation defined the independent variable as treatment of /s/ in word final position. The dependent variable was generalization as evidenced by a reduction in the use of the ingressive pattern with concomitant gains in the use of egressives. In the A phase, three baselines were administered. There was 0% accuracy in production of sibilants, demonstrating stability. Treatment was administered in the B phase using the nonword paradigm, with the phases of training and criteria for performance as described above. The child achieved 81% and 91% accuracy in imitation and spontaneous production, respectively. This demonstrated that learning took place day-to-day. Throughout the A and B phases, generalization was monitored. The pre- and posttreatment data are stylized in Figure 3, showing an increase in the use of untreated egressives in conjunction with a decrease in the use of untreated ingressives by context.

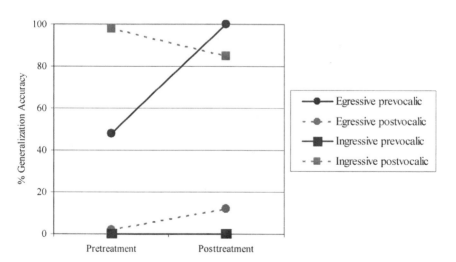

Figure 3. Generalized use of egressives versus ingressives by context, adapted from Gierut and Champion (2000).

Because a return to baseline following treatment was not desirable for this child, a control condition was added to document the causal effects of treatment on generalization learning. Liquids /l r/ served as the control sounds. They were identified from distributional gaps in the child's pretreatment phonology: liquids were excluded in word-initial position. Liquids were thus monitored in tandem with the treated and generalization classes, with baseline and posttreatment data being most relevant. Liquids remained essentially unchanged over the course of intervention. At pretreatment, they were 0% and 58% accurate in initial and postvocalic contexts respectively; at posttreatment, they were 0% and 50% accurate by respective context. This constitutes a stable production pattern as evaluated against the allowable ±10% variation. Because the accuracy and distribution of the control did not change as a result of treatment, experimental control was demonstrated in the AB manipulation. Changes in the complementary distribution of ingressives and egressives were thus a direct consequence of treatment.

Morrisette and Gierut (2002) used a staggered multiple baseline design in a study of the effects of word frequency and neighborhood density on children's phonological learning. Word frequency refers to the number of occurrences of a word in a language; neighborhood density is the number of phonetically similar counterparts to a word based on one phoneme substitutions, deletions, or additions. Together, these formed the independent variables of study, namely, treatment of sounds in high frequency, low frequency, high density, or low density words. Eight children were recruited to the conditions, being treated on either an errored fricative /f s/ or liquid /l r/, depending on the observed gaps in their pretreatment phonemic inventory. The dependent variable was generalization to treated and untreated target English phonemes that were phonotactically excluded pretreatment. Treatment followed the protocol outlined previously using 10 real words that were either of high/low frequency/density, depending upon a child's experimental assignment.

In a staggered application, the number of baselines administered in the A phase increases by 1 with successive legs of the design. Following baseline administration (and with a demonstration of baseline stability), treatment begins immediately. One advantage then of a staggered adaptation of the MBL is that a child is not held out from treatment for extended durations while other children in other legs of the design are in the process of intervention. In the Morrisette and Gierut study, there were two children corresponding to two legs of each frequency/density manipulation. The first child/leg always received 2 baselines and the second, 3 baselines. Figure 4 shows a schematic of a staggered sequence for children in the high frequency condition as one illustration (Morrisette, 2000). Across treatment, trial-by-trial learning and generalization were both demonstrated. In all, the results showed a gradient of generalization learning as defined by the breadth of change in treated, within- and across-classes; this is summarized in Table 3. Using optimality theoretic notation, the effects can be loosely translated into a constraint hierarchy, where high frequency >> low frequency, low density >> high density in promoting phonological change (Gierut, Morrisette & Champion, 1999). The results of this staggered MBL manipulation of psycholinguistic properties offered a set of testable predictions for evaluation in the linguistic domain. This reinforces the idea that learning data from children with phonological disorders can be used to evaluate the claims of linguistic and psycholinguistic theories, and potentially serves as an illustration for the design of future experimental studies.

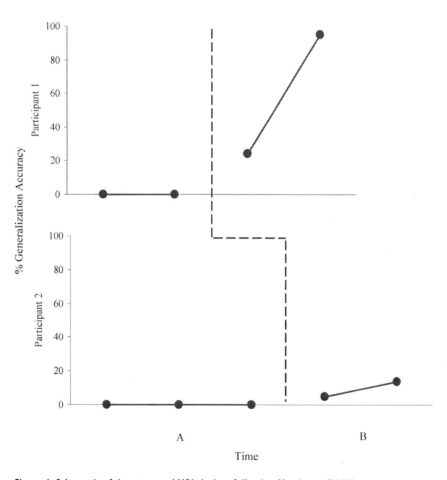

Figure 4. Schematic of the staggered MBL design, following Morrisette (2000).

Table 3. Gradient of generalization learning based on lexical frequency and density.

Generalization	High Frequency	Low Frequency	Low Density	High Density
Treated	Yes	No	Yes	No
Within-Class	Yes	Yes	No	No
Across-Class	Yes	Yes	No	No

A final mention in the discussion of design applications is the flexibility that is inherent to single-subject design. Because single-subject design is concerned with a given learner's problem and progress, it is possible to uniquely modify the design basics as long as the underlying assumptions are intact. Kearns (1986) has a comprehensive introduction to how flexible designs may be crafted. From his paper, one observation is that with design flexibility comes design complexity, with the use of one or more designs in combination with each other. This is a technique that characterizes much of our research as a way to enhance control across subjects, increase power through replication, and allow for the manipulation of multiple experimental comparisons (e.g., Gierut, Morrisette, Hughes & Rowland, 1996). One flexible complex design that is well suited to the study of phonology is an MBL across behaviors embedded within an MBL across subjects design (e.g., Gierut, 1996b). A hypothetical design implementation is shown in Figure 5. Consider a given learner, Subject 1, who is enrolled in an experimental manipulation of two properties of the grammar, a and b. These properties are manipulated in a time-lagged sequence, thereby constituting two legs of an MBL across behaviors design for this one learner. In addition to Subject 1, two other learners are recruited. Each of these subjects also has two properties of grammar that are of interest in the experimental manipulation. These learners are enrolled sequentially in the experimental manipulation, but not until Subject 1 has completed his or her experimental run. Thus Subjects 1, 2, and 3 constitute the three legs of the MBL across subjects component of the design. Notice that the combination of designs affords for six possible replications of effects within and across subjects, contributing to the generalizability of the results. If subject profiles and properties of grammar are similar across learners, then this constitutes a direct replication. However, the power of the experimental effect can be enhanced if there is variation in the properties that are manipulated across subjects. If the same result holds nonetheless, this now qualifies as a systematic replication. In the final section of this chapter, we focus on the hallmark finding of the Learnability Project that has derived from such single-subject experimental manipulations.

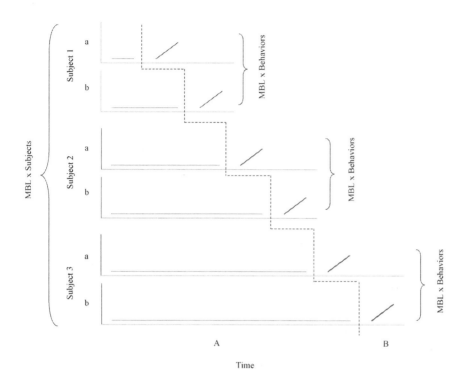

Figure 5. Schematic of the MBL across behaviors (a, b) combined with the MBL across subjects (1, 2, 3).

3   Complexity in phonological change

Three decades of research on the Learnability Project has converged upon a single finding. Specifically, complexity of the input governs phonological change, such that more complex structure promotes the greatest gains in children's sound systems. This effect has been replicated directly and systematically across participants, phonological systems, independent variables, and designs. While any given study of ours has utilized no more than 12 children, when the work is evaluated collectively, there is a consistent complexity effect that holds no matter the phenomenon being explored. Within single-subject design, the convergence of systematic replications is taken to be indicative of governing or higher order principles of learning (Parsonson & Baer, 1978). Our work thus has identified complexity as a higher order property that appears to be operative in phonology.

While it is not possible to document the results of every study that has contributed to this effect, we highlight three studies that draw from various strands of our research program. The interested reader is referred to available reviews and references therein that cite the complete range of linguistic, psycholinguistic, and clinical variables, which have been experimentally tested and shown to factor into the complexity effects (Dinnsen & Elbert, 1984; Gierut, 2001; 2007). There are reports from other independent labs and populations that concur with these findings; these too are cited in the review papers. We focus herein on illustrations of complexity associated with typological markedness, rule-based phenomena, and developmental age of sound mastery.

Typological markedness has obvious implications for learning. The prediction is that treatment of marked structure implies unmarked structure, but not vice versa. In an early investigation, Dinnsen and Elbert (1984) tested this prediction for children with phonological disorders, focusing on the relationship between fricatives and stops. Four children participated in a MBL design, with two receiving treatment on a stop and the other two, a fricative as the independent variables. The dependent variable was generalization to the related classes in untreated items. Results are stylized in Figure 6 (left panel) where it can be seen that a child treated on a stop showed gains in stops, but not fricatives. This stands apart from a child who was taught fricatives. This was the more efficacious condition because generalization extended to the treated class of fricatives and the untreated class of stops. Moreover, the results derived from treatment of relatively complex structure, in accord with predictions of markedness. Another instantiation of the effects of markedness can be found in Chapter 11 of this volume, in complement to demonstrations of complexity associated with implicational relationships involving the phonetic inventory (Tyler & Figurski, 1994), sonority (Gierut, 1999), voicing (McReynolds & Jetzke, 1986), and clusters (Elbert, Dinnsen & Powell, 1984) to cite a few.

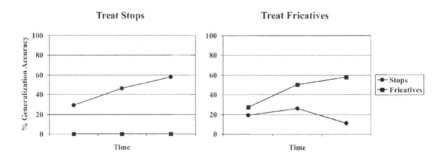

Figure 6. Generalization learning following treatment of unmarked fricatives versus marked stops, adapted from Dinnsen and Elbert (1984).

Another demonstration of complexity was culled in the context of a standard generative framework (Gierut et al., 1987). The question was whether differential generalization would be associated with the ambient or nonambient-like status of a child's underlying representations. Within generative phonology, nonambient-like underlying representations were attributed to a child in connection with phonotactic constraints. Ambient-like underlying representations were credited for dynamic sound changes that were neutralizing or allophonic. Following the theoretical reasoning, it was predicted that treatment of ambient-like underlying representations would be more facilitating since a child would have had greater underlying knowledge of the target phonemes, i.e., 'most knowledge.' It was expected that treating phonotactics would be more difficult since these target phonemes were unknown underlyingly, i.e., 'least knowledge.' A complex single-subject design using a multiple probe in conjunction with multiple baseline across subjects was used. Six children participated. The independent variable was starting point of treatment, most versus least knowledge. Half the children started treatment with most knowledge or rules; the other half started with least knowledge or phonotactics. The dependent variable was generalization to treated and untreated categories of a child's phonology. Stylized results are shown in Figure 7. When treatment was initiated with most knowledge, change occurred in target sounds affected by rules, but other sounds excluded from the inventory remained unchanged. By comparison, the more effective condition was associated with treatment of least knowledge. In this condition, treatment of phonotactics induced concomitant changes in rules, thus impacting the application of both static and dynamic properties of the phonology. In all, the findings suggest that expansion of the inventory promotes greater phonological generalization than does undoing errored applications of phonological rules. Interestingly, similar effects have been reported in the second language acquisition literature (Hammerly, 1982; Hardy, 1993).

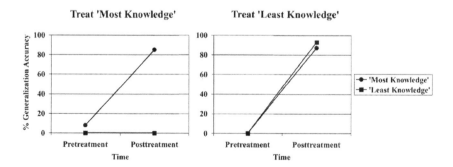

Figure 7. Generalization learning when treatment was initiated for 'most knowledge' versus 'least knowledge,' adapted from Gierut (1985).

A final illustration of complexity comes from development. A long held assumption is that earlier acquired sounds are 'easier' than later acquired sounds. This view is a holdover from Piagetian theory and the assumptions of maturational stage models. As applied to phonology, a stage model assumes that development follows a linear trend, such that sounds are acquired in fixed sequence in accord with maturational development. Another assumption is that early acquired sounds are easier to learn since they develop first. A further assumption is that early acquired sounds are prerequisite for later acquired sounds. These assumptions have been the cornerstone of clinical treatment for phonological disorders, where the conventional practice is to set the goals of treatment starting with the earliest sound a child produces in error (Van Riper, 1963; Winitz, 1975; Hodson, 1989). Interestingly, this recommendation had never been put to experimental test to determine the efficacy of teaching early as opposed to later acquired sounds. Two related studies were designed to address this question, using complementary single-subject designs (Gierut et al., 1996). One of the studies was a multiple baseline across 6 children, with half receiving treatment on an early acquired sound in error and the other half, a later acquired sound in error. Generalization was the dependent variable, with measures of gains in both early and later acquired sounds. Stylized results are shown in Figure 8. In the early acquired condition, generalization extended to

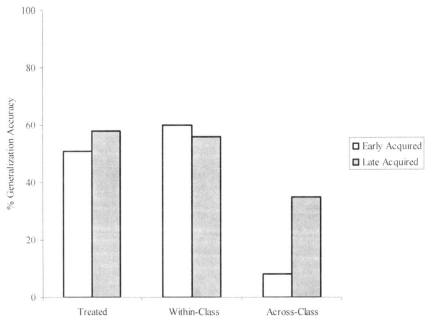

Figure 8. Generalization learning following treatment of early versus later acquired sounds, adapted from Gierut et al. (1999).

the treated sound and other members of the same manner class (i.e., within-class generalization). Likewise, the later acquired condition promoted the same kinds of treated and within-manner class gains. The teaching conditions were indistinguishable on these dimensions. The primary difference was based on across-class gains to untreated and unrelated manner classes. Specifically, later acquired sounds in treatment prompted system wide gains in the phonology across all affected manner classes, whereas the early acquired sounds did not. There were other benefits to treatment of later acquired sounds in that generalization was immediate in treatment, whereas change was delayed relative to early acquired sounds. Thus, the connection between early and easy was not beneficial to children's phonological learning. This effect has been demonstrated for learners with cognitive impairments who have phonological disorders as well (Dyer, Santarcangelo & Luce, 1987), suggesting further that ease may not be a cognitive necessity in learning.

Taken together, these examples illustrate how presumably more complex treatment targets are actually more efficacious in inducing change in children's phonologies. This effect is wholly consistent with models of language learnability as outlined in the context of universal grammar (Wexler & Culicover, 1980; Wexler, 1982). Children must be exposed to input that is outside the range of their own internal grammar in order to induce further language learning. In future research, it may be fruitful to reconsider the available findings on complexity from the view of optimality theory and the ranking of constraints. One hypothesis maintains that markedness constraints banning complex structure are highly ranked in children's grammar. Presumably, the highest ranked constraints would be demoted below Faithfulness in treatment, and consequently, this licenses the occurrence of complex structure. The puzzling question for optimality theory though is why should demotion of one high-ranked markedness constraint have consequences for so many other lower-ranked markedness constraints in the grammar? One option is to appeal to a fixed ranking among constraints. Given the extent of the generalization that is typically observed in learning studies, this may be problematic. The reason is that a host of seemingly unrelated constraints would need to be in a fixed ranking with each other to obtain the experimental effects. From the point of view of learning, it may be that the grammatical insights that a child gains in demotion of one high-ranked markedness constraint are so great as to motivate the demotion of other seemingly unrelated markedness constraints. Consequently, learning may take place so rapidly that it is impossible to capture the independent demotion of a host of individual constraints. This may require layered sets of studies to explore constraint-to-constraint relationships in treatment. Alternatively, the constraints of optimality theory may be too fine-grained as to be realized in an actual learning situation. This calls for added experimental studies of learning to complement learnability hypotheses that derive from theory. No matter what the outcome may be, the one fell swoop learning effect that derives from complexity will no doubt challenge and benefit theories of language, learning, and development.

Part II

Research reports: Opacity effects

4 A typology of opacity effects in acquisition*

Daniel A. Dinnsen
Indiana University

The phonological generalizations that are characteristic of children's early speech are generally assumed to reflect an initial state of relative unmarkedness and/or to be learned from the observable primary linguistic data. This chapter examines a number of emergent generalizations that do not fit well with standard expectations and that pose theoretical challenges. These generalizations have the special property of being opaque, i.e., they are either not surface-true or not surface-apparent. Most would consider such generalizations to be marked, and these particular generalizations were moreover not evident in the language to which the children were exposed. Optimality theory has had to invoke special machinery to account for opacity effects, and little is known about the incidence, emergence and loss of such generalizations in developing phonologies. This chapter presents data and analyses for several different emergent opacity effects and situates them in a larger typology. Primary attention is given to a case study involving the emergence and loss of an opaque generalization in the phonology of a child with a phonological delay (Child 142, age 4;3). Two independent error patterns in the presenting phonology were of special interest: Word-initial affricates deaffricated (Deaffrication), and word-initial alveolar stops assimilated in place to a following nonadjacent dorsal consonant (Place Assimilation). These error patterns interacted to yield perfectly transparent outputs ([tu] 'chew'; [kaɪɡoʊ] 'tiger'; [kɪkɪn] 'chicken'). However, following the child's enrollment in a clinical treatment experiment that was aimed at the elimination of Place Assimilation, the two error patterns interacted to yield opaque outputs: Place Assimilation persisted for those stops that were derived from Deaffrication ([kɪkɪn] 'chicken'), whereas nonderived target stops were immune to Place Assimilation ([taɪɡoʊ] 'tiger'). Subsequently and without further treatment, the remnants of Place Assimilation and Deaffrication were fully suppressed. Alternative optimality theoretic accounts of these and other acquisition facts are formulated and evaluated.

1   Introduction

Many of the phonological error patterns evident in children's early acquisition can be expressed as phonotactic generalizations. These generalizations represent the predictable properties of the children's pronunciation and are a central property of their grammars. A typical generalization might characterize restrictions on a child's phonetic inventory, the distribution of sounds, and/or substitution patterns. Depending on the theoretical framework one adopts, these generalizations are formulated as rules, processes or constraint hierarchies. Given the claims of Universal Grammar and assumptions about the initial state, very little learning would be required for such generalizations (e.g., Donegan & Stampe, 1979; Hayes, 2004; Prince & Tesar, 2004). However, if an error pattern changes over time or is lost, learning must be taking place, presumably on the basis of positive evidence from the primary linguistic data to which the child is exposed. Children's phonotactic generalizations should, therefore, be derivable from Universal Grammar or from observable facts in the target language being acquired.

Most phonological generalizations can be gleaned directly from the observable data and are transparent or surface-true. In such cases, the generalization holds without exceptions, and the factors that condition the generalization are present and observable on the surface. However, we know, especially from the early rule ordering literature within derivational phonology (Kiparsky, 1965; 1971; 1976), that phonological processes can interact and that sometimes those interactions result in generalizations that are opaque (i.e., not surface-true or not surface-apparent). In such cases, it might appear that (a) a process should have applied but did not (underapplication) or (b) a process applied but should not have because the conditioning factors are not present (overapplication). Opaque generalizations are interesting from both a theoretical and developmental perspective. To begin with, they are generally considered to be marked or hard to learn (e.g., Kiparsky, 1971). Despite this, opaque generalizations have been observed to occur in developing phonologies (see §4 and references therein). However, we know very little about how or why they emerge, especially in the course of acquiring a language which itself does not exhibit the opacity effect. The characterization of opacity effects has also posed a special challenge for optimality theory (Prince & Smolensky, 1993/2004; McCarthy, 2002b). The challenge has been met with varying degrees of success by different proposals, including (but not limited to) local constraint conjunction (e.g., Smolensky, 1995; Kirchner, 1996; Łubowicz, 2002), sympathy (McCarthy, 1999), comparative markedness (McCarthy, 2002a), output-to-output correspondence (Benua, 1995; 1997), and optimality theory with candidate chains (McCarthy, 2007). While some of these proposals have been examined relative to acquisition phenomena, the number of available case studies is relatively small, making it difficult to assess the range of occurring opacity effects in developing phonologies and even more difficult to evaluate the explanatory adequacy of these proposals.

This chapter brings together a range of emergent opacity effects with the intent of arriving at a fuller typology and evaluating some theoretical proposals within optimality theory. A substantial portion of the chapter is devoted to a consideration of a case study involving the emergence and loss of an opaque generalization in the phonology of a child acquiring English. This opaque generalization is not evident in English, but is an example of a process that is restricted to operate only in a derived environment. An optimality theoretic account of these acquisition facts will also be formulated. Two proposals for dealing with such opacity effects will be evaluated, specifically local constraint conjunction (Łubowicz, 2002) and comparative markedness (McCarthy, 2002a). While the primary focus will be on the changes in one child's phonology, other emergent opacity effects will also be analyzed to situate each in the larger typology. It will be argued that opacity effects are naturally occurring in the course of acquisition and that some proposals fare better than others in accounting for certain opacity effects. The chapter is organized as follows: In §2, the facts of the main case study are spelled out with a focus on a child's presenting phonology and the changes in that phonology as a result of treatment; §3 formulates and evaluates alternative optimality theoretic accounts for each of the observed stages; §4 presents analyses for a range of other emergent opacity effects in other children's phonologies and fills out the typology of opacity effects. The chapter concludes with a brief summary.

2   The case study

2.1   The presenting phonology

The case study reported here was drawn from a larger archival and experimental investigation of young children's phonological development (i.e., the Developmental Phonology Archive at Indiana University). Child 142 (age 4 years;3 months) was typically developing in all respects, except for evidence of a phonological delay. He scored within normal limits on all standardized tests of hearing, oral-motor mechanism and functioning, non-verbal intelligence, receptive vocabulary, and expressive and receptive language. He did, however, score at the 5th percentile on the *Goldman-Fristoe Test of Articulation* (Goldman & Fristoe, 1986). A comprehensive speech sample was also elicited in a spontaneous picture-naming task. The audio recordings were phonetically transcribed by a trained listener with 10% of all probes retranscribed for reliability purposes by an independent judge. The overall reliability measure was 95% agreement. Given that the focus of this case study is on word-initial place and manner characteristics of sounds, the reliability of the transcription of those sounds was also examined more specifically, revealing a disagreement in the transcription of only one word. The transcriptions were submitted to a phonological analysis that revealed a number of systematic error patterns, two of which are of special interest. One error pattern replaced word-initial affricates with simple alveolar stops (Deaffrication), and the other replaced word-initial alveolar stops with a dorsal consonant when a dorsal occurred later in the word (Place Assimilation). The relevant data are given in (1).

(1)   Child 142 (age 4;3)

    a)   Word-initial affricates replaced by simple alveolar stops (Deaffrication)

[tɪn]	'chin'	[dʌmp]	'jump'
[tu]	'chew'	[dip]	'jeep'
[tɪp]	'chip'	[dɛt]	'jet'

    b)   Affricates occur postvocalically

[wɔts]	'watch'	[bwɪːdz]	'bridge'
[pits]	'peach'	[bædz]	'badge'
[pʌntsɪn]	'punching'	[oʊwɪndzi]	'orange-i'

    c)   Word-initial alveolar stops assimilate to the place of a following dorsal consonant (Place Assimilation)

[gʌks]	'ducks'	[gʌki]	'duckie'
[gɔg]	'dog'	[gɔgi]	'doggie'
[kaɪgoʊ]	'tiger'	[kɪkɪt]	'ticket'

    d)   Fricatives occur word-initially

[sæni]	'Santa'	[sʌn]	'sun'
[soʊp]	'soap'	[sup]	'soup'
[sɔk]	'sock'	[sɪk]	'sick'

    e)   Affricates deaffricate and assimilate to the place of a following dorsal (Derived Assimilation)

[kik]	'cheek'	[kɪkɪn]	'chicken'
[kɔk]	'chalk'	[gækət̚]	'jacket'

    f)   Labial fricatives realized as coronals (Control error pattern)

[ɛwəsɪnts]	'elephant'	[seɪs]	'face'
[saɪz]	'five'	[gusi]	'goofy'
[wus]	'roof'	[kɔˀs]	'cough'

The forms in (1a) illustrate the Deaffrication error pattern in word-initial position, while those in (1b) show that (alveolar) affricates could occur in postvocalic
contexts. The contrast between affricates and stops was thus merged in favor of
simple stops in one well-defined context, namely in word-initial position. The
Deaffrication error pattern and its restriction to word-initial position are common
in children's early phonologies (Smit, 1993a; Chapter 9 in this volume). The
Place Assimilation error pattern is illustrated in (1c). Word-initial alveolar stops
were replaced by a dorsal consonant when a dorsal followed later in the word.
This error pattern is a typical instantiation of Regressive Consonant Harmony
as described in many other children's phonologies (Pater & Werle, 2003 and
references therein). The target of Place Assimilation was limited to alveolar stops
as can be seen by the forms in (1d). That is, alveolar fricatives could occur in
word-initial position in both assimilatory and non-assimilatory contexts. The
contrast between stops and fricatives was thus preserved in that context, and
fricatives showed no vulnerability to Place Assimilation. Deaffrication and
Place Assimilation also interacted as can be seen in (1e). That is, both processes were applicable when a word-initial affricate was followed by a dorsal
consonant. Under those circumstances, the word-initial affricate deaffricated and
also assimilated to the place of the following dorsal. While these error patterns
interacted, it is important to note that (unlike many other potential interactions)
this interaction did not obscure the generalizations associated with either error
pattern. Both generalizations were transparent in the presenting phonology. We
will see in a subsequent stage of development that the nature of the interaction
changed and rendered one of the generalizations opaque. It is also important to
keep in mind that these two processes were independently necessary. That is,
there were some words where Deaffrication alone was applicable (1a), and there
were other words where only Place Assimilation was applicable (1c). In these
situations, then, each process applied without any potential interference from
the other. However, if an affricate assimilated, it also deaffricated.

Finally, the forms in (1f) are illustrative of another independent error pattern affecting fricatives: As labial fricatives were replaced by coronals in all
contexts, the inventory of fricatives was limited to coronals. While the place
contrast among fricatives was merged, the contrast between fricatives and
stops was preserved. Because this error pattern did not interact in any way
with Deaffrication or Place Assimilation, it served as a control in the treatment
experiment (to be described below).

To describe the facts about Deaffrication and Place Assimilation in rule-
based derivational terms, we might propose two rules ordered in a feeding
relation as shown in the derivation in (2). A Deaffrication rule would be
formulated to operate on word-initial affricates, converting them into simple
alveolar stops. The Place Assimilation rule, which specifies dorsal consonants

as the trigger of assimilation and alveolar stops as the target, would be ordered after Deaffrication. As such, the output of Deaffrication could then serve as the input to Place Assimilation.

(2)   Rule-based derivational account

UR	/tʃu/	/taɪɡɚ/	/tʃik/
Deaffrication	tu	—	tik
Place assimilation	—	kaɪɡou	kik
PR	[tu]	[kaɪɡou]	[kik]

2.2   Treatment and learning patterns

Of the various error patterns evident in this child's speech, one was selected for treatment, namely Place Assimilation. Place Assimilation, as opposed to Deaffrication, was targeted in order to take advantage of an observed implicational relationship among certain error patterns, discussed in Dinnsen and O'Connor (2001a). One of the findings of their typological study was that the occurrence of certain error patterns involving manner features implied the occurrence of other error patterns involving place features. The implicational relationship appeared to be unidirectional in that problems with place features did not necessarily imply problems with manner features. Consequently, if errors in manner indeed depend in some way on the occurrence of errors in place, it is predicted that treatment that is successful at eradicating the place-related error pattern should result in the loss of the manner-related error pattern without direct treatment on the latter. In this case, then, the loss of Place Assimilation should result in the loss of Deaffrication. Treatment was designed to test this prediction by attempting to eradicate Place Assimilation.

Treatment was structured around a set of 8 nonwords of the shape /tVk/, /tVkV/, and /tVkVC/. The consonants in these nonwords were systematically varied for their voicing. The phonological characteristics of the nonwords were specifically designed to focus the child's attention on the occurrence of alveolar stops in the context before dorsals. Nonwords (rather than real words) were used for several reasons. First, this child was part of a larger experimental study in which it was important to control for individual differences in the words that children might know and for any potential influence of that knowledge on training and learning. Nonwords provide that control given that all children were unfamiliar with these nonwords prior to treatment. Nonwords have also been shown to offer an advantage for sublexical processing (e.g., Vitevitch, Luce, Charles-Luce & Kemmerer, 1997).

In an attempt to associate the nonwords with meaning, they were paired with pictures of imaginary figures engaged in novel activities. For an overview of similar treatment protocols, see Gierut (1989b). The child was seen for one-hour sessions three times a week. Treatment proceeded in two phases. In the first phase, the child produced the nonwords in imitation. The design of the experiment called for this phase to continue for a maximum of 7 sessions or until 75% accuracy on the treated nonwords was achieved in two consecutive sessions, whichever occurred first. This child met the criterion in the first two days of treatment. In the second phase, treatment then shifted to spontaneous production of the nonwords in association with the picture; a model was not provided as a prompt. The child was given feedback during this phase, but only the spontaneous productions were counted in assessing accuracy. This phase continued for a maximum of 12 sessions or until 90% accuracy was achieved in three consecutive sessions, whichever came first. For this child, the criterion was met in the first three days. Consequently, the actual time that this child was in treatment totaled 5 hours.

To assess change in the child's phonology, generalization probes were administered before, during, and following treatment. The probe list consisted of almost 600 untreated real words that sampled all aspects of the child's segmental phonology and especially his performance relative to the error patterns described in (1).

Figure 1 plots on the y-axis the percentage of words in the probe exhibiting each error pattern with time represented along the x-axis. Because some of the error patterns could interact in certain situations, distinct elements of each error pattern are plotted as a separate function. For example, the Deaffrication function relates to target words where Deaffrication alone is applicable (1a). Similarly, Place Assimilation refers to target words where that process alone is applicable (1b). The interaction of these two error patterns is reflected in the function labeled Derived Assimilation, where word-initial affricates could both deaffricate and assimilate (1e). Finally, the Fricative Substitution function refers to the error pattern affecting labial fricatives as described in (1f). Because of its presumed independence from the other error patterns, Fricative Substitution served as the control, and it was expected that this error pattern would persist with a high frequency of occurrence regardless of treatment. In comparison to the stability of the control error pattern, the changes that occur in the other error patterns can then be attributed, at least in part, to treatment and not maturation.

The first point in time represents the baseline performance prior to treatment. The subsequent points in time refer to phase shift (i.e., the point between imitation and spontaneous production training), immediate posttreatment, two-weeks posttreatment and two-months posttreatment.

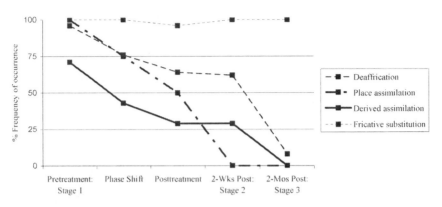

Figure 1. Generalization learning patterns.

The results reveal three identifiable stages. There is obviously some variation during these stages as reflected in the gradual decline of some of the functions. The nature of the variation centers around the fact that a process operates on some, but not other, words of the same phonological shape. Variation of this sort poses a separate set of challenges that will not concern us here.[1] We will instead define stages in terms of the observed extremes, i.e., the simple presence versus absence of an error pattern, without regard for the relative number of words affected. During the baseline period prior to treatment, all of the error patterns co-occurred and were evident in a high percentage of words. This accords with our claims about Child 142's presenting phonology and represents Stage 1 as described in (1). After treatment was initiated on Place Assimilation, all of the error patterns, except the control, began to decline. Of those error patterns that changed in response to treatment, Deaffrication was the most resistant, persisting until two-months posttreatment, albeit in a very small percentage of words (less than 10%) at that final sampling point. In contrast, the treated error pattern—Place Assimilation—declined the fastest, and was completely eradicated by two-weeks posttreatment. Words such as 'tiger', which had been realized with an assimilated production [kaɪgoʊ], changed to a relatively faithful production [taɪgʊ]. We thus take two-weeks posttreatment to represent Stage 2, identified primarily by the complete loss of Place Assimilation. The results as described to this point should not be surprising given the numerous prior studies that establish improved performance on treated (as opposed to untreated) sounds (e.g., Dinnsen & Elbert, 1984; Gierut, 1985).

The more interesting result at Stage 2 is the persistence of assimilation in words that could interact with Deaffrication (i.e., the Derived Assimilation function) despite the fact that the more basic Place Assimilation error pattern had been lost. That is, a word such as 'cheek' continued to be realized as [kik], while 'tiger' was realized faithfully. Stated differently, underlying simple alveolar stops were not affected by Place Assimilation, whereas alveolar stops derived from Deaffrication were. This asymmetry renders Place Assimilation opaque because only derived stops are subject to the error pattern. Underlying stops are immune to Place Assimilation. The opacity effect evident at Stage 2 should be compared to the transparency of Place Assimilation at earlier points where both underlying and derived alveolar stops were affected by the error pattern. It is the emergence of this opacity effect that is a focal point of this chapter.

We need to determine how and why Place Assimilation would have changed from a transparent generalization to an opaque generalization, especially given that the primary linguistic data provides no evidence for such a restriction. In derivational terms, the change from Stage 1 to Stage 2 might be attributed to a change in the status of the Place Assimilation rule. That is, if some version of Lexical Phonology (Kiparsky, 1982) were adopted, it might be claimed that Place Assimilation changed from a post-lexical rule that could apply to underlying and derived representations to a lexical rule that could only apply to phonologically derived representations. The problem remains that English provides no evidence that a learner could use to motivate the change or restriction in the Place Assimilation rule. In any event, Stage 2 is characterized by the persistence of Deaffrication and the emergence of an opacity effect for Place Assimilation.

The most significant fact marking Stage 3 (two-months posttreatment) is the loss of the opaque generalization (Derived Assimilation). That is, Place Assimilation no longer targeted deaffricated stops, and words such as 'cheek' were realized with a word-initial affricate. At this point, Deaffrication persisted in only a few words, none of which could have interacted with Place Assimilation. For all practical purposes, then, Deaffrication was marginal at that point. The decline and suppression of Deaffrication largely paralleled the loss of Place Assimilation as predicted by Dinnsen and O'Connor (2001a). While we cannot be entirely sure whether the loss of Deaffrication occurred concurrent with or subsequent to the loss of the opaque generalization, our preliminary assumption will be that both generalizations were lost at (or around) the same time.[2] This assumption is supported by the fact that at that point in time affricates were produced word-initially in all words where the two processes could have interacted and in over 90% of all other words. Again, in derivational terms, it would be claimed that the more restricted Place Assimilation rule and the Deaffrication rule were lost from the child's grammar.

The final observation in Figure 1 is that the control error pattern, which replaced labial fricatives with coronal fricatives, continued to occur in a high percentage of words. This error pattern was thus not affected by the other error patterns, treatment, or maturation. It properly served as a control error pattern.

By way of summary, the display in (3) highlights the crucial changes in the Place Assimilation error pattern over the three stages. Place Assimilation was perfectly transparent during Stage 1, affecting both underlying and derived alveolar stops. By two-weeks posttreatment (Stage 2), Place Assimilation no longer affected underlying alveolar stops but continued to operate on derived alveolar stops, rendering Place Assimilation opaque. All remnants of Place Assimilation were lost by two-months posttreatment (Stage 3).

(3)   Summary of changes to Place Assimilation

> Stage 1:   Underlying and derived alveolar stops targeted by Place Assimilation (Transparent)
>
> Stage 2:   Only derived alveolar stops targeted by Place Assimilation (Opaque)
>
> Stage 3:   Place Assimilation lost

3   Optimality theoretic accounts

This section formulates optimality theoretic accounts for each of the documented stages as well as the transition from one stage to the next. Two different proposals for dealing with opacity effects are considered, namely local constraint conjunction (Łubowicz, 2002) and comparative markedness (McCarthy, 2002a).

3.1   Stage 1: Transparent generalizations

Each of the error patterns at Stage 1 resulted in surface-true, transparent generalizations. This was so even in those cases where Deaffrication and Place Assimilation could interact. The interaction did not obscure either generalization. The relevant fact is that Place Assimilation effected assimilation of alveolar stops whether they were derived from Deaffrication or not.

The constraints relevant to the facts of this stage are given in (4).

(4)   Constraints and ranking

> a)   Markedness
>
> #-Agree: Word-initial alveolar stops are banned when followed by a nonadjacent consonant with a different place feature
>
> *#Affr: Word-initial affricates are banned
>
> *f: Labial fricatives are banned
>
> *s: Grooved coronal fricatives are banned

b)   Faithfulness

ID[place]:   Corresponding segments must have identical place features

ID[manner]: Corresponding segments must have identical manner features

c)   Ranking: #-AGREE, *#AFFR, *f >> ID[manner] >> *s >> ID[place]

In accord with assumptions about the initial state and the default ranking of constraints (Smolensky, 1996a), it is assumed that error patterns arise from the dominance of certain markedness constraints over antagonistic faithfulness constraints. Deaffrication, Place Assimilation and the control error pattern involve changes in manner and/or place features, suggesting that the faithfulness constraints ID[manner] and ID[place] are dominated by specific markedness constraints. Beginning with Deaffrication, we saw that the contrast between word-initial affricates and simple alveolar stops was neutralized in favor of the simple alveolar stop. A contextually conditioned markedness constraint such as *#AFFR banning word-initial affricates would compel a change to a less marked stop if that constraint dominated ID[manner].[3] For expository purposes, we will consider stops, fricatives and affricates to differ in manner, even though different features and geometric structures may ultimately be involved in their representations. Thus, any change from an affricate to a simple alveolar stop (or to a fricative) will be considered to violate ID[manner]. The tableau in (5) illustrates the ranking necessary to account for this one aspect of the error pattern.

(5)   Deaffrication

/tʃu/ 'chew'	*#AFFR	ID[manner]
a. tʃu	*!	
b. ☞ tu		*

We are assuming here and throughout that this child's input representations were target-appropriate. This is in accord with 'Richness of the Base' (Prince & Smolensky, 1993/2004), which precludes language-specific (or child-specific) restrictions on input representations. However, even if the input representation for this word were assumed to be identical to the occurring errored output representation, as might follow from lexicon optimization (Prince & Smolensky, 1993/2004; Itô, Mester & Padgett, 1995), the constraint hierarchy guarantees the selection of the attested output. By ranking *#AFFR over ID[manner], candidate (a) with an affricate incurs a fatal violation of the markedness constraint and is ruled out in favor of candidate (b) no matter what is assumed about the input representation.

In contrast to Deaffrication, where ID[manner] was violated, the control error pattern affecting fricatives preserved manner but resulted in a change in place. Labial fricatives were replaced by coronal fricatives (1f), and target coronal fricatives retained their place (1d). These facts require exploding the general context-free markedness constraint that bans fricatives into at least two component constraints: *f, which bans labial fricatives and *s, which bans coronal fricatives. These component constraints are independently necessary to account for observed individual differences in children's fricative inventories (Chapter 8 in this volume). By ranking *f over ID[manner], we can account for the non-occurrence of labial fricatives, and by ranking *s below ID[manner], we can account for the preservation of manner in the substitutes for labial fricatives and for the faithful occurrence of coronal fricatives. The dominance of ID[manner] over *s obviously departs from the initial-state ranking and reflects the learning that would have occurred based on the child's observation that coronal fricatives occurred in the primary linguistic data to which he was exposed. The change in place suggests that ID[place] is low-ranked, but we cannot tell just yet where it fits in the hierarchy. With the constraints that have been ranked thus far, the tableau in (6) illustrates how we can account for the control error pattern.

(6)   Control error pattern

/feɪs/ 'face'	*#AFFR	*f	ID[manner]	*s
a. feɪs		*!		
b. peɪs			*!	
c. tʃeɪs	*!		*	
d. ☞ seɪs				*

The faithful candidate (a) is eliminated by its violation of undominated *f. In terms of potential substitutes, candidate (b) with a labial stop preserves place but fatally violates ID[manner]. Candidate (c) with an initial affricate is an unlikely substitute and is eliminated by its violation of undominated *#AFFR (with an additional violation from ID[manner]). With all competitors being eliminated by higher-ranked constraints, candidate (d) is selected as optimal, even though it changes its place and violates *s.

Moving now to Place Assimilation, this error pattern also involves a change in a place feature, namely the change from an alveolar stop to a dorsal when followed by a dorsal consonant. Another contextually conditioned markedness constraint is needed: The constraint #-AGREE can compel the change by banning word-initial alveolar stops in that context, provided that this constraint also dominates the antagonistic faithfulness constraint ID[place]. This faithfulness constraint is an abbreviation for a set of constraints that refer to specific place features where, for example, preservation of dorsal place is more important than preservation of coronal place (e.g., de Lacy, 2002).[4] While #-AGREE would assign a fatal violation mark to the faithful candidate with this ranking, this is not sufficient to determine the repair whereby the initial consonant is replaced by a more marked dorsal that agrees in place with a following consonant. Other constraints are needed to rule out all but the assimilated candidate, and we still need to determine where in the hierarchy ID[place] must be ranked. The constraints and rankings considered thus far go some way toward achieving the desired result. The dominance of *#AFFR, which was established for the Deaffrication error pattern, is helpful here in ruling out substitutes with an initial affricate. Similarly, the undominated character of *f, required for the control error pattern, will eliminate candidates with labial fricatives as substitutes. Given that ID[place] can be violated, and given moreover that it has not played a role thus far, we will adopt the position, consistent with the assumption that faithfulness constraints are ranked as low as possible (e.g., Hayes, 2004), that ID[place] is ranked below *s. The tableau in (7) illustrates how these constraints and the hierarchy account for several details of this error pattern when the input includes a word-initial alveolar stop.

(7) Place Assimilation

/taɪgə/ 'tiger'	#-AGREE	*#AFFR	*f	ID[manner]	*s	ID[place]
a. taɪgoʊ	*!					
b. tʃaɪgoʊ		*!			*	
c. faɪgoʊ			*!		*	*
d. saɪgoʊ				*!	*	
e. ☞ kaɪgoʊ						*

Candidates (a), (b), and (c) are all eliminated by their violations of the high-ranked markedness constraints. Note that candidate (b) with an initial affricate does not violate #-AGREE as we are interpreting the constraint. The assumption is that Place Assimilation targets simple (non-branching) alveolar stops and not other coronals that differ from the trigger in terms of manner. This assumption is not crucial here, but we will see that it is important as we consider the facts of the subsequent stages. Recall, however, that coronal fricatives were immune to Place Assimilation (1d). Of the remaining candidates, candidate (d) with a coronal fricative incurs a fatal violation of ID[manner] (in addition to its violation of *s), resulting in the selection of candidate (e) as optimal, despite its violation of ID[place].

It is a simple matter now to see how the account works to yield transparent outputs for words where Deaffrication and Place Assimilation interact. The tableau in (8) considers the realization of a word such as 'cheek', adopting the constraints and ranking from above.

(8)   Transparent interaction of Deaffrication and Place Assimilation

/tʃik/ 'cheek'	#-AGREE	*#AFFR	*f	ID[manner]	*s	ID[place]
a. tʃik		*!				
b. tik	*!			*		
c. fik			*!	*		*
d. sik				*	*!	
e. ☞ kik				*		*

Just as in the prior tableau, candidates (a), (b), and (c) are eliminated by their violations of the undominated markedness constraints. The difference is that the remaining candidates (d) and (e) each violate ID[manner], resulting in a tie. The choice is thus passed down to the next stratum where *s assigns a fatal violation mark to candidate (d). The assimilated candidate (e) is selected as optimal, despite its violation of ID[place], because all other competitors have been eliminated by higher-ranked constraints. This tableau provides crucial evidence in support of our decision to rank ID[place] as low as possible in this hierarchy.

Summing up to this point, we have accounted for the error patterns in Child 142's presenting phonology in a way that is consistent with standard optimality theory. This is largely because the generalizations associated with the child's phonology were perfectly transparent. In particular, we saw that word-initial alveolar stops assimilated whether they corresponded to underlying stops or to stops derived from Deaffrication. However, we will see in the next section that this generalization became opaque and that optimality theory cannot account for the facts of Stage 2 without adopting certain theoretical innovations.

3.2   Stage 2: Emergence of opaque generalization (grandfather effect)

The two most relevant facts about Stage 2 (two-weeks posttreatment) that need to be accounted for are (a) that Place Assimilation ceased to have an effect on underlying alveolar stops, and (b) that Place Assimilation continued to affect alveolar stops derived from Deaffrication. The data in (9) illustrate these facts.

(9) Two-weeks posttreatment

    a) Underlying alveolar stops immune to Place Assimilation

        [dɔg]   'dog'   [taɪgʊ]   'tiger'

    b) Derived alveolar stops undergo Place Assimilation

        [kik]   'cheek'   [kɔk]   'chalk'

This represents the emergence of an opacity effect. That is, a process that had operated uniformly in the prior stage is now blocked from applying to a well-defined subset of identical segment types. Although it is standardly assumed that alveolar stops derived from Deaffrication are identical to alveolar stops that have not undergone any processes, the fact remains that at Stage 2 the only evidence of Place Assimilation was in words that were also subject to Deaffrication.[5]

To account for the simple loss or suppression of a process like Place Assimilation requires only that the child take note of the fact that alveolar stops could occur word-initially even when followed by a dorsal consonant. On the basis of such positive evidence and in accord with the constraint demotion algorithm (Tesar & Smolensky, 1998), the markedness constraint responsible for the error pattern (#-AGREE) would be demoted just below the highest-ranked constraint that the previous winner violated, namely just below ID[place]. The constraint hierarchy would otherwise retain the rankings from the previous stage. The tableau in (10) shows that the desired output can be selected by the new hierarchy, at least for words beginning underlyingly with simple alveolar stops.

(10) #-AGREE demoted: Place Assimilation suppressed (tentative)

/taɪgə/ 'tiger'	*#AFFR	*f	ID[manner]	*s	ID[place]	#-AGREE
a. ☞ taɪgʊ						*
b. tʃaɪgʊ	*!		*			
c. faɪgʊ		*!	*		*	
d. saɪgʊ			*!	*		
e. kaɪgʊ					*!	

The problem is that this new ranking fails to predict the persistence of the error pattern for alveolar stops derived from Deaffrication. This is illustrated in the tableau in (11). Note that the hierarchy predicts that the deaffricated, but unassimilated, candidate (b) would win, when the actually occurring output should have been candidate (e) (represented by '☞').

(11) Place Assimilation incorrectly blocked for derived alveolar stops

/tʃik/ 'check'		*#AFFR	*f	ID[manner]	*s	ID[place]	#-AGREE
a.	tʃik	*!					
b. ☞	tik			*			*
c.	fik		*!	*		*	
d.	sik			*	*!		
e. ☜	kik			*		*!	

Problems of this sort have been amply documented in fully developed languages. Those phenomena have variously been referred to as 'nonderived environment blocking' (e.g., Kiparsky, 1976; 1993a) or 'grandfather effects' (McCarthy, 2002a). One proposal for dealing with such effects extends optimality theory by invoking a special type of constraint conjunction whereby a low-ranked markedness constraint is conjoined with a faithfulness constraint and that locally conjoined constraint is ranked above the individual conjuncts (Łubowicz, 2002). With regard to the case at hand, the hierarchy in (10) and (11) would be modified by the combination of low-ranked #-AGREE and ID[manner] to yield the locally conjoined constraint, which we will label LC. This new constraint would be ranked above ID[manner]. The simple #-AGREE constraint would remain low-ranked. The locally conjoined constraint would only be violated by a candidate that violated both of the conjuncts, namely one with a word-initial alveolar stop that differed from the corresponding input in terms of manner and was followed by a dorsal later in the word. This is precisely the candidate that needed to be excluded in tableau (11) above. The tableau in (12) illustrates the local conjunction account for a word like 'cheek'. Note that LC assigns a fatal violation mark to candidate (b), which is deaffricated but not assimilated. Candidates (a) and (c) are also eliminated by the undominated markedness constraints. The remaining candidates each violate ID[manner], passing the choice down to *s, which assigns a fatal violation mark to candidate (d). The candidate that is both deaffricated and assimilated, namely candidate (e), is selected as optimal.

(12) Local conjunction account of opaque generalization

/tʃik/ 'check'		LC	*#AFFR	*f	ID[manner]	*s	ID[place]	#-AGREE
a.	tʃik		*!					
b.	tik	*!			*			*
c.	fik			*!	*		*	
d.	sik				*	*!		
e. ☞	kik				*		*	

We can see in tableau (13) that the local conjunction account also makes the correct prediction regarding the suppression of Place Assimilation for underlying alveolar stops.

(13) Local conjunction account of suppression of Place Assimilation

/taɪɡə/ 'tiger'	LC	*#AFFR	*f	ID[manner]	*s	ID[place]	#-AGREE
a. ☞ taɪɡʊ							*
b. tʃaɪɡʊ		*!		*			
c. faɪɡʊ			*!	*		*	
d. saɪɡʊ				*!	*		
e. kaɪɡʊ						*!	

While the faithful candidate (a) violates one of the conjuncts of LC, namely #-AGREE, it does not violate the other conjunct ID[manner] and therefore is considered to comply with LC. In fact, candidate (a) complies with all of the constraints, except for its violation of the lowest-ranked constraint #-AGREE. At that point, all of the other competing candidates have been eliminated, and the faithful candidate is selected as optimal.

Although the perfect transparency of the outputs from Stage 1 did not provide explicit evidence for LC, a slightly different ranking of these same constraints can account for the facts of this stage. The ranking for Stage 1 is given in (14). This ranking accords both with the assumption that conjoined constraints are universal and the requirement that a conjoined constraint such as LC is ranked above all of its individual conjuncts. This entails that locally conjoined constraints of this sort involving a markedness constraint must be ranked above simple markedness constraints in the initial state. With this ranking for Stage 1, the transition to Stage 2 would follow quite naturally by the demotion of #-AGREE below ID[place], as described above.

(14) Local conjunction account of Stage 1

LC >> #-AGREE, *#AFFR, *f >> ID[manner] >> *s >> ID[place]

While local constraint conjunction can account for the facts to this point, it must be recognized that many questions and concerns have been raised about local constraint conjunction, particularly concerning the conjunction of constraints from families as different as markedness and faithfulness. Some of those concerns relate to problems with the domain of conjunction, the conjoinability of constraints, the universality of locally conjoined constraints, strict domination, proliferation of constraints, and certain predictions that appear not to be empirically supported (e.g., McCarthy, 2002a).

As an alternative to local conjunction, McCarthy (2002a) has put forward a different theoretical innovation, namely 'comparative markedness'.[6] Comparative markedness modifies original conceptions of markedness by splitting up each conventional markedness constraint into two distinct versions of the same constraint. One version of a given constraint would assign a violation mark for an offending property that is fully faithful. Such a violation is considered 'old' in the sense that it carries over from the input representation. The other version of that same constraint would assign a violation mark for an offending property that differs from the fully faithful candidate (FFC). Such a violation is considered 'new' because it is not directly supplied by the input. The two versions of a given markedness constraint yield exactly the same combined violations of a conventional markedness constraint. The only real difference is that comparative markedness allows the violations to be partitioned into two non-overlapping sets with the marks being assigned separately by the different versions of the two freely permutable constraints.

With regard to the hierarchy discussed for Child 142, comparative markedness allows us to split #-AGREE into $_O$#-AGREE and $_N$#-AGREE as defined in (15).[7]

(15) Comparative markedness version of #-AGREE

$_O$#-AGREE: Word-initial alveolar stops that are shared with the FFC are banned when followed by a nonadjacent consonant with a different place feature

$_N$#-AGREE: Word-initial alveolar stops that differ from the FFC are banned when followed by a nonadjacent consonant with a different place feature

The two versions of #-AGREE would have been indistinguishable in Stage 1 because they were both undominated. However, the facts of Stage 2 reveal the independence of the two versions of the constraint. That is, in Stage 2, $_O$#-AGREE must be demoted below ID[place] for all the same reasons noted previously, but $_N$#-AGREE would remain undominated. The hierarchy for Stage 2 would thus be identical to that of Stage 1 (as in (4c)), except for the demotion of $_O$#-AGREE as shown in (16).

(16) Hierarchy for Stage 2 with comparative markedness

$_N$#-AGREE, *#AFFR, *f >> ID[manner] >> *s >> ID[place] >> $_O$#-AGREE

With this ranking, a fully faithful candidate that violates $_O$#-AGREE is protected or immune to Place Assimilation, but a candidate that is not fully faithful (i.e., is new) and that violates $_N$#-AGREE will be subject to Place Assimilation.

Accordingly, McCarthy (2002a) has dubbed this situation a 'grandfather effect'.

The tableau in (17) shows how Place Assimilation is blocked in nonderived environments. The only constraint that could compel a change from the fully faithful candidate (a) in this tableau is $_O$#-AGREE, and that constraint is at the bottom of this hierarchy. Candidate (a) does not incur a $_N$#-AGREE violation because the initial consonant is identical to the corresponding segment of the fully faithful candidate. Therefore, Place Assimilation is blocked, and the fully faithful candidate is selected as optimal.

(17) Place Assimilation blocked in nonderived environments

/taɪgə/ 'tiger'	$_N$#-AGREE	**#AFFR	*f	ID[manner]	*s	ID[place]	$_O$#-AGREE
a. FFC ☞ taɪgʊ							*
b. tʃaɪgʊ		*!		*			
c. faɪgʊ			*!	*		*	
d. saɪgʊ				*!	*		
e. kaɪgʊ						*!	

While the fully faithful candidate was protected from Place Assimilation in the above tableau, we can see in the next tableau in (18) that a derived candidate of the same shape (i.e., candidate (b)) would incur a fatal violation of $_N$#-AGREE because the initial consonant differs from the fully faithful candidate. The dominance of **#AFFR compels a change in underlying word-initial affricates. The assimilated candidate (e) is selected as optimal in this instance, despite its violation of ID[place].

(18) Place Assimilation operative in derived environments

/tʃik/ 'check'	$_N$#-AGREE	**#AFFR	*f	ID[manner]	*s	ID[place]	$_O$#-AGREE
a. FFC tʃik		*!					
b. tik	*!			*			
c. fik			*!	*		*	
d. sik				*	*!		
e. ☞ kik				*		*	

We have seen in this section that either of two innovations within optimality theory, local constraint conjunction or comparative markedness, can account for the emergence of the opacity effect associated with Place Assimilation.

The restriction of Place Assimilation to derived alveolar stops represents a generalization that was not observable in any primary linguistic data to which this child would have been exposed. The change that occurred was instead attributed to the principles of Universal Grammar embodied in the proposals of local constraint conjunction or comparative markedness. Under either proposal, a markedness constraint was demoted on the basis of positive evidence and another constraint (either LC or $_N$#-AGREE) remained undominated. That undominated constraint compelled Place Assimilation in just those cases where an alveolar stop was derived. In the next section, we will consider how these two proposals fare in accounting for the loss of the opacity effect.

3.3   Stage 3: Loss of opaque generalization

The central fact to be accounted for in Stage 3 is the complete suppression of any remnants of Place Assimilation, both with simple underlying and derived stops. Recall that Deaffrication was also lost, at least in words where both Deaffrication and Place Assimilation could interact. This suggests that Deaffrication was no longer producing any derived alveolar stops to which Place Assimilation could apply. Considering now the hierarchy for Stage 2 (employing either local conjunction as in (14) or comparative markedness as in (16)) as the starting point, the loss of these two error patterns would follow from the simple demotion of *#AFFR below ID[manner]. The resultant hierarchy under either proposal for Stage 3 is given in (19).

(19) Hierarchy for Stage 3

> Local constraint conjunction
> LC >> *f >> ID[manner] >> *#AFFR, *s >> ID[place] >> #-AGREE

> Comparative markedness
> $_N$#-AGREE, *f >> ID[manner] >> *#AFFR, *s >> ID[place] >> $_O$#-AGREE

In accord with the constraint demotion algorithm, the loss of the Deaffrication error pattern, by way of the demotion of *#AFFR, would follow from the child's recognition that affricates could occur word-initially. This would have the further consequence of eliminating the opaque generalization associated with Place Assimilation. At Stage 2, the high ranking of LC or $_N$#-AGREE compelled the place assimilation of derived alveolar stops. With the demotion of *#AFFR, no derived stops that could potentially be assimilated are created, and any violations assigned by LC or $_N$#-AGREE are largely gratuitous. The undominated character of LC or $_N$#-AGREE does rule out an unfaithful candidate with an alveolar stop in an assimilatory context, but such a candidate would have been eliminated anyway by lower-ranked faithfulness constraints. The tableaux in (20) show how the demotion of *#AFFR eliminates both Deaffrication and the remnants of Place Assimilation in a word like 'cheek'.

(20) Demotion of *#AFFR: Loss of Deaffrication and Place Assimilation

Local conjunction account

/tʃik/ 'cheek'	LC	*f	ID[manner]	*#AFFR	*s	ID[place]	#-AGREE
a. ☞ tʃik				*			
b. tik	*!		*				*
c. fik		*!	*			*	
d. sik			*!		*		
e. kik			*!			*	

Comparative markedness account

/tʃik/ 'cheek'	$_N$#-AGREE	*f	ID[manner]	*#AFFR	*s	ID[place]	$_O$#-AGREE
a. FFC ☞ tʃik				*			
b. tik	*!		*				
c. fik		*!	*			*	
d. sik			*!		*		
e. kik			*!			*	

Abstracting away from some of the details of these analyses, the table in (21) schematizes the essentials of an account for each stage in terms of local constraint conjunction and comparative markedness. Two markedness constraints are required: One of the markedness constraints, M1, serves the role of *#AFFR by favoring an unfaithful candidate that violates the other markedness constraint, M2 (corresponding to our #-AGREE). One or more faithfulness constraints are also necessary, abbreviated as F. In terms of local constraint conjunction, M2 must be conjoined with F to ensure that the unfaithful candidate that violates M2 is assigned an added violation not incurred by the faithful candidate that also violates M2. In terms of comparative markedness, M2 must be split into old and new versions, $_O$M2 and $_N$M2, respectively, to allow violations of M2 to be assessed independently depending on whether the candidate is fully faithful or derived.

(21) Stages of development

Stage	Local Conjunction	Comparative Markedness	Empirical effect
1 Transparent	LC(M2&F) | M1, M2 | F	M1, $_o$M2, $_N$M2 | F	Deaffrication & Place Assimilation (Derived and nonderived)
2 Opaque	LC(M2&F) | M1 | F | M2	M1, $_N$M2 | F | $_o$M2	Deaffrication & Place Assimilation (Derived only)
3 Transparent	LC(M2&F) | F | M1, M2	$_N$M2 | F | M1, $_o$M2	No Deaffrication or Place Assimilation

3.4   An alternative path of development

In the preceding section, the loss of the opaque generalization in the transition from Stage 2 to Stage 3 was attributed to the loss of the Deaffrication error pattern. This was achieved by the demotion of *#AFFR no matter whether we formulated the account in terms of local constraint conjunction or comparative markedness. For the most part, both accounts make sense, especially if we limit our consideration to an idealized situation involving the categorical presence versus absence of the processes. However, the variation evident during Stage 2 offers some insight into an alternative path of development that is not only possible but may even be a more accurate reflection of what was going on at both Stage 2 and Stage 3. This alternative path may also account for the loss of the opacity effect in a more direct fashion. These facts also have interesting implications for the evaluation of local constraint conjunction and comparative markedness.

Recall from Figure 1 that during Stage 2, 29% of the 'cheek'-type words deaffricated and assimilated (Derived Assimilation), and were realized as [kik]. Those words revealed the opacity effect inasmuch as all 'tiger'-type words were realized without assimilation at that point in time. The fact that only some 'cheek'-type words deaffricated and assimilated means that other words of the same phonological shape (approximately 70%) did not. The majority of those words, which we will refer to as 'chicken'-type words, were realized as [tɪkɪn]. That is, the 'chicken'-type words deaffricated but did not assimilate. This might not be surprising given that Deaffrication occurred in a large proportion of words during Stage 2 (62%). The forms in (22) exemplify some of the variation that occurred during Stage 2. We will refer to this set of circumstances as Stage 2'.

(22) Stage 2'

    a)   'tiger'-type words (No assimilation)

        [dɔg]   'dog'   [taɪgʊ]   'tiger'

    b)   'cheek'-type words (Deaffrication and assimilation)

        [kik]   'cheek'   [kɔk]   'chalk'

    c)   'chicken'-type words (Deaffrication but no assimilation)

        [tɪkɪn]   'chicken'   [dækɪt]   'jacket'

The hierarchies in (14) and (16) for Stage 2 can easily account for the facts in (22a-b), but not for those in (22c). Let us first consider how the comparative markedness account would have to be modified to account for the facts of Stage 2'. If some constraints were permitted to float or vary in their ranking (as Anttila and Cho (1998) have argued for other phenomena), $_N$#-AGREE could be ranked variably above and below ID[place]. That is, the sustained dominance of $_N$#-AGREE would account for Place Assimilation in some words, e.g., 'cheek'-type words as shown in (18) above. However, $_N$#-AGREE would also have to be ranked or demoted below ID[place] as in (23) below to account for the loss of assimilation in 'chicken'-type words. Deaffrication would persist with *#AFFR remaining undominated. If $_N$#-AGREE were permitted to float in its ranking as we are suggesting here, the claim would be that it is equally likely for it to be ranked above or below ID[place]. Interestingly, inspection of Figure 1 for Stage 2 reveals that of all the words that deaffricated (62%), close to half assimilated and the other half did not.

(23) Hierarchy for Stage 2': 'chicken'-type words

    *#AFFR, *f >> ID[manner] >> *s >> ID[place] >> $_O$#-AGREE, $_N$#-AGREE

The tableau in (24) illustrates how 'chicken'-type words would be realized if $_N$#-AGREE were permitted to float below ID[place].[8]

(24) Floating ɴ#-AGREE: 'chicken'-type words

/tʃɪkɪn/ 'chicken'	*#AFFR	*f	ID[manner]	*s	ID[place]	ɴ#-AGREE	o#-AGREE
a. FFC tʃɪkɪn	*!						
b. ☞ tɪkɪn			*			*!	
c. fɪkɪn		*!	*		*		
d. sɪkɪn			*	*!			
e. kɪkɪn			*		*!		

Interestingly, there is no similar way to modify the local constraint conjunction account to accommodate these facts, even with floating constraints. What would seem to be called for to account for the 'chicken'-type words is to demote LC below ID[place]. Such a ranking would make the correct claim that it is more important to preserve place than to have consonants agree in place, even if the initial consonant is a derived stop. The problem is that the principles that govern the conjunction of constraints require that the locally conjoined constraint dominate all of its individual conjuncts. This means that LC must dominate both #-AGREE and ID[manner]. Consequently, those constraints must also be demoted with LC. We also know that ID[manner] must continue to dominate *s because coronal fricatives were preserved in outputs. The hierarchy that would result from the demotion of LC and the other associated constraints is given in (25).

(25) Hierarchy for Stage 2': 'chicken'-type words (Local constraint conjunction fails)

   *#AFFR, *f >> ID[place] >> LC >> ID[manner] >> *s, #-AGREE

The tableau in (26) shows how this hierarchy fails to predict the realization of 'chicken'-type words in Stage 2'. The hierarchy would erroneously select candidate (d) when the actually occurring output is candidate (b). There is no way to rank these constraints to yield the attested outputs while also complying with the requirements of local constraint conjunction.

(26) Failure to account for 'chicken'-type words in Stage 2' (Local conjunction)

/tʃɪkɪn/ 'chicken'	*#AFFR	*f	ID[place]	LC	ID[manner]	*s	#-AGREE
a. tʃɪkɪn	*!						
b. ☜ tɪkɪn				*!	*		*
c. fɪkɪn		*!	*		*		
d. ☞ sɪkɪn					*	*	
e. kɪkɪn			*!		*		

It appears then that comparative markedness (but not local constraint conjunction) can account for the facts of both Stage 2 and Stage 2', while also providing plausible explanations for the transition to Stage 3. This alternative path of development and its explanation considered in this section draws on the observation that the opacity effect was being lost at a faster rate than Deaffrication. It would then not be surprising at Stage 3 that the opacity effect associated with Place Assimilation would be completely suppressed with only a few remnants of Deaffrication persisting at that point. The learning patterns displayed in Figure 1 certainly conform to these scenarios. In other words, using comparative markedness, the complete suppression of Place Assimilation can be due either to the demotion of *#AFFR (Stage 2) or through the loss of the opacity effect in advance of the loss of deaffrication by the demotion of $_N$#-AGREE below ID[place] (Stage 2'). As opposed to comparative markedness, LC fails to account for Stage 2', and this failure reveals an important difference in the empirical claims of local constraint conjunction and comparative markedness. That is, local constraint conjunction claims that the loss of the opacity effect depends necessarily on the loss of Deaffrication, but comparative markedness claims that the opacity effect can be lost independent of anything about Deaffrication.

The primary focus of this chapter has been on the emergence and loss of one particular type of opacity effect, namely a grandfather effect where phonologically derived representations undergo a process, but nonderived representations are immune to that process. While such effects are relatively common in fully developed languages, very few cases have thus far been identified from developing phonologies. Additionally, this particular instance of a grandfather effect emerged following treatment that was aimed at the suppression of Place Assimilation in nonderived environments. It is possible that a different learning pattern might have resulted if treatment had instead been aimed at the suppression of Place Assimilation in derived environments. Some evidence from second-language acquisition bearing on this issue is presented by Eckman, Elreyes and Iverson (2003) and is considered further in §4.2. Dinnsen and Farris-Trimble (Chapter 5 in this volume) reconsider one especially interesting case of a developmental grandfather effect that was first described by Leonard and Brown (1984) and that emerged spontaneously without treatment. Comparative markedness was needed to account for that case. A similar case is also reported by Barlow (2007b). We suspect that there are many other cases of grandfather effects in children's early phonologies that have simply gone without comment. Nevertheless, it will be important for future acquisition research to address this gap and further document opacity effects of this sort, if they do indeed exist. There are other types of opacity effects that are predicted to occur, and those predictions have been borne out, at least in fully developed languages. The next section considers some of the available evidence from acquisition regarding the occurrence and characterization of these other opacity effects.

4   Other emergent opacity effects

This section considers a broader range of occurring opacity effects in acquisition with the intent of establishing a fuller typology. Optimality theoretic analyses are formulated for each. Some of the cases might at first appear to pose problems for comparative markedness, but those problems are shown to disappear when examined more closely. Certain other cases of opacity are shown to be perfectly consistent with the predictions of either local constraint conjunction or comparative markedness. Finally, another type of opacity effect involving overapplication also occurs in acquisition and is shown to benefit from sympathy (McCarthy, 1999).

4.1   A presumed problem for comparative markedness

Łubowicz (2003) in her critique of comparative markedness spells out a hypothetical situation that should in principle be a problem for comparative markedness but not for local constraint conjunction. Her contention is that, while comparative markedness can easily distinguish between violations that are old or new relative to a fully faithful candidate, it cannot distinguish among new violations that arise from different processes. Local constraint conjunction, on the other hand, can distinguish between merged representations that are derived from one process versus another by employing multiple locally conjoined constraints that incorporate different conjuncts. A natural question is whether such situations ever actually occur. Early acquisition offers a fruitful venue to address this question because children often merge a number of contrasts by several different processes, and those derived representations might behave differently depending on their underlying source.

Dinnsen, Barlow and Morrisette (1997) report a relevant case involving a child with a phonological delay. Child LP18 (age 3;5) exhibited a number of interacting error patterns as exemplified in (27). One of those error patterns involved Place Assimilation (27a), similar to what we saw in the phonology of Child 142. One important difference was that Place Assimilation was triggered by labial consonants (rather than dorsals). Another difference was that the process applied both progressively and regressively. The factor that was common to both children's error patterns was that alveolar stops served as the target of assimilation. Two other independent error patterns also occurred and yielded alveolar stops. The forms in (27b) illustrate one of the error patterns where dorsals were replaced by alveolar stops (Fronting). The other error pattern (27c) replaced coronal fricatives with stops (Stopping). These latter two error patterns each interacted with Place Assimilation in different ways. While Fronting generally yielded alveolar stops, target dorsals were instead replaced by a labial when a labial occurred elsewhere in the word as shown in (27d). In derivational terms, this would be described as a feeding interaction with Fronting ordered before Place Assimilation to yield transparent outputs. Place Assimilation thus operated on both underlying and derived alveolar stops. Stopping, on the other hand, created the type of sounds targeted by Place Assimilation, but Place Assimilation was blocked, as shown in (27e). Again, in derivational terms, this would be described as a counterfeeding interaction with Place Assimilation ordered before Stopping to yield an opaque output. In this opacity effect, it looks like Place Assimilation should have applied but did not. The situation here relevant to Łubowicz's conjecture is that alveolar stops derived from one process (Fronting) behaved one way with respect to Place Assimilation, while alveolar stops derived from another process (Stopping) behaved in a different way relative to Place Assimilation.

(27) Child LP 18 (age 3;5)

    a) Alveolar stops assimilate to labials (Place Assimilation)

[bʌbi]	'tub-i'	[bʌbɪʔ]	'button'
[baɪbɨ]	'biting'	[bɪbi]	'muddy'

    b) Dorsals replaced by alveolar stops (Fronting)

[doʊʔ]	'coat'	[dædɪʔ]	'cracker'
[deɪt]	'gate'	[dɔḏi]	'sock-i'

    c) Alveolar fricatives replaced by stops (Stopping)

[dʌ̃ʔ]	'sun'	[dɪdɪ]	'scissors'
[du]	'zoo'	[noʊdi]	'noisy'

    d) Dorsals assimilate to labials (Fronting and Place Assimilation)

[bʌbi]	'cup-i'	[bæbi]	'baggie'
[bʌbi]	'gummy'	[bʊbi]	'book-i'

    e) Alveolar stops derived from Stopping do not assimilate (Place Assimilation blocked)

[dupi]	'soupy'	[dɪbɨ]	'zipping'
[doʊbi]	'soapy'	[dɪm]	'sleep'

If we were to formulate an account in comparative markedness terms, we would at least need the constraints in (28).

(28) Constraints

    a) Markedness

$_O$AGREE:	Alveolar stops that are shared with the FFC are banned when preceded or followed by a nonadjacent consonant with a different place feature
$_N$AGREE:	Alveolar stops that differ from the FFC are banned when preceded or followed by a nonadjacent consonant with a different place feature
*k:	Dorsal consonants are banned
*s:	Grooved coronal fricatives are banned

    b) Faithfulness

ID[place]:	Corresponding segments must have identical place features
ID[manner]:	Corresponding segments must have identical manner features

Employing essentially the same strategy as before in accounting for Place Assimilation, AGREE is split into $_O$AGREE and $_N$AGREE. The fact that the trigger of assimilation is labial and not dorsal in this case can be attributed to the dominance of the markedness constraint banning dorsals, *k. The dominance of the other markedness constraint (*s) bans coronal fricatives and leads to their replacement by stops. The faithfulness constraints preserving place and manner features are the same as before and must be ranked below $_O$AGREE, *k, and *s. The value of splitting AGREE into the two comparative markedness constraints is that it allows us to account for the differential behavior of underlying alveolar stops versus those alveolar stops derived from Stopping. That is, underlying alveolar stops in the context of a labial consonant would violate $_O$AGREE and compel assimilation, but alveolar stops derived from Stopping in the same context would incur a $_N$AGREE violation. By ranking $_O$AGREE above ID[place] and $_N$AGREE below ID[place], we could achieve the desired result. The lower ranking of $_N$AGREE protects alveolar stops derived from Stopping from undergoing Place Assimilation.

    It would seem, however, that a paradox would arise for comparative markedness with 'cup'-type words. That is, the dominance of *k would favor an alveolar stop and that alveolar stop would be new relative to the FFC. A new alveolar stop would not incur a violation of $_O$AGREE, and the lower ranking of $_N$AGREE would seem to incorrectly protect 'cup'-type words from assimilation. The tableaux in (29) show, however, that there is in fact no paradox. As a side note, many of the competing candidates considered here include voiced obstruents to more closely reflect this child's problem with voicing. That problem does not otherwise impact the analysis.

(29) Apparent paradox resolved

Ranking: $_O$AGREE, *k, *s >> ID[manner], ID[place] >> $_N$AGREE

/tʌbi/ 'tub-i'	$_O$AGREE	*k	*s	ID[manner]	ID[place]	$_N$AGREE
a. sʌbi			*!	*		
b. kʌbi		*!			*	
c. ☞ bʌbi					*	
d. FFC dʌbi	*!					

/kʌpi/ 'cup-i'	$_O$AGREE	*k	*s	ID[manner]	ID[place]	$_N$AGREE
a. sʌbi			*!	*	*	
b. FFC kʌbi		*!				
c. ☞ bʌbi					*	
d. dʌbi					*	*!

/soupi/ 'soapy'	$_O$AGREE	*k	*s	ID[manner]	ID[place]	$_N$AGREE
a. FFC soubi			*!			
b. koubi		*!		*	*	
c. boubi				*	*!	
d. ☞ doubi				*		*

The tableau for 'cup-i' reveals that $_N$AGREE actually makes the crucial choice in eliminating candidate (d), thus favoring as optimal the assimilated candidate (c). More specifically, candidates (c) and (d) both violate ID[place], passing the choice down to $_N$AGREE. The different behavior of the alveolar stops derived from Stopping is revealed in the tableau for 'soapy'. Notice that candidates (c) and (d) both violate ID[manner], but it is ID[place] that assigns the added fatal violation to candidate (c). While candidate (d) violates $_N$AGREE, the lower ranking of that constraint allows candidate (d) to survive as optimal.

It is perhaps not surprising that local constraint conjunction can also account for these facts. All of the same constraints as above would be required, except that $_O$AGREE and $_N$AGREE would be replaced by a simple version of AGREE and two locally conjoined constraints would have to be included in the hierarchy as shown in (30).[9]

(30) Constraints and Hierarchy (Local conjunction)

AGREE: Alveolar stops are banned when preceded or followed by a
              (nonadjacent) consonant with a different place feature

LC(A&P):   AGREE & ID[place]
LC(M&P):   ID[manner] & ID[place]

Ranking: LC(M&P), LC(A&P), *k, *s >> AGREE >> ID[place], ID[manner]

The two locally conjoined constraints warrant some comment. LC(A&P) assigns a fatal violation mark to a candidate with an alveolar stop derived from Fronting (e.g., candidate (d) in the tableau for 'cup-i'). The other locally conjoined constraint, LC(M&P), is typical of counterfeeding chain shifts and assigns a fatal violation mark to the assimilated candidate (c) in the tableau for 'soapy'. The tableaux in (31) illustrate these points and demonstrate that local constraint conjunction can also account for these facts.

(31) Local conjunction account

/tʌbi/ 'tub-i'	LC(M&P)	LC(A&P)	*k	*s	AGREE	ID[place]	ID[manner]
a. sʌbi				*!			*
b. kʌbi			*!			*	
c. ☞ bʌbi						*	
d. dʌbi					*!		

/kʌpi/ 'cup-i'	LC(M&P)	LC(A&P)	*k	*s	AGREE	ID[place]	ID[manner]
a. sʌbi	*!			*		*	*
b. kʌbi			*!				
c. ☞ bʌbi						*	
d. dʌbi		*!			*	*	

/soupi/ 'soapy'	LC(M&P)	LC(A&P)	*k	*s	AGREE	ID[place]	ID[manner]
a. soubi				*!			
b. koubi	*!		*			*	*
c. boubi	*!					*	*
d. ☞ doubi					*		*

This case is significant on at least two fronts. First, it demonstrates with acquisition data that actual cases do exist where it is necessary to distinguish between merged representations derived from different processes. Also, contrary to

Lubowicz's contention, comparative markedness can in fact account for such facts. Lubowicz is nevertheless correct that comparative markedness alone cannot distinguish among merged representations that are derived from different processes. We saw that, when necessary, other constraints in the hierarchy contributed to the different behavior of derived alveolar stops. For example, in the tableau for 'soapy', alveolar stops derived from Stopping incurred a $_N$AGREE violation, but that violation was less serious than the $_N$AGREE violation that was assessed to alveolar stops derived from Fronting (cf. the tableau for 'cup-i'). Stated differently, $_N$AGREE was ranked low enough that it never got to play a role when Stopping was involved, but it was decisive when Fronting was involved. Interestingly, the presumed limitation of comparative markedness ends up being a virtue of the proposal because comparative markedness forces additional distinctions, if any, to be made by other independently necessary constraints in the hierarchy.

The second point of significance is that this case represents very nearly the mirror image of Child 142 (Stage 2), at least in terms of the permutable ranking of $_O$AGREE and $_N$AGREE. That is, Child 142 required the ranking $_N$#-AGREE >> FAITH >> $_O$#-AGREE, and Child LP18 required the ranking $_O$AGREE >> FAITH >> $_N$AGREE. This is important to the evaluation of comparative markedness and the survey of opacity effects in acquisition because the phenomena on which any of these claims are based should ideally be comparable. To this end, we have shown that the typological variation associated with the phenomenon of Place Assimilation fully instantiates the logical possibilities: Child 142's Place Assimilation error pattern exhibited a transparency effect and a grandfather effect across time, and Child LP18's error pattern during a single point in time exhibited a transparency effect with respect to its interaction with Fronting and a chain shift opacity effect with respect to Stopping.

4.2 Grandfather effects (blocking in morphologically nonderived environments)

The grandfather effect associated with Child 142's Place Assimilation error pattern during Stage 2 involved a restriction to a phonologically derived environment. That is, Place Assimilation operated on representations derived from Deaffrication, but did not operate on otherwise identical nonderived underlying representations. Another type of grandfather effect involves the restriction of a process to morphologically derived environments. Restrictions of this sort are quite common in fully developed languages and are a hallmark of lexical phonology leading to the putative universal principle that certain phonological processes apply only in derived environments (Kiparsky, 1976; 1993a).

Combining morphemes is one way to create or derive an environment that can trigger a phonological process. Phonological processes are blocked from applying to identical representations that are tautomorphemic (nonderived), rendering the process opaque.

Grandfather effects involving morphologically derived environments also occur in acquisition. They emerge and are lost in a way very similar to that of Child 142. This has been documented cross-sectionally and longitudinally in second-language acquisition for Spanish, Korean, Japanese, and Catalan learners of English (e.g., Eckman & Iverson, 1997; Eckman et al., 2003; Cortes, Ota & Turk, 2004). All of these cases involve an allophonic process in the native language that must be suppressed in the target language where a phonemic split is called for. More specifically, two sounds that are allophones of the same phoneme in the native language must be split into separate phonemes in the target language. For example, a Spanish speaker learning English must reassociate his/her two allophones [d] and [ð] with two separate phonemes in the target language. Three characteristic stages of development have been observed in effecting a phonemic split: Stage 1 involves the wholesale transfer of the allophonic process into the target language. The process results in a systematic error pattern that is perfectly transparent, applying in derived and nonderived environments. As a result of this transfer, the sounds of interest do not contrast in any context in the native language or the interlanguage. For example, a Spanish speaker beginning to acquire English would produce 'ladder', 'leather', 'reading', and 'bathing' all with an intervocalic [ð]. Stage 2 involves the partial suppression of the transferred process with the introduction of a contrast in certain environments, namely only in morphologically non-derived environments. For example, then, a more advanced Spanish speaker learning English would continue to spirantize voiced obstruents in morphologically derived words like 'reading' and 'bathing', but the process would be blocked from applying in nonderived words such as 'ladder' and 'leather'. Thus, the contrast between /d/ and /ð/ emerges first in a nonderived environment while continuing to be neutralized in a derived environment.

The restriction of the process to morphologically derived environments is an interesting development because it is a restriction that could not have been inferred from any data in the target language. This partial suppression of the process constitutes a grandfather opacity effect because a process is triggered by a new, morphologically derived representation while being blocked from applying to an identical (old) representation supplied directly by the underlying representation. Stage 3 results in the complete suppression of the process with the contrast occurring in both derived and nonderived environments. Consequently, an even more advanced Spanish speaker learning English would maintain the contrast between /d/ and /ð/ in all contexts.

Eckman et al. (2003) entertain with skepticism a local conjunction account of these facts, but it is important to acknowledge that such an account does at least work. We will formulate here an alternative account in terms of comparative markedness. As McCarthy (2002a) has noted for the characterization of such phenomena in fully developed languages, correspondence theory can be extended to comparative markedness to allow not only input-output comparisons (as have been employed thus far in this chapter), but also output-output comparisons, which are required to capture the morphological effects. This entails distinguishing between old and new violations relative to an input and old and new violations relative to the base in the sense of Benua (1997). Essentially, then, each conventional markedness constraint is reinterpreted as four comparative markedness constraints. Considering the Spanish allophonic process of Spirantization, a conventional markedness constraint, *VdV, which bans intervocalic voiced obstruent stops, would be recast as in (32). We will adopt a generalized faithfulness constraint, FAITH, which demands identity between corresponding segments.

(32) Constraints

    IO-$_O$*VdV: Intervocalic voiced stops that are shared with the FFC are banned
    IO-$_N$*VdV: Intervocalic voiced stops that differ from the FFC are banned
    OO-$_O$*VdV: Intervocalic voiced stops that are shared with the base are banned
    OO-$_N$*VdV: Intervocalic voiced stops that differ from the base are banned

    FAITH: Inputs and outputs must be identical

With these constraints, Stage 1 is easily accounted for by ranking all of the markedness constraints over FAITH as shown in (33). This hierarchy is transferred from the native language and reflects the default ranking of constraints.

(33) Hierarchy for Stage 1 (Transfer from native language)

    OO-$_N$*VdV, IO-$_N$*VdV, OO-$_O$*VdV, IO-$_O$*VdV >> FAITH

The tableaux in (34) illustrate how the violations are assessed to yield intervocalic [ð] in both derived and nonderived representations. This stage is not especially interesting from the perspective of comparative markedness because original conceptions of markedness constraints would have yielded the same results. Note that the fully faithful candidate for 'ladder' incurs an IO-$_O$*VdV violation and an OO-$_O$*VdV violation. The latter violation is because a nonderived form of a word is a base of itself. The fully faithful candidate for 'reading' also incurs an IO-$_O$*VdV violation because all properties of the word are supplied directly from the input. This same candidate does not incur an OO-$_O$*VdV violation because it differs from the base in that the suffix provides the new crucial part of the environment for Spirantization. It thus incurs an OO-$_N$*VdV violation.

(34) Account of Stage 1 (Transparent outputs)

/lædər/ 'ladder'	OO-$_N$*VdV	IO-$_N$*VdV	OO-$_O$*VdV	IO-$_O$*VdV	FAITH
a. FFC lædər				*!	*
b. ☞ læðər					*

/lɛðər/ 'leather'	OO-$_N$*VdV	IO-$_N$*VdV	OO-$_O$*VdV	IO-$_O$*VdV	FAITH
a. FFC ☞ lɛðər					
b. lɛdər	*!	*			*

/beɪðɪŋ/ 'bathing'	OO-$_N$*VdV	IO-$_N$*VdV	OO-$_O$*VdV	IO-$_O$*VdV	FAITH
a. FFC ☞ beɪðɪŋ					
b. beɪdɪŋ	*!	*			*

/ridɪŋ/ 'reading'	OO-$_N$*VdV	IO-$_N$*VdV	OO-$_O$*VdV	IO-$_O$*VdV	FAITH
a. FFC ridɪŋ	*!			*	
b. ☞ riðɪŋ					*

The more interesting development is Stage 2 with the emergence of the grand-father effect. To account for the facts of this stage, it is necessary to demote IO-$_O$*VdV and OO-$_O$*VdV below FAITH, as shown in (35). This demotion (and the resultant hierarchy) is consistent with the constraint demotion algorithm and is based on positive evidence. That is, the learner must recognize the fact that voiced obstruent stops do occur intervocalically in monomorphs such as 'ladder', forcing the demotion of IO-$_O$*VdV. Additionally, because a word such as 'ladder' is a base of itself, the observation about the occurrence of intervo-calic voiced stops in such words also motivates the demotion of OO-$_O$*VdV. The demotion of these constraints yields a contrast between /d/ and /ð/ in monomorphs such as 'ladder' and 'leather'.

(35) Hierarchy for Stage 2 (OO-$_O$*VdV and IO-$_O$*VdV demoted)

OO-$_N$*VdV, IO-$_N$*VdV >> FAITH >> OO-$_O$*VdV, IO-$_O$*VdV

The persistence of the error pattern in derived environments obtains from the sustained dominance of OO-$_N$*VdV. This is revealed in the tableau for 'reading' in (36). While the fully faithful candidate (a) incurs a violation of low-ranked IO-$_o$*VdV (seemingly protecting it from change), it also incurs a fatal violation of undominated OO-$_N$*VdV. This violation is considered new relative to the base because [d] is not in an intervocalic context in the base. Candidate (b) with the spirant substitute is thus selected as optimal, only violating lower-ranked FAITH.

(36) Account of Stage 2 (Grandfather effect)

/lædər/ 'ladder'	OO-$_N$*VdV	IO-$_N$*VdV	FAITH	OO-$_o$*VdV	IO-$_o$*VdV
a. FFC ☞ lædər				*	*
b. læðər			*!		

/lɛðər/ 'leather'	OO-$_N$*VdV	IO-$_N$*VdV	FAITH	OO-$_o$*VdV	IO-$_o$*VdV
a. FFC ☞ lɛðər					
b. lɛdər	*!	*	*		

/beɪðɪŋ/ 'bathing'	OO-$_N$*VdV	IO-$_N$*VdV	FAITH	OO-$_o$*VdV	IO-$_o$*VdV
a. FFC ☞ beɪðɪŋ					
b. beɪdɪŋ	*!	*	*		

/ridɪŋ/ 'reading'	OO-$_N$*VdV	IO-$_N$*VdV	FAITH	OO-$_o$*VdV	IO-$_o$*VdV
a. FFC ridɪŋ	*!				*
b. ☞ riðɪŋ			*		

The transition to Stage 3 where the grandfather effect is lost is achieved by demotion of OO-$_N$*VdV below FAITH to yield the hierarchy in (37). This demotion is again based on positive evidence, namely the recognition that voiced obstruent stops occur intervocalically in morphologically derived environments.

(37) Hierarchy for Stage 3 (OO-$_N$*VdV demoted)

IO-$_N$*VdV >> FAITH >> OO-$_N$*VdV, OO-$_o$*VdV, IO-$_o$*VdV

The tableaux in (38) show how the error pattern is completely suppressed as a result of the demotion of OO-$_N$*VdV. While IO-$_N$*VdV remains undominated for lack of any evidence to depart from the default ranking, it plays no role in any of these words.

(38) Account of Stage 3 (Loss of grandfather effect)

/lædər/ 'ladder'	IO-$_N$*VdV	FAITH	OO-$_N$*VdV	OO-$_O$*VdV	IO-$_O$*VdV
a. FFC ☞ lædər				*	*
b. læðər		*!			

/lɛðər/ 'leather'	IO-$_N$*VdV	FAITH	OO-$_N$*VdV	OO-$_O$*VdV	IO-$_O$*VdV
a. FFC ☞ lɛðər					
b. lɛdər	*!	*	*		

/beɪðɪŋ/ 'bathing'	IO-$_N$*VdV	FAITH	OO-$_N$*VdV	OO-$_O$*VdV	IO-$_O$*VdV
a. FFC ☞ beɪðɪŋ					
b. beɪdɪŋ	*!	*	*		

/ridɪŋ/ 'reading'	IO-$_N$*VdV	FAITH	OO-$_N$*VdV	OO-$_O$*VdV	IO-$_O$*VdV
a. FFC ☞ ridɪŋ			*		*
b. riðɪŋ		*!			

The results from Eckman et al. (2003) are interesting on another front. As part of their investigation, they enrolled Spanish speakers learning English in an experimental study where some learners were taught the contrast between /d/ and /ð/ in derived environments, and others were taught the contrast in nonderived environments. Independent of the assigned experimental condition, all but one of the logically possible learning patterns emerged from the training. The one learning pattern that was conspicuously absent was that none of their subjects learned the contrast in a derived environment while continuing to merge it in the nonderived environment. This result would seem to run counter to the predictions of comparative markedness because it suggests that the old and new versions of a markedness constraint are not freely permutable. If they were truly permutable, we might have expected that training on the contrast in derived environments would have compelled the demotion of OO-$_N$*VdV without affecting IO-$_O$*VdV. We will see, however, in the next section that a celebrated case of typical first-language acquisition provides the crucial missing evidence in support of comparative markedness, namely an opacity effect where a process applies in a nonderived environment but is blocked in derived environments.

4.3 Chain shifts (blocking in morphologically derived and phonologically derived environments)

Smith (1973) in his diary study of a typically developing child, Amahl, provides evidence of a process that applies in a nonderived environment, but is blocked from applying in both a morphologically derived environment and a phonologically derived environment. Dinnsen and McGarrity (2004) formulate one possible account of this opacity effect employing output-to-output correspondence (Benua, 1995; 1997). In this section, we will formulate an alternative account of these facts in terms of comparative markedness.[10]

The data in (39) are from Amahl during an early stage of development (age 2;2–2;11). The forms in (39a) illustrate the Velarization error pattern, which replaced coronal stops with a dorsal when followed by a liquid consonant. This process applied in simple, nonderived forms of words. Interestingly, however, the process was blocked from applying when the consonantal sequence spanned a morpheme boundary, as the forms in (39b) show. The restriction on Velarization (i.e., that it must apply only in nonderived environments) results in an opacity effect that is not evident in the primary linguistic data to which Amahl would have been exposed. Velarization also interacted with another error pattern, Stopping, which replaced coronal fricatives with a stop. The forms in (39c) show that Velarization was also blocked from applying to coronal stops derived from Stopping. This constitutes another opacity effect where it looks like Velarization should have applied, but did not. This restriction on Velarization is also not inferable from the primary linguistic data to which Amahl would have been exposed. Both of these opacity effects involve chain shifts, which are just the reverse of a grandfather effect, at least when described in terms of comparative markedness.

(39) Amahl (Smith, 1973)

   a) Velarization in nonderived environments
[pʌgl̩]	'puddle'	[æŋkləz]	'antlers'
[bɔkl̩]	'bottle'	[bʌklə]	'butler'
[hæŋgl̩]	'handle'	[trɔglə]	'troddler'

   b) Velarization blocked in morphologically derived environments
[kwæːtliː]	'quietly'	(cf. [kwæːt]	'quiet')
[sɔftliː]	'softly'	(cf. [sɔft]	'soft')
[haːdliː]	'hardly'	(cf. [haːd]	'hard')
[taitliː]	'tightly'	(cf. [tait]	'tight')

   c)   Velarization blocked in phonologically derived environments

        [pʌdl̩]   'puzzle'

        [pɛntl]   'pencil'

        [wɪtl]   'whistle'

The constraints needed to account for these facts are given in (40). The general markedness constraint, *dl, which bans coronal stops when followed by a liquid consonant, relates to the Velarization error pattern and has been recast in comparative markedness terms. The markedness constraint banning coronal fricatives, *s, is highly ranked for Amahl (cf. the reverse ranking for Child 142). The faithfulness constraints preserving place and manner features are the same as those that we saw earlier in this chapter.

(40) Constraints

    IO-$_O$*dl: Alveolar stops that are shared with the FFC are banned before liquid consonants

    IO-$_N$*dl: Alveolar stops that differ from the FFC are banned before liquid consonants

    OO-$_O$*dl: Alveolar stops that are shared with the base are banned before liquid consonants

    OO-$_N$*dl: Alveolar stops that differ from the base are banned before liquid consonants

    *s: Grooved coronal fricatives are banned

    ID[place]:   Corresponding segments must have identical place features

    ID[manner]: Corresponding segments must have identical manner features

The hierarchy needed to account for these facts is given in (41).

(41) Hierarchy for Amahl

    OO-$_O$*dl, *s >> ID[manner], ID[place] >> IO-$_O$*dl, IO-$_N$*dl, OO-$_N$*dl

Our account of the facts and the motivation for the above hierarchy are illustrated in the tableaux in (42). The fact that 'puddle'-type words were subject to Velarization might make one think that IO-$_O$*dl would have been highly ranked to eliminate the fully faithful candidate. Our hierarchy shows, however, that it is ranked below the faithfulness constraints. 'Puddle'-type words do incur a violation of IO-$_O$*dl, but more importantly, they also incur a violation of OO-$_O$*dl because every word that is a monomorph is a base of itself. The violation assigned by OO-$_O$*dl is fatal, resulting in the selection of candidate (b). The reason that IO-$_O$*dl is ranked below the faithfulness constraints is to account for the fact that the fully faithful candidate is optimal in morphologically derived words like 'quietly'. This fully faithful candidate also violates

OO-$_N$*dl because it differs from its base ('quiet') in that the suffix contributes the new conditioning environment for Velarization. Therefore, OO-$_N$*dl must also be ranked below ID[place]. The fact that both of these markedness constraints are ranked below the faithfulness constraints would again follow from the constraint demotion algorithm. Their demotion is based on positive evidence about the occurrence of a place contrast in a morphologically derived environment. The velarized candidate (b) is thus eliminated by its fatal violation of ID[place]. Finally, if it had not been for 'puzzle'-type words, we might have thought that IO-$_N$*dl could have remained undominated. The fact is, however, that IO-$_N$*dl must be ranked below the faithfulness constraints to account for the fact that alveolar stops derived from Stopping are immune to Velarization. Notice that the two most likely competitors, candidates (b) and (c), both violate ID[manner]. The additional violation assigned to candidate (c) by ID[place] is fatal and thus favors the opaque candidate (b).

(42) Account of Amahl's opacity effects

/kwaɹjət/ 'quiet'	OO-$_O$*dl	*s	ID[manner]	ID[place]	IO-$_O$*dl	IO-$_N$*dl	OO-$_N$*dl
a. FFC ☞ kwæt							
b. kwæk				*!			

/kwaɹjətli/ 'quietly'	OO-$_O$*dl	*s	ID[manner]	ID[place]	IO-$_O$*dl	IO-$_N$*dl	OO-$_N$*dl
a. FFC ☞ kwætli					*		*
b. kwækli				*!			

/pʌdl̩/ 'puddle'	OO-$_O$*dl	*s	ID[manner]	ID[place]	IO-$_O$*dl	IO-$_N$*dl	OO-$_N$*dl
a. FFC pʌdl̩	*!				*		
b. ☞ pʌgl̩				*			

/pʌzl̩/ 'puzzle'	OO-$_O$*dl	*s	ID[manner]	ID[place]	IO-$_O$*dl	IO-$_N$*dl	OO-$_N$*dl
a. FFC pʌzl̩		*!					
b. ☞ pʌdl̩			*			*	*
c. pʌgl̩			*	*!			

Another example from a fully developed language where a phonological process is blocked from applying in a morphologically derived environment is provided by Harris (1990) for an English dialect of northern Ireland. Coronal stops dentalize before [r] in nonderived forms of words, but dentalization is blocked before [r] across a morpheme boundary.

4.4   Chain shifts (blocking in phonologically derived environments)

One of the most prevalent (or at least most commonly reported) type of opacity effect in first- and second-language acquisition is a chain shift (e.g., Jesney, 2005). One frequently occurring example of a chain shift in both typical and atypical first-language development involves the substitution of [θ] for target /s/ along with the substitution of [f] for target /θ/ (Dinnsen & Barlow, 1998). Importantly, /s/ is not replaced by [f]. This error pattern constitutes an opacity effect because, while [θ]'s corresponding to underlying nonderived /θ/'s are banned, [θ]'s derived from other phonological processes are preferred. The process that replaces [θ] is thus blocked from applying to phonologically derived [θ]'s. For a characterization of this particular chain shift and how it might arise in terms of comparative markedness, see Dinnsen and Farris-Trimble (Chapter 5 in this volume). An alternative account has also been formulated in terms of local constraint conjunction (Chapter 8, in this volume). For yet another alternative, see Jesney (2005).

An interesting case of a chain shift is reported by Bernhardt and Stemberger (1998: 651) for a typically developing child. Gwendolyn (before age 4;3) exhibited the typical English process of Degemination which breaks up geminate clusters by epenthesizing a vowel. For example, /nid+d/ 'needed' was realized as [nidəd]. That process interacted with an independent error pattern which replaced dorsals with a coronal stop (Fronting). The interaction is exemplified in words like /hʌg + d/ 'hugged' which were realized as [hʌdd]. Note that a geminate was derived from Fronting, but Degemination was blocked from applying to these phonologically derived geminates. In derivational rule-based terms, this might have been described by ordering Degemination before Fronting in a counterfeeding relation.

While Bernhardt and Stemberger have formulated an account of these facts in optimality theoretic terms, their account is somewhat unconventional in its reliance on underspecified representations (in violation of richness of the base). We therefore formulate here an alternative account in terms of comparative markedness. The relevant constraints are given in (43). For completeness, the general markedness constraint banning geminates, *GEM, is spelled out in all four of its comparative markedness subconstraints, primarily because the opacity effect also shows up in a morphologically derived environment. Fronting necessitates the undominated markedness constraint *k, which bans dorsals. The faithfulness constraint ID[place] is obviously antagonistic to *k and is always violated in the winning output. DEP militates against insertion and is clearly violated when geminates are underlying (not phonologically derived).

(43) Constraints

IO-$_O$*GEM: Geminates that are shared with the FFC are banned
IO-$_N$*GEM: Geminates that differ from the FFC are banned
OO-$_O$*GEM: Geminates that are shared with the base are banned
OO-$_N$*GEM: Geminates that differ from the base are banned
*k: Dorsal consonants are banned

ID[place]:   Corresponding segments must have identical place features
DEP: No insertion

The hierarchy required to account for Gwendolyn's chain shift is given in (44).

(44) Hierarchy for Gwendolyn's chain shift

*k, IO-$_O$*GEM, OO-$_O$*GEM >> DEP, ID[place] >> IO-$_N$*GEM, OO-$_N$*GEM

The tableaux in (45) show how comparative markedness can account for the different behavior of geminates, depending on whether they are underlying or phonologically derived. The fully faithful candidate in the tableau for 'needed' violates low-ranked OO-$_N$*GEM because the suffix provides crucial new information that was not present in the base. The lower ranking of that constraint would seem to protect it from Degemination, but more importantly, that candidate also fatally violates undominated IO-$_O$*GEM. That violation eliminates the fully faithful candidate in favor of candidate (b) with the epenthetic vowel. The tableau for 'hugged' reveals why both IO-$_N$*GEM and OO-$_N$*GEM must be low-ranked. The fully faithful candidate is eliminated by undominated *k. Of the two remaining candidates with derived coronal stops, candidate (c) with the epenthetic vowel fatally violates DEP, resulting in the selection of candidate (b) with the phonologically derived geminate as optimal. The winner violates IO-$_N$*GEM because of Fronting and OO-$_N$*GEM because of the new information provided by the suffix.

(45) Account of Gwendolyn's chain shift

/nidd/ 'needed'	*k	IO-$_O$*GEM	OO-$_O$*GEM	DEP	ID(place)	IO-$_N$*GEM	OO-$_N$*GEM
a. FFC nidd		*!					*
b. ☞ nidəd				*			

/hʌgd/ 'hugged'	*k	IO-$_O$*GEM	OO-$_O$*GEM	DEP	ID(place)	IO-$_N$*GEM	OO-$_N$*GEM
a. FFC hʌgd	*!						
b. ☞ hʌdd					*	*	*
c. hʌdəd				*	*!		

An alternative local conjunction account of these facts would conjoin the two faithfulness constraints DEP and ID[place] to eliminate the transparent candidate that is the result of Fronting and Degemination.

Another case of blocking in phonologically derived environments is reported by Applegate (1961) for three children (ages 4;0, 5;6, and 8;6), all from the same English-speaking family. One error pattern changed the second of two identical obstruent stops (with or without intervening consonants) into a glottal stop (Dissimilation). This process operated in nonderived words such as 'toot', which was realized as [tuw?]. It also operated in morphologically derived environments, even when a consonant intervened. For example, the past tense of 'take' was regularized to preserve the vowel quality of the stem and was realized as [teyki?]. Another independent error pattern also occurred and replaced fricatives with stops (Stopping). These two processes interacted such that stops derived from Stopping did not condition or undergo Dissimilation. For example, a target word with an initial fricative such as 'suit' was realized as [tuwt], showing that derived stops could not condition Dissimilation. Similarly, words such as 'takes' were realized as [teykt], showing that derived stops also did not undergo Dissimilation. In comparative markedness terms, the Dissimilation error pattern would require a markedness constraint banning the second of two identical consonants within a word. That constraint would need to be split into a new and old version with $_\text{O}$DISSIMILATION ranked above FAITH and $_\text{N}$DISSIMILATION ranked below FAITH. The Stopping error pattern would be undominated. The lower ranking of $_\text{N}$DISSIMILATION would insulate derived stops from Dissimilation.

Dinnsen (1993) documents another example of a chain shift evident in the speech of a child with a phonological delay. Child 27 (age 4;11) exhibited an alternation between word-final coronal stops and intervocalic glottal stops (e.g., [but] 'boot' ~ [bu?i] 'bootie'). Target coronal stops in intervocalic position in monomorphs were also replaced with a glottal stop (e.g., [wæ?ɚ] 'ladder'). This Weakening process thus applied in both morphologically derived and nonderived environments. Another independent Stopping error pattern replaced interdentals with a coronal stop (e.g., [tud] 'tooth'). Importantly, coronal stops derived from Stopping did not alternate with glottal stop (e.g., [tuti] 'toothy').

In another study, Dinnsen (1998) described three children (Child 9 (3;9), Child 23 (4;8), and Child 29 (4;11)) with phonological delays, all of whom exhibited some form of an error pattern involving Manner Assimilation. This error pattern replaced a consonant or glide with another consonant that agreed with a following (nonadjacent) consonant in terms of manner features (e.g., [nasal] or [continuant]). Manner Assimilation was, however, blocked when some other process created the type of sound targeted by Manner Assimilation.

For example, while glides might have been the target of Manner Assimilation, being realized as a nasal consonant when a nasal followed later in the word, glides that were derived from target liquid consonants were immune to Manner Assimilation.

Chain shifts of this sort have also been documented in second-language acquisition by Eckman et al. (2003). They found, for example, that, while some Spanish speakers learning English substitute [s] for /θ/, only underlying nonderived /s/'s become [z]'s before voiced consonants. Similarly, many Korean and Japanese learners of English substitute [s] for /θ/, but only palatalize underlying nonderived /s/ before high front vowels (e.g., [ʃimpasi] 'sympathy').

McCarthy (2002a) has proposed the following general comparative markedness schema for the characterization of chain shifts:

$$_O\text{MARKEDNESS} \gg \text{FAITH} \gg {}_N\text{MARKEDNESS}.$$

All of the chain shifts discussed in this subsection could receive an account consistent with this schema.

4.5   Overapplication opacity effects

All of the opacity effects described above in one way or another involved cases of underapplication. That is, it appeared that a process should have applied but did not, resulting in a generalization that was not surface-true. There are, however, other types of opacity effects in both fully developed languages and acquisition that involve overapplication, i.e., where it appears that a process applied, but should not have. In those cases, the generalization is opaque because it is not surface-apparent; the conditioning environment has been obscured by some other process. In rule-based derivational terms, this situation would typically arise from the interaction of two processes ordered in a counterbleeding relation.

This can be illustrated for acquisition by considering one of the children described by Weismer, Dinnsen and Elbert (1981). Child A (age 7;2) was typically developing in all respects, except for evidence of a phonological delay. This child exhibited two interacting processes: Vowels lengthened before voiced obstruents (Lengthening), and word-final obstruents were omitted (Deletion). Instrumental acoustic analyses revealed that these processes interacted when target words ended in a voiced obstruent, yielding long vowels before (omitted) voiced obstruents and short vowels elsewhere. The data in (46) illustrate the interaction. The forms in (46a) show that final obstruents were deleted and that vowels lengthened before omitted voiced (but not voiceless) obstruents. The forms in (46b) establish that there was a consonantal alternation and show that the stem-final obstruents did occur when not in word-final position. The transcriptions of these latter forms do not indicate vowel length, because no measurements were made for these words. However, since vowel length is one of the primary perceptual cues for postvocalic voicing differences in obstruents, the transcription of voicing is taken to reflect the fact that vowels were transparently long before the occurring voiced obstruents and short before voiceless.

(46) Child A (age 7;2)

    a)   Vowels lengthen before voiced obstruents

[kæ:]	'cab'	[ka]	'cop'
[kɪ:]	'kid'	[pæ]	'pat'
[dɔ:]	'dog'	[dʌ]	'duck'

    b)   Obstruents contrast in voice word-medially

[kæ:bi]	'cabby'	[kapoʊ]	'copper'
[kɪ:doʊ]	'kidder'	[pæti]	'patty'
[dɔ:gi]	'doggie'	[dʌki]	'ducky'

The lengthening of vowels before omitted voiced obstruents, even though the conditioning environment was not present phonetically, constitutes the opacity effect in these data. One consequence of this interaction is that this child exhibited a superficial vowel length contrast word-finally—a contrast that does not occur in English. In rule-based derivational terms, Lengthening would be ordered before Deletion in a counterbleeding relation.

    The characterization of this and other similar opacity effects poses a challenge for optimality theory that is different from what we have considered thus far. Local constraint conjunction and comparative markedness do not (nor were they ever intended to) account for this type of opacity. One leading proposal for dealing with overapplication effects is embodied in 'sympathy' (McCarthy, 1999; 2003a).

    Sympathy extends optimality theory by introducing a novel type of faithfulness constraint that demands similarity between two candidates, i.e., a particular failed candidate and an opaque output candidate. Briefly, the relevant failed candidate is considered the object of sympathy and is termed the flower candidate or the sympathetic candidate. The candidate that serves as the flower candidate is determined by another constraint. McCarthy (1999) has argued that the flower candidate is identified from a set of candidates that complies with and is defined by a low-ranked faithfulness constraint (i.e., the selector). The constraint that serves as the selector is determined language-specifically. By virtue of the selector constraint being low-ranked (i.e., dominated by a markedness constraint), many candidates that are consistent with the selector are failed candidates. The candidate of that set which is the most harmonic relative to the other constraints in the hierarchy serves as the flower candidate. The sympathy constraint has the effect of preserving some property of the flower candidate in another output candidate. If the flower candidate and the input representation happened to be different, and if the sympathy constraint outranked the conventional IO-faithfulness constraints, the optimal output candidate would be opaque, more closely resembling the flower candidate than the input representation.

Dinnsen, McGarrity, O'Connor and Swanson (2000) invoked an early version of sympathy to account for the acquisition facts for Child A. We update that account here to reflect some of the more recent refinements of the proposal (McCarthy, 2003a).

The constraints needed to account for these facts are given in (47). LENGTHEN abbreviates two markedness constraints that ensure that vowels are long before voiced consonants and are short elsewhere. NoCODA is a well-documented markedness constraint banning coda consonants. The dominance of this constraint compels deletion of final consonants. The faithfulness constraints that are antagonistic to LENGTHEN and NoCODA are ID[weight] and MAX, respectively. ✿SYM is the sympathy constraint that assigns a violation mark to candidates that do not preserve certain properties of the flower candidate.[11] Similarity to the flower candidate is enforced by requiring that every candidate's faithfulness violations be cumulative relative to the flower candidate. This means that a candidate must contain a superset of the violations incurred by the flower candidate. Any candidate that is not cumulative relative to the flower candidate is assigned a violation by ✿SYM.

(47) Constraints

LENGTHEN:	Short vowels are banned before voiced consonants; long vowels are banned elsewhere
NoCODA:	Coda consonants are banned
MAX:	No deletion
ID[weight]:	Corresponding vowels must be identical in terms of length (or weight)
✿SYM:	A candidate's faithfulness violations must be cumulative relative to the flower candidate

The constraint ranking needed to account for the opacity effect is given in (48). Notice that the faithfulness constraints are dominated by the markedness constraints in accord with the default ranking of constraints. The only departure from the default ranking is the dominance of ✿SYM.

(48) Constraint hierarchy

NoCODA, ✿SYM >> LENGTHEN >> MAX, ID[weight]

The account of the opacity effect is illustrated in the tableau for 'cab' in (49). Let us first establish which candidate is the flower candidate. The low-ranked faithfulness constraint MAX will serve as the selector constraint. The only candidates that are potential flower candidates because they comply with MAX are (a) and (b) and, of those, the most harmonic is candidate (b). Thus, candidate (b) is the flower candidate. Candidate (a) was eliminated as a flower candidate because it violated LENGTHEN, while the other candidate did not. With the flower candidate identified, we can discuss the hierarchy's evaluation of the full candidate set. NOCODA assigns fatal violation marks to the two candidates (a) and (b), and it is ❀SYM that will decide between the final two candidates. In order to see how ❀SYM evaluates candidates, we might first examine the lattice or partial ordering diagram in (50). This diagram reveals the shared and unshared faithfulness violations of the different candidates for a given input. At the top of the lattice is the fully faithful candidate. It obviously incurs no faithfulness violations. Each step down from the fully faithful candidate reflects one faithfulness violation. For example, candidate (c) without the final consonant incurs only a MAX violation. Similarly, the flower candidate (b) with a long vowel before a voiced consonant incurs just an ID[weight] violation. Importantly, the faithfulness violation of candidate (c) is not cumulative relative to the flower candidate; each incurs a nonoverlapping set of faithfulness violations. Candidate (d) at the bottom of the lattice incurs two faithfulness violations, one assigned by MAX and the other assigned by ID[weight]. Its violations are cumulative relative to the flower candidate because it has a superset of the flower candidate's faithfulness violations. With this sense of cumulativity, we can now see how ❀SYM assigns its violations. More specifically, the transparent candidate (c) with a short vowel incurs only one faithfulness violation, and that violation is not shared with the flower candidate. It is thus not cumulative relative to the flower candidate and is assigned a fatal violation by ❀SYM. The winning opaque candidate (d) violates LENGTHEN, but that violation is less serious given that all other competitors have been eliminated by the higher-ranked constraints.

(49) Account of overapplication opacity effect

				selector	
/kæb/ 'cab'	NOCODA	❀SYM	LENGTHEN	MAX	ID[weight]
a. kæb	*!	*	*		
b. ❀ kæːb	*!				*
c. kæ		*!		*	
d. ☞ kæː			*	*	*

(50) Partial ordering diagram for 'cab'

Other similar cases from acquisition involving overapplication are also cited in Dinnsen et al. (2000). For example, it has been observed that many children acquiring English devoice final obstruents. Interestingly, they also lengthened their vowels before voiced obstruents word-medially and before the devoiced obstruents, but not before the underlying voiceless obstruents. Similar results are also reported for fully developed languages (e.g., Slowiaczek & Dinnsen, 1985 and references therein). The account for these cases would be similar to that of Child A above. The difference would be that the low-ranked faithfulness constraint ID[voice] would serve as the selector, and MAX would be ranked above NOCODA. The similarity among these cases centers around the crucial ranking: ❀SYM >> LENGTHEN >> ID[weight].

These overapplication cases are important to acquisition and sympathy for several reasons. First, contrary to the standard assumption that opacity effects are hard to learn, overapplication opacity effects are predicted by sympathy to occur naturally in early stages of acquisition, even if the target language does not exhibit the opaque generalization. One reason for this prediction is that the default ranking of constraints in the initial state is for faithfulness constraints to be dominated by markedness. Sympathy depends on there being a low-ranked faithfulness constraint that could serve as the selector. The default ranking of constraints thus predisposes early acquisition to opacity effects of this sort because it makes many constraints available for this essential aspect of a sympathy account. Dinnsen et al. (2000) propose that ❀SYM, like other faithfulness constraints, is ranked below the markedness constraints in the initial state, accounting for the transparency of phonological generalizations in the earliest stages of acquisition. It is further argued that the sympathy constraint is ranked above the selector constraints in the initial state. The dominance of ❀SYM over the selector places ❀SYM at a point in the hierarchy where it is poised to exercise its influence to introduce an opaque generalization. That is, the opacity effect would emerge from the demotion of a markedness constraint just below ❀SYM but above the other faithfulness constraints. That demotion would be consistent with the constraint demotion algorithm and would be based on positive evidence if the child recognized some property of the target word that he had not recognized previously and that was not present in the prior transparent winner. For example, in the case of Child A, his opacity effect would emerge quite naturally from the recognition that vowels were long in target words such as 'cab'. The child would not necessarily have to take note of the occurrence of a coda consonant. His observation about vowel length draws on evidence that is certainly present in the primary linguistic data, but most of us would take that fact to be a secondary consequence of the voicing of the following consonant. Nevertheless, the observation of vowel length would force the demotion of LENGTHEN just below ✿SYM because that is the highest-ranked constraint that the previous transparent winner would have violated. Overapplication opacity effects thus occur in acquisition, and sympathy accounts for their occurrence and emergence, even when the target language does not exhibit the same opacity effect.[12]

The next section builds on our account of overapplication effects by documenting a different case where multiple error patterns interact to yield both an overapplication and an underapplication opacity effect.

4.6   An overapplication and underapplication interaction

Child 209 (age 3;5) exhibited two different types of opacity as a result of interacting error patterns. One opacity effect involved a conventional chain shift whereby /s/ was replaced by [θ], and /θ/ was replaced by [f]. The data in (51) illustrate the various parts of the chain shift in postvocalic contexts.

(51) Child 209 (age 3;5): Postvocalic chain shift

a)   Grooved coronal fricatives realized as interdentals

[mauθ]	'mouse'	[nouð]	'nose'
[bʌθi]	'bus-i'	[rouð]	'rose'
[dɛθ]	'dress'	[bʌð]	'buzz'
[aɪθ]	'ice'	[nɔɪði]	'noisy'

b)   Interdental coronal fricatives realized as labials

[mauf]	'mouth'	[mʌvu]	'mother'
[maufi]	'mouth-i'	[ʌvu]	'other'
[bæf]	'bath'	[vifi]	'wreath-i'

c)   Labial fricatives realized target-appropriately

[læf]	'laugh'	[ouvu]	'over'
[naɪf]	'knife'	[daɪv]	'drive'
[læfɪn]	'laughing'	[daɪvɪn]	'driving'
[tafɪn]	'coughing'	[weɪvɪn]	'waving'

The focus on postvocalic position allows us to observe the chain shift in a context where no other error pattern interacted with it. These data reveal an underapplication opacity effect in that, while interdentals were banned, they were also preferred as the substitute for other sounds. If we were to formulate an account for this opacity effect in derivational terms, we might order the rule that changes /θ/ to [f] (Labialization) before the rule that changes /s/ to [θ] (Dentalization). That order of application represents a counterfeeding relation. The opposite order would cause Dentalization to incorrectly feed Labialization. The empirically attested order makes it appear that the Labialization rule under-applied in words where [θ] was the substitute for /s/.

(52) Counterfeeding derivation for chain shift

UR	/maʊs/	/maʊθ/	/læf/
Labialization	—	maʊf	—
Dentalization	maʊθ	—	—
PR	[maʊθ]	[maʊf]	[læf]

Another independent error pattern replaced word-initial fricatives with a (voiced) stop. The data in (53) illustrate this Stopping error pattern. Note in (53a) that a voiced coronal stop was the substitute for a coronal fricative, and in (53b) that a voiced labial stop was the substitute for a labial fricative. While voice and manner distinctions were merged in word-initial position, place of articulation appeared to be preserved. On the basis of these data alone, it might be thought that the chain shift and stopping error patterns interacted in a perfectly transparent way. We will see, however, that target interdental fricatives behaved differently in word-initial position.

(53) Word-initial stopping (and voicing)

a) Grooved coronal fricatives realized as voiced coronal stops

[dʌn]	'sun'	[dupi]	'soupy'
[doʊp˺]	'soap'	[doʊ]	'sew'
[dæntə]	'santa'	[doʊpi]	'soapy'
[dɛvɪn]	'seven'	[dʌni]	'sunny'

b) Labial fricatives realized as voiced labial stops

[baɪv]	'five'	[bɛvʊ]	'feather'
[baɪjʊ]	'fire'	[boʊʔɛd]	'forehead'
[bʊʔ]	'foot'	[bɑd]	'frog'
[bʊti]	'foot-i'	[bɑdi]	'frog-i'

The data in (54) reveal an added dimension to the interaction of these error patterns. Note that target interdental fricatives in initial position were realized as a voiced labial stop—not as a coronal stop, which would have been the expected transparent output if place were preserved as above. It appears, then, that the chain shift was also operating even in word-initial position, but its application was partially obscured due to its interaction with Stopping.

(54) Word-initial interdentals realized as voiced labial stops: Overapplication opacity
effect

[bʌm]	'thumb'	[bʌmi]	'thumb-i'
[buθti]	'thirsty'	[bi]	'three'
[bif]	'thief'	[boʊn]	'throne'
[bʌndʊ]	'thunder'		

To account for these facts in derivational terms, it would be necessary to order
the chain shift Labialization rule before Stopping in a counterbleeding relation
as shown in (55). This represents an overapplication opacity effect because it is
not apparent from the output why the Labialization rule would have applied to
a stop. Note that the reverse order of the rules would cause Stopping to bleed
Labialization, making the empirically incorrect prediction that a coronal stop
would be the substitute for /θ/. While the Labialization rule must apply before
Dentalization, the order of the Dentalization rule and Stopping is not crucial
since either order yields the same result.

(55) Counterbleeding interaction

UR	/sʌn/	/θʌm/
Labialization	—	fʌm
Stopping	dʌn	bʌm
PR	[dʌn]	[bʌm]

To account for these error patterns and the two different opacity effects in
optimality theoretic terms, we might employ comparative markedness for
the chain shift and sympathy for the overapplication effect.[13] The constraints
relevant to the chain shift are given in (56). For a fuller discussion of these
constraints and the associated ranking arguments, see Chapter 5.

(56) Chain shift constraints

a) Markedness

*s:	Grooved coronal fricatives are banned
$_o$*θ:	Interdental fricatives that are shared with the FFC are banned
$_N$*θ:	Interdental fricatives that differ from the FFC are banned
*f:	Labial fricatives are banned

b) Faithfulness

ID[grooved]: Corresponding segments must have an identical [grooved]
feature

ID[place]:   Corresponding segments must have identical place features

Ranking: *s, $_o$*θ >> ID[grooved], ID[place] >> *f, $_N$*θ

The tableaux in (57) show how the chain shift would be accounted for in postvocalic contexts.

(57) Chain shift in postvocalic position

/maʊs/ 'mouse'	*s	$_0*\theta$	ID[grooved]	ID[place]	*f	$_N*\theta$
a. FFC maʊs	*!					
b. ☞ maʊθ			*			*
c. maʊf			*	*!	*	

/maʊθ/ 'mouth'	*s	$_0*\theta$	ID[grooved]	ID[place]	*f	$_N*\theta$
a. maʊs	*!		*			
b. FFC maʊθ		*!				
c. ☞ maʊf				*	*	

/læf/ 'laugh'	*s	$_0*\theta$	ID[grooved]	ID[place]	*f	$_N*\theta$
a. læs	*!		*	*		
b. læθ				*!		*
c. ☞ FFC læf					*	

The additional constraints relevant to the overapplication opacity effect are given in (58).

(58) Constraints for Stopping and overapplication effect

*#Fʀɪᴄ: Word-initial fricatives are banned
ID[manner]: Corresponding segments must have identical manner features
❀Sʏᴍ: A candidate's faithfulness violations must be cumulative relative to the flower candidate

Ranking: ❀Sʏᴍ, *s, $_0*\theta$, *#Fʀɪᴄ >> ID[grooved], ID[manner], ID[place] >> *f, $_N*\theta$

By ranking the contextually conditioned markedness constraint *#Fʀɪᴄ over the antagonistic faithfulness constraint ID[manner], we can account for the Stopping error pattern in word-initial position. The interaction of this error pattern with the chain shift can be handled by appealing to sympathy. Sympathy is especially relevant to the explanation of target interdentals. The sympathy constraint is interpreted as in the prior section (§4.5) and assigns violations to all candidates that are not cumulative with respect to the flower candidate. The flower candidate is determined in part by ID[manner], which serves as the selector. The candidates that are consistent with the selector include all of the fricative-initial candidates. Given the hierarchy for the chain shift, the most harmonic fricative for an input interdental would be a labial fricative; more serious violations are assigned to a fully faithful interdental ($_0*\theta$) and a grooved coronal fricative (*s). For a word-initial target interdental fricative, then, the highly ranked sympathy constraint essentially demands that the labial place feature of the flower candidate be preserved in the winning output candidate. On the other hand, for a word-initial target grooved fricative, the most harmonic fricative would be an interdental because a labial fricative includes an added ID[place] violation not incurred by the interdental. Given that the flower candidate in this instance includes an interdental fricative, then, the sympathy constraint would preserve its coronal place feature in the winning output. The partial ordering diagram in (59) shows the unfaithful mappings for a word-initial target /θ/ 'thumb'. It is easy to see from the display which candidates are cumulative relative to the flower candidate and which are not. More specifically, the troublesome transparent candidate [dʌm], which would otherwise have been selected as optimal, is ruled out by the sympathy constraint because its violations are not cumulative relative to the flower candidate.

(59) Partial ordering diagram for 'thumb'

The tableaux in (60) illustrate the interaction of these error patterns. Our account glosses over the voicing that occurs in word-initial position insofar as it is not central to the opacity effects observed here. For a discussion of word-initial voicing and other processes that are restricted to word-initial position, see Chapter 9.

(60) Chain shift and Stopping interaction

						selector				
/θʌm/ 'thumb'	⌾Sʏᴍ	*s	$_0*\theta$	*#Fʀɪᴄ	ID[grooved]	ID[manner]	ID[place]	*f	$_N*\theta$
a. FFC θʌm	*!		*	*					
b. ⌾ fʌm				*!			*	*	
c. dʌm	*!					*			
d. ☞ bʌm						*	*		

/sʌn/ 'sun'	☞Sym	*s	$*\theta_o$	*#Fric	ID[grooved]	ID[manner]	ID[place]	*f	$*\theta_N$
a. FFC sʌn	*!	*		*					
b. ☞ θʌn				*!	*				*
c. fʌn				*!	*		*	*	
d. ☞ dʌn					*	*			
e. bʌn					*	*	*!		

The case of Child 209 is interesting on both theoretical and clinical grounds. While it adds to the store of developmental overapplication effects and supports sympathy, it also differs in some ways from the other observed cases. First, it reveals that overapplication effects can and do interact with other opacity effects. It is at present unknown how common such interactions might be in either developing or fully developed languages. Again, as with the other cases discussed in this chapter, none of these opacity effects was evident in the primary linguistic data to which the child would have been exposed. Recall, too, that the overapplication cases from §4.5 yielded a superficial vowel length contrast. However, in the case of Child 209, the overapplication effect did not introduce a superficial contrast, but instead resulted in a wholesale merger with multiple sources for word-initial labial stops. Aside from the obvious target-appropriate underlying source for a labial stop, both underlying and derived labial fricatives also served as sources for word-initial labial stops. These different sources, in turn, pose a clinical question regarding which source to target for treatment. For example, if Child 209 were to be taught word-initial /f/, we might reasonably expect Stopping to be (partially) suppressed with the demotion of *#Fric below ID[manner], but such treatment would not be expected to have any beneficial consequence for the chain shift error pattern. That is, target interdentals in word-initial position would likely be produced as a labial fricative or a labial stop. Such a result would be consistent with the learning pattern of Child 142 described in §2 and §3 and Child T in Chapter 5. On the other hand, if Child 209 were to be taught a word-initial interdental fricative, we might expect not only that Stopping would be suppressed but also that some aspect of the chain shift would likely be resolved with target-appropriate realizations of word-initial interdental fricatives. For a discussion of some of the outcomes associated with treating chain shifts, see Chapters 6 and 8 and references therein. An empirical test of these predictions must await future experimental treatment studies.

5   Conclusion

It is well established that opacity effects are abundant and naturally occurring in fully developed languages. If children's grammars are governed by the same principles that govern fully developed languages, we might expect opacity effects to occur in developing phonologies as well. However, it has long been assumed that opaque generalizations are hard to learn (e.g., Kiparsky, 1971). Additionally, if children's grammars yield transparent generalizations in the earliest stages of acquisition, we might expect children to find it especially hard or counterproductive to acquire generalizations that are not present in the primary linguistic data to which they are exposed. As we have tried to show here, however, opacity effects of various kinds are naturally occurring in acquisition. Additionally, in all of the cases reviewed here, the generalizations that the children arrived at were not observable in English. Some recent proposals for the characterization of opacity effects were evaluated against these acquisition facts and were, for the most part, found to make correct predictions about the range of effects, their emergence and their loss. Comparative markedness probably enjoys a slight advantage over local conjunction, at least given the discussion in §3.4 relating to the characterization of Stage 2' for Child 142 and the analysis of another case study presented in Chapter 5. Sympathy also appears to provide an explanation for overapplication opacity effects as described in §4.5 and §4.6. The range of attested opacity effects was also shown to have parallels in fully developed languages. Our primary focus was on documenting the emergence of a grandfather effect that involved blocking in a phonologically nonderived environment (Child 142, Stage 2). The opposite opacity effect was also documented with a chain shift that involved blocking in a phonologically derived environment (§4.1, §4.4, and §4.6). A different type of grandfather effect was also considered which involved blocking in a morphologically nonderived environment (§4.2). The opposite opacity effect was also observed in a chain shift where a process was blocked in a morphologically derived environment (§4.3). These underapplication opacity effects were also contrasted with overapplication opacity effects in §4.5 and §4.6. It is, of course, not yet known whether children will instantiate the full range and prevalence of opacity effects that have been observed in fully developed languages. It is hoped that this survey will stimulate interest in identifying other opacity effects in first- and second-language acquisition to fill out the typology, replicate the effects observed here, and further evaluate theoretical proposals for their characterization.

Notes

* I would like to thank Judith Gierut, Ashley Farris-Trimble, Laura McGarrity, Nick Henriksen, Michele Morrisette, Amanda Edmonds, Paul Smolensky, John McCarthy, Andries Coetzee, and Arto Anttila for their many helpful comments and discussions about various aspects of this chapter. This work was supported in part by a grant to Indiana University from the National Institutes of Health (DC001694).

1 For a range of alternative accounts of variation, see Anttila and Cho (1998), Gierut, Morrisette and Champion (1999), Boersma and Hayes (2001), and Coetzee (2004).

2 This is not a trivial assumption because the relative timing of these events has implications for the theoretical account. It is in principle possible that other words not sampled in our study could have shown the effect of Deaffrication but not assimilation. The facts of Stage 2 begin to show such an effect and suggest that Derived Assimilation was being lost in advance of Deaffrication. That is, a greater percentage of words that could have undergone Derived Assimilation deaffricated but did not assimilate (e.g., words such as 'chicken' were realized as [tɪkɪn]). For a fuller discussion of this issue, see §3.4.

3 The long-standing observation for fully developed languages is that contrasts tend to be preserved in strong, perceptually salient contexts and neutralized elsewhere. Word-initial position is typically judged to be a strong, prominent context, at least in fully developed languages. We thus might not expect to see mergers limited to word-initial position. However, early stages of acquisition provide some evidence that prominence may shift from a default where word-final position and/or rhymes are the more prominent contexts for acquiring contrasts (Chapter 9 in this volume). One possible reason for the difference in prominence may be related to differences in the size of the lexicon for children versus adults. Consequently, the restriction to word-initial position in this and other constraints considered here may derive from other factors, allowing the constraints for children and adults to be the same.

4 This entails as well an antagonistic set of lower-ranked markedness constraints that disfavor the different place features.

5 The greater prevalence of Deaffrication relative to Derived Assimilation also means that some derived alveolar stops at that stage did not assimilate. Recall that we are not attempting to account for such variation and are instead focusing on the categorical occurrence of error patterns.

6 For a critical review of comparative markedness, see the various commentaries in the 2003 issue of *Theoretical Linguistics*, especially Łubowicz's (2003) critique and McCarthy's (2003b) reply to those commentaries.

7   The assumption would be that the other markedness constraints are also split up in the same way. However, because the data considered here provide no evidence for the distinction in those other constraints, both versions of each markedness constraint will be collapsed under one generic label.

8   In his proposal for comparative markedness, McCarthy (2002a:59) has pointed out that there is some question about the facts that would ever motivate a child to demote a new markedness constraint. Dinnsen and Farris-Trimble (Chapter 5 in this volume) offer a possible solution to this problem in the emergence of chain shift opacity effects. The situation is a little different in this case because $_O$#-AGREE has already been demoted. It thus may be that the demotion of $_N$#-AGREE is motivated simply by the child's recognition that all initial consonants contrast in place.

9   If we were to entertain an LC constraint AGREE & ID[manner] (LC(A&M)), it would need to be ranked below the two locally conjoined constraints and above AGREE.

10 McCarthy (2002a) formulates a comparative markedness account for one aspect of this problem, but he does not consider how it interacts with morphology. That interaction requires a slightly different analysis as formulated in this section. An account is also formulated in terms of local constraint conjunction (Dinnsen, O'Connor & Gierut, 2001).

11 This is an abbreviation for two subconstraints of ✿SYM: ✿CUMUL and ✿DIFF. ✿CUMUL demands that a candidate be cumulative relative to the flower candidate. This means that any candidate that does not have a superset of the flower candidate's faithfulness violations is assigned a ✿CUMUL violation. This is exemplified in the lattice (or partial ordering diagram) in (50), which shows the faithfulness violations incurred by the different candidates for a given input. The second subconstraint, ✿DIFF, is assumed to be universally ranked below ✿CUMUL. It essentially favors candidates that differ minimally from the flower candidate. Because ✿DIFF is not decisive in this type of opacity, the violations of ✿SYM in this example are ✿CUMUL violations.

12 For a different perspective on sympathy and the acquisition of an opaque generalization that is present in the target language, see Bermúdez-Otero (2003).

13 Sympathy was originally proposed to handle both overapplication and underapplication effects associated with counterbleeding and counterfeeding derivations, respectively. If sympathy were employed to account for both the overapplication and underapplication effects observed here, it would be necessary to appeal to two different selectors, ID[manner] and ID[grooved], respectively. Two sympathy constraints would also be necessary with each relativized to a specific selector. McCarthy (2007) has proposed an intriguing alternative to sympathy and some aspects of comparative markedness in his new framework 'optimality theory with candidate chains' (OTCC). Interestingly, in one of his Phonologyfest lectures at Indiana University (June, 2006), McCarthy reinterpreted the overapplication and underapplication effects in Child 209's phonology and showed that both could be handled within OTCC. The broader implications of his new framework for acquisition certainly warrant further consideration.

5 An unusual error pattern reconsidered*

Daniel A. Dinnsen & Ashley W. Farris-Trimble
Indiana University

Certain phonological error patterns in children's early speech have been judged to be 'unusual' or 'idiosyncratic'. The peculiarities associated with these error patterns pose a number of theoretical and clinical problems. This chapter reconsiders an especially challenging case of an unusual error pattern documented by Leonard and Brown (1984). T (age 3;8) replaced all word-final consonants (except for labial stops) with [s] but more importantly inserted [s] after word-final vowels. The purpose of this chapter is to show that optimality theory offers a fresh perspective on this error pattern and its subsequent course of development. The apparent unusualness of this error pattern is shown to be a natural consequence of constraint conflict. Additionally, empirical support from acquisition is provided for 'comparative markedness' (McCarthy, 2002a). The account is also argued to have implications for resolving another problem relating to the characterization of a common error pattern.

1   Introduction

Accounting for children's error patterns is a central goal of acquisition research, and accounting for acquisition is crucial for a theory to achieve explanatory adequacy. Many different phonological error patterns have been documented and characterized within the available theoretical frameworks. Most of these error patterns are commonly occurring in both typical and atypical development. It is also not difficult to find comparable phenomena in fully developed languages. Current theories of phonology have little difficulty accounting for these common error patterns. There are, however, other error patterns that are less common and pose a more serious challenge. These less common error patterns have been viewed as 'unusual' or 'idiosyncratic' largely because they appear to run counter to what we observe in fully developed languages and/ or to what we think we know about the principles that govern language and its acquisition (e.g., Ingram & Terselic, 1983; Camarata & Gandour, 1984; Leonard, 1985; Leonard & Leonard, 1985; Bedore, Leonard & Gandour, 1994; Bernhardt & Stoel-Gammon, 1996; Gierut & Champion, 2000; Morrisette, Dinnsen & Gierut, 2003; Dinnsen & Farris, 2004a). Some of these less common error patterns can result in a sound that does not occur in the target language or a sound substitute that is more marked than the target sound. Some of these error patterns might even appear to be entirely nonsystematic. Yet other error patterns might operate in phonological contexts that are generally assumed to be strong or perceptually salient and should otherwise resist mergers. Because of the peculiarities associated with these unusual error patterns, some theoreticians find it convenient to set these and other acquisition phenomena aside as irrelevant to general principles of phonology (e.g., Hale & Reiss, 1998). These error patterns also pose a number of clinical challenges. For example, it is unknown whether these error patterns are a reflection of a more severe disorder or even a deviant phonology that might be resistant to conventional remediation. The nature of these unusual error patterns, how they arise, their developmental course, and even their theoretical relevance have remained open questions.

This chapter reconsiders one especially challenging case of an unusual error pattern documented by Leonard and Brown (1984). The child in their study replaced most word-final consonants with a particular fricative but, more importantly, inserted that fricative after word-final vowels. Multiple rounds of treatment were required to deal with this error pattern, and treatment was only partially successful. Leonard and Brown's account of these facts has gone without challenge for at least twenty years now, despite the fact that it departs from several standard assumptions about acquisition and leaves a number of questions unanswered. The analytical challenges posed by this case are underscored all the more by considering the advances in phonological theory that have been made over the years but which have gone untapped in this case. Our main purpose will be to put forward and evaluate an alternative account of this unusual error pattern and its course of development within the current framework of optimality theory (e.g., Prince & Smolensky, 1993/2004; McCarthy & Prince, 1995; McCarthy, 2002b). Our solution will draw on general principles that are directly relevant to the characterization of fully developed languages and will take advantage of 'comparative markedness' (McCarthy, 2002a). One important consequence of our reanalysis will be that, while this error pattern might have appeared somewhat unusual, it is certainly not deviant in any sense and in fact is an expected result of conflicting constraints. The treatment results will also be shown to accord with general principles of learning. Finally, we will argue that our reanalysis of this unusual error pattern begins to offer some promise for resolving certain other problems for optimality theory.

The chapter is organized as follows. In §2, we summarize the essentials of Leonard and Brown's study and spell out the problem. §3 lays out an optimality theoretic analysis of the facts for each stage of development. In §4, we take up some issues that arise from our analyses, including speculation about how this unusual error pattern might have arisen and a consideration of the implications of our account for certain other problems in optimality theory and for claims about the nature of children's underlying representations. The chapter concludes with a brief summary.

2   Sketch of the case study

The child from Leonard and Brown's study, T (age 3 years;8 months), was a female with language-delays. Her presenting phonology included what has come to be a classic example of an unusual error pattern affecting word-final position. The data in (1) illustrate some of the peculiarities associated with this error pattern. First, the forms in (1a) exemplify the fact that all final consonants (except labial stops) were replaced by [s]. More importantly, the forms in (1b) show that [s] was inserted after word-final vowels. This aspect of the error pattern poses the most serious problem because a presumably unmarked open syllable is being transformed into a more marked closed syllable. Finally, the forms in (1c) show that word-final labial stops were produced target-appropriately and were thus immune to the error pattern.

(1)   T (3;8) baseline productions (Leonard & Brown, 1984)

   a)   Final consonants replaced by [s]

[mæs]	'Matt'	[gɜs]	'girl'
[dɔs]	'dog'	[mas]	'mouth'

   b)   Insertion of [s] after word-final vowels

[tus]	'two'	[bɔs]	'boy'
[as]	'eye'	[gɔs]	'go'

   c)   Final labial stops preserved

[kʌp]	'cup'	[gab̥]	'Gabe'
[hom]	'home'	[mam]	'mom'

Leonard and Brown argued that the most parsimonious account of these facts was to posit a highly restricted, child-specific set of underlying representations. That is, all words, except for those target words ending in a labial stop, were assumed to be represented underlyingly with a final /s/. It should be kept in mind that this assumption about T's underlying representations departs from the more widely held view among acquisition researchers that children's underlying representations are target-appropriate or at least correspond with target surface phonetic representations (e.g., Smith, 1973; Ingram, 1989). A more conventional approach would have required a set of rules to convert target-appropriate underlying representations into the errored phonetic representations. One consequence of Leonard and Brown's account is that no rules would be necessary because words were represented underlyingly the way they were pronounced.

T's presenting error pattern would be interesting in its own right, but she also received treatment that was intended to eradicate the error pattern, revealing an interesting course of phonological development with three distinct stages. The facts of the three stages are summarized in (2). Using traditional treatment methods, T was first taught /f/ in word-final position. The reason given for selecting this sound was that T was able to produce the sound in imitation, and it shared two features with her 'favorite sound' [s]: oral and continuant. This treatment regime was only partially successful and yielded a second identifiable stage of development. That is, treatment resulted in the addition of target-appropriate realizations of final labial fricatives, but the original error pattern persisted with the other words. Some vowel-final words also began to be produced correctly. In a further effort to eradicate the persisting error pattern, an additional round of treatment was initiated with a focus on introducing final /d/. The reason given for selecting this sound was again that T produced the sound in imitation, and it also shared two features with [s]: oral and non-labial. Again, treatment was only partially successful, yielding a third stage of development. That is, coronal stops began to be produced correctly in final position, but the insertion of final [s] in vowel-final words largely persisted. However, some vowel-final words also began to overgeneralize the effects of treatment with the insertion of a final [d] (rather than [s]).

This case, with its unusual error pattern and longitudinal development, poses a number of problems that are in need of an explanation. First, why would a consonant be inserted to close a presumably unmarked open syllable word-finally? Second, why would some but not other final consonants be immune to this error pattern during each of the different stages? Third, why did this error pattern change (and even overgeneralize) as it did? Finally, is it really more parsimonious to posit unique, child-specific underlying representations for this unusual error pattern? The remainder of this chapter is devoted to addressing these questions from the fresh perspective of optimality theory.

(2)   Summary of the facts for the three stages

Stage	Word-final production facts	Sound taught
1	Labial stops correct All other words end in [s]	final /f/
2	Labial stops & labial fricatives correct Some vowel-final words correct All other words end in [s]	final /d/
3	Coronal stops & all labials correct Some vowel-final words correct All other words end in [s] or [d] (overgeneralization)	

3   An optimality theoretic account

In this section, we formulate an optimality theoretic account of the facts for each of the three stages. The change from one stage to the next will be shown to follow from standard assumptions about learning through constraint demotion (e.g., Tesar & Smolensky, 1998). A crucial element of our account that distinguishes it from Leonard and Brown's is that no child-specific restrictions on underlying representations will need to be imposed.

3.1   Stage 1: Pretreatment baseline

We begin with an account of the more unusual aspect of the pretreatment error pattern, namely the insertion of a final [s] to target vowel-final words. On both cross-linguistic and developmental grounds, open syllables are usually considered unmarked relative to closed syllables; thus, although the realization of closed syllables as open is not uncommon or surprising, the opposite pattern—an open syllable realized as closed—is less expected. The fact is, however, that a number of languages (e.g., Yapese (Jensen, 1977; Pigott, 1999) and Arrernte (Breen & Pensalfini, 1999)) and some varieties of English (e.g., Bristol and Bostonian (McCarthy, 1993)), prefer the occurrence of a word-final consonant over a final vowel. This has given rise to the postulation of the markedness constraint FINAL-C, which bans word-final vowels (McCarthy, 1993; Swets, 2004). One way to satisfy this constraint while preserving underlying vowels would be to insert a consonant in final position. If FINAL-C were ranked above a generalized faithfulness constraint, FAITH, which militates against any changes relative to the underlying input representation, the greater demand to comply with FINAL-C would compel the insertion of a word-final consonant. We will return shortly to the issue of why it is specifically [s] that is inserted as opposed to some other consonant.

We tentatively adopt the constraints and ranking in (3) to account for this one aspect of T's error pattern.

(3)   Constraints and ranking (tentative)

> FINAL-C: Word-final vowels are banned
> FAITH: Inputs and outputs must be identical
> Ranking: FINAL-C
>
> |
>
>   FAITH

The tableau in (4) shows how a vowel-final word such as 'two' would be realized with a final [s]. We are assuming for the moment that the child could have internalized target-appropriate underlying representations for words with and without final vowels. This is in accord with 'richness of the base' (Prince & Smolensky, 1993/2004), which prohibits language-specific or child-specific restrictions on underlying representations. Even if this child had incorrectly internalized the input as identical to the errored output, as might be expected given lexicon optimization (e.g., Prince & Smolensky, 1993/2004; Itô, Mester & Padgett, 1995), the same candidate would be selected as optimal with this hierarchy. The important point is that there is no need to exclude vowel-final words from this child's set of underlying representations, and lexicon optimization is only relevant after the constraint hierarchy guarantees the actually occurring output. We will see in subsequent sections that it is neither necessary nor sufficient to impose child-specific restrictions on T's underlying representations.

(4)   Insertion of [s] for vowel-final words

/tu/ 'two'	FINAL-C	FAITH
a. tu	*!	
b. ☞ tus		*

The faithful candidate (a) fatally violates undominated FINAL-C and is eliminated from the competition. Candidate (b) thus survives as optimal even though it violates lower-ranked FAITH.

Target words with final consonants are predicted to be realized faithfully with this same constraint hierarchy and the assumption of target-appropriate input representations. For example, a fully faithful candidate of a target word with a final labial stop or coronal fricative incurs no violation of either constraint, compelling no changes. Any competitors that depart from the input representation would incur a violation of one of these constraints and would be eliminated. This is illustrated in the tableau in (5) for a word such as 'cup'.

(5)   Faithful realization of (some) consonant-final words

/kʌp/ 'cup'	Fɪɴᴀʟ-C	Fᴀɪᴛʜ
a. ☞ kʌp		
b. kʌ	*!	*
c. kʌs		*!

While this correctly accounts for T's realization of some consonant-final words, it makes the wrong prediction about many others. For example, target words with final coronal stops or labial fricatives were realized unfaithfully with a final [s]. This brings us to the second part of our solution, i.e., accounting for the substitution pattern associated with many consonant-final words.

T clearly favored some final consonants over others. Coronal stops and labial fricatives (among others) were banned from final position. It is difficult to see what features are shared by these banned sounds that would distinguish them from those labial stops and coronal fricatives that were tolerated word-finally. To determine which markedness constraint(s) might be responsible for the substitution pattern affecting some final consonants, it is worth noting first that the particular sound that replaced those final consonants was identical to the sound that was inserted at the end of vowel-final words, suggesting a common source. With some final consonants absolutely banned and with it being equally important that some consonant occur in final position as required by Fɪɴᴀʟ-C, the conflict between these opposing demands would have to be resolved by other constraints. We appeal to an exploded version of a general markedness constraint, NᴏCᴏᴅᴀ, which abbreviates a larger family of constraints banning different classes of coda consonants, a partial listing of which is given in (6).

(6)   Exploded version of NᴏCᴏᴅᴀ (NC)

    NC-t: Coda coronal stops are banned
    NC-s: Coda coronal fricatives are banned
    NC-p: Coda labial stops are banned
    NC-f: Coda labial fricatives are banned

       Tentative ranking: Fɪɴᴀʟ-C, NC-t, NC-f

                         |

                    Fᴀɪᴛʜ

                         |

                 NC-p, NC-s

By ranking some of the NoCODA constraints above FAITH and others below FAITH, certain final consonants are eliminated in favor of others. Undominated FINAL-C requires that some consonant be present word-finally. The lower ranking of the other NoCODA constraints renders their violations less serious. Thus, we can eliminate candidates with a final coronal stop or labial fricative by ranking NoCODA-t and NoCODA-f above FAITH. We can also account for the occurrence of final coronal fricatives and labial stops with the ranking of NoCODA-s and NoCODA-p below FAITH. This is illustrated in the following series of tableaux. No ranking argument can be established for FINAL-C relative to NoCODA-t and NoCODA-f. Any ranking of these three constraints above FAITH will yield the same result. We thus assume that they are equally ranked or unranked relative to one another.

(7)   Realizations of consonant-final words

/mæt/ 'Matt'		FINAL-C	NC-t	NC-f	FAITH	NC-p	NC-s
a.	mæt		*!				
b.	mæ	*!			*		
c.	mæf			*!	*		
d. ☞	mæs				*		*

/naɪf/ 'knife'		FINAL-C	NC-t	NC-f	FAITH	NC-p	NC-s
a.	naf			*!			
b.	na	*!			*		
c.	nat		*!		*		
d. ☞	nas				*		*

/bʌs/ 'bus'		FINAL-C	NC-t	NC-f	FAITH	NC-p	NC-s
a. ☞	bʌs						*
b.	bʌ	*!			*		
c.	bʌf			*!	*		
d.	bʌp				*!	*	

/kʌp/ 'cup'		FINAL-C	NC-t	NC-f	FAITH	NC-p	NC-s
a. ☞	kʌp					*	
b.	kʌ	*!			*		
c.	kʌt		*!		*		
d.	kʌs				*!		*

The first two of the tableaux in (7) begin to illustrate how the substitution pattern comes about for certain final consonants. The last two tableaux show how the fully faithful candidate survives as optimal in other cases. In all of these tableaux, FINAL-C eliminates the vowel-final candidates (b). While the other competitor candidates comply with FINAL-C, undominated NoCODA-t and NoCODA-f eliminate candidates with a final coronal stop or a labial fricative, whether faithful or not. This same constraint hierarchy also goes some way toward explaining why it was [s] rather than certain other consonants that was inserted after a final vowel. This is illustrated in the tableau in (8).

(8)   Final consonant insertion for vowel-final words

/tu/ 'two'	FINAL-C	NC-t	NC-f	FAITH	NC-p	NC-s
a. tu	*!					
b. tut		*!		*		
c. tuf			*!	*		
d. ☞ tus				*		*

The astute reader will observe that the first two tableaux in (7) and the one in (8) did not consider one very important candidate, namely one with a final labial stop. Such a candidate would incur a violation of low-ranked NoCODA-p, resulting in a tie with the intended and empirically attested winner with a final coronal fricative. This problem is illustrated in (9) by reconsidering the tableau in (8) with an expanded set of output candidates. While candidate (d) is correctly predicted to win, so is the wrong candidate (e), indicated by ☛.

(9)   False prediction of free variation

/tu/ 'two'	FINAL-C	NC-t	NC-f	FAITH	NC-p	NC-s
a. tu	*!					
b. tut		*!		*		
c. tuf			*!	*		
d. ☞ tus				*		*
e. ☛ tup				*	*	

We thus cannot account yet for why [s], rather than a labial stop, served as the substitute for certain consonant-final words or as the inserted segment for vowel-final words. This indeterminacy results from the assumption that NoCODA-p and NoCODA-s are equally ranked below FAITH. However, it might be suggested that this problem could be solved by simply imposing a ranking among the two dominated markedness constraints such that NoCODA-p outranked NoCODA-s. Such a ranking would have the desirable consequence of eliminating any unfaithful candidate with a final labial stop. However, this ranking cannot be motivated by the primary linguistic data to which T would have been exposed and, thus, there is no explanation for how the ranking might have arisen. It might be countered that NoCODA-p is ranked above NoCODA-s in accord with a putative universal scale among place features with labial place being more marked than coronal place (e.g., Prince & Smolensky, 1993/2004; Lombardi, 2001; de Lacy, 2002). One problem with such a proposal is that the facts of this case also require that NoCODA-t be undominated (i.e., ranked above NoCODA-p), in direct contradiction to a universal place scale. Such a scale must also be reconciled against opposing findings which require freely permutable place-referring constraints in both fully developed and developing phonologies (e.g., Hume & Tserdanelis, 2002; Morrisette et al., 2003). There appears to be no independent motivation for ranking NoCODA-p above NoCODA-s.

This brings us to the next part of our solution, i.e., accounting for the specific sound that was substituted or inserted. To address this aspect of the problem, we appeal to 'comparative markedness', which was put forward by McCarthy (2002a) as a refinement to optimality theory's account of other opaque phenomena in fully developed languages.[1] Comparative markedness modifies original conceptions of markedness by splitting up each conventional markedness constraint into two distinct versions of the same constraint. One version of a given constraint would assign a violation mark for an offending property that is fully faithful. Such a violation is considered 'old' in the sense that it carries over from the input representation. The other version of that same constraint would assign a violation mark for an offending property that differs in any way from the fully faithful candidate. Such a violation is considered 'new' because it is not directly supplied by the input. The two versions of a given markedness constraint yield exactly the same combined violations of a conventional markedness constraint. The only real difference is that comparative markedness allows the violations to be partitioned into two nonoverlapping sets with the marks being assigned separately by the different versions of the two freely permutable constraints.

Comparative markedness is relevant to the case at hand because it allows us to explain why a target labial stop could surface faithfully, but it could not be inserted and/or be the substitute for another sound. This requires splitting the constraint that disfavors final labial stops (NoCODA-p) into one that assigns a mark for an 'old' violation, $_O$NoCODA-p, and another that assigns a mark for a 'new' violation, $_N$NoCODA-p. By ranking $_O$NoCODA-p below FAITH, we claim that final labial stops that are faithful are protected or immune from change. McCarthy (2002a) has dubbed such a situation a 'grandfather effect'. By ranking $_N$NoCODA-p above FAITH, any unfaithful labial stop will be assessed a fatal violation mark and will be eliminated from the competition. Thus, although underlying labial stops will surface faithfully, labial stops that are inserted or employed as a substitute will be ruled out by high-ranking $_N$NoCoda-p. The revised hierarchy incorporating comparative markedness is given in (10). It can be assumed for the moment that all of the other markedness constraints are also split up into old and new versions. However, because this stage provides no evidence of differential behavior in the case of these other constraints, we abbreviate both versions of each constraint under one label. The component parts of the constraints will be differentiated as evidence necessitates in the subsequent stages.

(10) Revised hierarchy for Stage 1

$$\text{Final-C, } _N\text{NC-p, NC-t, NC-f}$$
$$|$$
$$\text{Faith}$$
$$|$$
$$_O\text{NC-p, NC-s}$$

The grandfather effect associated with target words ending in a labial stop is illustrated in the tableau in (11). The vowel-final candidate (b) is eliminated by Final-C. Candidates (c) and (d) with a final labial fricative and a coronal stop as a substitute incur fatal violations of NoCoda-f and NoCoda-t, respectively; thus, in the exploded versions of these markedness constraints, these candidates violate $_N$NoCoda-f and $_N$NoCoda-t, respectively. Those violations happen to be new relative to the fully faithful candidate (a). Candidate (e) with a final [s] is eliminated by Faith. This leaves the faithful candidate (a) to be correctly selected as optimal, even though it violates low-ranked $_O$NoCoda-p.

(11) Faithful realization of final labial stops: A grandfather effect

/kʌp/ 'cup'	Final-C	$_N$NC-p	NC-t	NC-f	Faith	$_O$NC-p	NC-s
a. FFC ☞ kʌp						*	
b. kʌ	*!				*		
c. kʌf				*!	*		
d. kʌt			*!		*		
e. kʌs					*!		*

The next two tableaux in (12) show how a candidate with a final [s] is preferred over other candidates, whether the [s] is inserted at the end of vowel-final words or substituted for a final consonant. In the first of these, the faithful candidate is eliminated by its violation of Final-C. Candidates (b), (c), and (d) incur fatal violations of $_N$NoCODA-p, NoCODA-f, and NoCODA-t. In fact, all of those violations are new relative to the fully faithful candidate. While candidate (e) with an inserted [s] violates FAITH and NoCODA-s, all other competitors have been eliminated by higher-ranked constraints. In the second of these tableaux, the vowel-final candidate is again eliminated by FINAL-C. Candidates (a), (b), and (c) are also eliminated by the same constraints as in the prior tableau. The difference in this case is that the fully faithful candidate (a)'s violation of NoCODA-f is a violation of $_O$NoCODA-f, given that the labial fricative is a part of the input representation. Candidate (e) with a final [s] as the substitute thus survives as optimal.

(12) Final [s] preferred whether inserted or substituted

/tu/ 'two'	FINAL-C	$_N$NC-p	NC-t	NC-f	FAITH	$_O$NC-p	NC-s
a. FFC tu	*!						
b. tup		*!			*		
c. tuf				*!	*		
d. tut			*!		*		
e. ☞ tus					*		*

/naɪf/ 'knife'	FINAL-C	$_N$NC-p	NC-t	NC-f	FAITH	$_O$NC-p	NC-s
a. FFC naf				*!			
b. nap		*!			*		
c. nat			*!		*		
d. na	*!				*		
e. ☞ nas					*		*

Summing up to this point, we have accounted for Stage 1 of T's seemingly unusual error pattern by appealing to two independently motivated but conflicting markedness constraints (FINAL-C and NoCODA). Comparative markedness also played a role in explaining the grandfather effect whereby labial stops were, on the one hand, immune to the error pattern and, on the other hand, were not viable substitutes for the other sounds that participated in the error pattern. Finally, in accord with richness of the base, we did not need to make any child-specific assumptions about underlying representations. The result is that this error pattern, while challenging on analytical grounds, does have an explanation within optimality theory. As a further test of the theory, we next turn to an account of the stages of development that emerged following treatment.

If our analysis is correct, we should expect to see a high degree of continuity preserved in T's grammar across stages.

3.2   Stage 2: After treatment on final /f/

Recall that in response to T's presenting phonology, she was first taught final /f/. One of the main results following this treatment was the target-appropriate realization of [f] in final position. The error pattern otherwise persisted as before for the other target sounds. This pattern follows naturally from our characterization of the prior stage's demotion of the markedness constraint that had banned final labial fricatives, namely NoCodA-f. However, labial fricatives could not serve as substitutes for other final consonants or be inserted after final vowels.

This reveals the emergence of another grandfather effect where labial fricatives were realized faithfully but continued to be banned as substitutes for other sounds. This is similar to the situation described for labial stops at Stage 1 and, accordingly, we propose a similar solution: $_N$NoCodA-f remains dominant over FAITH, whereas $_O$NoCodA-f is demoted below FAITH. It appears that T already had target-appropriate underlying representations for labial fricatives, especially given that no other final consonants were realized as [f]. In order, then, for labial fricatives to be realized target-appropriately, T had to begin with target-appropriate underlying representations of those and other final consonants, and $_O$NoCodA-f would have been demoted just below the highest-ranked constraint that the previous winner violated, namely just below FAITH. This is consistent with the constraint demotion algorithm (Tesar & Smolensky, 1998).

The constraint hierarchy for Stage 2 that resulted from this reranking is given in (13). The tableau in (14) employs the new hierarchy and illustrates the target-appropriate realization of final labial fricatives. To see the difference between the two stages, this tableau can be compared with the one for the same word from the prior stage (12).

(13) Constraint hierarchy for Stage 2

FINAL-C, $_N$NC-p, $_N$NC-f, NC-t

|

FAITH

|

$_O$NC-f, $_O$NC-p, NC-s

(14) Target-appropriate realization of final labial fricatives: Another grandfather effect

/naɪf/ 'knife'	FINAL-C	$_N$NC-p	$_N$NC-f	NC-t	FAITH	$_o$NC-f	$_o$NC-p	NC-s
a. na	*!				*			
b. FFC ☞ naf						*		
c. nas					*!			*
d. nap		*!			*			

While the above tableau shows that target labial fricatives in final position were immune to the error pattern because $_o$NoCoda-f was ranked below FAITH, we can see in the next tableau in (15) the effect of $_N$NoCoda-f in the selection of the segment inserted in vowel-final words. Specifically, it is $_N$NoCoda-f that eliminates candidate (b) with an unfaithful final labial fricative. The faithful candidate continued to be eliminated by undominated FINAL-C. The winning output is unfaithful because all the other competitors have been eliminated by higher-ranked constraints.

(15) Persistence of the error pattern for other words

/tu/ 'two'	FINAL-C	$_N$NC-p	$_N$NC-f	NC-t	FAITH	$_o$NC-f	$_o$NC-p	NC-s
a. FFC tu	*!							
b. tuf			*!		*			
c. tup		*!			*			
d. ☞ tus					*			*

The other result that immediately followed treatment on final /f/ was that some vowel-final words (approximately 50%) began to be produced target-appropriately. Neither we nor Leonard and Brown presume to have a good explanation for this particular result. The problem is that there is no obvious connection between vowel-final words and treatment on final /f/, except for the focus on final position itself. It is thus difficult to see why this treatment would have affected vowel-final words in a positive way and not other consonant-final words. Of course, we cannot exclude the possibility that T on her own might have taken note of the occurrence of vowel-final words. In fact, similar spontaneous improvements on untreated aspects of the phonology have been observed for many children and are deemed a desirable effect of treatment, even if no one can fully explain such effects. The other problem is that it is also unclear from Leonard and Brown's discussion whether some vowel-final words freely varied between correct and incorrect productions or whether certain vowel-final words were consistently produced in error while other vowel-final words were produced correctly. In either case, the target-appropriate realization of any vowel-final word would require a slightly different ranking of two constraints. Specifically, FINAL-C must be ranked below FAITH, at least sometimes for some words or word classes. The variation evident in Stage 2 may thus be similar to the variation that often occurs in language contact situations or in the course of historical change (Nagy & Reynolds, 1997). Some have accounted for this sort of variation by adopting a partial ordering among certain constraints (e.g., Anttila & Cho, 1998). Under such a proposal, FINAL-C and FAITH could have become unranked relative to one another in Stage 2, allowing FINAL-C to be ranked above FAITH sometimes and below FAITH other times with different empirical consequences corresponding to the different rankings. The remainder of the constraint hierarchy would have been unaffected. The tableau in (16) illustrates the alternate ranking that yields the faithful realization of some vowel-final words.

(16) Faithful realization of some vowel-final words

/tu/ 'two'	$_N$NC-p	$_N$NC-f	NC-t	FAITH	FINAL-C	$_o$NC-f	$_o$NC-p	NC-s
a. FFC ☞ tu					*			
b. tuf		*!		*				
c. tup	*!			*				
d. tus				*!				*

Again, it appears from these results that T internalized target-appropriate underlying representations for vowel-final words because no consonant-final words exhibited this same variation; that is, no consonant-final words were produced with a final vowel. At the very least, then, she knew underlyingly that there was a difference between vowel-final and consonant-final words.

Our account of Stage 2 (and its transition from Stage 1) appealed to a standard implementation of the constraint demotion algorithm with the demotion of the markedness constraint that had previously banned labial fricatives. Comparative markedness also played a role again in accounting for the emergence of another grandfather effect whereby labial fricatives came to be produced target-appropriately but were prevented from serving as substitutes for the other sounds that participated in the new version of the error pattern. Our account for the target-appropriate realization of some vowel-final words is perhaps less compelling, but is nonetheless within the realm of other accounts of variation and change. Again, there was no need to adopt any child-specific assumptions about underlying representations. In fact, the change from Stage 1 to Stage 2 supports the stronger claim that T internalized target-appropriate underlying representations.

Recall that the persistence of the error pattern during Stage 2 required a new round of treatment which focused on introducing final /d/. We now turn to an account of the facts resulting from that treatment.

3.3   Stage 3: After treatment on final /d/

There were two main results that emerged following treatment on final /d/: (a) coronal stops began to be produced correctly in final position, and (b) the error pattern affecting vowel-final words largely persisted (insertion of final [s]) with some overgeneralization involving the insertion of a final [d]. The proportion of correctly produced vowel-final words remained essentially the same across Stages 2 and 3. The changes for this stage follow naturally from the simple demotion of the constraint that banned final coronal stops, namely NoCODA-t. The rest of the constraint hierarchy would otherwise remain unchanged from the prior stage. The reranked hierarchy for Stage 3 is given in (17). Note that NoCODA-t has been demoted just below FAITH in accord with the constraint demotion algorithm.

(17) Constraint hierarchy for Stage 3

$$\text{FINAL-C, }_N\text{NC-p, }_N\text{NC-f}$$
$$|$$
$$\text{FAITH}$$
$$|$$
$$\text{NC-t, }_o\text{NC-f, }_o\text{NC-p, NC-s}$$

We first illustrate the result for target words that ended correctly in a coronal stop in (18). It is important to keep in mind that these same words were produced in error in the prior stage, ending with an [s]. Notice that candidate (a), the previous winner, is now eliminated because of its violation of FAITH. The constraint demotion algorithm called for the demotion of NoCODA-t below FAITH.[2] While the faithful candidate violates NoCODA-t, all of the other competitors are eliminated by higher-ranked constraints.

(18) Faithful realization of final coronal stops

/wʊd/ 'wood'		FINAL-C	$_N$NC-p	$_N$NC-f	FAITH	NC-t	$_o$NC-f	$_o$NC-p	NC-s
a.	wus				*!				*
b.	wup		*!		*				
c. ☞	wud					*			
d.	wu	*!			*				

We now turn to the characterization of the overgeneralization results and the variation in the error pattern affecting vowel-final words. Again, it is unclear from Leonard and Brown's discussion whether the variation across the two different inserted consonants ([s] and [d]) was the result of inter- or intra-word variation. However, if it turns out that either consonant could be inserted at the end of any given vowel-final word, this too can be seen as the result of demoting NoCoda-t below Faith. The stratum into which NoCoda-t was demoted also includes NoCoda-s. With these two conflicting constraints in the same stratum, there would be an unresolved tie between the two remaining unfaithful candidates, each of which violates one or the other of these two constraints. This free-variation is illustrated by the prediction of two winning candidates in the tableau in (19). The violations incurred by these two winning candidates both happen to be new relative to the fully faithful candidate.[3]

(19) Free variation between final [s] and [d]: Overgeneralization

/tu/ 'two'		Final-C	$_N$NC-p	$_N$NC-f	Faith	NC-t	$_o$NC-f	$_o$NC-p	NC-s
a.	FFC tu	*!							
b.	tup		*!		*				
c. ☞	tud				*	*			
d. ☞	tus				*				*

Target vowel-final words also continued to exhibit some of the same variation evident in Stage 2, namely variation between correct and incorrect productions. It is assumed that this variation is carried over from the partial ordering between Final-C and Faith.

Our account of Stage 3 employing comparative markedness preserved the constraint hierarchy from Stage 2, except for the principled demotion of the markedness constraint that had previously banned coronal stops. That demotion had the interesting consequence of accounting for the overgeneralization that occurred in certain words.

3.4 Summary account of the three stages

Our account of the facts of this case employed target-appropriate underlying representations throughout and a slightly different constraint hierarchy for each of the three stages. The changes to the constraint hierarchy were minimal with a single markedness constraint demoted on the basis of positive evidence at each stage in complete accord with the constraint demotion algorithm. The changes in the hierarchy are depicted in (20) by highlighting in bold the affected constraint at each stage.

(20) Changes to the constraint hierarchy over time

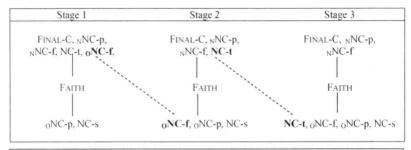

Stage 1	Stage 2	Stage 3
FINAL-C, $_N$NC-p, $_N$NC-f, NC-t, $_O$NC-f.	FINAL-C, $_N$NC-p, $_N$NC-f, **NC-t**	FINAL-C, $_N$NC-p, $_N$NC-f
FAITH	FAITH	FAITH
$_O$NC-p, NC-s	$_O$NC-f, $_O$NC-p, NC-s	**NC-t**, $_O$NC-f, $_O$NC-p, NC-s

FINAL-C and FAITH may have become unranked relative to one another during Stages 2 and 3 to account for the occurrence of some vowel-final words.

4   Discussion

In this section, we take up various issues that arise from our account of T's error pattern. We first consider how this error pattern might have arisen. We then turn to the implications of our account for the resolution of a problem relating to the characterization of another common type of error pattern. We also consider the implications of our account for assumptions about the nature of children's underlying representations. We conclude the discussion with some thoughts about why T's error pattern is not more common.

4.1   How might the unusual error pattern of Stage 1 have come about?

Optimality theory and comparative markedness offer some interesting suggestions about how T's pretreatment error pattern might have arisen. A basic assumption of the theory is that the initial state is characterized by a default ranking of markedness over faithfulness (Smolensky, 1996a). Our account of the pretreatment stage has some of the NoCODA markedness constraints ranked below FAITH, suggesting that one or more stages preceded the pretreatment stage. If FINAL-C and all of the NoCODA constraints were ranked above FAITH prior to Stage 1, all competing candidates would violate one or the other of these constraints. The conflict between these constraints had to be resolved in some way. One possibility, although unlikely, is that FINAL-C and NoCODA were unranked relative to one another and lower-ranked FAITH broke the tie by eliminating all unfaithful competitors. This would have resulted in fully faithful realizations (i.e., the complete absence of the error pattern) and would have absolutely negated any effect of the presumably undominated markedness constraints. While there are reports in the literature of 'progressive idioms' in which a child might produce a particular word correctly during an early stage of development and later produce that word incorrectly (e.g., Stampe, 1973), it is unlikely that T would have produced so many of these words correctly prior to Stage 1, especially given the persistence of the error pattern after the initial round of treatment. Another possibility is to impose a ranking among the conflicting markedness constraints. For example, all of the NoCODA constraints might have dominated FINAL-C, which in turn would have dominated FAITH. Such a ranking predicts that all consonant-final words would have been produced in error without a final consonant, but vowel-final words would have been realized target-appropriately because all consonant-final candidates would have been eliminated by the higher-ranked NoCODA constraints. The lower ranking of FINAL-C would have rendered its violations less serious, predicting that words would have been realized without a final consonant.

These possibilities are unlikely because they predict that the error pattern during an earlier stage would have either been nonexistent or more restricted than in the pretreatment stage. The only way to evidence the effect of both FINAL-C and the NoCODA constraints and to arrive at an initial state error pattern that is at least as extensive as T's pretreatment error pattern would be to demote one of the $_N$NoCODA constraints, e.g., $_N$NoCODA-s. It is not obvious why NoCODA-s would be demoted as opposed to some other $_N$NoCODA constraint. However, if frequency of occurrence in the input influences acquisition (e.g., Morrisette, 2000; Zamuner, Gerken & Hammond, 2004), the greater frequency of final coronal fricatives in English may have played some role in this instance. The demotion of an $_0$NoCODA constraint would have allowed an underlying final consonant to surface faithfully, but the lower ranking of that constraint would not have been sufficient to compel the insertion or replacement of a final consonant for all the other words. At the very least, then, $_N$NoCODA-s had to be demoted below FAITH, and $_0$NoCODA-s may or may not also have been demoted at the same time. The dominance of the other $_0$NoCODA constraints would have had the effect of first eliminating all underlying final consonants, including labial stops. At the same time, the demands of FINAL-C would have required that some consonant occur finally. The dominance of all the other $_N$NoCODA constraints would have also prevented any consonant but [s] from being inserted or substituted for those final consonants.

We thus speculate that prior to Stage 1, all final consonants (including target labial stops) were replaced by [s], and vowel-final words were also realized with a final [s]. Consequently, the constraint hierarchy for T might have had FINAL-C and all of the NoCODA constraints, except for $_N$NoCODA-s, ranked above FAITH as in (21).

(21) Hypothesized hierarchy for Stage 0: All words end in final [s]

$$\textsc{Final-C}, {}_{\text{ON}}\text{NC-p}, {}_{\text{ON}}\text{NC-f}, {}_{\text{ON}}\text{NC-t}, {}_{\text{O}}\text{NC-s}$$

$$|$$

$$\textsc{Faith}$$

$$|$$

$${}_{\text{N}}\text{NC-s}$$

If, as shown above, ${}_{\text{O}}\textsc{NoCoda}$-s were not demoted below $\textsc{Faith}$ with ${}_{\text{N}}\textsc{NoCoda}$-s at Stage 0, the claim would be that even underlying coronal fricatives were banned or deleted along with all other final consonants, but they were replaced by an identical segment due to the lower ranking of ${}_{\text{N}}\textsc{NoCoda}$-s. Such a characterization claims that, while final coronal fricatives might have been produced correctly, those correct productions came about for the wrong reasons. Similar phenomena involving correct productions for the wrong reasons have been identified for other children (e.g., Dinnsen, 1999; 2002). In any event, there is no way to know for sure when ${}_{\text{O}}\textsc{NoCoda}$-s might have been demoted.

Given our hypothesized hierarchy for Stage 0, the pretreatment hierarchy of Stage 1 would follow quite naturally from the simple demotion of ${}_{\text{O}}\textsc{NoCoda}$-p on the basis of positive evidence about the occurrence of final labial stops in the target system.

4.2   Chain shifts and comparative markedness[4]

Our speculation about how T's pretreatment error pattern might have arisen begins to resolve a problem that certain acquisition phenomena pose for comparative markedness theory. While comparative markedness allows for permutable rankings of 'old' and 'new' markedness constraints, McCarthy (2002a:59) acknowledges that it is unclear what facts about the target language would ever motivate a child to demote a new markedness constraint. In other words, what in the input would force the demotion of a constraint that allows for the realization of unfaithful segments? Here we can see from our speculation about Stage 0 that it may not be a fact about the target language per se that would have motivated the demotion of ${}_{\text{N}}\textsc{NoCoda}$-s, but rather the demotion of that constraint is an initial minimal response that allows maximal compliance with the default ranking of undominated conflicting markedness constraints. It is thus conceivable that a similar situation may be at the heart of a commonly occurring class of children's error patterns, namely chain shifts. One very common chain shift finds /s/ replaced by [θ], but target /θ/ replaced by [f] (e.g., Dinnsen & Barlow, 1998). In this chain shift, /f/ is realized target-appropriately. McCarthy

(2002a) has characterized chain shifts by the ranking of $_O$MARKEDNESS over FAITH over $_N$MARKEDNESS, as schematized in (22).

(22) Schema for chain shifts (McCarthy, 2002a)

Some of the constraints that we propose as relevant to the characterization of the s>θ>f chain shift are given in (23). These various markedness constraints belong to a family of constraints disfavoring fricatives generally. Each markedness constraint bans a different class of fricatives, and each is independently necessary to account for individual differences in children's fricative inventories. We assume in accord with comparative markedness that each of the markedness constraints in (23) is an abbreviation for two markedness constraints, one of which assigns a violation mark to an offending property if fully faithful (or old) and the other to an offending property that is not fully faithful (or new). The two faithfulness constraints demand featural identity between corresponding segments. The replacement of /s/ by [θ] involves a change in stridency or the loss of the feature [grooved]. The replacement of target /θ/ by [f] involves a change in place.

(23) Some constraints relevant to the s>θ>f chain shift

*s: Grooved coronal fricatives are banned
*θ: Interdental fricatives are banned
*f: Labial fricatives are banned

ID[grooved]: Corresponding segments must have an identical [grooved] feature
ID[place]:   Corresponding segments must have identical place features

To account for one part of this chain shift, namely the exclusion of [s] from a child's inventory, *s must be undominated. The idea of comparative markedness becomes crucial in that a fully faithful [θ] is absolutely banned by the ranking of $_O$*θ being ranked above faithfulness, but [θ] is permitted to surface as the substitute for another fricative due to the lower ranking of $_N$*θ. Finally, the target-appropriate realization of labial fricatives and their substitution for target interdentals follows from the dominance of faithfulness over *f. The substance of the hierarchy for a chain shift is given in (24), and the tableau is shown in (25).

(24) Substantive hierarchy for the s>θ>f chain shift

$$_{ON}*s, \; _o*\theta$$

$$|$$

$$ID[grooved], \; ID[place]$$

$$|$$

$$_{ON}*f, \; _N*\theta$$

(25) Account of the s>θ>f chain shift

/sup/ 'soup'	$_{ON}*s$	$_o*\theta$	ID[grooved]	ID[place]	$_{ON}*f$	$_N*\theta$
a. FFC sup	*!					
b. ☞ θup		*				*
c. fup		*		*!	*	

/θʌm/ 'thumb'	$_{ON}*s$	$_o*\theta$	ID[grooved]	ID[place]	$_{ON}*f$	$_N*\theta$
a. sʌm	*!		*			
b. FFC θʌm		*!				
c. ☞ fʌm				*	*	

In our view, an explanation of the nature of chain shifts and their advent/ development should not be sought solely in the target language; rather, the motivation for the demotion of $_N$MARKEDNESS may well reside elsewhere. That is, the motivation may reside in something about the hierarchy itself, specifically in the dominance of conflicting constraints and the need to maximally comply with those constraints. For example, the beginnings of a chain shift might arise from an initial state in which all fricatives are banned. Next, the child begins to recognize that fricatives can and do occur. Faithfulness to manner is thus becoming important, but the child still fails to take proper note of the details of those fricatives. A minimal response that maximally complies with these conflicting pressures would be to allow just one fricative to occur and for that fricative to serve as the substitute for all other fricatives. This could be achieved by simply demoting one member of the family of constraints banning fricatives generally. One likely member of that family might be *θ, which bans interdentals.[5] As a result of this demotion, the first fricatives to emerge would be interdentals and they would be realized faithfully and as substitutes for all other fricatives. The demotion of $_N*\theta$ alone would achieve this result and would be motivated by the child's observation that fricatives can occur. More importantly, it is the demotion of ${}_N*\theta$ that allows fuller compliance with all of the other constraints and leads to an initial phase of the substitution pattern. That is, an interdental fricative substitute satisfies faithfulness to manner while also complying with all of the other old and new markedness constraints banning fricatives. The 'faithful' realization of interdentals would be a spurious, but inevitable, result due to the continued dominance of ${}_O*\theta$ and the other markedness constraints. If instead ${}_O*\theta$ had been demoted, target /θ/ would have been realized faithfully but all the other fricatives would have been realized as stops, precluding the chain shift.

The other elements of the chain shift could emerge subsequent to the demotion of ${}_N*\theta$ with the addition to the inventory of [f], whether faithful or not, due to the demotion of ${}_N*f$ and/or ${}_O*f$. The choice of either of the *f constraints as the constraint to demote moves the child's phonology closer to the target system by adding a labial fricative to the inventory and introducing a place contrast among the occurring fricatives. However, the demotion of that particular constraint again is only a minimal response that allows maximal compliance with the prior hierarchy, i.e., it continues to ban grooved coronal fricatives and preserves manner. The only empirical consequence of the reranking is the introduction of a place distinction among fricatives, although the place distinction may not necessarily correspond to the target place distinction. The plausibility of this scenario is supported by the case studies reported by Gierut (1998b), which are reanalyzed by Dinnsen (2002). The hypothesized progression is described in the table in (26).

(26) The emergence of the s>θ>f chain shift

Stage	Facts	Ranking
0 (default)	All fricatives realized as stops	${}_{ON}*s, {}_{ON}*f, {}_{ON}*\theta \gg$ FAITH
1	Manner preserved, but all fricatives realized as [θ]	${}_{ON}*s, {}_{ON}*f, {}_O*\theta \gg$ FAITH $\gg {}_N*\theta$
2	s>θ>f	${}_{ON}*s, {}_O*\theta \gg$ FAITH $\gg {}_{ON}*f, {}_N*\theta$

If we are correct about the factors that bring about the demotion of ${}_N$MARKEDNESS, we will have filled in an important piece for comparative markedness generally and for the characterization of chain shifts in particular. We also find it significant that these factors came to light from consideration of T's unusual error pattern—one that some might have put aside as irrelevant to phonological theory.

4.3   The nature of children's underlying representations

Our account of T's error pattern has implications for claims about children's underlying representations generally. The standard assumption among acquisition researchers has long been that children's underlying representations are target-appropriate—even if their output productions are not (e.g., Smith, 1973; Ingram, 1989). Leonard and Brown clearly departed from that assumption by postulating a more restricted, child-specific set of underlying representations as the explanation for T's unusual error pattern. They claimed that T's underlying representations were limited in Stage 1 to a canonical shape that allowed words to end only in either a labial stop or the coronal fricative [s]. Other consonant-final and vowel-final words were disallowed underlyingly and were forced to conform to an underlying representation with a final /s/. It may not be so surprising that Leonard and Brown appealed to child-specific underlying representations at that time given that earlier theoretical approaches to phonology (at least in the description of fully developed languages) routinely provided for restrictions of this sort. In fact, an essential element of earlier phonological descriptions was to remove from underlying representations all of the predictable or redundant information and incorporate only those idiosyncratic, learned properties of pronunciation at the underlying level. However, on empirical grounds it is less clear why they might have felt the need to adopt child-specific underlying representations in this case. T's production facts did not fit very well with the type of evidence that has been adduced in support of child-specific representations. That is, her substitution errors were entirely systematic, and her production of final labial stops corresponded perfectly with the target system. After T received treatment on final /f/, she produced that sound correctly and evidenced no overgeneralization, suggesting that she already knew just which words needed to be realized with a final [f]. Even the emergence of some correct productions of vowel-final words during Stage 2 affected only target words with final vowels. Again, she must have known that those words ended underlyingly in vowels in order to realize them appropriately without treatment on that class of words. It was only after being taught final /d/ that T showed any overgeneralization. That overgeneralization was, however, limited to only a few words that had been produced in error with a final [s]. While overgeneralization can be taken as evidence of incorrectly internalized representations, our analysis showed that the same result could follow from target-appropriate underlying representations.

One of the more significant points that distinguishes our account from Leonard and Brown's and distinguishes optimality theory from earlier approaches is that we were able to account for the facts of all three stages without imposing child-specific restrictions on underlying representations at any point in time. Given richness of the base, the option of positing child-specific underlying representations for T's error pattern is unavailable. We had to allow for the possibility that her underlying representations could have been as rich and varied as target representations. We were thus forced to look to the constraint hierarchy for the source of the problem. If we had not been able to account for these facts in accord with richness of the base, one of the fundamental underpinnings of optimality theory would have been dealt a serious blow. However, it must be underscored that richness of the base does not preclude the possibility that individual lexical items might be internalized incorrectly. All that is required is that the full range of universal distinctions be available for input representations. Individual lexical items might not correspond with target representations, but the constraint hierarchy is ultimately responsible for the elimination of those distinctions that do not occur in the child's output.

4.4   If T's error pattern is not 'unusual', why does it not occur more often?

We have argued that T's unusual error pattern is really not all that unusual. If we are correct, some might wonder why this error pattern does not occur more often. There are several ways to approach this question, depending on what is meant by 'unusual'. Assuming for the moment that T's error pattern is indeed rare, its very occurrence might be considered unusual because it does not seem to fit well with other factors that are thought to influence language. For example, the error pattern might be considered implausible on phonetic grounds. Here the sense of 'unusual' is that the error pattern is unnatural or deviant in some way. Plausibility considerations of this sort have long been attractive, but almost always turn out to be tenuous at best. The fact is that some languages have 'crazy' rules (e.g., Bach & Harms, 1972) and/or rules that defy phonetic explanations (e.g., Dinnsen, 1980; Anderson, 1981; Hyman, 2001). If fully developed languages can tolerate unusual rules, then why should we be any more surprised about the occurrence of an unusual error pattern in a developing phonology? No one would suggest that languages with crazy rules are unnatural languages. While we know of no other published study documenting an error pattern identical to T's in the phonology of another child, Paul Fletcher (personal communication, February 2004) pointed out to us that he observed a similar error pattern in the speech of a child who came through his clinic. That child reportedly inserted a coronal stop (rather than [s]) after word-final vowels and substituted a coronal stop for other word-final consonants. An account of that case would only require a slightly different ranking of the constraints presented here. The NoCODA constraint banning coronal stops (NC-t) would have to be ranked below FAITH with the other NoCODA constraints ranked above FAITH. FINAL-C would remain dominant. This ranking bears a striking resemblance to the hypothesized ranking in (21) for T's Stage 0. Interestingly, in our larger project, we encountered a second female child with phonological delays—Child 191 (age 3;5)—who presented with an error pattern similar to that of T and Fletcher's case study. That is, she added [t] to the end of many vowel-final words and replaced final obstruents (except for labial stops) with [t]. The data in (27) reflect some of her baseline productions.

(27) Child 191 (age 3;5)

    a)   Insertion of [t] after vowel-final words
        [paɪᵗ] 'pie'   [boʊt] 'throw'   [doʊt] 'sew'   [boʊᵗ] 'blow'

    b)   Substitution of [t] for final obstruents
        [bæt] 'back'   [bɪt] 'pig'   [jɛt] 'yes'   [bʌt] 'buzz'
        [naɪt] 'knife'   [weɪt] 'wave'   [bit] 'peach'   [bɪt] 'bridge'
        [maʊt] 'mouth'   [wɑt] 'wash'   [dɑt] 'star'   [hɪt] 'hill'

    c)   Target-appropriate realization of final labial stops
        [tɪp] 'chip'   [tup] 'soup'   [tʌb] 'tub'   [toʊm] 'comb'

Given that some vowel-final words were produced without the insertion of a final consonant, the facts of this case and the account may more properly correspond with T's Stage 2 during which some variation began to emerge.

We suspect that other similar cases exist, but have not yet made their way into the published literature, possibly because earlier theoretical frameworks could not make sense of them. Moreover, given that the preference for final consonants is relatively rare in the languages of the world, it may not be surprising that T's error pattern is uncommon in developing phonologies.

Another approach to this question shifts the focus away from concerns about the prevalence of an error pattern and its presumed naturalness to typological considerations. The fact that some phenomenon occurs is sufficient to warrant an account that attempts to fit the error pattern into a larger typology of what is possible. Our claim that T's error pattern is not unusual is a typological claim. We have tried to show that T's error pattern follows naturally from general principles of grammar and acquisition, at least within optimality theory. No special assumptions or ad hoc mechanisms were needed to account for this error pattern.

Our rendering of T's unusual error pattern is only the most recent attempt to deal with such patterns. Earlier reports have documented several other error patterns that were claimed to be unusual or idiosyncratic (e.g., Ingram & Terselic, 1983; Camarata & Gandour, 1984; Gierut, 1986; Bedore et al., 1994; Dinnsen, 1999; Gierut & Champion, 2000; Dinnsen & Farris, 2004a). As developments in phonological theory have been brought to bear on each of these cases, many of these error patterns have been rendered more tractable and found to be consistent with general principles of phonology and acquisition. For example, some cases involving seemingly nonsystematic error patterns were found to be highly systematic when something as basic as complementary distribution was considered (e.g., Camarata & Gandour, 1984; Gierut, 1986; Dinnsen, 1999). Nevertheless, other unusual error patterns remain to be (re-)considered in light of yet newer theoretical advances. Given the wide ranging successes of optimality theory, it may be especially fruitful now to appeal to this perspective in reconsidering some of these more unusual error patterns with the hope that some new insights would emerge. Such reconsiderations would also serve as a further test of the claims of the new theory.

5   Conclusion

Our optimality theoretic reconsideration of T's unusual error pattern concluded that the error pattern was not so unusual after all. It was instead argued to be the natural result of constraint conflict. The conflict between the two independently motivated markedness constraints, FINAL-C and NoCODA, was at the heart of the problem. Comparative markedness received empirical support from these acquisition data and played a role in resolving the conflict between constraints and explaining the grandfather effects observed at different points in time. Additionally, in accord with richness of the base, we did not need to make any child-specific assumptions about underlying representations. Finally, the changes in the error pattern over time also followed from the constraint demotion algorithm. The result is that this error pattern, while challenging on analytical grounds, does have an explanation within optimality theory. That explanation also holds promise for resolving a problem relating to comparative markedness and the characterization of chain shifts.

Notes

*   We are especially grateful to Judith Gierut for her many contributions through-out this project and to Eric Bakovic, Jessica Barlow, Amanda Edmonds, Paul Fletcher, Greg Iverson, Larry Leonard, John McCarthy, Laura McGarrity, Heather Rice, Nick Henriksen, and members of the Learnability Project for their comments on various aspects of this chapter. This work was supported in part by grants to Indiana University from the National Institutes of Health (NIH DC001694 & DC00012).

1   For a critical review of comparative markedness, see the commentaries and McCarthy's reply in *Theoretical Linguistics* Vol. 29 (2003b).

2   If NoCoda-t were split into $_O$NoCoda-t and $_N$NoCoda-t (as would seem to be required by comparative markedness), the evidence from the target language could only motivate the demotion of $_O$NoCoda-t (not $_N$NoCoda-t). We will see, however, that the overgeneralization facts require the concomitant demotion of $_N$NoCoda-t. It is ultimately an empirical issue whether all markedness constraints are split into old and new versions. It may be that some markedness constraints such as NoCoda-t are unitary, unanalyzeable constraints. The relative unmarkedness of coronal stops might obviate the need for finer-grained distinctions within that class. The issue here is similar to the problem of whether the universal constraint set includes markedness constraints banning the least marked element in some markedness scale (e.g., de Lacy, 2002).

3   Alternatively, these two constraints could vary in their ranking relative to one another with NoCoda-t being ranked above NoCoda-s sometimes and NoCoda-s above NoCoda-t other times. Under any of these alternatives, both constraints must be ranked below Faith during this stage.

4   For an alternative account employing Local Constraint Conjunction, see Chapter 8 in this volume.

5   An equally plausible alternate path to this chain shift could also arise from the demotion of $_N$*f. The result would be that /f/ would be the first fricative in the system, and that fricative would serve as the substitute for all other fricatives.

6 Innovations in the treatment of chain shifts*

Michele L. Morrisette & Judith A. Gierut
Indiana University

Chain shift error patterns are of particular importance in acquisition because of their reported prevalence and resistance to traditional treatment methods. This chapter reports the results of an innovative approach to treatment for three children with phonological delays who evidence the chain shift error pattern. The treatment introduced all members of the chain /s θ f/ in minimal triplet forms. As a result of the treatment, the children evidenced a reduction in errors for the targets /s θ/. Interestingly, all of the children evidenced variation in production of these target phonemes as their productions changed over time. An optimality theoretic account of this developmental course of change is provided. The account appeals to the local conjunction of constraints and a partially ordered constraint hierarchy to explain the children's variation in productions at different points in time.

1 Introduction

Children's acquisition of the target phonology often results in interesting, but sometimes perplexing error patterns. One such pattern is known as a 'chain shift'. A chain shift typically involves three phonemes (e.g., A, B, C) which are linked to one another by a child's substitution pattern such that A is realized as B and B is realized as C, while C is produced accurately (A→B→C). What is remarkable about this chained relationship among phonemes is that the child exhibits the ability to produce the second segment in the chain (B as a substitute for A), but fails to produce this segment with any accuracy. There have been several documented cases of chain shifts in the literature and for children they often involve a chained relationship in the voiceless fricatives (e.g., Smit,

1993a; Dinnsen & Barlow, 1998; Gierut & Champion, 1999). Specifically, the target coronal fricative /s/ is realized as [θ], target /θ/ is realized as [f], and target /f/ is produced accurately.

This error pattern is of particular importance in acquisition due to its prevalence and reported resistance to phonological treatment. It has been estimated that 20% of children who are typically developing will exhibit a chain shift at some point in their phonological development (Dinnsen & Barlow, 1998). Moreover, for children with phonological delays, traditional treatment methods have shown only limited success in altering the chain shift error pattern (Dinnsen & Barlow, 1998; Gierut & Champion, 1999).

To date, there have been two documented courses of treatment for a chain shift in children with phonological delays. Dinnsen and Barlow (1998) report on Subject 33 (age 5 years;4 months) who evidenced a chain shift of s→ θ →f, as described above. Subject 33 was taught the phonemes /θ f/ in a conventional minimal pair treatment protocol as a participant in a larger study on phonological learning. The goal of minimal pair treatment is to reduce homonymy in a child's outputs by highlighting the phonemic contrasts at a featural level between target sounds in the language (Weiner, 1981; Saben & Ingham, 1991; Barlow & Gierut, 2002), in this case between the phoneme /θ/ and its substitute [f]. The treatment itself exposed the child to sets of minimal pair words differing only in the target phonemes to be contrasted (e.g., 'thin' v. 'fin'). One might expect that this treatment would have the effect of altering the chain shift by teaching the child to accurately produce the target /θ/, but results indicated that even after a full year of intervention, the pattern remained. This lack of change is quite remarkable, especially given the fact that the child evidenced the ability to produce the fricative [θ], albeit as a substitute for /s/, but failed to accurately generalize the use of the sound to target /θ/ words.

Gierut and Champion (1999) reported on two preschool children, Subject 74 (age 4;0) and Subject 90 (age 4;8), evidencing the same s→ θ →f chain shift. These children were enrolled in treatment on the singleton /s/. Given that /s/ would add a new phonological category for the children, Gierut and Champion hypothesized that treatment of this phoneme would interrupt the chain. Results indicated that one child, Subject 74, learned target /s/ as a result of the treatment, but continued to substitute [f] for target /θ/. The other child, Subject 90, learned to produce target /θ/ accurately, but continued to substitute [θ] for target /s/. Thus, each child corrected one part of the chain, but the other remained. Given these results, the authors suggested that it might be necessary to teach the contrast between all three phonemes in the chain at once in order to eliminate all aspects of the error pattern, hence, the purpose of this study.

In this chapter, our goal is two-fold: (1) to report the results of an innovative treatment protocol involving minimal triplets for three children with phonological delays evidencing the chain shift error pattern; and (2) to provide an optimality theoretic account of the developmental course of change observed for the children in this study. We begin in §2 with a description of the participants and their pretreatment chain shift error pattern. In §3 the nature of the minimal triplet treatment is detailed, followed by a summary of the children's learning in §4. In §5, we put forward a modified version of a previously proposed optimality theoretic account to explain the children's course of change. Interestingly, the result is a series of constraint demotions involving a partial ordering of constraints that accounts for intervening periods of variability in the children's productions. This course of change is longitudinally substantiated by LP127, who participated in the treatment. Finally, the chapter concludes in §6 with some directions for new research.

2   Participants and the chain shift error pattern

Three preschool children with functional phonological delays served as participants: one girl (LP127, age 4;2) and two boys (LP128, age 3;9; and LP131, age 4;8). The children scored within normal limits on measures of hearing (ASHA, 1985), receptive and expressive language skills (Dunn & Dunn, 1981; Hresko, Reid & Hammill, 1981; Newcomer & Hammill, 1988), nonverbal intelligence (Levine, 1986), and oral-motor structure and function (Robbins & Klee, 1987). However, demonstrating the children's phonological delay, they scored at or below the 10th percentile (M=6th percentile) relative to age- and gender-matched peers and excluded at least five sounds from all word positions on the *Goldman-Fristoe Test of Articulation* (Goldman & Fristoe, 1986). A more extensive sampling of each child's phonological system was collected on the Phonological Knowledge Protocol (PKP; Gierut, Elbert & Dinnsen, 1987; Gierut, 1998c; 1999). The PKP was designed to sample all target singletons and onset and coda clusters in English in at least five words per relevant word-position. In all, there are more than 600 forms elicited on the PKP allowing for a more in-depth analysis of children's productions. The PKP forms were elicited through a spontaneous picture naming task, digital audio-taped, and phonetically transcribed using narrow notation of the IPA. Approximately 10% of the data were re-transcribed by an independent listener and compared consonant-to-consonant to the original transcriptions in order to establish interjudge transcription reliability. On average, the listeners achieved 92% agreement.

Drawing from the pretreatment PKP sample, the chain shift error pattern is illustrated by the productions of target /s θ f/ for one child, LP131, as shown below in (1). Only one of the children's productions is provided given that the other two, LP127 and LP128, evidenced the exact same substitution pattern. Moreover, for ease of illustration, the focus of the chapter will be on the children's word-initial productions.[1]

(1)   LP131 (age 4;8) pretreatment

a)   Target /s/ realized as [θ] and [s̺]
      [θɔk] 'sock'   [s̺up] 'soup'   [s̺ændə] 'santa'
      [s̺oup] 'soap'   [s̺ʌn] 'sun'   [θevɪn] 'seven'

b)   Target /θ/ realized as [f]
      [fʌm] 'thumb'   [fiv] 'thief'   [fwouw] 'throw'
      [fʌmi] 'thumb-i'   [fus̺ti] 'thirsty' [fʌndu] 'thunder'

c)   Target /f/ realized as [f]
      [faɪjʊ] 'fire'   [fit] 'feet'   [feɪs̺] 'face'
      [faɾɪ̥] 'five'   [fɛdu] 'feather'   [fɪŋgʊ] 'finger'

Consistent with the typical s→θ→f chain shift, target /s/ is realized as [θ], target /θ/ is realized as [f], and target /f/ is produced accurately. However, it is important to note that, at this pretreatment point, all of the children in this study evidenced variation for target /s/ with dentalized [s̺] productions occurring 60% of the time, on average, and [θ] productions occurring 40% of the time, on average. Target /θ/ words were realized as [f] 100% of the time and /f/ was produced with 100% accuracy.

3   Minimal triplet treatment

The three children were enrolled in a single-subject multiple baseline across subjects design (McReynolds & Kearns, 1983). The children's entry into treatment was staggered following a baseline phase in which each consecutive child was administered one additional baseline in order to establish control across participants (i.e., LP127 = 1 baseline, LP128 = 2 baselines, LP131 = 3 baselines). The baselines were specifically designed to monitor the status of the children's productions for targets /s θ f/ and to ensure that the chain shift remained unchanged prior to the start of treatment.

The treatment for these three children targeted the three phonemes that constituted the members of the chain shift /s θ f/. The phonemes were contrasted in treatment through minimal triplets, or three words that differed only by the initial phoneme. As with minimal pair treatment, the goal was to emphasize the featural contrasts of the target segments. In all, there were a total of 12 treated words consisting of 4 sets of nonword triplets (e.g., /seɪb/, /θeɪb/, and /feɪb/). The triplets varied in canonical shape (i.e., CVC, CVCV, and CVCVC) to include both one- and two-syllable forms. Nonwords were selected for treatment over the use of real words because of the feasibility in identifying real word triplets. Moreover, the nonword treatment procedures used in this study were consistent with previous intervention studies for children with phonological delays and have been described elsewhere (Gierut, 1989b; Gierut & Champion, 2001). Briefly, the treated words were presented to children in the context of a story that was read on the first day of treatment each week. Each word was depicted in the story as a character, object, or action. Treatment then proceeded through two phases: imitation and spontaneous productions. During the imitation phase, children produced the treated words following the experimenter's model until they reached 75% accuracy for at least one of the target sounds across two consecutive treatment sessions or until they completed 7 sessions. During the spontaneous phase, children produced the treated words without a model until they reached 90% accuracy for at least one of the target sounds across three consecutive treatment sessions or until they completed 12 sessions. Treatment sessions were scheduled three times each week.

Within a given session, the children were presented with each of the 4 triplets in turn with the order of triplets and target sound presentation randomized within- and across-trials. For example, first the child was shown the three pictures corresponding to a given triplet (e.g., /seɪb/, /θeɪb/, and /feɪb/) and the child's production of each word was elicited in turn with feedback provided on the target sounds. After the last word in any given triplet, the experimenter reminded the child that these three words 'go together.' Then, the next triplet was presented (e.g., /soʊdən/, /θoʊdən/, and /foʊdən/), productions were elicited and feedback was provided. This continued until all triplets were presented for a predetermined number of trials within each session. Drill play activities were used to elicit the treated words and auditory and visual feedback were provided only for the target sound in each word. These procedures were consistent through both imitation and spontaneous phases of the treatment.

Importantly, the children were given equal exposure to each of the three target sounds in treatment and all of the children learned to produce the target sounds in the treated words during treatment sessions with a mean accuracy of 92%. On average, the children completed 18 sessions of treatment over a period of 57 days.

Although the children were able to accurately use the target sounds in the treated words, the true test of learning was to determine whether the children generalized the use of the target sounds to other untreated words in their lexicon. To examine this generalization learning, the PKP was administered to the children at posttreatment, and again at 2 months posttreatment. Children's percentage of errors for the target sounds /s θ/ was calculated and plotted at each of these points in time and served as the dependent variable of the study.

4   Generalization learning

A quantitative summary of the children's learning following the minimal triplet treatment is depicted in Figure 1 below. Given that the children all followed a similar path of learning, their data were collapsed. In Figure 1, the mean percentage of errors for target /s/ words and target /θ/ words, as sampled on the PKP, are plotted as a function of time.

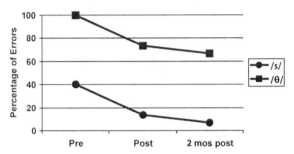

Figure 1. The children's mean percentage of errors for target /s θ/ plotted at pretreatment, posttreatment, and 2 months posttreatment.

The results indicate that, in all, the children evidenced learning for both phonemes /s θ/, as demonstrated by the suppression of errors on the sampled forms. For target /s/, recall that all of the children evidenced some accuracy at pretreatment with 40% of the words produced in error, as [θ], on average. Following the minimal triplet treatment, the children suppressed errors on target /s/ words to an average of 13%. For target /θ/ words, the children began with 100% of the words in error at pretreatment, producing [f] instead. By posttreatment, errors on target /θ/ words were reduced to 73%. At 2 months following the minimal triplet treatment, the children continued to suppress both types of errors. Children's errors on target /s/ words were reduced to 7%, whereas the children's errors on target /θ/ words were reduced to 67%.

Despite the fact that the children started the treatment with fewer errors on target /s/ words, the rate of suppression for errors on both target /s/ and target /θ/ words was virtually the same for the children in this study. This suggests that the minimal triplet treatment was effective in impacting both types of errors that constitute the chain shift. This differs from past studies where either no change was reported (Dinnsen & Barlow, 1998) or children only evidenced learning for one aspect of the chain (Gierut & Champion, 1999). Nevertheless, at 2 months posttreatment, two of the three children, LP128 and LP131, continued to evidence variability in target /θ/ productions with some targets produced as [θ] and others as [f]. One child, on the other hand, LP127, almost completely suppressed both error patterns by the 2 month follow-up point.

Interestingly, the children in this study appeared to suppress the errors in a similar manner across time, suggesting a developmental progression associated with remediation of the chain shift error pattern. At pretreatment, the children all evidenced variability in target /s/, but no suppression of the target /θ/ error pattern was observed. Given that all of the children presented with the variation for target /s/ at pretreatment, it seems likely that there was a preceding stage in their productions in which target /s/ was produced strictly as [θ] and target /θ/ as [f]. This is supported by other documented cases of chain shifts in the literature (Dinnsen & Barlow, 1998; Gierut & Champion, 1999) and, fortunately, we had the opportunity to document this preceding stage for one child in this investigation, LP127. This sampling point was collected three months prior to LP127's minimal triplet treatment and was obtained during her participation in a previous independent experimental investigation. The data from this additional point will be detailed in §5.

By posttreatment, all of the children evidenced suppression of errors on target /s/ and two of the three children evidenced suppression of errors for target /θ/. Interestingly, as the children suppressed errors for target /θ/, variation in their productions occurred with both [θ] and [f] being realized. This variation paralleled the variation for target /s/ forms observed at pretreatment. By 2 months posttreatment, all of the children had almost completely suppressed errors for target /s/, with one child, LP127, suppressing nearly all errors for target /s/ and target /θ/ words. For the remaining two children, target /θ/ words continued to be realized as either [θ] or [f] at 2 months posttreatment. By examining the individual differences for these children, it appears that LP127 progressed through the stages of suppression more rapidly than the other two children, but they all followed the same path shifting from variation in production of one phoneme to another.

5   OT account of error pattern suppression

To account for the longitudinal suppression of the chain shift error pattern, we will turn to an optimality theoretic account of the data across time. To illustrate each of the stages, one child, LP127, was selected from the three participants. This child was selected for two reasons. First, we had the opportunity to collect an earlier sampling point for this child that collectively yields four points in time, as described above. The four sampling points occurred on an average of every 2.5 months. Second, because this child was able to eliminate virtually all aspects of the chain by 2 months following the minimal triplet treatment, she illustrates a more complete view of the process of error pattern suppression.

At the first sampling point, 3 months prior to the child's pretreatment point in the minimal triplet treatment, LP127 evidenced the more typical version of the s→ θ →f chain shift, as shown below in (2). Target /s/ words were realized as [θ], as shown in (2a) and target /θ/ words were realized as [f], as shown in (2b), while target /f/ was produced accurately. The data for target /f/ words were eliminated from the illustration to conserve space.

(2)   LP127 (age 3;9) three months prior to pretreatment

    a)   Target /s/ realized as [θ]
        [θɔk] 'sock'   [θʌn] 'sun'   [θup] 'soup'

    b)   Target /θ/ realized as [f]
        [fif]   'thief'   [fʌndʊ] 'thunder' [fʌm] 'thumb'

To account for this typical s→ θ →f chain shift we will appeal to a local conjunction account in accord with the constraints and ranking proposed by Dinnsen in Chapter 8 in this volume, shown in (3) below.[2] As described by Dinnsen, the three markedness constraints oppose the production of the target fricatives /s θ f/, while the faithfulness constraints insist that the input and output correspond in manner or place features. The LC, or local conjunction constraint, is only relevant if both of the conjoined constraints ID[place] and ID[grooved] are violated, at which time the LC constraint is also violated.

(3)   Constraints

    a)   Markedness
        *s: Grooved coronal fricatives are banned
        *θ: Interdental fricatives are banned
        *f: Labial fricatives are banned

    b)   Faithfulness
        ID[manner]: Corresponding segments must have identical manner features
        ID[grooved]: Corresponding segments must have an identical [grooved] feature
        ID[place]: Corresponding segments must have identical place features
        LC: Local conjunction of ID[place] & ID[grooved]

The chain shift error pattern surfaces from the ranking of constraints shown in (4). ID[manner] is highly ranked and prohibits the substitution of a stop for one of the fricatives. This constraint was left out of the following tableaux in order to present a more concise analysis.

    In the tableau for 'sock', highly ranked *s and LC eliminate candidates (a) and (c). Candidate (c) violates *s with a grooved coronal fricative in the output, while candidate (a)'s fatal violation of the LC constraint results from the collective violations of lower-ranked ID[grooved] and ID[place]. Candidate (b) with [θ] as the output emerges as the optimal candidate, despite violations of lower-ranked *θ and ID[grooved]. In the tableau for 'thumb', candidate (c) is eliminated by a fatal violation of high-ranking *s. Candidate (b) suffers a similar fate by incurring a fatal violation of *θ. Candidate (a) violates ID[place] and *f, but because these constraints are lower-ranked this candidate survives as the winner.

(4) Constraint ranking for LP127 three months prior to pretreatment

ID[manner], *s, LC >> *θ >> ID[grooved], ID[place],*f

/sɔk/ 'sock'	*s	LC	*θ	ID[grooved]	ID[place]	*f
a.　fɔk		*!		*	*	*
b. ☞　θɔk			*	*		
c.　sɔk	*!					

/θʌm/ 'thumb'	*s	LC	*θ	ID[grooved]	ID[place]	*f
a. ☞　fʌm					*	*
b.　θʌm			*!			
c.　sʌm	*!				*	

LP127's production of target /s θ/ words at the next sampling point, which served as the pretreatment point for the minimal triplet treatment, are shown below in (5). Target /s/ was now realized as either [θ] or [s̬][3], as shown in (5a). This variability in production will be the next challenge for our ranking within OT. There was no change in target /θ/; it continued to emerge as [f], as shown in (5b).

(5) LP127 (age 4;2) pretreatment

　a)　Target /s/ realized as [θ] and [s̬]
　　　[θɔk] 'sock'　　[s̬ʌn] 'sun'　　[s̬up] 'soup'

　b)　Target /θ/ realized as [f]
　　　[fif] 'thief'　　[fʌndʊ] 'thunder' [fʌm] 'thumb'

To account for the change in target /s/ productions, it is not possible to simply demote *s in the ranking. This would lead to only one optimal output of [s] for target /s/. Rather, the observed variation can be explained by appealing to a 'partial ordering' of constraints where two constraints conflict and are permitted to vary in their ranking, with the grammar randomly choosing one of the possible rankings for each input to output mapping (Kiparsky, 1993b; Anttila & Cho, 1998; Legendre, Hagstrom, Vainikka & Todorova, 2002). The result is that, for each input to output mapping, the constraints have an equal opportunity to outrank one another. In this case, the constraints are *s and ID[grooved] and for one input to output mapping, *s may be ranked above ID[grooved], while for another, ID[grooved] may be ranked above *s. This partial constraint ranking is shown below in (6a) and (6b).

The tableaux in (6a) present the first scenario predicted by the partial constraint ranking, where *s is ranked above ID[grooved]. The tableaux in (6b) present the second scenario, where ID[grooved] is ranked above *s. We assume, along with others (e.g., Auger, 2001) that the constraints in a partial ranking occupy their own stratum. This will in some cases make it appear that certain constraints are crucially ranked when in fact no ranking argument can be established. Notice, for example, that LC is ranked above *s in (6a) even though *s could be undominated under this scenario. Similarly, the ranking of *θ below ID[grooved] in (6a) is also not crucial. For the input 'sock', candidate (a) is eliminated due to its fatal violation of the highly ranked LC constraint. This is consistent in both scenarios. The variation for the input /s/ emerges as candidates (b) and (c) are evaluated under the randomly selected rankings. In (6a), candidate (b) is the optimal candidate because candidate (c) fatally violates the higher-ranked *s, whereas in (6b) candidate (c) is optimal with candidate (b) fatally violating the higher-ranked ID[grooved]. In both scenarios, the rankings correctly predict the output [f] for /θ/. This is illustrated by the tableau for 'thumb'. Candidates (b) and (c) are eliminated because they violate the higher-ranked constraints *s, ID[grooved] and *θ, no matter the order. Candidate (a) only violates lower-ranked constraints, ID[place] and *f, surviving as the winning candidate.

(6)   Partial constraint ranking at pretreatment

ID[manner], LC >> {*s, ID[grooved]} >> *θ >> ID[place], *f

a)   Target /s/ realized as [θ]

/sɔk/ 'sock'	LC	*s	ID[grooved]	*θ	ID[place]	*f
a. fɔk	*!		*		*	*
b. ☞ θɔk			*	*		
c. ʂɔk		*!				

/θʌm/ 'thumb'	LC	*s	ID[grooved]	*θ	ID[place]	*f
a. ☞ fʌm					*	*
b. θʌm				*!		
c. ʂʌm		*!	*			

b) Target /s/ realized as [ʂ]

/sɔk/ 'sock'	LC	ID[grooved]	*s	*θ	ID[place]	*f
a. fɔk	*!	*			*	*
b. θɔk		*!		*		
c. ☞ ʂɔk			*			

/θʌm/ 'thumb'	LC	ID[grooved]	*s	*θ	ID[place]	*f
a. ☞ fʌm					*	*
b. θʌm				*!		
c. sʌm		*!	*			

Interestingly, it has been proposed that this partial ordering of constraints makes predictions about the reranking of constraints as change occurs (Anttila & Cho, 1998). In particular, this reranking can be modeled as a three-stage process. Given two constraints (C1 and C2), it is predicted that at Stage 1, C1 will outrank C2. At Stage 2, the two constraints are partially ordered resulting in variation in the output. At Stage 3, C1 would be reranked below C2. Considering the two constraints relevant to this case for LP127, *s and ID[grooved], we saw that at the first point in time *s was ranked above ID[grooved], while at the next point in time, the two constraints became partially ordered in the ranking. Thus, the stage predictions appear to hold for the first two sampling points for LP127 and subsequently predict that at the next point *s will be demoted below ID[grooved].

This prediction can be tested with data from the posttreatment point in time. LP127's productions immediately following the minimal triplet treatment are shown in (7) below. LP127 completely suppressed the /s/ error pattern with all target /s/ words realized as [s] as shown in (7a). As for the target /θ/, LP127 now evidenced variation in her productions with either [θ] or [f] being realized as the output, shown in (7b) below.

(7) LP127 (age 4;6) after treatment on /s θ f/

a) Target /s/ realized as [s]
    [sɔk]   'sock'   [s:ʌn] 'sun'   [sup]   'soup'

b) Target /θ/ realized as [θ] and [f]
    [θif]   'thief' [fʌndʊ] 'thunder' [fʌm] ~ [θʌm] 'thumb'

To account for the shift in productions that surfaced at posttreatment, it is necessary to again demote both *s and *θ in the ranking, while continuing to appeal to a partial constraint ranking in order to account for the variation in the target /θ/ productions. This is achieved by a partial ordering of *θ and ID[place]. The constraint ranking is shown below in (8a) and (8b).

The tableaux in (8a) present the first scenario predicted by the new partial constraint ranking, where *θ is ranked above ID[place]. The tableaux in (8b) present the second scenario, where ID[place] is ranked above *θ. In both cases, *s has been demoted below ID[grooved] to account for the accurate productions of target /s/ in the data at posttreatment. This is illustrated in the tableaux for 'sock', where the [f] candidate (a) is eliminated due to its violation of the highly ranked LC constraint. Candidate (b) is also eliminated because it violates ID[grooved]. Thus, candidate (c) is selected as optimal by only violating the lower-ranked and recently demoted *s constraint.

The demotion of *s below ID[grooved] supports the stage prediction by Anttila and Cho (1998) described above. The surprising fact is that while *s and *θ were demoted, *θ simultaneously became partially ordered with the faithfulness constraint ID[place], leading to variation in the output for target /θ/. For the input 'thumb', the [s] candidate (c) is eliminated from both sets of tableaux due to its fatal violation of highly ranked ID[grooved]. Variation for the input /θ/ emerges as candidates (a) and (b) are evaluated under the randomly selected rankings. In (8a), candidate (a) is the optimal candidate because candidate (b) fatally violates the higher-ranked *θ, whereas in (8b) candidate (b) is optimal with candidate (a) fatally violating the higher-ranked ID[place].

(8) Partial constraint ranking at posttreatment

ID[manner], LC >> ID[grooved] >> *s >> {*θ, ID[place]} >> *f

a) Target /θ/ realized as [f]

/sɔk/ 'sock'		LC	ID[grooved]	*s	*θ	ID[place]	*f
a.	fɔk	*!	*			*	*
b.	θɔk		*!		*		
c. ☞	sɔk			*			

/θʌm/ 'thumb'		LC	ID[grooved]	*s	*θ	ID[place]	*f
a. ☞	fʌm					*	*
b.	θʌm				*!		
c.	sʌm			*!	*		

b) Target /θ/ realized as [θ]

/sɔk/ 'sock'		LC	ID[grooved]	*s	ID[place]	*θ	*f
a.	fɔk	*!	*		*		*
b.	θɔk		*!			*	
c. ☞	sɔk			*			

/θʌm/ 'thumb'		LC	ID[grooved]	*s	ID[place]	*θ	*f
a.	fʌm				*!		*
b. ☞	θʌm					*	
c.	sʌm		*!	*			

Turning to the final point in time for LP127, shown in (9) below, we see that both error patterns have now been suppressed. Target /s/ words, shown in (9a), continued to be realized accurately as [s], as in the previous sampling. More importantly, the target /θ/ words, shown in (9b), were now correctly realized as [θ].

(9) LP127 (age 4;8) 2 months after treatment on /s θ f/: Stage 4

    a) Target /s/ realized as [s]
       [sɔk] 'sock'   [sʌn]   'sun'   [sup]   'soup'

    b) Target /θ/ realized as [θ]
       [θif] 'thief'   [θʊsti] 'thirsty'   [θæŋkju] 'thank you'

The reranking of constraints associated with this final point in time is in (10) below. The partial ordering between *θ and ID[place] has now been resolved as *θ stabilized in the ranking below ID[place]. This has the consequence of eliminating the variation seen at Stage 3. Now that the three markedness constraints *s, *θ, and *f have been demoted within the ranking and the partial ranking has been resolved, the chain shift error pattern has been eradicated.

(10) Constraint ranking at 2 months posttreatment

    ID[manner], LC >> ID[grooved] >> *s >> ID[place] >> *θ, *f

/sɔk/ 'sock'		LC	ID[grooved]	*s	ID[place]	*θ	*f
a.	fɔk	*!	*		*		*
b.	θɔk		*!			*	
c. ☞	sɔk			*			

/θif/ 'thief'		LC	ID[grooved]	*s	ID[place]	*θ	*f
a.	fif				*!		**
b. ☞	θif					*	*
c.	sif		*!	*			*

6   Conclusion

Treatment of minimal triplets targeting all members of the chain shift proved effective in reducing errors for both target /s/ and target /θ/ for the children in this investigation. For one child, the result was a complete suppression of errors, while the other two children continued to evidence errors on target /θ/ following treatment. Moreover, all of the children who received the treatment exhibited a similar path of change over time documenting a developmental course of change associated with the chain shift error pattern. In particular, this developmental account was illustrated for one child, LP127.

In accord with the data from LP127, a four stage process of constraint demotion is proposed in (11) to account for change associated with the chain shift error pattern. In Stage 1, the markedness constraint *s is crucially ranked above *θ. In Stage 2, both *s and *θ are demoted with *s and ID[grooved] partially ordered resulting in variation of target /s/ productions. In Stage 3, both *s and *θ are again demoted with *s now ranked below ID[grooved] and *θ in a partial ranking with the faithfulness constraint ID[place]. This results in variation of target /θ/ productions. Finally, in Stage 4, *θ is demoted below ID[place]. The four stages observed with this chain shift expand upon the three stages described §5. The additional stage can be attributed to the fact that two pairs of constraints enter into partial rankings.

(11)   Summary of constraint demotion for chain shift error pattern

Stage	Ranking of constraints
1	ID[manner], *s, LC >> *θ >> ID[grooved], ID[place],*f
2	ID[manner], LC >> {*s, ID[grooved]} >> *θ >> ID[place], *f
3	ID[manner], LC >> ID[grooved] >> *s >> {*θ, ID[place]} >> *f
4	ID[manner], LC >> ID[grooved] >> *s, ID[place] >> *θ, *f

While the stages were developed from LP127, data from the other two children, LP128 and LP131, who also received the minimal triplet treatment indicate that they progressed from Stage 2 at pretreatment to Stage 3 at posttreatment and remained at Stage 3 at 2 months posttreatment. Therefore, we were unable to predict how long a given child would remain in any given stage. Perhaps for the latter two children the treatment needed to be longer allowing more exposure to the target segments to promote constraint demotion. Alternatively, a different type of treatment may prove to be more beneficial for these children. One possibility, as suggested by Gierut and Champion (1999), is that it may be necessary to examine the children's perceptual knowledge of the phonological categories associated with the chain shift and capitalize on this information in treatment by incorporating metalinguistic tasks.

It is possible, however, that the stages proposed herein may be specific to change that ensued from the minimal triplet treatment. For all of the children in this investigation, suppression of errors for target /s/, and therefore demotion of *s, preceded suppression of errors for target /θ/ and demotion of *θ. In the Gierut and Champion (1999) study, however, Child 90 (see also Chapter 8 in this volume), progressed in the opposite manner. This suggests that Stages 2 and 3 may be reversed for some children with a chain shift. Data from this child also suggest an intervening stage between Stages 2 and 3 in which one of the markedness constraints *s or *θ would be independently demoted before the other enters into a partial ordering with ID[place].

The role of variation as it relates to change associated with the chain shift error pattern warrants further consideration. Although all of the children in this investigation evidenced variation in their productions as part of the learning process, it is not clear as to whether this finding generalizes to other children with the chain shift error pattern. Moreover, the appeal to a partial ordering of constraints is somewhat restrictive in accounting for this variation in that it predicts a 50–50 chance of the emergence of one phoneme over another in the child's output. While these percentages were roughly achieved by the children in this study at Stages 2 and 3, none of the children strictly shifted from 0% to 50% to 100% accuracy on the target phonemes over time. It is possible, however, that a larger sampling of the children's productions would have demonstrated this effect. Alternatively, a continuous ranking scale in which constraints are numerically weighted may offer insight (Boersma, 1998; Boersma & Hayes, 2001). This approach has the potential to allow for different degrees of variation and observed frequencies, but raises other problems related to falsifiability (McCarthy, 2002b).

Notes

*   We would like to extend our sincere gratitude to Daniel Dinnsen, Ashley Farris-Trimble, and Amanda Edmonds for their invaluable input on this chapter. We would further like to acknowledge Annette Champion, for participating in the data collection and analysis, and Rachel Dale, for transcription reliability. This work was supported by a grant to Indiana University from the National Institutes of Health (NIH DC001694).

1   For two of the three children, LP127 and LP128, the chain shift error pattern was restricted to the word-initial position, with word-medial and -final productions

of /s θ/ surfacing accurately. For the other child, LP131, the chain shift was evidenced across word positions.

2   An alternative to a local conjunction account of chain shifts is also available through comparative markedness (McCarthy, 2002a; 2003b; Chapters 4 and 5 in this volume). A partial ordering of constraints is equally successful within a comparative markedness account, but beyond the scope of this chapter. Briefly, at Stage 2, the variation in /s/ productions would be accounted for by the demotion of $_o$*s and a tied ranking between $_o$*s and ID[grooved]. At Stage 3, variation in /θ/ productions would be accounted for by the demotion of $_o$*θ and a tied ranking between $_o$*θ and ID[place].

3   We assume for the purposes of this chapter that [s] and dentalized [ş] are both correct realizations of target /s/ and are differentiated from [θ] by the feature [grooved], with [s ş] characterized as grooved and [θ] as not. However, as noted in Chapter 8 of this volume, it is further possible to differentiate [s] and dentalized [ş] by the feature [distributed] with [s] as nondistributed and dentalized [ş] as distributed.

Part III

Research reports: Developmental shifts and learning

7 Developmental shifts in children's correspondence judgments*

Judith A. Gierut & Daniel A. Dinnsen
Indiana University

External evidence is brought to bear on predictions about phono-logical acquisition that derive from optimality theory. Specifically, correspondence relationships among outputs, their rankings, and change in these rankings with development were examined from a psycholinguistic perspective. Thirty children, aged 3;0 to 5;10, were assigned to developmental groups characteristic of prototypic initial- and final-state grammars. Children participated in an experimental task whereby they judged the similarity of competing output forms which varied along the featural dimensions of place and manner. Results indicated that children judged output similarity on the basis of place, rather than manner, in the initial-, but not the final-state grammar. Moreover, in some specific instances, children of both developmental groups relied on the combined properties of place plus manner in their judgments of output similarity. These findings offer methodological and theoretical advances to the study of optimality theory by providing novel support for some central tenets.

1 Introduction

The facts of language acquisition are often brought to bear on the evaluation of linguistic theory. Acquisition plays an important role because it has the potential to contribute to a theory's descriptive and explanatory adequacy. A formal theory of language must account for the static structural properties of a linguistic system, as well as the dynamic changes that take place in that system over time, while maintaining continuity in the grammar (Chomsky, 1999). This documentation of continuitous change in grammar is precisely where acquisition comes in. For phonological theory, in particular, acquisition data have been central to the claims of many prominent frameworks. Beginning with structuralism, Jakobson's work exemplified universal typologies with the observed order of emergence of contrasts in children's early productions. Derivational theories, such as natural and generative phonology, accrued evidence from children's systematic production errors in describing rule-governed sound changes in the mapping between phonemic and phonetic representations (Smith, 1973; Ingram, 1976). Related nonlinear perspectives appealed to children's omissions and substitutions, respectively, in demonstration of prosodic structure (Gerken, 1996; Kehoe & Stoel-Gammon, 1997) and the underspecification of features in lexical representations (Stoel-Gammon & Stemberger, 1994). Most recently, the contemporary framework of optimality theory has amassed developmental data in the verification of aspects of language learnability and the universality of certain constraints (e.g., Barlow, 1997; Demuth, 1997; Pater, 1997; Gnanadesikan, 2004).

While phonological theory has clearly benefited from acquisition data, it is not without certain drawbacks. In order to make valid claims about linguistic structure and a speaker's competence, sufficient and representative production data must be obtained. Ferguson, Peizer and Weeks (1973) first acknowledged the inherent methodological difficulties associated with gathering production data from young children. They noted that, in any given sample, it cannot be guaranteed that a child will produce all of the relevant phones, contrasts, or alternations that may be of interest. A child may or may not produce certain segments or forms, and the examiner would not know why. On the one hand, gaps in the data could be accidental, due to a child's unwillingness to cooperate or to attend, or due to inadequate elicitation, sampling, or recording procedures. On the other hand, observed gaps could be real, reflecting the true internal structure of a child's phonology. Another complication is the fact that children's productions are notoriously variable. The reasons for this variability may again be traced to different sources, some of which are linguistically relevant and others, not. Variable outputs may be associated with motor immaturity and superficial performance limitations. Alternatively, variability may reflect newly emerging linguistic competence or the opposite, constraints on competence. Related to this is the potential interference of input on a child's productive outputs. Following a model, a child's productions may actually exceed his or her knowledge of the language, thereby providing an inflated view of competence.

Many different solutions for getting around these problems have been offered, but in keeping with linguistic theory, one particular suggestion stands out. This is the use of external evidence from psycholinguistic tasks in lieu of, or in complement to internal evidence from productions (Anderson, 1981). In studies of adults, psycholinguistic tasks have been routinely used to confirm the tenets of phonological theory (e.g., Fodor, Bever & Garrett, 1974; Lahiri & Marslen-Wilson, 1991). Yet, in development, these same procedures have been less widely adopted. There are only a few psycholinguistic experiments involving children that have been explicitly designed to evaluate phonological theory independent of, or in addition to production evidence (e.g., Treiman, 1985; Gierut, 1996a). It is interesting to contrast this with other studies of acquisition theory (cf. Chomsky, 1999) which frequently rely on psycholinguistic protocols. In evaluations of acquisition theory, the course or process of language development is the alternate focus of study as, for example, in establishing whether children attend to the whole word or its subconstituent parts in early word learning (Walley, Smith & Jusczyk, 1986; Gerken, Murphy & Aslin, 1995). A methodological asymmetry thus emerges in the study of children: psycholinguistic tasks are used to test theories of acquisition, but not theories of phonology, despite the intimate relationship between the two. In this paper, we seek to bridge the relationship between linguistics and psycholinguistics in acquisition. The broad goal is to evaluate predictions of linguistic theory as they pertain to phonological acquisition by appealing to psycholinguistic evidence. The theoretical framework to be examined is optimality theory (hereafter, OT; Prince & Smolensky, 1993/2004; McCarthy & Prince, 1995), and the psycholinguistic methodology to be used is a conceptual triad task. The sections that follow provide an overview of each to motivate the experimental study.

1.1   Developmental predictions of OT

OT has had a major influence on the formal study of the phonological systems of primary languages, with recent extensions to acquisition. This theory offers a fresh perspective on language because it maps the relationship between an internalized lexical representation and its corresponding spoken output through the ranking and parallel processing of constraints. This uniquely contrasts with conventional derivational frameworks that assumed a linearly ordered, sequential application of phonological rules to generate surface from underlying form. As it is currently formulated, OT offers at least two predictions about phonological acquisition. Both derive from the substantive nature of constraints and their apparent ranking relative to each other.

By way of overview, OT posits two different types of constraints: 'markedness constraints' and 'faithfulness constraints'. Markedness constraints express preferences for universally unmarked structure; that is to say, marked forms are to be avoided in a speaker's output. Faithfulness constraints are the antagonists of markedness constraints because these serve to preserve and maintain a close correspondence between representational strings. Faithfulness constraints can further manifest as two distinct types: those that explicitly map the relationship between properties of the input (i.e., underlying representation) and a given speaker's output, termed 'IO-faithfulness', and those others that express the relationship between a speaker's unique outputs of different but related forms, termed 'OO-faithfulness'. OT assumes that these different types of constraints operate simultaneously and in parallel to evaluate competing output candidates when provided an input representation. A further assumption is that constraints are universal, but their rankings may vary from language to language and grammar to grammar, thereby yielding observed cross-linguistic differences and individual variation. The constraints that specifically bear on acquisition involve IO- and OO-faithfulness and their ranking relative to markedness and to each other.

1.2   IO-faithfulness and markedness

The ranking of IO-faithfulness to markedness offers a first of the predictions for acquisition. IO-faithfulness stipulates that properties of the input representation must be preserved; that is, a child must be 'faithful' to the phonological characteristics of the ambient language if these constraints are high-ranked. On the other hand, markedness constraints, if undominated, promote a child's use of unmarked forms, and these may or may not resemble the target language. This sets up an opposition that must be rectified in the course of development. The explicit prediction is that, at the earliest stages of development, markedness will likely outrank IO-faithfulness (Smolensky, 1996a). That is, a child will tend to prefer unmarked outputs, regardless of the structural properties of the input language. With development, markedness constraints will be demoted, such that IO-faithfulness constraints come to dominate a child's productions (Tesar & Smolensky, 1998). This then appropriately aligns a child's grammar with the adult target. A range of common phonological patterns of acquisition have been examined to verify this purported developmental course including, for example, the emergence of closed syllables (Levelt & van de Vijver, 2004), fricatives (Bernhardt & Stemberger, 1998), and consonant clusters (Barlow & Dinnsen, 1998; O'Connor, 1999; Pater & Barlow, 2003; Goad & Rose, 2004). Thus far, the proposal has received broad descriptive and experimental support, affirming the ranking of markedness over IO-faithfulness in the initial-state, and the subsequent demotion of markedness at later states, of a child's unfolding grammar.

One crucial construct of OT—'emergence of the unmarked'—is also borne out by the predicted relationship between IO-faithfulness and markedness in acquisition. Emergence of the unmarked occurs when IO-faithfulness constraints outrank markedness constraints, yet unmarked forms are still realized in a child's output. In these situations, the effects of markedness are not expected to be observed given the ranking of constraints. Because IO-faithfulness is high-ranked, a child's outputs are expected to conform to the input; instead, what happens is that outputs conform to principles of markedness. In essence, emergence of the unmarked provides a glimpse of constraints and their rankings that should not otherwise be observed in a child's overt productions. Emergence of the unmarked provides further behavioral evidence that constraints are universal and continue to exist in the grammar, even though they may have been demoted. Emergence of the unmarked is believed to define the developmental process of acquisition specifically, and has been taken to be one critical test of an optimality theoretic account of linguistic phenomena generally (Gnanadesikan, 2004).

1.3   IO- and OO-faithfulness

There also exists a predicted relationship between IO- and OO-faithfulness that has potential implications for acquisition. OO-faithfulness was originally proposed to handle reduplication and truncation phenomena in fully developed systems given the necessity of correspondence relationships between outputs for base and reduplicated (or truncated) forms (Benua, 1995; McCarthy & Prince, 1995; Benua, 1997). For acquisition, the claim is that OO-faithfulness is ranked above IO-faithfulness at the initial stages of phonological development (McCarthy, 1998; Hayes, 2004). By this, a child is expected to closely match versions of his or her own unique output, rather than to attend to the details of the target input representation. With developmental change, OO-faithfulness must be demoted if IO-faithfulness and conformity to the adult grammar are to be achieved. To date, this hypothesized relationship between OO-and IO-faithfulness has received only in principle support; therefore, an example may be in order to best illustrate the projected developmental sequence.

Drawing from data presented in Weismer, Dinnsen, and Elbert (1981), consider Child C (age 3 years;10 months) who produced 'dog' as [dɔ]. This child violated faithfulness to the input because [g] did not surface in his output, but he obeyed markedness because an unmarked coda-less form was produced. Markedness outranked IO-faithfulness, as predicted. Importantly, Child C also produced the morphologically-related form 'doggie' as [dai]. Markedness and the prohibition of codas would not be applicable to 'doggie' since target /g/ is not in coda position. IO-faithfulness would obviously be violated since Child C's output did not match the target. There must be an alternate constraint operating—namely, OO-faithfulness—such that Child C maintained a close correspondence between his own unique outputs of 'dog' and 'doggie.' This then yields the predicted ranking of OO-faithfulness over IO-faithfulness in early development. Extending this, consider another child, Child A (age 7;2) who exhibited morphophonemic alternations, with 'dog' and 'doggie' being produced as [dɔ] and [dɔgi], respectively. As in the prior case, markedness would still dominate IO-faithfulness for Child A given the nonoccurrence of /g/ in coda position for the base morpheme 'dog'. However, for the derived form 'doggie', a change in the ranking of OO-and IO-faithfulness is necessitated. IO-faithfulness is not violated because Child A's output [dɔgi] directly matched the input. The close correspondence between base and derived forms that was observed in the first case of Child C is no longer maintained in this second case of Child A. OO-faithfulness would have to be demoted to allow for the latter child's mismatch between the morphologically-related outputs 'dog' and 'doggie'. Therefore, IO-faithfulness comes to outrank OO-faithfulness, which is characteristic of later stages of development. This example of Child A also serves to illustrate the independence of the rankings of markedness and OO-faithfulness relative to IO-faithfulness. Markedness may be demoted independent of a comparable change in the ranking of OO-faithfulness, and vice versa.

When taken together, OT thus offers an integrated set of predictions that bear on phonological acquisition, as summarized in (1). Specifically, in the initial-state grammar, markedness and OO-faithfulness are presumed to outrank IO-faithfulness; whereas, in the final-state grammar, IO-faithfulness is thought to outrank markedness and OO-faithfulness. The ranking relationships are formally denoted by double-angled brackets. Notice there is no explicit ranking of markedness relative to OO-faithfulness at either stage of development, as is formally indicated by the comma. In this study, we set out to document empirically a type of OO-faithfulness in phonological acquisition, and to evaluate experimentally the predicted differential rankings of the initial- and final-state grammar.

(1)   Initial-state grammar   markedness, OO-faithfulness >> IO-faithfulness

      Final-state grammar   IO-faithfulness >> markedness, OO-faithfulness

1.4   Psycholinguistic evidence

The purpose of gathering external evidence in evaluation of linguistic theory is to model the claims and premises of that theory in a domain outside of language as further validation of its correctness. External evidence from psycholinguistic tasks has the potential to achieve this by demonstrating the psychological reality of linguistic constructs and their potential utility in the cognitive processing of language. As applied in studies of acquisition, psycholinguistic evidence has typically been obtained using conceptual tasks, whereby a child evaluates the phonological similarity of experimental stimuli. These usually take one of two complementary formats: free classification or the triad task. The structure of these tasks is pertinent to our concerns because they are essentially analogs of the correspondence relationships defined by faithfulness constraints (both IO and OO) within OT.

To elaborate, in a free classification task, a child listens to a standard stimulus followed by a series of test stimuli, and is required to make binary 'yes–no' judgments about whether the test stimuli resemble the standard (Smith & Kemler, 1977). The task is administered as a game involving the selection of a character's favorite outputs when presented with a standard input. Data that emerge from free classification are thought to reflect general category membership; that is, which stimuli belong to the same phonological category. Free classification can further isolate that specific phonological property that is common to all members of the category. It cannot, however, discern priority relationships among categories, which is where the triad task takes over. In the triad task, a child listens to three phonologically unique stimuli, and is required to select those two that belong together (Treiman & Breaux, 1982). Again, in the guise of a game, a child sees identically pictured characters, is told the 'name' of each, and then must select those two that are 'friends'. This task involves choosing among different outputs in selection of the best match. Data that result from the triad task are taken to be indicative of precedence relationships among different categories, such that stimuli which share certain phonological properties will be preferred over others. Notice that free classification seems to be analogous to IO-faithfulness because the task involves comparison of an input to an output in selection of an optimal match. In complement, the triad task appears to mirror OO-faithfulness because competing outputs are evaluated in establishing the best fit.

In this experiment, given our interest in OO-faithfulness, we adapted the triad task to examine correspondence relationships between the subsegmental properties of place and manner in phonological acquisition of English. Place and manner were examined because these are basic and fundamental contrasts which have received considerable attention in the acquisition literature from a range of theoretical linguistic perspectives. We revisited these properties but from the perspective of OT. Two groups of children were recruited, presenting with characteristic rankings of either an initial- or final-state grammar, as defined within OT. One group of children had high-ranked markedness constraints prohibiting production of certain segments, whereas the other group had high-ranked IO-faithfulness constraints, permitting production of these same segments. This afforded an opportunity to evaluate potential changes in the status of OO-faithfulness that may be associated with changes in the grammar. Thus, the purpose of this experiment was to garner behavioral evidence in support of OO-faithfulness and its ranking relative to other types of constraints in acquisition, and to document changes in OO-faithfulness that may occur with development.

2   Method

2.1   Participants

Thirty children, ages 3, 4, and 5, were recruited through public announcement to area day care and school facilities. Entry criteria and presenting phonological characteristics were identical to those reported in Gierut (1996a) in a psycholinguistic study of underspecification. To briefly recapitulate, children were preliterate, monolingual English speakers with normal hearing. They exhibited developmental milestones at typically expected ages, including age-appropriate phonological development. The status of the children's phonological systems was established from production samples that included a standardized measure (i.e., *Goldman-Fristoe Test of Articulation* (Goldman & Fristoe, 1986)), and a structured probe of fricatives and stops (Gierut, 1985). The standardized measure ensured that children were performing within normal limits relative to age- and gender-matched peers. The structured probe further determined production accuracy of the specific sound classes to be manipulated in the triad task. Production samples were elicited through spontaneous naming of real words that were picturable and familiar to children. Target sounds of interest were probed in all relevant word positions. Production data were audiorecorded and phonetically transcribed by trained listeners using narrow notation of the IPA. Interjudge transcription reliability was computed point-to-point for consonants, with 95% agreement obtained.

Children produced ambient segments accurately, with exception of the nonstrident fricatives /θ ð/. Twelve of the 30 subjects did not produce or use /θ ð/; the remaining 18 subjects had accurate productions of these sounds. Fricatives, in general, and /θ ð/, in particular, are taken to be more marked, emerging later in development (Smit, Hand, Freilinger, Bernthal & Bird, 1990). Therefore, we used the observed differences in production of nonstrident fricatives to differentiate children into two independent developmental groups. Children without /θ ð/ resembled what OT would posit as an initial-state grammar, where a particular markedness constraint dominated an antagonistic IO-faithfulness constraint. This group (hereafter, 'initial-state grammar') opted for unmarked structure, instead of producing the required nonstrident fricative targets of the input. In comparison, children with /θ ð/ resembled a final-state grammar because they were entirely faithful to the target language given their accurate use of nonstrident fricatives. For this group (hereafter, 'final-state grammar'), IO-faithfulness outranked markedness. Notice that these production data established the apparent ranking relationship between IO-faithfulness and markedness as pertains specifically to the nonstridents /θ ð/. These data were not revealing of other IO-faithfulness relationships, or of the substantive properties of OO-faithfulness. Children either did or did not produce the nonstridents, with no morphologically-related alternating forms observed. Consistent with our purpose, phonological development was thus defined on linguistic grounds, rather than on the basis of children's chronological age. In fact, mean ages of children of the initial- versus final-state grammars were comparable, being 4;5 (range: 3;0 to 5;10) and 4;3 (range: 3;1 to 5;3), respectively.

2.2   Triad task

The triad task was adapted to evaluate children's perceived similarity of sounds as a potential reflection of OO-faithfulness. The task began with a brief pretraining period followed by the experimental manipulations. A child viewed three identical pictures of an animate character (e.g., clown, teddy bear, dinosaur) that were mounted in each of the corners of an equilateral triangular board. Instructions to the child were to listen to each character's name, and to point to those two characters that were 'friends'. The character names were prerecorded and presented at a comfortable listening level through desktop speakers. As the names were recited, the examiner pointed to each character's picture, beginning in the left position, then proceeding sequentially to the top and right, respectively. After the triplet of names was presented, there was a 5-second response interval during which time a child made his or her similarity judgment. Following this, the next triplet was presented, and the task continued in the same manner until completion. The main difference between the pretraining and experiment phases was in the stimuli (i.e., character names) being compared.

2.3   Experimental stimuli

The pretraining stimuli started out as concrete real names (e.g., 'Bob') and then shifted to nonword sequences (e.g., [pɪd]) so as to gradually orient a child to the kind of outputs they would be hearing in the experimental phase.

Also, on beginning trials, the pretraining stimuli preserved 2 of the 3 character names as an identical match as, for example, in the triplet 'Bob–Bob–Fred.' Subsequent trials introduced three phonologically unique character names, such as [pɪd]–[bɪd]–[rɪd], to illustrate to a child the more abstract judgments that would be required in the experimental phase. There were three blocks of pretraining trials, each consisting of six triplets. Criterion for advancement to the experimental phase was selection of the intended output pairs with 60% or greater accuracy on each block. All but one child passed the pretraining phase. The child who failed, aged 3;2, presented with an initial-state grammar and was dismissed from the study. This reduced the total number of participants to 29, with 11 in the initial-state and 18 in the final-state grammars.

The experimental stimuli were Consonant1–Vowel–Consonant2 nonword sequences. The use of nonwords is conventional to the triad task, as well as other psycholinguistic methodologies that have been used with children (e.g., Walley et al., 1986; Gerken et al., 1995). Nonwords permit the systematic experimental manipulation of linguistic variables and remove potential interferences often associated with the use of real words, such as word familiarity, word frequency, or word history affiliated with age of acquisition. In this study, onset position (i.e., C1) of the nonwords was the point of focus given its perceptual salience (Walley et al., 1986). Segments in the onset position were drawn from the set /θ s t ɸ f p/, in parallel to the prior study by Gierut (1996a).[1] The possible vowels that followed these onsets in the nonwords were /e i a o u/, representing extremes of the vowel space. Segments in the coda position of the nonwords (i.e., C2) were limited to /m n b d/ since these were present in the productive repertoires of all participants, and are generally early-acquired sounds.

The resulting pool of possible CVC nonwords was then organized into three stimulus sets consisting of minimal triplets that varied by onset position; these are shown in Table 1. Each nonword stimulus set evaluated a different OO-faithfulness relationship as the independent variables, to be described below. The stimulus sets were digitally recorded in citation form by a male talker. Nonwords were excised from the tape and evaluated acoustically for consistency in duration, intensity, and clarity; those items that were judged to be aberrant were discarded and re-recorded for suitable replacements. A listener, naive to the purpose of the study, phonetically transcribed the nonwords to ensure that they were accurate renditions of the intended forms. The nonword stimulus sets were then transferred to master audiotapes for use in the experiment.

2.4   Independent and dependent variables

Three stimulus sets were necessary to tease apart the logically possible relationships between place and manner in OO-correspondence, as displayed in Table 1.

Table 1. Experimental stimulus sets.

Onset Triplet and Replicant	Similarity Relationship			
	αPlace	αManner	αPlace αManner	ΔPlace ΔManner[1]
/θ t p/	/θ t/	/t p/		/θ p/
/ɸ t p/	/ɸ p/	/t p/		/ɸ t/
/θ s t/	/θ t/ or /s t/		/θ s/	
/ɸ f p/	/ɸ p/ or /f p/		/ɸ f/	
/θ ɸ s/		/θ ɸ/ or /s ɸ/	/θ s/	
/θ ɸ f/		/θ ɸ/ or /θ f/	/ɸ f/	

A first set of stimuli examined children's similarity judgments of αPLACE versus αMANNER; that is, same place as opposed to same manner. When faced with a triplet of unique phonological outputs, does a child establish OO-correspondences between pairs of items that share the same place, or between those others that share the same manner? The onset triplet /θ t p/ was used in this comparison, with /θ t/ sharing the same place (coronal), but /t p/ sharing the same manner (stop). A second onset triplet /ɸ t p/ was included for replication (Table 1). Notice that both of these triplets allowed for an unusual pairing of either /θ p/ or /ɸ t/, respectively, in the triad task. Such pairings are anomalous because the segments that are involved differ in both place and manner. Pairings of this type run counter to the aims of the triad task which seeks to establish similarity (not difference) relationships. Anomalous responding consequently reflected guessing on the part of a child (cf. Treiman & Breaux, 1982). As a matter of record, there was no significant difference in the proportion of guessing observed for children displaying initial- versus final-state grammars (t (27) = – 0.338, $p = 0.738$).

A second set of stimuli evaluated children's judgments of similarity based on αPLACEαMANNER versus αPLACE (Table 1). Again, when faced with unique outputs, does a child set up an OO-correspondence between items that share both place and manner, or is place alone sufficient? The onset triplet /θ s t/ provided for this comparison because /θ s/ have place and manner in common (coronal fricative); whereas pairings of /θ t/ or /s t/ are only alike in terms of place (coronal). The replicating triplet involved the onsets /ɸ f p/ as a further demonstration of these similarity relationships.

A third, related stimulus set considered children's similarity judgments of αPLACEαMANNER versus αMANNER (Table 1). Here, the question was whether a child forms OO-correspondences between items sharing place and manner properties, or whether shared manner is adequate in and of itself. The onset triplet /θ ɸ s/ was used. As in the previous set, /θ s/ represent shared place and manner; the pairs /s ɸ/ and /θ ɸ/ have only manner (fricative) in common. The onset triplet /θ ɸ f/ was the relevant replication.

To summarize, three stimulus sets served as the independent variables in examination of OO-faithfulness to (1) place versus manner, (2) the combination of place+manner versus place alone, and (3) the combination of place+manner versus manner alone. The dependent variable was children's judgments of the perceived similarity of the nonword triplets presented in the triad task. To measure this, each stimulus set was administered to each child who participated. A given stimulus set consisted of 20 trials, with 10 trials per onset triplet. Across stimulus sets, there were 60 total trials (i.e., 10 trials per triplet, 2 triplets per stimulus set, 3 stimulus sets). Stimulus sets were administered in random order over two consecutive days in 30-minute individualized sessions. During testing, a child was praised for staying on-task, but no feedback was given about response accuracy because there were no 'correct' OO-correspondences planned a priori.

3   Results and discussion

Results of the triad task were used to empirically establish OO-faithfulness in phonological acquisition, and to document changes in OO-faithfulness that ensued with development. OO-faithfulness was revealed through the findings associated with the independent manipulations of place and manner similarity; whereas, developmental change was apparent in the patterns of responding observed for children presenting with initial- versus final-state grammars. The mean proportion of children's responses to the conditions αPLACE versus αMANNER, αPLACEαMANNER versus αPLACE, and αPLACEαMANNER versus αMANNER are shown in Table 2 for each developmental group, along with

Table 2. Mean proportion of responding for initial- and final-state grammars.

		αPlace vs. αManner			αPlaceαManner vs. αPlace			αPlaceαManner vs. αManner		
		αPlace	αManner	ΔPlace ΔManner[1]	αPlace αManner	αPlace	αPlace	αPlace αManner	αManner	αManner
Onset Stimulus		/θ t/	/t p/	/θ p/	/θ s/	/θ t/	/s t/	/θ s/	/θ Φ/	/s Φ/
Replicating Stimulus		/Φ p/	/t p/	/Φ t/	/Φ f/	/Φ p/	/f p/	/Φ f/	/θ Φ/	/θ f/
Initial-State Grammar	M	.408*	.302	.289	.467*	.263	.272	.313	.312	.375
	SD	.090	.064	.092	.115	.121	.096	.106	.136	.098
Final-State Grammar	M	.353	.349	.299	.447*	.287	.264	.342	.314	.343
	SD	.106	.108	.064	.102	.108	.062	.100	.101	.112

[1] Anomalous pairing indicative of guessing
* $p < 0.05$

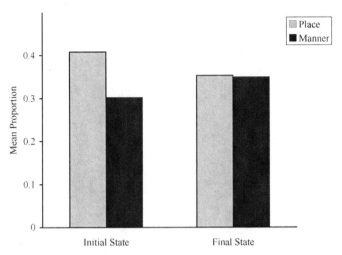

Figure 1. Mean proportion of αPLACE versus αMANNER judgments by children with initial- and final-state grammars. From Table 2, αPLACE pairs were /θ t/ and /ɸ p/, and αMANNER pairs, /t p/.

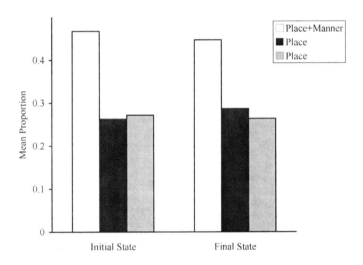

Figure 2. Mean proportion of αPLACEαMANNER versus αPLACE judgments by children with initial- and final-state grammars. From Table 2, αPLACEαMANNER pairs were /θ s/ and /ɸ f/; whereas αPLACE pairs were /θ t/ and /ɸ p/, or /s t/ and /f p/, as denoted by heavy and light shaded bars, respectively.

corresponding standard deviations. The data are also plotted in Figures 1, 2, and 3. For purposes of statistical comparison, these data were analyzed independently by group using one-way analyses of variance. Main effects that were statistically significant were further evaluated using post hoc analyses for planned pair-wise contrasts. Post hoc analyses established which of the dimensions of place and/or manner were relevant to children's similarity judgments. The alpha level for all comparisons was set at 0.05. In this section, the results are presented separately for each developmental group, and then integrated in discussion of the ranking of OO-faithfulness constraints as observed in the course of acquisition. The discussion also considers the implications of the present findings for the predictions that OT outlines for acquisition, and explores the mutually beneficial relationship between linguistics and psycholinguistics in theory building and testing.

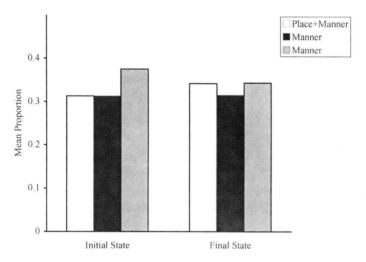

Figure 3. Mean proportion of αPLACEαMANNER versus αMANNER judgments by children with initial- and final-state grammars. From Table 2, αPLACEαMANNER pairs were /θ s/ and /ɸ f/; whereas αMANNER pairs were either /θ ɸ/, or /s ɸ/ and /θ f/, as denoted by heavy and light shaded bars, respectively.

3.1   Initial-state grammar

Children who presented with a characteristic initial-state grammar had no nonstrident fricatives in the sound system, such that markedness was claimed to outrank IO-faithfulness based on production facts. In terms of OO-faithfulness, performance on the triad task revealed two primary patterns.

A first pattern, shown in Figure 1, emerged from the comparison of αPLACE to αMANNER. The finding was children selected competing outputs that shared place properties significantly more often than those that shared manner character-istics (F (2, 10) = 4.594, p = 0.0228; planned pair-wise comparison (F (1, 10) = 6.077, p = 0.0229). When presented with the triplets /θ t p/ and /ɸ t p/, children made more total judgments based on place of articulation, choosing /θ t/ and /ɸ p/ as being most alike, respectively. From an OT perspective, this may be interpreted as OO-faithfulness to place outranking OO-faithfulness to manner.

A second pattern, displayed in Figure 2, was observed in the comparison of αPLACEαMANNER versus αPLACE alone. In this case, children significantly judged competing outputs that shared both place and manner as being most similar (F (2, 10) = 7.959, p = 0.0029; planned pair-wise comparison (F (1, 10) = 15.898, p = 0.0007). Children grouped pairs of coronal fricatives /θ s/ and labial fricatives / P f / most often in their similarity judgments of the triplets /θ s t/ and /ɸ f p/, respectively. In OT terms, this implies that OO-faithfulness to place and manner outranked OO-faithfulness to place. When taken together, these two statistically significant findings suggest a potential ranking of OO-faithfulness for the initial-state grammar, as in (2).

(2) OO-faithfulness[place+manner] >> OO-faithfulness[place] >> OO-faithfulness[manner]

The third manipulation involving judgments of αPLACEαMANNER versus αMANNER alone was not statistically significant for this group of children (F (2, 10) = 0.743, p = 0.4882). As in Figure 3, when asked to judge the triplets /θ ɸ s/ and /θ ɸ f/, children responded at chance. There was no discern-able preference for selecting outputs that agreed in both place and manner as opposed to those that only shared manner properties.

3.2   Final-state grammar

For children displaying characteristic final-state grammars, the produc-tion of nonstrident fricatives was accurate as in the ambient language, with IO-faithfulness presumed to outrank markedness. Analogous OO-faithfulness relationships that resulted from the triad task for this group are summarized in Table 2 and depicted as above in Figures 1, 2, and 3. In large part, the findings for the final-state grammar were identical to those reported for the initial-state grammar, with one exception. The difference was observed in the condition αPLACE versus αMANNER, as in Figure 1. For this comparison, children responded with no significant difference between place or manner (F (2, 17) = 1.205, p = 0.3121). When given the onset triplets /θ t p/ and /ɸ t p/, children were equally likely to select outputs that agreed in place, either /θ t/ or /ɸ p/, respectively, as they were to select outputs that agreed in manner, /t p/.

Apparently, there was no preference for the preservation of place over manner in competing outputs for those who presented with final-state grammars.

With reference to Figures 2 and 3, respectively, the remaining triad results were very much like those observed for the initial-state grammar. Children with final-state grammars significantly judged output similarity on the basis of the combined properties of place plus manner, rather than just using place alone ($F (2, 17) = 13.781$, $p = 0.0001$; planned pair-wise comparisons ($F (1, 17) = 27.202$, $p = 0.0001$). However, there was no preference in the selection of outputs with common place and manner properties as opposed to those with shared manner only ($F (2, 17) = 0.295$, $p = 0.7463$). Taken together, the statistically significant triad results for children with final-state grammars support a tentative ranking of OO-faithfulness relationships as in (3).

(3) OO-faithfulness[place+manner] >> OO-faithfulness[place]

3.3 Developmental change

When the triad results from the initial- and final-state grammars are compared, certain commonalties and differences emerge. In general, what was the same about the groups was the ranking of OO-faithfulness to place+manner above place, but not also above manner; and, what was distinct about the groups was the ranking of OO-faithfulness to place relative to manner. These observations serve to guide our discussion of the development of OO-faithfulness as it bears on the acquisition process, in particular, and OT, in general.

3.3.1 Conjoined constraints

As noted, OO-faithfulness to the combination of place and manner consistently outranked OO-faithfulness to place alone, regardless of the characteristics of children's sound systems. Both groups, initial- and final-state grammars, maintained this effect. That a combination of OO-constraints outranked one of its members thus appeared to remain static with development. Within the framework of OT, this effect of combining constraints has been termed 'local conjunction' (Smolensky, 1995). The notion of local conjunction originated in reference to IO-faithfulness in fully developed systems, where it has been argued that conjoined constraints will always assume a more dominant ranking over any of the related individual conjuncts. The findings from this study illustrate exactly this same ranking relationship for OO-faithfulness. This serves as a replication and validation of local conjunction within OT given its extension to a different type of faithfulness constraint, to alternate developing populations, and to the psycholinguistic domain.

One perplexing aspect of these findings, however, is that the effects of conjoining constraints did not also hold up in the experimental comparisons involving manner. Place+manner outranked place, but place+manner did not also outrank manner. This too was true for both initial- and final-state grammars. A relevant question is why this might have been the case. We offer three potential hypotheses associated with the interface of linguistic and psycholinguistic performance, perceptual salience, and competing dimensions of the experimental stimulus set. With reference to Table 1, recall that the triplets of the αPLACEαMANNER versus αMANNER comparison were /θ ɸ s/ and /θ ɸ f/, with 2 of the 3 segments being nonstrident fricatives /θ ɸ/, and all three of the segments being of the same manner. All other stimulus sets consisted of only one nonstrident sound, either /θ/ or /ɸ/, and introduced two different manner classes for comparison.

In light of this, one possible account of the lack of significant effects for manner may relate to the isomorphic relationship that has been observed between production and conceptual judgments in children. It has been shown that when children are able to produce a phonological distinction, they are also able to conceive this same distinction in psycholinguistic tasks, and vice versa (Gierut, 1996a; 1998b). For children with initial-state grammars, in particular, the fact that /θ ɸ/ were both excluded from the productive repertoire may have prevented an explicit output preference. While plausible, this hypothesis does not hold for at least two reasons. First, children with initial-state grammars were capable of making similarity judgments involving /θ ɸ/ in other stimulus sets. If productions were prerequisite, then consistent responding should not have been observed for other experimental conditions. Second, children exhibiting final-state grammars did use nonstrident fricatives productively, but still there were no significant preferences for conjoined constraints versus αMANNER alone.

An alternate hypothesis is that segments of the αPLACEαMANNER versus αMANNER stimulus set were not perceptually distinct. Acoustically, /θ ɸ f/ have the weakest and most diffuse spectral energy of all fricatives (Ladefoged & Maddieson, 1996). Perceptually, studies of phonetic confusions in children and in adults have shown greater errors to intra- as opposed to inter-class stimuli (Miller & Nicely, 1955; Graham & House, 1971). That is, more perceptual confusions result when comparing different places of articulation within the same manner category. It is the case that the triplets at issue, /θ ɸ s/ and /θ ɸ f/, were of the same manner but differed featurally by place. Yet, in the triad task, stimulus sets were to be revealing of featural similarity, not phonetic difference. Children were not asked to phonetically discriminate among places of articulation—labial, labiodental, interdental, alveolar. Moreover, if phonetic confusability were a relevant factor, then children should not have reliably judged other triplets that involved equally similar segments. Nonetheless, they responded consistently in their pairings of /θ s/ and /ɸ f/ when presented with other αPLACEαMANNER comparisons.

A third, and the most likely explanation relates to multiple competing features among segments of the stimulus set used in this comparison of αPLACEαMANNER to αMANNER. In this initial study of OO-faithfulness, we designed the experimental comparisons with primary (i.e., continuancy), and not also secondary (i.e., stridency) features in mind. Perhaps though, children did appeal to further secondary distinctions when making their similarity judgments, as in the following illustration for the triplet /θ ɸ s/ (a comparable situation obtains for the replicant /θ ɸ f/). When this triplet was presented in the triad task, a pairing of /θ s/ would yield, as originally predicted, an αMANNERαPLACE judgment since both segments are coronal fricatives. These segments have two properties in common. Consider, however, that an alternate pairing of /θ ɸ/ would also lead to a match of two properties: These segments are fricatives and they are nonstrident. This then sets up a potential OO conflict among multiply competing features that was not anticipated. At issue is whether OO-correspondences formed on the basis of place +manner are a more optimal match than those involving manner +manner. In this example, for the remaining pairing of /s ɸ/, both are fricatives, they do not agree in place or in stridency, and predictably, would be the least favored of this triplet. By this account, a lack of preference for the conjunction of αPLACEαMANNER versus αMANNER may be attributed to multiple competing properties of the outputs. This highlights a potential limitation in the use of external evidence in tests of linguistic theory even in the face of carefully crafted and controlled manipulations, and is one that will need to be addressed in subsequent studies.

3.3.2   OO-faithfulness to place

A primary difference that emerged between initial- and final-state grammars was in the rankings of αPLACE relative to αMANNER. In the initial-state grammar, OO-faithfulness to place dominated OO-faithfulness to manner; whereas in the final-state grammar, there was no difference between the two.

The observation that place took precedence over manner for the initial-state grammar is wholly consistent with other reports of children's productions and conceptual judgments of sounds. In particular, the substitution errors that children exhibit in their early productions are said to be more heavily influenced by the place characteristics of the target sound, rather than by its associated manner properties (Smit, 1993a). For instance, a child is more likely to substitute one labial for another, as in [p] for target /f/, instead of substituting one fricative for another, as in *[s] for /f/. Eventually, both place and manner are established target-appropriately in productions. In parallel to this, other psycholinguistic studies have reported that children, aged 5 and 7, reliably classified sounds by place, and by the conjunction of place and manner, when they are given cues of sound symbolism (Tomes & Shelton, 1989). By comparison, for manner, 7- but not 5-year-olds were able make these same classifications. When coupled with the present findings, the different sources of evidence converge on the prominence of place of articulation in phonological acquisition. The evidence also hints that the importance of place shifts with continued development.

For the final-state grammar, because there was no significant difference between OO-faithfulness to place versus manner, there remains a question of what exactly happened with the ranking of place. There are at least two mutually compatible possibilities that we advance for future study. On the one hand, the fact that these children did not show an explicit preference for place over manner may suggest that the two are equivalent and perhaps, even equally ranked at later stages of development. As the phonological system advances in complexity, OO-faithfulness to place may be demoted. For OT generally, a potential demotion of OO-faithfulness to place to be on par with manner is consistent with hypotheses about language learnability. Constraint demotion is considered the fundamental way in which change is induced in grammar, and it has been demonstrated computationally and descriptively for acquisition and for historical sound change (Tesar & Smolensky, 1998; Hayes, 2004). The results of this study submit the possibility of constraint demotion in OO-faithfulness, thereby making for a unified theoretical perspective on the learning mechanisms involved in the acquisition process. A further implication of this hypothesis pertains to a conceivable universal ranking of OO-faithfulness to place over manner. If OO-faithfulness to place had remained dominant and static from the initial- to final-state grammars, then this would have been indicative of a potential harmonic ranking, such that place would be presumed to always outrank manner. This, however, did not appear to be the case in light of the present psycholinguistic data.

On the other hand, concurrent with constraint demotion, OO-faithfulness to place may have become more fine-grained or well-defined for children with final-state grammars. This proposal would be consistent with related claims about IO-faithfulness and markedness regarding place. In particular, labial place is thought to outrank all others in IO-faithfulness (Kiparsky, 1994) and, as the reverse, the avoidance of labial place is thought to be a high-ranked markedness constraint in early development (Levelt, 1994; Goad, 1997). To evaluate the possibility that children with final-state grammars were beginning to distinguish labial place from other places in OO-correspondence, we examined the response preferences of individual children. If there were a preference for OO-faithfulness to labial place, then children would have exhibited different patterns of similarity judgments when presented with triplets consisting of primarily labial, as opposed to primarily coronal segments in the manipulation of αPLACE versus αMANNER. In fact, when presented with the labial-weighted triplet /ɸ t p/ of this comparison, 10 of 18 children made their judgments on the basis of place; whereas, for the coronal-weighted triplet /θ t p/, 11 of 18 children made judgments by manner. This suggests a place effect, such that at least some of the children responded differentially to labial- versus coronal-weighted triplets of this stimulus set. Children's responses were apparently split across place and manner dimensions given the specific segmental composition of the triplet. From an OT perspective, an implication is that OO-faithfulness to place may have been exploded in the final-state grammar, such that OO-faithfulness to labial place played a substantive role in the constraint rankings for this group. For future research, it will be important to explore these hypotheses about constraint demotion and constraint explosion in OO-faithfulness both cross-sectionally as in this study, as well as longitudinally.

3.4   Implications for OT

The integrated outcome of this experiment bears upon, and extends the predictions of OT to acquisition in mutually beneficial ways. For the contribution of OT to acquisition, this study demonstrated the psycholinguistic reality of OO-faithfulness in development. Children's ability to perform the triad task in a linguistically relevant way provided behavioral evidence of the operation of comparing competing output candidates in selection of an optimal production match. Prior to this, hypotheses about OO-correspondence relationships had not been empirically validated for developing systems. This demonstration was obtained in the absence of production evidence, conventional to the claims of OT, in general, or morphologically-related alternations, necessary to the claims of OO-faithfulness, in particular. This notwithstanding, it was still possible to establish constraints, their rankings, and changes in those rankings for children by using the triad task. This is a particularly useful finding in light of the methodological concerns associated with obtaining production data in the study of phonological acquisition. Moreover, if psycholinguistic evidence is accepted as revealing to OT as it has been for other theoretical linguistic frameworks (Lahiri & Marslen-Wilson, 1991), then it should be possible to extend the triad task in new directions. For children, the triad task may be adapted to sample other OO-faithfulness relationships besides place and manner, thereby bolstering the validity and furthering our understanding of these kinds of constraints in acquisition. For adults, the triad task may provide converging evidence of OO-faithfulness across linguistic and psycholinguistic domains. OO-faithfulness relations that have been posited by appealing to production facts should also be borne out by speakers' judgments of related, but competing outputs in triad tasks.

For the contribution of acquisition to OT, the results of this experiment have implications for possible elaboration of central constructs of the theory, particularly as related to emergence of the unmarked. Recall, as in (1), that emergence of the unmarked occurs specifically when IO-faithfulness constraints outrank markedness constraints. With this constraint ranking, a child's outputs are expected to closely correspond to the input; but instead, the effects of markedness are realized and unmarked forms are produced. Emergence of the unmarked thus allows for observation of what would be otherwise covert constraints and their rankings. In this study, we obtained a situation much akin to emergence of the unmarked, but with respect to OO-faithfulness. Consider that the results of the triad task provided a glimpse of output-to-output correspondences that should never have been detected from the facts of these children's productions. There were no morphophonemic alternations produced by children with either initial- or final-state grammars; yet, for both stages of development, OO-faithfulness relationships were attested. Moreover, for those with a final-state grammar, IO-faithfulness was highly ranked given ambient-like productions of nonstrident fricatives. With IO-faithfulness dominating, OO-faithfulness should again have been obscured; yet, here too, it was captured through the triad task. Thus, the psycholinguistic evidence provided for what we will term 'emergence of OO-faithfulness'. As used in a novel sense, emergence of OO-faithfulness can be described as an opportunity to view correspondence relationships among outputs psycholinguistically that are not also available productively. From the data gathered in this study, it is not yet possible to extend the notion of emergence of OO-faithfulness in a more conventional way to refer to explicit ranking relationships. This notwithstanding, an extension of this sort directly follows from, and is wholly consistent with the basic premises of OT. Just as IO-faithfulness comes to dominate markedness, OT predicts that IO-faithfulness will eventually outrank OO-faithfulness at later stages of development. Presumably then, OO-correspondences will remain in the grammar, but will not be reflected in a child's productions given a dominant ranking of IO-faithfulness. Consequently, this sets up a potential opportunity to realize the effects of OO-faithfulness even though these constraints may be low-ranked. This is precisely emergence of OO-faithfulness, in parallel to emergence of the unmarked. It remains for future research to identify such predicted cases of emergence of OO-faithfulness in developing and fully developed systems.

In addition to these noted extensions, other related research questions come to mind that warrant examination in subsequent studies. One such question relates to OO-correspondence relationships among morphologically-related forms. In this study, children were asked to judge the similarity of outputs involving minimal triplet base forms, but not also derived forms. As OO-faithfulness has been explicated for production, it may be necessary to evaluate output similarity among both base and derived nonwords; for example, as in correspondences among the triplets [mʌt]–[mʌs]–[mʌt+li] or [mʌt]–[mʌt+li]–[mʌs+li]. Judgments of such stimuli may be revealing of the actual structures taken to be similar, in parallel to subsegmental features. In a similar vein, it may be informative to replicate this study with children who are normally developing, but who also produce morphophonemic alternations in their outputs. This would complement the present participants who did not produce alternating outputs. While a replication of this sort would contribute to an integration of linguistic and psycholinguistic evidence, it may not be feasible given the practical difficulties of identifying a sufficient number of children who exhibit exactly the same pattern of alternation. Another question for further study relates to the role that specific places of articulation may play in OO-correspondence. In this study, the triplets for comparison were structured to sample only labial and coronal places. A possible expansion to include dorsal place may be warranted as, for example, in the presentation of /t k x/ in parallel to labial-weighted /t p ɸ/ and coronal-weighted /t p θ/ triplets. Children might be expected to respond similarly to coronal- and dorsal-weighted sets, but differentially to labial-weighted sets, as further indication that labial place holds special status in the grammar. A last, but perhaps most important question is how markedness, IO-faithfulness, and OO-faithfulness constraints and their rankings come together to intersect in developing systems. Like other investigations of children's productions, this study focused on a well-defined, albeit narrow, aspect of OT. It may be that, in order to address the broader question, details about specific constraints will first be required before the developmental predictions of OT may be integrated in a more cohesive way.

While not to minimize these contributions and extensions, a final word is in order about potential limitations of external evidence in evaluation of OT, specifically or linguistic theory, generally. It is important to keep in mind that external evidence is oftentimes experimental, requiring the manipulation of independent variables. Language, however, is an interdependent system, where certain structural relations depend on certain others. As was evidenced in this study, precedence relationships among place and manner were examined in independent experimental comparisons, but OT stipulates a dependency in such constraint rankings. For this reason, it was not always possible to establish a comprehensive, conclusive ranking of OO-faithfulness (as herein with regard to αMANNER). Also, external evidence is discerned from highly structured stimuli that vary systematically from manipulation to manipulation. In this study, each place/manner comparison involved different sets of triplets in examination of specific dimensions of similarity. It is not feasible to sample all combinations of all stimuli in any given experiment for such reasons as stimulus overexposure, response predisposition or bias, teaching to the task, or subject fatigue. In sum, potential mismatches between experimental outcomes and language itself underscore the need to appeal to internal and external evidence in tandem whenever possible. Ultimately, if linguistic theory is to reflect both the formal structure of language and a speaker's competence, it will be imperative to integrate multiple sources of evidence from linguistic and psycholinguistic domains.

4   Conclusion

This experiment extended the relationship between linguistic theory and phonological acquisition by applying the predictions of OT to development, with specific reference to OO-correspondence relationships. The results provided a demonstration of OO-faithfulness in prototypic initial- and final-state grammars of children's developing systems. Through use of a psycholinguistic task, it was possible to validate OO-faithfulness constraints, their potential rankings, and change in these rankings as children's grammars evolved. The findings also lend support for other central tenets of OT, including local conjunction, constraint demotion in language learnability, and constraint explosion. Perhaps of most importance, the outcome of this research offered both methodological and theoretical advances to the study of OT by applying psycholinguistic procedures of the triad task, and by introducing a construct of emergence of OO-faithfulness, respectively. As OT continues to be refined, there is no doubt that this framework will have an impact on our views of acquisition which, in turn, will likely lead to new discoveries about language itself.

Notes

*   We appreciate comments and discussion provided by Annette Hust Champion, Stuart Davis, Michele Morrisette, Kathleen O'Connor, and Holly Storkel. Aspects of data collection, management, and analysis were handled by Jessica Barlow, Jennifer Huljak, David Long, Michele Morrisette, Kathleen O'Connor, and Jennifer Taps, with special thanks to Annette Hust Champion and Holly Storkel for their central contributions. This research was supported in part by a grant to Indiana University from the National Institutes of Health (NIH DC001694).

1   The nonambient onset /ɸ/ was pertinent to the prior experiment on underspecification (Gierut, 1996), and in the present study, it rounded out logical place–manner relationships. Perhaps, it is of interest to note that none of the children of this study evidenced /ɸ/ in their productions. Consistent with an OT framework, it would be claimed that all children, regardless if displaying an initial- or a final-state grammar, maintained a highly ranked markedness constraint prohibiting nonstrident labial fricatives.

8   Recalcitrant error patterns[*]

Daniel A. Dinnsen
Indiana University

Children typically suppress their phonological error patterns on their own without explicit instruction, although some error patterns may persist longer than others. For children with phonological delays or disorders, clinical intervention may be required to help eradicate those error patterns. However, treatment does not always meet with success. Certain error patterns appear to be especially recalcitrant, devolving into new overgeneralization errors and/or requiring multiple rounds of treatment. The theoretical and clinical challenge is to explain why some error patterns persist longer than others and/or why some error patterns respond well to treatment, while others do not. Optimality theory offers a fresh perspective on this issue through its characterization of children's error patterns. Various error patterns that are common to both typical and atypical development but that differ in their persistence and resistance to treatment are shown to follow from characteristic constraint hierarchies. This characterization is shown to have the further consequence of revealing the constitution of specific error patterns and explaining the course of development.

1   Introduction

The typical course of phonological development is for children to suppress their error patterns on their own over time without explicit instruction. The fact that some error patterns persist longer than others is often attributed to different rates of development for achieving motor control of the various mechanisms involved in speech production (e.g., Locke, 1983; Kent, 1992). Such accounts, while plausible in many instances, have always had difficulty explaining those other cases in which children produce a sound in error after having produced it correctly at an earlier point in time (recidivisms), or they

247

produce a target sound in error but at the same time use that troublesome sound as the substitute for some other sound (chain shifts). The persistence of error patterns and their ultimate suppression is even more of an issue for children with phonological delays or disorders. These children often require clinical intervention to move this process along. The expectation is that treatment will provide the child with the essential information that is needed to suppress those error patterns, and it often does (Gierut, 1998c). There are, however, a number of common error patterns that appear to be especially recalcitrant or persistent, requiring extended treatment that may result in only limited success or may even regress into new overgeneralization errors. This resistance to treatment by some error patterns, but not others, has remained a mystery to clinicians and has largely been ignored as an issue in phonological theory. With the advent of optimality theory (e.g., Prince & Smolensky, 1993/2004; McCarthy & Prince, 1995; McCarthy, 2002b) comes a fresh perspective on this issue which may be more enlightening both clinically and theoretically. One reason for this optimism is that optimality theory forces a very different characterization of children's error patterns. Until recently, these phonological errors have been attributed to a wide variety of grammatical factors, including the presence/absence of rules and/or a more restricted (or coarsely coded) set of underlying representations, the substance of which can vary across children and over the course of development (e.g., Elbert & Gierut, 1986; Ingram, 1989; Dinnsen, 1999). Despite the range of descriptive devices available in derivational phonology, it is somewhat surprising that the unifying properties of recalcitrant error patterns have remained elusive. Optimality theory approaches the same problem of describing children's error patterns without two of the descriptive tools often invoked in previous literature: rules and restrictions on underlying representations. Error patterns result instead from intricate hierarchies of universal constraints. Because the set of constraints is presumed to be finite and the same for all children, our focus is narrowed to the discovery of the permissible constraint hierarchies. This sharper focus may help to limit the domain of inquiry and should allow us to get at the internal composition or anatomy of children's error patterns. In clinical terms, this perspective's potential contribution would allow more accurate diagnosis that leads to more effective treatment options with a predictable learning path. Also, the ability of a theory to properly differentiate between those error patterns that are suppressed early in development or respond well to treatment versus those that persist or resist treatment should add to the value of that theory. To the extent that these same error patterns also occur and persist in the speech of younger, typically-developing children (e.g., Dinnsen, O'Connor & Gierut, 2001), additional insight is gained into the process of acquisition generally.

Optimality theory is thus positioned to receive a special, previously unattained measure of support from this developmental and clinical issue.

With this background in mind, we will examine a number of published case studies involving children (age 3 years;0 months to 7;0) with phonological delays who would have received conventional clinical treatment for certain common error patterns. All of the children in these studies exhibited highly unintelligible speech, scoring at or below the fifth percentile on a standardized articulation test (e.g., Goldman & Fristoe, 1986). These children also scored within normal limits relative to age-matched peers on all other tests of oral-motor functioning and general language abilities. Consistent with the classification 'phonological delay' (e.g., Elbert & Gierut, 1986; Leonard, 1992), there was no known organic basis for the presenting speech problems. The data presented in this chapter are drawn from the cited studies with some supplemental forms added from the original source (the Developmental Phonology Archive at Indiana University). Our focus will be on the optimality theoretic characterization of those error patterns prior to and following treatment. It will be argued that optimality theory offers an explanation for the relative resistance of different error patterns to treatment. The accounts of the error patterns will also be shown to fit well with the observed stages of development and the transition from one stage to the next as a result of treatment.

The chapter is organized as follows. In this first section, we illustrate the basic approach of optimality theory to the characterization of a simple error pattern which responded well to treatment and was fully suppressed after treatment. In the remainder of the chapter, we turn to the characterization of certain other error patterns that have proven more problematic for treatment. More specifically, in §2, we consider some problems associated with the treatment of a classic chain shift error pattern for two children. In §3, we examine a representative case in which treatment on one error pattern results in new overgeneralization errors. In §4, we take up the problem of why treatment sometimes fails to generalize to the full class of sounds affected by an error pattern. §5 deals with a similar problem of why treatment might fail to generalize to all contexts affected by a particular error pattern. Finally, §6 concludes with a brief summary.

The schema in (1) highlights the standard approach of optimality theory to the characterization and treatment of an error pattern. The assumption is that the initial state or default ranking of constraints is markedness over faithfulness (e.g., Smolensky, 1996a). Error patterns arise when this ranking differs from that of the adult. Acquisition proceeds by the demotion of the markedness constraints on the basis of positive evidence (e.g., Tesar & Smolensky, 1998; Hayes, 2004; Prince & Tesar, 2004). When this process fails to progress for whatever reason, treatment can be initiated to induce the reranking of the constraints; this treatment focuses the child's attention on some property of the target system that must be preserved in violation of a highly ranked markedness constraint in the child's phonology. Suppression of the error pattern requires that the highly ranked markedness constraint be demoted below the previously violated faithfulness constraint.

(1) Schema for error patterns, treatment, and learning

We now turn to a case study of a child with phonological delays who instantiates this schema. Child 31 (age 4;5) is one of several children who participated in an experimental treatment study (Gierut, 1998b). The data in (2) are from the period immediately prior to treatment. The forms in (2a) illustrate the fact that labial fricatives were excluded from the child's inventory and were replaced by coronal fricatives. The forms in (2b) show that target coronal fricatives were indeed realized as coronals (albeit with some distortion or dentalization).

(2) Child 31 (age 4;5) pretreatment (Gierut, 1998b)

　　a) Target labial fricatives realized as coronals
　　　　[ṣæt] 'fat'　　[ṣaɪjʊ] 'fire'　　[ṣɛz̪oʊ] 'feather'

　　b) Target coronals realized as coronals
　　　　[ṣup] 'soup'　　[ṣoʊp] 'soap'　　[ṣɛzɪn] 'seven'

The constraints relevant to the characterization of these facts are given in (3). The two markedness constraints, *s and *f, belong to a family of constraints disfavoring fricatives generally, but each is independently necessary to account for the individual differences that can occur. For example, some children (such as Child 31) exclude labial fricatives from their inventories, requiring *f to be ranked above an antagonistic faithfulness constraint. Other children exclude instead grooved coronal fricatives, such as [s] or dentalized [s̪] (e.g., Ferguson, 1977), requiring *s to be highly ranked. We will employ the monovalent articulatory feature [grooved] in referring to these sibilants as an alternative to the feature [strident] (e.g., Ladefoged & Maddieson, 1996).[1] The two faithfulness constraints, ID[manner] and ID[place], demand identity between input and output representations in terms of place and manner features. Faithfulness to place (ID[place]) is apparently not all that important to this child given that labials are replaced by coronals. However, preservation of manner (ID[manner]) does appear to be important given that the offending fricative is replaced by another fricative rather than by a stop.

(3) Constraints

Markedness

*f:	Labial fricatives are banned
*s:	Grooved coronal fricatives are banned

Faithfulness

ID[manner]:	Corresponding segments must have identical manner features
ID[place]:	Corresponding segments must have identical place features

The ranking of the constraints in (4) accounts for the pretreatment facts. Notice in the two tableaux that candidate (a) with a stop substituted for an input fricative fatally violates the undominated faithfulness constraint ID[manner] and is eliminated from the competition. The undominated markedness constraint *f eliminates candidate (b) with a labial fricative, independent of the input fricative. This results in the selection of candidate (c) with a coronal fricative as optimal, despite its violations of the lower-ranked constraints ID[place] and *s in the first tableau, and its violation of low ranking *s in the second tableau. It is assumed for now that *s is ranked below the two faithfulness constraints to account for the fact that target grooved coronal fricatives were produced correctly (except for their dentalization). The dentalization effect is not of central concern here, but it is likely attributable to some highly ranked markedness constraint disfavoring non-distributed (coronal) fricatives, such as [s].

(4) Constraint ranking for pretreatment stage

ID[manner], *f >> ID[place] >> *s

/fæt/ 'fat'	ID[manner]	*f	ID[place]	*s
a. pæt	*!			
b. fæt		*!		
c. ☞ şæt			*	*

/sup/ 'soup'	ID[manner]	*f	ID[place]	*s
a. tup	*!			
b. fup		*!	*	
c. ☞ şup				*

Given our schema in (1) and our characterization of this particular error pattern, the main problem for this child is the dominance of the markedness constraint *f. Treatment aimed at the demotion of that constraint below ID[place] should result in correct productions. To this end, this child received traditional treatment (e.g., Fey, 1988; Gierut, 1998c) on /f/ in word-initial position. As the data in (5) show, labial fricatives were acquired in untreated words following treatment on that class of sounds with no effects on target coronal fricatives.

(5)   Child 31 (age 4;10) after treatment on /f/

    a)   Target labial fricatives realized as labials
        [fæt˺] 'fat'   [faɪjoʊ] 'fire'   [fɛðoʊz]   'feather'

    b)   Target coronals realized as coronals
        [s̪up] 'soup'   [s̪oʊp] 'soap'   [s̪ɛvɪn]   'seven'

The new ranking in (6) accounts for the posttreatment facts and entails the demotion of *f just below the highest-ranked constraint that the previous winner violated, namely just below ID[place]. This reranking is consistent with the constraint demotion algorithm of Tesar and Smolensky (1998) and preserves all other aspects of the prior hierarchy. Notice in the new tableau for 'fat' that the faithful candidate (b) now survives as optimal with all other competitors eliminated by their violations of the more highly ranked faithfulness constraints.

(6)   Constraint ranking for posttreatment stage

    ID[manner] >> ID[place] >> *s, *f

/fæt/ 'fat'	ID[manner]	ID[place]	*s	*f
a. pæt	*!			
b. ☞ fæt				*
c. s̪æt		*!	*	

With this as the archetypical characterization of an error pattern and its subsequent suppression as a result of treatment, why is it that certain other error patterns appear so much more resistant to treatment? In the remainder of this chapter, we will focus on some of those more problematic error patterns and the associated treatment results.

2   Chain shift error patterns

One of the most challenging and interesting error patterns, both clinically and theoretically, is a chain shift. Chain shifts are common in fully developed languages (e.g., Kirchner, 1996; Moreton & Smolensky, 2002) and as error patterns in children's developing phonologies (e.g., Dinnsen, Barlow & Morrisette, 1997; Bernhardt & Stemberger, 1998; Dinnsen & Barlow, 1998; Dinnsen et al., 2001; Dinnsen & O'Connor, 2001b; Jesney, 2005). One typical chain shift for children replaces /s/ with [θ], but target /θ/ is itself replaced by [f]. Chain shifts pose a theoretical challenge, especially for optimality theory (McCarthy, 1999; 2002a). The theory must account for an opacity effect in which [θ] is preferred as a substitute for one sound but is at the same time dispreferred as a correspondent of itself. Chain shifts are opaque due to the non-surface-true character of their resultant generalizations. In addition to this theoretical challenge, chain shifts pose a clinical challenge: they are resistant to treatment. In an experimental study, Gierut and Champion (1999) documented some of the problems associated with the treatment of this error pattern for two children who were taught /s/ in word-initial position. As we will see, the two children continued to have problems after treatment, albeit different problems. The question is: What is it about the chain shift error pattern that makes it so recalcitrant, and why would the same treatment have these two different effects?

We will begin by considering an optimality theoretic characterization of the chain shift for the two children from the Gierut and Champion study prior to treatment. We will then formulate an account of the different posttreatment facts to see how the children's phonologies changed.

The data in (7) are from Child 74 (age 4;0), but are also illustrative of the same chain shift error pattern for the other child from that study, Child 90 (age 4;8). The forms in (7a) exemplify the fact that /s/ did not occur and was replaced by [θ]. The forms in (7b) show that target /θ/ was replaced by [f]. Finally, the forms in (7c) show that target /f/ was realized correctly.

(7) Child 74 (age 4;0) pretreatment (Gierut & Champion, 1999)

    a) Target /s/ realized as [θ]
        [θup]   'soup'   [θɔk]   'sock'   [θʌn]   'sun'

    b) Target /θ/ realized as [f]
        [fʌmi]   'thumb (dimin.)'   [fʌndʊ]   'thunder'   [fʊθi]   'thirsty'

    c) Target /f/ realized as [f]
        [fæt]   'fat'   [faɪv]   'five'   [feɪθ]   'face'

The constraints relevant to the characterization of this chain shift are given in (8). They include all of the constraints considered in §1 with a few additions. The markedness constraint *θ disfavors interdentals such as /θ ð/ and is another member of the family of constraints militating against fricatives. It is independently necessary and would be highly ranked for those many children who exclude interdentals from their inventories (e.g., Smit, Hand, Freilinger, Bernthal & Bird, 1990). While interdentals are not excluded from the phonetic inventories of children with this particular chain shift, we will see that this constraint compels the replacement of target interdentals. In terms of faithfulness, we have expanded our considerations to include two additional constraints. ID[grooved] demands that corresponding segments be identical in terms of the feature [grooved] (roughly equivalent to the feature [strident]). The replacement of /s/, which is grooved, by [θ], which is not grooved, would represent a violation of this constraint. However, given that neither [θ] nor [f] is grooved, the substitution of [f] for target /θ/ would not violate this constraint. This latter substitution pattern would, of course, violate ID[place] because of the change in place features. The other new faithfulness constraint in this display, LC, represents the local conjunction of the two independent faithfulness constraints ID[place] and ID[grooved]. Local conjunction of constraints (Smolensky, 1995) is one of several different proposals for achieving opacity effects, especially those associated with chain shifts (e.g., Kirchner, 1996; Moreton & Smolensky, 2002).[2] The locally conjoined constraint is violated if and only if all of its individual conjuncts are violated. Thus if /s/ were replaced by [f], which entails changes in both the place and grooved features, the locally conjoined constraint would be violated. On the other hand, if /s/ were replaced by [θ], or if /θ/ were replaced by [f], the change would involve just one feature, violating only one of the conjuncts and would thus not violate the locally conjoined constraint.

(8) Constraints

*s:	Grooved coronal fricatives are banned
*θ:	Interdental fricatives are banned
*f:	Labial fricatives are banned

ID[manner]:	Corresponding segments must have identical manner features
ID[grooved]:	Corresponding segments must have an identical [grooved] feature
ID[place]:	Corresponding segments must have identical place features
LC:	Local conjunction of ID[place] & ID[grooved]

The ranking in (9) illustrates how these constraints interact to yield a chain shift error pattern. As we saw earlier, to account for the fact that fricatives are replaced by fricatives (and not by stops), ID[manner] must be highly ranked to eliminate any candidates with a stop substitute. To simplify the tableaux, this constraint (along with lower-ranked inactive markedness constraints and their offending candidates) will be left out of this and all subsequent tableaux. The undominated character of *s eliminates candidate (c) in both of the tableaux in (9), independent of the input. In the tableau for 'soup', we see additionally that candidate (a) fatally violates LC. This results in the selection of the [θ] candidate (b) as optimal. In the tableau for 'thumb', we see that the faithful candidate is eliminated by its violation of *θ, permitting candidate (a) with [f] to survive as optimal, even though it violates the lower-ranked constraints ID[place] and *f.

(9) Constraint ranking for pretreatment chain shift stage[3]

ID[manner], *s, LC >> *θ >> ID[grooved] >> ID[place] >> *f

/sup/ 'soup'	*s	LC	*θ	ID[grooved]	ID[place]	*f
a. fup		*!		*	*	*
b. ☞ θup			*	*		
c. sup	*!					

/θʌm-i/ 'thumb (dimin.)'	*s	LC	*θ	ID[grooved]	ID[place]	*f
a. ☞ fʌmi					*	*
b. θʌmi			*!			
c. sʌmi	*!			*		

With this as the characterization of the chain shift error pattern for both Child 74 and Child 90, we can now turn to the impact that treatment on /s/ had on this error pattern. Both children were taught /s/ in word-initial position. We first consider the posttreatment results for Child 74 given in (10).

(10) Child 74 (age 4;4) after treatment on /s/

   a) Target /s/ realized as [s]
       [sup]   'soup'   [sɔk]   'sock'   [sʌn]   'sun'

   b) Target /θ/ realized as [f]
       [fʌm]   'thumb'   [fʌndʊ]   'thunder'   [fʊsti]   'thirsty'

It appears that treatment was only partially effective for this child. That is, while the problem with /s/ was eliminated (10a), the forms in (10b) show that one part of the chain shift persisted, namely the labialization error pattern in which target /θ/ was realized as [f].

To achieve these results in accord with the constraint demotion algorithm, the child had to recognize the occurrence of /s/ and rerank the constraints as shown in (11). It should be noted that this requires *s to be demoted just below the highest-ranked constraint that the child's previous winner violated, in this case just below *θ. The constraint hierarchy is otherwise the same for both stages of development. The tableau for 'soup' now shows that candidates (a) and (b) incur fatal violations of LC and *θ, respectively, and are thus eliminated, allowing the faithful candidate (c) to win. The tableau for 'thumb' shows how the labialization error pattern continues with this new ranking; the faithful candidate (b) is eliminated by *θ, and candidate (c) with [s] is eliminated by *s, which leaves candidate (a) with a labial fricative to be selected as optimal.

Given the persistence of the labialization error pattern, Child 74 would likely benefit from further treatment with a different focus, at the very least redirected toward the demotion of *θ.

(11) Constraint ranking for Child 74 posttreatment

ID[manner], LC >> *θ >> *s, ID[grooved] >> ID[place] >> *f

/sup/ 'soup'	LC	*θ	*s	ID[grooved]	ID[place]
a. fup	*!			*	*
b. θup		*!		*	
c. ☞ sup			*		

/θʌm/ 'thumb'	LC	*θ	*s	ID[grooved]	ID[place]
a. ☞ fʌm					*
b. θʌm		*!			
c. sʌm			*!	*	

Let us now turn to the results of treatment for Child 90, who also began with the same chain shift and was treated on /s/. The data in (12) reveal rather different results. As we see in (12a), target /s/ continued to be produced in error, being realized as [θ]. However, as the forms in (12b) show, /θ/ came to be produced target-appropriately, effectively suppressing the labialization part of the error pattern.

(12) Child 90 (age 5;0) after treatment on /s/

a) Target /s/ realized as [θ]
    [θup] 'soup'   [θɔk] 'sock'   [θʌn] 'sun'

b) Target /θ/ realized as [θ]
    [θʌmi] 'thumb (dimin.)'   [θif] 'thief'   [θwoʊw] 'throw'

To account for these results, the original constraint hierarchy in (9) had to undergo a different reranking, as shown in (13). The only difference here is that *θ—and not *s—is demoted just below the highest-ranked constraint that the previous winner violated, namely just below ID[place]. This reranking is presumably motivated by the child's recognition that /θ/ can occur. With *s remaining undominated, candidate (c) with an [s] incurs a fatal violation and is eliminated, again independent of the input. In the tableau for 'soup', we see that candidate (a) with a labial fricative is also eliminated by the undominated locally conjoined constraint, permitting the [θ] candidate (b) to survive as optimal. The tableau for 'thumb' shows how the target-appropriate realization of /θ/ is achieved. That is, *θ is ranked low enough that it exercises no force.

(13) Constraint ranking for Child 90 posttreatment

ID[manner], *s, LC >> ID[grooved] >> ID[place] >> *θ, *f

/sup/ 'soup'	*s	LC	ID[grooved]	ID[place]	*θ
a. fup		*!	*	*	
b. ☞ θup			*		*
c. sup	*!				

/θʌm-i/ 'thumb (dimin.)'	*s	LC	ID[grooved]	ID[place]	*θ
a. fʌmi				*!	
b. ☞ θʌmi					*
c. sʌmi	*!		*		

We do not claim to have an explanation for why treatment on /s/ would have motivated Child 90 to demote *θ as opposed to *s, except that both markedness constraints are essential components of this same chain shift and both must ultimately be demoted if the error pattern is to be fully eradicated. Also, while any treatment plan might be designed to focus the child's attention on some property of a sound, there is no guarantee that the child will conceptualize the new information exactly as the treatment plan intended. It thus may be that Child 90 took away from treatment only that a coronal fricative was being presented, ignoring the grooved character of that fricative, and then demoted one of the two available markedness constraints consistent with that observation. Given that one critical part of the chain shift remained for this child after treatment (just as the other component remained for Child 74), another round of treatment would be warranted, but this time it would be appropriate for treatment to remain focused on the demotion of *s. In some sense, progress was being made in eradicating the chain shift as evidenced by the demotion of *θ.

However, it might be that treatment on /s/ was aborted prematurely, especially if the goal were to demote *s and fully eradicate the chain shift.

While this chain shift error pattern proved to be relatively resistant to treatment for these two children, it was not entirely immune. That is, changes did occur, but essential elements of the original error pattern persisted. The fact that these two children both began with the same error pattern, but responded differently to the same treatment, was attributed to the principled demotion of either one of two active markedness constraints: either *s or *θ. The fact that the error pattern was not fully eradicated was attributed to the sustained dominance of one of the two markedness constraints. We will return to a general characterization of this class of error patterns after connecting it with another, seemingly different problem. In the following section, we move to the situation in which treatment can result in new overgeneralization errors.

3   Overgeneralization error patterns

One standard clinical expectation is that treatment should move the child's phonology forward, bringing it into greater conformity with the target system. It is deemed undesirable for treatment to introduce new errors. Despite this, treatment often has just that effect, i.e., solving one problem while creating another. Aside from the clinical dilemma that such U-shaped learning poses, it also presents significant challenges for phonological theory. The problem arises in optimality theory largely because of the constraint rankings and rerankings that would seem to be required to account for the introduction of overgeneralization errors. That is, the occurrence and correct production of a target sound in the child's speech is typically indicative of the ranking of faithfulness over markedness. For that correct production to then revert to an error in a subsequent stage would presumably require a reranking of the constraints in which markedness comes to outrank faithfulness. Such rerankings would, however, entail the assumption that children take advantage of counterfactual, negative evidence, contrary to the more standard assumption that learning requires positive evidence. We will show here that optimality theory can account for such facts without compromising those standard assumptions.

One of the children from the Gierut (1998b) treatment study exhibited what appears to be a typical example of overgeneralization as a result of treatment. The data in (14) are from Child 33 (age 5;7) prior to any treatment. It can be observed in (14a) that /θ/ did not occur in the child's inventory and was replaced by a labial fricative. The forms in (14b) show that the coronal fricative /s/ occurred, albeit with some distortion/dentalization.

(14) Child 33 (age 5;7) pretreatment (Gierut, 1998b)

   a) Target /θ/ realized as [f]

      [fʌm]   'thumb'   [fif]   'thief'   [fʌndə] 'thunder'

   b) Target /s/ realized as [ṣ]

      [ṣoʊp] 'soap'   [ṣoʊ] 'sew'   [ṣɔk] 'sock'

The constraints described in the previous sections are relevant to this case as well. The ranking of constraints needed for Child 33 is given in (15). Just as in our characterization of a chain shift, ID[manner] and LC are among the undominated constraints. (We will leave ID[manner] out of the tableau because we will only consider candidates with fricatives. Likewise, we will leave low-ranked *f out of the tableau because it plays no role here.) The most important element of this hierarchy is the dominance of *θ over *s, accounting for the nonoccurrence of [θ].[4] Consistent with the permutability of these markedness constraints in different phonologies, it happens in this case that *θ is undominated.

(15) Constraint ranking for pretreatment stage

ID[manner], LC, *θ >> *s >> ID[grooved] >> ID[place] >> *f

/θʌm/ 'thumb'	LC	*θ	*s	ID[grooved]	ID[place]
a. ☞ fʌm					*
b. θʌm		*!			
c. ṣʌm			*!	*	

/soʊp/ 'soap'	LC	*θ	*s	ID[grooved]	ID[place]
a. foʊp	*!			*	*
b. θoʊp		*!		*	
c. ☞ ṣoʊp			*		

In the tableau for 'thumb', we account for the nonoccurrence of [θ] and its replacement with a labial fricative. The faithful candidate (b) is eliminated by its violation of undominated *θ. Candidate (a) with a labial fricative is selected as the substitute because the other competitor candidate (c) is eliminated by its violation of *s. In the tableau for 'soap', candidates (a) and (b) are eliminated by their violations of LC and *θ, respectively, resulting in the selection of candidate (c) as optimal.

Given our characterization of the pretreatment error pattern, the focus of treatment should be on the demotion of the undominated markedness constraint *θ. This child was in fact taught /θ/ in word-initial position and, as the results in (16a) show, /θ/ came to be produced target-appropriately. Unfortunately, as the forms in (16b) show, target /s/ shifted to [θ]—a new overgeneralization error.

(16) Child 33 (age 5;10) after treatment on /θ/

    a) Target /θ/ realized as [θ]
        [θʌm] 'thumb'   [θi] 'thief'   [θʌndə] 'thunder'

    b) Target /s/ realized as [θ]
        [θoup] 'soap'   [θou] 'sew'   [θɔk] 'sock'

In order to account for the suppression of the original labialization error pattern and the coincident introduction of the new overgeneralization error, this child had to take note of the occurrence of /θ/ and rerank the constraints as in (17). More specifically, *θ is demoted just below the highest-ranked constraint that its previous winner violated, namely just below ID[place]. The tableau for 'thumb' shows how /θ/ came to be produced target-appropriately with this reranking. With the demotion of *θ and the rest of the hierarchy remaining unchanged, *s accrues greater force. As the tableau for 'soap' shows, the dominance of *s accounts for the nonoccurrence of [s] (whether plain or dentalized). The resulting hierarchy (specifically candidate (a)'s violation of LC) forces the selection of [θ] as the substitute for /s/. This tableau also shows that another round of treatment would be warranted for this child. That is, the focus of treatment could profitably be shifted to the demotion of *s.

(17) Constraint ranking for posttreatment overgeneralization stage

ID[manner], LC >> *s >> ID[grooved] >> ID[place] >> *θ, *f

/θʌm/ 'thumb'	LC	*s	ID[grooved]	ID[place]	*θ
a. fʌm				*!	
b. ☞ θʌm					*
c. sʌm		*!	*		

/soup/ 'soap'	LC	*s	ID[grooved]	ID[place]	*θ
a. foup	*!		*	*	
b. ☞ θoup			*		*
c. soup		*!			

A novel consequence of our optimality theoretic account of this case is that the apparent regression associated with the new overgeneralization errors actually represents a positive step forward. That is, constraints are being demoted as they should be, and the reranking has the further beneficial consequence of revealing another highly ranked, partially hidden (relatively inactive) markedness constraint (*s). That constraint was hidden in the sense that it exercised little or no force as a result of the dominance of other constraints. Upon the demotion of one of those more highly ranked constraints (*θ), the hidden constraint was made more active and revealed. Hidden constraints of this sort ultimately need to be demoted below the relevant faithfulness constraint, and treatment that is properly refocused on that constraint would likely contribute toward this end. This underscores the importance of arriving at an accurate diagnosis, which entails fleshing out the child's actual constraint hierarchy to be sure that all relevant markedness constraints have been demoted. It was, however, not possible for us to be entirely certain about Child 33's pretreatment constraint hierarchy until we saw the results of treatment. That is, the relatively inactive *s constraint might otherwise have been thought to be ranked lower in the pretreatment hierarchy (cf. Child 31). Analyses based on data from a single slice of time are often limited in this regard. If treatment does not result in new overgeneralization errors (as we saw, for example, for Child 31 in §1), we can be more confident that the inactive markedness constraint is indeed dominated by an antagonistic faithfulness constraint. On the other hand, the introduction of overgeneralization errors following treatment can be taken as indicative of an earlier stage of development and a constraint hierarchy more closely resembling the default ranking of markedness over faithfulness. For a similar optimality theoretic characterization of other overgeneralization phenomena in typical and atypical development, see Dinnsen (2002) and Dinnsen, O'Connor and Gierut (2001).

Our accounts of chain shifts and overgeneralization errors share a number of commonalities that distinguish them from the more tractable type of error pattern considered in §1. First, it might be noted that the pre- and posttreatment pronunciation facts for Child 33 (the overgeneralization case) bear a striking resemblance to the posttreatment pronunciation facts for the two children who presented with a chain shift. The similarity of the facts and of the account of these cases points to a possible developmental connection between these error patterns such that overgeneralization might be an expected result of an earlier chain shift. Unfortunately, we have no information about Child 33's earlier phonology to know whether a chain shift occurred, nor do we know whether Child 74 and Child 90 exhibited overgeneralization errors at later points in time. In any event, if these error patterns are indeed connected in this way, their resistance to treatment is underscored all the more. That is, several rounds of treatment will likely be necessary to eradicate a chain shift, and those rounds of treatment will likely require several additional rounds of treatment to eradicate any possible overgeneralization errors.

The theoretical essentials of chain shifts and overgeneralization errors are schematized in (18) (cf. (1) for the more tractable error patterns). Chain shifts and other error patterns that result in overgeneralization are characterized in their initial stages in the same way, namely by two conflicting markedness constraints, M1 and M2, both of which are ranked above an antagonistic faithfulness constraint. The markedness constraints conflict in that different rankings relative to one another would have different empirical consequences. Treatment that is aimed at demoting one of those markedness constraints can only hope to enjoy limited success in that the other markedness constraint will likely remain highly ranked (Stage 2). The sustained dominance of that markedness constraint will either result in new overgeneralization errors or the persistence of some part of the original error pattern. It is precisely this property that warrants another round of treatment that is aimed at the demotion of that active markedness constraint and leads to a third stage of development. The more tractable error patterns, on the other hand, can achieve the end state in one step as schematized in (1).

(18) Schema for chain shifts and overgeneralization errors

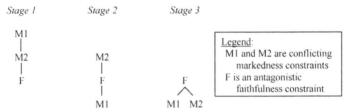

4   Complementary error patterns

Another standard clinical expectation is that treatment on one sound affected by an error pattern should generalize to other sounds affected by that same error pattern (Gierut, 1998c). It thus should be possible to fully suppress an error pattern without teaching the child all of the sounds affected by that error pattern. Some treatment studies have, however, documented the need to treat the fuller class of sounds affected by one putative process (e.g., Elbert & McReynolds, 1985; Saben & Ingham, 1991). In this section, we attempt to show why, from the perspective of optimality theory, treatment on one sound affected by some error patterns might fail to generalize to other sounds affected by the same process.

Final consonant omission is a revealing example of a common error pattern thought to be the result of a unified process (Smit, 1993a). The data in (19)

illustrate this error pattern for one of the four children from the Elbert and McReynolds treatment study, namely Child 1 (age 3;11). It can be observed that word-final obstruent stops and fricatives were systematically omitted. The three other children who participated in that study also exhibited the same error pattern prior to any treatment.

(19) Child 1 (age 3;11) pretreatment (Elbert & McReynolds, 1985)[5]

   a) Word-final stops omitted

     [bɪ] 'bib'   [kæ] 'cat'   [da] 'dog'

   b) Word-final fricatives omitted

     [fɪ] 'fish'   [du] 'goose'   [kæ] 'calf'

The Elbert and McReynolds study bears directly on the issue of generalization to other untreated sounds because each of the children in that study received treatment on one sound affected by final consonant omission. Two of the children were taught a final stop, while the other two were taught a final fricative. The results of treatment are summarized in (20). Interestingly, the error pattern was effectively suppressed only with regard to the class of sounds treated. While treatment on final stops resulted in the occurrence of final stops, final fricatives continued to be omitted. Similarly, while treatment on final fricatives resulted in the occurrence of final fricatives, final stops continued to be omitted.

(20) Results of treatment (adapted from Elbert & McReynolds, 1985)

Teach word-final	Generalize to	Pronunciation of 'bib' & 'fish'
Stops	Stops, but not fricatives	[bɪb] [fɪ]
Fricatives	Fricatives, but not stops	[bɪ] [fɪʃ]

These results suggest that final obstruent omission is not a unified process governed by a single, highly ranked markedness constraint such as NoCODA (Prince & Smolensky, 1993/2004). Instead, it appears that final stops and fricatives are each subject to independent markedness constraints, as in (21). By exploding NoCODA in this way, either or both of the constituent constraints can be ranked above or below the faithfulness constraint MAX, which militates against deletion.

(21) Constraints

   NoCODA-STOPS: Coda stops are banned

   NoCODA-FRICS: Coda fricatives are banned

   MAX: No deletion

The ranking needed to account for the pretreatment stage is given in (22). Notice that both of the markedness constraints are ranked above the antagonistic faithfulness constraint MAX, accounting for the nonoccurrence of final stops and fricatives. The dominance of these two markedness constraints and their complementary character makes their ranking relative to one another indeterminate. With both constraints ranked above MAX, the same result would obtain no matter how the two markedness constraints are ranked relative to one another.

(22) Constraint ranking for pretreatment stage of final obstruent omission

NoCODA-STOPS, NoCODA-FRICS >> MAX

/bɪb/ 'bib'	NoCODA-STOPS	NoCODA-FRICS	MAX
a. bɪb	*!		
b. ☞ bɪ			*

/fɪʃ/ 'fish'	NoCODA-STOPS	NoCODA-FRICS	MAX
a. fɪʃ		*!	
b. ☞ fɪ			*

For those children who were taught a final stop, reranking of only one of the markedness constraints is motivated, resulting in the demotion of NoCODA-STOPS, as shown in (23). Notice that NoCODA-FRICS remains highly ranked. This particular ranking results in the suppression of the error pattern with regard to final stops, but the persistence of the error pattern with regard to final fricatives. An additional round of treatment would be warranted, this time aimed at the demotion of the other markedness constraint NoCODA-FRICS.

(23) Constraint ranking after treatment on final stops

NoCODA-FRICS >> MAX >> NoCODA-STOPS

/bɪb/ 'bib'	NoCODA-FRICS	MAX	NoCODA-STOPS
a. ☞ bɪb			*
b. bɪ		*!	

/fɪʃ/ 'fish'	NoCODA-FRICS	MAX	NoCODA-STOPS
a. fɪʃ	*!		
b. ☞ fɪ		*	

For those other children who were taught a final fricative, it is NoCODA-FRICS that is demoted, leaving NoCODA-STOPS undominated. Again, the error pattern persists for the untreated class of sounds, necessitating an additional round of treatment, this time aimed at final stops.

Our explanation for why treatment might fail to generalize to all sounds affected by a particular error pattern can be schematized as in (24). The claim is that some error patterns are characterized by multiple, nonoverlapping (complementary) markedness constraints, M1 and M2, both of which can dominate an antagonistic faithfulness constraint (Stage 1). The undominated and complementary character of these markedness constraints means that different rankings relative to one another will have no different empirical consequence. When both markedness constraints outrank the faithfulness constraint, the error pattern will appear to be a unitary process affecting all relevant sounds in that same context. However, the independence of the two markedness constraints means that treatment aimed at the demotion of either one of them would in all likelihood result in only partial success, leaving the other markedness constraint to dominate faithfulness. The independence of the two markedness constraints also means that there is no clinical advantage to be gained by focusing treatment on the demotion of one as opposed to the other. The sustained dominance of one of the complementary markedness constraints entails an intermediate Stage 2 with a more restricted set of sounds participating in the error pattern. An additional round of treatment with a different focus may be necessary to demote that markedness constraint, leading to the end state (Stage 3) where both markedness constraints are dominated by faithfulness.

(24) Schema for complementary errors

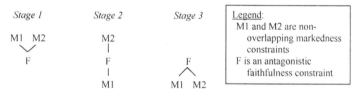

Our characterization of this error pattern and the schema in (24) extends to a seemingly different and classic problem in second language acquisition, namely the problem of effecting a phonemic split. It is well known that second language learners have extreme difficulty associating allophones of a single phoneme from their native language with separate phonemes in the target language (Lado, 1957). The relevance of allophonic phenomena and the difficulty of suppressing them can be seen if complementary distribution of sounds is achieved by two or more highly ranked, independent markedness constraints, each disfavoring a different sound in some context(s). In order to eradicate the error pattern associated with the transfer of an allophonic process, each of the individual markedness constraints must be demoted. Under this view, an allophonic rule is not a simple, unitary process that could be readily suppressed, but rather reflects a hierarchy of constraints involving multiple, highly ranked markedness constraints, the demotion of which requires the learner to recognize different facts about different sounds and contexts. The difficulty of effecting a phonemic split for children with phonological delays has also been documented by Gierut (1986; 1989a) and Gierut and Champion (2000) and has been characterized in these same optimality theoretic terms for typical and atypical development in Dinnsen (2002) and in Dinnsen, O'Connor and Gierut (2001).

5   Implicationally-related errors

Another common clinical expectation is that treatment on an error pattern in one context should generalize to other contexts, suppressing the error pattern in all contexts without direct treatment on each affected context (e.g., Gierut, 1998c). While this expectation is warranted in many instances, it also often happens that treatment fails to have this effect. That is, the new sound might be acquired in only one, more limited word position, usually the treated context. In such cases, the error pattern persists in the untreated contexts. The issue here is why treatment of a given error pattern might have these two different results in two different contexts, one highly desirable and the other less so. As we will see below, optimality theory offers an answer to this question through its appeal to fixed rankings or stringency relations among certain constraints (see de Lacy, 2002; McCarthy, 2002b for a fuller discussion of such constraints and rankings).

This problem can be illustrated by considering the results of treatment for two children who presented with the common error pattern of velar fronting and were each taught the new target sound in a different word position. In its most general form, this error pattern involves the context-free replacement of target velar consonants by coronals (e.g., Smit, 1993a). The data in (25) exemplify this error pattern for one of the two children of interest, namely Child 25 (age 4;10) from Forrest, Dinnsen and Elbert (1997). The pretreatment facts relating to this error pattern were essentially the same for the other child, Child 16 (age 4;2) from Dinnsen, Chin and Elbert (1992).[6]

(25) Child 25 (age 4;10) pretreatment (Forrest et al., 1997)

  a) Word-initial velars realized as coronals
      [dʌm] 'gum'   [det] 'gate'   [dot] 'goat'

  b) Postvocalic velars realized as coronals
      [bɪd] 'big'   [bed] 'bag'   [hʌd] 'hug'

If velar fronting were truly a unitary process unaffected by context, it should be possible to fully suppress this error pattern by teaching a child a velar in any single context, thereby demoting the markedness constraint that bans velars. The results of treatment should be uniform across children, independent of the word position in which the velar consonant is taught. There is, however, some evidence that different contexts may be more or less facilitative for learning velars as a new sound. A contextual asymmetry in the velar fronting error pattern has been identified in a number of cross-sectional studies (e.g., Smit, 1993a; Stemberger, 1996; Stoel-Gammon, 1996; Inkelas & Rose, 2003; Morrisette, Dinnsen & Gierut, 2003). More specifically, velar fronting has been found to occur in both word-initial and postvocalic positions or simply in word-initial position; phonologies with velar fronting only in postvocalic position have not been reported. Thus, velars tend to be acquired in postvocalic contexts before they are acquired in word-initial position, which allows this error pattern to persist in word-initial position without occurring postvocalically. Translating this implicational universal into claims about markedness, velars would be considered marked relative to coronals, but they are more marked (harder to learn) word-initially and less marked (easier to learn) postvocalically. This contextual asymmetry is acknowledged to be at odds with many observed contextual asymmetries in fully developed languages where word-initial position is presumed to be an unmarked context for the preservation of contrasts (e.g., Beckman, 1998). We will return to this point below.

This contextual asymmetry in the acquisition of velars offers at least two treatment options, each with different predictions about the suppression of the error pattern. Adopting a more conventional clinical and developmental perspective, treatment might be designed to teach the child a velar in the presumably easier word-final position, especially because it is that postvocalic context where velars are naturally first acquired. While this might result in the suppression of the error pattern in that context, the error pattern would likely persist in word-initial position because that is the more marked context for velars. Child 16 serves as an instantiation of this prediction. That is, in an effort to suppress her context-free velar fronting error pattern, she was taught velars word-finally using conventional minimal pair treatment procedures (Gierut, 1998c; Barlow & Gierut, 2002). Treatment resulted in the target-appropriate realization of velars in only a few words and only in postvocalic contexts. As predicted, the error pattern persisted word-initially. The other treatment option would be to teach velars in the presumably more difficult, marked word-initial position. Given the implicational relationship that holds for the different contexts of this error pattern, suppression of the error pattern in word-initial position should result in the suppression of the error pattern in the untreated postvocalic contexts. Child 25 serves to instantiate this prediction. In an effort to suppress his context-free velar fronting error pattern, he was taught velars word-initially, again using the same form of minimal pair treatment. Treatment resulted in the suppression of the error pattern word-initially and in the untreated postvocalic position. Velars were thus acquired in the treated context and were generalized to untreated contexts.

Optimality theory is capable of directly expressing the markedness claims associated with the contextual asymmetries of this error pattern and the two different treatment results with the constraints in (26). The two markedness constraints, *#k and *k, both disfavor velars but the first of the two is a more specific instance of the other. These constraints are in a fixed ranking such that the more specific *#k universally outranks *k. The claim would be that velars are disfavored generally, but they are especially bad (or marked) in word-initial position. As these markedness constraints are formulated here, any candidate that violates *#k will also violate *k, but the reverse does not hold. Consequently, a candidate with a postvocalic velar would violate *k, but not *#k. As we will see, this differs crucially from our formulation of the markedness constraints in (21), which were defined over complementary classes of sounds or environments and thus had no shared violations or interactions. The faithfulness constraint, ID[place], is the same as seen previously and would be violated if velar fronting were to occur in any context.

(26) Constraints[7]

*#k:	Word-initial dorsal consonants are banned
*k:	Dorsal consonants are banned
ID[place]:	Corresponding segments must have identical place features

These constraints and their permissible rankings yield the typology in (27). Notice that only three of the four possibilities can occur. Both the substance of these constraints and the fixed ranking of *#k over *k preclude option (d) where fronting would occur postvocalically but not word-initially.

Our explanation for why treatment on velar fronting might or might not generalize across contexts takes advantage of the fixed ranking that holds among the markedness constraints in this instance. Recall that treatment aimed at word-initial velars (Child 25) generalized to treated and untreated contexts, eradicating the error pattern in all word positions. The child's recognition that velars can occur word-initially necessitates the demotion of the more specific constraint *#k below ID[place], and the fixed ranking (or shared violation) in turn forces the demotion of the more general version of the constraint *k (e.g., Prince & Tesar, 2004). The demotion of *#k alone would be empirically indistinguishable from the sustained dominance of both markedness constraints and is thus unmotivated. On the other hand, the failure to generalize to all contexts (Child 16) follows from treatment that focuses the child's attention on the occurrence of velars postvocalically, which only motivates the demotion of the general markedness constraint *k. The child's observation about the occurrence of postvocalic velars would have no necessary impact on the more specific markedness constraint *#k, permitting it to remain undominated in its ranking with, as a consequence, the persistence of the error pattern in word-initial position.

(27) Typology for velar fronting

Context for velar fronting	Ranking	Pronunciation of 'gum' and 'big'
Everywhere	*#k >> *k >> ID[place]	[dʌm] [bɪd]
Initially, but not postvocalically	*#k >> ID[place] >> *k	[dʌm] [bɪg]
Nowhere	ID[place] >> *#k >> *k	[gʌm] [bɪg]
Postvocalically, but not initially	Impossible	[gʌm] [bɪd]

The partial suppression of velar fronting in the case of Child 16 might at first appear to resemble the partial suppression of other error patterns that we considered earlier. There is, however, an important difference. Consider again the error pattern of final obstruent omission, which was only partially suppressed as a result of treatment. The internal composition or anatomy of that error pattern differed from that of velar fronting in terms of how the constraints were exploded or partitioned. The markedness constraint responsible for final obstruent omission (NoCODA) was exploded into two independent and complementary constraints defined on nonoverlapping classes of sounds: final stops or final fricatives. That particular partitioning, as opposed to any of the other logical possibilities, was motivated on the basis of the independent behavior of the two classes of sounds with regard to the learning results following treatment. The constraint responsible for velar fronting (*k) might also have been exploded into two complementary constraints, one defined on word-initial position and the other on postvocalic position. That particular partitioning could, however, be eliminated as a possibility because it was contradicted by the learning results. That is, if complementary constraints had been involved, demotion of either of the two putative constraints should have been independent of the other, resulting in the unattested case where velar fronting would occur postvocalically but not initially. The learning results in the suppression of velar fronting revealed instead that the markedness constraint responsible for that error pattern was exploded and that the constituent constraints were in a fixed ranking. The theoretical significance of this is that it is the learning results following treatment that can help to reveal the substance of these universal constraints and tell us what is and is not a possible constraint.

As we have seen here, the context (or the position within a word) that is used to teach a new sound facilitates different degrees of success in eradicating an error pattern altogether. Word-initial position played an especially helpful role in the teaching of velar consonants, resulting in the full suppression of the velar fronting error pattern in all contexts. Although this might not be surprising given the salience of word-initial position for signaling many contrasts, contextual salience does not necessarily correspond (or may inversely correspond) with the context where a contrast first emerges. Note the tendency for the velar/coronal place contrast to first emerge in the presumably less salient postvocalic context. Inkelas and Rose (2003) attempt to offer an explanation for this developmental disparity based on a combination of factors, including anatomical considerations (i.e., a child's large tongue size relative to a small oral cavity) and enhanced articulation associated with a prosodically strong context, both of which are hypothesized to lead to coronal release for a target velar in word-initial position. Such an explanation must, however, be reconciled against those other cases where children do just the opposite, namely substitute a velar for a coronal in word-initial position (e.g., Morrisette et al., 2003).

No doubt some contrasts emerge first in word-initial position; however, in order to fully eradicate the error patterns associated with the absence of those contrasts elsewhere, it may be necessary to teach the new sound in a different, implicationally more marked context. The acquisition of the voice contrast within the obstruent series might be a relevant case. On cross-linguistic typological grounds, it has long been held that a voice contrast in final position implies a voice contrast in earlier word positions, but not vice versa (e.g., Dinnsen & Eckman, 1975; Lombardi, 1999). This means that word-final position would be considered more marked than word-initial position for the occurrence of a voice contrast. For children (or second language learners) who present with the absence of a voice contrast in all word positions, we might expect that teaching the voice contrast in final position should generalize to the other less marked word positions without directly teaching the contrast in those other contexts. This prediction awaits experimental evaluation. There is, however, some evidence from Amahl's natural acquisition of the voice contrast (Smith, 1973) that runs counter to this prediction (e.g., Dinnsen, 1996; Dinnsen et al., 2001; Kager, van der Feest, Fikkert, Kerkhoff & Zamuner, 2003). Based on these studies, it appears that the voice contrast is acquired first in word-final position and only later extends to other word positions. These developmental facts suggest that word-initial position may in fact be the more marked context for the preservation of the voice contrast. If so, we might then expect that teaching the voice contrast in word-initial position should promote the acquisition of the contrast in other less marked contexts.

Some of the contextual asymmetries observed in the acquisition of contrasts run counter to those asymmetries observed for the preservation of contrasts in fully developed languages. While we are simply trying to establish here some of the facts relevant to acquisition, these differences will ultimately need to be reconciled in a fuller account. For example, it may not be necessary to expand the constraint set, as we have done here with markedness constraints defined on word-initial position, or to attribute different constraints to children and adults (e.g., Boersma, 1998). The difference may instead reside in a developmental change that occurs in what constitutes a prominent or salient context (see Chapter 9 in this volume). That is, in early stages of development, the default may be for children to appeal to syllable rhymes as the more prominent and accessible contexts (Brooks & MacWhinney, 2000). As the lexicon grows with the addition of new words, and as it changes in its organization of those words, there is a need to shift prominence and perceptual salience to include other prosodic structures, such as syllable onsets and word edges (e.g., Metsala & Walley, 1998). Such an approach of course raises many other issues, not the least of which is specifying the critical degree of lexical neighborhood density that would be required to motivate the shift in prominence. The consequence of this approach is that the constraint set would remain more limited and be the same for both children and adults. Positional faithfulness constraints would be relativized to strong or prominent positions as has been standardly assumed, but the substance of those contexts would be supplied by processing demands and the organizational structure of the lexicon, which changes over time and differs for children and adults. Similarly, contextual markedness constraints would be relativized to weak contexts, but again the substance of those contexts would be determined by considerations of the lexicon.

The general characteristics of implicationally-related error patterns like velar fronting and their associated treatment options can be schematized as in (28). The claim is that some error patterns entail multiple markedness constraints, M1 and M2, which are in a fixed ranking relative to one another. If treatment is focused solely on the demotion of the more general constraint M2, the error pattern will only be partially suppressed because the more specific constraint M1 can remain dominant (Stage 2). A further round of treatment aimed at the demotion of M1 would be necessary to fully eradicate the error pattern. The other treatment option for children who present in Stage 1 with implicationally-related error patterns is to focus treatment on the demotion of M1. The fixed ranking of M1 over M2 forces the concomitant demotion of M2 (e.g., Prince & Tesar, 2004). This should fully eradicate the error pattern and result directly in Stage 3 without necessitating an intermediate stage. This differs from the characterization of complementary errors in terms of the relationship between M1 and M2. Complementary errors entail independent markedness constraints that do not conflict or interact with one another. Implicationally-related errors, on the other hand, entail markedness constraints that potentially interact and may be in a fixed ranking relative to one another.

(28) Schema for implicationally-related error patterns

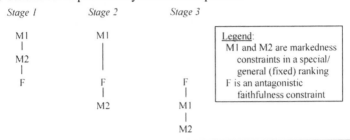

Treatment options	Consequences
Demote M2 below F	M1 remains active and requires additional treatment
Demote M1 below F	Error pattern eradicated in all contexts

Our characterization of this particular error pattern and the different treatment results extend to other implicationally-related error patterns with comparable treatment effects (e.g., Gierut, 1999; Dinnsen & O'Connor, 2001a; Dinnsen, 2002).

6   Conclusion

In sum, at least four general points emerge from our optimality theoretic consideration of children's error patterns and their learning following treatment. First, we have seen that error patterns in many instances need not and should not be viewed as the result of unitary processes. Instead, different error patterns correspond to characteristic constraint hierarchies. These different hierarchies were schematized in (1) for simple or tractable error patterns, (18) for chain shifts and overgeneralization errors, (24) for complementary error patterns and (28) for implicationally-related error patterns. Second, optimality theory offers an explanation for the relative resistance of different error patterns to treatment. That is, the more tractable error patterns are those governed by a single markedness constraint as schematized in (1). These errors are tractable because the problem can be solved by the demotion of that one constraint on the basis of positive evidence. All of the more problematic error patterns are governed by multiple markedness constraints, each of which must be demoted in order to fully eradicate the error pattern. The resilience of an error pattern and its resistance to treatment will be a necessary, unavoidable consequence of those error patterns in which the markedness constraints can be freely ranked relative to one another, as in chain shifts, overgeneralization errors and complementary errors. Third, treatment success is enhanced if it is the highest-ranked markedness constraint that is demoted. This is especially evident for implicationally-related error patterns as we saw in the prior section. That is, the demotion of the higher-ranked markedness constraint in a fixed ranking results in the demotion of the other markedness constraint and the full suppression of the error pattern. There is even some value in demoting the highest-ranked markedness constraint in the other cases. While demotion of that highest-ranked constraint may not fully eradicate the error pattern, it does at least reveal a previously hidden markedness constraint and an associated error pattern that should respond to a new, refocused round of treatment. The fourth point that emerges is that the learning results from treatment help to reveal the substance of the constraints. This was most evident in the comparison of complementary errors and implicationally-related errors. The explosion or analyzability of any constraint requires knowing what the component constraints are, and the learning results following treatment forced a particular partitioning of what might have seemed to be a general constraint. This is important because, even though the constraints of optimality theory are presumed to be universal, we are in the business of trying to discover the substance of those universal constraints.

Earlier rule-based approaches would find it difficult to arrive at a comparable explanation for these facts. On the one hand, all of the error patterns considered here (including both tractable and resistant errors) would likely be attributed to the same property of grammar, namely the presence of some phonological rule that ultimately must be lost if the error pattern is to be suppressed. The rules associated with these error patterns do not possess any obvious substantive characteristics that might allow some rules to be grouped together as resistant versus those that are more suppressible. This lack of a discernable difference among the rules suggests that all of the error patterns should respond to treatment in the same way. We have seen, however, that this is not the case. For example, in some cases (e.g., Child 31 and Child 25), simple rule loss would be the response to treatment. Treatment would induce rule complication in other cases (e.g., Child 1 and Child 16). In yet other cases, treatment would result in rule loss with coincident rule addition to yield a new overgeneralization error pattern (e.g., Child 33). Under such an approach, why only sometimes a rule would be added to a child's grammar when another rule is being lost must remain an open question. Finally, a rule-based approach might attempt to attribute the resistance of chain shift error patterns (e.g., Child 74 and Child 90) to the fact that two ordered rules are involved, and only one of those rules is lost as a result of treatment. The idea would be that it is the sheer number of rules involved in this error pattern that makes it so resistant to treatment. But this would not explain comparable difficulties in eradicating other error patterns where presumably a single rule is involved.

While our focus in this chapter has been on common error patterns of children with phonological delays, we would also expect our account and associated claims to extend to early normal development. The fact is that all of the error patterns considered here also occur in the speech of younger, typically developing children, and all of them persist to varying degrees (e.g., Smit, 1993a). Aside from the need for treatment on the part of only some children and the role that treatment plays in initiating change, the characterization of the presenting error patterns and the course of development should be much the same for both groups of children. Given the prevalence and developmental character of these error patterns, a question naturally arises concerning the implications of our account for other less common (or 'idiosyncratic') error patterns, which are sometimes taken as indicative of a truly disordered or 'deviant' phonology (e.g., Leonard, 1973; Leonard & Brown, 1984; Leonard, 1992). This question must await a fuller exploration, but we might speculate that even uncommon error patterns arise from the same set of universal constraints with similar intricate hierarchies, which reflect any one of the many possible rankings and rerankings that might follow from an initial state or default ranking. We might even expect idiosyncratic error patterns to respond to treatment in the same way that more common error patterns do. That is, some idiosyncratic error patterns should be more recalcitrant or resistant to treatment, while others should be more tractable, depending on the details of the constraint hierarchy (c.f. Leonard, 1973; Dodd & Iacano, 1989). See Chapter 5 for an optimality theoretic reconsideration of a classic case of an unusual error pattern and the course of development following treatment. Finally, having arrived at a principled means for differentiating among recalcitrant and tractable error patterns, we are now in a better position to begin to evaluate alternate treatment methods that may be more or less effective in eradicating error patterns of these different types (e.g., Gierut, 1998c). For example, all of the treatment studies summarized here taught the child just one sound in one context, as required by the experimental design. Our characterization of these error patterns suggests that this plan for treatment will be effective for only some error patterns (e.g., Child 31 and Child 25). Other error patterns will ultimately require that multiple new sounds or contexts be taught, depending on the details of the constraint hierarchy. For example, we now know that children who exhibit omission of final obstruents will likely need to be taught both a stop and a fricative in final position in order to fully suppress the error pattern. These characterizations thus have some clinical utility in planning treatment (selecting treatment sounds and treatment contexts) and predicting the learning path.

Notes

* I am especially grateful to Judith Gierut and Laura McGarrity for their ongoing discussions about all aspects of this work. I would also like to thank John McCarthy, Amanda Edmonds, Ashley Farris-Trimble, Nick Henriksen, and Michele Morrisette for their many helpful contributions. This work was supported by a grant to Indiana University from the National Institutes of Health (NIH DC001694).

1 It is assumed that [s], dentalized (or distorted) [s̪], and [θ] are differentiated from one another in terms of the features [grooved] and [distributed]. As formulated here, *s would be violated by a candidate with a plain (nondistributed) [s] or a dentalized (distributed) [s̪], both of which are grooved. These sibilants are differentiated from interdentals, which are not grooved.

2 For a fuller discussion of the (de)merits of local conjunction and other proposals for achieving opacity effects (including sympathy and comparative markedness), see McCarthy (1999; 2002a), Łubowicz (2003), and references therein. For a discussion about the natural emergence of opacity effects in the course of acquisition, see Dinnsen, McGarrity, O'Connor & Swanson (2000) and Chapter 4 in this volume.

3 Other rankings of these constraints are compatible with the facts of this stage. However, an effort has been made throughout the chapter to avoid the stipulation of crucial rankings, unless otherwise motivated. Additionally, constraints have been ranked to reflect as much as possible the default ranking of markedness over faithfulness and to provide for continuity in the transition from one stage to the next. For example, we have no evidence based on the facts of this stage that *θ must outrank ID[grooved], except that the ranking reflects the default ranking and the requirement that faithfulness constraints be ranked as low as possible (e.g., Hayes, 2004; Prince & Tesar, 2004).

4 While other rankings can account for this particular stage, we will see that this ranking is necessary to account for the subsequent overgeneralization.

5 The phonology of this child (who has also been identified as MB) is described more fully in Dinnsen and Maxwell (1981) and Dinnsen and Elbert (1984).

6 In contrast to Child 25, this child was credited with some emerging pretreatment knowledge of velars due to the fact that she produced a few words with a target-appropriate velar. It should, however, be noted that those words were morphologically complex, and the velar consonants occurred only in word-medial, morpheme-final position, e.g., [waki] 'rock (dimin.)'. Those same morphemes alternated with a coronal consonant in absolute word-final position. For an optimality theoretic account of similar alternations, see Dinnsen and McGarrity (1999; 2004). In any event, we will see that the apparent advantage afforded by this minimal knowledge was ultimately not helpful to the child in her learning of velars.

7   This account employs a contextual markedness constraint (*#k); however, an alternative account is also available that appeals instead to a positional faithfulness constraint relativized to postvocalic position. Under that scenario, it would be the positional faithfulness constraint and the context-free version of the faithfulness constraint that are in a special/general relation. Whether contextual markedness or positional faithfulness is employed, the contextual restrictions incorporated in any of these constraints do not correspond with standard assumptions about contextual asymmetries in fully developed languages. For more on this, see the discussion later in this section and in Morrisette, Dinnsen and Gierut (2003) and Chapter 9 in this volume.

9   The prominence paradox*

Daniel A. Dinnsen & Ashley W. Farris-Trimble
Indiana University

Phonological contrasts tend to be preserved or enhanced in prominent
contexts and are often merged or lost in weak contexts. One issue for
the continuity hypothesis (Pinker, 1984) is whether children and adults
treat prominent contexts in the same way. This chapter addresses this
question by documenting what appears to be a prominence paradox:
Fully developed languages preserve contrasts in one set of contexts,
but children tend to acquire those contrasts first in the complementary
set of contexts. An optimality theoretic solution to the paradox is put
forward that draws upon psycholinguistic evidence of a developmental shift in contextual prominence. The consequence is that the theory
can retain a universal constraint set that is limited and identical for both
children and adults. Additionally, purported typological asymmetries
in the transition from initial- to final-state grammars can be integrated
in a theoretically uniform and psychologically valid way.

1   Introduction

Research on the phonologies of fully developed languages has identified certain
contexts within a word to be preferred for signaling meaning differences and
phonemic contrasts. Contrasts thus tend to be preserved in those contexts
while being merged or neutralized in others. Some examples of contexts that
have been shown to resist mergers include word-, foot- and syllable-initial
position (Beckman, 1998; Lombardi, 1999; de Lacy, 2002; Smith, 2002).
These contexts are considered to be strong, perceptually salient, privileged,
or prominent. Conversely, contexts that are vulnerable to neutralization tend not
to be initial and include word- or syllable-final position or foot-medial position.
These non-initial contexts are considered to be weak or nonprominent. The
languages of the world provide many examples of phonological processes that

are restricted to neutralize voice, place, or manner contrasts in these presumably weak contexts.

The facts relating to contextual prominence and the preservation/merger of contrast converge to yield a typological hypothesis—'the prominence hypothesis'—which maintains that there are languages that exhibit a particular contrast in: (a) both a strong and a weak context, (b) a strong, but not a weak context, or (c) neither a strong nor a weak context. This hypothesis makes the further asymmetric prediction that there should be no language that exhibits a particular contrast in a weak context while merging it in a strong context. Thus, while languages can differ in the presence/absence of a contrast as well as in whether they maintain that contrast in a weak context, they apparently cannot differ by what counts as a strong context for a given contrast. This suggests that contextual prominence is universal and that all languages will preserve/ neutralize contrasts in accord with the prominence hypothesis above. Extending this hypothesis to acquisition, continuity considerations would predict further that children at any single point in time will display the same typology for contextual prominence seen in fully developed languages. This means that children would be expected to first acquire a contrast, if at all, in a strong position and only later in weak positions. We might also expect children to evaluate the relative prominence of contexts in the same way that adults do, arriving at the same designations for what constitutes a strong/weak context. Any departures from these predictions would represent a paradox for the prominence hypothesis. One of the main purposes of this chapter is to document cases where children maintain contrasts in what would be considered a weak context (from the perspective of fully developed languages) while neutralizing them in so-called strong contexts, precisely what would seem to be excluded by both the prominence hypothesis and continuity considerations. This paradox, if real, is important to optimality theory because it challenges one of its basic tenets, namely that the constraint set is universal and the same for children and adults. The developmental facts would seem to require a set of constraints that is quite different from those required for fully developed languages. We will, however, offer a solution to this problem that draws, in part, on psycholinguistic evidence of a developmental shift in prominence, allowing the constraint set to remain the same for children and adults.

The chapter is organized as follows: In §2, we present a range of developmental phenomena that runs counter to expectations of fully developed languages. More specifically, different children are shown to neutralize a variety of contrasts in word-initial position while maintaining those contrasts elsewhere. Our solution to this apparent paradox is presented in §3. In §4, we present further independent support for our solution and consider some of its implications. §5 concludes the chapter with a brief summary.

2   Problematic developmental facts

This section presents evidence from the Developmental Phonology Archive and the published literature showing that at least some children merge voice, place, and manner contrasts in word-initial position while maintaining those contrasts in other contexts. It will also be shown that some children even omit initial consonants while retaining them in other contexts. This is just the opposite of what has been observed in fully developed languages.[1] These facts will come as no surprise to acquisition researchers because the phenomena depicted here are quite common in the early phonologies of children with typical and atypical phonological development. However, what is surprising is that little or no theoretical attention has been given to reconciling this disparity between developing and fully developed languages.

2.1   The voice contrast

Of the many contrasts in English that children must acquire, probably the greatest research attention has been given to the voice contrast. While the English laryngeal distinction is often referred to in terms of the feature [voice], convincing arguments have been made for the alternative view that the distinction in English is one of aspiration associated with the feature [spread glottis] (e.g., Iverson & Salmons, 1995). We will, nevertheless, use the term 'voice' throughout simply because that is what appears in much of the acquisition literature and is how the children's outputs are typically transcribed. Unfortunately, because most of the available studies have focused exclusively on a single context, either word-initial or word-final position, it is not possible to determine from those studies in which contexts the voice contrast first arises. For a summary review of the descriptive and instrumental findings from some of the classic studies, see Weismer (1984) and Dinnsen, McGarrity, O'Connor and Swanson (2000). Suffice it to say, the implementation of the voice contrast in any context poses a challenge for children, whether typically developing or not. Nevertheless, the prominence hypothesis predicts that this contrast will be acquired more easily in strong contexts. There are a few studies that have traced the development of the voice contrast across contexts (e.g., Smith, 1973; Dinnsen, 1996; Kager, van der Feest, Fikkert, Kerkhoff & Zamuner, 2003). The general finding from these and other studies is that the voice contrast emerges first in word-final position. At that point in time, word-initial voiced and voiceless obstruents are realized as voiced (or more properly as voiceless unaspirated), resulting in the merger of the laryngeal distinction in initial position. The developmental facts relating to the contextual merger of the voice contrast are important because they are at odds with the common phenomenon of word-final or syllable-final devoicing observed in many languages (e.g., Catalan, German, Polish). The developmental facts also run counter to the observed implicational relationship in fully developed languages which finds that the maintenance of a voice contrast in final position implies the presence of a voice contrast in initial position (e.g., Dinnsen & Eckman, 1975).

The data in (1) exemplify the general developmental finding about the emergence of the voice contrast in final position. These data were drawn from the Developmental Phonology Archive and are from Child 180 (age 5 years; 5 months). Note in (1a) and (1b) that word-initial voiced and voiceless labial stops are realized as voiced, merging the voice contrast in that context. The forms in (1c) and (1d) show that the voice contrast is maintained word-finally.

(1)   Child 180 (age 5;5)

    a)   Word-initial target /p/ realized as [b]
        [bɪd]   'pig'   [bits]   'peach'
        [beɪnt] 'paint'   [baɪ]   'pie'
        [bænts] 'pants'

    b)   Word-initial target /b/ realized as [b]
        [bɪd]   'big'   [but]   'boot'
        [bæd]   'bag'   [bɛd]   'bed'
        [bʌs]   'bus'

    c)   Word-final target /p/ realized as [p]
        [soʊp] 'soap'   [sup]   'soup'
        [sɪp]   'chip'   [sʌp]   'cup'
        [sip]   'sleep'

    d)   Word-final target /b/ realized as [b]
        [wɛb]   'web'   [tɑb]   'cob'
        [sʌb]   'tub'   [wʌb]   'rub'
        [stʌb] 'scrub'

2.2   The place contrast

Children with typical and atypical phonological development often exhibit a range of problems with their acquisition of English place contrasts. Two of the most common contextually restricted error patterns involving place features are Consonant Harmony (e.g., Smith, 1973; Stoel-Gammon & Stemberger, 1994; Goad, 1997; Pater & Werle, 2001; Chapter 4 in this volume) and Velar Fronting (e.g., Ingram, 1974; Stoel-Gammon, 1996; Bernhardt & Stemberger,

1998; Inkelas & Rose, 2003; Chapter 8 in this volume). Consonant Harmony is a regressive assimilatory neutralization process affecting place features and is often restricted to word-initial position (e.g., 'take' realized as [kek]). The sounds that are vulnerable to assimilation tend to be word-initial coronal stops. The trigger of assimilation tends to be a postvocalic labial or dorsal consonant. This error pattern has the effect of merging the place contrast in word-initial position while allowing it to be preserved in the triggering postvocalic context.[2]

The other common contextually conditioned error pattern affecting place features, Velar Fronting, is a nonassimilatory neutralization process restricted to word-initial position. This process is illustrated by the data in (2) from Child 173 (age 5;11). Note in (2a) and (2b) that the place contrast between coronals and dorsals is merged in favor of a coronal in word-initial position. The forms in (2c) and (2d) show that the place contrast between coronals and dorsals is preserved in word-final position.

(2) Child 173 (age 5;11)

  a) Word-initial target /k/ realized as [t]
      [tɔb]   'cob'   [toʊm] 'comb'
      [toʊt] 'coat'   [tʌp]   'cup'
      [tʌt]   'cut'

  b) Word-initial target /t/ realized as [t]
      [toʊz] 'toes'   [tijʊ] 'tear'
      [tʌb]   'tub'   [tʌŋ]   'tongue'
      [taɪgʊ] 'tiger'

  c) Word-final target /k/ realized as [k]
      [s̥ɔk]   'sock'   [bæk]   'back'
      [bʊk]   'book'   [wɔk]   'rock'
      [dʌk]   'duck'

  d) Word-final target /t/ realized as [t]
      [but]   'boot'   [itˈ]   'eat'
      [fʊtˈ] 'foot'   [tʌt]   'cut'
      [baɪt] 'bite'

Inkelas and Rose (2003) have commented on the disparity of this restriction on Velar Fronting relative to restrictions in fully developed languages and attempted to explain why children's Velar Fronting error pattern would be restricted to word-initial position. Their explanation was based on a combination of factors, including anatomical considerations (i.e., young children's presumably large tongue size relative to a small oral cavity) and enhanced articulation associated with a prosodically strong context, all of which is hypothesized to lead to coronal release for a target velar in word-initial position. Such an explanation must, however, be reconciled against those other cases where children do just the opposite, namely substitute a velar for a coronal (Coronal Backing) in word-initial position (e.g., Morrisette, Dinnsen & Gierut, 2003). Additionally, we might expect the purported anatomical factors leading to this error pattern to be attenuated as children get older and the size of the tongue body and oral cavity normalize; yet, this error pattern is quite common in older children with phonological delays.

The place error patterns discussed in this section are at odds with well known restrictions on place features in fully developed languages. The presumed prominence of onsets in word-initial position is expected to resist place mergers in that context, especially if place is licensed in codas (e.g., Steriade, 1995). Additionally, the well supported observation in fully developed languages that coda position is vulnerable to place mergers has given rise to markedness constraints banning place features in that context (e.g., Coda Condition; Itô, 1989).

2.3   The manner contrast

Among the manner classes of English that pose the greatest problem for children are fricatives, affricates, and liquids. When these sounds come into the child's system, they are often acquired first in final position. This has been documented for fricatives (e.g., Ferguson, 1978), the rhotic liquid /r/ (e.g., Smit, 1993a), and affricates (e.g., Smit, 1993a; Chapter 4 in this volume). In those cases, the same manner class is produced in error in word-initial position, merging a manner contrast in that context. As with place features (§2.2), the mergers can be attributed to assimilatory and nonassimilatory processes. For example, several different types of manner assimilation have been reported by Dinnsen (1998). Those cases all found the target of assimilation to be restricted to word-initial position and the trigger to be a specified manner of a postvocalic consonant (e.g., 'yellow' realized as [lɛlo]). A commonly occurring nonassimilatory manner merger restricted to word-initial position would be Deaffrication (e.g., 'chew' realized as [tu], cf. 'peach' realized as [pits]). This process was also documented for Child 142 (age 4;3) in Chapter 4 in this volume.

As a further illustration of a nonassimilatory merger of the stop/fricative contrast in word-initial position, we present data from Child 110 (age 6;0) in (3). Note in (3a) and (3b) that word-initial labial stops and fricatives are realized as a stop. The forms in (3c) and (3d) show, however, that the stop/fricative contrast is preserved in final position.

(3) Child 110 (age 6;0)

    a) Word-initial target /v/ realized as [b]
       [bənɪjə]   'vanilla'   [bæd]   'van'
       [bæʔətaĩ] 'valentine' [bæʔwum] 'vacuum'
       [bɛzəbouˢ] 'vegetable'

    b) Word-initial target /b/ realized as [b]
       [bæt]   'back'   [bʊt]   'book'
       [bɛd]   'bed'   [bʌs]   'bus'
       [baɪʔ]   'bite'

    c) Word-final target /v/ realized as [v]
       [weɪv]   'wave'   [glʌv]   'glove'
       [tsoʊv]   'stove'   [tʃaɪv]   'drive'
       [ʃeɪv]   'shave'

    d) Word-final target /b/ realized as [b]
       [wɛb]   'web'   [wʌb]   'rub'
       [tɔb]   'cob'   [tʌb]   'tub'
       [woʊb]   'robe'

The contextual restriction to word-initial position in these manner mergers runs counter to observed restrictions in fully developed languages. If a language preserves a manner contrast anywhere, it is expected to be in initial position. Likewise, if a language merges a manner contrast anywhere, it is expected to be in coda position. For example, Korean merges its distinction between stops, fricatives, and affricates in codas (Ahn, 1998).

2.4   Initial consonant omission

Each of the phenomena described above represented a commonly occurring error pattern that involved a merger of a single voice, place, or manner distinction in word-initial position. Another type of error pattern restricted to word-initial position that results in a wholesale merger of contrasts is Initial Consonant Omission (e.g., Rockman, Dinnsen & Rowland, 1983; Ingram, 1989; Gierut, 1989b; Howell & Dean, 1994; Schwartz & Goffman, 1995; Savinainen-Makkonen, 2000). This process appears to be unattested in fully developed languages, and its contextual restriction is just the opposite of that associated with constraints or processes in fully developed languages in which consonants are prohibited in coda position.

    The data in (4) are drawn from Rockman, Dinnsen and Rowland (1983) and exemplify the error pattern of Initial Consonant Omission for one child with a phonological delay. The forms in (4a) reveal that a broad range of consonants were omitted in initial position.[3] The forms in (4b) show that those same consonants were retained in postvocalic contexts.

(4)   Child RDR (age 4;0)

   a)   Initial consonants omitted

[ɛnsəl]	'pencil'	[up]	'soup'
[aɪk]	'bike'	[ɛtsəs]	'catches'
[æn]	'man'	[aʊd]	'loud'
[ʌtʃ]	'touch'	[imeɪk]	'remake'
[oʊn]	'don't'	[æt]	'that'
[aʊ]	'now'		

   b)   Postvocalic consonants retained

[hip]	'keep'	[ɜdaʊs]	'birdhouse'
[ibeɪk]	'rebake'	[ɪək]	'milk'
[æmɚ]	'hammer'	[igo]	're-go'
[itɪŋ]	'eating'	[ɛnsəl]	'pencil'
[idu]	'redo'	[ætʃəs]	'matches'
[inu]	'renew'	[ɪdʒ]	'bridge'
[ɪʃ]	'fish'		

One of the other studies cited above in this subsection is especially interesting because it reports longitudinal evidence of Initial Consonant Omission for 6 typically developing children (age 1;3–2;5) acquiring Finnish (Savinainen-Makkonen, 2000). These errors are striking because they occur in stressed syllables, which might be thought to resist mergers. However, Schwartz and Goffman (1995) found in their English study that omissions were more common in stressed as opposed to unstressed syllables.

   While the error pattern of Initial Consonant Omission does not appear to be as prevalent as the other error patterns considered in §2 (only around 5% of the children in our archive exhibited some form of this error pattern), it serves to show that word-initial position behaves as if it were weak relative to final position. That is, initial position is rendered vulnerable to mergers—even wholesale mergers—and postvocalic or final position is preferred for the preservation of contrasts.

2.5   Other comparable case studies

The works cited above are just a few of the available case studies that document children's merger of a contrast in word-initial position while maintaining that contrast elsewhere. The appendix at the end of this chapter provides a partial listing of other comparable developmental studies. Several of the children cited in the appendix exhibited multiple error patterns that merged different distinctions in initial position and are thus mentioned more than once. The significance of this point will be made clear when we consider the further implications of our account in §4.6.

Before moving on to our account, it should be noted that the reported mergers above and in most other acquisition studies are based on impressionistic phonetic transcriptions. When instrumental acoustic analyses have been employed in some studies to validate children's presumed mergers, it has sometimes been found that some of those children were preserving subtle acoustic distinctions that were otherwise not discernable by the transcriber (e.g., Kornfeld & Goehl, 1974; Maxwell & Weismer, 1982; Hoffman, Stager & Daniloff, 1983; Weismer, 1984; Forrest, Weismer, Milenkovic & Dougall, 1988; Hoffman & Damico, 1988; Forrest, Weismer, Hodge, Dinnsen & Elbert, 1990; Forrest, Weismer, Elbert & Dinnsen, 1994; Scobbie, 1998; Cohn & Kishel, 2002; 2003). Caution is thus called for in the interpretation of any claims of a merger, whether based on impressionistic phonetic transcription or instrumental studies that fail to find a systematic phonetic distinction. It is, however, important to keep in mind that the situation is exactly the same for presumed mergers in fully developed languages, which are also based largely on impressionistic phonetic transcriptions. A host of instrumental studies have found that subtle acoustic differences were being maintained by some speakers of certain languages, contrary to widely held assumptions (e.g., Dinnsen & Charles-Luce, 1984; Dinnsen, 1985; Port & O'Dell, 1985; Slowiaczek & Dinnsen, 1985; Charles-Luce, 1987). In any event, subtle, but systematic phonetic distinctions (whether in developing or fully developed languages) can be taken as evidence that the speaker has at least some knowledge of an underlying distinction. However, the phonetic implementation of that distinction may be sufficiently weak that it has no communicative function or perceptual salience and thus results in a merger.

3   An optimality theoretic account

3.1   Contextual mergers in optimality theory

Before we formulate an account of the developmental facts from the prior section, let us first briefly review how optimality theory typically deals with contextual mergers in fully developed languages. Two different approaches making essentially the same typological predictions have been advanced. One approach relies on a positional faithfulness constraint to preserve a contrast in a prominent context (e.g., Beckman, 1998; Lombardi, 1999). What serves as a prominent context is stipulated and may be specific to the property to be preserved. The positional faithfulness constraint is ranked above a general antagonistic markedness constraint which in turn is ranked above a context-free faithfulness constraint. German serves as a standard example of a language that maintains a voice contrast in onsets while merging that contrast in codas. The prominence of onsets and their resistance to mergers with regard to laryngeal features is captured by stipulating the contextual restriction to onsets in the definition of a laryngeal faithfulness constraint (e.g., ID-Onset[laryngeal]). By ranking the general markedness constraint *Laryngeal below the positional faithfulness constraint, the [voice] feature would be preserved in onsets but banned in all other contexts. The following schema serves to illustrate how the merger of the voice contrast is achieved in codas in fully developed languages: ID-Onset[laryngeal] >> *Laryngeal >> ID[laryngeal].

The alternative approach to contextual mergers relies instead on a highly ranked markedness constraint that is formulated to ban a marked property in a specific context, i.e., one that is nonprominent or weak. For example, the markedness constraint relevant to the merger of the voice contrast in codas, *Voiced-Coda, simply bans voiced obstruents in codas (e.g., Kager, 1999). By ranking ID[laryngeal] between *Voiced-Coda and the context-free *Laryngeal, a contrast is permitted to occur in a prominent onset context but not in the weak coda context. The schema for this alternative approach would entail the following constraints and ranking: *Voiced-Coda >> ID[laryngeal] >> *Laryngeal. No matter which approach (or combination of approaches) one adopts, the assumption is that constraints from the same family are generally asymmetric in their substantive formulation.[4] That is, if some constraint bans a feature in codas, the expectation is that there should be no constraint banning that same feature in the specific context of onsets. Similarly, if some positional faithfulness constraint demands featural identity between corresponding input and output segments in the prominent context of onsets, no positional faithfulness constraint relating to the same feature would be restricted to the complementary context of codas.

Either of these general approaches fails to account for the developmental facts from the prior section. One possible solution might be to give up the asymmetric character of constraints and postulate the existence of additional constraints from the same family with the stipulation of opposite or complementary contextual restrictions. For example, a positional faithfulness account of children's acquisition of the laryngeal contrast might seem to require an additional highly ranked faithfulness constraint stipulating the preservation of the voice contrast in codas while allowing it to be merged in word-initial position due to a lower-ranked markedness constraint. The hypothetical constraint that is called for might be ID-CODA[laryngeal], but that constraint is the complement of what is needed for fully developed languages, namely ID-ONSET[laryngeal]. The same issue arises with regard to constraints involving place and manner contrasts. We could, of course, expand the constraint set to include constraints defined on complementary contexts, but the permutable rankings of these constraints would predict a wider range of variation than has been observed in fully developed languages. This constitutes a serious drawback for this approach.

The facts of fully developed and developing phonologies leave little doubt about the need for contextual restrictions of some kind in the substantive formulation of constraints. The real issue is whether those restrictions need to be stipulated, as has been assumed, and whether the restrictions are the same for developing and fully developed languages. In the next section, we put forward a solution that allows us to derive prominence and retain a universal constraint set that is the same for children and adults.

3.2   The solution

One element of our solution introduces two new families of competing markedness constraints that have the effect of deriving prominence (rather than stipulating it). Under this proposal, what serves as a prominent context is derived from the ranking of competing universal markedness constraints given in (5). These markedness constraints assign or license prominence in certain prosodic domains. For example, one such markedness constraint from the INITIALPROM family holds at the level of the syllable and would assign prominence to syllable onsets (and only that subsyllabic constituent); the other competing markedness constraint from the FINALPROM family would assign prominence to the complementary subsyllabic constituent, namely rhymes. A candidate incurs a violation of these constraints if it fails to have prominence in the licensed context or if it includes prominence in a context that does not license prominence.

(5)   Prominence-assigning markedness constraints

> INITIALPROM: The initial constituent of a syllable, foot, or prosodic word
>   must be prominent
> FINALPROM: The final constituent of a syllable, foot, or prosodic word must
>   be prominent
>
> Default ranking: FINALPROM >> INITIALPROM

Depending on how these markedness constraints are ranked, one or the other context, but not both, would be realized with prominence. It is assumed that no more than one constituent of a particular prosodic domain can be prominent. This is similar to the restriction that a foot can have no more than one head, and every foot must have a head. We further assume, for reasons to be discussed below, that the default ranking of these markedness constraints results in rhymes being prominent in the initial state. Clearly, the ranking of these two prominence-assigning markedness constraints must change over time if the well established prominence of onsets in fully developed languages is to be accounted for. We hypothesize that one possible explanation for the reranking of prominence-assigning constraints may draw on increases in the size of the lexicon and the need to differentiate words in more densely packed lexical neighborhoods. This hypothesis accords with the widely held developmental perspective that the lexicon undergoes a restructuring that leads to more elaborate, detailed representations (e.g., Walley, Metsala & Garlock, 2003). Additionally, some psycholinguistic studies have documented a developmental shift in the prominence of subsyllabic structures with the early salience of rhymes giving way to more enhanced onsets (see §4.1 for some highlights from relevant studies and Munson and Babel (2005) for a more thorough review).

Given that the lexicon under normal circumstances does not get smaller as time goes on, no fact would ever motivate a further reranking of the prominence-assigning constraints. Consequently, once onsets have become prominent due to the first reranking of the prominence-assigning markedness constraints, the ranking of these constraints essentially becomes fixed with onsets remaining prominent in fully developed languages.

With the prominence-assigning markedness constraints determining what is prominent, positional faithfulness constraints can then take advantage of that licensed prominence at any stage of development by simply specifying that the constraint holds only in a prominent context. We will be formulating our solution in terms of positional faithfulness, but it could as well be recast in contextual markedness terms.[5] The formulation of positional faithfulness constraints can in turn be constrained or simplified in that the prominence of a specific context would not need to be stipulated; instead, the constraint would simply specify that it is sensitive to prominence at some higher prosodic level (e.g., the syllable, foot, or word).

The following serves as a generic account of the contextual mergers described in §2. The constraints in (6) are defined in general terms, but they can be instantiated with any of the relevant voice, place, or manner features. Similarly, the prominence-assigning constraint INITIALPROM in (5) above should be interpreted as referring to a family of constraints holding at the level of the syllable, foot, or word. This constraint assigns prominence to the initial constituent of a prosodic category (e.g., either the onset of a syllable, the initial syllable of a foot, or the initial foot of a word). The other family of prominence-assigning constraints, FINALPROM, in (5) refers to the complementary class of constituents within a given prosodic domain (e.g., the syllable rhyme, the final syllable of a foot, or the final foot of the word).

(6)   Generic constraints

    a)   Faithfulness
       ID-PROM[feature]:   Corresponding segments in prominent contexts must have identical voice, place, or manner features
       ID[feature]:   Corresponding segments must have identical voice, place, or manner features

    b)   Segmental/featural markedness
       *FEATURE: Voice, place, or manner features are banned

Let us now reconsider the case of Child 173, who merged the place contrast word-initially, but maintained it word-finally in rhymes. The prominence-assigning markedness constraints are interpreted in this instance as holding at the syllable level and require that either syllable onsets or syllable rhymes, but not both, be prominent. All candidates will thus violate one or the other of these constraints. Any single candidate with both a prominent onset and a prominent rhyme or a candidate with neither a prominent onset nor a prominent rhyme is especially disfavored, violating both constraints. By appealing to the default ranking of FINALPROM over INITIALPROM, all candidates that have initial prominence or that lack final prominence are assigned fatal violations, independent of the segmental content of the candidate. The remaining candidates with final prominence clearly violate INITIALPROM, but the lower ranking of that constraint makes those violations less serious. The positional faithfulness constraint is defined in terms of prominence at the syllable level and demands that input and output segments in the prominent part of the syllable be identical in terms of place features. Given that the hierarchy for Child 173 designates rhymes to be prominent, the highly ranked positional faithfulness constraint will assign fatal violations to all candidates that are unfaithful in terms of place features in the rhyme. Place is thus preserved in rhymes.

    The merger of place in word-initial position comes about from the violation of a context-free markedness constraint banning dorsals, i.e., *k. Given that onsets are not prominent according to this child's grammar, the positional faithfulness constraint does not contribute to preserving place in onsets.

The tableaux in (7) show how place is preserved word-finally when the rhymes are prominent. Notice that phonetically identical candidates differ in the location of prominence. The prominent part of a candidate is indicated in boldface.

(7)   Place contrast preserved word-finally

/bʊk/ 'book'	FINALPROM	ID-PROM[place]	INITIALPROM	*k	ID[place]
a. bʊk	*!			*	
b. ☞ bʊk			*	*	
c. bʊt	*!				*
d. bʊt		*!	*		*
e. bʊt	*!		*		*
f. bʊk	*!		*	*	

/but/ 'boot'	FINALPROM	ID-PROM[place]	INITIALPROM	*k	ID[place]
a. but	*!				
b. ☞ but			*		
c. buk	*!			*	*
d. buk		*!	*	*	*

The tableaux in (8) demonstrate how the merger of the place contrast is achieved in nonprominent word-initial position.

(8)   Place contrast merged word-initially

/kɔb/ 'cob'	FINALPROM	ID-PROM[place]	INITIALPROM	*k	ID[place]
a. kɔb	*!			*	
b. kɔb			*	*!	
c. tɔb	*!	*			*
d. ☞ tɔb			*		*

/tʌb/ 'tub'	FINALPROM	ID-PROM[place]	INITIALPROM	*k	ID[place]
a. tʌb	*!				
b. ☞ tʌb			*		
c. kʌb	*!	*		*	*
d. kʌb			*	*!	*

The above account is a particular instantiation of what would be required generally for the cases presented in §2. If our hypothesis about prominence-assigning constraints is correct, we might also expect a child to evidence a shift in prominence from the default ranking to the reverse ranking with little else in the grammar changing. Possible reasons for this shift are discussed below, but independent of the factors motivating the shift, the reranking of the prominence-assigning constraints would be manifest by a change in the contexts where a contrast is preserved/merged. The following section presents a case from the Developmental Phonology Archive instantiating this prediction and illustrating the independence of the prominence-assigning constraints.

3.3   A longitudinal shift in prominence

Child 96 (age 4;2) presented with a phonology that resembled that of the children from §2 in that she maintained a manner contrast between /d/ and /ð/ in postvocalic contexts, but merged the distinction in word-initial position. The postvocalic domain vis-à-vis prominence-assigning constraints will be discussed below. The data in (9) illustrate that early stage of development in which postvocalic position would have represented a prominent, contrast-preserving context for this child.

(9)   Child 96 (age 4;2): Manner contrast merged word-initially, but preserved postvocalically

| [dɪʔ] | 'that' | [dʌn] | 'done' | [ʌðʊr] | 'other' | [wædʊr] | 'ladder' |
| [dɛm] | 'them' | [dijʊr] | 'deer' | [mʌðʊr] | 'mother' | [mʌdi] | 'muddy' |

The data in (10) are from the same child five months later. Between these two intervals and as part of a larger experimental treatment study, the child was taught the word-initial cluster /skw/. Following that treatment, she showed no evidence of having generalized the cluster to untreated words. Additionally, several fricatives continued to be excluded from her inventory. However, some improvements were observed in word-initial affricates and /r/. Of greatest interest is the observation that /ð/ both improved and got worse at the same time. On the one hand, postvocalic /ð/, which in the earlier stage had been produced correctly and contrasted with /d/, merged with [d] in the later stage. The manner contrast was thus merged in postvocalic position. On the other hand, word-initial /ð/, which had been produced in error in the earlier stage, was produced correctly in the later stage, introducing a new manner contrast in that context. Postvocalic position no longer represented a prominent context for this child, but word-initial position came to behave as a prominent context, allowing the manner contrast to be preserved in that context.

(10) Child 96 (age 4;7): Manner contrast merged postvocalically, but preserved word-initially

| [ðæt] | 'that' | [dʌn] | 'done' | [ʌdʊr] | 'other' | [wædʊr] | 'ladder' |
| [ðɛm] | 'them' | [diʊr] | 'deer' | [mʌdʊr] | 'mother' | [mʌdi] | 'muddy' |

This case is interesting because the contexts in which the distinction between /d/ and /ð/ was merged and preserved were just the opposite in the two stages of development. Postvocalic position appears to have shifted from a prominent, contrast-preserving context to a nonprominent neutralizing context. This entailed a concomitant change in the prominence of word-initial position. As we will see below, this shift in prominence can be achieved quite simply by reranking the prominence-assigning constraints. But, what might have motivated this reranking? While treatment did not result in improvements for the treated cluster, it may well be that the shift in prominence was triggered by the treatment itself, which was focused on word-initial position. Little else of the constraint hierarchy changed across the two stages of development. The few segmental changes that did occur were limited to word-initial position and are not obviously related to the changes associated with /ð/. The independence of the prominence-assigning constraints is supported by the fact that the contrast between /d/ and /ð/ remained contextually restricted, albeit in different contexts, during both points in time.

The reference to postvocalic position in either stage of development involves a mix of different prosodic domains. On the one hand, postvocalic position refers to the coda of a syllable (especially a monosyllable), but it also refers to the onset of the second syllable of a foot. Our account thus needs to capture the prominence and unity of both postvocalic contexts in the earlier presenting stage. The prominence of a coda consonant in a monosyllabic word can be achieved by ranking FINALPROM over INITIALPROM in the domain of the syllable. However, for the onset of the second syllable to be prominent, FINALPROM would also need to dominate INITIALPROM, but in this instance, in the domain of the foot. The consequence of this latter ranking is that the entire final syllable of a two-syllable word is rendered prominent. The two different prosodic domains of the FINALPROM constraint converge to assign prominence to a consonant in postvocalic position, regardless of whether that consonant is the onset of the second syllable of a two-syllable word (foot prominence) or whether that consonant is in the rhyme of a monosyllabic word (syllable prominence). We will thus collapse the two different domains of FINALPROM into one unified constraint in our account of this case.

Our account of the early presenting stage for Child 96 is similar to that required for the other cases in §2. The relevant faithfulness and markedness constraints from §3.2 are instantiated here by manner features (shown in (11)). The tableaux in (12) illustrate our account of the merger of the manner contrast in word-initial position during that early stage. Given the ranking of FINALPROM over INITIALPROM, word-initial position would not be a prominent context. The highly ranked positional faithfulness constraint would thus not help in this instance to preserve the manner contrast in word-initial position. The markedness constraint banning interdental fricatives (*θ) is, however, decisive in the selection of the merged output.[6]

(11) Constraints and ranking

    a) Faithfulness

        ID-PROM[manner]: Corresponding segments in prominent contexts must have identical manner features

        ID[manner]: Corresponding segments must have identical manner features

    b) Markedness

        *θ: Interdental fricatives are banned

        Ranking: FINALPROM, ID-PROM[manner] >> INITIALPROM, *θ >> ID[manner]

(12) Manner contrast merged word-initially

/ðɛm/ 'them'	FINALPROM	ID-PROM[manner]	INITIALPROM	*θ	ID[manner]
a. dɛm	*!	*			*
b. ☞ dɛm			*		*
c. ðɛm	*!			*	
d. ðɛm			*	*!	

/dʌn/ 'done'	FINALPROM	ID-PROM[manner]	INITIALPROM	*θ	ID[manner]
a. dʌn	*!				
b. ☞ dʌn			*		
c. ðʌn	*!	*		*	*
d. ðʌn			*	*!	*

The tableaux in (13) show how the manner contrast is preserved in postvocalic contexts. The dominance of FINALPROM over INITIALPROM renders postvocalic positions prominent. The highly ranked positional faithfulness constraint is sensitive to prominence and is responsible for preserving the manner distinction in that prominent postvocalic context.

(13) Manner contrast preserved postvocalically

/mʌdi/ 'muddy'	FINALPROM	ID-PROM[manner]	INITIALPROM	*θ	ID[manner]
a.　　mʌdi	*!				
b. ☞ mʌdi			*		
c.　　mʌði	*!			*	*
d.　　mʌði		*!	*	*	*

/mʌðʊr/ 'mother'	FINALPROM	ID-PROM[manner]	INITIALPROM	*θ	ID[manner]
a.　　mʌdʊr	*!				*
b.　　mʌdʊr		*!	*		*
c.　　mʌðʊr	*!			*	
d. ☞ mʌðʊr			*	*	

Our account of the subsequent stage of development for Child 96 is identical to that of the prior stage, except for a change in the ranking of the prominence-assigning constraints. FINALPROM must be demoted below INITIALPROM to render word-initial position prominent. Note, as before, that in the case of monosyllabic words, INITIALPROM holds at the level of the syllable and assigns prominence to the word-initial onset consonant. In the case of bisyllabic words, INITIALPROM holds at the level of the foot and assigns prominence to the entire initial syllable of the foot. Importantly, the onset of the second syllable is no longer prominent. The tableaux given in (14) show how the manner contrast is preserved in word-initial position. With INITIALPROM assigning prominence to word-initial position, the highly ranked positional faithfulness constraint ensures that the manner contrast is preserved in that context.

(14) Manner contrast preserved word-initially

/ðɛm/ 'them'	INITIALPROM	ID-PROM[manner]	FINALPROM	*θ	ID[manner]
a.　　dɛm		*!	*		*
b.　　dɛm	*!				*
c. ☞ ðɛm			*	*	
d.　　ðɛm	*!			*	

/dʌn/ 'done'	INITIALPROM	ID-PROM[manner]	FINALPROM	*θ	ID[manner]
a. ☞ dʌn			*		
b.　　dʌn	*!				
c.　　ðʌn		*!	*	*	*
d.　　ðʌn	*!			*	*

In (15) we show how the manner contrast came to be merged in postvocalic contexts. With the shift in prominence to word-initial position, the positional faithfulness constraint is no longer relevant to postvocalic position and thus does not contribute to the preservation of manner in that context. The markedness constraint banning interdental fricatives does, however, get to play a role and results in a merger of the manner distinction in postvocalic position. This merger represents an apparent regression from a previously correct production to an erred production.[7] While a new error was introduced as a result of the shift in prominence, the fact is that new correct productions were also introduced at the same time in word-initial position. A simple trade-off does not appear to be involved here because the child's system has changed in a way that brings it into greater conformity with the typological properties of fully developed languages.

(15) Manner contrast merged postvocalically

/mʌdi/ 'muddy'	INITIALPROM	ID-PROM[manner]	FINALPROM	*θ	ID[manner]
a. ☞ mʌdi			*		
b. mʌdi	*!				
c. mʌði			*	*!	*
d. mʌði	*!	*		*	*

/mʌðʊr/ 'mother'	INITIALPROM	ID-PROM[manner]	FINALPROM	*θ	ID[manner]
a. ☞ mʌdʊr			*		*
b. mʌdʊr	*!	*			*
c. mʌðʊr			*	*!	
d. mʌðʊr	*!			*	

Summing up this case, the longitudinal development of Child 96 provides valuable support for the independence of the prominence-assigning constraints by showing that they can rerank while leaving much of the constraint hierarchy intact. The result of that reranking yields a phonology that looks more like those fully developed languages in which word-initial position is a prominent, contrast-preserving context with other contexts allowing mergers.

3.4   The course of development

Our account of the prominence paradox makes certain predictions about the course of development. Four fundamental and distinct stages can be discerned from an initial state to the end state. The constraint hierarchies for these stages are schematized in (16).

(16) Schema for stages of development

Stage	Facts	Ranking
1	Contrast merged in all contexts	FINALPROM, *FEATURE >> INITIALPROM, ID-PROM[feature], ID[feature]
2	Contrast preserved in final position, but merged in all other contexts	FINALPROM, ID-PROM[feature] >> INITIALPROM, *FEATURE >> ID[feature]
3	Contrast preserved in initial position, but merged in all other contexts	INITIALPROM, ID-PROM[feature] >> FINALPROM, *FEATURE >> ID[feature]
4	Contrast preserved in all contexts	INITIALPROM, ID-PROM[feature], ID[feature] >> FINALPROM, *FEATURE

The cases from §2 represent an early stage of development, but certainly not the initial state given that contrasts were preserved in some contexts. An even earlier stage of development (Stage 1) is assumed to have preceded the stage relating to the cases in §2. Stage 1 would have exhibited the default ranking of the prominence-assigning markedness constraints, but the positional faithfulness constraint would have been dominated by an antagonistic markedness constraint in accord with the default ranking of markedness over faithfulness. The default ranking of these various constraints would result in the absence of the particular contrast in all contexts, even prominent ones. Such a stage is typified by those many children who exclude one or more sound classes from their phonetic inventories.

Stage 2 involves the introduction of a featural contrast in a limited set of contexts—specifically in those contexts that are assigned prominence by default. This stage is characteristic of the cases in §2. Stage 2 would follow from Stage 1 by the simple demotion of a context-free markedness constraint banning a voice, place, or manner feature. That markedness constraint would be demoted below the antagonistic positional faithfulness constraint based on positive evidence and in accord with the requirement that general faithfulness constraints be ranked as low as possible (e.g., Hayes, 2004; Prince & Tesar, 2004). While this would result in a contrast being preserved in a prominent context and merged elsewhere, the affected contexts are just the opposite of what would be expected for the preservation/merger of contrasts in fully developed languages.

The change from Stage 2 to Stage 3 is illustrated by Child 96 and involves the reranking of the prominence-assigning constraints to yield a shift in prominence. The resultant designation of prominence is more in accord with the facts of fully developed languages. In this stage, a contrast is preserved in what is conventionally taken as a strong, prominent context while being merged elsewhere.

Stage 4 represents the end state for languages with a featural contrast in all contexts. Such a stage would follow from Stage 3 by the demotion of the context-free markedness constraint below the antagonistic context-free faithfulness constraint. Interestingly, Child 96 (4;9) also evidenced the transition from Stage 3 to Stage 4 at 2 months posttreatment, having acquired the manner contrast in all contexts.

Each of these individual stages has been amply documented in published cross-sectional or typological acquisition studies. Parts of the developmental progression have also been documented here and in other longitudinal studies, but no single study has yet exemplified all four stages in a given child. The hypothesized transition from the initial state to the end state does at least provide for plausible and minimal changes in the constraint hierarchy. Of course, we cannot necessarily expect to witness each of the intervening stages in all cases. Instantiating a child's particular developmental trajectory depends in part on the investigator's sampling intervals and the target language facts that a child might choose to take note of. The important point is that no child is predicted to proceed by reversing the order of any of these stages. This prediction is perhaps clearest when considering the logically possible alternative to the developmental profile of Child 96. That is, if a child were to present with a Stage 3 phonology in which a particular contrast occurred word-initially and was merged elsewhere, the contexts for the preservation/merger of that contrast should not switch in a subsequent stage (characteristic of Stage 2).[8] This hypothesis is more difficult to evaluate when a markedness constraint banning codas (NoCoda) remains highly ranked and only later is demoted below an antagonistic faithfulness constraint. Under those circumstances, there would have been no opportunity for contrasts to occur in coda position during the early stages. Contrasts would then arise first in onsets. After the demotion of NoCoda, contrasts could arise in codas, much later than they appeared in onsets. This cannot be taken as a challenge to our hypothesis if codas were not available to compete with onsets for new contrasts. For a further discussion of this issue, see §4.4. As additional longitudinal studies become available, it should be possible to more fully evaluate this developmental hypothesis.

4   Discussion

This section highlights other independent support for our hypotheses and considers some issues that arise from those proposals.

4.1   Psycholinguistic support

The facts considered thus far in this chapter have largely involved conventional internal linguistic evidence regarding children's synchronic grammars. However, two recent psycholinguistic studies are especially relevant to our proposals about the early prominence of rhymes and the reranking of prominence-assigning markedness constraints. Both studies provide external evidence of a developmental shift in the prominence of children's subsyllabic structures. In the first study, Brooks and MacWhinney (2000) report results from two experiments that were designed to test the effects of interfering primes in different age groups. They compared the effects of auditorily presented words with onset prime and rhyme prime in a picture-naming task. Thirty participants in four age groups (5 years, 7 years, 9+ years and college undergraduates) were divided into two groups. Participants were asked to name a picture after being presented auditorily with a stimulus word which was either identical to the picture, phonologically related, phonologically unrelated, or neutral. Of the phonologically related words, half of the participants received words that shared an onset with the picture word and half that shared a rhyme with the picture word. The 5-year-old children's picture naming was faster when they were presented with a rhyme prime word than with an onset prime word. 7-year-old children showed equal facility for the two sets of words, while older children and adults' productions were better facilitated by onset prime words. Brooks and MacWhinney conclude that there is a developmental change in speech production strategies—as children grow older, they restructure their lexicons in order to facilitate incremental production. As a default, though, young children's productions are most strongly influenced by the rhyme.

In another series of experiments, Coady and Aslin (2004) performed nonword repetition tasks with two groups of 12 children, ages 2;6 and 3;6. Both groups of children more accurately repeated 2- and 3-syllable nonwords that contained high frequency phonemes than they did nonwords that contained low frequency phonemes. However, in a second study, Coady and Aslin found that only the older set of children more accurately repeated nonwords in which the frequency difference occurred only in syllable onsets. The younger children showed no difference in accuracy in these words. Coady and Aslin concluded that while all the children were sensitive to the relative frequency of segments, only the older children were sensitive to more fine-grained frequency differences in onset position.

We take the findings of a developmental shift in the prominence of subsyllabic structures to reflect our proposed reranking of the prominence-assigning constraints and to be supportive of our claim that the default is for rhymes to be prominent in the early stages of acquisition.

4.2   Other evidence for the prominence of rhymes

Acquisition researchers have long recognized the perceptual salience of final position for young children (e.g., Slobin, 1973; Echols & Newport, 1992). Another piece of evidence for the default prominence of rhymes relates to the fact that vowels tend to be produced more accurately than onset consonants in the early stages of acquisition (e.g., Pollock & Keiser, 1990; Otomo & Stoel-Gammon, 1992; Pollock & Berni, 2003).

There is also some evidence that the prominence of rhymes persists for some phenomena, even after there has been a general shift of prominence to onsets for other phenomena. This is exemplified by onset structures that are dependent on an aspect of rhyme structure. That is, on the basis of cross-linguistic and developmental evidence, it has been observed that the occurrence of certain onset clusters in a language depends on the occurrence of complex (branching) rhymes in that language (e.g., Lleó & Prinz, 1996; Baertsch, 2002; Kirk & Demuth, 2003; Pan & Snyder, 2003; Kehoe & Hilaire-Debove, 2004; Levelt & van de Vijver, 2004). A promising optimality theoretic proposal for capturing this dependency is embodied in the 'split margin hierarchy' (Baertsch, 2002). Under this proposal, the occurrence of an onset stop+liquid cluster depends on the occurrence of a coda liquid consonant. The developmental prediction would also be that a stop+liquid cluster cannot be acquired without first having acquired a coda liquid consonant. For an overview and critique of the split margin hierarchy, see Chapter 13 in this volume. Independent of the theoretical account that one might adopt, the persistent dependency of onsets on rhymes can be seen as a possible remnant of the early developmental prominence of rhymes.

4.3   Lexical restructuring and richness of the base

Our proposal about the reranking of the prominence-assigning constraints was tied, in part, to the widely held view among acquisition researchers that children's lexical representations and the organization of their lexicons undergo a restructuring in the early stages (Treiman & Breaux, 1982; Charles-Luce

& Luce, 1990; 1995; Treiman & Zukowski, 1996; Metsala & Walley, 1998; Storkel, 2002; Walley et al., 2003). The general assumption has been that children begin with more holistic, syllable-sized representations. Those representations are presumed to be coarsely coded, underspecified, or otherwise unanalyzable. As new words are added to the lexicon and more and more words need to be differentiated, representations begin to restructure, becoming more elaborated or more fully specified. This developmental perspective might seem at odds with a basic tenet of optimality theory, namely richness of the base. The assumption of optimality theory is that input representations are universal and are thus the same for children and adults. Children's underlying representations should not be subject to change—contrary to what has typically been assumed by acquisition researchers. These seemingly incompatible positions can, however, be reconciled within optimality theory without violating richness of the base. That is, even during the earliest stages of acquisition, highly elaborate, adult-like, unchanging input representations can be adopted, if the markedness constraints that militate against structure outrank the faithfulness constraints. This is assumed to be the default ranking of constraints, and it mimics what would appear to be simple, underspecified representations. Over time, as markedness constraints are demoted on the basis of positive evidence, more elaborate representations are permitted to surface, revealing the rich base. Under this view, then, it is not the representations that change, but rather the constraint hierarchy. In this way, changes in the constraint hierarchy can be equated with apparent lexical restructuring. Consequently, when we talk about the reranking of the prominence-assigning constraints being triggered by lexical restructuring, this should more properly be interpreted to mean that the prominence-assigning constraints reranked in response to other changes in the constraint hierarchy that yielded the effect of lexical restructuring.

4.4   Prominent rhymes and final consonant omission

One of our central claims is that rhymes are rendered prominent in the initial state as a result of the default ranking of the prominence-assigning constraints. This might, however, seem at odds with the fact that many children in the early stages of acquisition omit coda consonants. Why would a child omit coda consonants if rhymes were truly prominent? This is reconciled by appealing to the independent and freely permutable markedness constraint NoCoda, which bans coda consonants. When NoCoda is ranked above the antagonistic faithfulness constraint, Max, which militates against deletion, coda consonants would be omitted, even if FinalProm were ranked above InitialProm. It is important to keep in mind that the prominence-assigning constraints conflict with one another, but they do not conflict with other segmental/featural markedness or faithfulness constraints. There is thus no antagonism between the prominence of rhymes and the presence/absence of coda consonants. The situation we are entertaining here is analogous to our characterization of a Stage 1 grammar from our discussion of the developmental trajectory in §3.4. Recall that Stage 1 involved the absence of one or more contrasts in all contexts, including those that were prominent. On the other hand, when NoCoda is demoted below Max, coda consonants would be preserved independent of the ranking of the prominence-assigning constraints. Importantly, the early demotion of NoCoda during the stages when rhymes are prominent (Stages 1 and 2) should result in the emergence of segmental contrasts first in rhymes. It is, of course, possible that NoCoda could be demoted late in the course of acquisition—after many segmental contrasts had already been established in onsets. In such a situation, it might mistakenly appear that our predictions were not supported because rhymes would lag behind onsets in the order and number of acquired contrasts. However, to properly evaluate our hypothesized developmental trajectory, it is important to identify a child who has demoted NoCoda early in the course of acquisition—before onsets and codas compete for featural contrasts (Stage 1).

4.5 Apparent counterexamples

The general observation for fully developed languages has been that syllable onsets and word-initial position are strong, prominent contexts that favor the preservation of contrasts. There is, however, some evidence that the prominence of a context may be dependent on the contrast to be preserved. For example, Steriade (2001) has argued on perceptual grounds that the transition from a vowel to a following consonant makes postvocalic position a preferred context for the preservation of an apical contrast between plain and retroflex consonants. She has observed that there are three basic types of languages relevant to this particular contrast, namely (a) those that maintain an apical contrast in both a post- and prevocalic context (e.g., Djinang), (b) those that maintain the contrast in postvocalic, but not prevocalic contexts (e.g., Murinbata and Miriwung), and (c) those that maintain the contrast in neither post- nor prevocalic contexts (e.g., English). Importantly, no language has yet been identified that maintains an apical contrast prevocalically without also maintaining that contrast postvocalically. Thus, while the details of the typology for an apical contrast may differ from most other contrasts, the same contextual asymmetry still holds such that the occurrence of a contrast in a certain context (i.e., a presumably weak context) implies its occurrence in other (stronger) contexts, but not vice versa. The only difference, then, in this case is in what constitutes a strong context for this particular contrast. We speculate further about this issue in §4.6 below.

Because there is otherwise a fairly uniform interpretation of what constitutes a prominent context for most distinctive features, a corollary of the prominence hypothesis would be that a strong context should exhibit as many or more distinctions than its weak counterpart. While this expectation is generally borne out, Parker (2001) has identified a potential counterexample in Chamicuro, where the inventory of consonants is more limited in the presumably strong context of syllable onsets while being more extensive in the weaker context of syllable codas: Codas can include glottal consonants while onsets cannot. Parker attributes this anomaly to a violable universal markedness constraint that demands that onsets have place, thus preventing placeless glottal consonants from occurring in onsets while allowing them (and other consonants) to occur in codas. Even though these facts might at first seem to run counter to the prominence hypothesis, Parker's arguments for this constraint are grounded in the attraction of marked structure to prominent positions (e.g., Zoll, 1998; Smith, 2002). Parker assumes that consonants with place features are structurally more complex (i.e., more marked) than placeless glottals and that onsets are prominent. This analysis meets with several difficulties, among them the unexpected defective distribution of an unmarked sound as well as the fact that the distribution of glottals has been argued to depend on language-specific differences in their relative sonority (de Lacy, 2002).

4.6   Some unresolved issues

While our proposals in this chapter solve certain problems, they also raise other questions and point to some promising areas in need of further research. For example, our proposal about the reranking of the prominence-assigning constraints raises questions about the nature of the evidence needed to trigger the reranking. We speculated that the reranking might be triggered by increases in the size of the lexicon. However, this hypothesis requires further experimental evaluation. If supported, it will also be important to determine the locus and threshold for change within the lexicon or within the constraint hierarchy. More psycholinguistic research is also called for to determine whether there is a developmental shift in the prominence of other prosodic constituents beyond the onset and rhyme. These questions highlight the need for more studies that are specifically designed to focus on the interaction between children's error patterns and the structure and organization of their lexicons.

Another issue that arises is whether some contexts are invariably prominent for certain featural contrasts. As we have formulated our proposal, the prominence-assigning constraints are freely permutable, at least to a certain extent, predicting that complementary contexts can be prominent either at different stages of development or in different children. This prediction was borne out for Child 96 as shown in §3.3. However, returning to Steriade's (2001) claims about the salience of postvocalic contexts for apical contrasts, it would appear that the prominence of that context may not change for that contrast (although she presented no developmental data on this point). If it were to turn out that certain contexts are invariably prominent for certain contrasts, it may be desirable to distinguish those from others that are vulnerable to a shift in prominence. This might be done by postulating positional faithfulness constraints that are restricted to those specific invariant features and contexts.

Most of the examples presented in this chapter have involved the contextual preservation/merger of a single distinctive feature. However, one prediction that follows from a ranked set of the prominence-assigning constraints is that a given context should affect several different features in the same way at a single point in time. This prediction is certainly supported by those many children who exhibit multiple independent error patterns that merge different contrasts in the same context (e.g., Child 142 and Child 209 in Chapter 4, as well as numerous examples in the appendix to this chapter). As a further test of this prediction, it will be important to determine whether there are cases where a child might, for example, merge one contrast in initial position and merge a different contrast in final position. If such cases were found, it would be necessary to modify our proposal. One possible approach to this problem might be to reformulate the prominence-assigning constraints with each relativized to specific features. It is unclear at present whether such an elaboration is necessary or desirable.

The prominence paradox is just one of several known disparities between developing and fully developed languages. Our proposal for dealing with this disparity may hold promise for resolving others. For example, one routinely cited difference relates to the phenomenon of long distance consonant harmony commonly observed in developing (but not fully developed) phonologies. The widely held assumption is that assimilation is local with the trigger and target being adjacent (Ni Chiosain & Padgett, 2001). The nonlocal character of children's consonant harmony processes challenges this assumption. Feature geometry with its hierarchical organization of features and autonomous tiers offers a structural means for characterizing limits on assimilatory processes. However, standard conceptions of feature geometry (e.g., Clements & Hume, 1995) only reinforce the disparity by integrating consonant and vowel features into a single geometry with vowel features as dependents of consonant place features. Such a configuration is intended to allow phonetically nonadjacent vowels to participate in harmony processes. More specifically, the assimilating vowel features are assumed to be on their own tier and would not incur line-crossing violations with intervening consonants. Those same geometries preclude place assimilation among nonadjacent consonants because the assimilating consonant features would incur a line-crossing violation with the intervening vowel.

To get around this problem, some have suggested that children's geometries may be simpler than those of adults, being configured with consonant and vowel features on entirely independent segregated tiers (e.g., McDonough & Myers, 1991; Macken, 1992). Such a proposal would allow phonetically nonadjacent consonants to be autosegmentally adjacent on the consonant tier and thus vulnerable to assimilation. This proposal would at least be consistent with standard locality expectations. Continuity considerations and richness of the base would, however, argue against any claims that children's geometries are inherently different from those of adults.

A possible alternative (similar to our solution to the prominence paradox) might be to postulate two competing markedness constraints that license particular geometric configurations in output candidates. One such constraint (INTEGRATEDGEOM) would require that vowel place features be licensed by a consonantal place node, favoring integrated geometries along the lines of Clements and Hume (1995). The other competing constraint (SEGREGATEDGEOM) would demand that consonant and vowel features be fully segregated, favoring geometries of the sort adopted by McDonough and Myers (1991) and Macken (1992). The default ranking of these constraints would find SEGREGATEDGEOM to dominate INTEGRATEDGEOM in the initial state. The default ranking would provide for the long distance consonant harmony effects during the early stages of development, and the reverse ranking would preclude such effects in fully developed languages. The trigger for the reranking might again be motivated by increases in the size of the lexicon and the need for greater differentiation within and across words. Once the geometry-licensing constraints have been reranked, that aspect of the hierarchy would remain stable. Our speculation about the resolution of this particular disparity between developing and fully developed languages clearly requires a more thorough examination, but it does at least illustrate how the insights of our solution to the prominence paradox can be extended to other cases.

5   Conclusion

The main purpose of this chapter was to show that children's error patterns are often restricted to word-initial position, merging a range of contrasts in that context, while maintaining those contrasts elsewhere within the word. The contextual restrictions on these processes are quite different from those observed for phonological processes in fully developed languages. Word-initial position is generally presumed to be a strong, prominent context that resists mergers in fully developed languages; other contexts are weaker and are thus vulnerable to mergers. This discrepancy between developing and fully developed languages represents what we have termed the 'prominence paradox' and undermines any claims of continuity (e.g., Pinker, 1984). A theory such as optimality theory with its strong universal claims is especially challenged to reconcile the discrepancy between these developmental facts and those of fully developed languages.

Our solution was to introduce two new competing families of prominence-assigning markedness constraints. One family (INITIALPROM) assigns or licenses prominence in the initial constituent of a syllable, foot, or prosodic word. The other competing family (FINALPROM) assigns prominence to the complementary final constituent of those same prosodic categories. The ranking of those constraints determines which prosodic constituents are prominent and thus likely to preserve contrasts. It was proposed that the default is for FINALPROM to be ranked over INITIALPROM. That ranking accounts for the early prominence of rhymes and final position and the emergence of many contrasts in those contexts. The reverse ranking of these constraints accounts for the prominence of onsets and initial position in fully developed languages. One likely trigger for the reranking of the prominence-assigning constraints was hypothesized to be a change in the size and organization of the lexicon in accord with experimental results revealing a developmental shift in the prominence of prosodic structures. Other factors may as well be responsible for reranking the prominence-assigning constraints, e.g., treatment that focuses the child's attention on word-initial position. With prominence determined from the ranking of the prominence-assigning constraints, the other positional faithfulness (or contextual markedness) constraints that depend on prominence can take advantage of that licensed prominence to preserve (or neutralize) a contrast.

One result of our proposal is that the constraint set can remain the same for developing and fully developed languages. As has been standard within optimality theory, the difference between these linguistic systems resides in the ranking of the constraints. Consequently, one of the most striking differences between developing and fully developed languages (vis-à-vis the prominence paradox) has in large part been obviated. The difference simply arises when developing phonologies rely on the default ranking of the universal prominence-assigning constraints, and fully developed languages rely on the reverse ranking of those constraints.

Appendix: Children's word-initial mergers

Word-initial Phenomenon	Participant	Source
affrication	Child A (3;3)	Hua & Dodd (2000)
chain shift	John (5;0)	Powell et al. (1999)
cluster affrication	S1 (5;0)	Grunwell (1982)
coda clusters acquired before onset clusters	9 subjects (1;0–1;11)	Levelt, Schiller & Levelt (1999/2000)
	5 subjects (0;9–2;1)	Lleó & Prinz (1996)
	9 subjects (1;7–2;7)	Kirk & Demuth (2003)
consonant deletion	1 (1;10); 2 (2;4); 3 (2;5)	Goldstein & Cintron (2001)
	SF (3;6); CS (5;1); YW (4;8); YL (5;11)	So & Dodd (1994)
	Oskar (4;5)	Nettelbladt (1983)
	Daniel (0;11–1;4)	Stoel-Gammon & Cooper (1984)
consonant harmony	Daniel (0;11–1;4)	Stoel-Gammon & Cooper (1984)
	Jennifer (4;4)	Edwards & Bernhardt (1973)
	Joe (4;6)	Lorentz (1976)
	Dylan (4;6–5;0)	Bernhardt (1994)
	Tom (6;0); Jim (4;6)	Compton (1970)
	Jennika (1;3–1;4)	Ingram (1974)
	126 (3;11); 132 (3;9)	Dinnsen & O'Connor (2001a)
	CS (5;1)	So & Dodd (1994)
coronal backing	LP76 (4;3)	Morrisette, Dinnsen & Gierut (2003)
deaffrication	Keith (5;2)	Powell et al. (1999)
	5 subjects	Grunwell (1977)
	Pamela (7;2)	Grunwell (1975)
	BN (5;2)	Pollack & Rees (1972)
deaspiration	Jim (4;6); Tom (6;0)	Compton (1970)
	Linn's girl (1;10)	Linn (1971)
debuccalization	Larissa; Blair; Sean; Chrissie	Bernhardt & Stemberger (1998)
	Albert (4;0)	Nettelbladt (1983)
dentalization	John (5;0)	Powell et al. (1999)
desonorization	9 (3;9)	Dinnsen & O'Connor (2001b)
	S3 (6;3)	Grunwell (1977)
devoicing	Graham (9;0)	Grunwell (1988)

	5 (3;8); 9 (3;9); 23 (4;8)	Dinnsen & O'Connor (2001b)
gliding	Graham (9;0)	Grunwell (1988)
	S1 (5;0); S5 (8;0)	Grunwell (1977)
	Larry	Bernhardt (1994)
lateralization	Chad (5;9)	Powell et al. (1999)
nasal gliding	S4 (6;11)	Grunwell (1977)
nasal harmony	Ethel I	Hinckley (1915)
	Sally and Suzy (3;10)	Powell et al. (1999)
nasal substitution	Marcy (3;3)	Bernhardt (1994)
retroflex fronting	Child A (3;3); Child B (4;3)	Hua & Dodd (2000)
rhoticism	Martin (6;3)	Grunwell (1975)
spirantization	OC (5;0)	So & Dodd (1994)
	DE	Stoel-Gammon & Dunn (1985)
	126 (3;11)	Dinnsen & O'Connor (2001a)
	Larissa	Stemberger (1993)
stopping	Child B (4;3)	Hua & Dodd (2000)
	Albert (4;0)	Nettelbladt (1983)
	Stephen (4;7–4;10)	Chiat (1989)
	Graham (9;0)	Grunwell (1988)
	Rosey (6;8)	Grunwell & Pletts (1974)
	Pamela (7;2)	Grunwell (1975)
	John (5;0)	Powell et al. (1999)
	Dylan (4;6–5;0); Stuart	Bernhardt (1994)
velar fronting	Ruth Hills (2;0)	Hills (1914)
	Jim (4;6)	Compton (1970)
	Darryl; Gwendolyn	Bernhardt & Stemberger (1998)
	Sally (3;10)	Powell et al. (1999)
	Rosey (6;8)	Grunwell & Pletts (1974)
	S3 (6;3); S4 (6;11); S5 (8;0); S6 (5;6); S7 (7;2)	Grunwell (1977)
	BN (5;2)	Pollack & Rees (1972)
	Larissa	Stemberger (1993)
voicing	Joan Velten (pre 1;11)	Velten (1943)
	Dylan (4;6–5;0); Stuart	Bernhardt (1994)
	Caroline (2;4)	Celce-Murcia (1978)
	Hilde (1;3)	Vanvik (1971)

Notes

*   We are especially grateful to Judith Gierut, John McCarthy, Nola Stephens, Amanda Edmonds, and Nick Henriksen for their helpful comments and assistance with various aspects of this chapter. This work was supported by grants to Indiana University from the National Institutes of Health (NIH DC001694 & DC00012).

1   See, however, Walter (2002) for evidence that some fully developed languages treat final position as prominent.

2   Aside from Consonant Harmony's restriction to word-initial position, this process has the further peculiarity that the trigger and target are not adjacent (i.e., a vowel intervenes). For a discussion of some proposals that attempt to reconcile the locality issue, see, for example, McDonough and Myers (1991), Macken (1992), Gierut, Cho and Dinnsen (1993) and Goad (1997).

3   Standard transcription practices for English would likely not include a glottal stop before a word-initial vowel. It thus may be that initial consonants were not omitted, but instead were replaced by a glottal stop. The point remains that voice, place, and manner distinctions were merged in that context.

4   There are some exceptions to this general claim motivated by typological considerations. For example, while the markedness constraint NoCoda (Prince & Smolensky, 1993/2004) bans closed syllables, a conflicting markedness constraint Final-C (McCarthy, 1993) demands that a word-final syllable be closed. The asymmetric character of markedness constraints is also challenged by constraints making the same demand in complementary contexts. For example, while Onset (Prince & Smolensky, 1993/2004) bans onsetless syllables, Final-C requires that a syllable be closed word-finally.

5   A contextual markedness alternative to positional faithfulness would rely on the prominence-assigning markedness constraints in the same way. The difference would be that a context-sensitive markedness constraint would incorporate prominence by specifying that some feature is banned in the non-prominent part of a syllable, foot, or prosodic word. A context-free version of that markedness constraint would also be necessary to ban that same feature in all contexts. By ranking a context-free faithfulness constraint between these two markedness constraints, a contrast would be preserved in prominent contexts and merged in non-prominent contexts.

6   The markedness constraint banning interdentals is just one of several markedness constraints banning other fricatives. The independence of these markedness constraints is supported by the different distributional restrictions on fricatives in this child's phonology. Those fricatives excluded from the child's inventory would require the relevant markedness constraints to be undominated.

7   For a discussion of other cases of regression and an optimality theoretic account of the facts, see Chapter 8 in this volume and Dinnsen and Gierut (2008).

8   A possible counterexample to this claim is presented in Chapter 14 in this volume, Child SGL.

Part IV

Research reports:
Acquisition of consonant clusters

10 Syllable onsets in developmental perception and production*

Judith A. Gierut
Indiana University

Holly L. Storkel
University of Kansas

Michele L. Morrisette
Indiana University

This chapter addresses longstanding questions about children's knowledge of phonological structure and how this structure is used to acquire the productive phonology. Onsets of syllables were the primary focus, in evaluation of three levels of internal structure: surface structure associated with number of segments, representational structure associated with hierarchical complexity and organizational structure associated with syllable well-formedness. Three sets of experiments were conducted to sample children's judgments of the perceived similarity of onset-internal structure as related to their productive use of that same structure. To achieve this, two groups of preliterate preschoolers were enrolled: those with typical versus delayed phonological development. Results showed that children have graded knowledge of onset-internal organization and representation, and this was uniform across groups, despite obvious differences in the productive sound system. These findings bear on our understanding of the nature of children's representations and the relationship between perception and production, and hold implications for models of language development.

1   Introduction

The syllable has played a central role in the study of language acquisition. Since its first citation as a possible bootstrap to the acquisition process (Gleitman & Wanner, 1982; Peters, 1983), the syllable has been crucial to our understanding of phonological and lexical development from the dual perspectives of perception and production. We know, for example, that even in the earliest stages of development, infants 2 months of age differentially attend to different types of syllables in the input (Jusczyk, Bertoncini, Bijeljac-Babic, Kennedy & Mehler, 1990). By 9 months of age, their ability to differentiate syllables sharpens, such that they preferentially attend to those that share the same initial consonant as compared to overlaps in subsequent vowel-consonant sequences (Jusczyk, Goodman & Baumann, 1999). The focus on syllables is also evident in children's production of the first 50 words. Children produce sounds that they had not attempted previously when these occur in the context of often-used 'stable' syllabic frames, but not when in novel syllable shapes (MacNeilage & Davis, 1990; Schwartz & Goffman, 1995). It is noteworthy that this early reliance on the syllable persists across a broad developmental span. It has commonly been reported that preschoolers make systematic syllable reduction errors, deleting unstressed syllables in their outputs, e.g., 'banana' [nænə] (Gerken, 1996; Kehoe & Stoel-Gammon, 1997). Moreover, in clinical treatment of syllable errors, preschoolers with phonological delays exhibit differential patterns of learning depending on the type of syllable that is taught (Gierut, 1999; Gierut & Champion, 2001). In still other metalinguistic tasks, preliterate children have been shown to reliably count the number of syllables in a word, rather than the corresponding number of segments (Liberman, Shankweiler, Fischer & Carter, 1974). Even into adolescence, the adult-like precision of children's outputs is reportedly implemented in syllable-sized units (Nittrouer, Studdert-Kennedy & McGowan, 1989; Nittrouer, 1993). The syllable has thus emerged as a robust unit of language acquisition from a variety of converging perspectives.

Despite its apparent developmental significance, there is a paucity of research on children's knowledge of the internal structure of syllables, or how such knowledge may be used to promote the language learning process. Thus far, the only internal components of the syllable that have established psychological reality in development are the onset and the rhyme (Treiman, 1985; Jusczyk et al., 1999). Short of these demonstrations, few studies have gone on to further examine constituents of the syllable and their reflection in children's productive phonologies. These concerns are especially relevant because they bear on two longstanding debates about the nature of children's representations and the relationship between perception and production, respectively. With regard to the former, the finding that children attend to syllable-sized units has been taken as evidence that the early representation of words is holistic in nature (Ferguson & Farwell, 1975; Menyuk & Menn, 1979; Vihman, 1996; Jusczyk, 1997; Boysson-Bardies, 1999). That is, a word like 'cat' may be coarsely coded for Consonant-Vowel composition (e.g., CVC) or generic manner (e.g., Stop-Vowel-Stop), but may be otherwise lacking in phonological substance (Charles-Luce & Luce, 1990; Logan, 1992; Storkel, 2002). Children's representations presumably become more fully delineated with subsequent increases in vocabulary size and/or the emergence of literacy (Walley & Metsala, 1990; Walley, 1993; Metsala & Walley, 1998). This contrasts with opposing views that posit rich, detailed phonological representations from the outset of development (Dollaghan, 1994; Swingley & Aslin, 2000; 2002; Coady & Aslin, 2003). Nevertheless, because the constituent structure of syllables has not been fully explored, support for holistic representations in its strongest form is currently lacking. Manipulations of the internal structure of syllables would be one way in which to empirically establish whether or not children have access to fine-grained phonological details for use in the formation of representations.

This may be further extended to inform the second issue regarding the relationship between perception and production. Some have proposed that children's attention to syllable-sized units in the input promotes rapid lexical acquisition (Jusczyk, Luce & Charles-Luce, 1994; Morgan & Demuth, 1996; Metsala, 1999). Consistent with this, others have suggested that the focus on syllables helps to reveal the structure of the phonological system of the ambient language (Ingram, 1978; Peters, 1983). By 'spotlighting' syllables in the input, children are then able to transfer and use this information in their corresponding outputs (cf. Peters & Strömqvist, 1996). In other words, perception of structure apparently facilitates production and acquisition of that same structure. Nevertheless, the hand-in-hand integration of perception with production remains a noted gap in the acquisition literature (Gerken, 1994). But again, if the constituents of syllables were evaluated from dual perspectives, it would be possible to establish a relationship between what children know about syllable-internal structure and how this potentially informs their productive phonology.

The purpose of this chapter is to pursue these questions by specifically examining the onset as a constituent of the syllable in two groups of preschoolers: those with typical versus delayed productive phonologies. The tack we take is to sample children's judgments of the perceived similarity of onset structure when these same children do or do not produce the target onsets in question. This thereby brings together perception with production for two groups of children. Three sets of experiments are reported to establish children's knowledge of onsets at three distinct levels of structure as the independent variables. As will be defined herein, the 'surface level' of structure is indicative of the number of segments; the 'representational level' reveals the hierarchical complexity of onsets; and the 'organizational level' further reflects onset well-formedness. The predictions that follow from the existing literature are two-fold. Namely, children will evidence minimal knowledge of the internal structure of onsets, consistent with prominent views about the holistic nature of their representations. Moreover, children with typical phonological development are expected to have greater (albeit limited) insight to onset structure given their productive advances relative to children with delayed development. We begin with a description of the representation of onsets to operationalize the variables of interest; this is followed by a review of what children may know about the details of onset subconstituent structure. We then consider the literature related to perception of onsets for insight to possible relationships between representational and perceptual information, as these may differentially inform children's similarity judgments.

2   Representation of syllable onsets

Syllables are thought to consist of three primary constituents: the onset, nucleus or vowel, and coda. Of these, the onset is least controversial in terms of its internal structure and the principles that govern this structure (Davis, 1992; Clements & Hume, 1995). It is also the case that the onset constitutes a prominent position for the preservation of phonological contrasts. This is true in perception and production, and for fully developed and developing linguistic systems (Stoel-Gammon & Cooper, 1984; Walley, Smith & Jusczyk, 1986; Jusczyk et al., 1990; Beckman, 1998; Smith, 2002; Dinnsen & Farris, 2004b; cf. Slobin, 1973; Echols & Newport, 1992; Treiman & Zukowski, 1996; Brooks & MacWhinney, 2000). The onset thereby provides an optimal context for experimentally establishing children's knowledge and use of syllable-internal structure.

Figure 1 (a through e) depicts a conventional representation of the syllable onset for fully developed systems following from linguistic theory (see Clements & Hume, 1995 for review). The Greek symbol sigma designates the syllable itself, which dominates the onset as its constituent. Within the onset, there is further subconstituent structure, which serves to define and differentiate the simple singleton (1a) from the affricate (1b), true cluster (1c), adjunct cluster (1d) and 3-element cluster (1e), as shown here for English. The motivation for this representation of onset-internal structure comes from a broad set of cross-linguistic data that relate to the phonological patterns of fully developed primary languages. The motivating patterns include, but are not limited to rules of syllabification and stress that appeal to syllables as opposed to sounds, gemination and lengthening effects, assimilatory processes that promote the spreading or loss of distinctive features, edge and anti-edge effects that are specifically associated with assimilatory effects of affricates, and root and morphological patterns of Semitic languages such as Arabic. In addition to internal linguistic evidence, there is external support for the structure of onsets that comes from historical sound change, slip-of-the-tongue phenomena, spelling errors, language games and ludlings. The reader is referred to Kenstowicz (1994) for a general overview of the facts that motivate the syllable. Blevins (1995) provides a complementary review of the data that motivate this particular structural depiction of onsets. Blevins also considers the advantage of this representational structure relative to alternative proposals in accounting for the linguistic facts (see also Clements & Hume, 1995). In addition to the internal and external evidence that is summarized in these reviews, a number of related papers provide behavioral evidence in support of the representation of onsets as adopted herein (e.g., McCay, 1972; Vitz & Winkler, 1973; Santa, Santa & Smith, 1977; Stemberger & MacWhinney, 1984; Stemberger & Treiman, 1986; Bagemihl, 1995; Hume & Johnson, 2001).

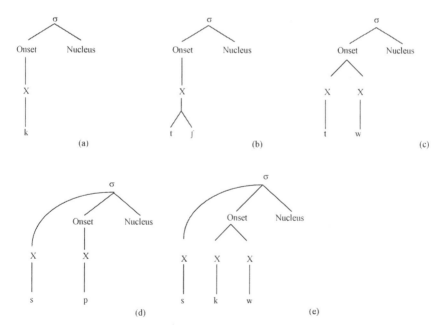

Figure 1. Representational structure of (a) singleton, (b) affricate, (c) true cluster, (d) adjunct cluster and (e) 3-element cluster.

316 *Optimality Theory, Phonological Acquisition and Disorders*

The five onset types of English shown in Figure 1 are our specific focus; thus, we limit the discussion to descriptions of these. As can be seen, there are distinct points of overlap among the different representations, which motivate our definitions of surface, representational and organizational levels of structure.

2.1 Surface structure

An obvious point of structural overlap among onsets relates to number of segments. As in Figure 1, permissible onsets of English may consist of 1, 2, or 3 sounds. This is captured structurally by the number of timing or X-slots to accommodate each of the corresponding numbers of segments. It should be noted that the onset is an optional constituent of the syllable to provide for vowel-initial forms such as 'at.' Along this dimension, the singleton (1a) and affricate (1b) are alike because each consists of one X-slot. Likewise, the true (1c) and adjunct clusters (1d) are alike, each with two X-slots, whereas the 3-element cluster (1e) stands apart. Structural resemblances at the surface level are summarized in Table 1.

Table 1. Structural similarity of syllable onsets.

Onset Type	Surface Level	Representational Level	Organizational Level
	Total Number of Segments	Occurrence of Branching	Conformity to Sonority Sequencing Principle
Singleton /k/	1	No	Yes
Affricate /tʃ/	1	Yes, segmental level	Yes
True cluster /tw/	2	Yes, onset level	Yes
Adjunct cluster /sp/	2	No	No
3-element cluster /skw/	3	Yes, onset level	No

2.2 Representational structure

Onsets may also be related in their hierarchical representation, most notably pertaining to the occurrence of branching. Branching in representational structure is indicative of increased linguistic complexity (Lleó & Prinz, 1997). The simplest onset is nonbranching (1a), and includes all singletons of English with exception of the affricates /tʃ/ and /dʒ/. While affricates (1b) are singletons, they are admittedly more complex given that production involves closed stricture followed by turbulent release. Complexity associated with the contour nature of affricates is captured through branching that is hierarchically located at the level of the segment. True clusters (1c) also require branching to conjoin consecutive sound sequences, but hierarchically, the location of branching is at the level of the onset. As in Table 1, affricates and true clusters are similar in their branching representational structure, whereas singletons stand apart. Adjunct (1d) and 3-element clusters (1e) can also be defined by branching in representational structure, but only when further related to the organizational principles that dictate the well-formedness of onsets.

2.3   Organizational structure

The organization of onsets is governed by the Sonority Sequencing Principle (Clements, 1990). The Sonority Sequencing Principle was identified over a century ago (Sievers, 1881; Jespersen, 1904), and has since been shown to be a robust cross-linguistic universal or 'preference condition' (Bybee, 2001). Its function is to delineate the sequential order of segments that can constitute a permissible onset. In particular, the Sonority Sequencing Principle states that onsets must rise in sonority to the nucleus, with sonority being a relative measure that is directly correlated with intensity (i.e., acoustic energy) and inversely correlated with intraoral air pressure (Parker, 2002). Sounds that are highly sonorous are produced with greater intensity and lower intraoral air pressure. Conversely, sounds that are low in sonority are produced with less intensity and greater intraoral air pressure. Onsets are well-formed and in conformity with the Sonority Sequencing Principle when segments align from least to most sonorous from the edge of a syllable. On a continuum, stops and affricates are least sonorous, followed by fricatives, nasals, liquids, glides, and vowels (Parker, 2002). Thus, singletons from any of these classes, when followed by a vowel (as in 1a, b), are considered well-formed onsets. Likewise, clusters that consist of consecutive segments of low, followed by high sonority (1c) also abide by the Sonority Sequencing Principle. Following from the continuum, clusters consisting of a stop followed by a liquid (e.g., /kr/) or glide (e.g., /kw/) are well-formed in English. Sequences of a fricative followed by either a liquid (e.g., /sl/), nasal (e.g., /sm/) or glide (e.g., /sw/) are also well-formed, in accord with the Sonority Sequencing Principle.

There is one well-defined exception to the Sonority Sequencing Principle that affects English as well as many other languages. It involves s+obstruent stop sequences, where a more sonorous fricative precedes a less sonorous stop (1d, e). According to the Sonority Sequencing Principle, it should be just the reverse. This observation has given rise to a distinction between 'true' clusters, which conform to the Sonority Sequencing Principle versus 'adjunct' clusters, which do not (Selkirk, 1982; Davis, 1992; Harris, 1994). For English, the distinction between true and adjunct clusters is further motivated by language-specific evidence associated with the phonotactics of the language. English does not allow homorganic clusters (where consecutive segments share the same place, but have a different manner of articulation), except in the case of adjuncts (e.g., */pw-/ but /st-/). English also does not allow obstruent+obstruent sequences, again except in the case of adjuncts (e.g., */ft-/ but /st-/). These and other data from native speakers' intuitions about the syllabification of s+obstruent stop sequences have motivated an alternate representational structure (Clements & Keyser, 1983). In particular, for s+obstruent stop sequences (whether adjuncts or 3-element clusters), /s/ is posited as an appendix of the syllable, external to the onset. This can be seen in Figure 1d and e, where /s/ occupies one timing slot that is directly linked to the syllable node, and is not structurally part of the onset itself. In the case of an adjunct then, onset subconstituent structure consists of just one nonbranching segment. Notably, this representation closely resembles that of a nonbranching singleton (cf. 1d and a, respectively). Likewise, in the case of a 3-element cluster, onset subconstituent structure consists of two segments with branching; this representation looks much like that of a true cluster (cf. 1e and c, respectively). Thus, at an organizational level, the adjunct and 3-element cluster are alike in their violation of the Sonority Sequencing Principle, with the more sonorous /s/ appended directly to the syllable node. They stand apart from other singletons and true clusters that conform to the Sonority Sequencing Principle. However, at a representational level, the adjunct and singleton are alike given the lack of subconstituent branching; and likewise, 3-element and true clusters are alike given the presence of subconstituent branching. Table 1 summarizes these points of organizational and representational similarity.

In summary, the onset as a constituent of the syllable is free to vary in at least three dimensions related to surface, representational, and organizational levels of structure. For present purposes, we have operationalized surface structure as the number of segments in syllable-initial position. Representational structure is operationalized as the presence or absence of branching within the onset of the syllable itself. Organizational structure is operationalized in reference to conformity to the Sonority Sequencing Principle, given its important role in specifying the arrangement of segments in a well-formed onset. These three dimensions were manipulated as the independent variables in tapping children's knowledge of onset-internal structure. An important consideration though is whether there is any prima facie evidence to suggest that children can even access such structure, either in perception or production.

3   Acquisition of syllable onsets

Data from children's productions shed most light on their potential knowledge of onset-internal structure at surface, representational and organizational levels. Three sets of findings can be viewed as indirect evidence of their knowledge. First, normative studies show differences in the order of acquisition of singletons as opposed to true clusters (Smit, Hand, Freilinger, Bernthal & Bird, 1990; Smit, 1993a; 1993b). One consonant emerges before sequences of two, and simple (nonbranching) onsets emerge before those that branch. That is to say, children acquire singletons first, before affricates or clusters. These observations bear on surface and representational levels of subconstituent structure. Second, production of affricates is prerequisite to production of clusters, with branching being identified as the crucial condition in this elaboration of onsets (Lleó & Prinz, 1996; 1997; Gierut & O'Connor, 2002). The claim that derives is that branching at the level of the segment (as in production of affricates) must be in place before children can implement branching at the level of the onset (as in production of true clusters). This again relates to the representational level of onset structure. Third, adjuncts are reportedly among the first clusters produced by children (Smit, 1993b). Children also employ different learning strategies in their acquisition of adjuncts as opposed to other true clusters (Gierut, 1999; Gierut & Champion, 2001; Barlow, 2001b). These patterns of learning suggest that adjuncts are acquired like singletons as opposed to other true clusters. This is taken as support of their exceptional status relative to the Sonority Sequencing Principle, and thereby bears on children's knowledge of the organizational structure of onsets.

By comparison, in perception, surface structure associated with number of segments is the only dimension that has been explored. As noted previously, children's ability to count the number of segments in an onset is a skill that emerges coincident with learning to read (Liberman et al., 1974). Children not only have difficulty counting segments, but they also have difficulty identifying whether two onsets are alike, even following direct training (Treiman & Breaux, 1982). Moreover, children's ability to identify like sounds in an onset increases in difficulty when these are presented in clusters as opposed to singletons (Treiman & Zukowski, 1996). By this, /b/ in 'broom' and 'bloom' will be more difficult for children to identify than /b/ in 'big' and 'ball.' In the former case, /b/ is a member of an onset cluster, whereas in the latter, it is an onset singleton. Other related perceptual work has shown that children view clusters as one unit, not two (Menyuk, 1972; Barton, Miller & Macken, 1980), which implies once again that number of segments is not their central focus.

In all, the evidence in support of children's knowledge of the internal structure of onsets is inferential at best. Moreover, it is unclear whether such acquisition patterns actually reflect children's insight to the details of the sub-constituent structure of onsets, or whether they might derive from perceptual sensitivity to the raw signal.

4   Perception of syllable onsets

A number of classic psychoacoustic studies have evaluated the perception of onsets by adults (e.g., Miller & Nicely, 1955; Peters, 1963; Shepard, 1972; Singh, Woods & Becker, 1972; Black, Singh & Janocosek, 1974; see also Graham & House, 1971 for children). The focus has been almost exclusively on English singletons, yielding plots of the perceptual space of consonants as derived from multidimensional scaling. Most reports focus on consonant confusability, but a few have also evaluated listeners' judgments of perceptual similarity, as is the intent of the present work. This distinction is relevant because of reported asymmetries in listeners' confusions among sounds and their corresponding subjective judgments of sound similarity (Greenberg & Jenkins, 1964; Shepard, 1972; Luce & McLennan, 2003). Similarity judgments are thought to be indicative of a listener's 'cognitive (analogical) hypotheses' about underlying structure, whereas confusability studies inform basic processes of 'speech discrimination' (Shepard, 1972).

Two perceptual studies stand out in their independent examination of onset singletons (Singh et al., 1972) and onset clusters (Black et al., 1974). The study of singletons is relevant because the methods elicited perceptual similarity judgments, and the results incorporated reanalyses of developmental data. The study of clusters is germane because, to our knowledge, it is the only published work on perceptual confusability of clusters (cf. Newman, Sawusch & Luce, 1997; Luce & McLennan, 2003).

Singh et al. (1972) identified five dimensions as relevant to listeners' judgments of onset singleton similarity. In rank order, these are the properties sibilant[1], plosive, place (front/back or anterior/nonanterior), voicing, and nasality. The first three of these dimensions are directly pertinent to the onset singletons shown in Figure 1a and b. Notice that all onsets under consideration were voiceless, and none involved a nasal. As applied specifically to these singletons, /k/ is nonsibilant, plosive, and back; whereas /tʃ/ is sibilant, nonplosive, and back. Thus, on perceptual grounds, /k/ and /tʃ/ are similar in terms of their shared property, back. This is summarized in Table 2. All of the remaining onsets in Figure 1 are clusters of one sort or another. A question that immediately comes to mind is whether perception of singletons can be uniformly extended to clusters, even though the latter are comprised of sound sequences. This extension might be based, for example, on alignment of sounds at the left-edge of a syllable, as in the /t/ in /tw/ or /s/ in /sp/ and /skw/ (Figure 1c, d, e). If we accept this premise and apply the properties sibilant, plosive and place to the remaining set of onsets shown in Figure 1, then /tʃ/ and /s/ (in /sp/ and /skw/) are alike on perceptual grounds in terms of the shared property, sibilant (cf. Shepard, 1972). Likewise, /k/ and /t/ (in /tw/) are alike perceptually in terms of the shared property, plosive. For completeness, Table 2 lists these perceptual relationships. These follow from Table 18 of Singh et al. (1972). This extension notwithstanding, it remains to be empirically determined whether perceptual data for singletons is generalizable to clusters. For preliminary insight, we turn to the available report on perception of clusters.

Table 2. Perceptual confusability of sounds that comprise the different onset types, as based on Singh et al. (1972: Table 18). Confusability of clusters was based on the first sound of the sequence, e.g., /t/ in /tw/.

Onset Type	Sibilant	Plosive	Place
Singleton /k/	No	Yes	Nonanterior
Affricate /tʃ/	Yes	No	Nonanterior
True cluster /tw/	No	Yes	Anterior
Adjunct cluster /sp/	Yes	No	Anterior
3-element cluster /skw/	Yes	No	Anterior

Black et al. (1974) examined sibilant and nonsibilant clusters of English in two independent studies of confusability. Results for both kinds of clusters indicated that the second member of the sequence was the primary contributor to perceptual confusions. For nonsibilant (stop) clusters (e.g., /gr/, /gl/, /gw/), the second member of the sequence /w/, /l/, or /r/ was most influential. For example, /dw/, /gw/, /tw/, and /kw/ were judged as confusable, despite having different initial segments. These were unique from the set of /dr/, /gr/, /tr/, and /kr/ as confusable, with the same pattern observed for consonant+/l/ clusters. Likewise, in examination of sibilant clusters, the second member of the sequence was most informing of confusability, as based on the voicing, nasality or labiality of that second sound. Given this, it might not be entirely appropriate to predict the confusability of clusters based on the left-edge alignment of sounds, as we did in Table 2. Luce and colleagues (Newman et al., 1997; Luce & McLennan, 2003) raise precisely this question in a recent series of reports. Their findings have led them to conclude that the perceptual similarity of sounds as singletons is not in one-to-one correspondence with those same sounds as clusters (cf. Treiman & Zukowski, 1996 for children). They further propose that clusters are not processed from left-to-right in serial order of sounds, but rather are adjoined as a psycholinguistic unit. Stevens (cf. Kornfeld, 1978 for children) makes related observations from the perspective of production in his discussions of the effects of context on the acoustic, articulatory and aerodynamic properties of sounds as singletons versus clusters. Admittedly, the data on perception of clusters are limited and emerging, but the evidence seems to suggest that their perception is unique from that of singletons, even though the two types of onsets may be comprised of seemingly identical segments. Given the paucity of research thus far, this developmental investigation takes on added significance in that it will contribute to the available data on singletons and clusters, albeit from perceptual and/or representational perspectives.

To reiterate our purpose then, three sets of experiments were conducted to evaluate children's judgments of the perceived similarity of onsets. Five types of onsets of English were considered, including the singleton, affricate, true cluster, adjunct, and 3-element cluster. These were systematically manipulated at the surface, representational, and organizational levels of onset-internal structure as the independent variables. Two groups of preliterate preschoolers participated, having either typical or delayed productive phonologies, with the intent to evaluate children's knowledge of the subconstituent structure of onsets relative to their corresponding productive phonologies. The broader goal was to inform two long-standing issues of debate associated with the nature of children's representations and the relationship between perception and production in development, both of which continue as pertinent to the development of optimality theory.

5   General methods

5.1   Participants and their productive phonologies

Seventy-eight children between the ages of 3 and 7 were recruited through public announcement. Because we were interested in including children who did, as well as those who did not, produce specific onset types, recruitment was extended to preschools and day care facilities, as well as centers for the remediation of childhood language delays. For the same reason, it was necessary to recruit a broader age range given the standard time-frame for identification of such delays (Shriberg, Kwiatkowski, Best, Hengst & Terselic-Weber, 1986). In this sense then, development was defined in terms of children's productive phonological systems, rather than their chronological age (cf. Gierut, 1996a).

To be eligible for participation, children had to be preliterate monolingual speakers of English as established by parent report. Children also had to have normal hearing at 20 dB HL at 1000, 2000 and 4000 Hz (ASHA, 1997), and pass the pretraining phase of the experimental task (see procedures below). Of the 78 recruits, 28 children failed to meet one or more of these entry criteria ($M = 52$ months; range $= 37$–72). Sixteen of the 28 children who were lost to attrition failed at pretraining ($M = 49$ months; range $= 37$–72). The result was that 50 participants enrolled, 25 boys and 25 girls, with an average age of 54 months (range $= 38$–77).

Once eligibility was established, children participated in two production tasks. The first was a standardized measure to determine the typical or delayed status of the productive phonology. If a child scored at or above the 50th percentile on the *Goldman-Fristoe Test of Articulation* (Goldman & Fristoe, 1986) relative to age- and gender-matched peers, he or she was assigned to the group of typically developing children. Scores less than the 13th percentile on this same measure warranted placement in the group of children with phonological delays. Of the 50 participants, 21 children were classified as typically developing, with a mean *Goldman-Fristoe* score in the 72nd percentile; their mean age was 55 months (range $= 38$–71). The remaining 29 children evidenced phonological delays, with a mean *Goldman-Fristoe* score in the 5th percentile; mean age of this group was 54 months (range $= 41$–77). There was no significant difference in chronological age of the groups, $t(48) = -.48$; $p = .64$. There was also no correlation between age and *Goldman-Fristoe* performance, $r = .042$; $p = .77$. That is, younger children did not necessarily score more poorly than older children due to our inclusion of those with typical and with delayed development. There was, however, a statistically significant difference between groups in articulation performance on the standardized measure, $t(48) = -20.68$; $p < .01$.

The second production task was a phonological probe of the target sounds and sound sequences to be employed as experimental stimuli, following from Figure 1. Specifically, production of obstruent stops, affricates, true clusters, adjuncts, and 3-element clusters were sampled in 80 real words that were picturable and familiar to children. These were drawn from the PKP and OCP, as described in Chapter 2 of this volume. Each target was elicited in the word-initial position of at least five different words following spontaneous naming procedures established in the production literature (cf. Gierut, Elbert & Dinnsen, 1987; Gierut, 1998a). Mean production probe accuracy for children with typical development was 86% and for those with delayed development, 29%. Production probe accuracy of the groups was statistically significant $t(48) = -10.66$; $p < .01$. For the most part, children with delayed phonological development evidenced substitutions, coupled with deletion errors in the case of clusters, such that targeted sounds and sound sequences were uniformly realized as stops. The result was that the five different onset types were generally merged (i.e., neutralized) into a single phonological category in production.

In both production tasks, a child's responses were digitally recorded and independently transcribed by two judges trained in the use of the International Phonetic Alphabet. Interjudge transcription reliability was established for 18% of randomly selected participants. Mean point-to-point consonant agreement between judges was 95% (range = 93 to 100%, with 2,435 consonants transcribed).

In addition to the production tasks, children with phonological delays were evaluated for adequacy of their oral-motor structure and function (Robbins & Klee, 1987). This was intended to rule out possible oral-motor deviations or inadequacies as a source of children's production errors. The mean score for oral-motor structure was 24 ($SD = 0$), which fell within the expected age-referenced normative range of 20–24 for typical structural development. The mean oral-motor function score was 110 ($SD = 3$), which was also within the expected range of 104–112 for typical functional development. Children thus performed within expected oral-motor limits for their age, confirming the non-organic (functional) nature of their phonological delay.

5.2   Procedures

5.2.1   Oddity task

Following Treiman and Breaux (Treiman & Breaux, 1982; Bradley & Bryant, 1983), an oddity task was used to sample children's judgments of the perceived similarity of onsets. This is a constrained classification task that has been closely linked to lexical access in acquisition (Walley et al., 1986; Walley, 1993; Gerken, Murphy & Aslin, 1995; De Cara & Goswami, 2003). It is revealing of the relative similarity among representational structures without introducing significant demands on children's memory or attention. The oddity task, as an evaluation of perceptual similarity, is said to correspond to a listener's cognitive hypotheses about underlying linguistic structure (Greenberg & Jenkins, 1964; Shepard, 1972; Treiman & Zukowski, 1996; Luce & McLennan, 2003).

As adapted herein, the oddity task was administered individually to each child in game format. The child was seated at a table, with the examiner's position offset to the right and behind the child. In this position, the child was unable to directly view the examiner's face. The child was shown an equilateral triangular game board with identical pictures of animate characters (e.g., three identically pictured clowns) mounted in each of the corners. The child was instructed to listen to each character's 'name,' and then to select the two characters that were 'friends.' Character 'names' were prerecorded and delivered over desktop speakers at a comfortable listening level. A child's attention was drawn to each character in turn, with the examiner pointing in sequence—left, then top, then right—to the pictures on the game board, in sync with the delivery of the auditory stimulus 'names.' A child's response was simply pointing to 2 of 3 pictures in each trial. The spatial location corresponding to the 'names' of the characters was systematically varied across trials to prevent perseverative pointing. The only feedback provided was in the form of general encouragement to attend to the task.

5.2.2 Pretraining

Prior to experimental administration, children were required to complete and pass a pretraining task, which was modeled after the procedures used by Treiman and Breaux (1982). The purpose of pretraining was to familiarize a child with the general procedures without biasing them toward specific classifications or classification strategies. The intent was to ensure that children would in fact respond to taped stimuli, that they understood a pointing response was required, and that judgments were to be based on stimulus similarity. Pretraining mirrored the experimental protocol in instructions and format, but the visual and auditory stimuli differed. None of the experimental stimuli were introduced in pretraining. Task difficulty was gradually incremented in two phases, with corrective feedback provided.

Phase 1 of pretraining was intended to draw a child's attention to stimulus similarity in the most direct and straightforward way. To do this, children were presented with two identical CV items in each stimulus triplet. For example, the triplet /mæ/, /mæ/, /læ/ consists of two occurrences of /mæ/; likewise, /fʌ/, /rʌ/, /rʌ/ contains two occurrences of /rʌ/. A child was required to make an exact match of sonorants in 4 of 6 such comparisons. If successful, Phase 2 of pretraining was instated. If unsuccessful, an intermediate phase with live voice presentation of the stimuli with assisted pointing was introduced. This then was followed by a second unassisted administration of the prerecorded Phase 1 trials. If criterion was still not achieved for Phase 1 of pretraining, a child was dismissed from participation following the eligibility criteria outlined above.

Phase 2 of pretraining was intended to show a child that similarity judgments were to be made even if the stimuli were not identical. This more closely resembled the experimental trials because each CV of a given triplet was unique. For example, the triplet /mæ/, /næ/, /ʃæ/ consists of unique sounds, but this notwithstanding, /m/ and /n/ are both nasals. Another example is

/nʌ/, /ʃʌ/, /mʌ/, where /n/ and /m/ are again both nasals. A child was required to make same manner (i.e., nasal) matches in 4 of 6 such comparisons in order to advance to the experimental trials. If this was not achieved, a child was given a second chance at Phase 2 trials. Those who met criterion on a second administration proceeded to the experimental phase; those who failed were dismissed.

5.3   Stimulus materials

Character 'names' used in the oddity task were CV syllables. These were constructed to sample the five onset types displayed in Figure 1 in varying vowel contexts. We first describe the rationale for choosing the CV composition of the stimuli. This is followed by the procedures we used to generate the stimuli for experimental use.

5.3.1   Consonant composition

The specific consonants associated with each onset type were singleton /k/, affricate /tʃ/, true cluster /tw/, adjunct /sp/, and 3-element cluster /skw/. These were chosen in consideration of developmental predictions, experimental control associated with stringent foils, and perceptual confusability independent of onset-internal representational structure.

First, in terms of development, we anticipated that children with phonological delays would likely produce these sounds and sequences in error based on normative orders of sound acquisition (Smit et al., 1990; Smit, 1993a; 1993b), but that typically developing children would not. This was indeed exemplified by the phonological probe data. Moreover, because children with phonological delays merged the five onset types into a single phonological category in production, we expected that their performance on the oddity task might be at chance levels since, in production, these onsets were undifferentiated. In comparison, children with typical phonological development, who maintained productive distinctions among the onsets, might respond more systematically in accord with onset-internal structure. This then allowed for our examination of perceived structural similarity given the presence or absence of those same structures in children's outputs.

Second, to ensure that the variables being manipulated were the same dimensions being used by children in their similarity judgments, we implemented 'stringent foils', following recommendations in the literature on the development of categories (see Murphy, 2002 for review). A stringent foil is one that is as similar as possible to the items of a test set, without also being a member of that set. Stringency relative to onset-internal structure was defined herein from an acoustic perspective. Specifically, the onset-internal structure of the test consonants required that all be initiated with a transient and that all be voiceless (Stevens, 1998). This was true even for the adjunct /sp/ and 3-element cluster /skw/, bearing in mind that /s/ is appended to, but not part of the onset internally. Thus, test consonants were acoustically alike, but underlyingly different in terms of their subconstituent structure. It should be recognized that the acoustic characteristics of transients do vary by place of articulation and also context in the case of clusters; therefore, transients were not identical in an absolute sense, cf. Stevens (1998).

As an additional precaution, test consonants were selected to allow us to begin to determine if children's similarity judgments were based on shared perceptual characteristics of the stimuli as opposed to shared structural characteristics. This can best be illustrated by comparing Table 1, which shows the similarity of different onsets based on points of structural overlap and Table 2, which shows similarity based on tentative projections of perceptual confusability. Keep in mind that Table 2 should be interpreted with caution because these estimates of confusability were gleaned only from singleton data, as reported by Singh et al. (1972). As noted above, this extension may not be entirely accurate, but pertinent data are still forthcoming. Nonetheless, the data that are available provide us with a first step in advancing differential predictions about onset similarity as based on an appeal to structural versus perceptual information. This further allows for a potential examination of the bases of children's patterns of response.

There is one last point that is also worth mentioning about the consonant composition of the stimuli. In particular, studies of perceptual confusability show a 3% average error rate in children's perception of sounds as different when, in fact, these sounds are the same (Graham & House, 1971). This bears specifically on the test onsets /sp/ and /skw/, which both have /s/ as the first sound of the sequence. Based on prior reports, we might not expect that all children will uniformly recognize that this particular test pair has a common first element (Treiman & Baron, 1981; Treiman & Zukowski, 1996).

When these considerations are taken together, the end result is that the consonants we selected made it possible for us to begin to trace the source of children's similarity judgments as being due to their knowledge of onset-internal structure versus the perceptual confusability of the sounds that comprised that structure. We will return to this point again in the presentation of results and in discussion, given the theoretical import of this distinction between perception and representation in development (Jones & Smith, 1993).

5.3.2   Vowel composition

Each onset was combined with each of five vowels /i e ɑ o u/. Only long vowels of English were used for consistency with phonotactics of the language. Vowels were appended to the test consonants to form an exhaustive list of 25 syllables (e.g., /ki/, /ke/, /kɑ/, /ko/, /ku/; /tʃi/, /tʃe/, /tʃɑ/, /tʃo/, /tʃu/; etc.). For the most part, the resulting syllables were nonce items for children. Consistent with prior similarity studies (Treiman & Baron, 1981), nonsense syllables allowed a child to focus on the phonological properties of the input, rather than on meaning. It should be noted, however, that three real words, which might have been known by children, resulted from these CV combinations. These were 'key', 'coo,' and 'chew.' (Other real words that derived would have been unfamiliar to children, e.g., 'spa', 'coupe', 'spay,' cf. Moe, Hopkins & Rush, 1982). Child lexical databases show the frequency of these words to be 11, 2, and 2, respectively (Moe et al., 1982); thus, they are of low frequency in the lexicons of children. This notwithstanding, we took care to avoid presenting real word pairs or triplets in given experimental manipulations. Recall also that characters pictured in the oddity task were semantically unrelated to their 'names', albeit real or nonce test syllables.

5.3.3   Preparation of stimuli

Multiple exemplars of the CV syllables were produced in citation form by a female talker and digitally recorded for purposes of creating master stimulus tapes. The resulting productions were excised and edited using a waveform program (Milenkovic & Read, 1992). From these, one representative token of each of the 25 syllables was selected for use on the master tapes. Care was taken to choose syllables with comparable vowel durations so that children's judgments would not be inadvertently influenced by stimulus length. Across the 25 syllables identified for the master tapes, mean vowel durations were /i/ 369 ms, /e/ 370 ms, /ɑ/ 375 ms, /o/ 376 ms and /u/ 370 ms. Other factors considered in syllable selection were clarity, loudness, intonation and quality (Munson, 2001). Syllables were further submitted to two independent listeners, who phonetically transcribed the stimuli to ensure that they were perceived as intended.

The resulting set of 25 syllables was then used to create the experimental blocks specific to each individual study; these are shown in the appendix. In any given block, there were 10 trials, with a 5s interstimulus interval between trials to allow for a child's pointing response. Trials consisted of triplets of syllables, as called for by the oddity task. Within a trial, there was a 1s interstimulus interval between delivery of each syllable of the triplet. In all, five sets of triplets were used per block, with each set presented twice in the block and order randomized. Thus, in each study, three onset types, paired with each of the five vowels, were systematically manipulated to obtain children's similarity judgments. Studies were administered in individual 20 minute sessions, and families could choose to enroll their child in more than one study. Order of experimental runs was semi-randomized across participating children.

5.4   Data analyses

Subjects analyses were completed for each study. Data were submitted to a 2 Group (typical vs. delayed) x 3 Comparison (different onset types of an experiment triplet) repeated measures analysis of variance with Huynh-Feldt correction for sphericity (Huynh & Feldt, 1976). Significant main effects were followed by planned pair-wise comparisons, with Huynh-Feldt correction for sphericity and Bonferroni correction for multiple comparisons. Corrected p-values are reported for all pair-wise comparisons. In all cases, significant main effects were explored by comparing each pairing to all others (i.e., 3 comparisons). We were unable to complete complementary items analyses on the data (cf. Clark, 1973; 1976; Cohen, 1976; Keppel, 1976; Smith, 1976; Wike & Church, 1976; Raaijmakers, Schrijnemakers & Gremmen, 1999). Recall that, in any given study, there were just five different items; this did not render sufficient power. The items did, however, constitute the exhaustive set of the representational possibilities of onsets in English, bearing on the issue of generalizability. It should be noted that items analyses are often precluded in developmental work that is dependent on children's similarity judgments (e.g., Treiman & Baron, 1981; Treiman & Breaux, 1982) due to limited attention, cooperation or fatigue and task demands that constrain the feasible size of the stimulus set.

6   Experiment 1

The purpose was to determine whether children have access to the internal properties of onsets when these are introduced in combination, in an overlapping and additive way. The hypothesis was that if fine-grained structural details of syllables were indeed elusive to children, then perhaps conjoining these details would serve to underscore and draw attention to their relevance (Gerken et al., 1995; cf. Restle, 1959). In Study 1.1, combined surface+organizational structures were evaluated, and in Study 1.2, representational+organizational structures were tested. It was not possible to evaluate the full complement of logical possibilities (i.e., surface+representational structures) because the phonotactics of English are limited to the five general types of onsets shown in Figure 1. In essence, a manipulation of this type would be a within- as opposed to an across-onset-type comparison, e.g., evaluating the similarity of one nonbranching singleton relative to another (Singh et al., 1972).

6.1   Study 1.1

6.1.1   Participants

Forty-five children participated: 20 with typical phonologies ($M = 55$ months; range = 38–71) and 25 with delayed ($M = 55$ months, range = 45–77).

6.1.2   Methods

Procedures were as described. The experimental triplet used in this manipulation consisted of the singleton, affricate, and adjunct. Children were to judge the similarity of these onsets based on their internal structure as the dependent variable. Table 3 reports structural similarities among members of this triplet (cf. Table 1), along with a tentative projection of their perceptual confusability. Recall that the perceptual relationships follow from Table 2 as derived from listeners' judgments of singletons, and therefore must be interpreted with reservation (cf. Klatt, 1973; Black et al., 1974; Luce & McLennan, 2003). Nonetheless, it serves as a possible starting point for examining the role of structure versus perception in children's judgments.

Table 3. Onset triplets of Experiment 1. Structural and perceptual overlap, following from Tables 1 and 2 respectively, are indicated with '+'.

Study	Onset Triplet	Structural Overlap			Perceptual Overlap		
		Surface	Representational	Organizational	Sibilant	Plosive	Place
1.1	Singleton /k/	+	+	+			+
	Affricate /tʃ/	+		+	+	+	+
	Adjunct /sp/		+		+	+	
1.2	Affricate /tʃ/		+	+	+	+	
	True Cluster /tw/	+	+	+			+
	Adjunct /sp/	+			+	+	+

With regard to onset-internal structure, Table 3 shows that the singleton and affricate are alike at both the surface and organizational levels: each consists of one segment and conforms to the Sonority Sequencing Principle. In comparison, the singleton and adjunct have only representational structure in common, since both are nonbranching. The affricate and adjunct are structurally anomalous because they share no points of overlap; however, on perceptual grounds, these might be viewed as confusable because of their sibilant, nonplosive characteristics. As based on structural resemblances, the independent variables were thus conjoined surface+organizational structure versus representational structure (vs. anomalous structure).

6.1.3   Results

Data analysis was as described. Figure 2 (panel (a)) shows the mean proportion of similarity judgments for each of the three logically possible onset pairings for the two groups of children, typical and delayed. There were no significant main effects of group, $F(1, 43) = 1.73, p = .19$ or comparison, $F(2, 86) = .92$, $p = .40$; nor was the Group x Comparison interaction significant, $F(2, 86) = .39, p = .67$. Further post hoc pair-wise comparisons were not warranted given the lack of statistical significance. In this study then, dually conjoined surface+organizational structure did not enhance children's similarity judgments of onsets. Perceptual confusability of the onsets also did not appear to have an effect on children's judgments. They were just as likely to pair confusable onsets (e.g., affricate and adjunct) as they were to pair nonconfusable onsets (e.g., singleton and adjunct). The findings ran counter to our predictions based on structure, and cannot be attributed alternatively to perceptual confusions.

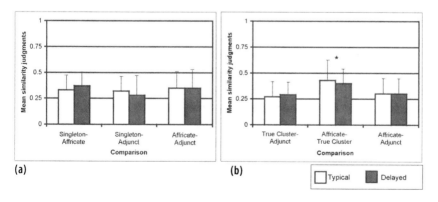

Figure 2. Mean proportion of similarity judgments for the logically possible onset pairings by children with typical and delayed phonological systems for Experiment 1.

6.2   Study 1.2

6.2.1   Participants

Thirty-five children participated, 20 with typical and 15 with delayed phonological development. Mean ages were 55 months (range = 38–71) and 51
months (range = 45–70), respectively.

6.2.2   Methods

Procedures were as described. The experimental triplet included the affricate,
true cluster, and adjunct as independent variables; the dependent variable
was structural similarity as before. Table 3 shows that, in terms of onset configuration, the affricate and true cluster are alike in both representational and
organizational structure: both branch and accord with the Sonority Sequencing
Principle, respectively. The true cluster and adjunct share only surface similarity with a common number of segments. The affricate and adjunct have no
common properties, being structurally anomalous; yet, as in the prior study,
these might be interpreted as being perceptually confusable. Following from
the structural relationships then, the independent variables were conjoined
representational+organizational structure versus surface structure (vs. anomalous structure).

6.2.3   Results

Data were analyzed as described, with results shown in panel (b) of Figure
2. There was no significant main effect of group, $F(1, 33) < 1, p > .10$, but
there was a significant main effect of comparison, $F(2, 66) = 5.25, p = .008$.
The interaction of Group x Comparison was not significant, $F(2, 66) = .16$,
$p = .85$. Planned pair-wise comparisons showed that children selected the
affricate and true cluster as being similar more often than they chose the true
cluster–adjunct pairing, $F(1, 66) = 8.88, p = .01$. That is to say, combined
representational+organizational structure was more salient than surface structure alone. The affricate and true cluster were also chosen more often than
the anomalous (but perceptually confusable) affricate–adjunct pairing, $F(1,
66) = 6.71, p = .04$. Children's selection of the true cluster paired with the
adjunct, following from a common number of segments, was no different
from the anomalous affricate–adjunct pair, $F(1, 66) = .15, p > .10$. In this study
then, the combination of representational+organizational structures served to
inform children's similarity judgments, independent of the purported perceptual
confusability of the onsets.

6.3 Discussion

The results of Experiment 1 demonstrated that children were able to access the internal properties of syllable onsets when provided with certain combinations of structure. The conjunction of representational+organizational structure was utilized in children's judgments of similarity, but surface+representational structure was not. Children's reliance on representational + organizational properties was also preferred over a single surface level property associated with number of segments. This is consistent with prior research and the (non)salience of segmental number in development (e.g., Liberman et al., 1974; Treiman & Baron, 1981; Walley, 1993). Perhaps more important, the representational+organizational combination, as exemplified through children's pairing of the affricate and true cluster, was favored even though there were a variety of other structural and perceptual differences. To illustrate, the affricate consists of just one segment, whereas the true cluster is comprised of two. And, while both have a branching representation, the hierarchical location of branching differs: the affricate branches at the segmental level, whereas the true cluster branches at the onset level (cf. Figure 1b and c, respectively). Further, the affricate and true cluster differ in their acoustic and articulatory properties (Klatt, 1973; Stevens, 1998; Chang, Plauché & Ohala, 2001). Perceptually, the affricate is a sibilant, nonplosive and nonanterior, whereas the true cluster is a nonsibilant, plosive and anterior (Table 2). Notice, in particular, that the affricate and true cluster are distinct from each other in all three dimensions that have been reported as contributing to singleton perceptual confusability (Singh et al., 1972). These differences did not override the apparent importance of structural similarity based on branching coupled with conformity to the Sonority Sequencing Principle. Finally, this pattern of results obtained for children with and without phonological delay, suggesting that insight to specific properties of onsets were available regardless of whether these same onsets occurred in children's productive sound systems.

7   Experiment 2

The purpose was to evaluate the independent contribution of surface, representational, and organizational structure in children's judgments of the similarity of onsets. In complement to the combined effects shown in Experiment 1, this next set of studies examined whether individual levels of onset structure were available to children. If so, our prediction was that one level of structure would emerge as higher order and perhaps most basic in development. Studies 2.1 and 2.2 were complementary. In Study 2.1, surface, representational and organizational levels of structure were pitted against each other when the experimental triplet was in conformity to the Sonority Sequencing Principle; in Study 2.2, it was just the reverse, with the triplet in violation of the principle. The reverse instantiations further served to evaluate the potential strength of independent levels of structure in children's similarity judgments.

7.1   Study 2.1

7.1.1   Participants

Forty-five children enrolled, 20 with typical ($M = 55$ months; range $= 38–71$) and 25 with delayed ($M = 55$; range $= 45–77$) phonological systems.

7.1.2   Methods

Procedures and dependent variable were identical to Experiment 1. The experimental triplet consisted of the singleton, true cluster, and adjunct. Structural and perceptual points of overlap among members of the triplet are shown in Table 4. Based on onset-internal structure, the true cluster and adjunct share surface similarity, each consisting of two segments. The singleton and adjunct share representational similarity given that both are internally nonbranching. The singleton and true cluster share organizational similarity in conformity to the Sonority Sequencing Principle; this pair is also potentially confusable in their nonsibilant, plosive characteristics. Following from onset-internal structure, the independent variables were surface versus representational versus organizational structure.

Table 4. Onset triplets of Experiment 2. Structural and perceptual overlap, following from Tables 1 and 2 respectively, are indicated with '+'.

Study	Onset Triplet	Structural Overlap			Perceptual Overlap		
		Surface	Representational	Organizational	Sibilant	Plosive	Place
2.1	Singleton /k/		+	+	+	+	
	True Cluster /tw/	+		+	+	+	+
	Adjunct /sp/	+	+				+
2.2	True Cluster /tw/	+	+				+
	Adjunct /sp/	+		+	+	+	+
	3-element /skw/		+	+	+	+	+

7.1.3 Results

Data were analyzed as described, with results shown in panel (a) of Figure 3. There was no main effect of group, $F(1, 43) < 1, p > .10$, but there was a main effect of comparison, $F(2, 86) = 7.61, p = .001$. The interaction of Group x Comparison failed to reach significance, $F(2, 86) = .25, p = .76$. Planned pair-wise comparisons indicated that children judged the singleton and true cluster as having a common organizational structure more often than they chose the singleton and adjunct as having a shared representational structure, $F(1, 86) = 14.69, p = .001$. Likewise, they used organizational similarity in choosing the singleton–true cluster pair more often than surface similarity in selection of the true cluster–adjunct pair, $F(1,86) = 6.49, p = .04$. Finally, there was no significant difference in their grouping of the adjunct with the singleton or with the true cluster, following from representational and surface overlap, respectively, $F(1, 86) = 1.65, p = .60$. In all, the organizational level associated with conformity to the Sonority Sequencing Principle emerged as the underlying property that guided children's similarity judgments. This not-withstanding, their choice of the singleton and true cluster as similar coincides with estimates of perceptual confusability; but this, of course, assumes that clusters are processed serially from left-to-right, which may not be correct (cf. Klatt, 1973; Black et al., 1974; Luce & McLennan, 2003). Nevertheless, if this assumption is accepted, then children's reliance on onset-internal structure cannot be disambiguated from perception.

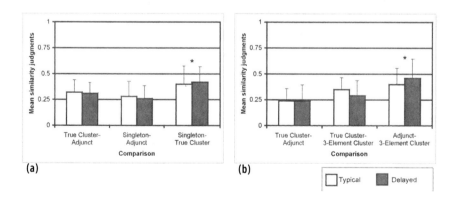

Figure 3. Mean proportion of similarity judgments for the logically possible onset pairings by children with typical and delayed phonological systems for Experiment 2.

7.2   Study 2.2

7.2.1   Participants

Forty-five children participated, 20 with typically developing and 25 with delayed phonological systems. Their mean ages were 55 (range = 38–71) and 54 months (range = 41–77), respectively.

7.2.2   Methods

Procedures and dependent variable were the same as in prior studies. The experimental triplet consisted of the true cluster, adjunct, and 3-element cluster. Table 4 shows that the true cluster and adjunct are alike in surface structure with the same number of segments. The true cluster and 3-element cluster are alike in representational structure since both have onset-internal branching. Finally, the adjunct and 3-element cluster are alike in organizational structure because both violate the Sonority Sequencing Principle. The latter might also be viewed as perceptually confusable, given the sibilant, nonplosive nature of /s/ as the first segment of these sequences. From an onset-internal perspective, the independent variables were again surface versus representational versus organizational structure.

7.2.3   Results

Results are displayed in panel (b) of Figure 3 for both groups of children, with data analyzed as before. There was no significant main effect of group, $F(1, 43)$ = 2.65, p = .11; but there was a main effect of comparison, $F(2, 86)$ = 11.99, p = .0001. The Group x Comparison interaction was not significant, $F(2, 86)$ = 1.17, p = .31. Planned pair-wise comparisons revealed that children judged the adjunct and 3-element cluster as being similar more often than the adjunct and true cluster, $F(1, 86)$ = 23.77, p = .0003. The former reflects organizational similarity, whereas the latter reflects surface similarity. Children also paired the adjunct and 3-element cluster more often than the true and 3-element clusters, even though the latter agree on representational grounds, $F(1, 86)$ = 7.97, p = .02. There was no significant difference in judgments based on surface similarity (between the adjunct and true cluster) as compared to representational similarity (between the true and 3-element clusters), $F(1, 86)$ = 4.21, p = .14. At first glance, Study 2.2 appears to replicate the utility of the Sonority Sequencing Principle in children's judgments of onset similarity, albeit from a reverse instantiation. Nevertheless, as in Study 2.1, the role of the onset-internal structure cannot be fully disentangled from perception in children's choice of the adjunct and 3-element cluster as being similar.

7.3 Discussion

The collective results of Experiment 2 suggested that onset organization, as based on the Sonority Sequencing Principle, may have been reliably used by children in judgments of onset similarity. This, however, is not without a caveat because similarity from the view of onset-internal structure was in harmony with projected interpretations of perceptual confusability. We therefore entertain the results from both vantages.

On the structural side, onset organization emerged as primary relative to other internal aspects of structure. This was demonstrated in three ways. First, there were no group differences between children with typical and delayed phonological development, underscoring the relevance of onset organization independent of production. Second, onset organization was used singly and in combination with representational (i.e., branching) structure (Experiment 1). Organizational information was therefore separable from representational, but the reverse was not also true. Thus far, branching has not emerged as an independent property upon which children based their judgments. This implies a potential precedence relationship such that organizational structure may take priority over representational structure in development. It may be that representational information is relevant in and of itself, but only under well-defined circumstances. For instance, if the presumed higher order organizational structure were removed as a possible dimension of overlap, perhaps children would resort to (secondary) representational structure in judging the similarity of onsets; this will be considered in Experiment 3. A third way that the primacy of organizational structure was supported was by its equivalence. That is, children judged onset similarity in conformity to, and violation of the Sonority Sequencing Principle. They appeared to know what was and what was not a well-formed onset of English. Yet, there is again an (unavoidable) alternative given the phonotactics of the language, which brings us then to an examination of the perceptual side of the results. In particular, onsets that violate the Sonority Sequencing Principle are obligatorily defined by a more sonorous /s/ at the left edge of the syllable, e.g., adjunct /sp/ or 3-element cluster /skw/. As phonetically transcribed, the adjunct and 3-element cluster necessarily share an identical segment /s/. Thus, it might be thought that children judged similarity on the basis of (perceptual) segmental identity and not (underlying) instantiations of the Sonority Sequencing Principle. A similar hypothesis can be advanced for Study 2.1, with respect to children's judgments of the singleton /k/ and true cluster /tw/, with both being nonsibilant plosives (cf. Chang et al. (2001) for counterevidence). This notwithstanding, there are a number of pieces of evidence that work against a perceptual hypothesis. As summarized in the introduction, speech does not seem to be literally processed in a left-to-right fashion, and this appears to have consequences for the perception and processing of sounds as singletons and as clusters (Black et al., 1974; Luce & McLennan, 2003). The implication is that /s/, /sp/, and /skw/ may not be perceptually identical, despite having a seemingly common consonant. This receives added support based on acoustic, articulatory and aerodynamic evidence indicating that the properties of /s/ change with context, as in /sp/ versus /skw/ (Stevens, 1998). Turning to development, /s/ apparently has low perceptual salience, with errors persisting to 9 years of age and potentially contributing to language delay as a causal factor (Smit et al., 1990; Leonard, McGregor & Allen, 1992; Leonard, 1998). It is also the case that preliterate children are not very good at making judgments of segmental identity (Treiman & Breaux, 1982; Walley, 1993). The difficulty of this task apparently increases when clusters are involved (Treiman & Zukowski, 1996). Even with training, children in the second grade are still unreliable in their decisions about the common phonemes of syllables (Treiman & Baron, 1981). Children also err in discrimination tasks by judging sounds as different when, in fact, the sounds are identical (Graham & House, 1971). Finally, on linguistic grounds, /s/ in the adjunct and 3-element cluster is not onset-internal material since it is appended directly to the syllable node (Figure 1d, e). These facts aside, if /s/ were being used by children to judge onset similarity, we might expect this to be a robust pattern of responding because perceptual information is the first way in to representational structure (Murphy, 2002). If this is the case, (perceptual) segmental identity is the most apparent and obvious form of onset overlap. This too will be considered in Experiment 3.

8   Experiment 3

The purpose was to further constrain and limit the dimensions of structural overlap among onsets. The hypothesis was that, if the range of structural overlap were reduced, then children would opt to use alternate levels of structure in their similarity judgments. That is, a decrease in the choice set size would predictably force a child to rely on other onset-internal characteristics that might not have been revealed in prior manipulations. In Study 3.1, organizational structure was removed as a variable, and in Study 3.2, surface level structure was subbed out. In Study 3.3, we take this further by parceling out both surface and representational information. As we have noted before, it was not possible to implement the full complement of logical possibilities due to the phonotactics that limit the onset types of English. Such manipulations would have been either within-onset-type comparisons (e.g., one nonbranching singleton vs. another) or they would have required the use of stimuli that do not occur in language (e.g., singletons that violate the Sonority Sequencing Principle). A secondary intent of Experiment 3 was to tease apart whether children's judgments might alternatively be based on the possible perceptual confusability of certain stimuli.

8.1   Study 3.1

8.1.1   Participants

Thirty-five children enrolled, 20 with typical ($M = 55$ months; range $= 38$–71) and 15 with delayed ($M = 51$ months; range $= 45$–70) phonological development.

8.1.2   Method

Procedures and dependent variable remained the same. The experimental stimulus set consisted of the singleton, affricate and true cluster, as in Table 5. Notably, these all conform to the Sonority Sequencing Principle, thus organizational structure was held constant. The singleton and affricate share a common surface structure, both consisting of one segment. The affricate and true cluster share a common representational structure, with the occurrence of branching. The singleton and true cluster do not overlap (save for organization, which was held constant); but, as in Study 2.1, this pair might be taken as perceptually confusable given its nonsibilant plosive characteristics. In terms of onset-internal structure, the independent variables were thus surface versus representational structure.

Table 5. Onset triplets of Experiment 3. Structural and perceptual overlap, following from Tables 1 and 2 respectively, are indicated with '+'.

Study	Onset Triplet	Structural Overlap			Perceptual Overlap		
		Surface	Representational	Organizational	Sibilant	Plosive	Place
3.1	Singleton /k/	+		+	+	+	+
	Affricate /tʃ/	+	+	+			+
	True Cluster /tw/		+	+	+	+	
3.2	Affricate /tʃ/		+		+	+	
	Adjunct /sp/			+	+	+	+
	3-element /skw/		+	+	+	+	+
3.3	Affricate /tʃ/	+	+		+	+	
	True Cluster /tw/	+	+				+
	3-element /skw/	+			+	+	+

8.1.3   Results

Panel (a) of Figure 4 displays the results for both groups of children. The main effect of group did not achieve significance, $F(1, 33) = .24, p = .63$; the main effect of comparison was significant, $F(2, 66) = 4.63, p = .01$; and there was again no significant interaction of Group x Comparison, $F(2, 66) = .35, p = .71$. Planned pair-wise comparisons indicated that children grouped the affricate and true cluster as being structurally alike on representational grounds more often than they grouped the singleton and true cluster, $F(1, 66) = 9.23, p = .01$. An affricate–true cluster pairing was not significantly different from an affricate–singleton pairing, $F(1,66) = 2.73, p = .31$. Nor was there a significant difference in children's selection of the singleton with either the affricate or with the true cluster, $F(1, 66) = 1.92, p = .51$. These results show that children used representational structure associated with branching in their similarity judgments, but only when the apparent higher order organizational structure was held constant across onsets. Children's selection of the affricate and true cluster as being similar was not attributable to the perceptual confusability of these onsets. As noted before, the affricate is a nonanterior, nonplosive sibilant whereas the true cluster begins with an anterior, plosive nonsibilant. Notably, children did not pair the singleton and true cluster, even though these were projected to be most perceptually confusable (as in Study 2.1). This then demonstrates that onsets that were alike on structural grounds were selected in lieu of onsets that were alike on perceptual grounds.

8.2   Study 3.2

8.2.1   Participants

Thirty-five children participated, 20 with typical development ($M = 55$ months; range $= 38$–71) and 15 with phonological delays ($M = 50$ months; range $= 41$–70).

8.2.2   Method

Procedures and dependent variable were identical to prior experiments. The experiment triplet consisted of the affricate, adjunct, and 3-element cluster. Each onset differs from the others in number of segments, 1, 2, and 3, respectively; hence, surface level structure was removed as a dimension of structural overlap. As in Table 5, the affricate and 3-element cluster both have a branching

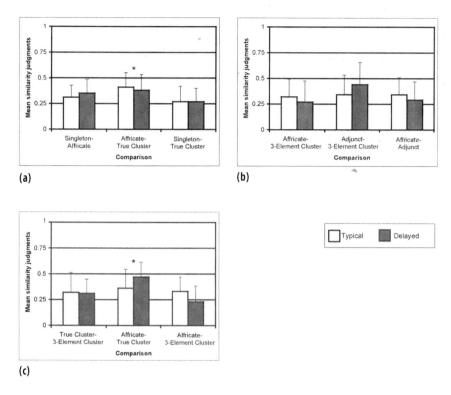

Figure 4. Mean proportion of similarity judgments for the logically possible onset pairings by children with typical and delayed phonological systems for Experiment 3.

representation, whereas the adjunct and 3-element cluster both violate the Sonority Sequencing Principle. The latter pair also have an /s/ edge for further examination of the robustness of segmental identity in children's similarity judgments, following from Study 2.2. Finally, the affricate and adjunct share no common underlying structure and thus were anomalous. The independent variables then were representational versus organizational (vs. anomalous) structure.

8.2.3 Results

Data were analyzed consistent with previous experiments, with results shown in panel (b) of Figure 4. There was no significant main effect of group, $F(1, 33) < 1, p > .10$ or comparison, $F(2, 66) = 1.63, p = .20$. The interaction of Group x Comparison also lacked significance, $F(2, 66) = 1.19, p = .31$. The lack of significance associated with these findings suggests that children did not take advantage of either representational or organizational structure, nor did they appear to resort to a purely perceptual strategy in their judgments. In contrast to Study 2.2, the adjunct /sp/ and 3-element cluster /skw/ were not consistently selected, even though they have a common /s/ edge. It should be noted that children with delayed phonological development did choose this pair more often than the other possibilities, but this was not statistically reliable. Nonetheless, if (perceptual) segmental identity were guiding children's judgments, then this might have been especially apparent because the dimensions of structural overlap had been reduced in this study (cf. Markman, 1989); yet, this was not the case.

8.3   Study 3.3

8.3.1   Participants

There were 35 children in this study, 20 with typical and 15 with delayed phonological systems. Mean ages in months were 55 (range = 38–71) and 50 (range = 41–70), respectively.

8.3.2   Method

Procedures and dependent variable were the same as in prior studies. The experimental triplet included the affricate, true cluster, and 3-element cluster. Table 5 shows that each onset of the triplet varies in number of segments, such that surface level information was eliminated as a point of structural similarity. Also, each onset has branching structure; thus representational structure was held constant. The only relevant distinguishing dimension was conformity to the Sonority Sequencing Principle, as exemplified by the affricate–true cluster pair. This pair, however, is not considered perceptually confusable given its uniqueness along the dimensions sibilant, plosive and back. Thus, on structural grounds, the Sonority Sequencing Principle was the only property manipulated as the independent variable.

8.3.3   Results

Data were analyzed as in prior experiments, with results shown in panel (c) of Figure 4. There was no main effect of group, $F(1, 33) < 1, p > .10$, but there was a main effect of comparison, $F(2, 66) = 4.29, p = .02$. The Group x Comparison interaction failed to reach significance, $F(2, 66) = 2.31, p = .11$. Planned pair-wise comparisons showed that children grouped the affricate with the true cluster given conformity to the Sonority Sequencing Principle, even though this pair is apparently perceptually unique. This pairing occurred more often than a grouping of the affricate with the 3-element cluster, $F(1, 66) = 7.98$, $p = .02$. By comparison, there was no significant difference in children's pairing of the true cluster with the affricate as opposed to the 3-element cluster, $F(1, 66) = 4.33$, $p = .12$. Likewise, there was no difference between the pairing of the 3-element cluster with the affricate or with the true cluster, $F(1, 66) = .56$, $p > 1.0$. The Sonority Sequencing Principle again emerged as a critical dimension in children's similarity judgments, independent of perception.

8.4   Discussion

The collective results of Experiment 3 were especially revealing of the role of representational structure and its relationship to other internal properties of onsets. Specifically, children (albeit typical or delayed) used representational structure to define onset similarity under the conjunction of two well defined conditions: (a) when higher order organizational information was removed as a possible dimension of comparison and (b) when lower order surface information was left as the only other alternative on which to base their judgments. These structural conditions did not intersect with the projected perceptual confusability of the sounds that comprised the onsets. Thus, when children were forced to choose between representational or surface structure (because preferred organizational structure was unavailable), they seemed to opt for the use of representational information to guide their similarity judgments. This was exemplified in Study 3.1 by children's use of branching as opposed to number of segments in their pairing of the affricate with the true cluster. Interestingly, however, when children had to choose between the seemingly most salient properties of onset organization or representation (because the least relevant surface structure was unavailable), they did not reliably employ one or the other. This was realized in Study 3.2 when children had to select either onsets that violated the Sonority Sequencing Principle by pairing the adjunct with the 3-element cluster, or onsets that branched by pairing the affricate with the 3-element cluster. It is significant, however, that in the latter case, organizational structure was associated with violations of (as opposed to conformity to) syllable well-formedness (cf. Gómez & Gerken, 1999 for infants' attention to violations of an artificial grammar). This may well have promoted the apparent antagonism between organizational and representational structure. Nonetheless, well-formedness as defined by the Sonority Sequencing Principle emerged once again in Study 3.3 as a higher order property of syllables in development.

9   General discussion

This research addressed two questions: what do children know about the constituent structure of syllables, and how does that knowledge inform the productive phonology? The focus was specifically on syllable onsets, with evaluation of children's knowledge of surface structure associated with number of segments, representational structure associated with internal branching, and organizational structure associated with the Sonority Sequencing Principle. More generally, these properties are revealing of segmental composition, hierarchical complexity, and onset well-formedness, respectively. The inclusion of preliterate preschoolers with typical versus delayed phonological systems provided the venue for exploring how knowledge of structure mapped onto productive use of that same structure. In answer to the primary questions, the general results showed that children not only had knowledge of the fine-grained details of onset-internal structure, but that there was no difference between what children with typical and delayed sound systems knew, despite obvious differences in their productive phonologies. These findings do not fully accord with predictions that follow from the existing literature in support of globally holistic representations and differential knowledge associated with differences in production, respectively. When set within a broader theoretical context, the findings bear on longstanding debates about the nature of children's representations and the relationship between perception and production. They also hold implications for models of phonological development, particularly those that aim to account for language delay.

9.1   Nature of children's representations

The results supported in part the relevance of the syllable, and onset in particular, in development. The evidence comes from the mere fact that children completed the oddity task, making systematic judgments about the similarity of unique onset types. Further evidence attesting to the importance of the syllable was the finding that surface structure (associated with number of segments) was not used by children in their similarity judgments. This was not unexpected given that segmental counting and identification prove to be difficult for children, even following explicit training (Treiman & Breaux, 1982). Thus, consistent with the experimental intent, properties of syllables as opposed to sounds as units were the locus of children's attention. At first glance, this would appear to be in sync with prior claims that children rely on larger (holistic) units of structure in the course of acquisition. However, our results stand apart in their demonstration that some aspects of the subconstituent structure of syllables were accessible and functional. This was evidenced by the fact that children used abstract properties associated with the representation and organization of onsets in their similarity judgments. For the most part, this was independent of the purported perceptual confusability of the stimuli. Three new observations emerged about children's insights to onset-internal structure.

First, the Sonority Sequencing Principle served as a primary dimension that defined onset structure for children. This organizational principle is universal among languages in establishing the permissibility of syllables. The implication is that children did not extract just any detail about onsets, but rather honed in specifically on that which is characteristic of all languages. Their appeal to the Sonority Sequencing Principle appeared to be robust because children used this property when presented on its own and in combination with other aspects of internal structure. They seemed to rely on the Sonority Sequencing Principle to also demarcate onsets that were and were not well-formed. Typically, in development, this ability to classify information equivalently comes with increased experience, knowledge of and familiarity with a category (Murphy, 2002). At the earliest stages, a child's default response is to identify members of a category by their defining properties, instead of by exclusionary properties; e.g., what a category is as opposed to what it is not. In this case, the equivalent application of the Sonority Sequencing Principle by children implies that it may have been known and operative for some length of time.

A second observation was that children's knowledge of onset-internal structure was graded. Following from above, organizational information associated with the Sonority Sequencing Principle was the most salient aspect of structure. This was succeeded by representational information associated with the occurrence of branching, with children having least knowledge then of the segmental composition of onsets. Of significance was the fact that the higher order properties of onsets functioned in both complementary and antagonistic ways. For the most part, children routinely chose to use organizational, in lieu of representational structure. However, when first order information about well-formedness was unavailable, they opted for the use of secondary information about branching. But, when forced to choose between the 'best of the best', children did not reliably use either organizational or representational information. This outcome is consistent with other studies of language acquisition, which have reported competition (or conflict) effects when optimal structural variables are pitted against each other (Gierut, Morrisette & Champion, 1999). The pattern of results also extends beyond the study of acquisition to research on language structure and processing (Smolensky, 1997b; Luce & Large, 2001). Such competition/conflict/cancellation effects have been interpreted as one way to confirm the relative domain and ranking of linguistic variables. For our purposes then, children's relative knowledge of onset structure may be ranked as organizational, then representational (i.e., Sonority Sequencing Principle >> Branching >> Segment number).

A third observation was that, although children had insight to certain abstract properties of onset-internal structure, they also lacked knowledge of other details. As reported, the number of segments was of little utility to children; in addition, they did not have complete knowledge of representational branching. Recall that children identified resemblances among onsets with branching representations, as in the parallel structure of affricates, true clusters, and 3-element clusters (Table 1 and Figure 1b, c and e, respectively). Yet, they did not further attend to the precise location of branching within these representations. They ignored differences in branching at the level of the segment (for the affricate) compared to branching at the level of the onset (for the true cluster). The occurrence of branching, but not its location was all that seemed relevant. That is to say, children apparently knew about representational complexity, but not necessarily how this complexity was internally arranged. Interestingly, this fits with other facts of phonological acquisition. For instance, Lleó and Prinz (1996; 1997; see also Gierut & O'Connor, 2002) found that branching segments are precursors to branching onsets in development. Apparently, once a child learns about branching, this form of structural complexity can be spread throughout the phonology, being applied generally to various locations in the phonological hierarchy. Kehoe (2001) made a similar observation with regard to acquisition of stress, noting that preschool children are aware of which stress patterns are more or less complex, but do not know precisely what makes them complex. Another parallel case comes from Thompson and Newport's (2003) evaluation of adults' abilities to learn an artificial language. In the optimal learning condition, adults capitalized on variability and complexity of the input to master the structure of the miniature linguistic system, but they were unable to pinpoint just exactly which cues aided them most in the learning task (see also Gómez, Lany & Chapman, 2003).

From these results, it seems that children have fine-grained, but graded knowledge of the constituents of syllables, but they still have not achieved adult-like knowledge. This then raises at least two questions about the nature of children's representations for future research.

One outstanding issue bears on debates about whether children's linguistic representations are holistic versus analyzable. While we have demonstrated that preschool children may have insight to certain details of onset-internal structure, it was not possible to determine whether this knowledge was present from the outset (Pinker, 1984; Chomsky, 1999; Swingley & Aslin, 2000; 2002), or whether their initial representations had been gradually restructured to date (Walley & Metsala, 1990; Metsala & Walley, 1998; Storkel, 2002). In this regard, it will be important to trace the longitudinal emergence of children's knowledge of onset structure. A possible way to achieve this is to document the developmental time course of those aspects of structure that are not yet known by children. From the present studies, children's knowledge of branching location and surface level information might be appropriate places to start. Extending this, it may also be fruitful to examine children's knowledge of other subconstituent properties of syllables. For example, each segment of the onset is further comprised of hierarchically arranged subsegmental (featural) properties of place, voice, and manner (Gerken et al., 1995; Gierut, 1996a). Examinations of subsegmental relative to subsyllabic information may ultimately yield unique heterochronic trajectories for a full range of linguistic units that children must come to know in the course of language acquisition. This will serve to better inform our understanding of the nature of, and potential change in children's representations.

Another outstanding issue bears on debates about the role of perception in representational development. Consider that in 2 of 7 studies reported herein, the projected perceptual confusability of the stimuli coincided with predictions about structural similarity as derived from the onset representation (Table 2). Recall that in Study 2.1, /k/ and /tw/ were judged as similar, both being plosives; in Study 2.2, /sp/ and /skw/ were paired, both being initiated with /s/. In these two studies, perceptually confusable onsets were also structurally similar, making it impossible to discern whether children were relying on perception or the representation to inform their judgments. It would not be unlikely that both sources of information contributed to their response patterns. These cases notwithstanding, a perceptually-driven response strategy cannot account for the full set of data. Recall that listeners' perceptual confusions are primarily influenced by the properties sibilant, plosive, and place (Table 2; Singh et al., 1972). Consequently, if perception were solely responsible for the collective results, we might have predicted that sibilants /tʃ/, /sp/, and /skw/ would pattern alike, as would the back sounds /k/ and /tʃ/ or the plosive sounds /k/ and /tw/. However, for the most part, children paired /tʃ/ with /tw/, despite their reported perceptual, acoustic, aerodynamic and articulatory uniqueness (Singh et al., 1972; Black et al., 1974; Newman et al., 1997; Stevens, 1998; Chang et al., 2001). Although both /tʃ/ and /t/ of /tw/ are initiated with a transient, in the case of the affricate, the transient is so brief that the strong prolonged turbulence of the release apparently takes over as its more salient characteristic. This apparently contributes to why /tʃ/ is perceptually similar to sibilants instead of stops. One might ask then why /tʃ/ and /tr/ have been reported as perceptually similar in other studies (e.g., Kornfeld, 1978; Barton et al., 1980). After all, /tr/ is initiated with the stop /t/, just as is /tw/. The reason again relates to the acoustic properties of the cluster /tr/. As reported by

Klatt (1973) and others (Haggard, 1973; Hawkins, 1973; Davidsen-Nielsen, 1974), a number of contextual changes take place when a voiceless stop is followed by a liquid. Specifically, voice onset time of the stop is lengthened, which in turn lowers the F1 onset frequency; these are now cues to a voiced, not a voiceless stop. The longer voice onset time is accompanied by turbulence prior to the first glottal pulse of the vowel; this results in the stop burst being affricated. An open glottis provides for more airflow, which translates to greater acoustic energy and perceived loudness. Thus, contextual changes in the duration of voice onset time, turbulence of the stop burst and loudness converge to influence the percept of /tr/ as an affricate. These same changes do not take place in the case of /tw/. This serves to underscore the point that sounds as singletons and those same sounds as clusters seem to take on entirely different complexions, which in turn influences their perception and processing (Black et al., 1974; Luce & McLennan, 2003). Thus, when the results are taken together, a representational account appears to offer a more parsimonious description. As directions for future research, it will be important to examine how perception and the development of representations interact. We know, for example, that learners' perceptions are sharply modified as knowledge of a category is gained, such that previously arbitrary attributes become enhanced and are made to be relevant (Goldstone, 1994; Goldstone & Steyvers, 2001). As extended to the linguistic domain, studies directed at exploring the mutual contributions of perceptual to representational learning, and vice versa, are warranted. Perhaps a more provocative and challenging question that arises from this discussion is whether it is even necessary to posit linguistic (or other symbolic) representations (Cole & Hualde, 1998). Some have argued that not enough attention has been paid to the rich perceptual context in which language is grounded, and further that there are a myriad of cues available in the input to allow a child to compute linguistic structure on-line (Bates & MacWhinney, 1987; Jones & Smith, 1993). As Murphy (2002) notes, the origins of any higher order (linguistic) category must start in perception. Such questions lie at the heart of current developmental research, and it is only through continued study and debate that we will gain an understanding of how perceptual and representational information are coordinated in development.

9.2   Relationship between perception and production

The way in which knowledge of syllables was reflected in children's productive phonologies was revealed by the comparative findings from children with typical versus delayed phonological development. Across experiments, the two groups performed alike, with no differences in their judgments of perceptual similarity. While null results obtained in our examination of syllable structure, other studies of featural structure have shown differential performance among groups, as associated with the productive sound system (Gierut, 1996a; 1998b; Gierut, Morrisette & Storkel, 2003). As one example, typically developing children who produced a distinction between /θ/ and /s/ judged featural similarity in terms of the relevant property, stridency. In contrast, those who did not use /θ/ and /s/ in production also did not use stridency in their similarity judgments. That group differences emerged at a featural, but not a syllabic level of structure may further support the syllable as a basic unit in acquisition. If the syllable were established right from the start as a relevant property of sound systems, then a child would be quite familiar with this unit, perhaps evidencing advanced knowledge of its internal structure. By comparison, other units, such as the distinctive features that make up the internal structure of segments, may be fuzzy or less well known. This hypothesis again calls for an evaluation of multiple levels of structure in tandem, so as to discern possible relationships between subsyllabic and subsegmental structure in acquisition.

The null result is nonetheless interesting because it implies that children may have comparable knowledge of the structure of syllables, no matter their productive outputs. For the typically developing group, children's knowledge and use of that knowledge were in perfect agreement: they perceived and produced the full range of permissible onset types in a manner that was consistent with the ambient language. However, for the group with phonological delays, children appeared to know more than they said; that is, their knowledge was not reflected in their performance. This observation is similar to widely reported perception–production mismatches that have been noted for younger typically developing children (e.g., Yeni-Komshian, Kavanagh & Ferguson, 1980a; 1980b), thereby supporting the delayed status of the group. Yet, the asymmetry presents a number of challenges, which bear directly on explanatory accounts of phonological delay.

From a bottom-up perspective, it has been argued that children with phonological delays have perceptual limitations as the source of their productive errors. These may be general deficits that crosscut the phonological system (Travis & Rasmus, 1931; Winitz, 1969), or they may be specific, such that the sounds children misperceive are precisely those they misproduce (Locke, 1980a; Hoffman, Stager & Daniloff, 1983; Groenen, Maassen, Crul & Thoonen, 1996). By this account, we might have expected that children with phonological delays would have had both perception and production lags relative to those with typical development. This was not supported by the data because the group with delayed development was perceptually on par with those developing typically. Others have suggested that phonological delays are due to an immature motor system (Dworkin & Culatta, 1985; Vihman, 1996; Hale & Reiss, 1998; cf. Forrest, 2002 for a critical review of this perspective). From this vantage, we would predict that there would be constraints on articulation, but children's knowledge of language structure would be intact. This accords with the perception–production asymmetry that was observed; but importantly, recall that the children who participated in this research had functional phonological delays. They performed on par with age-matched typically developing peers on tests of oral-motor structure and function, and thus evidenced no physical limitations. Bottom-up accounts of phonological delay associated with, for example, hearing loss (Shriberg et al., 1986; Shriberg & Kwiatkowski, 1994) can also be set aside in light of the criteria for inclusion that was used herein.

Turning then to top-down accounts, a primary theme has been that phonological delays are due to nonadult-like mental representations, following from standard generative approaches to linguistic description associated with the application of static and/or dynamic rules (Macken, 1980; Dinnsen, 1984; Gierut et al., 1987; Ingram, 1989; Dinnsen, 2002). By these accounts, we might have expected children with phonological delays to exhibit nonadult-like ('different') knowledge of syllables on tasks of perceptual similarity, which would have resulted in corresponding errored productions. This was not the case because children with phonological delays had knowledge of the structure of syllable onsets that was both target- and developmentally-appropriate. This suggests that their internal representations were intact. In a related vein, an alternate claim is that perception–production asymmetries are encoded in children's representations, but this is accomplished by either positing two distinct lexical entries, one for perception and one for production, within a two lexicon framework, or by diacritically marking (e.g., differentially 'tagging') lexical entries for each domain, within a one lexicon framework (Maxwell, 1984 for review). In general, these solutions have been challenged on the basis of parsimony, falsifiability, and continuity in development (Straight, 1980; Iverson & Wheeler, 1987; Gerken, 1994).

At present then, there appears to be no clear resolve of the observed perception–production asymmetries following from available models of phonological delay. Moreover, general theories of language acquisition have yet to identify a breakthrough in understanding mismatches between perception and production (Naigles, 2002; 2003; Tomasello & Akhtar, 2003). The present findings, however, suggest at least two lines of study as possible directions for future research. First, the fact that children with phonological delays had knowledge of syllables, but that this did not transfer to their productions has implications for our understanding of bootstrapping as a mechanism of language learning. The general assumption is that children enter into the language learning process by bootstrapping onto salient and relevant linguistic structure that is available in the speech stream. If we were to acknowledge the syllable as one type of phonological bootstrap (Gleitman & Wanner, 1982), then the results from children with phonological delays appear to challenge its role in facilitating the acquisition process. While these children were able to access the syllable as a relevant unit, once the information was available, either they did not use it (elusion), could not use it (inability), or didn't know how to use it (confusion). Possible reasons might be associated with domain-general limitations on children's abilities to encode and decode information, or domain-specific limitations associated with the relationship between form and meaning. Thus far, the data are inconsistent regarding the cognitive resources of children with phonological delays (Dodd, Leahy & Hambly, 1989; Felsenfeld, Broen & McGue, 1992; Powell, Elbert & Dinnsen, 1999; Chiat, 2001), and this highlights one needed line of continued study. Regarding the connection between form and meaning, perhaps the structure of syllables was easy for the children to extract from the input, but their ability to map this structure onto the contrastive function of onsets in the language was more difficult (cf. Chiat, 1979; Jusczyk, 1992; cf. Barlow & Gierut, 2002), similar to what has been observed across other modules of grammar (Naigles, 2002). Related to this, it may be important to examine more generally the way in which known bootstrapping devices factor directly into language learning. For example, it is not yet known whether children's ability to extract key linguistic structures from the input directly influences the rate at which these structures are acquired, their sequential order of emergence, or their accuracy (Morgan & Demuth, 1996; cf. Fernald & McRoberts, 1996). To address such questions, it will be necessary to trace the emergence of linguistic structure in children's perception and to concurrently monitor its surfacing in production. This will allow us to more carefully pinpoint the precise abilities that are being tapped under these differential modes of performance.

As a second line of study in the attempt to rectify the perception and production dichotomy, it may be beneficial to appeal to distributed computational models of language acquisition and learnability. In this regard, constraint-based accounts such as optimality theory (Prince & Smolensky, 1993/2004; McCarthy, 2002b) may offer new insight, as they accord well with the present data. The essence of this approach lies in constraints that are posited to derive optimal correspondence relationships between input and output, with a shift away from the status of underlying representations. The basic premise is that constraints are universal and available to all learners, but they are violable. Constraints are also neutral to perception and production, but it is their ranking (and violability) that differentiates among languages and stages of development. As applied to the present results, children with typical and delayed development would presumably differ only in their ranking of constraints associated with the structure of syllable onsets, perhaps, for example, properties of the Sonority Sequencing Principle or branching (Féry & van de Vijver, 2003). For those with phonological delays, there would be further differences in the violation of these constraints as they operate in perception as opposed to production. To date, the relationship between perception and production has been hypothetically modeled within optimality theory (Smolensky, 1996b; Pater, 1998); what is now called for is an empirical instantiation of the proposal (cf. Gierut, 2004). This would have the further advantage of aiding theory development because thus far the primary evidence that has accrued in favor of this model has come from children's productions (Kager, Pater & Zonneveld, 2004; cf. Jusczyk, Smolensky & Allocco, 2002). For future research, it will be necessary to draw complementary data from children's perception and production in validation of optimality theory as a model of language acquisition.

10   Conclusion

The goal of this research was to contribute a more fully delineated view of children's knowledge of linguistic structure and its utility in the language learning process. By examining a prominent unit of acquisition, that being the syllable, in both perception and production, we were able to begin to identify the details of structure that are available to children. The results supported the crucial role of universal principles of syllable well-formedness in children's knowledge of structure, and further demonstrated that other aspects of syllable complexity, as associated with branching representational structure, were also available. Children's insight to these abstract properties of syllables occurred in the absence of their attending to superficially transparent relationships among sounds. The implication that derives is that children are able to extract certain fine-grained details about linguistic structure, which contrasts with commonly held views that their knowledge of phonology remains largely unanalyzed until lexical size increases substantially. Yet, despite the accessibility of structure, children did not necessarily implement the same level of detail in their productive outputs. Those with and without productive phonological delays evidenced one and the same knowledge of structure, but their sound systems were quite different. This highlights the perennial mismatch between perception and production in acquisition, but more importantly, raises questions about phonological bootstrapping and the causes and models of phonological delay. These issues encourage several new lines of research that will likely lead to a greater understanding of the language learning process.

Appendix: Experimental stimulus sets.

Experiment 1

Study 1.1

spi	ki	tʃi
ka	spa	tʃa
tʃu	ku	spu
spo	tʃo	ko
tʃa	ka	spa
ke	tʃe	spe
ko	spo	tʃo
spu	tʃu	ku
tʃi	ki	spi
spe	tʃe	ke

Study 1.2

tʃi	spi	twi
spa	tʃa	twa
two	spo	tʃo
twi	tʃi	spi
spe	twe	tʃe
tʃa	spa	twa
twu	spu	tʃu
tʃe	twe	spe
spo	tʃo	two
tʃu	spu	twu

Experiment 2

Study 2.1

spu	ku	twu
twi	ki	spi
two	spo	ko
ka	twa	spa
spe	ke	twe
spa	twa	ka
twu	ku	spu
twe	spe	ke
spi	twi	ki
ko	spo	two

Study 2.2

skwa	twa	spa
twi	spi	skwi
spo	two	skwo
twe	skwe	spe
spa	skwa	twa
skwo	spo	two
spu	twu	skwu
spi	skwi	twi
twe	spe	skwe
skwu	twu	spu

Experiment 3

Study 3.1

twa	tʃa	ka
tʃi	ki	twi
two	ko	tʃo
tʃe	twe	ke
tʃa	ka	twa
ku	twu	tʃu
twe	ke	tʃe
tʃi	twi	ki
two	ko	tʃo
ku	tʃu	twu

Study 3.2

tʃe	spe	skwe
spu	skwu	tʃu
skwo	spo	tʃo
spi	tʃi	skwi
skwu	tʃu	spu
tʃe	skwe	spe
skwa	spa	tʃa
skwi	tʃi	spi
spo	skwo	tʃo
tʃa	spa	skwa

Study 3.3

twi	skwi	tʃi
skwe	tʃe	twe
tʃu	skwu	twu
skwo	two	tʃo
tʃa	twa	skwa
twe	tʃe	skwe
tʃu	skwu	twu
tʃi	twi	skwi
skwa	tʃa	twa
two	skwo	tʃo

Notes

* We would like to thank Paul Luce (University at Buffalo, SUNY) and Rochelle Newman (University of Maryland) for sharing the details of their ongoing research. This work was supported in part by grants from the National Institutes of Health to Indiana University (NIH DC001694) and to the University of Kansas (NIH DC004781, DC008095, & DC006545).

1   The sibilants of English are /s z ʃ tʃ dʒ/.

11 Experimental instantiations of implicational universals in phonological acquisition

Judith A. Gierut
Indiana University

This chapter reports the results of four experiments testing the predictions of two purported universals associated with onset clusters. A first prediction is that the occurrence of true clusters implies the occurrence of affricates, as based on the patterns of first language acquisition (Lleó & Prinz, 1996; 1997). A second is that the occurrence of Consonant+Liquid clusters implies the occurrence of a contrast between /l r/, as based on the patterns of second language acquisition (Archibald & Vanderweide, 1997; Archibald, 1998). Eleven children with functional phonological disorders participated in single-subject treatment manipulations, where they were taught the more versus less marked structures. Generalization learning was monitored in the implicated categories. In direct and systematic replications across studies, children's generalization learning supported the predicted link between clusters and affricates, but not liquids. The results are interpreted within an optimality theoretic framework as documentation of the process of constraint demotion.

1 Introduction

The study of language universals continues to play a major role in shaping the direction of research on language acquisition. There has been a concerted effort to apply language universals to children's developing sound system dating to Jakobson (1941/68). The intent has been to document systematic orders of sound emergence and to predict errors in children's early outputs. Universals are thought to aid in this regard because there appear to be common cross-linguistic patterns of phonological development, such that children seem to acquire the same sounds in similar progressions and they tend to make the same kinds of simplification errors. Universals are also relevant from an applied perspective in phonological learning because markedness relationships help set the goals of treatment for children with phonological disorders. Whereas unmarked properties may define the necessary prerequisites for expansion of a sound system, it is actually the marked properties that enhance the overall efficacy of clinical treatment (Chapters 3 and 8 in this volume). The general findings have shown that treatment of a marked element promotes learning of the unmarked, with the latter acquired for 'free' in the absence of direct intervention. Thus, greater gains result from treatment of marked properties of grammar.

Despite these contributions, the extension of language universals to phonological acquisition has been met with some criticism. There are at least three challenges that have been raised in the literature, and it is these that we aim to remedy in the design of the present set of experiments. One criticism relates to the individual differences that are characteristic of phonological development. Even though cross-sectional and cross-linguistic normative studies (Locke, 1983; Smit, Hand, Freilinger, Bernthal & Bird, 1990) may give an appearance of an orderly progression of sound learning, the complementary longitudinal evidence suggests otherwise (Vihman, Ferguson & Elbert, 1986; Vihman & Greenlee, 1987). From this vantage, it is often the case that an individual child's inventory will go against the predictions of markedness (Ingram, 1988a; 1988b; Gruber, 1999). This has been taken as counterevidence against the validity of universals in acquisition. Other less rigid interpretations have argued that universals were never intended as predictive of a serial path of learning, but serve only to demarcate general boundaries of phonological acquisition (Leonard, Newhoff & Mesalam, 1980; Ohala, 1980). In the face of such opposing viewpoints, the interplay between observed commonalities and individual differences in development is an issue that remains unsolved. It is in this regard that optimality theory (OT) has made significant advances. By positing a universal set of constraints, it is possible to model the common tendencies in phonological development; yet, because constraints are violable and differentially ranked to yield unique grammars, it is possible to capture individual variability. Thus, OT offers a theoretical framework for potentially reconciling one of the longstanding debates in the acquisition literature. We capitalize on this by appealing to OT in analysis of children's phonological learning as predicted by language universals as one goal of this research.

A second problem with the application of language universals to phonological acquisition is the time course relative to the sampling of children's learning. For obvious reasons, it is not possible to establish the precise moment at which a child may acquire a particular sound using conventional language sampling procedures given the typical rapid rate of phonological learning (Locke, 1983). Consequently, it is only possible to achieve a rough estimate of phonological learning. To complicate things further, children's learning is typically sampled in the context of play activities, which are loosely scripted to elicit a range of target sounds (e.g., Tyler, 1996). Even under the best circumstances, it cannot be guaranteed that a child will actually say the intended words due to any number of reasons from lack of interest or familiarity, to fatigue or distraction (Olswang & Bain, 1994). While it is possible to add structure to sampling procedures, this introduces other methodological problems. It is reportedly difficult to systematically elicit the kinds of data that are required to support linguistic claims (e.g., minimal pairs or morphophonemic alternations) from toddlers (Ferguson & Farwell, 1975). Given these logistical concerns, one might ask whether it is even fruitful to test the validity of universals in development. This is where the study of children with phonological disorders comes into play. These children present with functional errors, such that they perform within the expected range on the usual developmental milestones except for slowed sound development (Chapter 2 in this volume). In this respect, they resemble their much younger peers; yet, because the children are preschoolers, they are able to complete complex sampling tasks that are needed in support of conventional linguistic analyses. Thus, the data are richer but indicative of typical phonological learning. Another advantage is that clinical treatment is needed to alleviate phonological disorders. Treatment may be structured as an experiment, such that the treated sound serves as the independent variable and the learning that follows as the dependent variable (Chapter 3 in this volume). As such, it is possible to conduct experimental tests of universals in acquisition by manipulating marked versus unmarked phonological properties and measuring the generalization that results; this was a second goal of the present studies.

A final challenge in the extension of universals to development relates to the scope of study. Some have argued that the patterns found in acquisition may be tangential to the facts of fully developed languages (Kenstowicz & Kisseberth, 1979; Anderson, 1981; Hale & Reiss, 1998). The reason is that development itself is likely to be influencing, or at least interacting with linguistic structure. If there are differences in the realization of universals by children as compared to adults, these cannot be attributed unambiguously to the effects of grammar because the developmental process is in play. Consequently, it may be more appropriate to search for universals within the context of acquisition; that is, to identify developmentally specific implicational relationships. Similar sets of questions can be raised with respect to the study of phonological disorders. Here, the concern is that learning occurs through clinical teaching and this may or may not be comparable to learning that takes place naturalistically. It may be more appropriate then to test universals in like populations as, for example, in comparisons of children with phonological disorders and second language learners since both are able to benefit from instructional programs (Eckman, 1993; Archibald, 1995). This latter set of recommendations is particularly interesting because they motivate a new two-pronged approach to the study of universals in acquisition. One line of study derives from patterns of typical phonological acquisition to be evaluated against the sound systems of children with phonological disorders. This provides the needed 'developmentally matched' comparison since the learners in both cases are children; hence, any effects of the developmental process are held constant in the interpretation of evidence. A second line of study draws upon patterns of second language acquisition to again be evaluated against the sound systems of those with phonological disorders. This provides the complementary 'instruction matched' comparison since both sets of learners receive instruction; here, any interference of treatment is held constant in data interpretation. As our third goal then, we adopted this framework in examining two implicational proposals, one stemming from observations in typical development and the other, from second language acquisition. The proposals are related in that both make predictions about the prerequisites to, and acquisition of onset clusters. The general purpose was to experimentally test the validity of each through treatment of children with phonological disorders, and to account for the observed learning from an OT perspective. In this way, we aim to establish the robustness of the purported universals, while controlling for some of the apparent limitations in the extension of universals to language acquisition. This chapter is organized by experiment. For each study, the motivating data for the universal are presented, along with a possible OT analysis of the observed effects. The OT analysis serves a secondary purpose in generating a set of predictions about learning; these are put to test in the clinical treatment manipulations. The background to each study is then followed by the methods and results, where the universal is revisited for its accuracy. The experiments are brought together in a final discussion of the generalizability of the observed patterns of learning for typical development, second language acquisition, and clinical treatment.

2   Experiment 1

With respect to typical phonological development, Lleó & Prinz (1996; 1997; hereafter L&P) reported on children's cross-linguistic and cross-sectional acquisition of onset clusters. Their goal was to trace the emergence of syllable structure in typically developing toddlers learning German or Spanish as a first language. Across studies, nine children (ages 0;9 to 2;2 years;months) participated, with naturalistic speech samples obtained over time. From the data, a developmental sequence of syllable expansion was identified; namely, children chronologically acquired the structures Consonant-Vowel > CVC > CVCC > CCVCC. Perhaps the most intriguing observation was that children produced onsets using simple singletons first before they used affricates, with these occurring in advance of clusters. Based upon this, L&P hypothesized that branching was a phonological trigger that motivated the expansion of syllable structure in acquisition. Specifically, they proposed that branching at the level of the segment is prerequisite to branching at the level of the onset. Alternatively, the occurrence of onset clusters implies affricates, which in turn implies singletons, but not the reverse. Onset clusters are thereby marked relative to affricates (and also singletons). This thereby constitutes the relevant implicational relationship to be tested in Experiment 1.

L&P offered a parameterization account of their data following from a metrical model of the syllable, with an appeal to the Sonority Sequencing Principle and minimal sonority difference. As reinterpreted within OT, their data presuppose an interaction between the markedness constraint *COMPLEX and a general FAITH constraint. As shown in (1), *COMPLEX bans the occurrence of branching structure in syllable onset position, whereas FAITH necessitates that the output is identical in structure to the input. In modeling the course of development observed by L&P, *COMPLEX would outrank FAITH in the first stage of learning. This ranking captures the exclusion of all complex onsets, albeit clusters or affricates, in children's outputs. Over time, *COMPLEX would be exploded into its constituent constraints: *COMPLEXONSET prevents the occurrence of onset clusters, and *COMPLEXSEGMENT restricts the use of affricates. These two markedness constraints must be in a fixed ranking with each other, with FAITH interleaved, to achieve the course of acquisition that was reported by L&P. Specifically, to provide for the emergence of affricates at Stage 2 of development, *COMPLEXSEGMENT would be demoted below FAITH, with *COMPLEXONSET remaining highly ranked. For acquisition of clusters to occur at a later Stage 3, *COMPLEXONSET would subsequently be demoted below FAITH, but still ranked above *COMPLEXSEGMENT.

(1) Constraints and hierarchy following from L&P's developmental data

*COMPLEX	Branching structure is banned in syllable onset position
*COMPLEXONSET	Clusters are banned in syllable onset position
*COMPLEXSEGMENT	Affricates are banned in syllable onset position
FAITH	Inputs and outputs must be identical

Stage 1:	*COMPLEX >> FAITH
Stage 2:	*COMPLEXONSET >> FAITH >> *COMPLEXSEGMENT
Stage 3:	FAITH >> *COMPLEXONSET >> *COMPLEXSEGMENT

Importantly, the longitudinal changes that derived from this possible OT analysis were put to test in Experiment 1. The purpose was to evaluate the purported implicational relationship between clusters and affricates in the emerging sound systems of children with functional phonological disorders. This group thus served as the 'developmentally matched' counterpart to L&P's data. Children who participated entered the study with a phonology characteristic of Stage 1. Half the group was taught the less marked affricate in treatment and the other half, a more marked onset cluster. In validation of L&P's universal, we predicted that treatment of an affricate would induce changes consistent with a Stage 2 phonology, such that *COMPLEXSEGMENT would be demoted but *COMPLEXONSET would not. Children of this group were predicted to learn affricates but not clusters. In comparison, we expected that treatment of a cluster would yield a Stage 3 system and consequently, greater learning. Because of the fixed ranking, the demotion of *COMPLEXONSET would necessarily result in the demotion of *COMPLEXSEGMENT, resulting in children's acquisition of both clusters and affricates. Importantly, the relatively unmarked affricates were expected to emerge in the absence of direct intervention. Based on L&P's observations and in line with the OT account, we did not anticipate children would learn clusters to the exclusion of affricates.

2.1   Participants and their phonological systems

Four children with functional phonological delays participated. Mean age of the children was 3;4 (range 3;1 to 3;10), with two being male and two female. Children performed within expected limits on a diagnostic battery that included measures of hearing acuity, oral-motor structure and function, intelligence, receptive vocabulary, and receptive and expressive language use. By parent report, children were prereaders. There were no other known or overt developmental lags among the group, except for observed delays in phonological acquisition.

A standard clinical measure of the sound system, the *Goldman-Fristoe Test of Articulation* (Goldman & Fristoe, 1986), was administered to all children. Children scored at or below the 16th percentile (range -1 to 16th percentile) relative to their typically developing peers, matched for age and gender. Interpretively, this means that 84% of typically developing children were performing better than the study population in terms of production accuracy. In addition to standardized testing, a detailed phonological sample was obtained using the Phonological Knowledge Protocol (PKP; Gierut, 1985). The PKP taps production of English singleton consonants in relevant word positions, using picture stimuli that are familiar to children. The PKP is designed to elicit minimal pairs for purposes of establishing the phonemic status of sounds, and morphophonemically related forms to allow for potential alternations. A complementary Onset Cluster Probe (OCP; Gierut, 1998a and Chapter 2 in this volume) was administered to obtain data about children's production of 2- and 3-element target clusters and adjuncts. The OCP samples both true cluster and adjunct sequences, with at least five picturable exemplars per target. Both phonological probes were elicited using a spontaneous naming task. Additional details about the phonological probe measures can be found in Chapter 2 in this volume.

Children's probe responses were digitally recorded and phonetically transcribed by trained listeners, and interjudge reliability of phonetic transcriptions was computed. There was 95% mean agreement among independent listeners on consonant transcriptions (range 92–99% agreement), with 885 consonants transcribed. These data provided the corpora for the phonological analyses, where particular attention was given to children's use of affricates and 2-element true clusters since these were crucial to the lawful relationship being tested.

Phonological analyses revealed that, on average, children excluded 9 ambient singletons from their phonemic inventories across contexts (range 7–11). This was confirmed by the lack of minimal pairs and 0% production accuracy on the probe measures. The participants did not produce any ambient 2-element true clusters or 3-element sequences. This was determined by 0% accurate production of target clusters on the OCP. It should be noted that some children produced adjunct sequences, /sp- st- sk-/. It has been shown that adjuncts have exceptional status in language generally (Selkirk, 1982; Goldsmith, 1990; Harris, 1994), but of most importance for children with phonological delays, adjuncts appear to inhibit generalization learning (Gierut, 1999; Gierut & Champion, 2001). For this reason, adjuncts were set aside in the experimental manipulation and interpretation of treatment, which was also consistent with the procedures of L&P.

Table 1 summarizes the phonemic inventories and clusters of participating children. For experimental purposes, the phonological data established that children had 0% pretreatment baseline accuracy and use of target affricates and 2-element true clusters.

Table 1. Descriptive phonological data.

Experiment	Child	CA[a]	GFTA[b]	Condition	Treated Target	Target Exclusions	True Clusters (accuracy)
1	154	3;2	16	Marked	tw-	/θ ð ʃ tʃ dʒ l r/	0%
	164	3;10	-1	Marked	kw-	/θ ð ʃ tʃ dʒ l r/	0%
	147	3;1	8	Unmarked	tʃ-	/f v θ ð z ʃ tʃ dʒ l r/	0%
	150	3;2	10	Unmarked	dʒ-	/ŋ θ ð s z ʃ tʃ dʒ l r/	0%
2	136	3;9	-1	Marked	br-	/ŋ v θ ð ʃ tʃ dʒ l r/	0%
	144	3;5	1	Marked	bl-	/ŋ f v θ ð tʃ dʒ l r/	0%
	125	4;0	<-1	Unmarked	l r	/ŋ f v θ ð s z ʃ tʃ dʒ l r/	0%
	133	4;0	<-1	Unmarked	l r	/ŋ k g f v θ ð s z ʃ tʃ dʒ l r/	0%
3	123	3;9	8	Unmarked	l r	/θ ð r k g f v s z ʃ tʃ dʒ/[c]	0%
	129	3;4	<-1	Unmarked	l r	/ŋ k g f θ ð z ʃ tʃ dʒ r h/	0%
	130	3;9	4	Unmarked	l r	/ŋ v θ ð z ʃ r f/[d]	0%

[a]Chronological age.
[b]*Goldman-Fristoe Test of Articulation* (Goldman & Fristoe, 1986).
[c]The phonemes /k g f v s z ʃ tʃ dʒ/ were positionally restricted in this child's inventory.
[d]The phoneme /f/ was positionally restricted in this child's inventory.

2.2   Experimental design and methods

A staggered single-subject multiple baseline design was applied across pairs of children. The basic setup involved periods of no treatment followed by treatment. In the no treatment phase, baseline data were obtained to demonstrate stability of responding prior to any experimental manipulations. Treatment was then instated sequentially, such that a first child was enrolled, while a second continued to be monitored, with the number of pretreatment baseline administrations increasing by one with each successive child. The underlying assumptions of this design are three-fold: (1) baseline performance is to remain constant until the instatement of treatment for a given child; (2) stability of the baseline across children and over time reflects experimental control over extraneous or interfering variables (e.g., maturation); and (3) phonological gains are expected only during treatment so as to establish a causal link between the manipulation of treatment and children's phonological learning (see Chapter 3 in this volume for more detail).

The independent variables were determined in accord with L&P's implicational proposal. Children were assigned to 1 of 2 treatment conditions directed at production of either more marked clusters or less marked affricates. The dependent variable was children's generalization to both marked and unmarked properties. The operational definition of generalization was a child's production of the target property in a word that called for that property. For example, a child was credited with an affricate if an affricate of any type were produced in target words like 'cheese' [tʃiz] or 'catch' [kets]. Likewise, a child was credited with a cluster if a sequence of consonants were used for target words like 'sweep' [swip] and 'clean' [kwin]. Thus, generalization was based on the extension of specific kinds of structure from treatment, and not necessarily production accuracy. This is in keeping with independent characterizations of phonological acquisition, and follows from previous literature (Weiner, 1981; Fey, 1992b; Gierut & O'Connor, 2002). Moreover, the definition is consistent with an OT framework, where constraints are ranked in favor (or disfavor) of particular structural characteristics of outputs. In this way, our definition of generalization was framed to evaluate constraint demotion as a consequence of the experimental manipulation of treatment. Generalization learning was probed longitudinally in untreated real words and contexts using items from the PKP and OCP. Probes were administered at baseline, during and immediately following treatment.

Treatment followed the protocol described in Chapter 3 in this volume. Briefly, there were two successive phases of instruction that continued to pre-established time and/or performance based criteria. During the imitation phase, a child produced the treated items following an adult model until achieving 75% accuracy of production over 2 consecutive sessions or 7 total sessions, whichever occurred first. Treatment then shifted to the spontaneous phase, where a child produced the treated items independently until 90% accuracy over 3 consecutive sessions, or 12 total sessions, whichever occurred first. In both phases of treatment, corrective feedback was provided to a child in the form of praise for target-appropriate responses and enhanced modeling for errored outputs. Treatment was conducted three times weekly in 1-hour sessions regardless of a child's experimental assignment to a marked or unmarked condition. Thus, all children received the same amount and type of instruction.

The stimuli that were used to elicit the targeted phonological property in treatment were 16 nonwords, following the protocol outlined in Chapter 3 in this volume. The theoretical rationale for using nonwords is, in part, associated with Slobin's operating principle of new versus old information (Slobin, 1971), and the effects of phonotactic probability on production accuracy in language acquisition (Vitevitch & Luce, 1998; 1999). The methodological rationale is associated with maintaining constancy of the visual input across participants, and uniformity among children in familiarity and age-of-word-acquisition of the treated items. Nonwords were phonotactically permissible sequences, created such that the treated phonological property assumed the onset position of (C)CVC, (C)CVCV and (C)CVCVC forms. Nonwords were embedded in the story line of children's books, with meaning associated with the pictured characters and actions. Examples of the treated items are shown in (2).

(2) Example of nonwords used in treatment of unmarked affricates versus nonliquid clusters

    a) Sample affricate forms   b) Sample cluster forms
       [tʃɪd]   [kwɪd]
       [tʃoʊnu]   [kwoʊnu]
       [tʃiməd]   [kwiməd]

2.3   Results

Figure 1 displays the pre- to posttreatment correspondences for the groups of children who were taught clusters and affricates, respectively. Recall that, by L&P's proposal, treatment of a cluster constituted the marked teaching condition, with the affricate being less marked. Further, by the OT account, the marked teaching condition was predicted to be more efficacious given the fixed ranking between *COMPLEXONSET and *COMPLEXSEGMENT. Beginning then with the marked manipulation, Figure 1 shows that treatment of clusters resulted in children's generalization to other clusters. This was reflected in a mean post-treatment correspondence score of 68% relative to 0% baseline, denoted by the hatched bars. Following treatment, children produced a variety of cluster types ranging from those with a small sonority difference (e.g., /sm- sn-/) to those with a larger sonority difference (e.g., /tw- kw-/). Treatment of a cluster had the further effect of inducing generalization in children's use of affricates (denoted by the shaded bars): the mean posttreatment correspondence score was 40%, even though affricates were never taught. For these children, the demotion of *COMPLEXONSET in treatment of marked clusters led to the spontaneous demotion of *COMPLEXSEGMENT, consistent with a Stage 3 grammar, as in (1). Thus, treatment of clusters had the predicted effect of inducing generalization to both marked and unmarked structures, which lends credence to L&P's implicational proposal and the corresponding OT account.

    In the unmarked manipulation, a different set of findings emerged. Figure 1 shows that children treated on affricates evidenced generalization to this class. The gains were modest at best, with a mean pre-post correspondence score of 7%. This is remarkable because affricates were directly treated. Moreover, in the criterial sessions of treatment, children produced affricates to 49% mean accuracy in imitation, and 93% mean accuracy in spontaneous phases of instruction. This demonstrates that affricates were learned, but did

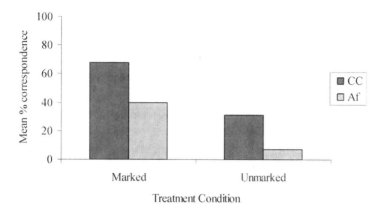

Figure 1. Mean correspondences in generalization to consonant clusters and affricates by experimental condition.

not generalize from treatment. It is of further significance that treatment of affricates resulted in generalization to clusters, with a mean of 31% correspondence from pre- to posttreatment. For these children, exposure to an affricate in treatment prompted acquisition of the more marked category of clusters. These findings are consistent with L&P's observation that children who produced onset clusters also produced affricates, but the generalization pattern was not entirely as predicted: treatment of an unmarked affricate presumably should not have induced changes in marked clusters, and children treated on affricates did not evidence a Stage 2 grammar as predicted by an OT account as in (1). We consider two possible reasons for the apparent asymmetries.

A first is associated with (falsely) assumed limits that are imposed on predictions of learning (Gierut, 2007). Specifically, L&P posited branching structure as a trigger of syllable expansion, with branching segments prerequisite for branching onsets. In this experiment, the rationale for teaching affricates in the unmarked condition was to induce the prerequisite structure. Treatment thereby delineated the particular structure to be taught; it was not designed to constrain or inhibit what would be learned (Chapter 3 in this volume). Following L&P, the findings suggest that by learning affricates in treatment, children were setting the foundation for continued phonological learning. They then built on their newfound knowledge of branching structure to further elaborate the complexity of syllables. Consequently, clusters were acquired in the process. While plausible, this scenario does not accommodate anticipated differences in generalization based on markedness, at least upon first glance. Qualitatively, treatment of unmarked affricates produced the same kind of change as did marked clusters. Importantly, however, there were quantitative differences that emerged between the teaching conditions as seen in the comparison of the data displayed in Figure 1. Whereas unmarked affricates promoted generalization in the range of 7 to 31%, marked clusters prompted gains in the range of 40 to 68%. The quantitative differences thus imply a psychologically real difference associated with markedness. Consistent with the predictions of L&P, the proposed OT account, and the more general clinical literature, treatment of the marked yielded greater generalization learning.

A second consideration is theoretical in nature and bears on the claims of the OT analysis in (1). In particular, some of the assumptions of the learning algorithm may not be obligatory. *COMPLEX may not need to be exploded into its constituent constraints, which then nullifies a fixed ranking of *COMPLEXONSET >> *COMPLEXSEGMENT. In the unmarked experimental condition, once children demoted *COMPLEX below FAITH, then any type of branching structure was permissible in the grammar. This effect is wholly consistent with the construct of generalization in that exposure to one instantiation of branching structure (affricates) prompted learning of other like structures (clusters). Successive stages of learning, i.e., first affricates, then clusters, were not observed. It should be cautioned, however, that the particular experimental design we used is not intended to document *when* particular structures emerge but rather, which structures generalize from treatment. To more fully explore the time course of learning, an alternative design such as a multiple probe may be called for (Kearns, 1986).

Taken together, the experimental data from children with phonological disorders served as a 'developmental match' to L&P's descriptive data from first language learning. The findings were generally consistent with L&P's proposal that the occurrence of clusters implied the occurrence of affricates, but not vice versa. There was somewhat of a departure though from L&P's proposal in that the marked and unmarked conditions yielded quantitative, but not qualitative differences in generalization learning. From the view of OT, this suggests a possible modification in L&P's hypothesis specific to purported stages of learning. As exemplified by the experimental data, branching may emerge step-by-step or in one fell swoop, as in marked versus unmarked treatments respectively (see also L&P for typical development). The consequence is that an explosion of *COMPLEX and the fixed rankings associated with the constraint family may not be uniform across development, as might be expected but also as allowed for within OT. In Experiment 2, we eliminate the possibility that the observed variability may somehow be due to the influences of direct instruction. The second study reports a complementary 'instruction matched' manipulation, whereby a purported universal from second language learning was tested against the performance of children enrolled in clinical treatment.

3   Experiment 2

In a study of second language learning, Archibald (Archibald & Vanderweide, 1997; Archibald, 1998) set out to predict accuracies and error rates in the interlanguages of 8 adult native speakers of Korean learning English. The approach followed that of Broselow and Finer (1991) and Eckman and Iverson (1993), with descriptive and instrumental phonetic data collected. Of particular interest was the learners' use of onset clusters and liquids. Korean does not allow branching onsets as does English, and while [r] and [l] occur in Korean, they are in complementary distribution. [l] occurs postvocalically with [r] elsewhere, thereby supporting the conventional interpretation of /r/ as phonemic in the language. Not surprisingly, Koreans have difficulty learning clusters (namely Consonant+Liquid sequences) and liquids of English. Whereas prior work focused on L1–L2 transfer effects, Archibald explored the possibility that the phonological representations of the learners were at issue. In this regard, he argued that a phonemic contrast between /l r/ was prerequisite to learners' acquisition of liquid clusters. Once learners altered the phonotactics of the grammar by allowing /l r/ to occur, this paved the way for use of the full sonority sequencing scale in the mastery of clusters generally, and liquid clusters in particular. Archibald captured the effects as an implicational universal: learners who accurately produced liquid clusters maintained a laterality distinction, but not vice versa. Clusters are therefore marked relative to the laterality contrast. This implicational law is the focus of Experiment 2.

   In account of the co-occurrence, Archibald appealed to phonological government within a feature geometry model (Rice & Avery, 1993) coupled with derived sonority. He argued that L2 learners must build up nodes of the L1 geometry in accord with the target language being learned. For Korean learners, this necessitated expansion of the Spontaneous Voice node to include approximant and lateral as dependents, i.e., the /l r/ contrast. With the representational change and prerequisite structure in place, general principles of sonority kick in to permit Consonant+Liquid sequences. It is possible to reinterpret Archibald's data within the more contemporary framework of OT, as in (3). The markedness constraint *LIQUID prohibits the occurrence of /l r/ in the grammar, and a general FAITH constraint demands correspondence between the output and input at a first stage of learning. Subsequently, there is an explosion of *LIQUID to provide for the differential exclusion of liquids as contrastive phonemes (via *LIQUIDPHONEME) as opposed to liquids in clusters (via *LIQUIDSEQUENCE), with FAITH intervening. In parallel to the OT interpretation offered in (1), the family of *LIQUID constraints must be in a fixed ranking to comply with the implicational predictions. *LIQUIDPHONEME is demoted at Stage 2, thereby allowing contrastive use of /l r/, but *LIQUIDSEQUENCE stays ranked above FAITH, thereby banning the use of liquids in clusters. At Stage 3, liquids are allowed as phonemes and in clusters, as both markedness constraints are demoted below FAITH. This then yields three stages of acquisition as the predicted results of Experiment 2.

(3) Constraints and hierarchy for Archibald's data from second language acquisition

> *LIQUID   Liquids are banned
> *LIQUIDSEQUENCE Consonant+Liquid clusters are banned
> *LIQUIDPHONEME Contrastive use of /l r/ is banned
> FAITH   Inputs and outputs must be identical
>
> Stage 1:   *LIQUID >> FAITH
> Stage 2:   *LIQUIDSEQUENCE >> FAITH >> *LIQUIDPHONEME
> Stage 3:   FAITH >> * LIQUIDSEQUENCE >> * LIQUIDPHONEME

Thus, the purpose of the second study was to evaluate Archibald's proposal by manipulating treatment of liquid clusters versus the liquid contrast in two groups of children with phonological disorders. Following from (3), we expected that treatment of a marked liquid cluster would promote generalization learning consistent with a Stage 3 grammar with children acquiring liquid clusters and the liquid contrast. In comparison, treatment of the unmarked laterality distinction would accord with a Stage 2 system, such that children would learn the liquids but generalization would not extend to liquid clusters. Under either manipulation, generalization to liquid clusters was not expected in the absence of the laterality distinction.

3.1   Participants, design, and methods

The procedures were essentially the same as in Experiment 1. Four children (ages 3;5 to 4;0) participated, three boys and one girl, with their corresponding phonological data shown in Table 1. None of the children produced clusters of any type, nor did they produce a liquid contrast, establishing 0% baseline performance for the phonological properties of interest. For the descriptive data, reliability of consonantal transcriptions was 93% mean agreement among independent listeners (range 88–97%), with 790 consonants transcribed.

Children were assigned to 1 of 2 experimental conditions, treatment of a marked Consonant+Liquid cluster or treatment of the unmarked liquid contrast. The independent variable thus was treatment of marked versus unmarked structure. As before, the dependent variable was percent correspondence in use of liquid clusters and the liquid contrast. The methods and timing of the generalization samples remained the same as in the prior study. Treatment also followed the same protocol, with one caveat associated with the unmarked condition. Because Archibald's proposal implicates the laterality contrast, children were taught a phonemic distinction between /l r/ using minimal pairs. This procedure departs somewhat in that two sounds were being introduced, and minimal pairs served as stimulus items, with examples shown in (4).

(4) Example of nonwords used in treatment of a liquid contrast versus liquid cluster

    a) Sample contrast forms   b) Sample cluster forms
          [lib]–[rib]   [blib]
          [lɛmoʊ]–[rɛmoʊ]   [blɛmoʊ]
          [lunəd]–[runəd]   [blunəd]

3.2 Results

Pre- to posttreatment correspondence data are shown in Figure 2 for the marked and unmarked treatment conditions, respectively. Notice that children who received treatment of a marked liquid cluster evidenced gains in production of the treated class. The average gain in use of liquid clusters was 20% above 0% baseline performance (hatched bars). Qualitatively, the clusters learned were limited to Consonant+Liquid sequences, i.e., /bl- ʃr- fl-/. On the one hand, the scope of learning may seem appropriate since liquid clusters were after all the target of treatment; but on the other hand, the shallow learning departs from findings in the clinical literature. Previous research has shown that treatment of clusters with a small sonority difference (i.e., Consonant+Liquid sequences) triggers broad generalization to clusters of all greater differences as a highly efficacious teaching condition (Gierut, 1999). By this, the marked treatment manipulation of the present study did not yield comparable levels of learning.

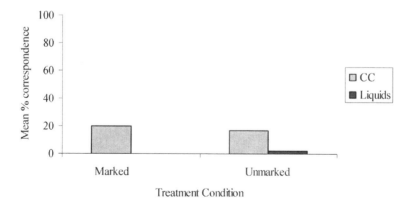

Figure 2. Mean correspondences in generalization to consonant clusters and liquids by experimental condition.

There was another anomaly in the data. Contrary to Archibald's proposal, children who were taught (and learned) liquid clusters did not learn the liquid contrast. None of the children treated on liquid clusters acquired a phonemic distinction between /l r/ (shaded bars). This pattern of learning should have been excluded by the implicational proposal; this thereby constitutes an apparent violation of the law. It is even more significant that the unmarked treatment manipulation resulted in an identical set of findings. As shown in Figure 2, treatment of the /l r/ contrast as the unmarked targets did not result in generalization to liquids. In fact, there was just one correspondence with just one of the liquids that was produced by one child in the entire corpus of data, i.e., [loʊloʊ] 'yellow.' The phonotactic exclusion remained, even though the children learned minimal pairs during treatment to 85% (imitation phase) and 87% (spontaneous phase) mean accuracy in the criterial phases of instruction. As before, children treated on the liquid distinction generalized to liquid clusters, with 17% mean pre- to posttreatment correspondence. While liquid clusters were learned, the range was limited to Consonant+/r/ sequences /br- tr- dr- fr- θr-/. Notice again that this pattern of change violates Archibald's proposal because liquid clusters were acquired to the exclusion of the liquid phonemes.

The finding that children employed sounds in clusters without also using those same sounds as singletons may appear unusual at first glance. This however is not an uncommon phenomenon in the acquisition literature (Kent, 1982; Smit, 1993a; 1993b; Gierut & O'Connor, 2002). One thought is that seemingly obvious links between levels of structure are not fully elucidated in the early stages of development. Another idea is that ease of production may be facilitated in certain (cluster) contexts. With respect to the current study, there is another possible reason for the asymmetry that may be related to the methods. Specifically, because Archibald's proposal required a distinction between /l r/, children were required to learn and generalize two new phonemes. This departs from the other manipulations reported thus far, where the goals of treatment focused on adding just one new structure to the grammar. It is quite possible that the acquisition of the liquid contrast was a more challenging task, hence the lack of generalization and the violations of Archibald's proposal. To eliminate this possibility, we therefore designed a third study where children were taught one liquid as the contrast to a known liquid of their repertoire.

4   Experiment 3

Prior research has shown that contrastive information is especially help-ful to children's learning from a more general cognitive perspective (Au & Laframboise, 1990). For phonology, in particular, contrast treatment using minimal pairs has received strong support as an efficacious teaching method for children with phonological disorders (Weiner, 1981; see also Barlow & Gierut, 2002 for review). Within the minimal pair method of treatment, there is a gradient of efficacy. One of the most efficacious pairings involves the presentation of two new sounds in contrast to each other (Gierut, 1998c). This was the set up we used in Experiment 2, which oddly resulted in the lack of generalization learning of liquids. Another efficacious pairing involves presenting one new sound in contrast to a sound that is already in the child's repertoire (Gierut, 1989b). This was the paradigm we adopted herein. The purpose of Experiment 3 was to modify the learning task in acquisition of phonemic distinctions through minimal pairs as a possible way of reducing the cognitive load. By teaching children one new liquid in comparison to another known liquid in their inventory, the task more closely resembles the other experimental manipulations. Thus, the independent variable was presentation of a liquid in minimal pairs to induce the laterality distinction, as a complementary unmarked treatment condition. As before, the dependent variable was pre- to posttreatment correspondences in production of the liquid contrast and liquid clusters. Predicted generalization learning also followed from above, such that treatment of the unmarked liquid was expected to lead to the liquid contrast but not liquid clusters.

4.1   Participants, design, and methods

Three children (ages 3;4 to 3;9) served as participants; their relevant phono-logical data are shown in Table 1. Notice that the inclusionary criteria were expanded such that children were required to have at least one liquid in the phonemic inventory. The liquid in the inventories of these children was /l/. Aside from this deviation, the methods, design, and procedures were identi-cal to those reported previously for Experiment 2. Reliability of consonantal transcriptions was established for the descriptive data, with 93% mean agree-ment among independent listeners (range 88–96%) based on 604 consonants transcribed.

4.2   Results

The learning data are shown in Figure 3. It can be seen that treatment of the liquid /r/ in comparison to a known liquid /l/ did not aid in children's acquisition of the laterality distinction (shaded bars). Mean correspondence accuracy in production of the known liquid /l/ was 26% from pre- to posttreatment; however, the contrastive phoneme /r/ was in correspondence only at 2%. As in Experiment 2, there was just one occurrence of [r] in the data, coming from 1 of the 3 children, [rʌbɪn] 'rubbing.' Thus, the modification in the learning task did not impact the results. Of greater significance was the finding that children generalized to the more marked liquid clusters, without also generalizing to the liquids. This occurred with 12% correspondence from pre- to posttreatment. The effect was exactly as reported in Experiment 2, adding to the robustness of the findings. Thus, across two experiments and seven children, liquid clusters occurred in the absence of a liquid contrast such that Archibald's hypothesis was not borne out.

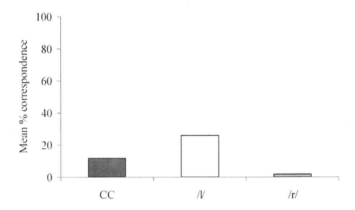

Figure 3. Mean correspondences in generalization to liquid clusters, /l/ and /r/.

When Experiments 2 and 3 are taken together, the findings do not support an implicational or even co-occurrence relationship between liquid clusters and a phonemic distinction between /l r/. Whereas children of both studies acquired liquid clusters, they did not learn to use liquids contrastively. This demonstrated that production of the liquid contrast was not prerequisite to the acquisition of liquid clusters for children with phonological disorders. The absence of the liquid contrast, coupled with the lack of differential learning by experimental conditions, as replicated within and across studies add up to seriously challenge the validity of Archibald's claims. The implications for OT are obvious: markedness constraints against production of clusters (albeit liquid or nonliquid) are independent of constraints against production of liquids.

5   Experiment 4

The power of an experimental effect is demonstrated by its applicability to the population at-large. In group designs, generalizability is accomplished by increasing sample size; the more participants, the more robust the effect. In single-subject designs, the underlying assumptions of the model are based on the uniqueness of an individual. Power is not achieved by recruiting more participants, but rather by direct and systematic replication (Chapter 3 this volume). Thus far, we have reported direct replications in that the same patterns of results occurred across participants of a given experiment. However, systematic replications are more compelling because they require the same pattern of results to occur across participants of different experiments. This shows the strength of control that a particular variable has on behavior under a number of circumstances. The goal of Experiment 4 was to bring together the results of the prior studies as post hoc demonstrations of systematic replication. Across studies, children's phonologies were essentially the same at pretreatment (see Table 1). Namely, they did not produce clusters (liquid or nonliquid sequences), affricates or liquids. Consequently, it was possible to measure generalization to these categories independent of a particular treatment manipulation. In light of the results thus far, we anticipated that there would be a systematic replication of L&P's proposal, but not Archibald's.

5.1   Methods

Table 1 shows that children excluded the phonological properties of interest to both of the purported universals, and serves as the starting point for an examination of systematic replications. In Experiment 1, children did not have clusters or affricates (pertinent to the test of L&P's proposal), but they also excluded liquids. Consequently, generalization to liquids by this group provides for a systematic replication of Archibald's claims. Likewise, in Experiments 2 and 3, children excluded liquids and liquid clusters (pertinent to the evaluation of Archibald's proposal), but because affricates were also missing from these children's systems, there was the possibility to systematically replicate L&P's claims. To explore this, we relied on the probe data that had been collected in the course of each of the experiments. The data were used to compute pre- to posttreatment mean percent correspondences of liquids and affricates respectively, for the participants of all three experiments.

5.2   Results

Figure 4 displays plots of affricate and liquid generalization for completeness and comparative purposes, recognizing that portions of these data had already been reported for the individual experiments. Recall that, across experiments, all 11 children showed generalization to clusters as shown. Thus, we might expect, by L&P's proposal, that they all would also learn affricates, and by Archibald's, the liquid contrast. As can be seen, there was a systematic replication of the relationship between clusters and affricates in Experiments 2 and 3, consistent with the direct replications of Experiment 1. Across all three experiments, children learned the affricates, which attests to the robustness of L&P's claims. The strength of this pattern has now been replicated directly and systematically, in typical and delayed phonological acquisition, under descriptive and experimental conditions.

Figure 4 shows the opposite effect for the purported relationship between clusters and the liquid contrast. When examined systematically or directly, the laterality distinction was not evident in children's learning. The phonemic distinction between /l r/ was not acquired in Experiment 1, which is in keeping with the results of Experiments 2 and 3. While clusters were produced, liquids surfaced only occasionally in the data sets. Moreover, the instances of occurrence were isolated and restricted to /l/ to the exclusion of /r/. The data thereby falsify Archibald's claim of the necessity of a laterality distinction for clusters, in extension to phonological acquisition or treatment.

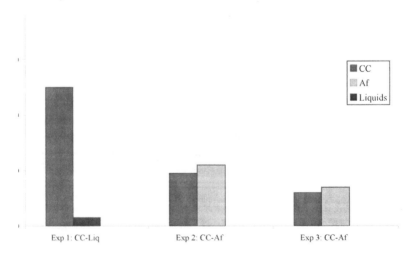

Figure 4. Systematic replications of the relationship between liquid clusters and liquids (Experiment 1) and clusters and affricates (Experiments 2 and 3).

6   Conclusions

Universal properties of phonological systems have served an important purpose in furthering our understanding of the acquisition process from theoretical and applied perspectives. The research reported herein tackled some prior concerns that had been raised about the suitability of extending universals to developing systems. This was achieved by testing a set of purported universals culled from typical and second language acquisition against the experimental results of treatment of children with phonological disorders. In all, the experimental data supported the coupling of clusters and affricates in acquisition, consistent with reports of typical development. Treatment of branching structure prompted generalization to like structure. Within OT, possible accounts of these effects involved either the demotion of a single unexploded markedness constraint *COMPLEX, or alternatively a family of markedness constraints that were in a fixed ranking, and militated against branching onsets and against branching segments. In comparison, the experimental data did not support the co-occurrence of liquid clusters and a liquid contrast, as observed in second language learning. Together, these results highlight three themes to guide future research.

One point of interest is the consistency between typical and delayed phonological development in children. As this volume has attempted to show, children with phonological disorders are not very different from their typically developing counterparts, even though they may be older and learn language through direct instruction. The commonalities suggest that the implicational patterns observed in one child population may be applicable to another child population. This opens the door for more integrated approaches to descriptive and experimental evaluations of co-occurring patterns (universals) in phonological acquisition (Schwartz, Leonard, Folger & Wilcox, 1980; Dinnsen, 1992; Leonard, 1992).

From the reverse perspective, another striking observation is the clear difference between children with phonological disorders and second language learners. It has been argued that the research questions that bear on second language learners and children with phonological disorders are similar in theoretical and applied respects (Eckman, 1993). Our results suggest that while the underlying issues may be the same, the answers to those questions may emerge as very different. It does not appear that the instructional methods are a central contributor to these differences; rather it seems that the developmental process itself is most influential. For children with phonological disorders, development is still in its dynamic phases; whereas for second language learners, development has had its impact on cognitive and experiential advances. It may be the consequences of development then that differentiate the groups. In future research, it may not be the intent to replicate behavioral effects across populations, despite converging experimental questions and conditions. Instead, the findings from second language acquisition may serve only as a springboard for research on phonological disorders in children, and vice versa.

Finally, this report has provided an experimental instantiation of the process of constraint demotion in phonological acquisition. To date, such demonstrations have been limited (Dinnsen, 2002; Jusczyk, Smolensky & Allocco, 2002; Chapters 4, 5, 6, and 8 in this volume). Nevertheless, one concern that emerged is that the experimental designs employed thus far may not be sensitive enough to capture the longitudinal changes predicted by the learning algorithm. As a result, the experimental data cannot fully disambiguate between alternate linguistic accounts (e.g., Experiment 1). Yet, from a reverse perspective, it is also possible that the algorithmic predictions of learning are overly sensitive when compared to children's actual learning trajectories. A consequence is that the longitudinal predictions that derive from a linguistic account may not appear to be behaviorally instantiated. Under either scenario, for future research, it will be important to appeal to a range of designs and a convergence of different types of evidence in manipulations and validations of OT analyses. Attention should also be given to converging phonological gains in children's grammars in an effort to better document the heterochronic and/or tandem nature of phonological change. Together, these efforts may help to more carefully delineate the individual differences from the universal patterns in children's phonological learning.

12 Gapped s-cluster inventories and faithfulness to the marked*

Ashley W. Farris-Trimble & Judith A. Gierut
Indiana University

Markedness hierarchies have played a key role in contemporary theories of both phonology and acquisition. In fully developed languages, implicational markedness hierarchies suggest that languages will have harmonically complete inventories (Prince & Smolensky, 1993/2004); however, this is not always the case. Gapped inventories, which include marked and unmarked items but lack items of intermediate markedness, are predicted not to occur, but despite the claims of markedness, such inventories exist (e.g., de Lacy, 2002; 2006). If children's grammars are believed to parallel adult grammars, a question that follows naturally is whether children produce gapped inventories as they learn languages with harmonically complete inventories. The current chapter addresses this question by exploring children's acquisition of word-initial s-clusters. It is shown that, though the target English s-cluster inventory is harmonically complete, gapped inventories occur with relatively high frequency in children's early stages of acquisition. These results force us to rethink markedness and its role in the acquisition process. The notion of faithfulness to the marked within optimality theory is used to account for the presence of gapped inventories.

1   Introduction

Claims about markedness and markedness hierarchies have pervaded all contemporary theories of both phonology and acquisition. In fully developed languages, markedness hierarchies suggest the existence of harmonically complete inventories; that is, any inventory with a marked element should also contain the full set of less marked elements on the same scale (Prince & Smolensky, 1993/2004). Markedness in fully developed languages, then, is a tool used to

377

explain implicational relationships and typological frequency. In developing languages, on the other hand, markedness is often used to predict or account for the order of acquisition of speech sounds (e.g., Jakobson, 1941/68; Cairns, 1969; Pertz & Bever, 1975; Smit, 1993b), whereby a child cannot acquire a more marked sound without also having acquired less marked sounds first (Jakobson, 1941/68; Smit, 1993b).

The predictions of markedness hierarchies in fully developed languages, particularly the prediction that languages should have harmonically complete inventories, do not always hold. Gapped inventories—those which include highly marked and highly unmarked items but lack items of intermediate markedness—are predicted not to occur, but despite the claims of markedness, such inventories have been shown to exist in many fully developed languages (de Lacy, 2002; 2006). Such findings challenge theoretical proposals for dealing with markedness hierarchies and have direct implications for theories of acquisition. Based on markedness predictions, children should acquire sounds or sound sequences in a markedness relationship from least to most marked. Thus, although unexpected given markedness predictions, the question of whether children produce gapped inventories as they learn languages with harmonically complete inventories is clearly of interest.

Languages and language inventories that do not follow predictions related to markedness hierarchies have often presented problems for the architecture of optimality theory, particularly as one of the primary components of optimality theory is based on markedness. Two main architectural variants have been proposed in dealing with markedness hierarchies: fixed rankings (Prince & Smolensky, 1993/2004) and stringency theory (Prince, 1997; de Lacy, 2002; 2004; 2006). Fixed rankings are those in which a set of constraints are in a strict hierarchy, such that constraints against more marked segments or structures always outrank constraints against less marked segments or structures. On the other hand, constraints in a stringent ranking are freely permutable, but are formulated such that any constraint that bans or preserves a segment or structure must also ban or preserve more marked segments or structures. While fixed rankings capture the implicational component of a markedness hierarchy with their ranking, stringently-formulated constraints capture the same component in their formulation. Stringency theory has been argued to be better able to deal with gapped inventories of the sort discussed herein. One goal of this chapter, then, is to compare fixed hierarchies and stringent constraints.

The current chapter addresses these questions by exploring children's acquisition of word-initial s-clusters and by presenting a theoretical account of this acquisition. In the following sections, a database of 110 children is first examined to establish the patterns of s-cluster acquisition in a wide range of children. Possible exceptions to the claim that children acquire s-clusters in a fixed order are then investigated in more detail. This is a particularly interesting question given that gapped inventories have been demonstrated in singleton hierarchical inventories (de Lacy, 2002; 2006), but not previously in cluster hierarchical inventories. It will be shown that, while the target English s-cluster inventory is harmonically complete, gapped inventories are actually quite common in children's early stages of acquisition. These results force a reconceptualization of markedness and its role in acquisition. Moreover, employing faithfulness to the marked makes certain theoretical predictions about the types of inventories that can and cannot occur. We explore those predictions and compare them to the empirical data. We will demonstrate that our theoretical predictions and empirical evidence converge on the characterization of a number of possible grammars, including a gapped inventory. Moreover, the theoretical predictions highlight an impossible grammar—a disharmonic inventory—which is shown not to occur in the acquisition process. Thus our theoretical accounts are able to predict and account for the possible inventories in children's acquisition of s-clusters, as well as accounting for why some logically possible inventories never occur or only occur as the result of other processes. We will conclude that both fixed rankings and stringent constraints can account for gapped inventories as long as the theory-neutral notion of faithfulness to the marked is observed.

The chapter is organized as follows. In §2, we offer some background on the role of markedness in acquisition, a discussion of why we chose s-clusters as the focus of study, and a more detailed discussion of what constitutes a gapped inventory. In §3 and §4 we present a series of studies, first offering a general pseudo-order of s-cluster acquisition, and then breaking the order of acquisition results down in greater detail. In §5, we offer an optimality theoretic account of one gapped inventory from the study; in §6 we consider an alternative analysis. A general discussion of our findings and their implications is given in §7.

2   Background

2.1   The role of markedness in acquisition

As mentioned above, a frequently observed fact about child phonological acquisition is that markedness guides much of the acquisition process. This is claimed to be the case both in order of acquisition and in common errors and substitutions. For instance, in a large-scale study of the acquisition of singletons and clusters, Smit and colleagues (Smit, Hand, Freilinger, Bernthal & Bird, 1990; Smit, 1993b) attribute the order of acquisition of both singletons and onset clusters to rules governed by markedness; they also note that unmarked sounds are more likely to be used correctly and as substitutes for errored sounds. Prosodic or syllable structure errors and repairs have been attributed to markedness considerations (e.g., Demuth, 1995; Levelt & van de Vijver, 2004). Even word stress acquisition order and errors have been discussed in terms of markedness (e.g., Zonneveld & Nouveau, 2004). Moreover, the child is able to access knowledge of which structures are marked and which are unmarked based on a universal, innate knowledge of markedness (Davidson, Jusczyk & Smolensky, 2004). For example, it has been shown (Pertz & Bever, 1975) that children are able to predict parts of a universal hierarchy of onset clusters even when those portions of the hierarchy do not exist in their native languages, thus accessing an underlying awareness of markedness relations.

Within the realm of word-initial clusters, the focus of the current chapter, it has been argued that children acquire clusters in a hierarchical order based on markedness, whereby the least marked cluster is acquired first, and the child adds more marked clusters linearly (Greenlee, 1973; 1974; Smit, 1993b). Researchers have also appealed to markedness in explaining the substitutions most commonly made when onset clusters are produced in error. In one common error pattern, many children reduce onset clusters to the least sonorous member, creating a syllable with the least marked sonority profile (Ohala, 1996; Barlow, 1997; Ohala, 1999). Within OT, a number of proposals have been put forth to deal with the acquisition of onset clusters in general. In most of these accounts, the hierarchical pattern predicted by markedness relations has been translated into constraints that also have fixed hierarchical relationships. Pater and Barlow (2003) use a fixed ranking of sonority constraints intermingled with other constraints banning marked segments to account for the error patterns they describe. The constraints they appeal to—the 'margin hierarchy' family of *X-Ons constraints—are universally ranked and thus universally favor onsets with low sonority. Pater and Barlow use this fixed ranking of constraints in explaining why children typically reduce an onset cluster to its least sonorous member; when this is not the case, they explain other reduction patterns with reference to markedness constraints that ban, for instance, dorsals. Other researchers have applied different theories of markedness to similar problems: Gnanadesikan (1997; 2004) explains G's reduction of onset clusters by appealing to a universal tendency to have high sonority segments in moraic positions; markedness constraints, then, favor low-sonority segments in non-moraic (i.e., onset) positions. Goad and Rose (2004) argue that onset clusters are organized in a head-dependent relationship, and that some children's reduction patterns can be explained by the reduction of a cluster to its head. Though markedness hierarchies are used to describe children's error patterns in the studies described, no study has attempted to account for order of s-cluster acquisition. Thus, the literature on cluster acquisition is incomplete.

2.2   Why s-clusters?

The s-clusters permitted in English are shown in (1). English allows s-clusters whose second segments include four manners and three places of articulation.

(1)   English s-clusters

	s+stop	s+nasal	s+liquid	s+glide
coronal	st	sn	sl	
labial	sp	sm		sw
dorsal	sk			
sonority difference	-1	+1	+2	+3

In onset clusters, sonority difference (the difference in the sonority of the first and second members of the clusters) is often used to determine markedness (Clements, 1990; Davis, 1990; Gierut, 1999). Clusters with the greatest sonority difference are considered least marked. A generic sonority scale is given in (2).

(2)   Sonority scale

Stop < Fricative < Nasal < Liquid < Glide < Vowel
 0   1   2   3   4   5

S-clusters were chosen as the focus of attention because they allow the greatest range of variation along the sonority scale. That is, stops, nasals, liquids, and glides are all allowed as the second member of an onset s-cluster, creating s-clusters with various degrees of sonority difference. An s+nasal cluster has a sonority difference of +1, s+liquid of +2, and s+glide of +3. These clusters, then, are increasingly less marked. Based on markedness and sonority difference, children would be expected to acquire the s-clusters with the greatest sonority difference, s+glide, first. They would then add s+liquid clusters, and finally s+nasal.

On the other hand, s+stop clusters have a negative sonority difference; the fricative [s] is more sonorous than the following stop. This violates an important phonological principle, the Sonority Sequencing Principle (SSP; Clements, 1990). The SSP states, in part, that onsets should rise in sonority towards the nucleus. However, s+stop clusters fall in sonority. This makes the status of s-clusters as 'true clusters' versus 'adjunct clusters' (in which only one member of the cluster is in the onset slot of the syllable) debatable (Selkirk, 1982; Kenstowicz, 1994; Barlow, 1997). The relative markedness of s+stop clusters is also at issue (e.g., Gierut, 1999; Barlow, 2001b; Morelli,

2003; Goad & Rose, 2004). Because s+stop clusters have such a tenuous status, their acquisition may not be comparable to that of the other s-clusters. For the purposes of this study, then, we only discuss clusters that abide by the SSP: s+nasal, s+liquid, and s+glide.

2.3   Gapped inventories

An inventory of sounds or sound sequences that contains a marked element and an unmarked element, but lacks an element of intermediate markedness, is known as a gapped inventory. While markedness hierarchies predict that gapped inventories should not occur, they have been shown to occur in a number of languages and across a range of sounds and sound positions (de Lacy, 2002; 2004; 2006). De Lacy (2002) presented examples of gapped inventories in the voiced and voiceless stop and fricative series and the nasal series. For instance, in the voiceless stop series, the markedness scale is k >> p >> t >> ?. Nhanda, a Pama-Nyungan language, allows all four of these sounds in onset position, and thus has a harmonically complete inventory. On the other hand, Hawaiian, which lacks onset [t], and Tlingit, which lacks onset [p], both have gapped voiceless stop inventories in onset position.

No study has yet examined gapped cluster inventories. In terms of the s-clusters discussed in this chapter, a gapped s-cluster inventory would contain s+nasal clusters (most marked) and s+glide clusters (least marked), but not s+liquid clusters.

3   Study 1: Pseudo-order of s-cluster acquisition

There exists no large-scale documentation focusing specifically on the order of s-cluster acquisition. Though Smit (1993b) includes s-cluster acquisition in her extensive study of the acquisition of clusters, most of the s-clusters are not distinguished in her results, though she does note that /sl/ is acquired later than the other s-clusters. Templin (1957) concludes that 75% of all subjects in her cross-sectional normative study had acquired the s+nasal clusters by age 4 years;0 months, while it was only by age 7;0 that 75% of subjects had acquired the s+liquid and s+glide clusters, a result different from that of Smit (1993b). The current study examines the s-cluster acquisition of 110 children with phonological delays, allowing for a broad cross-sectional view of the order of acquisition. In order to make claims about the relevance of s-cluster acquisition to competing theoretical views, the order of s-cluster acquisition must first be determined. One goal of this study, then, is to document the order of s-cluster acquisition of 110 children in the Learnability Project archive.

In past studies, order of acquisition has been projected in two ways. Specific trajectories have been drawn from longitudinal studies, in which the order of acquisition of sounds in a given child can be compared to the order of acquisition of the same sounds in other children. On the other hand, cross-sectional data have also been used in determining trajectories of acquisition (e.g., Shriberg & Kwiatkowski, 1994; Gierut & O'Connor, 2002). In this type of analysis, the sound that has been acquired by the greatest number of children is also assumed to be the earliest acquired. Study 1 employs the second type of trajectory, and may thus be called a 'pseudo-order' of acquisition, as it does not necessarily reflect the order of acquisition of any particular child. In the following sections, we will extend this analysis to a small number of more in-depth examinations of individual learning trajectories as a point of validation. Possible limitations of these approaches will be discussed below.

3.1   Participants

Longitudinal data from 110 children in the Learnability Project archival database were examined in order to determine which children presented with s-clusters as well as the singletons of which they are comprised. This particular sample included 86 boys and 24 girls. Their mean age was 4;4, with a range of 3;0 to 7;4, and their mean score on the *Goldman-Fristoe Test of Articulation* (Goldman & Fristoe, 1986) was at the 3rd percentile.

3.2   Data collection

Data from the Phonological Knowledge Protocol (PKP; Gierut, 1985) and the Onset Cluster Probe (OCP; Gierut, 1998a and Chapter 2 in this volume) were used in this study. Only the probes elicited prior to any experimental manipulations were considered in this study, thereby allowing an account of the children's phonologies with no influence from treatment.

3.3   Data analysis

Pretreatment data were analyzed in order to determine which children could be credited with producing a particular s-cluster. Following the established literature (Dinnsen, 1984; Stoel-Gammon, 1985; Gierut & O'Connor, 2002), a conjunction of relational and independent criteria was used. The independent criterion guarantees that the child produces the cluster regardless of target; the relational criterion provides evidence that the child produces the cluster target-appropriately. The two criteria do not always overlap; their conjunction allows for a relatively conservative measure of cluster production in the developmental grammar.

To be credited with a given s-cluster, children were required to produce the cluster at least twice for any target and with at least 20% accuracy for the target. If a child met only one of the criteria, or failed to meet either of them, s/he was not credited with the cluster. That is, a child may produce [sn] twice, meeting the independent criterion, but if both occurrences were produced for target /sl/, the child fails to meet the relational criterion. Likewise, a child who meets the relational criterion by producing one target-appropriate [sn] cluster would fail to be credited with the cluster if s/he did not produce it at least twice in the entire sample. Words produced in imitation or which varied across multiple productions were not included in the calculations. Words transcribed with sound approximations, such as [ˢneɪk] 'snake', were counted as accurate. Any word in which either member of the cluster was omitted or substituted, such as [neɪk] or [sjeɪk] 'snake', or in which the cluster was broken by an epenthetic vowel, as in [səneɪk] 'snake', was not considered accurate.

Each child's data were coded as having or lacking each of the possible two-element s-clusters. However, as this study focuses mainly on the influence of sonority on cluster production, the two s+nasal clusters were aggregated in the analysis. That is, children had to meet criteria for either [sn] or [sm] to be credited with an s+nasal cluster. [sl] was the only s+liquid cluster included and [sw] the only s+glide cluster. Given three cluster types and a binary +/- coding for each type, this yielded the seven possible combinations discussed in §4.

In order to determine the influence of singleton accuracy on cluster production, the inventories of the singletons that make up s-clusters were also analyzed, following the same conjunction of independent and relational criteria; a child was required to produce the singleton at least twice and with at least 20% target accuracy to be credited with the singleton.

3.4   Results

Of the 110 children whose data were examined, 80 (72%) presented with no s-clusters. Of these 80 children, 29 produced no English onset clusters whatsoever, while the other 51 presented with some onset cluster other than a true s-cluster. These 80 children's data will henceforth be set aside because they do not contribute to the purpose of the study, and the focus will be on the data from the 30 children who met criteria for at least one s-cluster type. Of these 30 children, 26 (87%) presented with an s+nasal cluster, 7 (23%) presented with an s+liquid cluster, and 22 (73%) presented with an s+glide cluster. This is represented in Figure 1. Overall, s+nasal clusters were produced with the greatest frequency of occurrence across children, followed by s+glide clusters. Both were produced with much greater frequency than the s+liquid clusters. Thus the pseudo-order of s-cluster acquisition predicts that s+nasal and s+glide are acquired before s+liquid, with essentially no difference between s+nasal and s+glide clusters. This order clearly does not parallel the strict application of order-of-acquisition predictions made by the sonority view of markedness. That is, [sl] is not the most marked cluster in the sonority difference hierarchy, yet it seems to be the latest acquired. Similarly, [sn] and [sm] clusters are presumably the most marked clusters, but are among the earliest acquired.

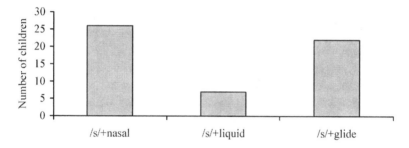

Figure 1. Pseudo-order of s-cluster acquisition.

It might be argued that some children's restrictions on certain clusters may have been influenced by restrictions on singleton segments. To explore this possibility, data regarding each of the subconstituent singletons were also examined. Again, the focus is on the 30 children who produced some type of s-cluster. Of these, all 30 (100%) met criteria for singleton [s], singleton nasal, and singleton [w], and 16 of 30 (53%) met criteria for singleton [l]. It is clear that singleton [l] was the least robust segment in the inventories of these children, yet more than half of them had acquired it. With respect to the relationship between the singletons and clusters, no child in the study produced a sound in a cluster that was not also produced in the singleton form.[1] However, production of a singleton does not guarantee that the singleton will be produced in a cluster. For example, there is an interesting asymmetry between singleton occurrence and its application in clusters that relates to the liquid [l]. More than twice as many children produced singleton [l] than produced s+liquid clusters. For the children in this study, then, having the singleton sound was a necessary but not a sufficient prerequisite for using that sound in a cluster.

The data reported thus far are presented in (3). The top rows of the table list the number of children who produced the singleton segments accurately, while the bottom rows list the number of children who produced the s-clusters accurately. These data can be summarized with several conclusions. First, the children in this study produced clusters with much less frequency than they produced their subconstituent singletons. They also produced singleton nasals, glides, and [s] with greater frequency than they produced singleton [l]. They further produced s+nasal clusters with slightly greater frequency than s+glide clusters; most importantly, both s+nasal and s+glide clusters were produced with far greater frequency than s+liquid clusters. These facts together indicate that within the s-cluster series, [sl] is the cluster that occurs least often in phonologically delayed children, and, according to the pseudo-order, is latest acquired. This is in agreement with Smit (1993b), who showed that [sl] was the latest-acquired s-cluster for the children in her study. It appears that children may acquire s-clusters in a gapped order—that is, they acquire less marked clusters (e.g., s+glide) and more marked clusters (e.g., s+nasal) before they acquire clusters of intermediate markedness (e.g., s+liquid). However, there is another possible explanation. Perhaps the pseudo-order actually obscures the real order of acquisition. It is possible, for instance, that the seven children in the data set who have acquired [sl] have acquired no other s-cluster. If this were the case, then we could no longer argue that [sl] is the latest acquired cluster.

(3) Number of children presenting with word-initial s-cluster types and subconstituent singletons

Sound	n	Proportion (N = 30)
[s]	30	100%
nasal	30	100%
[l]	16	53%
[w]	30	100%
s+nasal	26	87%
s+liquid	7	23%
s+glide	22	73%

In the next section, the data from the 30 children who produced at least one s-cluster will be examined in more detail to look for evidence of a particular order of cluster acquisition. The greater detail of this second study will more fully justify the pseudo-order of acquisition as a true developmental trajectory for a subset of children. Likewise, the detailed study will determine whether the children follow an acquisition pattern based on the sonority hierarchy.

4   Study 2: Course of acquisition

Study 2 is a more in-depth analysis of the pseudo-order of s-cluster acquisition. The purpose of this study was to focus on the occurrence of different s-cluster types evidenced by the 30 children in a combinatorial way in order to determine whether the individuals' patterns of acquisition are those predicted by the pseudo-order in the previous study. To achieve this, each child's cluster production data were examined in order to determine which s-cluster type or types had been acquired. The data in (4) show the number of children who presented with each of the logically possible combinations of cluster types. Most of the different combinations of cluster types were evidenced by at least one child; the notable exceptions were three possible combinations, all of which included the s+liquid cluster: s+liquid only, s+liquid and s+nasal, and s+liquid and s+glide.

(4)   Number of children who produced each s-cluster combination (gapped inventories in bold)

Cluster Type	n	Proportion (N=30)
Nasal only	8	27%
Liquid only	0	
Glide only	4	13%
Nasal and liquid	0	
Nasal and glide	**11**	**37%**
Liquid and glide	0	
Nasal, liquid and glide	7	23%

Though research reported above would indicate that as children develop, they add increasingly more marked structures to their phonological inventories (Greenlee, 1973; 1974; Smit, 1993b), this does not seem to be the case in this data set. The children of this study acquired s-cluster types in a variety of sequences. Two children acquired s+nasal clusters first, while three acquired s+glide clusters first. When children added a second cluster, they added whichever of the s+nasal or s+glide clusters they had not already acquired, such that no child acquired an s+liquid cluster without having also acquired the other two s-clusters.

After examining the individual acquisition trajectories of the 30 children who had acquired some s-cluster types, it is clear that 11 of the 30 children (37%) fell into the gapped inventory cell—that is, 11 children acquired s+nasal clusters and s+glide clusters, but not s+liquid clusters. These results confirmed the results of Study 1: Gapped inventories do occur during the acquisition of the harmonically complete s-cluster inventory, and over a third of the children in the study who had acquired any s-cluster at all were at this gapped stage. The gapped distribution, in fact, was the most common pattern of the study. Moreover, it seems possible that most children go through a stage in which they produce s+nasal and s+glide clusters without producing s+liquid clusters. That is to say, it is likely that most children acquiring English have a gapped s-cluster inventory at some point during the acquisition process. This is particularly interesting when recalling that these children are in the process of acquiring a harmonically complete inventory.

Thus it appears that while a fixed sonority scale may serve as a possible account of children's onset cluster substitution or reduction patterns (Pater & Barlow, 2003), the same approach does not work for generating an order of acquisition. These gapped sequences appear to reflect a counterexample to the idea that structures are universally acquired from least marked to most marked, thereby requiring an alternative theoretical account. To evaluate these possibilities, in §5 of this chapter, we examine the theoretical consequences of the acquisition patterns of the children studied thus far, with a focus on a case study.

5   Analysis: Stringency vs fixed rankings

In this section, we present accounts of two possible types of inventories: gapped inventories (which our analysis correctly predicts to occur) and disharmonic inventories (which our analysis correctly predicts not to occur, with some qualifications). Fixed rankings are compared to stringent rankings in accounting for the types of inventories that do and do not occur. Harmonic inventories, which do occur in the data and are easily accounted for by both of the analyses, will not be explicitly discussed.

5.1   Gapped inventories

Smolensky (1996a) was the first of many to attribute the evidence of markedness in child acquisition to the high ranking of markedness constraints in the initial-state grammar. It is now assumed by many acquisition researchers that in the initial state, all markedness constraints are ranked above all faithfulness constraints, making it more important for a child's output to be unmarked than for it to be faithful to the input (cf. Hale & Reiss, 1998). As shown in §1, markedness constraints conforming to markedness hierarchies are commonly accepted. However, the identity of the antagonistic faithfulness constraints has not been sufficiently explored. While most researchers have accepted the presence of hierarchical markedness constraints, the above description of gapped s-cluster inventories and the following optimality theoretic accounts offer evidence that the key to solving the gapped inventory problem is the combination of markedness constraints banning marked elements and faithfulness constraints preserving them. We will show that this can be done with either stringent constraints or fixed rankings; the common important factor is faithfulness to the marked.

In this section we offer an analysis of one of the children discussed above who fell into the gapped inventory category: Child 102 (5;4–5;7). This child scored at the 4th percentile on the *Goldman-Fristoe Test of Articulation* (Goldman & Fristoe, 1986). The data in (5a) and (5b) illustrate that he produced s+nasal and s+glide clusters target-appropriately, while the data in (5c) show that s+liquid clusters were produced as [sw].

(5)   Child 102 (5;4–5;7): Gapped inventory

    a)   s+nasal clusters produced correctly
        [sniz]   'sneeze'   [smoʊk]   'smoke'
        [sneɪk]   'snake'   [smɛl]   'smell'

    b)   s+glide clusters produced correctly
        [swɛtsʊt] 'sweatshirt'   [swɪŋᵍ]   'swing'
        [swip]   'sweep'   [swit]   'sweet'

    c)   s+liquid clusters produced as [sw]
        [swɪp]   'sleep'   [swɛpʊ]   'slipper'
        [swɛd]   'sled'   [swiz]   'sleeve'

Though Child 102 did not produce [l] following [s] in an onset cluster, he did produce singleton [l] (6a) and even [l] in other onset clusters (6b), including three-element clusters (6c). Because of these productions, any presumed solution explicitly banning [l] from the child's output will not be considered.

(6)   Child 102 (5;4–5;7): Production of [l]

    a)   Singleton /l/ correctly produced
        [lɛg]   'leg'   [lif]   'leaf'
        [jɛloʊ]   'yellow'   [kʌlʊ]   'color'
        [hɪl]   'hill'   [kɔl]   'call'

b) /l/ in other onset clusters correctly produced

[pleɪt] 'plate'   [blæk]   'black'

[glu]   'glue'   [flaɪ]   'fly'

c) /l/ in three-element clusters correctly produced

[splæθ] 'splash'   [splɪt]   'split'

[splɪnʊ] 'splinter'   [splæsən]   'splashing'

As mentioned in the introduction, most optimality theoretic analyses of onset cluster acquisition (including error patterns) have relied upon a hierarchy of constraints in a strict domination relationship. That is, a series of constraints on sounds or sound sequences is in a fixed ranking such that constraints against the most marked segments/structures outrank constraints against less marked segments/structures. The example most relevant for the current work is the set of *X-ONS constraints used in Pater and Barlow (2003). A similarly formulated set of constraints for a fixed hierarchy analysis of onset s-clusters is shown in (7). These constraints (as well as the stringent constraints) could be formulated in a number of ways.[2] The constraints presented here are used simply because they are the most transparent.

(7) Fixed hierarchy: Constraints and ranking

a) Markedness:

*sn: Initial s+nasal clusters are banned

*sl: Initial s+liquid clusters are banned

*sw: Initial s+glide clusters are banned

b) Faithfulness:

MAX: No deletion

DEP: No insertion

UNIFORMITY: No coalescence

IDENT: Corresponding segments must be identical

c) Ranking:

MAX, DEP, UNIFORMITY >> *sn >> *sl >> IDENT >> *sw

The *s+segment markedness constraints are a subset of a larger group of constraints subsumed under *COMPLEX, which bans all clusters. The constraints used here are specific to each of the different s-cluster types, and based on claims about the universal markedness of small sonority differences, they are in a fixed ranking: *sn >> *sl >> *sw. Of the faithfulness constraints, there are a number of constraints that ban different possible alternatives to disallowed input clusters: MAX bans deletion of one of the cluster members, while DEP bans epenthesis to break up the cluster. UNIFORMITY (McCarthy, 1999) bans the coalescence of members of a cluster into a single segment. All of these constraints are present and active in the grammars discussed below, but as there is no deletion, insertion, or coalescence, they must be high-ranked and will be left out of all of the following tableaux. These constraints, though, serve to ban candidates not shown in the tableaux: those candidates that differ from the input in not having an s-cluster. Finally, IDENT is a generalized faithfulness constraint that requires correspondence between the input and the output; the substitution of [sw] for /sl/ violates IDENT. A tentative ranking places this single faithfulness constraint between *sl and *sw, so that input /sw/ sequences are preserved but input /sl/ sequences are not, as in (8).

(8) Fixed ranking with generalized IDENT

/sneɪk/ 'snake'	*sn	*sl	IDENT	*sw
a. ☞ sneɪk	*!			
b. sleɪk		*!	*	
c. ☜ sweɪk			*	*

/slip/ 'sleep'	*sn	*sl	IDENT	*sw
a. slip		*!		
b. ☞ swip			*	*
c. snip	*!		*	

/swit/ 'sweet'	*sn	*sl	IDENT	*sw
a. ☞ swit				*
b. snit	*!		*	
c. slit		*!	*	

In these tableaux, the fully faithful candidate for each input competes against several other onset s-clusters of greater or lesser markedness. As can be seen from the tableaux for 'snake' and 'sleep', there is no way to rank a generalized faithfulness constraint such that it bans the output s+liquid cluster without also banning the s+nasal cluster. The leftward-pointing manual indicator indicates that the first tableau predicts the wrong output [sweɪk] for the input 'snake'. This occurs because IDENT must be ranked below *sl in order to ban [sl] from Child 102's outputs, but this also serves to ban [sn] from the output as well. That is, s+nasal clusters are more marked than s+liquid clusters, and fixed rankings cannot ban a construction without also banning other more marked constructions on the same hierarchy. A fixed ranking with a generalized faithfulness constraint does not allow for Child 102's outputs.

According to our analysis, the fixed rankings successfully used by other researchers (Pater & Barlow, 2003; Gnanadesikan, 2004) to account for children's substitution patterns would fail to account for children like Child 102 who evidence gapped s-cluster inventories. There is, however, an alternative. Within OT, stringency theory (Prince, 1997; de Lacy, 2002; 2004; 2006) deals with just such gapped inventories. Rather than fixed rankings, stringency theory appeals to freely permutable markedness and faithfulness constraints. In this theory, a markedness constraint can ban a particular structure, but it must also ban every related structure that is more marked. On the other hand, stringent faithfulness constraints can preserve any given structure, but must also preserve every related structure that is more marked. Constraints in a stringency relationship are freely permutable, and the interaction of stringent markedness and stringent faithfulness constraints can allow for gapped inventories.

The stringent markedness constraints and ranking for Child 102 are shown in (9). Again the *COMPLEX constraint is split into constraints banning individual cluster types, but now these constraints are formulated in a stringent manner. Since clusters of a smaller sonority difference are more marked than clusters of a larger sonority difference, s+nasal, the s-cluster with the smallest sonority difference, is banned by all of the stringently formulated markedness constraints. The s+liquid cluster, which is less marked, is banned by fewer of the stringency constraints, while the s+glide cluster is banned by only one of the constraints, and that constraint also bans both the s+liquid and s+glide cluster. That constraint, *sn-sl-sw, is in parentheses here because, as it bans all s-clusters, it must be extremely low-ranked for Child 102.

(9)   Stringent markedness constraints

*sn:	Initial s+nasal clusters are banned
*sn-sl:	Initial s+nasal and s+liquid clusters are banned
(*sn-sl-sw:	Initial s+nasal, s+liquid, and s+glide clusters are banned)

Similarly, stringent faithfulness constraints (in (10)) preserve a marked element and everything more marked. Thus ID[sn] preserves the marked s+nasal cluster; ID[sn-sl] preserves less marked s+liquid and everything else more marked, here s+nasal. Again, the constraint ID[sn-sl-sw] is in parentheses; this constraint, which preserves all s-clusters, must be low-ranked for Child 102, as he did not produce all s-clusters correctly.[3]

(10)   Stringent faithfulness constraints

ID[sn][4]:	Corresponding segments in an s+nasal cluster must be identical
ID[sn-sl]:	Corresponding segments in an s+nasal or s+liquid cluster must be identical
(ID[sn-sl-sw]:	Corresponding segments in an s+nasal, s+liquid, or s+glide cluster must be identical)

Using these constraints, an analysis for Child 102's phonology is shown in the tableaux in (11).

(11) Stringent account of Child 102's gapped inventory

/sneɪk/ 'snake'	ID[sn]	*sn-sl	*sn	ID[sn-sl]
a. ☞ sneɪk		*	*	
b. sleɪk	*!	*		*
c. sweɪk	*!			*

/slip/ 'sleep'	ID[sn]	*sn-sl	*sn	ID[sn-sl]
a. slip		*!		
b. snip		*!	*	*
c. ☞ swip				*

/swit/ 'sweet'	ID[sn]	*sn-sl	*sn	ID[sn-sl]
a. ☞ swit				
b. snit		*!	*	
c. slit		*!		

Because Child 102 produced [sn] target-appropriately, the faithfulness constraint that applies only to [sn], ID[sn], must be high-ranked. The ranking *sn-sl between ID[sn] and ID[sn-sl] ensures that s+nasal and s+glide clusters are produced target-appropriately, while s+liquid clusters are reduced to [sw]. This is in line with another prediction of stringency theory: the 'gap' in the inventory or cluster sequence is produced as the next less marked sound in the hierarchy. The fact that Child 102 reduced s+liquid clusters to [sw] complies with this prediction.

Thus far it has been shown that stringently formulated markedness and faithfulness constraints can account for the gapped s-cluster inventory found with such prevalence in Study 2, while an account based on a fixed ranking of markedness constraints in a strict domination relationship cannot. What is it that allows stringently formulated constraints to solve the problem? Fundamentally, the solution must preserve s+nasal clusters while banning s+liquid clusters, even though s+nasal clusters are more marked. Stringently formulated constraints allow this because a constraint requiring faithfulness to [sn] can be ranked higher than the constraint banning [sn]. The previous fixed ranking account was unable to do this because only the markedness constraints were split into a fixed ranking. By splitting the faithfulness constraints in a fixed ranking, however, is it possible to find a ranking that would preserve [sn] and ban [sl] and in so doing salvage the fixed ranking account?

There are two possible ways to split a single faithfulness constraint into a family of faithfulness constraints. The highest-ranked constraint of the faithfulness series could preserve either the least marked or the most marked element of the series. An analysis with a split faithfulness constraint in a fixed ranking, and with high-ranking faithfulness to the unmarked, is clearly unable to account for the data; in an analysis such as this, the constraint that bans [sn] is the highest-ranked and therefore the strongest of the markedness constraints, while the constraint necessary to preserve that cluster is the lowest-ranked and thus the weakest of the faithfulness constraints. A fixed ranking of both markedness and faithfulness constraints with greatest faithfulness to the unmarked structures, then, cannot account for Child 102's gapped inventory.

There is a second option, though, in splitting faithfulness constraints into a fixed ranking. If markedness constraints ban the most marked segments and structures, and faithfulness constraints are typically thought of as antagonistic to markedness constraints, then it would seem that the highest-ranked of a series of faithfulness constraints should preserve the most marked structure. This essentially requires faithfulness to the marked, a theory de Lacy describes as fully compatible with either stringent constraints or constraints in a fixed ranking (Kiparsky, 1994; Jun, 1995; Goad, 1997; de Lacy, 2002; 2006). Such an account would involve the markedness constraints in (7), in addition to the faithfulness constraints also in a fixed ranking such that the highest-ranked constraint preserved the most marked segment. The necessary faithfulness constraints and ranking would be as in (12).

(12) Fixed-ranking faithfulness constraints

ID[sn]:   Corresponding segments in an s+nasal cluster must be identical
ID[sl]:   Corresponding segments in an s+liquid cluster must be identical
ID[sw]:   Corresponding segments in an s+glide cluster must be identical

Ranking: ID[sn] >> *sn >> *sl >> ID[sl] >> ID[sw] >> *sw

This allows a ranking of ID[sn] above *sn, preserving an input /sn/. The same ranking, however, allows for *sl above ID[sl], which successfully bans [sl]. Finally, the low ranking of ID[sw] over *sw ensures both that input /sw/ is preserved in the output and that input /sl/ is realized as less marked [sw]. The tableaux in (13) demonstrate that this ranking does account for Child 102's gapped inventory.

(13) Fixed hierarchy with faithfulness to the marked

/sneɪk/ 'snake'	ID[sn]	*sn	*sl	ID[sl]	ID[sw]	*sw
a. ☞ sneɪk		*				
b. sleɪk	*!		*			
c. sweɪk	*!					*

/slip/ 'sleep'	ID[sn]	*sn	*sl	ID[sl]	ID[sw]	*sw
a. slip			*!			
b. ☞ swip				*		*
c. snip		*!		*		

/swit/ 'sweet'	ID[sn]	*sn	*sl	ID[sl]	ID[sw]	*sw
a. ☞ swit						*
b. snit		*!			*	
c. slit			*!		*	

The four analyses discussed above each have their own key features within OT, but only two of them can account for the gapped inventories observed in the data. The table in (14) presents the four types of accounts, the key feature of each theory, and whether or not each is capable of accounting for gapped inventories.

(14) Summary of analyses

Optimality theoretic analysis	Key feature	Gapped inventory
Fixed ranking, Generalized Faith	Bans marked items	✗
Fixed ranking, Split Faith to Unmarked	Bans marked items, preserves unmarked items	✗
Fixed ranking, Split Faith to Marked	Bans marked items, **preserves marked items**	✓
Stringency	Bans marked items, **preserves marked items**	✓

As is highlighted in bold in (14), the two analyses that do account for the gapped inventory—stringency and fixed rankings with faithfulness to the marked—share one feature that the others do not: the preservation of marked items. It is not necessary that the constraints be freely permutable or stringently formulated to be able to account for a gapped inventory; what is vital is the interplay between markedness constraints that ban marked items and faithfulness constraints that preserve them. This is one of the highlights of stringency theory, and faithfulness to the marked is one of its most important innovations (de Lacy, 2002; 2006). However, as de Lacy points out, faithfulness to the marked can be achieved without stringency; it simply requires some assumptions about the architecture of faithfulness constraints that have not been commonly adopted or frequently discussed in previous literature.

5.2   Disharmonic inventories

An important feature of stringency theory and, by extension, faithfulness to the marked, is the hypothesis that no language should have a disharmonic inventory, that is, an inventory which contains marked segments or structures but lacks the least marked segment or structure on that hierarchy (de Lacy, 2002). As de Lacy notes, 'banning incidental processes, the least marked element cannot be eliminated by neutralization in the present theory' (de Lacy, 2002:238). The following section shows that this prediction is borne out, but that 'incidental processes' do occasionally allow for an inventory that appears to be disharmonic. In the example of s-cluster inventories, an inventory containing only [sl], only [sn], or both [sn] and [sl] is disharmonic, as each of these inventories lack the least marked s-cluster, [sw]. We will account for the children in the study who had acquired only [sn], as well as a child who acquired only [sl], as reported in the literature (Allerton, 1976).

As de Lacy (2002) argues, the fact that the lowest-ranked segment or structure on a hierarchy cannot be excluded from the inventory is a property of 'harmonic ascent' (Moreton, 2004). Harmonic ascent means that an output may not be unfaithful unless it is as a result of conforming to a markedness constraint. Since no s-cluster is less marked than [sw], then there is no reason for [sw] to be realized unfaithfully. As a result of this property, if any s-cluster occurs at all, then [sw] must occur. This property can be captured with both fixed rankings and stringently-formulated constraints. The tableaux in (15) show that a fixed ranking account of s-cluster acquisition cannot yield an inventory in which [sn] and [sl] occur but [sw] does not. Even if the markedness constraint *sw is ranked above the faithfulness constraint ID[sw], their low position in the hierarchy means that /sw/ cannot surface as any other s-cluster, as outputs [sn] and [sl] are ruled out by higher-ranked constraints. Again, a high-ranking set of faithfulness constraints such as MAX, DEP, and UNIFORMITY is assumed and therefore is not shown in the tableaux. With these constraints high-ranked, no ranking of the s-cluster constraints is possible such that [sw] is banned but another s-cluster is allowed to occur.

(15) Fixed ranking correctly predicts no grammar lacking least marked [sw]

/sneɪk/ 'snake'	ID[sn]	*sn	ID[sl]	*sl	*sw	ID[sw]
a. ☞ sneɪk		*				
b. sleɪk	*!			*		
c. sweɪk	*!				*	

/slip/ 'sleep'	ID[sn]	*sn	ID[sl]	*sl	*sw	ID[sw]
a. ☞ slip				*		
b. swip			*!		*	
c. snip		*!	*			

/swit/ 'sweet'	ID[sn]	*sn	ID[sl]	*sl	*sw	ID[sw]
a. ☞ swit					*	
b. snit		*!				*
c. slit				*!		*

The tableaux in (16) show the same result from a stringency perspective. Here, even if we rank *sn-sl-sw relatively high, the stringent formulation of the constraints means that an output [sw] for the input /sw/ will always incur a subset of the markedness violations for output [sn] or [sl]. The result is the same as above: There is no way to rank the constraints such that [sw] is ruled out but [sn] and/or [sl] is allowed.

(16) Stringent ranking correctly predicts no grammar lacking least marked [sw]

/sneɪk/ 'snake'	*sn-sl-sw	ID[sn-sl]	*sn	ID[sn-sl-sw]	*sn-sl	ID[sn]
a. ☞ sneɪk	*		*		*	
b. sleɪk	*	*!		*	*	*
c. sweɪk	*	*!		*		*

/slip/ 'sleep'	*sn-sl-sw	ID[sn-sl]	*sn	ID[sn-sl-sw]	*sn-sl	ID[sn]
a. ☞ slip	*				*	
b. snip	*	*!	*	*	*	
c. swip	*	*!		*		

/swit/ 'sweet'	*sn-sl-sw	ID[sn-sl]	*sn	ID[sn-sl-sw]	*sn-sl	ID[sn]
a. ☞ swit	*					
b. snit	*		*!	*	*	
c. slit	*			*!	*	

Another interesting prediction of the theory as it relates to harmonic ascent is that because [sw] is the least marked and thus most harmonic cluster, it is the best substitute for another more marked cluster. That is, no child should substitute, for instance, [sn] for /sl/. Such a substitution would violate harmonic ascent.[5] We saw this above in the analysis of Child 102, who substituted least marked [sw] for /sl/. In fact, of the 11 children in the study who produced gapped inventories, all of them substituted a less marked form, such as [sw] or [fw], for /sl/.

Though the tableaux in (15) and (16) show that disharmonic inventories are not predicted, this seems to be at odds with the data. As reported in §4, 8 of 30 children who produced some s-cluster produced only [sn], exhibiting what appear to be disharmonic inventories. Moreover, though no child in the study acquired only [sl], there is a case in the literature (Allerton, 1976) of a child who acquired [sl] before any other s-cluster, also exhibiting a disharmonic inventory. This is where it is crucial to note de Lacy's qualification 'barring incidental processes.' The inventories which include only [sn] or only [sl] turn out to be a result of these 'incidental processes.' The example discussed below is from a child who produced only [sl], as this appears to be a less common and more interesting inventory. However, a similar account would hold for any of the children who had acquired only [sn].

Allerton (1976) discusses a child, J, who acquired the [sl] cluster before any other cluster, even using [sl] as a substitute for /kl/, /pl/, and /fl/. For an input /sn/ cluster, J produced [s], and for an input /sw/ cluster, he produced [f]. Both of these productions are examples of coalescence, in which the manner quality of the first cluster segment and the place quality of the second segment are preserved.[6] For J, coalescence was the 'incidental process' that resulted in a disharmonic inventory. In the analysis of Child 102, it was assumed that faithfulness constraints such as MAX, DEP, and UNIFORMITY were high-ranked, thus banning incidental processes like deletion, epenthesis, or coalescence. However, in the case of J, ranking one of these faithfulness constraints low enough in the hierarchy allows the unfaithful production of certain clusters (e.g., s+nasal and s+glide) but not others (e.g., s+liquid).

The tableaux in (17) illustrate a fixed ranking account of J's grammar. Here, the constraint that militates against coalescence, UNIFORMITY, is ranked below *sw. In the tableaux for inputs /sn/ and /sw/, the high-ranked markedness constraints *sn and *sw force these inputs to be realized unfaithfully; the low ranking of UNIFORMITY then privileges the coalesced candidates as the best unfaithful outputs. In the tableau for input /sl/, however, the ranking of ID[sl] above *sl requires faithfulness to the input rather than allowing coalescence.

(17) Fixed ranking account of J's s-cluster acquisition

/s_1n_2eɪk/ 'snake'	*sn	ID[sn]	ID[sl]	*sl	*sw	UNIFORMITY	ID[sw]
a.　s_1n_2eɪk	*!						
b.　s_1l_2eɪk			*		*!		
c.　s_1w_2eɪk			*		*!		
d. ☞ $s_{1,2}$eɪk			*			*	

/$s_1l_2$ip/ 'sleep'	*sn	ID[sn]	ID[sl]	*sl	*sw	UNIFORMITY	ID[sw]
a. ☞ $s_1l_2$ip				*			
b.　$s_1w_2$ip			*!		*		
c.　$s_1n_2$ip	*!		*				
d.　$s_{1,2}$ip			*!			*	

/$s_1w_2$it/ 'sweet'	*sn	ID[sn]	ID[sl]	*sl	*sw	UNIFORMITY	ID[sw]
a.　$s_1w_2$it					*!		
b.　$s_1n_2$it	*!						*
c.　$s_1l_2$it				*!			*
d. ☞ $f_{1,2}$it						*	*

This same result is possible with a stringent ranking, as in (18). Here, the constraint *sn-sl-sw must be ranked above UNIFORMITY to ensure the unfaithful outputs for input /sn/ and /sw/; again, low-ranking UNIFORMITY chooses the coalesced candidates as the best unfaithful outputs. (Note that the constraint ID[sn-sl-sw] would be ranked below UNIFORMITY but is excluded from this exposition.) For an input /sl/, the ranking of ID[sn-sl] over *sn-sl-sw requires the faithful output rather than a coalesced output.

(18) Stringent account of J's s-cluster acquisition

/s_1n_2eɪk/ 'snake'	*sn	ID[sn-sl]	*sn-sl-sw	UNIFORMITY	*sn-sl	ID[sn]
a.　s_1n_2eɪk	*!		*		*	
b.　s_1l_2eɪk		*	*!		*	*
c.　s_1w_2eɪk		*	*!			*
d. ☞ $s_{1,2}$eɪk		*		*		*

/$s_1 l_2$ip/ 'sleep'	*sn	ID[sn-sl]	*sn-sl-sw	UNIFORMITY	*sn-sl	ID[sn]
a. ☞ $s_1 l_2$ip			*		*	
b. $s_1 w_2$ip		*!	*			
c. $s_1 n_2$ip	*!	*	*		*	
d. $s_{1 2}$ip		*!		*		

/$s_1 w_2$it/ 'sweet'	*sn	ID[sn-sl]	*sn-sl-sw	UNIFORMITY	*sn-sl	ID[sn]
a. $s_1 w_2$it			*!			
b. $s_1 n_2$it	*!		*		*	
c. $s_1 l_2$it			*!		*	
d. ☞ $f_{1 2}$it				*		

Thus J is not a counterexample to the predictions made by the faithfulness to the marked accounts. If one assumes a particular sonority hierarchy coupled with markedness and faithfulness constraints relative to that hierarchy, then it is possible to predict that no disharmonic inventory will occur. However, other possible processes and the faithfulness constraints that allow those processes may result in apparent disharmonic inventories.

In sum, an analysis appealing to faithfulness to the marked, whether couched in fixed rankings or stringency, correctly predicts the grammars that do and do not occur. Faithfulness to the marked accounts for gapped inventories, but correctly predicts that disharmonic inventories will only occur if some other process intervenes.

6   An alternative explanation

The account of the gapped inventories above relies on the assumption that the gaps are systematic and due to a particular ranking of constraints referring to a markedness hierarchy. However, it is appropriate to ask whether there are alternative explanations for the gapped inventories that were evidenced by 11 of 30 children in the current study. A potential alternative explanation for some of the gapped inventories is presented below.

Of the 11 children with gapped s-cluster inventories, 7 did not produce singleton [l] on the pretreatment sampling. A child's production of a sound in a cluster is not necessarily dependent on his production of the same sound as a singleton (e.g., O'Connor, 1999). Similar asymmetries have been observed in fully developed languages (Bolognesi, 1998). However, the fact that these children did not produce [l] in singletons or clusters may imply a restriction on the sound [l] in general (e.g., a high-ranked constraint *l), and not specifically the [sl] cluster. If this were the case, we could not claim that these gapped inventories are exceptions to predictions made by the markedness hierarchies; rather, they would simply be a reflection of a single segmental markedness constraint.

While this alternative may be valid at the first pretreatment stage, it does not hold at later stages in time. This is best illustrated by the longitudinal data of children who fail to produce both singleton [l] and the [sl] cluster at pretreatment. Of 7, 5 acquired singleton [l] (as defined by the previously stated relational and independent criteria) at a stage in longitudinal data collection, but none acquired [sl] at any point in the longitudinal sample. These five children thus conform to the gapped inventory pattern, exhibiting systematic gaps in clusters without the concomitant gap in the singleton series, at a later stage in time. The remaining two children did not acquire either [l] or [sl] during the longitudinal sampling. In the absence of evidence, these two children do not negate the previous claims; their phonologies are simply inconclusive relative to the issues at hand.

These two children notwithstanding, the four others who did produce [l] at pretreatment and the five who acquired [l] at a later stage seem to exhibit systematic gaps in their s-cluster inventories. Though they were capable of producing [l], and several even produced [l] in other onset clusters, they failed to produce [sl] sequences, though they did produce s+nasal and s+glide sequences. Given that a strict analysis based on the sonority hierarchy does not predict any gapped inventories, their existence clearly necessitates a reconsideration of the role of markedness and sonority in acquisition.

7   Discussion

This study of the acquisition of word-initial s-clusters has filled in a lacuna in the literature. Previous studies examined the order of acquisition of onset clusters, but not specifically initial s-clusters. In accord with Smit (1993b), the data reported herein show that s+nasal and s+glide clusters are acquired at about the same time, and that their order of acquisition in relation to one another is not fixed. On the other hand, s+liquid clusters seemed to be latest acquired for essentially every child in this study. Because children are predicted to acquire sounds and sound sequences in an order based on markedness, and because the markedness of onset clusters is typically defined in terms of sonority difference, children who had acquired s+glide and s+nasal clusters, but not s+liquid clusters, were said to have acquired gapped s-cluster inventories. Given the large number of children who presented with this pattern, and the fact that no child produced [sl] without also producing all the other s-initial clusters, it was argued that the gapped stage is common to most children acquiring English. An optimality theoretic account of the asymmetry showed that both stringent constraints and fixed rankings can account for gapped inventories, as long as the key assumption of faithfulness to the marked is maintained; moreover, these accounts correctly predicted that disharmonic inventories will not occur unless some other process intervenes.

The previous discussion leaves at least three outstanding issues. The first involves the relative markedness of s-clusters: Why is it that /sl/ is the latest acquired cluster, even though it is not the most marked based on the SSP and minimal distance? From a broader perspective, is there a contradiction in the use of faithfulness constraints that make use of markedness relations? And finally, how common are gapped inventories in acquisition?

7.1   The markedness of /sl/

The first question deals with why /sl/ in particular is such a late-acquired cluster. If acquisition is predicted to proceed from least to most marked, it seems to follow that [sl] must be a highly marked onset cluster. This marked-ness, however, does not derive strictly from the SSP and the minimal distance between the fricative [s] and the liquid [l].

Some researchers have attempted to explain the late acquisitions of certain sounds and sound sequences from an articulatory perspective, arguing that the most marked sounds are those that are most difficult to produce (e.g., Hawkins, 1973; 1979). This explanation does not necessarily account for the late acquisi-tion of /sl/. Child 102, for instance, had acquired both [s] and [l] in singletons and even in other clusters, including highly marked and complex three-element clusters. He was capable, then, of the articulatory gestures necessary to produce those sounds. Moreover, it has even been argued that clusters facilitate the production of some liquids (Swisher, 1973; Kent, 1982; Sheldon & Strange, 1982), calling into question the articulatory difficulty of clusters like [sl].

Other attempts to account for the late acquisition of /sl/ have relied upon statistical regularities in languages like frequency or neighborhood density. Sounds and sound sequences that occur in words with high frequencies or that occur in words with many similar sounding neighbors are often argued to be earlier acquired (Ingram, 1988a; Beckman & Edwards, 2000). Farris and Gierut (2005) explored the statistical characteristics of the English s-clusters. They found that the [sl] cluster occurred in words which were more frequent than words which contained the [sn] cluster. Moreover, the [sl] cluster occurred in the set of words with the highest density compared to the words which contained all the other s-clusters. These results predict that [sl] should be a relatively early-acquired cluster, contrary to the results of the current study. Statistical characteristics, then, cannot explain why /sl/ is the latest acquired s-cluster.

Another relevant observation about the acquisition patterns of s-clusters in this study is that the earlier acquired s-clusters—s+nasal and s+glide clusters—both consist of clusters whose second member is an early-acquired singleton, while the latest acquired cluster—the s+liquid cluster—has as its second member a late-acquired singleton. While this may be a relevant and important observation, it introduces a further problem. Even outside the realm of onset clusters, the markedness hierarchy predicts that more sonorous segments are more marked in syllable-initial position (Prince & Smolensky, 1993/2004). The fact that [n] and [w] are earlier acquired than initial [l], and that final [n] and [w] are earlier acquired than final [l] (Templin, 1957; Smit et al., 1990) also raises difficulties for the dual assumptions of the margin hierarchy (discussed in §2.1) and acquisition from least to most marked.[7] As in the Allerton (1976) case above, the introduction of constraints outside the margin hierarchy (e.g., *l), might help account for this problem; however, the markedness hierarchy alone cannot explain the order of acquisition of singleton segments any better than it can explain the order of acquisition of clusters. This seems to be a broader problem with the theory: If we assume certain hierarchies of markedness, and we assume that children should acquire least marked segments and sequences first, then we arrive at an impasse when the markedness hierarchies and the children's acquisition patterns do not match.

It may be the case that in order to account for the late acquisition of the /sl/ cluster, a more multifaceted definition of markedness is necessary, particularly in relation to initial s-clusters. The formal definition of the markedness of clusters has always relied heavily upon minimal distance and the sonority scale (Clements, 1990; Davis, 1990; Gierut, 1999). OT, as a formal theory of phonology, draws upon the phonological structures already in place, e.g., the sonority scale, when defining constraints. Given this assumption, the markedness hierarchy most relevant to the acquisition of s-clusters is one related to the sonority distance of the two members; in light of the present data, however, this account seems insufficient. One possible solution, which would preserve the important predictions of the sonority scale, is to explore why it is that the s+nasal cluster is the earliest-acquired s-cluster, even though it is the most marked in terms of the SSP. Some researchers have argued that the s+nasal cluster can pattern with s+stop adjunct clusters and thus that they behave differently from s+liquid and s+glide clusters (Barlow, 1997). Under this hypothesis, one could argue that children with 'gapped' inventories represent s+nasal clusters differently from s+liquid and s+glide clusters. If this is the case, then it may be possible to explain the acquisition of s+nasal clusters by means of different constraints or mechanisms (possibly as adjunct clusters), and that the remaining s+liquid and s+glide clusters are being acquired in the order predicted by minimal distance and the SSP, with s+liquid clusters acquired last. A future line of research may be devoted to an experimental validation of this theory. In the end, what is needed is an account of the markedness of s-clusters that is both theoretically motivated and explanatorily adequate.

7.2   Is faithfulness to the marked legitimate?

A second unexplored issue has to do with the theory of faithfulness to the marked. Faithfulness constraints have typically been seen simply as constraints requiring correspondence between the input and the output, while it is the job of markedness constraints to ban output segments or structures that are typologically marked. Faithfulness constraints compare the underlying and surface levels of representation, while markedness constraints deal only with the surface level. By creating faithfulness constraints that require greater faithfulness to marked structures, we are forced to ask the question of whether the component of the grammar that deals with faithfulness has access to information about what is marked versus unmarked in the grammar. That is, do the faithfulness constraints in Con have knowledge of markedness hierarchies? Markedness constraints in a fixed ranking do not cause this problem—by virtue of being markedness constraints it is assumed that they are privy to markedness hierarchies. However, by embedding markedness into faithfulness constraints (whether stringently formulated or in a fixed ranking), we are, in a way, giving markedness access to the underlying level of representation rather than just the surface level. It seems as though faithfulness constraints, as only requiring correspondence between the input and output, should be blind to other considerations, such as markedness. However, in order to formulate the faithfulness constraints as they have been formulated here, certain assumptions about how to incorporate the theory of markedness into faithfulness constraints must be made. The viability of this approach in general remains to be seen.

7.3   The frequency of gapped inventories in acquisition

The fact that gapped s-cluster inventories seem quite common in the acquisition process, and indeed may reflect an entire stage that most children go through, raises the question of whether evidence exists for other gapped inventories in the child acquisition data. Future research might look for evidence of other gapped inventories in acquisition, for instance gaps in the place or manner hierarchies. A large-scale study of gapped inventories in child acquisition could lend insight into the existence of certain types of markedness constraints, the initial state ranking of these constraints, and possible demotion strategies.

7.4 Conclusion

We have shown that not only do gapped inventories occur, but they are not simply a fluke of a few fully developed languages. They occur during the acquisition process, and they occur across a large proportion of children acquiring a harmonically complete inventory of s-clusters. The use of acquisition data in assessing competing theories is vital to determining the adequacy of each theory. We have argued here that with faithfulness to the marked, both stringent and fixed rankings within optimality theory can account for gapped inventories. This evidence, then, provides the strongest sort of support for faithfulness to the marked—accounts conforming to this concept achieve explanatory adequacy.

Notes

* Thanks are especially due to Daniel Dinnsen, as well as to Michele Morrisette, Stuart Davis, Paul de Lacy, Amanda Edmonds, John McCarthy, and Holly Storkel for valuable comments and suggestions, Nola Stephens for help with data mining and analysis, and Abigail Scott for editorial assistance. This work was supported in part by grants to Indiana University from the National Institutes of Health (NIH DC001694 and DC00012).

1 It must be acknowledged that some children do produce sounds in clusters when those same sounds do not occur as singletons (e.g., O'Connor, 1999), that the same asymmetry can occur in adult languages (Bolognesi, 1998), and that the production of some sounds may be facilitated in the context of a cluster (e.g., Curtis & Hardy, 1959; Kent, 1982; Sheldon & Strange, 1982).

2 A number of possible formulations for these constraints exist. For instance, we might consider a formulation based on sonority difference (e.g. MinDist=1 >> MinDist=2 >> MinDist=3, etc.). From another perspective, these constraints could even be thought of as a series of locally conjoined constraints, the conjunction of *Complex and the margin hierarchy *Glide/Ons >> *Liquid/Ons >> *Nasal/Ons. However, this ranking would indicate that s+glide clusters are the most marked. While this constraint formulation and ranking could still capture the gapped inventory, it misses the minimal distance generalization discussed in §2. In any case, we are not as concerned with the formulation of the constraints as we are with their effects on hierarchical inventories.

3   This constraint is relevant for other participants; it would be a high-ranked constraint for the seven children who produce all three s-clusters. Likewise, the constraint *sn-sl-sw would be high-ranked for those 80 of 110 children in this study who did not produce any s-cluster at all.

4   The relevant IDENT constraints listed here are IDENT-IO constraints. They militate against the loss of any of the features in the bundle of feature specifications that make up a given s-cluster.

5   Thanks to Paul de Lacy (personal communication) for calling our attention to this important point.

6   The production of [s] for /sn/ could also be a deletion of the /n/; however, as [f] for /sw/ is clearly an example of coalescence, a more cohesive analysis is achieved by assuming that J's production of /sn/ is also an example of coalescence.

7   Another view of markedness and order of acquisition can be found in Rice and Avery (1993; 1995) and Rice (1996). In their feature geometric model, each new step in the acquisition process involves the specification of additional structure. Under this view, the coronal nasal [n] has the nodes Place and Sonorant Voicing; the liquid [l] has the additional node Continuant. The representation of glides in this representation is unclear; however, they may involve the additional specification of a Peripheral node under Place (Rice, 1996) or the specification of a V-Place node (Archibald & Vanderweide, 1997). This, then, might explain why /sl/ is later acquired than /sn/, but does not explain why /sw/ is earlier acquired than /sl/.

13 A typological evaluation of the split-margin approach to syllable structure in phonological acquisition*

Jessica A. Barlow
San Diego State University

Judith A. Gierut
Indiana University

This chapter evaluates the typological predictions of the split-margin approach to syllable structure, an elaboration of the Margin Hierarchy which distinguishes different sonority preferences of subsyllabic structure. Specifically, the *M_1 hierarchy applies to singleton onsets, showing a low sonority preference, while the *M_2 hierarchy applies to the second member of complex onsets and to codas, both showing a high sonority preference. Further, the constraints *COMPLEX (no complex onsets) and NoCODA are argued to be encapsulations of the *M_1 and *M_2 hierarchies, respectively, rather than separate constraints. This account of the relationship between the second member of an onset and a coda consonant predicts that languages that permit onset clusters (CCV) also allow codas (CVC), but not vice versa. To test the prediction that CCV implies CVC, we conducted independent and relational analyses of singleton and cluster data from English- and Spanish-speaking children. We identified 16 children who produced consonant + liquid clusters (CLV) and determined whether they also produced coda liquids (CVL). Results generally did not support the prediction, though there was some evidence for a tendency in this direction. In light of this, we entertain alternative explanations for those sound systems which diverge from the predicted pattern, such as the need to view NoCODA as separate from the Margin hierarchies, and alternative representational structures for initial clusters and word-final segments.

1   Introduction

This chapter addresses the proposed relationship between the second member of an onset cluster and coda consonants in language (Baertsch, 1998; 2002; Baertsch & Davis, 2003; Davis & Baertsch, 2005) and the predictions it has for phonological acquisition. By way of background, both onset clusters and coda consonants reflect relatively marked properties of language. Cross-linguistically, Consonant-Vowel (CV) syllables are least marked, in that they have a single consonant in the prevocalic margin, and a single vowel in the nucleus, which makes up the rhyme. Increased complexity occurs with branching subsyllabic structure, such as a branching onset (i.e., consonant cluster) or a branching rhyme (e.g., a consonant in the postvocalic margin, or coda), as illustrated in (1) (Blevins, 1995).

(1) Simple onset-rhyme (CV) structure and complex branching onset and branching rhyme (CCVC) structure

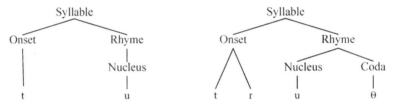

Within optimality theory, independent constraints are responsible for determining whether a grammar allows certain types of syllable structure. For example, the relative ranking of *COMPLEX determines whether a language will allow consonant clusters or not; the ranking of NoCODA determines whether a language will allow codas; and the ranking of ONSET will determine whether a language will allow onsetless syllables. In addition, the relative ranking of independent families of constraints (*M/α and *P/α; see below) based on the sonority hierarchy (shown in (2)) determines what types of segments may occur in the onset, nucleus, and coda for a given language.

(2) Sonority scale (least to most) (Baertsch, 2002; see also Steriade, 1982; Blevins, 1995)

Obstruent < nasal < /l/ < /r/ < high vowel/glide < non-high vowel

Specifically, the Sonority Sequencing Principle (Clements, 1990) guides syllable formation, generally requiring that the nucleus (or peak) of a syllable must be the most sonorous, while the edges (or margins) of the syllable are relatively lower in sonority. The role of sonority in syllable organization was incorporated into optimality theory in terms of prominence scales that identify well-formedness of syllables (Prince & Smolensky, 1993/2004). The Peak (P) of a syllable is more prominent (more sonorous) than the Margin (M), and the P and M hierarchies determine which segments may serve as ideal syllable peaks or margins. Accordingly, the P hierarchy, formulated as a family of constraints that are universally ranked, will select a vowel as an optimal peak of a syllable, while the M hierarchy, also a universally ranked family of constraints, will select a consonant as an optimal margin. The two hierarchies are ranked as in (3) and (4):

(3) Peak hierarchy (Prince & Smolensky, 1993/2004)

*P/α: α may not occur in the syllable peak
*P/Obstruents >> *P/Nasals >> *P/[l] >> *P/[r] >> *P/[+hi] >> *P/[+lo]

(4) Margin hierarchy (Prince & Smolensky, 1993/2004)

*M/α: α may not occur in the syllable margin
*M/[+lo] >> *M/[+hi] >> *M/[r] >> *M/[l] >> *M/Nasals >> *M/Obstruents

Thus, certain segments serve as better peaks, while certain other segments serve as better margins. Of the vowels, a low vowel is a better peak than a high vowel; of the consonants, an obstruent is a better margin than a sonorant.

The P and M hierarchies were incorporated into optimality theory in order to account for, among other things, the syllabification patterns of languages that allow consonants to serve as syllable peaks in certain contexts (e.g., Imdlawn Tashlhiyt Berber; Dell & Elmedlaoui, 1985; 1988; Prince & Smolensky, 1993/2004). A central component of the framework of optimality theory is constraint violability, which, in the case of sonority and syllabification, is particularly adept at accounting for the fact that a language may allow an obstruent to be syllabified in the peak when no other more sonorous sound is available for that position, or why another language may allow more sonorous sounds, such as glides, to surface in syllable margins. Thus, constraint violability allows for variation to occur both within and across languages in terms of what is an allowable margin or peak.

In general, appealing to these hierarchies, in combination with the syllable structure constraints *COMPLEX, ONSET, and NOCODA, has been relatively effective in accounting for restrictions on syllable structure cross-linguistically (cf. Goad & Rose, 2004, for alternative accounts). For example, the P and M hierarchies account for cluster reduction patterns observed cross-linguistically (e.g., Lamontagne & Rice, 1995; Zec, 1995; Hammond, 1999), as well as in phonological acquisition (e.g., Ohala, 1996; Barlow, 1997; Pater & Barlow,

2003; Barlow, 2003c; Gnanadesikan, 2004), whereby generally the least sonorous segment (often an obstruent) is the preferred onset.

Yet, these constraints alone cannot adequately predict the clusters that do occur in a given language, as Baertsch (1998; 2002) notes; additional sonority scales and information about sonority distance must be stipulated outside of the constraint ranking for a given grammar. That is, while the interaction of the markedness constraints *Complex, NoCoda, and Onset with faithfulness constraints (e.g., Max) generally accounts for clusters that are disallowed in particular grammars, this interaction does not adequately predict those that are allowed.

Also yet to be explained adequately is the asymmetry observed with respect to what segments may serve as an onset singleton versus what may serve within an onset cluster. One would expect that onset singletons would include all the segments that may occur within an onset cluster (and, likely others); this, however, is not necessarily the case. Davis and Baertsch (2005) consider Campidanian Sardinian as an example of a language that shows an unusual distribution for the rhotic /r/. Specifically, no words in Sardinian may begin with the rhotic as a singleton onset, though it may occur as the second member in a complex onset, as in [krai] 'key,' [primu] 'first', and [prus] 'more'. Prior accounts of this sound system (Bolognesi, 1998) made the unusual assumption that [r] was extraprosodic, despite its location in the middle of a syllable. Regardless, this unusual distribution of the rhotic does suggest some structural difference between singleton onsets and the second member of a complex onset. Davis and Baertsch (2005) characterize this as 'Bolognesi's paradox':

(5) Bolognesi's paradox: If an element can be a second member of an onset cluster, then why can't it appear as a singleton onset?

Further, the nature of the coda is not well explained in the research on syllable structure. It is clear that codas must be less sonorous than the peak of a syllable, given that they are optimally consonants rather than vowels; but, as numerous researchers have observed (e.g., Blevins, 1995; Zec, 1995; Orgun, 2001), language typologies indicate that sonorant codas appear to be less marked than obstruent codas. In fact, Baertsch and Davis (2003) describe the Siberian Turkic language Yakut as an example of a sound system that allows [r] and [j] to occur in coda position, but not in syllable-initial position (word-initially or internally).

What is more, there appears to be a parallel distribution between the second member of a complex onset and a singleton coda (or the first member of a complex coda), as noted by Baertsch (1998; 2002). Within an onset cluster, the second segment is more sonorous than the first segment, and is typically a glide or liquid (e.g., for English) (see also Côté, 1997; Green, 2003). Along the same lines, the first segment following the nucleus of the syllable typically is a glide or liquid. In fact, Campidanian Sardinian is such an example. This language, which shows an asymmetry for the patterning of [r] in onset position, also allows the rhotic to occur in coda position: [ar.ba] 'white' (Davis & Baertsch, 2005). Similarly, the Indo-Aryan language Gujarati allows [w] to occur in coda position, and as the second member of an onset, yet only the obstruent allophone [v] surfaces in syllable-initial position.

In addition, Baertsch and Davis (2003) cite syllable phonotactics as further evidence for the link between the second member of an onset cluster and singleton codas. English lacks syllables in which these two segments are identical (Fudge, 1969; Clements & Keyser, 1983; Davis, 1988). Forms such as *[plɪl] do not occur, while forms such as [lɪlt] do. Thus, the singleton [l] in onset position appears to pattern differently from [l] in clusters and codas.

This relationship between segments of subsyllabic constituents has been acknowledged and incorporated into accounts of sonority and syllable structure, with representations such as that proposed by Selkirk (1982), as illustrated in (6). (See also Cairns & Feinstein, 1982; Gilbers, 2001, for comparable syllable structure accounts.)

(6) Selkirk's (1982) proposed syllable organization based on featural properties of segments

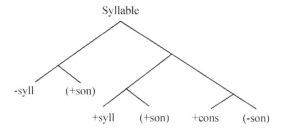

Thus, while the asymmetry in preferred sonority between the onset and the coda constituents has been acknowledged widely in the literature, it was not addressed satisfactorily within optimality theoretic terms in any formalized or consistent way.

1.1   The split-margin approach to syllable structure

The facts summarized in the previous section motivated Baertsch to formalize the relationship between the second member of the onset and the coda via modification of Prince and Smolensky's (1993/2004) Margin and Peak hierarchies and a modification of syllable organization (Baertsch, 2002; Baertsch &

Davis, 2003). She proposed that there are two different M hierarchies, M_1 and M_2, defined in (7) and (8), respectively, which govern the relative sonority of segments within subsyllabic constituents. The M_1 hierarchy is identical to that of Prince and Smolensky's M/α hierarchy, while the M_2 hierarchy is identical to their P/α hierarchy, but governs segments within the onset and coda (M) constituents, rather than the nucleus (P).

(7) M_1 hierarchy

 $*M_1/\alpha$: α may not occur in M_1 position
 $*M_1/[+lo] >> *M_1/[+hi] >> *M_1/[r] >> *M_1/[l] >> *M_1/Nasals >>$
  $*M_1/Obstruents$

(8) M_2 hierarchy

 $*M_2/\alpha$: α may not occur in M_2 position
 $*M_2/Obstruents >> *M_2/Nasals >> *M_2/[l] >> *M_2/[r] >> *M_2/[+hi] >>$
  $*M_2/[+lo]$

With this modification to the M hierarchy, Baertsch also proposed the syllable structure shown in (9), which is a modification of the structure shown in (6). Constituents within parentheses are optional (at least for many languages). Thus, if a syllable contains an onset, it must include an M_1 constituent, which, following from the M_1 hierarchy is optimally an obstruent. An M_2 segment within the onset would be optional, but, if present, it would optimally be a sonorant. The M_2 margin and the Peak margin would interact in such a way that a low vowel would be parsed in the nucleus rather than the margin. Similarly, if a syllable contains a coda, it must include an M_2 constituent, which, following from the M_2 hierarchy, would optimally be a sonorant. An M_1 segment within the coda, likewise, would optimally be an obstruent.

(9) Baertsch's (2002) proposed syllable organized based on M_1 and M_2 hierarchies

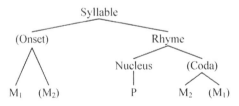

As stated previously, Prince and Smolensky's (1993/2004) proposed M hierarchy predicted that segments with a lesser degree of sonority would be preferred in

coda position, despite typological facts (Blevins, 1995; Zec, 1995). By incorporating the syllable organization shown in (9), Baertsch's proposed M_2 hierarchy, ranked with respect to relevant faithfulness constraints and the P/α hierarchy, can better account for the cross-linguistic preference for high sonority codas.

This modification to Prince and Smolensky's M hierarchy also more readily accounts for distributional patterns of liquids in languages such as Campidanian Sardinian (described previously), accounts of which had previously ignored the parallel patterning of the second member of the onset and coda singletons. Specifically, in Campidanian Sardinian, [r] may occur in M_2 positions, but not M_1.

To account for the occurrence (and absence) of clusters in a given language, Baertsch proposed local conjunction (Smolensky, 1997a) of the individual M_1 and M_2 constraints, where the domain of the conjunction is the adjacent M_1 and M_2 segments within a syllable. Thus, the conjunction of $*M_1/$Obstruent and $*M_2/$[r] (represented as $*Obs_1\&*[r]_2$ for ease of exposition; Baertsch & Davis, 2003) disallows an onset cluster of an obstruent (in M_1) followed by [r] (in M_2), or a coda cluster of [r] (in M_2) followed by an obstruent (in M_1). A single hierarchy of the conjoined constraints thus accounts for the occurrence of both complex onsets and complex codas. As Baertsch suggests, the exhaustive ranking of these conjoined constraints with respect to faithfulness constraints determines what are acceptable onset and coda clusters as well as acceptable onset and coda singletons.

The conjoined constraints are intrinsically ranked with respect to one another due to the universal ranking of the individual constraints within each hierarchy (Baertsch, 2002; Baertsch & Davis, 2003). For example, since $*M_1/$Obstruent is the lowest ranked constraint in the M_1 hierarchy, and $*M_2/$[+lo] is the lowest ranked constraint in the M_2 hierarchy, the conjunction of the two constraints is the lowest ranking of all the conjoined $*M_1$ and $*M_2$ constraints (Davis & Baertsch, 2005). Further, the conjoined constraints also outrank their component constraints, following general assumptions of constraint conjunction (Smolensky, 1997a; Davis & Baertsch, 2005). Thus, the conjoined constraint $*Obs_1\&*[r]_2$ outranks both $*M_1/$Obstruent and $*M_2/$[r], as in (10):

(10) $*Obs_1\&*[r]_2 \gg *M_1/$Obstruent, $*M_2/$[r]

The ranking of multiple conjoined constraints that share one component is determined by the ranking of the component constraints that differ (Baertsch & Davis, 2003; Davis & Baertsch, 2005). For example, $*Obs_1\&*Nas_2$ must always outrank $*Obs_1\&*[r]_2$, because $*M_2/$Nasal outranks $*M_2/$[r]. A partial ranking is shown in (11).

(11) … >> *Obs$_1$&*Nas$_2$ >> *Obs$_1$&*[l]$_2$ >> *Obs$_1$&*[r]$_2$ >> *Obs$_1$&*[+hi]$_2$ >>…

The partial ranking of the conjoined constraints relevant to the current study is shown in (12) (Baertsch & Davis, 2003: 10):

(12) Partial ranking of conjoined M$_1$ and M$_2$ constraint hierarchies

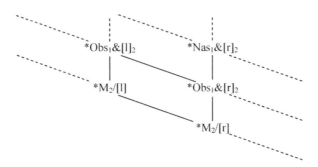

To account for the patterning of /r/ in Campidanian Sardinian, which, recall, may only occur in M$_2$ contexts, Davis and Baertsch (2005) assumed that *M$_1$/[r] ranks above relevant faithfulness constraints, which are in turn ranked above *Obs$_1$&*[r]$_2$ and *M$_2$/[r] as in (13):

(13) Ranking for Campidanian Sardinian

   *M$_1$/[r] >> F$_{AITH}$ >> *Obs$_1$&*[r]$_2$ >> *M$_2$/[r]

This can also account for the fact that many languages have codas to the exclusion of complex onsets (Baertsch & Davis, 2003). For those languages, the conjoined constraints which rule out clusters would be ranked above the relevant faithfulness constraints, while the entire *M$_2$ hierarchy would be ranked below them.

1.2 Typological predictions

One interesting issue that has emerged as a result of this proposed account is whether or not the constraints *C$_{OMPLEX}$ and N$_O$C$_{ODA}$ are necessary in the set of universal constraints (Baertsch & Davis, 2003). It is possible that the M$_1$ and M$_2$ hierarchies might be sufficient, and that *C$_{OMPLEX}$ and N$_O$C$_{ODA}$ are simply abbreviations of these elaborate constraint hierarchies. In other words, Baertsch and Davis argue that the job of *C$_{OMPLEX}$ is achieved with conjunction of the *M$_1$ and *M$_2$ hierarchies, while N$_O$C$_{ODA}$ is an encapsulation of the *M$_2$ hierarchy alone. Further, they observe:

> ... [I]f a conjoined $*M_1 \& *M_2$ constraint is ranked below FAITH so as to permit the $M_1 \& M_2$ onset cluster, then, necessarily, by the logic of constraint conjunction, the corresponding $*M_2$ conjunct must be even lower ranked which allows for that single M_2 segment in a coda. (11)

Based on the assumptions of constraint conjunction (Smolensky, 1997a), the conjunction of the M_1 and M_2 hierarchies predicts an implicational relationship between onset clusters and codas, as previously observed by Kaye and Lowenstamm (1981). Thus, it is predicted that no language would allow a complex $(M_1 - M_2)$ onset without also allowing a coda (M_2) consonant.[1]

Further, in acquisition, it is predicted that a child would acquire an M_2 coda segment before any complex onset with the corresponding M_2 segment. Numerous studies of acquisition do indicate that children acquire CVC syllables prior to onset clusters (e.g., Lleó & Prinz, 1996; Levelt, Schiller & Levelt, 1999). Baertsch and Davis (2003) cite further evidence of this prediction based on one child's longitudinal acquisition of Dutch as reported in Fikkert (1994). They note that this child, Jarmo, acquired sonorants in coda position and as the second member of an onset cluster (in other words, in M_2 contexts) at Stage III (using Fikkert's staging), prior to his acquisition of liquids as singletons in (M_1) onset position.

This provides some support for the typological predictions of the split-margin approach; however, a problem with this account is that what it means to have 'acquired' either onset clusters or sonorant codas is not specified. That is, the extent to which these structures occurred in Jarmo's productions is not specified. In fact, Fikkert (1994) notes specifically that both nasals and liquids appear in Jarmo's productions during Stage III, but that the nasals are 'frequently subject to deletion,' while the 'liquids are more often deleted than realized' (1994: 136–7). This begs the question of how we define 'acquisition' in order to test the predictions of the split-margin approach. How are these predictions satisfied? Is a single occurrence of a cluster or coda in a child's productions sufficient for evaluation of the predictions? Or must the child show more consistent use, with high degrees of accuracy and/or contrastive properties in the child's sound system?

Defining terms like 'acquired' and 'mastered' is of course a common problem in studies of phonological acquisition, and differences in how these terms are defined are partly responsible for the wide-ranging differences in, for example, normative studies of acquisition of English sounds (Templin, 1957; Sander, 1972; Smit, 1986; Smit, Hand, Freilinger, Bernthal & Bird, 1990; Goldman & Fristoe, 2000). This in turn makes it difficult to evaluate predictions like those of Baertsch and Davis. The goal of the present study, then, is to evaluate their predictions by appealing to different types of evidence from the sound systems of children learning English and Spanish.

2   Methods

As stated above, Baertsch and Davis (Baertsch, 1998; 2002; Baertsch & Davis, 2003; Davis & Baertsch, 2005) have suggested that *COMPLEX and NOCODA may be unnecessary constraints within the framework of optimality theory, noting that the split-margin hierarchies may be sufficient for predicting and accounting for the typological variation that occurs with respect to syllable structures. With this assumption is the prediction that a language cannot allow complex onsets unless it also allows coda consonants. Specifically, by virtue of the inherent ranking of conjoined constraints with respect to their component constraints, a language cannot allow a segment to occur in M_2 position in a complex onset unless that same segment is allowed in M_2 position in a coda. Should we find evidence to the contrary, this will require a reconsideration of assumptions about whether NOCODA should be included in the inventory of universal constraints, independent of the split-margin hierarchies.

In what follows, we describe our tests of this prediction. We conducted independent and relational analyses of longitudinal singleton and cluster data from English- and Spanish-speaking children. We identified 16 children who produced consonant + liquid (CLV) clusters and determined whether they also produced coda liquids (CVL). Specific details of participant characteristics and analysis procedures are described below.

2.1   Participants

The data come from 16 children (age 3 years;0 months-8;6) with phonological delays who participated in larger-scale studies at Indiana University or San Diego State University. Data from 11 monolingual English-speaking children were drawn from the archives of the Learnability Project at Indiana University. Children from this database had performed within normal limits on all measures of hearing, oral-motor structure and function, nonverbal intelligence, and expressive and receptive language, but showed a mean performance at the 2nd percentile on the *Goldman Fristoe Test of Articulation* (Goldman & Fristoe, 1986), characterizing them as phonologically delayed (Gierut & O'Connor, 2002).

Data from three additional monolingual English- and two monolingual Spanish-speaking children were drawn from archives of the Phonological Typologies Project at San Diego State University. These children also performed within normal limits on all measures of hearing, oral-motor structure and function, nonverbal intelligence, and expressive and receptive language

(Barlow, 2003d; 2003e; 2007a; 2007b). The English-speaking children showed a mean performance at the 5th percentile on the *Goldman-Fristoe Test of Articulation 2* (Goldman & Fristoe, 2000), which characterized them as phonologically delayed. The Spanish-speaking children were characterized as phonologically delayed based on parent/teacher report, due to the lack of standardized measures for Spanish-speaking children of the Southern California area (see also Gutiérrez-Clellen & Kreiter, 2003; Barlow, 2003c; 2005a).

2.2   Data and analyses

The data for the 11 English-speaking children of the Learnability Project come from spontaneous productions on single-word phonological probes that targeted consonant singletons and 2- and 3-element word-initial consonant clusters of the English language, totaling 375 tokens (Gierut, 1985; 1998a). The data from these 11 children were examined across time: prior to treatment, immediately following treatment, and at two additional points in time following treatment (typically 2 weeks and 2 months). For further details, see Chapter 2 in this volume.

The data from the remaining 3 English-speaking children from the Phonological Typologies Project likewise come from their spontaneous productions on a single-word phonological probe that targeted consonant singletons and 2- and 3-element clusters of the English language, totaling 256 tokens (Barlow, 2003a). The data from the 2 Spanish-speaking children, also drawn from the Phonological Typologies Project, come from their spontaneous productions on a single-word phonological probe that targeted consonant singletons and 2-element clusters of the Spanish language, totaling 134 tokens (Barlow, 2003b; 2005a). The data from these 5 children were examined across time: prior to treatment, immediately following treatment, and at 2 weeks and 2 months posttreatment.

The phonological probes used in both projects targeted all the relevant consonants of the adult language multiple times in all relevant contexts, allowing for multiple opportunities for minimal pairs. Further, consonant singletons were targeted in inflected and uninflected forms (e.g., [g] in *dog/doggie* or [l] in *call/calling* for English, and [l] in *nopal/nopalito* 'cactus'/'little cactus' for Spanish), allowing for potential morphophonemic alternations.

All productions of the children from both projects were digitally recorded and transcribed by listeners trained in narrow transcription with the IPA. An independent judge transcribed a portion of probe data for each child (25% of the English data, 20% of the Spanish data). Mean point-to-point interjudge reliability was 93% for the English data and 85% for Spanish.

The children's productions at each point in time were analyzed separately using methodology similar to that of a previous typological study of cluster acquisition by Gierut and O'Connor (2002), which incorporated independent and relational analysis procedures (Dinnsen, 1984; Dinnsen & Chin, 1994; Lleó & Prinz, 1997; Archibald, 1998). In essence, each point in time represented a separate grammar, allowing for multiple opportunities to evaluate the relationship between clusters and codas for each child, and resulting in multiple different cluster-coda relationships to be evaluated. Specifically, a given child's grammar at a given point in time was evaluated for the presence of consonant + /l/ (C/l/) and consonant + /r/ (C/r/) onset clusters relative to the occurrence of final /l/ or /r/ (where /r/ as a singleton or in a cluster corresponds to the approximant /ɹ/ in English or the tap /ɾ/ in Spanish). Thus, a given grammar could have C/l/ clusters or C/r/ clusters or both. For each child's sound system, the liquids /l/ and /r/ were evaluated independently of one another, instead of as a class, given their differing degrees of sonority in both languages (recall the sonority scale in (2)).

Independent analyses characterized a child's productions regardless of accuracy with respect to the adult target system. For these analyses, children's productions at a given point in time were analyzed for a minimum two-time occurrence of singleton /l/, singleton /r/, and C/l/ and C/r/ onset clusters. This established whether the child used these structures phonetically. Productions of singletons /l/ and /r/ were evaluated for use across word positions, including the M_2 context, the coda. The children's productions of singleton /l/ and /r/ also were evaluated for use in minimal pairs in order to determine whether they used these structures phonemically. Specifically, a child had to produce two unique sets of minimal pairs for /l/ and /r/ in order for those sounds to be considered phonemes in the child's system. Phonemic use of singletons /l/ and /r/ was evaluated across word positions.

Relational analyses, which evaluated the children's productions in terms of accuracy relative to the target system, involved a calculation of overall accuracy on target singleton /l/, singleton /r/, and C/l/ and C/r/ onset clusters. Accuracy scores allow us to establish that the clusters and singletons were consistently used relative to the target system at a given point in time. Accuracy on C/l/ and C/r/ onset clusters was evaluated in syllable-initial position (which was usually word-initial position). Accuracy on singletons /l/ and /r/ was determined across word positions, as well as in coda position, for specific evaluation of the M_2 context as before.

The two types of analyses therefore permitted a comprehensive evaluation of the prediction that a language cannot allow a segment to occur in M_2 position in a complex onset unless that same segment is allowed in M_2 position in a coda. The following predictions were tested:

1) C/l/V → CV/l/: a consonant + /l/ cluster implies an /l/ coda, and

2) C/r/V → CV/r/: a consonant + /r/ cluster implies an /r/ coda.

Due to the nature of the data, particularly those of the English-speaking children, coda productions were evaluated primarily in word-final position, due to the lack of elicited forms that targeted word-internal coda consonants. We consider implications of this limitation of the data analysis in the Discussion section. The data of Spanish-speaking children do include multiple forms that target word-internal coda consonants.

We evaluated the data in three different ways. The first was a more conservative evaluation of the data that used the combined independent and relational analyses following the methodology of Gierut and O'Connor (2002). For this analysis, a child had to show a minimum two-time occurrence of a liquid, use of the liquid in two minimal pairs, and a minimum 20% accuracy on that liquid as a singleton in final position. In addition, an accuracy score of 80% was necessary for each CL cluster. This more stringent criterion was followed in order to reduce the possibility of false counterexamples to the predicted relationship between onset clusters and codas, and thus allowed a more conservative evaluation of the data (Gierut & O'Connor, 2002).

The second type of analysis was less stringent, and considered results of the independent analyses only. Specifically, we looked at which structures (CL clusters or final liquids) occurred a minimum of two times within each grammar and whether they satisfied Baertsch and Davis' predictions about the cluster-coda relationship. The third type of analysis was also less stringent, and considered results of the relational analyses only. Specifically, we compared accuracy scores on clusters and liquids for those grammars that supported versus those that violated Baertsch and Davis' prediction.

Testing the predictions in this way, using both independent and relational analyses, allowed for more and less conservative evaluations of Baertsch and Davis' predictions of the split margin hierarchy and the need for NoCODA in the constraint hierarchy.

3   Results

From the data of the 16 children, a total of 64 different points in time were evaluated. Of those, the children evidenced CL clusters at only 52 points in time; the 12 remaining points in time will not be considered further. Within those 52 different points in time, 19 showed a minimum two-time occurrence of C/l/ only, 12 had C/r/, while 21 had both. Together, these accounted for 40

C/l/V → CV/l/ relationships (19 + 21 = 40) and 33 C/r/V → CV/r/ relationships (12 + 21 = 33), totaling 73 cluster-coda relationships to be evaluated.

3.1   Combined independent and relational analyses

Of the 73 cluster-coda relationships evaluated, only 11 of them (represented by four children across time: LP100, LP102, LP104, and LP110) showed accuracy levels at or above 80% for C/l/ clusters, while only 6 (represented by two children across time: LP98 and LP105), showed accuracy levels at or above 80% for C/r/ clusters.

For the 11 grammars with C/l/ clusters at or above 80% accuracy, only three satisfied the remaining criteria (two-time occurrence of /l/, use of /l/ in two minimal pairs, and minimum 20% accuracy in final position): LP100 (at two different points in time) and LP110 (at one point in time). The remaining 8 did not satisfy the combined criteria.

For the six grammars with C/r/ clusters at or above 80% accuracy, only two satisfied the remaining criteria (again, two-time occurrence of /r/, use of /r/ in two minimal pairs, and minimum 20% accuracy in final position): LP105 (at two different points in time). LP98 did not satisfy the combined criteria at any point in time.

Adopting these strict criteria for evaluating the predictions of the split-margin approach, only 17 out of 73 grammars could even be evaluated. Of those, only 5 (or 29%) supported the prediction that CL implied final L, for either liquid. Perhaps, though, the criteria used for determining whether a child had 'acquired' CL clusters and liquid codas were too strict.

3.2   Independent analyses alone

We next considered a less conservative evaluation of the data, in terms of the results of independent analyses alone, and based simply on those grammars that showed a minimum two-time occurrence of CL clusters and final liquids. An interesting observation is that, of the 73 cluster-coda relationships evaluated, 23 (or 32%) had C/l/ or C/r/ clusters to the exclusion of final /l/ or /r/ (respectively), while 50 (68%) had C/l/ or C/r/ clusters and their corresponding final liquids.

There were also notable differences in terms of cluster type. There were 40 grammars with a two-time occurrence of C/l/; of those, 6 (or 15%) did not have final /l/. There were 33 grammars with a two-time occurrence of C/r/; of those, 17 (or 52%) did not have final /r/ (refer to Figure 1). Thus, even this criterion alone provides compelling evidence against the prediction that the occurrence of CL clusters necessarily implies the occurrence of their corresponding final liquids; nevertheless, the data support a tendency in that direction, at least for the C/l/V → CV/l/ prediction.

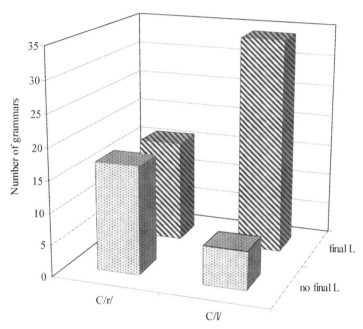

Figure 1. Classification of inventories with CL clusters with or without final liquids (totaling 73 comparisons).

3.3 Relational analyses alone: Individual differences and group trends

We can also consider the data in terms of a less conservative evaluation of the relational analyses alone, this time based simply on the accuracy scores of CL clusters and final liquids. With respect to the prediction that C/l/ implied final /l/, there were 40 grammars to be evaluated, as with the independent analyses described in the previous paragraph. Of these, 6 showed 0% accuracy for final /l/, as stated before. In fact, one child (LP110) had an accuracy of 70% on C/l/ clusters, yet showed 0% accuracy on final /l/. Another child (LP104) showed an accuracy of 93% on C/l/ clusters, yet showed 0% accuracy on final /l/. Similarly, of the 33 grammars that had C/r/ clusters, 17 showed 0% accuracy on final /r/. And, one child (LP73) had an accuracy of 58% on C/r/ clusters, yet showed 0% accuracy on final /r/, while another child had an accuracy of 51% on C/r/ clusters, yet showed 0% accuracy on final /r/.

We also considered the overall accuracy scores on C/r/, C/l/, final /r/, and final /l/ according to presence versus absence of the final liquid across all 73 cluster coda-relationships (Figure 2). In terms of the prediction that C/l/ clusters imply final /l/, the 34 grammars that supported that prediction showed an average accuracy of 62% on C/l/ clusters, and 60% on final /l/. In comparison, the 6 grammars that violated the prediction showed an average accuracy of 33% on the C/l/ clusters (and, of course, 0% on final /l/). Similarly, in terms of the prediction that C/r/ clusters imply final /r/, the 16 that supported the prediction had an average accuracy of 68% on C/r/ clusters, and 75% on final /r/. Those 17 grammars that violated the prediction showed an average accuracy of 26% on C/r/ clusters (and, as before, 0% on final /r/).

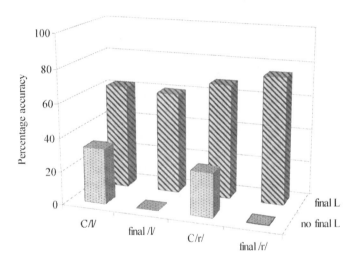

Figure 2. Percentage of accuracy on CL clusters and final L, according to classification of cluster type and presence or absence of the final liquid.

Thus, in terms of accuracy scores alone, and based on group averages rather than individual grammars, the children did show a much higher accuracy on CL clusters when they also had final liquids. This would appear to provide some support for Baertsch and Davis' prediction that CL clusters imply final liquids. However, one other matter must be considered, and that is the children's overall accuracy of singleton liquids, regardless of word position.

Consider again those 34 grammars (described above) that had C/l/ clusters and final /l/. Recall that they showed an average accuracy of 60% on final /l/. This same group of grammars also showed an average accuracy of 64% on singleton /l/ across word positions (refer to Figure 3). On the other hand, those 6 grammars with C/l/ clusters and no final /l/ showed an average accuracy of 23% on /l/ across word positions. Now consider those 16 grammars (described above) that had C/r/ clusters and final /r/. Recall that they showed an average accuracy of 75% on final /r/. This same group of grammars also showed an average accuracy of 80% on singleton /r/ across word positions. Compare this with those 17 grammars with C/r/ clusters and no final /r/, who showed an average accuracy of 10% on /r/ across word positions. It appears that the higher accuracy on final liquids may simply be a reflection of a higher accuracy on liquids generally, rather than anything to do with the proposed cluster-coda relationship.

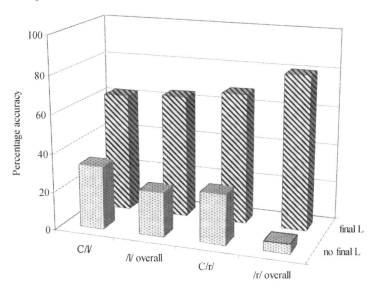

Figure 3. Percentage of accuracy on CL clusters and liquids (regardless of word position), according to classification of cluster type and presence or absence of the final liquid.

To summarize the results of this study, no matter how the data are considered— in terms of the results of combined independent and relational analyses, in terms of independent analyses alone, or in terms of relational analyses alone—there is not sufficient support for the claim that the occurrence of CL clusters implies the occurrence of final liquids, for either liquid. We consider the implications of these findings and directions for future research in the next section.

4   Discussion

The goal of this study was, in essence, to determine if NoCoda is a necessary constraint of the grammar within the framework of optimality theory. As discussed in the Introduction, the split-margin approach proposed by Baertsch (2002) has been shown to be effective in accounting for numerous aspects of syllable organization across a number of languages. Further, it allows for a more formalized account of the parallel patterning of codas and second members of complex onsets, which has been lacking in prior accounts of syllable organization within optimality theory.

The exclusion of NoCoda from the constraint hierarchy as proposed by Baertsch and Davis (2003) led to the prediction that a language cannot allow a segment to occur in M_2 position in a complex onset unless that same segment is allowed in M_2 position in a coda. We tested this prediction with respect to the acquisition of the liquids /l/ and /r/ for children learning English or Spanish.

Recall that one of the problems with testing this prediction with acquisition data related to the methodology that is used for characterizing a structure as 'acquired' or not, and this was particularly the case with the account of Jarmo from Fikkert (1994). Because of this, we evaluated the 16 children's sound systems across several points in time (resulting in 73 cluster-coda relationships to be tested), drawing from a variety of different types of evidence in order to test the prediction from a variety of perspectives.

Our first type of evaluation, which used a combination of independent and relational analyses, was the most conservative of our procedures, and was found to be perhaps too restrictive in our evaluation of the prediction. Specifically, of the 73 cluster-coda relationships evaluated, only 17 of them satisfied the strict criterion of 80% accuracy on C/l/ or C/r/ clusters. And of those 17, only 6 showed a two-time occurrence of the final liquid, use of the final liquid in two minimal pairs, and minimum 20% accuracy in final position. Thus, only 6 (35%) of the 17 grammars showed support for Baertsch and Davis' prediction.

Because these strict criteria limited the total number of grammars to be evaluated, we conducted additional analyses that used less conservative criteria to define 'acquisition.' Our independent analyses, which defined acquisition as simply a two-time occurrence of the structures in question, identified 50 (68%) grammars which supported the prediction and 23 (32%) that did not. Thus, the majority of grammars showed support for Baertsch and Davis' prediction, but there were clearly cases of grammars that did not.

We also conducted relational analyses of the data using less conservative criteria. We found that those grammars that satisfied the prediction (as based on the independent analyses) showed higher overall accuracy on CL clusters than those that did not satisfy the prediction. This seemed to be evidence in support of Baertsch and Davis' prediction. However, we also found that those grammars that satisfied the prediction also had higher accuracy on liquids generally, which makes the support for their prediction less compelling.

Our evaluations of the 73 cluster-coda relationships in the present study showed a tendency for sound systems that had CL clusters to also have final liquids. On face value, though, this is not sufficient support for the cluster-coda prediction. That is, how could we account for those children's sound systems that did not satisfy the prediction, using the tools of optimality theory as proposed by Baertsch and Davis? If NoCODA is not part of the constraint hierarchy, then a grammar that allows, for instance, C/r/ clusters to occur must also allow /r/ to occur in the coda.

Given the assumptions about the ranking of conjoined constraints with respect to their component constraints, $*Obs_1 \& *[r]_2$ must always outrank $*M_1$/Obstruent and $*M_2$/[r]. Further, for a grammar to allow C/r/, faithfulness constraints (such as MAX and DEP) must outrank $*Obs_1 \& *[r]_2$. It follows, then, that these faithfulness constraints must also outrank $*M_1$/Obstruent and $*M_2$/[r], thereby allowing [r] to occur in the coda. Without also including NoCODA to prohibit coda consonants, grammars such as those in the current study cannot be accounted for. Thus, the results of this study provide evidence that NoCODA is necessary in the inventory of universal constraints within optimality theory.

One limitation of this retrospective study is that the coda consonants evaluated in the English-speaking children's data were in word-final position only, due to insufficient numbers of word-internal codas targeted in the English probes. A number of cross-linguistic studies of phonological acquisition have provided evidence that word-final consonants pattern differently from word-internal coda consonants (Goad & Brannen, 2000; 2003; Barlow, 2005b), and this has led some researchers to propose that word-final consonants pattern as onsets early on in acquisition (Goad & Brannen, 2000; 2003; see also Piggott, 1999; Harris & Gussmann, 2002). This would correspond to an M_1 position, rather than M_2, following the split-margin approach. It is possible that, had the data included children's attempts at word-internal coda consonants, there would have been more support for the proposed cluster-coda implicational relationship.

It is also possible that those grammars that had CL clusters to the exclusion of liquid codas may have represented those CL clusters as something other than true branching onsets. A number of studies, including those that take into account acoustic properties of children's productions, as well as those that test children's performance on perceptual tasks, have provided evidence to suggest that children may represent consonant clusters as complex segments (similar to affricates) rather than complex onsets (e.g., Menyuk, 1972; Barton, Miller & Macken, 1980; Barlow & Dinnsen, 1998; Gierut & O'Connor, 2002). If this were the case, then those complex segments would occupy the M_1 position in Baertsch's (2002) proposed syllable structure. Further, complex segments (like affricates) appear to be necessary precursors to acquisition of complex onsets (Lleó & Prinz, 1997; Gierut & O'Connor, 2002); thus, it would not seem unreasonable that a child might first represent CL clusters as complex segments prior to representing them as complex onsets. If the children in the current study who had CL clusters but no liquid codas did in fact represent these CL clusters as complex segments instead, then this would not necessarily be evidence against the cluster-coda implicational relationship. It may in fact be the case that children represent all clusters as complex segments until their inventory of M_2 coda consonants develops. This in turn may allow the child to bootstrap this information to the M_2 onset position, which may mark the point at which CL clusters pattern as true branching onsets. Of course, relying on perceptual data (i.e., phonetic transcriptions) alone will make it difficult to empirically test such claims as this. Perhaps this perceptual data, in combination with acoustic and psycholinguistic information, may provide converging evidence for the representation of CL clusters as complex segments, as well as evidence for the cluster-coda implicational relationship proposed by Baertsch and Davis (2003). For now, though, it appears that there is still a role to be played by NoCoda, despite the improvements to the theory that may be evident with the split-margin approach.

Notes

*   Special thanks to (past and present) members of the Learnability Project and the Phonological Typologies Project for help with data collection and analysis. Thanks also to Lew Shapiro and Peter Torre III for feedback on aspects of this work. This research was supported in part by grants from the National Institutes of Health to San Diego State University (NIH DC05754) and Indiana University (NIH DC001694).

1   Blevins (1995) shows evidence of languages that have CCV syllables to the exclusion of codas, contrary to Baertsch and Davis' predictions. The latter note, however, that each of these exceptions noted in Blevins's typological study is subject to debate as regards syllable organization. For example, Mazateco is one such language that Blevins cites as having CCV but no CVC syllables, yet other researchers have analyzed the CCV forms as complex segments (more akin to affricates) rather than complex onsets (Steriade, 1994).

14 Constraints on consonant clusters in children with cochlear implants*

Steven B. Chin
Indiana University School of Medicine

This study examines synchronic and longitudinal variation in the realization of initial consonant clusters by children who are profoundly deaf and use cochlear implants. Productions were elicited in a picture-naming task from 10 children who had used their cochlear implants for between 5 and 7 years (first interval) and then again from the same children after they had used their implants for between 8.5 and 11.5 years (second interval). At both intervals, realization patterns for initial clusters were similar to those for children with normal hearing: null realizations and realizations with epenthetic vowels occurred only rarely, single-segment realizations with one of the target segments intact generally respected sonority principles, and two-segment realizations with at least one incorrect target segment reflected general constraints on singleton segments. Variation among children in number of output segments, the role of sonority in reduction, and relationships between segmental and featural faithfulness could be accounted for by differences in rankings of basic faithfulness constraints (e.g., MAX, DEP) and markedness constraints (e.g. *COMPLEX, *r). Comparison of individual realizations from the first interval and from the second interval revealed considerable variation, including change from incorrect to correct productions, maintenance of correct productions, maintenance of incorrect productions, and change from correct to incorrect productions. Change in the expected direction can be accounted for by a straightforward and relatively system-wide reranking of markedness constraints with respect to faithfulness constraints. In some cases, however, the introduction of indeterminate ranking as a developmental stage can result in unexpected variation and apparent regression in individual lexical items.

1   Introduction

The effects of profound hearing loss on the ability to produce spoken language is generally considered to be minimal in the case of adults who lose their hearing after acquiring language (Leder & Spitzer, 1990). For children who are prelingually deafened, however, hearing loss affects not only the ability to perceive spoken language, but also the ability to learn to produce it. Cochlear implantation is now a standard treatment in cases of profound deafness (pure tone average thresholds ≥ 90 dB HL) in both adults and children. A cochlear implant is an electronic device, part of which is surgically implanted into the cochlea and the remaining part worn externally. The implant functions as a sensory aid, converting mechanical sound energy into a coded electric stimulus that bypasses damaged or missing hair cells of the cochlea, directly stimulating surviving auditory neural elements. By nature, cochlear implants are primarily intended as auditory prostheses, providing users with better perception of sound, including both environmental sounds and speech sounds. They were originally developed for use by adults with postlingual hearing loss, and it was soon noted that in addition to providing access to the speech of interlocutors, cochlear implants also allowed users to monitor and, if necessary, adjust their own speech. In addition, many have believed that the ultimate benefits of cochlear implantation would accrue to 'children, particularly young children' (Berliner, Eisenberg & House, 1985). Perhaps most important, cochlear implants would provide profoundly deaf children with the auditory environment to acquire and to use a spoken language.

Cochlear implants with a single channel for stimulation were standard for both adults and children into the mid-1980s, but clinical trials in children of the Nucleus 22-channel cochlear implant were initiated in the United States in 1986, and in 1990, the device received approval for use in children from the U.S. Food and Drug Administration (FDA). Since then, multiple-channel cochlear implants have been the norm for both adults and children. Most serious research on the effects of cochlear implantation on the development of speech production in children dates from the time of the clinical trials of the Nucleus-22 and has continued into the present time, along with succeeding generations of both hardware and software.

Consistent with the nature of FDA clinical trials, most of the early research on the effects of cochlear implantation on spoken language development in children was based on batteries of tests of both speech perception and speech production that emphasized breadth, rather than depth. Such research has provided evidence that cochlear implants provide benefits to the acquisition of sound systems that are superior to other sensory aids such as tactile aids and traditional hearing aids, generally in terms of either articulation (Kirk & Hill-Brown, 1985; Tobey & Hasenstab, 1991; Tobey, Pancamo, Staller, Brimacombe & Beiter, 1991; Serry, Blamey & Grogan, 1997; Sehgal, Kirk, Svirsky, Ertmer & Osberger, 1998; Serry & Blamey, 1999) or speech intelligibility (Osberger, Maso & Sam, 1993; Osberger, Robbins, Todd, Riley & Miyamoto, 1994; Dawson, Blamey, Dettman, Rowland, Barker, Tobey, Busby, Cowan & Clark, 1995; Svirsky, Sloan, Caldwell & Miyamato, 2000). With respect to specific areas of phonological acquisition—in this case, consonant clusters—very little research has appeared.

In an early study, Kirk and Hill-Brown (1985) measured both imitative and spontaneous production in children using the House/3M single-channel cochlear implant. They noted slight but statistically nonsignificant improvements in imitated word-initial clusters from before implantation to 6 months after implantation, as well as from before implantation to 1 year after. Similar small and nonsignificant improvements were also noted for word-initial clusters produced in spontaneous speech. In a study reported by Tobey and Hasenstab (1991), it was concluded that cochlear implantation benefited the development of segmental phonology—including consonant clusters—although the specific benefit to clusters was not reported. Chin and Finnegan (2002) provided evidence that children with cochlear implants implement similar strategies as children with normal hearing when dealing with consonant clusters, and that children with implants who use oral communication (spoken language exclusively, without the use of accompanying sign language) produced more adult-like consonant clusters than children who use total communication (spoken language accompanied by formal sign language).

There is ample evidence in the literature that consonant clusters are a relatively difficult aspect of phonological acquisition for children with normal hearing, and that they are generally acquired later than most singleton consonants (Ingram, 1989; Smit, Hand, Freilinger, Bernthal & Bird, 1990; Chin & Dinnsen, 1992; Smit, 1993b). It is also generally accepted—if not conclusively proven—that the same holds for children with cochlear implants. Moreover, it is a commonplace in the field of pediatric cochlear implantation that the population of children who use cochlear implants exhibits wide-ranging variation in acquisition of language, including phonology (although generally in terms of percent correct).

The phonetic and phonological information available to a child with a cochlear implant is both quantitatively and qualitatively different from that available to a child with normal hearing. The design of the electrode array of a cochlear implant is intended to replicate the tonotopic character of the basilar membrane in order to stimulate neural elements at different frequencies; however, the array does not extend fully to the apex of the basilar membrane and in fact stimulates only at the higher frequencies characteristic of the basal end. This means that the perception of sound with a cochlear implant is at a higher pitch than with acoustic hearing. Additionally, because of a finite number of active electrodes and a diminished population of neuronal elements in the cochlea, not all of the characteristics of the incoming signal are captured.

A basic tenet of much of modern linguistic theory has been that the data available for language acquisition by children is degraded and impoverished. However, in spite of poverty of the stimulus (Chomsky, 1980), children with normal hearing will learn 'perfectly' the language present in their environment. Hearing with a cochlear implant (that is, electrical hearing rather than acoustic hearing) represents an even further degradation and impoverishment of the linguistic data available to a child and represents an acquisition environment that is unique in the history of humans and language. The case of children who use cochlear implants provides a unique opportunity to address the question of how robust language learning is in the presence of radically degraded and impoverished auditory input.

Research on the phonological systems of children who use cochlear implants has tended to ignore the context of linguistic systems in general (e.g., developed linguistic systems or the developing phonologies of children with normal hearing), and the tendency has been to view production errors and variation only in terms of the deafness, the cochlear implant, or demographic factors surrounding deafness and the cochlear implant. Because of its strong emphasis on the universality of constraints and its attribution of variation to differences in constraint rankings, optimality theory offers an excellent context in which to examine the phonological systems of cochlear implant users within a wider context. The current study examines the details of variation in consonant cluster realization in a group of 10 children with cochlear implants. Data from the children were collected at two different intervals, and both between-subjects variation and longitudinal within-subjects variation is examined within the framework of optimality theory.

2   Methods

2.1   Participants

Participants were 10 children with cochlear implants who were seen at the Indiana University Medical Center (Indianapolis, Indiana, USA). All children had used a cochlear implant for at least 5 years and lived in households in which English was the primary language. Table 1 shows summary demographic data for each of the 10 children. Age at onset of deafness ranged from 0.0 to 2.1 years ($M = 0.6$ years, $SD = 0.7$ years, median = 0.4 years), age at fitting with a cochlear implant ranged from 1.4 to 6.1 years ($M = 3.6$ years, $SD = 1.4$ years, median = 3.5 years), and better-ear unaided pure-tone average hearing thresholds (PTAs) prior to implantation ranged from 96.7 to 120.1 dB HL ($M = 111.2$ dB HL, $SD = 7.0$ dB HL, median = 113.4 dB HL). Data from each child were collected at two different intervals. At the first interval, chronological age ranged from 6.4 to 11.1 years ($M = 9.2$ years, $SD = 1.6$ years, median = 9.0 years), and length of cochlear implant use ranged from 5.0 to 7.1 years ($M = 5.7$ years, $SD = 0.8$ years, median = 5.4 years). At the second interval, age at testing ranged from 9.8 to 16.1 years ($M = 13.5$ years, $SD = 2.0$ years, median = 13.5 years), and length of cochlear implant use ranged from 8.4 to 11.5 years ($M = 10.0$ years, $SD = 0.9$ years, median = 10.0 years). Six of the children used oral communication exclusively, and four used total communication, a combination of speech and sign, generally Signing Exact English (Gustason & Zawolkow, 1993). All 10 children used the Nucleus 22 multichannel cochlear implant. Two of the devices implemented the Multipeak (MPEAK) processing strategy, and the other eight the Spectral Peak (SPEAK) strategy (see Wilson, 2000).

Table 1. Summary demographic data for 10 children.

Code[1]	Sex[2]	Mode[3]	Processor[4]	Onset[5]	PTA[6]	Age Fit[7]	Test 1[8]	Length 1[9]	Test 2[10]	Length 2[11]
SGB	F	Total	MPEAK	1.0	120.1	4.9	10.9	6.0	15.0	10.1
SGJ	M	Oral	SPEAK	0.8	116.7	5.0	10.7	5.7	15.0	10.0
SGK	F	Total	MPEAK	0.0	103.3	3.8	10.9	7.1	15.3	11.5
SGL	M	Oral	SPEAK	0.0	106.7	3.5	8.6	5.1	13.4	9.8
SGM	M	Oral	SPEAK	2.1	113.4	2.6	9.3	6.7	13.3	10.7
SHJ	M	Oral	SPEAK	0.0	116.7	1.4	6.4	5.0	9.8	8.4
SIF	M	Total	SPEAK	1.4	113.4	2.2	8.2	6.0	12.1	9.8
SIV	F	Oral	SPEAK	0.0	111.7	2.6	7.6	5.0	11.4	8.8
SIW	M	Total	SPEAK	0.8	113.4	3.5	8.6	5.1	13.5	10.0
SIZ	F	Oral	SPEAK	0.0	96.7	6.1	11.1	5.0	16.1	9.9

[1]Randomly-assigned triliteral participant indicator.
[2]Sex of participant: F = female, M = male.
[3]Communication mode.
[4]Cochlear implant processing strategy.
[5]Age at onset of deafness in years.
[6]Best unaided preimplantation pure-tone average threshold in dB HL.
[7]Age at fitting with cochlear implant in years.
[8]Age at first interval testing in years.
[9]Length of cochlear implant use at first interval in years.
[10]Age at second interval testing in years.
[11]Length of cochlear implant use at second interval in years.

2.2   Materials

Productions of initial consonant clusters at both intervals were elicited in an isolated-word picture-naming task. Elicited words included both root forms (e.g., *clock*) and quasi-diminutive derived forms (e.g., *clocky*). From each of the children one production of each of the following words containing a word-initial consonant cluster was elicited: *blue, brush, brushy, drum, drummy, flag, frog, froggy, glove, glovey, green, clock, clocky, crying, plane, stove, stovey, sleep, tree*. All productions were audio-recorded and phonetically transcribed individually and then in consensus by the author and a speech-language patholo-gist. In total, 189 productions of initial consonant clusters were elicited at the first interval and 189 productions at the second interval (difficulties during elicitation resulted in one token missing at each interval).

3   Results and discussion

3.1   Cross-sectional results

This section examines variation between subjects at the first testing interval. Of the 189 clusters elicited at the first testing interval, 55% were produced correctly (i.e., two correct segments); 84% were produced with two segments (without regard to correctness of either segment); 29% were produced with two segments, at least one of which was incorrect; 10% were produced with a single segment only (either a correct segment or not); and 6% were produced with epenthesis. Percent correct clusters for individual children ranged from 0% to 89%. Although there was considerable variation among children in their percent correct scores, a moment's reflection shows that there are only two possible loci of this variation: the number of segments and the nature of the segments. In optimality theoretic terms, all of the variation thus hinges on the degree to which the output representations are segmentally and featurally faithful to the input representations.

3.1.1   Segmental faithfulness

All 189 realizations of two-segment clusters produced by the 10 children contained between 1 and 3 segments. There were no null realizations (i.e., with zero segments, cf. Greenlee, 1974), and no realizations with more than 3 segments. Forms could thus be realized with two segments, one segment, or three segments (with an epenthetic vowel). Examples of these oppositions are shown in Table 2. Each phonetic transcription is followed by an indicator of the child who produced the form, consisting of an arbitrary triliteral code and an interval indicator; for example, SIF-1 indicates child SIF at the first interval.

Table 2. Differences in segmental faithfulness.

Two Segments	One Segment	Three Segments	Gloss
[blu] (SIF-1)		[bəlu] (SGK-1)	'blue'
[bɹʌtʃ] (SIV-1)	[bʊtʃ] (SIW-1)		'brush'
[dɹʌm] (SIV-1)		[dəwʌm] (SGJ-1)	'drum'
[kʰlɑki] (SHJ-1)	[lɑːhi] (SIW-1)		'clocky'
[glʌv] (SGL-1)	[hʌb̥] (SGK-1)	[gəlʌv] (SGJ-1)	'glove'
[glʌvi] (SGL-1)	[nɔb̥i] (SIW-1)	[gəlʌvi] (SHJ-1)	'glovey'
[gɹin] (SHJ-1)	[ɹin] (SIF-1)	[gəɹiːn] (SIZ-1)	'green'
[stoʋ̥i] (SHJ-1)	[tɔʋ̥i] (SIW-1)		'stovey'

With respect to segmental faithfulness, realizations with two segments are faithful to their inputs, because for every input segment, there is a corresponding output segment, and for every output segment, there is a corresponding input segment. On the other hand, one-segment realizations and segments showing epenthesis are not faithful to their inputs. For one-segment realizations, every output segment has a corresponding input segment, but not every input segment has an output segment. The opposite is true for epenthetic realizations: every input segment has a corresponding output segment, but not all output segments have corresponding input segments.

The faithfulness constraints that are of concern to differences in segmental faithfulness are shown in (1) (Kager, 1999). Realizations with two segments incur no violations of these faithfulness constraints, whereas one-segment realizations and epenthetic realizations do.

(1) Faithfulness constraints

MAX: No deletion
DEP: No insertion

That some outputs have fewer segments than the input (i.e., one-segment outputs) or contain an epenthetic vowel is accounted for by a markedness constraint prohibiting clusters in the output (Pater & Barlow, 2003):

(2) Markedness constraint

*COMPLEX: Branching structure is banned in syllable onset position

Whereas one-segment and epenthetic outputs violate, respectively, Max and Dep in (1), outputs with two segments violate the markedness constraint *Complex in (2). In terms of constraint rankings, children who allow two-segment outputs rank faithfulness constraints such as Max and Dep more highly than the markedness constraint *Complex, whereas systems with one-segment or epenthetic outputs rank the markedness constraint *Complex more highly than the faithfulness constraints. The tableau in (3) shows the constraint ranking for a system in which a two-segment onset cluster is realized faithfully.

(3)   SGL-1

/glʌv/ 'glove'	Max	Dep	*Complex
a. ☞ glʌv			*
b. hʌḅ	*!		
c. gəlʌv		*!	

The tableau in (3) shows that the optimal output candidate in the case of SGL is the faithful [glʌv], because the only constraint that it violates is the relatively low ranked markedness constraint *Complex. The second candidate, [hʌḅ], has just a single segment in the onset and thus violates the highly ranked Max, which prohibits deletion. The third candidate, [gəlʌv], demonstrates epenthesis and thus violates the highly ranked Dep, which prohibits insertion. The relative ranking of Max and Dep does not appear to be crucial in the case of SGL-1. In contrast to systems allowing two-segment onsets, systems with one-segment outputs for two-segment inputs incur violations of the faithfulness constraint Max, because not every input segment has a corresponding output. On the other hand, one-segment outputs incur no violations of the other faithfulness constraint Dep or of the markedness constraint *Complex. Thus, for systems with one-segment realizations of clusters, Max must be ranked relatively low. The tableau in (4) illustrates the relevant ranking for [hʌḅ] 'glove' from SGK-1.

(4)   SGK-1

/glʌv/ 'glove'	*Complex	Dep	Max
a. glʌv	*!		
b. ☞ hʌḅ			*
c. gəlʌv		*!	

The higher ranking of *Complex with respect to Max eliminates the faithful (two-segment) candidate [glʌv], leaving both [hʌḅ], with a singleton onset, and [gəlʌv], with epenthesis, as viable candidates. However, the faithfulness constraint DEP is ranked higher than the faithfulness constraint MAX and thus eliminates the epenthesized candidate [gəlʌv]. The two constraints *COMPLEX and DEP appear to be independent in this system, and their relative ranking is not crucial. Both must be ranked above MAX in order to eliminate the two-segment and epenthesized candidates.

Epenthetic forms contain segments in the output that have no correspondences in the input, thus incurring violations of DEP. In systems with epenthetic forms, then, DEP must be low-ranked, relative to *COMPLEX and MAX, as shown in the tableau in (5):

(5)   SIZ-1

/gɹin/ 'green'		*COMPLEX	MAX	DEP
a.	gɹin	*!		
b.	gin		*!	
c. ☞	gəɹi:n			*

The relative ranking of *COMPLEX and MAX is not crucial in such systems.

3.1.2   Featural faithfulness

Segmental faithfulness constraints such as MAX and DEP require that input segments have corresponding output segments and vice versa (i.e., inputs and outputs must have the same number of segments) but do not prohibit input-output mismatches in terms of the featural composition of segments. The data in Table 3 are examples of pairs that are similar in their segmental faithfulness but dissimilar in their featural faithfulness (with respect to the initial cluster).

Table 3. Featural faithfulness vs. featural unfaithfulness.

Featurally Faithful	Featurally Unfaithful	Gloss
a. [dɹʌmi] (SIV-1)	[d̪wʌmi] (SGJ-1)	'drummy'
b. [bɹʌʃ] (SHJ-1)	[bwʌʃ] (SGK-1)	'brush'
c. [tʰɹi:] (SIV-1)	[tʰwi:] (SGB-1)	'tree'
d. [flɛg] (SIF-1)	[fwɛd] (SIW-1)	'flag'
e. [kʰɹaɪŋ] (SIF-1)	[hwaɪ] (SIW-1)	'crying'

Output forms in both the first and second columns show two and only two consonants in their word-initial onsets, so that in all cases, segmental faithfulness is preserved, such that the faithfulness constraints MAX and DEP are ranked higher than the markedness constraint *COMPLEX. Featurally unfaithful forms, such as those in the second column of Table 3, violate a faithfulness constraint IDENT (Barlow & Dinnsen, 1998; Barlow, 2001b), defined as in (6).

(6) IDENT: corresponding segments must be identical

In cases such as those in the second column of Table 3, the faithfulness constraint IDENT must be outranked by markedness constraints prohibiting the appearance of segments with specific features in the output. For the outputs in the second column of Table 3, these markedness constraints are those in (7).

(7) Markedness constraints

   *r: Rhotic consonants are banned
   *l: Lateral consonants are banned
   *k: Dorsal consonants are banned

For outputs in the first column of Table 3, IDENT will outrank the markedness constraints in (7). The tableau in (8) shows the ranking for SIV-1's phonology, which includes the segmentally faithful and featurally faithful output [dɹʌmi], and the tableau in (9) shows the ranking for SGJ-1's segmentally faithful but featurally unfaithful form (with respect to the input /ɹ/) [d̪wʌmi].

(8) SIV-1

/dɹʌmi/ 'drummy'	MAX	DEP	IDENT	*COMPLEX	*r
a. ☞ dɹʌmi				*	*
b. dwʌmi			*!	*	
c. dʌmi	*!				
d. dəɹʌmi		*!			*

As the tableau in (8) shows, in SIV-1's phonological system, all faithfulness constraints (MAX, DEP, IDENT) are ranked higher than all markedness constraints (*COMPLEX, *r). This ranking rejects both segmentally faithful but featurally unfaithful candidates like [dwʌmi], as well as reduced forms like [dʌmi] and epenthesized forms like [dəɹʌmi]. The rankings of the faithfulness constraints with respect to each other, as well as of the markedness constraints with respect to each other, do not appear to be crucial.

(9) SGJ-1

/dɹʌmi/ 'drummy'	*r	MAX	DEP	IDENT	*COMPLEX
a. dɹʌmi	*!				*
b. ☞ dwʌmi				*	*
c. dʌmi		*!			
d. dəɹʌmi	*!		*		

As the tableau in (9) shows, *r is ranked relatively high in SGJ-1's system, because the faithful output [dɹʌmi] is not optimal. On the other hand, both IDENT and *COMPLEX must be ranked relatively low, since two-segment onsets are allowed, and [ɹ] is not possible in SGJ-1's output.

The high-ranking markedness constraint *r accounts for the absence of [ɹ] not only in clusters, but also as singletons, as shown in the tableau in (10).

(10) SGJ-1

/ɹoz/ 'rose'	*r	MAX	DEP	IDENT	*COMPLEX
a. ɹoʊz	*!				
b. ☞ woʊẓː				*	

For the featurally unfaithful forms in (d) and (e) of Table 3, the constraint rankings will be similar to those just described, with the markedness constraints *l and *k more highly ranked than the faithfulness constraint IDENT.

Markedness constraints such as *r are interpreted as prohibitions against occurrences of specific segments in outputs. A somewhat different case occurs when a segment occurs in some outputs but not in others, as illustrated by the data in (11).

(11) SGK-1

     a)   Outputs with [ɹ]
         [ɹi] 'rake'   [ɹeɪdi] 'rakey'   [ɹoʊṣi] 'rosey'

     b)   Outputs without [ɹ]
         [bwʌʃ] 'brush'   [dʒwʌm] 'drum'   [fwɔhi] 'froggy'

In the case of SGK-1, [ɹ] is permitted in outputs if it is the sole consonant in an onset but is not permitted if it shares the onset with another consonant. This can be interpreted as a constraint on how similar two consonants in the onset can be to each other; in this case, we interpret this as a constraint on the minimal sonority difference required between two onset consonants (Steriade, 1982; Clements, 1990). Although various proposed hierarchies of sonority differ in details, most researchers would agree on the basic characterization shown in (12).

(12) Basic Sonority Hierarchy (where > means 'is more sonorous than')

> Vowel > Glide > Liquid > Nasal > Obstruent
>   1   2   3   4   5

The faithful counterparts to the forms shown in (11b) are all of the form obstruent + liquid, and using the scale in (12), we can calculate the sonority difference as the difference between 5 (obstruent) and 3 (liquid), or 2. The actual outputs in (11b), however, have a sonority difference of 3, that is, the difference between 5 (obstruent) and 2 (glide). We can thus conclude that for SGK-1, the minimal sonority difference permissible between output consonants in an onset cluster is 3. This can be expressed as the markedness constraint in (13).

(13) *DIFF[SON] < 3: No sonority differences between onset consonants less than 3

The constraint *DIFF[SON] < 3 prohibits clusters whose constituents differ in sonority by less than 3 steps on the sonority hierarchy. Thus, although obstruent + glide sequences have a sonority difference of 3 and are thus allowed, sequences such as obstruent + liquid, with a sonority difference of 2, or liquid + glide, with a sonority difference of 1, are prohibited. The tableau in (14) illustrates the constraint ranking for a system such as that of SGK-1.

(14) SGK-1

/ɹozi/ 'rosey'	*DIFF[SON] < 3	MAX	DEP	IDENT	*COMPLEX	*r
a. ☞ ɹouʂi						*
b. wouʂi				*!		

/bɹʌʃ/ 'brush'	*DIFF[SON] < 3	MAX	DEP	IDENT	*COMPLEX	*r
a. bɹʌʃ	*!				*	*
b. ☞ bwʌʃ				*	*	

In the tableau for 'rosey', the faithful [ɹouʂi] is the optimal candidate, because *r is ranked lower than IDENT. In the tableau for 'brush', the unfaithful candidate [bwʌʃ] is the more optimal, because the constraint *DIFF[SON] < 3 is ranked higher than IDENT.

3.1.3 Reduction

A ranking of [*COMPLEX, DEP >> MAX] characterizes systems in which reduced versions of input clusters are more optimal outputs than either two-segment or epenthesized versions. High-ranked *COMPLEX and DEP, along with the relatively low ranking of MAX allow outputs with fewer segments than inputs, but these constraints alone do not specify the exact feature composition of the single output segment.

Where there is feature identity between a single output segment and one of the input segments, a commonly observed pattern is that the less sonorous (Clements, 1990) of the input segments survives to output. This has been observed in the phonology of children with normal hearing (Chin, 1996; Ohala, 1999) and appears to account for several diachronic changes in adult languages (Vennemann, 1988). According to the common pattern, input clusters consisting of two segments that differ in sonority have outputs consisting of the segment with lower sonority, that is, the one farther to the left on the hierarchy in (12). This is consistent with the Sonority Dispersion Principle (Clements, 1990; see also Chin, 1996; Ohala, 1999), by which structures with a maximum sonority slope from onset to nucleus are preferred. Thus, stop + liquid inputs have stop outputs, fricative + liquid inputs have fricative outputs, and fricative + stop clusters have stop outputs. Examples from the children with cochlear implants are shown in (15).

(15) Examples of cluster reduction

  a) Stop + Liquid Reductions
      SIW-1:   [bʊtʃ]   'brush'
      SIZ-1:   [kʰakki]   'clocky'

  b) Fricative + Liquid Reductions
      SGB-2:   [fak]   'frog'
      SIZ-2:   [fɔgi]   'froggy'

  c) Fricative + Stop Reductions
      SGK-1:   [toḇ]   'stove'
      SIW-1:   [tɔv̥i]   'stovey'

Constraints on the types of segments that can occur in syllable margins such as those exemplified in (15) are interpretable as a family of markedness constraints, *M/λ, as in (16) (from Prince & Smolensky, 1993/2004).

(16) *M/λ: λ must not be parsed as a syllable Margin (i.e., associated to Onset or Coda)

The set of markedness constraints inherent in *M/λ reflects the sonority hierarchy. Examination of the hierarchy in (12) reveals a dichotomy between obstruents and sonorants, such that all obstruents are lower in sonority, whereas all sonorants (nasals, liquids, glides, vowels) are higher in sonority. Output forms such as those in (15a-b) can be analyzed as reflecting a relatively simple hierarchy based on the obstruent vs. sonorant dichotomy, such as in (17) (Barlow, 1997):

(17) *M/SONORANT >> *M/OBSTRUENT

The tableau in (4) shows that the ranking [*COMPLEX, DEP >> MAX] accounts for systems that exhibit reduced clusters in outputs. The more refined hierarchy in the tableau in (18) is an account of one of the examples in (15a) and reflects the fact that in cases of reduced clusters, some reductions are more optimal than others (violations are noted in word-initial position only).

(18) SIZ-1

/klɑki/ 'clocky'		*COMPLEX	DEP	*M/SONORANT	*M/OBSTRUENT	MAX
a.	klɑkki	*!				
b. ☞	kʰɑkki				*	*
c.	lɑkki			*!		*
d.	kʰəlɑkki		*!			

In (18), the high-ranking markedness constraint *COMPLEX and the faithfulness constraint DEP eliminate the segmentally faithful candidate and epenthesized candidate, respectively. The two remaining candidates both exhibit reduction and so violate the faithfulness constraint MAX. It is only the relative ranking of *M/SONORANT above *M/OBSTRUENT that determines the form with the sonorant to be a nonoptimal candidate and the form with the obstruent to be the optimal one.

The constraint ranking in (18) is sufficient to define the circumstances under which an input cluster containing an obstruent and a sonorant will have a corresponding obstruent output. Such cases are illustrated in (15a-b). The forms in (15c), however, represent obstruent+obstruent inputs with single obstruent outputs, on which the markedness constraint *M/SONORANT has no bearing. The full set of individual steps in the sonority hierarchy in (12) suggests an expansion of *M/λ beyond [*M/SONORANT >> *M/OBSTRUENT]. A version applicable to onset singletons suggested by Pater (1997) is shown in (19), where G = glide, L = liquid, N = nasal, and F = fricative.

(19) *G-ONS >> *L-ONS >> *N-ONS >> *F-ONS

The hierarchy in (19) specifies that glides are the least optimal onset, whereas stops are the most optimal (there being no constraint against stop onsets). Thus, given a form such as in (15c), the constraint hierarchy in (19) accounts for the fact that the stop, rather than the fricative, is realized in the output, as shown in the tableau in (20).

(20) SIW-1

/stovi/ 'stovey'		*Complex	Dep	*G-Ons	*L-Ons	*N-Ons	*F-Ons	Max
a.	stovi	*!						
b. ☞	tɔy̥i							*
c.	sovi						*!	*
d.	sətovi		*!					

The Sonority Dispersion Principle, under which cluster reduction is to the less sonorous segment, accounts for a large number of single-segment output forms in the data from children with cochlear implants. In several cases, however, single-segment outputs reflect reduction to the more sonorous segment of the input cluster. These are given in (21).

(21) Reduction to More Sonorous Segment

    a)   Stop + Liquid
          SIW-1:   [laʔ]   'clock'
          SIW-1:   [laːhi] 'clocky'
          SGB-1:   [lakʼ] 'clock'
          SIF-1:   [ɹin]   'green'

    b)   /s/ + Liquid
          SGK-1:   [lip̬]   'sleep'

Cases such as those in (21) represent conflicts with the sonority pattern (Pater & Barlow, 2003). The Sonority Dispersion Principle and the constraint hierarchy in (12) would predict outputs with initial velar stops in (21a) and an alveolar fricative in (21b). The forms in (21a) reflect the constraint *k, and the form in (21b) reflects the constraint *FRICATIVE, both given in (22) (see also Pater & Barlow, 2003).

(22) Markedness constraints

    *k: Dorsal consonants are banned
    *FRIC: Fricatives are banned

Constraints such as those in (22) have wide-ranging effects in children's language, underlying such commonly-observed phenomena as 'velar fronting' and 'stopping' (Stoel-Gammon & Dunn, 1985). In systems that follow the sonority pattern, such constraints would be ranked below the hierarchy of constraints in (12), whereas in systems exhibiting forms such as those in (21), they rank above the sonority based hierarchy and disrupt its effects. For the form [ɹin] in (21a), the tableau in (23) shows how *k is ranked above the relevant margin constraint.

(23) SIF-1

/gɹin/ 'green'	*k	*L-Ons
a.　　　gin	*!	
b.　☞　ɹin		*

3.2　Longitudinal results

Of the 189 clusters elicited at the second interval, 51% were produced correctly (i.e., two correct segments); 83% were produced with two segments (without regard to correctness of either segment); 32% were produced with two segments, at least one of which was incorrect; 12% were produced with a single segment only (either a correct segment or not); 5% were produced with epenthesis; and <1% ($n = 1$) were produced as null. Percent correct clusters for individual children ranged from 16% to 74%. A comparison of these with those from the first interval seems to indicate that as a group, the children's productions regressed slightly. Percent correct went from 55% at the first interval to 51% at the second interval, although a paired t-test of mean clusters correct at the first and second interval indicated a nonsignificant difference, $t = .542$, n.s. Outputs with two segments (regardless of the correctness of either segment) showed a slight decrease from 84% to 83%. Additionally, the maximum individual percent correct fell from 89% to 74%. On the other hand, the minimum individual percent correct rose from 0% to 16%.

As is common with developing systems, there were some indications that productions became more adult-like, some indications that productions remained the same, and some indications that productions became less adult-like. The data in (24) are examples of productions that became more adult-like:

(24) Data from SIW-2

First Interval	Second Interval	Gloss
[laːhi]	[kʰlɑki]	'clocky'
[hwãĩ]	[kɹãĩ]	'crying'
[neːv̥]	[gləv]	'glove'
[nɔb̥i]	[glʌvi]	'glovey'
[bwˇi]	[gɹin]	'green'

Some of the data in (24) were cited previously in (21) as an example of the dominance of the markedness constraint *k that disrupted the sonority pattern for cluster reduction. The tableau in (25) shows a relevant part of SIW's grammar at the first interval (only word-initial violations of *k are included).

(25) SIW-1

/klɑki/ 'clocky'	*k	*L-Oɴꜱ	Mᴀx
a. klɑki	*!		
b. kɑki	*!		*
c. ☞ lɑːhi		*	*

SIW's faithful output at the second interval indicates demotion of both *k and *L-Oɴꜱ, as shown in the tableau in (26).

(26) SIW-2

/klɑki/ 'clocky'	Mᴀx	*k	*L-Oɴꜱ
a. ☞ kʰlɑki		*	
b. kɑki	*!	*	
c. lɑːhi	*!		*

In most cases, outputs that were correct at the first interval had corresponding correct outputs at the second interval. Forms from SGL in (27) illustrate the many instances in which both segmental and featural faithfulness in initial clusters were maintained longitudinally.

(27) Data from SGL

First Interval	Second Interval	Gloss
[pʰleɪn]	[pʰleɪn]	'plane'
[blu]	[blu]	'blue'
[tɹi]	[tʰɹi]	'tree'
[dɹʌm]	[dɹəm]	'drum'
[kʰɬak]	[kʰlæk]	'clock'
[glʌv]	[glʌv̥]	'glove'
[fɹɑg]	[fɹɑg]	'frog'

Forms like those listed in (27) indicate relatively well-advanced phonological development at the first interval, which remained stable over the 4.7 years between intervals. Nevertheless, as the data in (28) indicate, there were some exceptional cases.

(28) Additional Data from SGL

First Interval	Second Interval	Gloss
[dɹʌmi]	[tʰəmi]	'drummy'
[flæg]	[pʰwæg]	'flag'

Two questions raised by the data in (27) and (28) are first, whether errors of the type shown in (28) are random or characteristic, and second, whether SGL's grammar at the second interval is the same as at the first interval. The case of 'drum' in (27) vs. 'drummy' in (28) would seem to be a slip of the tongue: first, the output [tʰəmi] is the only example of a reduced cluster from either interval, and there are no further examples at either interval of an output [tʰ] for an input /d/. In 'flag' in (28), there are two unfaithful segments: output [pʰ] corresponding to input /f/ and output [w] corresponding to input /l/. At SGL's first interval, there is evidence of a constraint against labial fricatives such as formulated in (29).

(29) *f: Labial fricatives are banned

The constraint was particularly active in postvocalic position at the first interval, but by the second interval, output forms were faithful with respect to the continuancy of labials. This is shown in the data in (30), which contains all elicited instances of postvocalic [f].

(30) Postvocalic [f] from SGL

First Interval	Second Interval	Gloss
[lip͡f]	[lif]	'leaf'
[lip͡vi]	[lifi]	'leafy'
[naɪp͡f]	[naɪf]	'knife'
[naɪpi]	[mefi]	'knifey'

In fact, the relevant facts are that at the first interval, all postvocalic labiodental fricatives were incorrect and all initial labiodentals were correct, and at the second interval, all postvocalic labiodentals were correct and some initial labiodentals were incorrect. Because labiodentals in initial position and those in postvocalic position appear to have developed independently, it is possible that there are actually two relevant markedness constraints:

(31) Markedness constraints against labiodentals

*Vf: Postvocalic labial fricatives are banned
*#f: Word-initial labial fricatives are banned

The development of correct postvocalic labiodentals at the second interval is evidence for a demotion of *Vf to a place below IDENT in the constraint hierarchy. Note that longitudinally, correct initial labiodentals precede correct postvocalic labiodentals. This acquisition order is in contrast to the proposal of Dinnsen and Farris-Trimble (Chapter 9 in this volume), who argue that children first acquire contrasts in postvocalic position. Only later are contrasts acquired in initial position. The pattern exhibited by SGL is contrary to this general pattern, and one question raised by these data is whether this contrary pattern is in some way related to SGL's deafness and use of a cochlear implant. At present, we leave this as an open question awaiting further data from other children.

Additionally, evidence of both stop outputs and fricative outputs in initial position at the second interval speaks for a degree of continuing indeterminacy in the relative ranking of IDENT and *#f. In some cases, a higher ranked IDENT preserves a continuant input, as illustrated in the tableau in (32). In other cases, however, a higher ranked *#f results in unfaithful outputs, as shown in the tableau in (33).

(32) SGL-2

/fɹɑg/ 'frog'	IDENT	*#f
a. ☞ fɹɑg		*
b. pɹɑg	*!	

(33) SGL-2

/flæg/ 'flag'	*#f	IDENT
a. flæg	*!	
b. ☞ pʰwæg		*

As noted above, at SGL's first interval, all initial labiodental fricatives were correct, so that the constraint ranking was [IDENT >> *#f], and 'flag' was realized as [flæg]. The second interval data would appear to indicate a weakening of this strict ordering, resulting in [IDENT, *#f], sometimes realized as [IDENT >> *#f], as in (32), sometimes as [*#f >> IDENT], as in (33). Some researchers (Anttila & Cho, 1998; Cho, 1998) have suggested that a diachronic reranking is a three-stage process, so that reranking from [C1 >> C2] to [C2 >> C1] involves an intermediate indeterminate stage [C1, C2] at which variation is observed. With [IDENT >> *#f] as the first stage for SGL, and [IDENT, *#f] as the second stage, it might be concluded that the third stage is [*#f >> IDENT].

From the available data, however, it would be imprudent to call this third stage the final stage, at least because this ranking is not adult-like. In all likelihood, the situation is more complicated than a simple three-stage reranking, and it may be the case that longitudinal development in children with cochlear implants is not as straightforward a progression as that observed in children who have normal hearing. Again, we await further longitudinal data to support a definitive answer.

4   Conclusion

Children who use cochlear implants form a group that is unique in the history of research on language and language acquisition. Because hearing for these children is electrical rather than acoustic and mechanical, their auditory input is unlike any that has always been assumed in studies of how children acquire language. Although cochlear implants are primarily an aid to hearing, observation and research have shown that they are equally useful in supporting the production of spoken language, as well as the acquisition of spoken language in congenitally deaf children. Children with cochlear implants provide a unique opportunity to assess the effects of differences in the quality of auditory input on the acquisition of spoken language.

An oft-cited observation regarding both the perception and production of spoken language in children with cochlear implants is the wide variation found in all types of outcome measures. Independent research in language acquisition, speech-language pathology, and clinical linguistics has shown, however, that wide variation is found even among children who have normal hearing. The reliance on scores (e.g., percent correct) from standard assessment measures has amplified the impression of variability in fields such as pediatric cochlear implantation, and the search for predictive independent variables is a characteristic hallmark of current research in this area. All manner of factors such as age at the time of implantation, socio-economic status, and working memory have been suggested as predictors of success with a cochlear implant.

On the other hand, research programs such as optimality theory examine the variability itself, and offer the opportunity to determine exactly how variable the variability in fact is. For example, children in the current study ranged from 0 to 89 percent correct on their production of initial consonant clusters at the first interval, implying that they were highly variable. Yet, given that there are perhaps hundreds of ways to be wrong but only one way to be right, optimality theory provides a framework for asking whether the children's productions were so variable that they used all of the hundreds of ways to be wrong. A closer examination under these circumstances reveals that children's errors were not simply random, but rather constrained by how language and language acquisition actually work, and, in fact, more or less in the ways that optimality theory predicts.

Finally, the population of children with cochlear implants is both relatively new and relatively small, so that the amount of data available for analysis of the type illustrated here is also relatively small (from both cross-sectional and longitudinal points of view). As relevant data collection becomes both more widespread and more theoretically focused, we may hope that more definitive answers to the issues raised here will be forthcoming.

Notes

*   I am grateful to Cara Lento Kaiser and Amy P. Teoh for assistance with phonetic transcription. This work was supported by grants to Indiana University from the National Institute on Deafness and Other Communication Disorders (R01 DC005594 & R03 DC003852).

Part V

Epilogue

15 On the convergence of theory and application

Daniel A. Dinnsen & Judith A. Gierut
Indiana University

We close the volume with a few summary remarks highlighting our findings, their theoretical and applied implications, and unresolved issues that warrant further study. Throughout this volume, we have seen that optimality theory has contributed to and benefited from the description and experimental manipulation of children's phonological errors. On the descriptive side, children's error patterns were characterized by interleaving markedness and faithfulness constraints in an intricate hierarchy. This default ranking of markedness over faithfulness is responsible for the simplification errors that are observed in the children's early speech. The substantive details of the ranking pinpoint the sounds and contexts that are vulnerable to error, and project the sounds that are used as substitutes. The ranking also provides for a highly restricted, subset grammar in the initial state. The theoretical and practical value of starting with such a grammar is that the child can then use positive evidence from the available input to motivate changes in the grammar over time. A child's observation that a sound or sound sequence can in fact occur has the consequence of identifying the markedness constraint that had been responsible for an error and compels the minimal demotion of that markedness constraint, resulting in the eradication of the error pattern. In this way, optimality theory makes clear and testable predictions about aspects of learning in the course of acquisition. Those predictions have largely been borne out in the experimental work that we report, but there are instances where generalization learning proceeded in some unpredictable ways (Chapter 11). Conversely, some previously perplexing developmental trajectories involving overgeneralization errors have been shown to follow naturally from highly ranked, conflicting markedness constraints (Chapters 1, 5, and 8). The consequence is that overgeneralization errors can actually be seen as representing a step in the right direction as the constraint hierarchy is approaching conformity with the target system. Thus, our descriptive studies have highlighted the ways in which acquisition informs optimality theory and how optimality theory clears up some of the puzzles of acquisition.

An important finding of our research is that children's error patterns often do not simply reflect a subset of the generalizations about sounds and sound sequences of the target language. Many of the generalizations that children arrive at are not observable in the primary linguistic data to which they are exposed. These generalizations are moreover opaque (i.e., not surface-true or not surface-apparent). A wide variety of developmental opacity effects were documented and analyzed in Part II. Contrary to standard expectations that opacity effects are marked and hard to learn, opaque generalizations appear to be widespread in developing phonologies and emerge naturally (with or without treatment) in the early stages of acquisition. For example, we saw in Chapter 5 that T presented with a grandfather effect prior to her having received clinical treatment, and that another grandfather effect emerged after the first round of treatment. We also saw in Chapter 4 in the case of Child 142 that a grandfather effect can emerge from an earlier stage of transparency. The significance of these findings is that phonological theory needs to provide not only for the characterization of occurring opacity effects, but also for their natural emergence in the early stages of phonological acquisition, even when those effects do not occur in the target language. Toward this end, we saw that optimality theory can account for opacity effects by extending the theory to include local constraint conjunction (Chapters 4 and 6), comparative markedness (Chapters 4 and 5), and/or sympathy (Chapter 4). We probably do not need all of these extensions because they overlap in their coverage in several instances. It is somewhat more challenging, however, to explain how the ranking of constraints comes about when the end result is an opaque generalization. This is especially problematic, for example, for comparative markedness in its accounts of the emergence of counterfeeding chain shifts. More specifically, while comparative markedness characterizes such opacity effects by the ranking $_O$MARKEDNESS >> FAITH >> $_N$MARKEDNESS, the problem is that there is no observable fact in the target language that would have motivated the demotion of the $_N$MARKEDNESS constraint in the first place. We offer some speculative thoughts in Chapter 5 about other factors that might precipitate the demotion of $_N$MARKEDNESS, but this obviously remains an open issue. Nevertheless, what is clear from this set of chapters is that opacity effects arise naturally along the path to faithfulness; opaque generalizations are thus faithfulness-improving.

For the future, there is no doubt that developmental opacity effects will take on added significance and raise new questions given McCarthy's (2007) proposed revisions to optimality theory as embodied in Optimality Theory with Candidate Chains (OTCC). While this new version of optimality theory retains many of the core elements of the original theory (e.g., the hierarchical ranking of markedness and faithfulness constraints and their standard evaluation of output candidates), it also introduces some new architectural elements that have the effect of eliminating the need for local constraint conjunction, sympathy, and an aspect of comparative markedness. Many of the opacity effects that we have considered will necessitate a very different account within OTCC, and those accounts will need to be evaluated against the longitudinal facts of acquisition. However, one element of comparative markedness that is retained within OTCC is the account of opaque generalizations involving grandfather effects. Recall that the schema for grandfather effects is $_N$MARKEDNESS $>>$ FAITH $>>$ $_O$MARKEDNESS. From a developmental perspective, the emergence of grandfather effects makes perfect sense. That is, the demotion of $_O$MARKEDNESS from an initial-state ranking is straightforward and would be based on positive evidence. Also, the sustained dominance of $_N$MARKEDNESS explains why certain sounds cannot serve as substitutes and why certain other sounds continue to participate in an error pattern that has otherwise been eradicated. The opacity effects that will need to be reconsidered are those previously described in derivational terms as counterfeeding and counterbleeding interactions.

At least two theoretical innovations have been introduced within OTCC to handle these cases. One innovation is a 'candidate chain', which involves an elaborated sense of the candidates that are evaluated by a constraint hierarchy. A candidate chain is a series of steps or unfaithful mappings that an input might go through to yield a conventional output candidate. There are several requirements for a valid chain. Each of the steps must involve minimal (gradual) changes, and each step must be harmonically-improving based on the language-specific hierarchy of constraints. For each input, there will be several competing candidate chains. Many candidate chains will be eliminated in the standard evaluation process due to their violations of faithfulness and markedness constraints. However, in order for an opaque output to win in some language, a new family of constraints has been introduced as a second innovation; these are 'precedence constraints' (abbreviated PREC). PREC constraints assign a violation mark to chains when a particular step in the chain is not preceded, or is followed by another specific step. These constraints thus demand a particular order or precedence of unfaithful mappings in a chain. If a PREC constraint is ranked high enough in the hierarchy, it can effectively eliminate the chain that results in a transparent output, thus favoring the chain that ends with an opaque output. One issue for acquisition is how the PREC constraints come to be ranked high enough to favor opaque outputs. We suspect that the default ranking of PREC constraints places them relatively high in the hierarchy. However, a metacondition of the new theory requires that a PREC constraint must be ranked below the corresponding faithfulness constraint that establishes the precedence relationship. A question then arises: What fact of the target language would motivate a child to demote a markedness constraint below the PREC constraint rather than just below the highest-ranked faithfulness constraint that the previous winner violated? One possible answer might be that a PREC constraint and its associated faithfulness constraint behave as a cohesive unit that cannot be separated by intervening constraints.

In complement to phonological description, our experimental findings have shown that some error patterns are more difficult than others to remediate (Chapters 6 and 8). Those that are more difficult involve opacity effects (e.g., chain shifts), but also allophonic phenomena, which are transparent. What unifies these situations is the independence of multiple constraints, each of which must be demoted. If treatment is designed around the demotion of just one markedness constraint, additional rounds of treatment will likely be necessary. Chapter 6 experimentally supported this point by implementing a novel treatment protocol aimed at the demotion of multiple markedness constraints, all of which were associated with the truly recalcitrant chain shift error pattern. The success of that treatment protocol suggests that other recalcitrant error patterns involving multiple independent constraints might also benefit from a similar treatment design. Our optimality theoretic characterization of developmental conspiracies in Chapter 1 also shows that the hierarchy for conspiracies can be used to select words for treatment. Certain types of words are predicted to be especially effective in eradicating error patterns because they can force the demotion of multiple constraints simultaneously. Along the same lines, error patterns that are governed by implicationally-related constraints in a harmonic scale of some sort can be effectively eradicated by focusing treatment on the most marked structure (or highest-ranked markedness constraint). This then forces the demotion of lower-ranked markedness constraints. This was documented in Chapters 8 and 11. Results of this latter sort are suggestive of a fixed ranking among certain constraints (cf. Chapter 12 in this volume).

Across chapters, there were a number of convergences in the comparison of developing and fully developed phonologies. For the most part, we find that these two types of sound systems are governed by the same principles and constraints. This was especially evident in Part IV in our studies of consonant clusters. Additionally, many of the same general phenomena can be found in both developing and fully developed phonologies, e.g., inventory restrictions, allophonic and neutralization processes, alternations, conspiracies, output-to-output correspondence, and opacity effects. However, as described in Chapter 9, there are at least some superficial differences in terms of what can serve as a prominent or strong context. That is, fully developed languages tend to treat initial position as prominent, while children in the early stages of development tend to treat final position as prominent. We argued that this paradox might be resolved by appealing to a new family of conflicting markedness constraints that assign or license prominence in different contexts. The default ranking is for FINALPROM to outrank INITIALPROM. Predictably, the reranking of these constraints is triggered by an increase in the size of the lexicon and/or by treatment. Another disparity that was only briefly touched upon in Chapter 9 is the fact that young children often exhibit long-distance consonant harmony, but fully developed languages do not. Following in the lines of our prominence-assigning constraints, we speculated that optimality theory might add a family of conflicting markedness constraints that license different geometric configurations (e.g., segregated versus integrated geometries). The default ranking of these constraints in the initial state would favor segregated geometries that would allow Consonant Harmony; the reverse ranking would favor integrated geometries that would preclude Consonant Harmony. The reranking of these constraints might also be motivated by changes in the size of the developing lexicon.

Part IV of the volume was devoted exclusively to issues involving consonant clusters. The many problems that children have with clusters in the early stages of acquisition offer special opportunities to evaluate descriptively and experimentally the various principles that have been claimed to govern clusters. Several different implicational laws and markedness hierarchies were evaluated with mixed results. On the one hand, strong support was provided for the markedness of clusters relative to affricates (Chapter 11) and for the Sonority Sequencing Principle across all the chapters of Part IV. On the other hand, the developmental results from Chapter 13 did not support the split-margin hierarchy (Baertsch, 2002), which claims that onset clusters depend on codas. It was suggested, however, that the split-margin hierarchy might be salvaged if the universal constraint set retains NoCODA as an independent constraint. The finding of Chapter 12 that children have gaps in their inventories of s-clusters raises fundamental questions about markedness generally and the appropriateness of fixed rankings versus stringency. The systematic gaps in children's inventories of s-clusters are an intriguing finding in their own right that raise questions about whether fully developed languages might exhibit similar gaps in their s-cluster inventories (cf. Farris-Trimble, 2007). This holds potential as yet another vantage for comparing developing and fully developed languages.

One contribution of the volume that may be easy to overlook is the methodological innovations that have been highlighted across the various chapters. The obvious way to study phonological systems is by gathering production data of the kind required in support of conventional linguistic claims. However, eliciting such data from children is no small feat. In this regard, the child-friendly, easy to administer probes described in Chapter 2 and applied in nearly every other chapter of the volume provide an invaluable research tool. Demonstrations that extend the probe to new populations, as in Chapter 14 in the study of the phonological systems of children with cochlear implants, serve to illustrate how the measures may be explored and modified in new ways. Other methodological innovations highlighted in the volume are more experimental in nature and likewise, have potential for use in other applications. The experimental manipulation of linguistic and psycholinguistic variables using single-subject designs is noteworthy in this regard (Chapter 3), as the designs are particularly well suited to the study of individual grammars and to the process of change through constraint demotion within optimality theory.

One of the most interesting, but also challenging, findings to emerge from the application of single-subject designs in optimality theoretic studies relates to the effects of complexity on change in grammars. As summarized in Chapter 3, when children are presented with complex linguistic input, this induces system-wide change in grammar that appears to take place in a 'one fell swoop' fashion. The puzzle is how this change could occur given the current architecture of optimality theory and corresponding hypotheses about learnability through incremental constraint demotion. There are at least two possible starting points for exploring this question. One emphasizes the experimental design itself, in applying alternate setups that allow for a focus on time as opposed to behavioral change. The multiple probe design in particular may be worth looking at as it is sensitive to dependencies in behavior change. A possible application of the design for optimality theory is the examination of concurrent change among multiple constraints, whether related or unrelated. This may afford a closer look at what changes and when it changes for new insight into the 'one fell swoop' claims of learning. A second research emphasis turns to optimality theory itself and the specific claim that phonological learning is an incremental, one-change-at-a-time process. There is considerable evidence to suggest that human learning in general, and development in particular, is a dynamic and heterochronic process (Smith & Thelen, 1993; Thelen & Smith, 1994). Changes that take place in a given subsystem can enhance, detract, or have no effect on the properties of other subsystems. Within optimality theory, the focus has almost exclusively been on isolated phonological phenomena that are explored at a single point in time. In continued studies, it will be necessary to broaden the scope of study to explore how optimality theory crosscuts a developing sound system. One way this may be achieved is through statistical modeling of the coordinated effects of developmental change across children's grammars. An added benefit is that this line of study might help to validate the network structure that underlies optimality theory's simultaneous evaluation of candidates in constraint application.

Other experimental paradigms that might have utility in future research on optimality theory are based on the assessment of similarity of structure, as described in Chapters 7 and 10. These procedures are intriguing because they allow for the disambiguation of the underlying variables that contribute to systematic language patterns. Clearly, the study of phonological systems assumes that the core contribution is linguistic in nature. However, by pitting phonological dimensions against predictions of similarity that derive from other perceptual or acoustic sources, it becomes possible to discern the salience of competing variables. For future research, it may be relevant to expand the scope of comparison to include, for example, similarities that derive from markedness, strata of constraints, or even order of acquisition. Through such studies, it may be possible to pinpoint exactly what learners are extracting from the phonological input.

While theoretical implications for optimality theory have been prominently displayed throughout the volume, it is important also to highlight the clinical implications of the research reported herein. Through descriptive characterizations of children's phonological systems from an optimality theoretic perspective, a number of new findings have emerged. Of particular mention is the observation that certain error patterns systematically co-occur (Chapters 4 and 8). This is an observation that has been noted previously in the clinical literature, but due to inherent limitations of prior analysis frameworks, it was not possible to glean that co-occurrences are also implicational, such that certain error patterns predict certain others. The clinical value of this finding is that one error pattern can be isolated as critical for treatment, which when corrected, will lead to the eradication of other subordinate errors. This works to enhance the efficacy of clinical treatment because it reduces the set of treatment goals, maximizes the amount of phonological gain, and minimizes time in treatment. For speech-language pathologists and other practitioners, it will be important to stay abreast of descriptive reports that outline superordinate–subordinate relationships such as these to assist in planning intervention. This does not mean to say, however, that it will also be necessary for the practicing clinician to learn how to 'do' optimality theory. Certainly, tutorials are available, which some may find informative (Barlow & Gierut, 1999; Gierut & Morrisette, 2005). Nonetheless, clinicians should find the relevant clinical recommendations readily accessible in published reports because of their familiarity with the error patterns at hand, albeit through conventional diagnostic evaluations. The key then is being able to extract the recommendations from the literature for direct application.

Another clinical contribution that derives from the research reported in this volume follows from the experimental manipulations of treatment. While the research goals of most of the chapters were to test various tenets of optimality theory, the applied consequence of the findings bears on generalization learning as it is realized in clinical settings. In this context, generalization is the reflection of a successful intervention program. The differential learning patterns that obtain under contrasting experimental conditions serve to inform the plan of successful treatment. As in our prior work, the differential generalization that has obtained is consistent with the view that 'what' is treated may be more important than 'how' it is treated (Gierut, 2005). Moreover, phonological complexity continues to be a primary variable in target selection, but interestingly, the notion of complexity may actually encompass a broader domain, extending beyond such conventional phonological considerations as markedness. Following from Chapters 7 and 10, it will be important for future research to explore the effects and interactions of perceptual complexity in phonological treatment along with psycholinguistic variables that bear on children's ability to recognize spoken words. Such clinical studies will no doubt spawn theoretical questions to be taken up by optimality theory, such as whether related variables that lie outside of a phonological core per se are to be incorporated into the model and how.

Two additional issues that warrant attention from a clinical perspective follow from the findings reported in several different chapters. Specifically, in the analysis of gapped cluster inventories, Chapter 12 reveals the pervasive role of faithfulness in children's emerging grammars, in complement to the developmental mainstream concentration on the demotion and role of markedness in acquisition. This calls for treatment studies to focus on the interplay between both types of constraints in the examination of generalization learning. Likewise, in the use of classification paradigms, Chapters 7 and 10 placed emphasis on output-to-output correspondences, in complement to the primary focus on input-output relationships in acquisition work. This shift bears on clinical issues associated with children's ability to self-monitor their productions as a possible criterion that has been used to determine dismissal from treatment. It also bears on children's morphophonological skills, which have been reported as delayed in certain clinical populations (Dunn & Till, 1982). Treatment research that takes advantage of output correspondences may lead to new insights about these clinical issues.

On balance, the study of children with functional phonological disorders has afforded a new interpretation to the characterization of development in the study of language. Traditionally, chronological age is taken as synonymous with development, and as such, studies have focused on language development in toddlers, preschoolers, and so on. In this volume, we have advanced an alternate view based on the broader conceptualization of development as synonymous with change. In this way, our studies of children have placed emphasis on the composition of their grammars as defining where they are in the course of development. Children with similar grammars are evaluated in tandem, even though they may be of different ages or from different populations. This tack is consistent with the underlying theme of converging trajectories, as data from multiple sources feed the same questions in the study of language for a unified interpretation of results. Moreover, from observed differences that arise, it is possible to cull the points of uniqueness, thereby delimiting what is most basic to language from other systems, developmental processes, and/or disorders. The chapters in this volume serve as a sample of our research team's recent work on phonological acquisition and disorders from the perspective of optimality theory. We hope to have shown that the sound systems of children with phonological disorders provide a novel and rich landscape for the investigation and evaluation of theoretical linguistic claims. Toward this end, optimality theory has lent new and intriguing insights into acquisition that have real consequences for the clinical assessment and treatment of linguistic disorders. Phonological theory will no doubt continue to evolve and as such, it will necessitate innovations in analyses, methodologies, and applications. Our goal is to continue to encourage broad interdisciplinary collaboration, as modeled by the successes of our research team, in finding the synchrony and mutual benefits between phonological theory, acquisition, and disorders.

References

Ahn, S.-C. (1998). *An Introduction to Korean Phonology*. Seoul, Korea, Hanshin Publishing Co.

Aitchison, J. (2000). *The Seeds of Speech: Language Origin and Evolution*. Cambridge, UK, Cambridge University Press.

Allerton, D. J. (1976). Early phonotactic development: Some observations on a child's acquisition of initial consonant clusters. *Journal of Child Language* 3: 429–33.

Amayreh, M. M. and Dyson, A. T. (1998). The acquisition of Arabic consonants. *Journal of Speech, Language, and Hearing Research* 41: 642–53.

American Speech-Language-Hearing Association Audiologic Assessment Panel 1996. (1997). *Guidelines for audiologic screening*. Rockville, MD, ASHA.

Anderson, S. R. (1981). Why phonology isn't natural. *Linguistic Inquiry* 12: 493–539.

Angluin, D. (1980). Inductive inference of formal languages from positive data. *Information and Control* 45: 117–35.

Anttila, A. and Cho, Y.-m. Y. (1998). Variation and change in optimality theory. *Lingua* 104: 31–56.

Applegate, J. R. (1961). Phonological rules of a subdialect of English. *Word* 17: 186–93.

Archibald, J., Ed. (1995). *Phonological Acquisition and Phonological Theory*. Hillsdale, NJ, Erlbaum.

Archibald, J. (1998). Second language phonology, phonetics and typology. *Studies in Second Language Acquisition* 20: 189–211.

Archibald, J. and Vanderweide, T. (1997). Second language syllable structure: Phonological government and typological universals. *Calgary Working Papers in Linguistics* 19: 23–43.

ASHA (1985). Guidelines for identification audiometry. *ASHA* 27: 49–52.

Au, T. K.-f. and Laframboise, D. E. (1990). Acquiring color names via linguistic contrast: The influence of contrasting terms. *Child Development* 61: 1808–23.

Auger, J. (2001). Phonological variation and optimality theory: Evidence from word-initial vowel epenthesis in Vimeu Picard. *Language Variation and Change* 13: 253–303.

Bach, E. and Harms, R. (1972). How do languages get crazy rules? In R. Stockwell and R. Macaulay (eds) *Linguistic Change and Generative Theory*. 1–21. Bloomington, Indiana University Press.

Baertsch, K. S. (1998). Onset sonority distance constraints through local conjunction. In M. C. Gruber, D. Higgins, K. S. Olson and T. Wysocki (eds) *CLS 34, Part 2: The Panels*. 1–15. Chicago, Chicago Linguistic Society.

Baertsch, K. S. (2002). An optimality theoretic approach to syllable structure: The split margin hierarchy. Unpublished doctoral dissertation. Bloomington, Indiana University.

Baertsch, K. S. and Davis, S. (2003). The split margin approach to syllable structure. *ZAS Papers in Linguistics* 32: 1–14.

Bagemihl, B. (1995). Language games and related areas. In J. A. Goldsmith (ed.) *The Handbook of Phonological Theory*. 697–712. Cambridge, MA, Blackwell.

Baker, C. L. (1979). Syntactic theory and the projection problem. *Linguistic Inquiry* 10: 533–81.

Barlow, J. A. (1997). A constraint-based account of syllable onsets: Evidence from developing systems. Unpublished doctoral dissertation, Indiana University, Bloomington.

Barlow, J. A. (2001a). A preliminary typology of initial clusters in acquisition. *Clinical Linguistics & Phonetics* 15: 9–13.

Barlow, J. A. (2001b). The structure of /s/ sequences: Evidence from a disordered system. *Journal of Child Language* 28: 291–324.

Barlow, J. A. (2003a). *Assessment of English Phonology*. San Diego, CA, Phonological Development Laboratory, School of Speech, Language, and Hearing Sciences, San Diego State University.

Barlow, J. A. (2003b). *Assessment of Spanish Phonology-Revised*. San Diego, CA, Phonological Development Laboratory, School of Speech, Language, and Hearing Sciences, San Diego State University.

Barlow, J. A. (2003c). Asymmetries in the acquisition of consonant clusters in Spanish. *Canadian Journal of Linguistics* 48: 179–210.

Barlow, J. A. (2003d). The stop-spirant alternation in Spanish: Converging evidence for a fortition account. *Southwest Journal of Linguistics* 22: 51–86.

Barlow, J. A. (2003e). Variation in cluster production patterns by Spanish-speaking children. The 28th Annual Boston University Conference on Language Development, Boston.

Barlow, J. A. (2005a). Phonological change and the representation of consonant clusters in Spanish: A case study. *Clinical Linguistics & Phonetics* 19: 659–79.

Barlow, J. A. (2005b). Sonority effects in the production of consonant clusters by Spanish-speaking children. In D. Eddington (ed.) *Selected Proceedings from the 6th Conference on the Acquisition of Spanish and Portuguese as First and Second Languages*. 1–14. Somerville, MA, Cascadilla Proceedings Project. Available: http://www.lingref.com/cpp/casp/6/index.html.

Barlow, J. A. (2007a). Constraint conflict in the acquisition of heterosyllabic clusters in Spanish. In S. Colina and F. Martínez-Gil (eds) *Optimality-Theoretic Studies in Spanish Phonology*. 525–48. Philadelphia, John Benjamins.

Barlow, J. A. (2007b). Grandfather effects: A longitudinal case study of the phonological acquisition of intervocalic consonants in English. *Language Acquisition* 14: 121–64.

Barlow, J. A. and Dinnsen, D. A. (1998). Asymmetrical cluster development in a disordered system. *Language Acquisition* 7: 1–49.

Barlow, J. A. and Gierut, J. A. (1999). Optimality theory in phonological acquisition. *Journal of Speech, Language, and Hearing Research* 42: 1482–98.

Barlow, J. A. and Gierut, J. A. (2002). Minimal pair approaches to phonological remediation. *Seminars in Speech and Language* 23: 57–68.

Barton, D., Miller, R. and Macken, M. A. (1980). Do children treat clusters as one unit or two? In E. V. Clark (ed.) *Papers and Reports on Child Language Development*. 105–37. Stanford, Department of Linguistics, Stanford University.

Bates, E. and MacWhinney, B. (1987). Competition, variation, and language learning. In B. MacWhinney (ed.) *Mechanisms of Language Acquisition*. 157–93. Hillsdale, NJ, Lawrence Erlbaum.

Bauman-Wangler, J. A. (2000). *Articulatory and phonological impairments: A clinical focus*. Boston, Allyn and Bacon.

Beckman, J. N. (1998). Positional faithfulness. Unpublished doctoral dissertation. University of Massachusetts, Amherst.

Beckman, M. E. and Edwards, J. (2000). Lexical frequency effects on young children's imitative productions. In M. Broe and J. Pierrehumbert (eds) *Papers in Laboratory Phonology V*. 207–17. Cambridge, UK, Cambridge University Press.

Bedore, L. M., Leonard, L. B. and Gandour, J. (1994). The substitution of a click for sibilants: A case study. *Clinical Linguistics & Phonetics* 8: 283–93.

Bellugi, U. and St. George, M., Eds. (2001). *Journey from Cognition to Brain to Gene: Perspectives from Williams Syndrome*. Cambridge, MA, MIT Press.

Benua, L. (1995). Identity effects in morphological truncation. In J. Beckman, L. W. Dickey and S. Urbanizes (eds) *University of Massachusetts Occasional Papers 18: Papers in Optimality Theory*. 77–136. Amherst, MA, GLSA.

Benua, L. (1997). Transderivational identity: Phonological relations between words. Unpublished doctoral dissertation. University of Massachusetts, Amherst.

Berliner, K. I., Eisenberg, L. S. and House, W. F. (1985). The cochlear implant: An auditory prosthesis for the profoundly deaf child. *Ear and Hearing* 6(Suppl.): 4S.-5S.

Bermúdez-Otero, R. (2003). The acquisition of phonological opacity. Unpublished manuscript, Newcastle upon Tyne. [Available on Rutgers Optimality Archive].

Bernhardt, B. (1994). Nonlinear phonological intervention: Group and case study results. Paper presented at the Canadian Association of Speech-Language Pathologists and Audiologists Annual Conference, Winnipeg, Manitoba.

Bernhardt, B. and Stemberger, J. P. (1998). *Handbook of Phonological Development from the Perspective of Constraint-based Non-linear Phonology*. San Diego, Academic Press.

Bernhardt, B. and Stoel-Gammon, C. (1996). Underspecification and markedness in normal and disordered phonological development. In C. E. Johnson and J. H. V. Gilbert (eds) *Children's Language*. 33–53. Mahwah, NJ, Erlbaum.

Bernthal, J. E. and Bankson, N. W. (2004). *Articulation and phonological disorders*. Boston, Allyn & Bacon.

Bird, H., Franklin, S. and Howard, D. (2001). Age of acquisition and imageability ratings for a large set of words, including verb and function words. *Behavior Research Methods, Instruments, & Computers* 33: 73–9.

Black, J. W., Singh, S. and Janocosek, E. (1974). Multidimensional analysis of the perceptual uniqueness of 31 English consonant clusters. *Ohio State University Research Foundation Technical Report* 16.

Blevins, J. (1995). The syllable in phonological theory. In J. A. Goldsmith (ed.) *The Handbook of Phonological Theory.* 206–44. Oxford, Blackwell.

Boersma, P. (1998). *Functional Phonology: Formalizing the Interaction Between Articulatory and Perceptual Drives.* The Hague, Holland Academic Graphics.

Boersma, P. and Hayes, B. (2001). Empirical tests of the gradual learning algorithm. *Linguistic Inquiry* 32: 45–86.

Bolognesi, R. (1998). The phonology of Campidanian Sardinian. Unpublished doctoral dissertation. University of Amsterdam.

Boysson-Bardies, B. (1999). *How Language Comes to Children: From Birth to Two Years.* Cambridge, MA, MIT Press.

Bradley, L. and Bryant, P. E. (1983). Categorizing sounds and learning to read: A causal connection. *Nature* 301: 419–21.

Breen, G. and Pensalfini, R. (1999). Arrernte: A language with no syllable onsets. *Linguistic Inquiry* 30: 1–25.

Brentari, D. (1998). *A prosodic model of sign language phonology.* Cambridge, MA, MIT Press.

Brooks, P. J. and MacWhinney, B. (2000). Phonological priming in children's picture naming. *Journal of Child Language* 27: 335–66.

Broselow, E., Chen, S.-I. and Wang, C. (1998). The emergence of the unmarked in second language phonology. *Studies in Second Language Acquisition* 20: 261–80.

Broselow, E. and Finer, D. (1991). Parameter setting in second language phonology and syntax. *Second Language Research* 7: 35–59.

Busk, P. L. and Marascuilo, L. A. (1992). Statistical analysis in single-case research: Issues, procedures, and recommendations, with applications to multiple behaviors. In T. R. Kratochwill and J. R. Levin (eds) *Single-Case Research Design and Analysis.* 159–85. Hillsdale, NJ, Lawrence Erlbaum Associates.

Bybee, J. L. (2001). *Phonology and Language Use.* Cambridge, UK, Cambridge University Press.

Cairns, C. E. (1969). Markedness, neutralization and universal redundancy rules. *Language* 45: 863–85.

Cairns, C. E. and Feinstein, M. H. (1982). Markedness and the theory of syllable structure. *Linguistic Inquiry* 13: 193–225.

Camarata, S. M. and Gandour, J. (1984). On describing idiosyncratic phonologic systems. *Journal of Speech and Hearing Disorders* 49: 262–6.

Celce-Murcia, M. (1978). The simultaneous acquisition of English and French in a two-year-old child. In E. M. Hatch (ed.) *Second Language Acquisition: A Book of Readings.* Rowley, MA, Newbury House.

Chang, S. S., Plauché, M. C. and Ohala, J. J. (2001). Markedness and consonant confusion asymmetries. In E. Hume and K. Johnson (eds) *The Role of Speech Perception in Phonology.* 79–102. New York, Academic Press.

Charles-Luce, J. (1987). An acoustic investigation of neutralization in Catalan. Unpublished doctoral dissertation, Indiana University.

Charles-Luce, J. and Luce, P. A. (1990). Similarity neighbourhoods of words in young children's lexicons. *Journal of Child Language* 17: 205–15.

Charles-Luce, J. and Luce, P. A. (1995). An examination of similarity neighbour-hoods in young children's receptive vocabularies. *Journal of Child Language* 22: 727–35.

Chen, L.-M. and Kent, R. D. (2005). Consonant-vowel co-occurrence patterns in Mandarin-learning infants. *Journal of Child Language* 32: 507–34.

Chiat, S. (1979). The role of the word in phonological development. *Linguistics* 17: 591–610.

Chiat, S. (1989). The relation between prosodic structure, syllabification and segmental realization: Evidence from a child with fricative stopping. *Clinical Linguistics & Phonetics* 3: 223–42.

Chiat, S. (2001). Mapping theories of developmental language impairment: Premises, predictions and evidence. *Language and Cognitive Processes* 16: 113–42.

Chin, S. B. (1996). The role of the sonority hierarchy in delayed phonological sys-tems. In T. W. Powell (ed.) *Pathologies of Speech and Language: Contributions of Clinical Phonetics and Linguistics*. 109–17. New Orleans, LA, International Clinical Phonetics and Linguistics Association.

Chin, S. B. and Dinnsen, D. A. (1991). Feature geometry in disordered phonologies. *Clinical Linguistics & Phonetics* 5: 329–37.

Chin, S. B. and Dinnsen, D. A. (1992). Consonant clusters in disordered speech: Constraints and correspondence patterns. *Journal of Child Language* 19: 259–85.

Chin, S. B. and Finnegan, K. R. (2002). Consonant cluster production by pediatric users of cochlear implants. *The Volta Review* 102: 157–74.

Cho, Y.-m. Y. (1998). Language change and reranking of constraints. In R. M. Hogg and L. van Bergen (eds) *Historical Linguistics 1995: Volume 2: Germanic lin-guistics. Selected Papers from the 12th International Conference on Historical Linguistics, Manchester, August 1995*. Amsterdam, John Benjamins.

Chomsky, N. (1980). *Rules and Representations*. New York, Columbia University Press.

Chomsky, N. (1999). On the nature, use, and acquisition of child language. In W. C. Ritchie and T. K. Bhatia (eds) *Handbook of Child Language Acquisition*. 33–54. New York, Academic Press.

Chomsky, N. and Halle, M. (1968). *The Sound Pattern of English*. New York, Harper & Row.

Clark, H. H. (1973). The language-as-fixed-effect fallacy: A critique of language statistics in psychological research. *Journal of Verbal Learning and Verbal Behavior* 12: 335–59.

Clark, H. H. (1976). Discussion of Wike and Church's Comments. *Journal of Verbal Learning and Verbal Behavior* 15: 257–66.

Clements, G. N. (1990). The role of the sonority cycle in core syllabification. In J. Kingston and M. Beckman (eds) *Papers in Laboratory Phonology 1: Between the Grammar and Physics of Speech*. 283–333. Cambridge, MA, Cambridge University Press.

Clements, G. N. and Hume, E. (1995). The internal organization of speech sounds. In J. A. Goldsmith (ed.) *The Handbook of Phonological Theory*. 245–306. Cambridge, MA, Blackwell.

Clements, G. N. and Keyser, S. J. (1983). *CV Phonology: A Generative Theory of the Syllable*. Cambridge, MA, MIT Press.

Coady, J. A. and Aslin, R. N. (2003). Phonological neighbourhoods in the developing lexicon. *Journal of Child Language* 30: 441–69.

Coady, J. A. and Aslin, R. N. (2004). Young children's sensitivity to probabilistic phonotactics in the developing lexicon. *Journal of Experimental Child Psychology* 89: 183–213.

Coetzee, A. (2004). What it means to be a loser: Non-optimal candidates in optimality theory. Unpublished doctoral dissertation. University of Massachusetts, Amherst.

Cohen, J. (1976). Random means random. *Journal of Verbal Learning and Verbal Behavior* 15: 261–2.

Cohn, A. C. and Kishel, E. (2002). Development of initial consonant clusters in English: A case study of fraternal twins. The Eighth Conference on Laboratory Phonology, New Haven, CT.

Cohn, A. C. and Kishel, E. (2003). Phonological neutralization of covert contrast: Evidence from fraternal twins acquiring initial clusters in English. *2003 Child Phonology Conference*. University of British Columbia.

Cole, J. S. and Hualde, J. I. (1998). The object of lexical acquisition: A UR-free-model. *Chicago Linguistic Society* 34: 447–58.

Compton, A. (1970). Generative studies of children's phonological disorders. *Journal of Speech and Hearing Disorders* 35: 315–39.

Cortes, S., Ota, M. and Turk, A. (2004). Production of English intervocalic /d/ by Catalan speakers in derived and non-derived words. The Ninth Conference on Laboratory Phonology, University of Illinois, Urbana-Champaign.

Côté, M.-H. (1997). Phonetic salience and consonant cluster simplification. *MIT Working Papers in Linguistics* 30: 229–62.

Cruttenden, A. (1978). Assimilation in child language and elsewhere. *Journal of Child Language* 5: 373–8.

Curtis, J. F. and Hardy, J. C. (1959). A phonetic study of misarticulation of /r/. *Journal of Speech and Hearing Research* 2: 244–57.

Curtiss, S. (1977). *Genie: A Psycholinguistic Study of a Modern-Day 'Wild Child'*. New York, Academic Press.

Davidsen-Nielsen, N. (1974). Syllabification in English words. *Journal of Phonetics* 2: 15–45.

Davidson, L., Jusczyk, P. W. and Smolensky, P. (2004). The initial and final states: Theoretical implications and experimental explorations of Richness of the Base. In R. Kager, J. Pater and W. Zonneveld (eds) *Constraints in Phonological Acquisition*. 321–68. Cambridge, UK, Cambridge University Press.

Davis, B. L. and MacNeilage, P. F. (1995). The articulatory basis of babbling. *Journal of Speech and Hearing Research* 38: 1199–211.

Davis, S. (1988). *Topics in syllable geometry (Doctoral dissertation, University of Arizona, 1985)*. New York, Garland.

466   *Optimality Theory, Phonological Acquisition and Disorders*

Davis, S. (1990). Italian onset structure and the distribution of *il* and *lo*. *Linguistics* 28: 43–55.

Davis, S. (1992). The onset as a constituent of the syllable: Evidence from Italian. In M. Ziolkowski, M. Noske and K. Deaton (eds) *Papers from the 26th Regional Meeting of the Chicago Linguistic Society, Vol. 2: The Parasession on the Syllable in Phonetics and Phonology.* 71–9. Chicago, Chicago Linguistic Society.

Davis, S. and Baertsch, K. S. (2005). The onset-coda connection and the case of Campidanian Sardinian. Paper presented at the 79th Annual Meeting of the Linguistic Society of America, Oakland, CA.

Dawson, P. W., Blamey, P. J., Dettman, S. J., Rowland, L. C., Barker, E. J., Tobey, E. A., Busby, P. A., Cowan, R. C. and Clark, G. M. (1995). A clinical report on speech production of cochlear implant users. *Ear and Hearing* 16: 551–61.

De Cara, B. and Goswami, U. (2003). Phonological neighborhood density effects in a rhyme awareness task in 5-year old children. *Journal of Child Language* 30: 695–710.

de Lacy, P. (2002). The formal expression of markedness. Unpublished doctoral dissertation. University of Massachusetts, Amherst.

de Lacy, P. (2004). Markedness conflation in optimality theory. *Phonology* 21: 145–99.

de Lacy, P. (2006). *Markedness: Reduction and Preservation in Phonology.* Cambridge, UK, Cambridge University Press.

Dell, F. and Elmedlaoui, M. (1985). Syllabic consonants and syllabification in Imdlawn Tashlhiyt Berber. *Journal of African Languages and Linguistics* 7: 105–30.

Dell, F. and Elmedlaoui, M. (1988). Syllabic consonants in Berber: Some new evidence. *Journal of African Languages and Linguistics* 10: 1–17.

Demuth, K. (1995). Markedness and development of prosodic structure. In J. Beckman (ed.) *Proceedings of the North Eastern Linguistic Society 25.* Amherst, MA, GLSA, University of Massachusetts.

Demuth, K. (1997). Multiple optimal outputs in acquisition. *University of Maryland Working Papers in Linguistics* 5: 53–71.

Dinnsen, D. A. (1980). Phonological rules and phonetic explanation. *Journal of Linguistics* 16: 171–91.

Dinnsen, D. A. (1984). Methods and empirical issues in analyzing functional misarticulation. In M. Elbert, D. A. Dinnsen and G. Weismer (eds) *Phonological Theory and the Misarticulating Child (ASHA Monographs No. 22).* 5–17. Rockville, MD, ASHA.

Dinnsen, D. A. (1985). A re-examination of phonological neutralization. *Journal of Linguistics* 21: 265–79.

Dinnsen, D. A. (1992). Variation in developing and fully developed phonologies. In C. A. Ferguson, L. Menn and C. Stoel-Gammon (eds) *Phonological Development: Models, Research, Implications.* 191–210. Timonium, MD, York Press.

Dinnsen, D. A. (1993). Underspecification and phonological disorders. In M. Eid and G. K. Iverson (eds) *Principles and Prediction: The Analysis of Natural*

Language: Papers in Honor of Gerald Sanders. 287–304. Philadelphia, John Benjamins.

Dinnsen, D. A. (1996). Context-sensitive underspecification and the acquisition of phonemic contrasts. *Journal of Child Language* 23: 57–79.

Dinnsen, D. A. (1998). On the organization and specification of manner features. *Journal of Linguistics* 34: 1–25.

Dinnsen, D. A. (1999). Some empirical and theoretical issues in disordered child phonology. In W. C. Ritchie and T. K. Bhatia (eds) *Handbook of Child Language Acquisition.* 647–74. New York, Academic Press.

Dinnsen, D. A. (2002). A reconsideration of children's phonological representations. In B. Skarabela, S. Fish and A. H. J. Do (eds) *Proceedings of the 26th Boston University Conference on Language Development.* 1–23. Somerville, MA, Cascadilla Press.

Dinnsen, D. A. (2004). On the emergence and loss of opacity effects in acquisition. The Ninth Conference on Laboratory Phonology, University of Illinois, Urbana-Champaign.

Dinnsen, D. A. and Barlow, J. A. (1998). On the characterization of a chain shift in normal and delayed phonological acquisition. *Journal of Child Language* 25: 61–94.

Dinnsen, D. A., Barlow, J. A. and Morrisette, M. L. (1997). Long-distance place assimilation with an interacting error pattern in phonological acquisition. *Clinical Linguistics & Phonetics* 11: 319–38.

Dinnsen, D. A. and Charles-Luce, J. (1984). Phonological neutralization, phonetic implementation and individual differences. *Journal of Phonetics* 12: 48–60.

Dinnsen, D. A. and Chin, S. B. (1993). Individual differences in phonological disorders and implications for a theory of acquisition. In F. R. Eckman (ed.) *Confluence: Linguistics, L2 Acquisition and Speech Pathology.* 139–54. Amsterdam, John Benjamins.

Dinnsen, D. A. and Chin, S. B. (1994). Independent and relational accounts of pho-nological disorders. In M. Yavaş (ed.) *First and Second Language Phonology.* 135–48. San Diego, CA, Singular.

Dinnsen, D. A., Chin, S. B. and Elbert, M. (1992). On the lawfulness of change in phonetic inventories. *Lingua* 86: 207–22.

Dinnsen, D. A., Chin, S. B., Elbert, M. and Powell, T. W. (1990). Some constraints on functionally disordered phonologies: Phonetic inventories and phonotactics. *Journal of Speech and Hearing Research* 33: 28–37.

Dinnsen, D. A. and Eckman, F. R. (1975). A functional explanation of some phonological typologies. In R. E. Grossman, L. J. San and T. J. Vance (eds) *Functionalism.* 126–34. Chicago, Chicago Linguistic Society.

Dinnsen, D. A. and Elbert, M. (1984). On the relationship between phonology and learning. In M. Elbert, D. A. Dinnsen and G. Weismer (eds) *Phonological Theory and the Misarticulating Child (ASHA Monographs No. 22).* 59–68. Rockville, MD, ASHA.

Dinnsen, D. A. and Farris, A. W. (2004a). Constraint conflict: The source of an unusual error pattern. The 10th meeting of the International Clinical Phonetics and Linguistics Association, Lafayette, LA.

Dinnsen, D. A. and Farris, A. W. (2004b). Grammar continuity and the prominence paradox. The 78th Annual Meeting of the Linguistic Society of America, Boston, MA.

Dinnsen, D. A. and Gierut, J. A. (2008). Optimality theory. In M. J. Ball, M. Perkins, N. Müller and S. Howard (eds) *Handbook of Clinical Linguistics*. 439–51. Cambridge, MA, Blackwell.

Dinnsen, D. A. and Maxwell, E. M. (1981). Some phonology problems from functional speech disorders. *Innovations in Linguistics Education* 2: 79–98.

Dinnsen, D. A. and McGarrity, L. W. (1999). Variation and emerging faithfulness in phonological acquisition. In A. Greenhill, H. Littlefield and C. Tano (eds) *Proceedings of the 23rd Annual Boston University Conference on Language Development*. 172–83. Somerville, MA, Cascadilla Press.

Dinnsen, D. A. and McGarrity, L. W. (2004). On the nature of alternations in phonological acquisition. *Studies in Phonetics, Phonology and Morphology* 10: 23–41.

Dinnsen, D. A., McGarrity, L. W., O'Connor, K. M. and Swanson, K. A. B. (2000). On the role of sympathy in acquisition. *Language Acquisition* 8: 321–61.

Dinnsen, D. A. and O'Connor, K. M. (2001a). Implicationally-related error patterns and the selection of treatment targets. *Language, Speech and Hearing Services in Schools* 32: 257–70.

Dinnsen, D. A. and O'Connor, K. M. (2001b). Typological predictions in developmental phonology. *Journal of Child Language* 28: 597–628.

Dinnsen, D. A., O'Connor, K. M. and Gierut, J. A. (2001). The puzzle-puddle-pickle problem and the Duke-of-York gambit in acquisition. *Journal of Linguistics* 37: 503–25.

Dodd, B. J. (1995). *Differential diagnosis and treatment of children with speech disorder*. London, Whurr.

Dodd, B. J. and Iacano, T. (1989). Phonological disorders in children: Changes in phonological process use during treatment. *British Journal of Disorders of Communication* 24: 333–52.

Dodd, B. J., Leahy, J. and Hambly, G. (1989). Phonological disorders in children: Underlying cognitive deficits. *British Journal of Developmental Psychology* 7: 55–71.

Dollaghan, C. A. (1994). Children's phonological neighbourhoods: Half empty or half full? *Journal of Child Language* 21: 257–72.

Donegan, P. J. and Stampe, D. (1979). The study of natural phonology. In D. A. Dinnsen (ed.) *Current Approaches to Phonological Theory*. 126–73. Bloomington, IN, Indiana University Press.

Dunn, C. and Till, J. A. (1982). Morphophonemic rule learning in normal and articulation-disordered children. *Journal of Speech and Hearing Research* 25: 322–33.

Dunn, L. M. and Dunn, L. M. (1981). *Peabody Picture Vocabulary Test–Revised*. Circle Pines, MN, American Guidance Service.

Dunn, L. M. and Dunn, L. M. (1997). *Peabody Picture Vocabulary (Third Edition)*. Circle Pines, MN, American Guidance Service, Inc.

Dworkin, J. P. and Culatta, R. A. (1985). Oral structure and neuromuscular characteristics in children with normal and disordered articulation. *Journal of Speech
and Hearing Disorders* 50: 150–6.

Dyer, K., Santarcangelo, S. and Luce, S. C. (1987). Developmental influences
in teaching languages forms to individuals with developmental disabilities.
Journal of Speech and Hearing Disorders 52: 335–47.

Echols, C. H. and Newport, E. L. (1992). The role of stress and position in determining first words. *Language Acquisition* 2: 189–220.

Eckman, F. R. (1981). On the naturalness of interlanguage phonological rules.
Language Learning 31: 195–216.

Eckman, F. R., Ed. (1993). *Confluence: Linguistics, L2 Acquisition and Speech
Pathology*. Philadelphia, John Benjamins.

Eckman, F. R., Elreyes, A. and Iverson, G. K. (2003). Some principles of second
language phonology. *Second Language Research* 19: 169–208.

Eckman, F. R. and Iverson, G. K. (1993). Sonority and markedness among onset
clusters in the interlanguage of ESL learners. *Second Language Research* 9:
234–52.

Eckman, F. R. and Iverson, G. K. (1997). Structure preservation in interlanguage phonology. In S. J. Hannahs and M. Young-Scholten (eds) *Focus on
Phonological Acquisition*. 183–207. Amsterdam, John Benjamins.

Edwards, M. L. and Bernhardt, B. (1973). Phonological analyses of the speech of
four children with language disorders. Unpublished manuscript, The Scottish
Rite Institute for Childhood Aphasia, Stanford University.

Elbert, M., Dinnsen, D. A. and Powell, T. W. (1984). On the prediction of phonologic generalization learning patterns. *Journal of Speech and Hearing Disorders*
49: 309–17.

Elbert, M., Dinnsen, D. A., Swartzlander, P. and Chin, S. B. (1990). Generalization
to conversational speech. *Journal of Speech and Hearing Disorders* 55: 694–9.

Elbert, M., Dinnsen, D. A. and Weismer, G., Eds. (1984). *Phonological Theory and
the Misarticulating Child (ASHA Monographs No. 22)*. Rockville, MD, ASHA.

Elbert, M. and Gierut, J. A. (1986). *Handbook of Clinical Phonology: Approaches to
Assessment and Treatment*. San Diego, College-Hill Press.

Elbert, M. and McReynolds, L. V. (1979). Aspects of phonological acquisition
during articulation training. *Journal of Speech and Hearing Disorders* 44:
459–71.

Elbert, M. and McReynolds, L. V. (1985). The generalization hypothesis: Final
consonant deletion. *Language and Speech* 28: 281–94.

Emmory, K. (2002). *Language, Cognition, and the Brain: Insights from Sign
Language Research*. Mahwah, NJ, Erlbaum.

Farris, A. W. and Gierut, J. A. (2005). Statistical regularities of the input as predictive of phonological acquisition. Poster presentation. *Symposium on Research in
Child Language Disorders*. Madison, WI, June 9–11.

Farris-Trimble, A. W. (2007). A typology of s-cluster inventories. Paper presented at
the Association of Linguistic Typology VII, Paris, France.

Felsenfeld, S., Broen, P. A. and McGue, M. (1992). A 28-year follow-up of adults with a history of moderate phonological disorder: Linguistic and personality results. *Journal of Speech and Hearing Research* 35: 1114–25.

Felsenfeld, S., Broen, P. A. and McGue, M. (1994). A 28-year follow-up of adults with a history of moderate phonological disorder: Educational and occupational results. *Journal of Speech and Hearing Research* 37: 1341–53.

Felsenfeld, S., McGue, M. and Broen, P. A. (1995). Familial aggregation of phonological disorders: Results from a 28-year follow-up [Letter to the editor]. *Journal of Speech and Hearing Research* 38: 1091–107.

Ferguson, C. A. (1977). New directions in phonological theory: Language acquisition and universals research. In R. W. Cole (ed.) *Current Issues in Linguistic Theory*. 247–99. Bloomington, IN, Indiana University Press.

Ferguson, C. A. (1978). Fricatives in child language acquisition. In V. Honsa and M. J. Hardman-de-Bautista (eds) *Papers on Linguistics and Child Language*. 93–115. The Hague, Netherlands, Mouton.

Ferguson, C. A. and Farwell, C. B. (1975). Words and sounds in early language acquisition: English initial consonants in the first fifty words. *Language* 51: 419–39.

Ferguson, C. A., Peizer, D. B. and Weeks, T. E. (1973). Model-and-replica phonological grammar of a child's first words. *Lingua* 31: 35–65.

Fernald, A. and McRoberts, G. (1996). Prosodic bootstrapping: A critical analysis of the argument and the evidence. In J. L. Morgan and K. Demuth (eds) *Signal to syntax: Bootstrapping from speech to grammar in early acquisition*. 365–88. Mahwah, NJ, Lawrence Erlbaum.

Féry, C. and van de Vijver, R. (2003). *The Syllable in Optimality Theory*. Cambridge, UK, Cambridge University Press.

Fey, M. E. (1988). Generalization issues facing language interventionists: An introduction. *Language, Speech and Hearing Services in Schools* 19: 272–81.

Fey, M. E. (1992a). Articulation and phonology: An addendum. *Language, Speech and Hearing Services in Schools* 23: 277–82.

Fey, M. E. (1992b). Articulation and phonology: Inextricable constructs in speech pathology. *Language, Speech and Hearing Services in Schools* 23: 225–32.

Fikkert, P. (1994). *On the Acquisition of Prosodic Structure*. The Hague, Holland Academic Graphics.

Fodor, J. A., Bever, T. G. and Garrett, M. F. (1974). *The Psychology of Language*. New York, McGraw Hill.

Forrest, K. (2002). Are oral-motor exercises useful in the treatment of phonological/articulatory disorders? *Seminars in Speech and Language* 23: 15–26.

Forrest, K., Dinnsen, D. A. and Elbert, M. (1997). Impact of substitution patterns on phonological learning by misarticulating children. *Clinical Linguistics & Phonetics* 11: 63–76.

Forrest, K., Weismer, G., Elbert, M. and Dinnsen, D. A. (1994). Spectral analysis of target-appropriate /t/ and /k/ produced by phonologically disordered and normally articulating children. *Clinical Linguistics & Phonetics* 8: 267–81.

Forrest, K., Weismer, G., Hodge, M., Dinnsen, D. A. and Elbert, M. (1990). Statistical analysis of word-initial /k/ and /t/ produced by normal and phonologically disordered children. *Clinical Linguistics & Phonetics* 4: 327–40.

Forrest, K., Weismer, G., Milenkovic, P. H. and Dougall, R. N. (1988). Statistical analysis of word-initial voiceless obstruents: Preliminary data. *Journal of the Acoustical Society of America* 84: 115–23.

Fudge, E. C. (1969). Syllables. *Journal of Linguistics* 5: 253–86.

Gathercole, S. E. and Baddeley, A. D. (1996). *The Children's Test of Nonword Repetition*. San Antonio, TX, Harcourt Brace.

Gerken, L. (1994). Child phonology: Past research, present questions, future directions. In M. A. Gernsbacher (ed.) *Handbook of Psycholinguistics*. 781–820. New York, Academic Press.

Gerken, L. (1996). Prosodic structure in young children's language production. *Language* 72: 683–712.

Gerken, L., Murphy, W. D. and Aslin, R. N. (1995). Three- and four-year-olds' perceptual confusions for spoken words. *Perception & Psychophysics* 57: 475–86.

Gierut, J. A. (1985). On the relationship between phonological knowledge and generalization learning in misarticulating children. Unpublished doctoral dissertation. Indiana University, Bloomington. [Also available from the Indiana University Linguistics Club].

Gierut, J. A. (1986). Sound change: A phonemic split in a misarticulating child. *Applied Psycholinguistics* 7: 57–68.

Gierut, J. A. (1989a). Developing descriptions of phonological systems: A surrebuttal. *Applied Psycholinguistics* 10: 469–73.

Gierut, J. A. (1989b). Maximal opposition approach to phonological treatment. *Journal of Speech and Hearing Disorders* 54: 9–19.

Gierut, J. A. (1990). Differential learning of phonological oppositions. *Journal of Speech and Hearing Research* 33: 540–9.

Gierut, J. A. (1996a). Categorization and feature specification in phonological acquisition. *Journal of Child Language* 23: 397–415.

Gierut, J. A. (1996b). An experimental test of phonemic cyclicity. *Journal of Child Language* 23: 81–102.

Gierut, J. A. (1998a). Natural domains of cyclicity in phonological acquisition. *Clinical Linguistics & Phonetics* 12: 481–99.

Gierut, J. A. (1998b). Production, conceptualization and change in distinctive featural categories. *Journal of Child Language* 25: 321–42.

Gierut, J. A. (1998c). Treatment efficacy: Functional phonological disorders in children. *Journal of Speech, Language, and Hearing Research* 41: S85–100.

Gierut, J. A. (1999). Syllable onsets: Clusters and adjuncts in acquisition. *Journal of Speech, Language, and Hearing Research* 42: 708–26.

Gierut, J. A. (2001). Complexity in phonological treatment: Clinical factors. *Language, Speech and Hearing Services in Schools* 32: 229–41.

Gierut, J. A. (2004). An experimental validation of an OT solution to the comprehension-production dilemma. The 10th meeting of the International Clinical Phonetics & Linguistics Association, Lafayette, LA.

Gierut, J. A. (2005). Phonological intervention: The how or the what? In A. G. Kamhi and K. E. Pollock (eds) *Phonological disorders in children: Assessment and intervention*. 201–10. Philadelphia, Brookes.

Gierut, J. A. (2007). Phonological complexity and language learnability. *American Journal of Speech-Language Pathology* 16: 6–17.

Gierut, J. A. and Champion, A. H. (1999). Interacting error patterns and their resistance to treatment. *Clinical Linguistics & Phonetics* 13: 421–31.

Gierut, J. A. and Champion, A. H. (2000). Ingressive substitutions: Typical or atypical phonological pattern? *Clinical Linguistics & Phonetics* 14: 603–17.

Gierut, J. A. and Champion, A. H. (2001). Syllable onsets II: Three-element clusters in phonological treatment. *Journal of Speech, Language, and Hearing Research* 44: 886–904.

Gierut, J. A., Cho, M.-H. and Dinnsen, D. A. (1993). Geometric accounts of consonant-vowel interactions in developing systems. *Clinical Linguistics & Phonetics* 7: 219–36.

Gierut, J. A., Elbert, M. and Dinnsen, D. A. (1987). A functional analysis of phonological knowledge and generalization learning in misarticulating children. *Journal of Speech and Hearing Research* 30: 462–79.

Gierut, J. A. and Morrisette, M. L. (2005). The clinical significance of optimality theory for phonological disorders. *Topics in Language Disorders* 25: 266–79.

Gierut, J. A., Morrisette, M. L. and Champion, A. H. (1999). Lexical constraints in phonological acquisition. *Journal of Child Language* 26: 261–94.

Gierut, J. A., Morrisette, M. L., Hughes, M. and Rowland, S. (1996). Phonological treatment efficacy and developmental norms. *Language, Speech and Hearing Services in Schools* 27: 215–30.

Gierut, J. A., Morrisette, M. L. and Storkel, H. L. (2003). Children's representations: What they know and how they know it. The 28th Annual Boston University Conference on Language Development, Boston, MA.

Gierut, J. A. and O'Connor, K. M. (2002). Precursors to onset clusters in acquisition. *Journal of Child Language* 29: 495–517.

Gierut, J. A., Simmerman, C. L. and Neumann, H. J. (1994). Phonemic structures of delayed phonological systems. *Journal of Child Language* 21: 291–316.

Gilbers, D. (2001). Conflicting phonologically based and phonetically based constraints in the analysis of liquid-nasal substitutions. *Clinical Linguistics & Phonetics* 15: 23–8.

Gilhooly, K. J. and Logie, R. H. (1980a). Age-of-acquisition, imagery, concreteness, familiarity, and ambiguity measures for 1,944 words. *Behavior Research Methods, Instruments and Computers* 12: 395–427.

Gilhooly, K. J. and Logie, R. H. (1980b). Meaning-dependent ratings of imagery, age-of-acquisition, familiarity, and concreteness for 387 ambiguous words. *Behavior Research Methods, Instruments and Computers* 12: 428–50.

Gleitman, L. R. and Wanner, E. (1982). Language acquisition: The state of the state of the art. In E. Wanner and L. R. Gleitman (eds) *Language Acquisition: The State of the Art*. 3–48. Cambridge, UK, Cambridge University Press.

Gnanadesikan, A. (1995). Deriving the sonority hierarchy from ternary scales. Annual Meeting of the Linguistic Society of America. New Orleans.

Gnanadesikan, A. (1997). Phonology with Ternary Scales. Unpublished doctoral dissertation. University of Massachusetts, Amherst.

Gnanadesikan, A. (2004). Markedness and faithfulness constraints in child phonology. In R. Kager, J. Pater and W. Zonneveld (eds) *Constraints in Phonological Acquisition*. 73–108. Cambridge, MA, Cambridge University Press.

Goad, H. (1997). Consonant harmony in child language: An optimality theoretic account. In S. J. Hannahs and M. Young-Scholten (eds) *Focus on Phonological Acquisition*. 113–42. Philadelphia, John Benjamins.

Goad, H. and Brannen, K. (2000). Syllabification at the right edge of words: Parallels between child and adult grammars. *McGill Working Papers in Linguistics* 15: 1–26.

Goad, H. and Brannen, K. (2003). Phonetic evidence for phonological structure in syllabification. In J. van de Weijer, V. van Heuven and H. van der Hulst (eds) *The Phonological Spectrum, Vol. II: Suprasegmental Structure*. 3–30. Amsterdam, John Benjamins.

Goad, H. and Rose, Y. (2004). Input elaboration, head faithfulness, and evidence for representation in the acquisition of left-edge clusters in West Germanic. In R. Kager, J. Pater and W. Zonneveld (eds) *Constraints in Phonological Acquisition*. 109–57. Cambridge, UK, Cambridge University Press.

Goldin-Meadow, S. (2003). *The resilience of language: What gesture creation in deaf children can tell us about how all children learn language.* New York, NY, Psychology Press.

Goldman, R. and Fristoe, M. (1986). *Goldman-Fristoe Test of Articulation.* Circles Pines, MN, American Guidance Service.

Goldman, R. and Fristoe, M. (2000). *Goldman-Fristoe Test of Articulation-2.* Circle Pines, MN, American Guidance Service, Inc.

Goldsmith, J. A. (1990). *Autosegmental and Metrical Phonology.* Cambridge, MA, Blackwell.

Goldstein, B. and Cintron, P. (2001). An investigation of phonological skills in Puerto Rican Spanish-speaking 2-year-olds. *Clinical Linguistics & Phonetics* 15: 343–61.

Goldstone, R. L. (1994). Influences of categorization on perceptual discrimination. *Journal of Experimental Psychology: General* 123: 178–200.

Goldstone, R. L. and Steyvers, M. (2001). The sensitization and differentiation of dimensions during category learning. *Journal of Experimental Psychology: General* 130: 116–39.

Gómez, R. and Gerken, L. (1999). Artificial grammar learning by one-year-olds leads to specific and abstract knowledge. *Cognition* 70: 109–35.

Gómez, R., Lany, J. and Chapman, K. (2003). Dynamically guided learning. The 28th Annual Boston University Conference on Language Development, Boston, MA.

Graham, L. W. and House, A. S. (1971). Phonological oppositions in children: A perceptual study. *Journal of the Acoustical Society of America* 49: 559–66.

Green, T. (2003). Extrasyllabic consonants and onset well-formedness. In C. Féry and R. van de Vijver (eds) *The Syllable in Optimality Theory*. 238–53. Cambridge, UK, Cambridge University Press.

Greenberg, J. H. and Jenkins, J. J. (1964). Studies in the psychological correlates of the sound system of American English. *Word* 20: 157–77.

Greenlee, M. (1973). Some observations on initial English consonant clusters in a child two to three years old. *Papers and Reports on Child Language Development (Stanford University)* 6: 97–106.

Greenlee, M. (1974). Interacting processes in the child's acquisition of stop-liquid clusters. *Papers and Reports on Child Language Development (Stanford University)* 7: 85–100.

Groenen, P., Maassen, B., Crul, T. and Thoonen, G. (1996). The specific relation between perception and production errors for place of articulation in developmental apraxia of speech. *Journal of Speech and Hearing Research* 39: 468–82.

Gruber, F. A. (1999). Variability and sequential order of consonant normalization in children with speech delay. *Journal of Speech, Language, and Hearing Research* 42: 460–72.

Grunwell, P. (1975). The phonological analysis of articulation disorders. *British Journal of Disorders of Communication* 10: 31–42.

Grunwell, P. (1977). The analysis of phonological disability in children. Unpublished doctoral dissertation, University of Reading.

Grunwell, P. (1981). *The Nature of Phonological Disability in Children*. New York, Academic Press.

Grunwell, P. (1982). *Clinical Phonology*. Rockville, MD, Aspen Publications.

Grunwell, P. (1988). Phonological assessment, evaluation and explanation of speech disorders in children. *Clinical Linguistics and Phonetics* 2: 221–52.

Grunwell, P. and Pletts, M. M. K. (1974). Therapeutic guidelines from linguistics: A case study. Unpublished manuscript.

Gustason, G. and Zawolkow, E. G. (1993). *Signing Exact English*. Los Alamitos, CA, Modern Sign Press.

Gutiérrez-Clellen, V. F. and Kreiter, J. (2003). Understanding child bilingual acquisition using parent and teacher reports. *Applied Psycholinguistics* 24: 267–88.

Haas, W. (1963). Phonological analysis of a case of dyslalia. *Journal of Speech and Hearing Disorders* 28: 239–46.

Haggard, M. (1973). Abbreviations of consonants in English pre- and post-vocalic clusters. *Journal of Phonetics* 1: 1–8.

Hale, M. and Reiss, C. (1998). Formal and empirical arguments concerning phonological acquisition. *Linguistic Inquiry* 29: 656–83.

Hammerly, H. (1982). Contrastive phonology and error analysis. *International Review of Applied Linguistics* 20: 17–32.

Hammond, M. (1999). *English Phonology*. Oxford, UK, Oxford University Press.

Hardy, J. E. (1993). Phonological learning and retention in second language acquisition. In F. R. Eckman (ed.) *Confluence: Linguistics, L2 Acquisition and Speech Pathology*. 235–48. Amsterdam, John Benjamins.

Harris, J. (1990). Derived phonological contrasts. In S. Ramsaran (ed.) *Studies in the Pronunciation of English: A Commemorative Volume in Honour of A. C. Gimson*. 87–105. London, Routledge.

Harris, J. (1994). *English Sound Structure*. Cambridge, MA, Blackwell.

Harris, J. and Gussmann, E. (2002). Word-final onsets. University College London. Available: http://roa.rutgers.edu/files/575–0203/575–0203-HARRIS-0–0.PDF.

Hawkins, S. (1973). Temporal coordination of consonants in the speech of children: Preliminary data. *Journal of Phonetics* 1: 181–217.

Hawkins, S. (1979). Temporal coordination of consonants in the speech of children: Further data. *Journal of Phonetics* 7: 235–67.

Hayes, B. (2004). Phonological acquisition in optimality theory: The early stages. In R. Kager, J. Pater and W. Zonneveld (eds) *Constraints in Phonological Acquisition*. 158–203. Cambridge, UK, Cambridge University Press.

Hersen, M. and Barlow, D. H. (1976). *Single Case Experimental Designs: Strategies for Studying Behavior Change*. New York, Permagon Press.

Hills, E. C. (1914). The speech of a child two years of age. *Dialect Notes* 4: 84–100.

Hinckley, A. (1915). A case of retarded speech development. *Pedagogical Seminary* 22: 121–46.

Hodson, B. W. (1989). Phonological remediation: A cycles approach. In N. Creaghead, P. W. Newman and W. Secord (eds) *Assessment and Remediation of Articulatory and Phonological Disorders*. 323–33. Columbus, OH, Charles E. Merrill.

Hoffman, P. R. and Damico, S. K. (1988). Cluster-reducing children's identification and production of /sk/ clusters. *Clinical Linguistics & Phonetics* 2: 17–27.

Hoffman, P. R., Stager, S. and Daniloff, R. G. (1983). Perception and production of misarticulated /r/. *Journal of Speech and Hearing Disorders* 48: 210–4.

Houlihan, K. and Iverson, G. K. (1979). Functionally-constrained phonology. In D. A. Dinnsen (ed.) *Current Approaches to Phonological Theory*. 50–73. Bloomington, IN, Indiana University Press.

Howell, J. and Dean, E. (1994). *Treating Phonological Disorders in Children: Metaphon–Theory to Practice*. London, Whurr.

Hresko, W. P., Reid, D. K. and Hammill, D. D. (1981). *The Test of Early Language Development*. Austin, TX, Pro-Ed.

Hresko, W. P., Reid, D. K. and Hammill, D. D. (1999). *Test of Early Language Development (Third Edition)*. Austin, TX, Pro-Ed.

Hua, Z. and Dodd, B. J. (2000). Development and change in the phonology of Putonghua-speaking children with speech difficulties. *Clinical Linguistics & Phonetics* 14: 351–68.

Hudson, R. (1994). About 37% of word-tokens are nouns. *Language* 70: 331–9.

Hume, E. and Johnson, K., Eds. (2001). *The Role of Speech Perception in Phonology*. New York, Academic Press.

Hume, E. and Tserdanelis, G. (2002). Labial unmarkedness in Sri Lankan Portuguese Creole. *Phonology* 19: 441–58.

Huynh, H. and Feldt, L. S. (1976). Estimation of the Box correction for degrees of freedom from sample data in randomized block and split-plot designs. *Journal of Educational Statistics* 1: 69–82.

Hyman, L. (2001). On the limits of phonetic determinism in phonology: *NC revisited. In E. Hume and K. Johnson (eds) *The Role of Speech Perception in Phonology*. 141–85. New York, Academic Press.

Ingram, D. (1974). Fronting in child phonology. *Journal of Child Language* 1: 233–42.

Ingram, D. (1976). *Phonological Disability in Children*. London, Edward Arnold.

Ingram, D. (1978). The role of the syllable in phonological development. In A. Bell and J. B. Hooper (eds) *Syllables and Segments*. 143–55. Amsterdam, North-Holland.

Ingram, D. (1988a). The acquisition of word-initial [v]. *Language and Speech* 31: 77–85.

Ingram, D. (1988b). Jakobson revisited: Some evidence from the acquisition of Polish. *Lingua* 75: 55–82.

Ingram, D. (1989). *Phonological Disability in Children (Second Edition)*. London, Cole and Whurr.

Ingram, D., Christensen, L., Veach, S. and Webster, B. (1980). The acquisition of word-initial fricatives and affricates in English by children between 2 and 6 years. In G. H. Yeni-Komshian, J. F. Kavanagh and C. A. Ferguson (eds) *Child Phonology, Vol. 1: Production*. 169–92. New York, Academic Press.

Ingram, D. and Terselic, B. (1983). Final ingression: A case of deviant child phonology. *Topics in Language Disorders* 3: 45–50.

Inkelas, S. and Rose, Y. (2003). Velar fronting revisited. In B. Beachley, A. Brown and F. Conlin (eds) *Proceedings of the 26th Annual Boston University Conference on Language Development*. 334–45. Somerville, MA, Cascadilla Press.

Itô, J. (1989). A prosodic theory of epenthesis. *Natural Language & Linguistic Theory* 7: 217–59.

Itô, J., Mester, A. and Padgett, J. (1995). Licensing and underspecification in optimality theory. *Linguistic Inquiry* 26: 571–613.

Iverson, G. K. and Salmons, J. C. (1995). Aspiration and laryngeal representation in Germanic. *Phonology* 12: 369–96.

Iverson, G. K. and Wheeler, D. (1987). Hierarchical structures in child phonology. *Lingua* 73: 243–57.

Jakobson, R. (1941/68). *Child Language, Aphasia, and Phonological Universals*. The Hague, Mouton.

Jamieson, D. G. and Rvachew, S. (1992). Remediating speech production errors with sound identification training. *Journal of Speech-Language Pathology and Audiology* 16: 201–10.

Jensen, J. (1977). *Yapese Reference Grammar*. Honolulu, University of Hawaii Press.

Jesney, K. C. (2005). Chain shift in phonological acquisition. Unpublished master's thesis, University of Calgary.

Jespersen, O. (1904). *Lehrbuch der Phonetik*. Berlin, Germany, B. G. Teubner.

Jimenez, B. C. (1987). Acquisition of Spanish consonants in children aged 3–5 years, 7 months. *Language, Speech and Hearing Services in Schools* 18: 357–63.

Johnston, J. R. (1988). Generalization: The nature of change. *Language, Speech and Hearing Services in Schools* 19: 314–29.

Jones, S. S. and Smith, L. B. (1993). The place of perception in children's concepts. *Cognitive Development* 8: 113–39.

Jun, J. (1995). Perceptual and articulatory factors in place assimilation: An optimality theoretic approach. Unpublished doctoral dissertation, University of California, Los Angeles.

Jusczyk, P. W. (1992). Developing phonological categories from the speech signal. In C. A. Ferguson, L. Menn and C. Stoel-Gammon (eds) *Phonological Development: Models, Research, Implications*. 17–64. Timonium, MD, York Press.

Jusczyk, P. W. (1997). *The Discovery of Spoken Language*. Cambridge, MA, MIT Press.

Jusczyk, P. W., Bertoncini, J., Bijeljac-Babic, R., Kennedy, L. J. and Mehler, J. (1990). The role of attention in speech perception by infants. *Cognitive Development* 5: 265–86.

Jusczyk, P. W., Goodman, M. B. and Baumann, A. (1999). Nine-month-olds' attention to sound similarities in syllables. *Journal of Memory and Language* 40: 62–82.

Jusczyk, P. W., Luce, P. A. and Charles-Luce, J. (1994). Infants' sensitivity to phonotactic patterns in the native language. *Journal of Memory and Language* 33: 630–45.

Jusczyk, P. W., Smolensky, P. and Allocco, T. (2002). How English-learning infants respond to markedness and faithfulness constraints. *Language Acquisition* 10: 31–73.

Kager, R. (1999). *Optimality Theory*. Cambridge, MA, Cambridge University Press.

Kager, R., Pater, J. and Zonneveld, W., Eds. (2004). *Constraints in Phonological Acquisition*. Cambridge, UK, Cambridge University Press.

Kager, R., van der Feest, S., Fikkert, P., Kerkhoff, A. and Zamuner, T. (2003). Representations of [voice]: Evidence from acquisition. Voicing in Dutch Workshop, Leiden, The Netherlands.

Kamhi, A. G. and Pollock, K. E., Eds. (2005). *Phonological Disorders in Children: Assessment and Intervention*. Philadelphia, Brookes.

Kaye, J. D. and Lowenstamm, J. (1981). Syllable structure and markedness theory. In A. Belletti, L. Brandi and L. Rizzi (eds) *Theory of Markedness in Generative Grammar: Proceedings of the 1979 GLOW Conference*. 287–315. Pisa, Italy, Scuola Normale Superiore di Pisa.

Kazdin, A. E. (1976). Statistical analyses for single-case experimental designs. In M. Hersen and D. H. Barlow (eds) *Single-Case Experimental Designs: Strategies for Studying Behavior Change*. 265–316. New York, Pergamon Press.

Kearns, K. P. (1986). Flexibility of single-subject experimental designs, Part II: Design selection and arrangement of experimental phases. *Journal of Speech and Hearing Disorders* 51: 204–13.

Kehoe, M. (2001). Prosodic patterns in children's multisyllabic word productions. *Language, Speech and Hearing Services in Schools* 32: 284–94.

Kehoe, M. and Hilaire-Debove, G. (2004). The structure of branching onsets and rising diphthongs: Evidence from acquisition. In *Proceedings of the 28th Annual*

Boston University Conference on Language Development. 282–93. Somerville, MA, Cascadilla Press.

Kehoe, M. and Stoel-Gammon, C. (1997). Truncation patterns in English-speaking children's word productions. *Journal of Speech, Language, and Hearing Research* 40: 526–41.

Kehoe, M. M. and Stoel-Gammon, C. (2001). Development of syllable structure in English-speaking children with SLI. *Journal of Child Language* 28: 393–432.

Kenstowicz, M. (1994). *Phonology in Generative Grammar.* Cambridge, MA, Blackwell.

Kenstowicz, M. and Kisseberth, C. W. (1979). *Generative Phonology: Description and Theory.* New York, Academic Press.

Kent, R. D. (1982). Contextual facilitation of correct sound production. *Language, Speech and Hearing Services in Schools* 13: 66–76.

Kent, R. D. (1992). The biology of phonological development. In C. A. Ferguson, L. Menn and C. Stoel-Gammon (eds) *Phonological Development: Models, Research, Implications.* 65–90. Timonium, MD, York Press.

Keppel, G. (1976). Words as random variables. *Journal of Verbal Learning and Verbal Behavior* 15: 263–5.

Kiparsky, P. (1965). Phonological change. Unpublished doctoral dissertation. Massachusetts Institute of Technology, Cambridge.

Kiparsky, P. (1971). Historical linguistics. In W. O. Dingwall (ed.) *A Survey of Linguistic Science.* 576–642. University of Maryland, Linguistics Program.

Kiparsky, P. (1973). 'Elsewhere' in phonology. In S. Anderson and P. Kiparsky (eds) *A Festschrift for Morris Halle.* 93–106. New York, Holt, Rinehart, and Winston.

Kiparsky, P. (1976). Abstractness, opacity and global rules. In A. Koutsoudas (ed.) *The Application and Ordering of Grammatical Rules.* 160–86. The Hague, Netherlands, Mouton.

Kiparsky, P. (1982). Lexical phonology and morphology. In I.-S. Yang (ed.) *Linguistics in the Morning Calm.* 1–91. Seoul, Korea, Hanshin.

Kiparsky, P. (1993a). Blocking in non-derived environments. In S. Hargus and E. Kaisse (eds) *Phonetics and Phonology, Vol. 4: Studies in Lexical Phonology.* 277–313. San Diego, Academic Press.

Kiparsky, P. (1993b). The phonological basis of sound change. Stanford Workshop on Sound Change, Stanford University.

Kiparsky, P. (1994). Remarks on markedness. Handout from TREND 2. Stanford University.

Kirchner, R. (1996). Synchronic chain shifts in optimality theory. *Linguistic Inquiry* 27: 341–50.

Kirchner, R. M. (1999). An effort-based approach to consonant lenition. Unpublished doctoral dissertation, University of California, Los Angeles.

Kirk, C. and Demuth, K. (2003). Onset/coda asymmetries in the acquisition of clusters. In B. Beachley, A. Brown and F. Conlin (eds) *Proceedings of the 27th Annual Boston University Conference on Language Development.* 437–48. Somerville, MA, Cascadilla Press.

Kirk, K. I. and Hill-Brown, C. (1985). Speech and language results in children with a cochlear implant. *Ear and Hearing* 6(Suppl.): 36S-47S.

Kirk, S. A., McCarthy, J. J. and Kirk, W. D. (1968). *Illinois Test of Psycholinguistic Abilities-Revised*. Chicago, University of Illinois Press.

Kisseberth, C. W. (1970). On the functional unity of phonological rules. *Linguistic Inquiry* 1: 291–306.

Klatt, D. (1973). Voice onset time, frication, and aspiration in word-initial consonant clusters. *MIT Research Laboratory of Engineering Quarterly Progress Report* 109: 124–35.

Kornfeld, J. and Goehl, H. (1974). A new twist to an old observation: Kids know more than they say. *Chicago Linguistic Society* 4: 210–9.

Kornfeld, J. R. (1978). Implications of studying reduced consonant clusters in normal and abnormal child speech. In R. N. Campbell and P. T. Smith (eds) *Recent Advances in the Psychology of Language: Formal and Experimental Approaches*. 413–23. New York, Plenum Press.

Kratochwill, T. R. (1978). *Single-Subject Research*. New York, Academic Press.

Kratochwill, T. R. and Levin, J. R. (1992). *Single-Case Research Design and Analysis: New Directions for Psychology and Education*. Hillsdale, NJ, Lawrence Erlbaum Associates, Inc.

Kučera, H. and Francis, W. N. (1967). *Computational Analysis of Present-Day American English*. Providence, RI, Brown University.

Ladefoged, P. and Maddieson, I. (1996). *The Sounds of the World's Languages*. Malden, MA, Blackwell.

Lado, R. (1957). *Linguistics Across Cultures*. Ann Arbor, University of Michigan Press.

Lahiri, A. and Marslen-Wilson, W. (1991). The mental representation of lexical form: A phonological approach to the recognition lexicon. *Cognition* 38: 245–94.

Lamontagne, G. and Rice, K. (1995). A correspondence account of coalescence. In J. N. Beckman, L. W. Dickey and S. Urbanczyk (eds) *Papers in Optimality Theory (University of Massachusetts Occasional Papers 18)*. 211–24. Amherst, MA, Graduate Linguistic Student Association, University of Massachusetts.

Landau, B. and Gleitman, L. R. (1985). *Language and experience: Evidence from the blind child*. Cambridge, MA, Harvard University Press.

Leben, W. (1973). Suprasegmental phonology. Unpublished doctoral dissertation. Cambridge, MA, Massachusetts Institute of Technology.

Leder, S. B. and Spitzer, J. B. (1990). A perceptual evaluation of the speech of adventitiously deaf adult males. *Ear and Hearing* 11: 169–75.

Legendre, G., Hagstrom, P., Vainikka, A. and Todorova, M. (2002). Partial constraint ordering in child French syntax. *Language Acquisition* 10: 189–227.

Leonard, L. B. (1973). The nature of disordered articulation. *Journal of Speech and Hearing Disorders* 38: 156–61.

Leonard, L. B. (1985). Unusual and subtle phonological behavior in the speech of phonologically disordered children. *Journal of Speech and Hearing Disorders* 50: 4–13.

Leonard, L. B. (1992). Models of phonological development and children with phonological disorders. In C. A. Ferguson, L. Menn and C. Stoel-Gammon (eds) *Phonological Development: Models, Research, Implications.* 495–507. Timonium, MD, York Press.

Leonard, L. B. (1998). *Children with Specific Language Impairment.* Cambridge, MA, MIT Press.

Leonard, L. B. and Brown, B. L. (1984). Nature and boundaries of phonologic categories: A case study of an unusual phonologic pattern in a language-impaired child. *Journal of Speech and Hearing Disorders* 49: 419–28.

Leonard, L. B. and Leonard, J. S. (1985). The contribution of phonetic context to an unusual phonological pattern: A case study. *Language, Speech and Hearing Services in Schools* 16: 110–8.

Leonard, L. B., McGregor, K. K. and Allen, G. D. (1992). Grammatical morphology and speech perception in children with and without specific language impairment. *Journal of Speech and Hearing Research* 35: 1076–83.

Leonard, L. B., Newhoff, M. and Mesalam, L. (1980). Individual differences in early child phonology. *Applied Psycholinguistics* 1: 7–30.

Leonard, L. B. and Ritterman, S. I. (1971). Articulation of /s/ as a function of cluster and word frequency of occurrence. *Journal of Speech and Hearing Research* 14: 476–85.

Leopold, W. F. (1947). *Speech Development of a Bilingual Child: Sound Learning in the First Two Years.* Evanston, IL, Northwestern University.

Levelt, C. C. (1994). *On the Acquisition of Place (HIL Dissertation, 8).* The Hague, Netherlands, Holland Academic Graphics.

Levelt, C. C., Schiller, N. O. and Levelt, W. J. M. (1999). A developmental grammar for syllable structure in the production of child language. *Brain and Language* 68: 291–9.

Levelt, C. C., Schiller, N. O. and Levelt, W. J. M. (1999/2000). The acquisition of syllable types. *Language Acquisition* 8: 237–64.

Levelt, C. C. and van de Vijver, R. (2004). Syllable types in cross-linguistic and developmental grammars. In R. Kager, J. Pater and W. Zonneveld (eds) *Constraints in Phonological Acquisition.* 204–18. Cambridge, MA, Cambridge University Press.

Levine, M. N. (1986). *Leiter International Performance Scale: A Handbook.* Chicago, Stoelting.

Lewis, B. A. and Freebairn, L. (1992). Residual effects of preschool phonology disorders in grade school, adolescence and adulthood. *Journal of Speech and Hearing Research* 35: 819–31.

Liberman, I. Y., Shankweiler, D., Fischer, F. W. and Carter, B. (1974). Explicit syllable and phoneme segmentation in the young child. *Journal of Experimental Psychology* 18: 201–12.

Linn, S.-C. (1971). Phonetic development of Chinese infants. *Acta Psychologica Taiwanica* 13: 191–5.

Lleó, C. and Prinz, M. (1996). Consonant clusters in child phonology and the directionality of syllable structure assignment. *Journal of Child Language* 23: 31–56.

Lleó, C. and Prinz, M. (1997). Syllable structure parameters and the acquisition of affricates. In S. J. Hannahs and M. Young-Scholten (eds) *Focus on Phonological Acquisition.* 143–63. Philadelphia, John Benjamins.

Locke, J. L. (1980a). The inference of speech perception in the phonologically disordered child, Part I: A rationale, some criteria, the conventional tests. *Journal of Speech and Hearing Disorders* 45: 431–44.

Locke, J. L. (1980b). The inference of speech perception in the phonologically disordered child, Part II: Some clinically novel procedures, their use, some findings. *Journal of Speech and Hearing Disorders* 45: 445–68.

Locke, J. L. (1983). *Phonological Acquisition and Change*. New York, Academic Press.

Logan, J. S. (1992). A computational analysis of young children's lexicons. Bloomington, Speech Research Laboratory, Indiana University.

Lombardi, L. (1999). Positional faithfulness and voicing assimilation in optimality theory. *Natural Language & Linguistic Theory* 17: 267–302.

Lombardi, L. (2001). Why place and voice are different: Constraint-specific alternations in optimality theory. In L. Lombardi (ed.) *Segmental Phonology in Optimality Theory: Constraints and Representations*. 13–45. Cambridge, UK, Cambridge University Press.

Lorentz, J. P. (1976). An analysis of some deviant phonological rules of English. In D. M. Morehead and A. E. Morehead (eds) *Normal and Deficient Child Language*. 29–60. Baltimore, MD, University Park Press.

Łubowicz, A. (2002). Derived environment effects in optimality theory. *Lingua* 112: 243–80.

Łubowicz, A. (2003). Local conjunction and comparative markedness. *Theoretical Linguistics* 29: 101–12.

Luce, P. A. (1986). Neighborhoods of words in the mental lexicon (Tech. Report No. 6). Bloomington, Speech Research Laboratory, Indiana University.

Luce, P. A. and Large, N. R. (2001). Phonotactics, density, and entropy in spoken word recognition. *Language and Cognitive Processes* 16: 565–81.

Luce, P. A. and McLennan, C. (2003). Fundamentals of spoken word recognition. *The Journal of the Acoustical Society of America* 114: 2421.

Luce, P. A. and Pisoni, D. B. (1998). Recognizing spoken words: The neighborhood activation model. *Ear and Hearing* 19: 1–36.

Łukaszewicz, B. (2007). Reduction in syllable onsets in the acquisition of Polish: Deletion, coalescence, metathesis and gemination. *Journal of Child Language* 34: 53–82.

Macken, M. A. (1980). The child's lexical representation: The 'puzzle-puddle-pickle' evidence. *Journal of Linguistics* 16: 1–17.

Macken, M. A. (1992). Where's phonology? In C. A. Ferguson, L. Menn and C. Stoel-Gammon (eds) *Phonological Development: Models, Research, Implications*. 249–69. Timonium, MD, York Press.

MacNeilage, P. F. and Davis, B. L. (1990). Acquisition of speech production: Frames, then content. In M. Jeannerod (ed.) *Attention and Performance XIII: Motor Representation and Control*. 453–75. Hillsdale, NJ, Erlbaum.

Marascuilo, L. A. and Busk, P. L. (1988). Combining statistics for multiple-baseline AB and replicated ABAB designs across subjects. *Behavioral Assessment* 10: 1–28.

Marascuilo, L. A. and Serlin, R. C. (1988). *Statistical Methods for the Social and Behavioral Sciences*. New York, W. H. Freeman.

Markman, E. M. (1989). *Categorization and Naming in Children*. Cambridge, MA, MIT Press.

Marslen-Wilson, W. and Warren, P. (1994). Levels of perceptual representation and process in lexical access: Words, phonemes and features. *Psychological Review* 101: 653–75.

Martin, S. M. and Gierut, J. A. (2004). Sublexical effects in phonological treatment. The 25th Annual Symposium on Research in Child Language Disorders, University of Wisconsin, Madison.

Maxwell, E. M. (1984). On determining underlying phonological representations of children: A critique of current theories. In M. Elbert, D. A. Dinnsen and G. Weismer (eds) *Phonological Theory and the Misarticulating Child (ASHA Monographs No. 22)*. 18–29. Rockville, MD, ASHA.

Maxwell, E. M. and Weismer, G. (1982). The contribution of phonological, acoustic and perceptual techniques to the characterization of a misarticulating child's voice contrast for stops. *Applied Psycholinguistics* 3: 29–43.

McCarthy, J. J. (1993). A case of surface constraint violation. *Canadian Journal of Linguistics* 38: 169–95.

McCarthy, J. J. (1998). Morpheme structure constraints and paradigm occultation. In M. C. Gruber, D. Higgins, K. S. Olson and T. Wysocki (eds) *CLS 34/2: The Panels*. 125–50. Chicago, IL, Chicago Linguistic Society.

McCarthy, J. J. (1999). Sympathy and phonological opacity. *Phonology* 16: 331–99.

McCarthy, J. J. (2002a). Comparative markedness. Unpublished manuscript, University of Massachusetts, Amherst. [Available on Rutgers Optimality Archive].

McCarthy, J. J. (2002b). *A Thematic Guide to Optimality Theory*. Cambridge, UK, Cambridge University Press.

McCarthy, J. J. (2003a). Sympathy, cumulativity and the Duke-of-York gambit. In C. Féry and R. van de Vijver (eds) *The Syllable in Optimality Theory*. 23–76. Cambridge, UK, Cambridge University Press.

McCarthy, J. J. (2003b). What does comparative markedness explain, what should it explain, and how? *Theoretical Linguistics* 29: 141–55.

McCarthy, J. J. (2007). *Hidden Generalizations: Phonological Opacity in Optimality Theory*. London, Equinox Publishing.

McCarthy, J. J. and Prince, A. (1995). Faithfulness and reduplicative identity. In J. N. Beckman, L. W. Dickey and S. Urbanczyk (eds) *University of Massachusetts Occasional Papers 18: Papers in Optimality Theory*. 249–384. Amherst, GLSA.

McCay, D. G. (1972). The structure of words and syllables: Evidence from errors in speech. *Cognitive Psychology* 3: 210–27.

McDonough, J. and Myers, S. (1991). Consonant harmony and planar segregation in child language. Unpublished manuscript, UCLA and University of Texas, Austin.

McReynolds, L. V. and Jetzke, E. (1986). Articulation generalization of voiced-voiceless sounds in hearing-impaired children. *Journal of Speech and Hearing Disorders* 51: 348–55.

McReynolds, L. V. and Kearns, K. P. (1983). *Single-Subject Experimental Designs in Communicative Disorders*. Baltimore, MD, University Park Press.

Menn, L. (1976). Pattern, control and contrast in beginning speech: A case study in the development of word form and word function. Unpublished dissertation, University of Illinois.

Menn, L. (1978). Phonological units in beginning speech. In A. Bell and J. B. Hooper (eds) *Syllables and Segments*. 157–71. Amsterdam, North-Holland.

Menyuk, P. (1972). Clusters as single underlying consonants: Evidence from children's production. In A. Rigault and R. Charbonneau (eds) *Proceedings of the Seventh International Congress of Phonetic Sciences*. 1161–5. The Hague, Netherlands, Mouton.

Menyuk, P. and Menn, L. (1979). Early strategies for the perception and production of words and sounds. In P. Fletcher and M. Garman (eds) *Studies in Language Acquisition*. 49–70. Cambridge, UK, Cambridge University Press.

Metsala, J. L. (1999). The development of phonemic awareness in reading-disabled children. *Applied Psycholinguistics* 20: 149–58.

Metsala, J. L. and Walley, A. C. (1998). Spoken vocabulary growth and the segmental restructuring of lexical representations: Precursors to phonemic awareness and early reading ability. In J. L. Metsala and L. C. Ehri (eds) *Word Recognition in Beginning Literacy*. 89–120. Hillsdale, NJ, Erlbaum.

Milenkovic, P. H. and Read, C. (1992). *CSpeech*. Madison, University of Wisconsin.

Miller, G. A. and Nicely, P. E. (1955). An analysis of perceptual confusions among some English consonants. *Journal of the Acoustical Society of America* 27: 338–52.

Moe, A. J., Hopkins, C. J. and Rush, R. T. (1982). *The Vocabulary of First-Grade Children*. Springfield, IL, Charles C. Thomas.

Morelli, F. (2003). The relative harmony of /s+stop/ onsets. In C. Féry and R. van de Vijver (eds) *The Syllable in Optimality Theory*. New York, Cambridge University Press.

Moreton, E. (2004). Non-computable functions in optimality theory. In J. J. McCarthy (ed.) *Optimality Theory in Phonology: A Reader*. 141–64. Malden, MA, Blackwell.

Moreton, E. and Smolensky, P. (2002). Typological consequences of local constraint conjunction. In L. Mikkelsen and C. Potts (eds) *Proceedings of the West Coast Conference on Formal Linguistics 21*. 306–19.

Morgan, J. L. and Demuth, K., Eds. (1996). *Signal to Syntax: Bootstrapping from Speech to Grammar in Early Acquisition*. Mahwah, NJ, Erlbaum.

Morrisette, M. L. (1999). Lexical characteristics of sound change. *Clinical Linguistics & Phonetics* 13: 219–38.

Morrisette, M. L. (2000). Lexical influences on the process of sound change in phonological acquisition. Unpublished doctoral dissertation. Indiana University, Bloomington.

Morrisette, M. L., Dinnsen, D. A. and Gierut, J. A. (2003). Markedness and context effects in the acquisition of place features. *Canadian Journal of Linguistics* 48: 329–55.

Morrisette, M. L. and Gierut, J. A. (2002). Lexical organization and phonological change in treatment. *Journal of Speech, Language, and Hearing Research* 45: 143–59.

Munson, B. (2001). Phonological pattern frequency and speech production in adults and children. *Journal of Speech, Language, and Hearing Research* 44: 778–92.

Munson, B. and Babel, M. E. (2005). The sequential cueing effect in children's speech production. *Applied Psycholinguistics* 26: 157–74.

Munson, B., Edwards, J. and Beckman, M. E. (2005). Relationships between nonword repetition accuracy and other measures of linguistic development in children with phonological disorders. *Journal of Speech, Language, and Hearing Research* 48: 61–78.

Munson, B., Swenson, C. L. and Manthei, S. C. (2005). Lexical and phonological organization in children: Evidence from repetition tasks. *Journal of Speech, Language, and Hearing Research* 48: 108–24.

Murphy, G. L. (2002). *The Big Book of Concepts*. Cambridge, MA, MIT Press.

Nagy, N. and Reynolds, B. (1997). Optimality theory and variable word-final deletion in Faetar. *Language Variation and Change* 9: 37–55.

Naigles, L. R. (2002). Form is easy, meaning is hard: Resolving a paradox in early child language. *Cognition* 86: 157–99.

Naigles, L. R. (2003). Paradox lost? No, paradox found! Reply to Tomasello and Akhtar (2003). *Cognition* 88: 325–9.

National Institute on Deafness and Other Communication Disorders. (1994). *National strategic research plan*. Bethesda, MD, Department of Health and Human Services.

Nettelbladt, U. (1983). *Developmental Studies of Dysphonology in Children*. Lund, Sweden, CWK Gleerup.

Newcomer, P. L. and Hammill, D. D. (1988). *Test of Language Development–2 Primary*. Austin, TX, Pro-Ed.

Newcomer, P. L. and Hammill, D. D. (1997). *Test of Language Development – Primary (Third Edition)*. Austin, TX, Pro-Ed.

Newman, R. S., Sawusch, J. R. and Luce, P. A. (1997). Similarity scaling for consonants and consonant clusters in initial position. *The Journal of the Acoustical Society of America* 101: 3111.

Ni Chiosain, M. and Padgett, J. (2001). Markedness, segment realization, and locality in spreading. In L. Lombardi (ed.) *Segmental Phonology in Optimality Theory: Constraints and Representations*. 118–56. Cambridge, UK, Cambridge University Press.

Nippold, M. A. (2001). Phonological disorders and stuttering in children: What is the frequency of co-occurrence? *Clinical Linguistics & Phonetics* 15: 219–28.

Nittrouer, S. (1993). The emergence of mature gestural patterns is not uniform: Evidence from an acoustic study. *Journal of Speech and Hearing Research* 36: 959–72.

Nittrouer, S., Studdert-Kennedy, M. and McGowan, R. S. (1989). The emergence of phonetic segments: Evidence from the spectral structure of fricative-vowel syllables spoken by children and adults. *Journal of Speech and Hearing Research* 32: 120–32.

Nusbaum, H. C., Pisoni, D. B. and Davis, C. K. (1984). Sizing up the Hoosier mental lexicon (Progress Report No. 10). In. 357–76. Bloomington, IN, Speech Research Laboratory, Indiana University.

O'Connor, K. M. (1999). On the role of segmental contrasts in the acquisition of clusters. In K. S. Baertsch and D. A. Dinnsen (eds) *Indiana University Working Papers in Linguistics 1: Optimal Green Ideas in Phonology.* 109–26. Bloomington, IN, IULC Publications.

Ohala, D. (1996). Cluster reduction and constraints in acquisition. Unpublished doctoral dissertation. University of Arizona.

Ohala, D. (1999). The influence of sonority on children's cluster reductions. *Journal of Communication Disorders* 32: 397–422.

Ohala, J. J. (1980). The application of phonological universals in speech pathology. In N. Lass (ed.) *Speech and Language: Advances in Basic Research and Practice.* 75–97. New York, Academic Press.

Olswang, L. B. and Bain, B. (1994). Data collection: Monitoring children's treatment progress. *American Journal of Speech-Language Pathology* 3: 55–66.

Orgun, C. O. (2001). English r-insertion in optimality theory. *Natural Language and Linguistic Theory* 19: 737–49.

Osberger, M. J., Maso, M. and Sam, L. K. (1993). Speech intelligibility of children with cochlear implants, tactile aids, or hearing aids. *Journal of Speech and Hearing Research* 36: 186–203.

Osberger, M. J., Robbins, A. M., Todd, S. L., Riley, A. I. and Miyamoto, R. T. (1994). Speech production skills of children with multichannel cochlear implants. In I. J. Hochmair-Desoyer and E. S. Hochmair (eds) *Advances in Cochlear Implants.* Vienna, Manz.

Otomo, K. and Stoel-Gammon, C. (1992). The acquisition of unrounded vowels in English. *Journal of Speech and Hearing Research* 35: 604–16.

Pan, N. and Snyder, W. (2003). Acquisition of /s/-initial clusters: A parametric approach. In *Proceedings of the 28th Annual Boston University Conference on Language Development.* 436–46. Somerville, MA, Cascadilla Press.

Parker, S. (2001). Non-optimal onsets in Chamicuro: An inventory maximised in coda position. *Phonology* 18: 361–86.

Parker, S. (2002). Quantifying the sonority hierarchy. Amherst, University of Massachusetts.

Parsonson, B. S. and Baer, D. M. (1978). A tale of two paradigms. In T. R. Kratochwill (ed.) *Single Subject Research: Strategies for Evaluating Change.* 101–14. New York, Academic Press.

Pater, J. (1997). Minimal violation and phonological development. *Language Acquisition* 6: 201–53.

Pater, J. (1998). From phonological typology to the development of receptive and productive phonological competence: Applications of minimal violation. *Rutgers Optimality Archive 296.*

Pater, J. (2004). Bridging the gap between receptive and productive development with minimally violable constraints. In R. Kager, J. Pater and W. Zonneveld (eds) *Constraints in Phonological Acquisition.* 219–44. New York, Cambridge University Press.

Pater, J. and Barlow, J. A. (2003). Constraint conflict in cluster reduction. *Journal of Child Language* 30: 487–526.

Pater, J. and Werle, A. (2001). Typology and variation in child consonant harmony. In C. Féry, A. Green and R. van de Vijver (eds) *Proceedings of HILP 5*. 119–39. Potsdam, University of Potsdam.

Pater, J. and Werle, A. (2003). Direction of assimilation in child consonant harmony. *Canadian Journal of Linguistics* 48: 385–408.

Pertz, D. and Bever, T. G. (1975). Sensitivity to phonological universals in children and adolescents. *Language* 51: 149–62.

Peters, A. M. (1983). *The Units of Language Acquisition*. New York, Cambridge University Press.

Peters, A. M. and Strömqvist, S. (1996). The role of prosody in the acquisition of grammatical morphemes. In J. L. Morgan and K. Demuth (eds) *Signal to Syntax: Bootstrapping from Speech to Grammar in Early Acquisition*. 215–32. Mahwah, NJ, Lawrence Erlbaum.

Peters, R. W. (1963). Dimensions of perception of consonants. *The Journal of the Acoustical Society of America* 35: 1985–9.

Piggott, G. (1999). At the right edge of words. *The Linguistic Review* 16: 143–85.

Pinker, S. (1984). *Language Learnability and Language Development*. Cambridge, MA, Harvard University Press.

Pollack, E. and Rees, N. S. (1972). Disorders of articulation: Some clinical applications of distinctive feature theory. *Journal of Speech and Hearing Disorders* 37: 451–61.

Pollock, K. E. and Berni, M. C. (2003). Incidence of non-rhotic vowel errors in children: Data from the Memphis Vowel Project. *Clinical Linguistics & Phonetics* 17: 393–401.

Pollock, K. E. and Keiser, N. J. (1990). An examination of vowel errors in phonologically disordered children. *Clinical Linguistics & Phonetics* 4: 161–78.

Port, R. F. and O'Dell, M. L. (1985). Neutralization of syllable-final voicing in German. *Journal of Phonetics* 13: 455–71.

Powell, T. W. (1991). Planning for phonological generalization: An approach to treatment target selection. *American Journal of Speech-Language Pathology* 1: 21–7.

Powell, T. W. and Elbert, M. (1984). Generalization following the remediation of early-and later-developing consonant clusters. *Journal of Speech and Hearing Disorders* 49: 211–8.

Powell, T. W., Elbert, M. and Dinnsen, D. A. (1991). Stimulability as a factor in the phonologic generalization of misarticulating preschool children. *Journal of Speech and Hearing Research* 34: 1318–28.

Powell, T. W., Elbert, M. and Dinnsen, D. A. (1999). A follow-up study of the linguistic and intellectual abilities of children who were phonologically disordered. In B. Maassen and P. Groenen (eds) *Pathologies of Speech and Language: Advances in Clinical Phonetics and Linguistics*. 82–90. London, Whurr.

Powell, T. W., Miccio, A. W., Elbert, M., Brasseur, J. A. and Strike-Roussos, C. (1999). Patterns of sound change in children with phonological disorders. *Clinical Linguistics & Phonetics* 13: 163–82.

Prince, A. (1997). Stringency and anti-Paninian hierarchies. Handout from LSA Institute, University of Michigan, Ann Arbor.

Prince, A. and Smolensky, P. (1993/2004). *Optimality Theory: Constraint Interaction in Generative Grammar*. Malden, MA, Blackwell.

Prince, A. and Tesar, B. (2004). Learning phonotactic distributions. In R. Kager, J. Pater and W. Zonneveld (eds) *Constraints in Phonological Acquisition*. 245–91. Cambridge, UK, Cambridge University Press.

Raaijmakers, J. G. W., Schrijnemakers, J. M. C. and Gremmen, F. (1999). How to deal with 'The language-as-fixed-effect fallacy': Common misconceptions and alternative solutions. *Journal of Memory and Language* 41: 416–26.

Restle, F. (1959). Additivity of cues and transfer in discrimination of consonant clusters. *Journal of Experimental Psychology* 57: 9–14.

Rice, K. (1996). Aspects of variability in child language acquisition. In B. Bernhardt, J. Gilbert and D. Ingram (eds) *Proceedings of the UBC International Conference on Phonological Acquisition*. 1–14. Somerville, MA, Cascadilla Press.

Rice, K. and Avery, P. (1993). Segmental complexity and the structure of inventories. *Toronto Working Papers in Linguistics* 12: 131–54.

Rice, K. and Avery, P. (1995). Variability in a deterministic model of language acquisition: A theory of segmental elaboration. In J. Archibald (ed.) *Phonological Acquisition and Phonological Theory*. 23–42. Hillsdale, NJ, Erlbaum.

Rice, M. and Wexler, K. (2001). *Rice/Wexler Test of Early Grammatical Impairment*. San Antonio, TX, Harcourt Brace.

Robbins, J. and Klee, T. (1987). Clinical assessment of oropharyngeal motor development in young children. *Journal of Speech and Hearing Disorders* 52: 271–7.

Rockman, B. K., Dinnsen, D. A. and Rowland, E. J. (1983). A case of initial consonant deletion: Phonological issues and implications. Paper presented at the American Speech-Language and Hearing Association, Cincinnati.

Roid, G. H. and Miller, L. J. (1997). *Leiter International Performance Scale – Revised*. Chicago, Stoelting.

Saben, C. B. and Ingham, J. C. (1991). The effects of minimal pairs treatment on the speech-sound production of two children with phonologic disorders. *Journal of Speech and Hearing Research* 34: 1023–40.

Sander, E. K. (1972). When are speech sounds learned? *Journal of Speech and Hearing Disorders* 37: 55–63.

Santa, J. L., Santa, C. and Smith, E. E. (1977). Units of word recognition: Evidence for the use of multiple units. *Perception & Psychophysics* 22: 585–91.

Savinainen-Makkonen, T. (2000). Word-initial consonant omissions–A developmental process in children learning Finnish. *First Language* 20: 161–85.

Schwartz, R. G. and Goffman, L. (1995). Metrical patterns of words and production accuracy. *Journal of Speech and Hearing Research* 38: 876–88.

Schwartz, R. G. and Leonard, L. B. (1982). Do children pick and choose? An examination of phonological selection and avoidance in early lexical acquisition. *Journal of Child Language* 9: 319–36.

Schwartz, R. G., Leonard, L. B., Folger, M. K. and Wilcox, M. J. (1980). Early phonological behavior in normal-speaking and language disordered children:

Evidence for a synergistic view of linguistic disorders. *Journal of Speech and Hearing Disorders* 45: 357–77.

Scobbie, J. M. (1998). Interactions between the acquisition of phonetics and phonology. *Papers from the Regional Meetings, Chicago Linguistic Society* 34: 343–58.

Sehgal, S. T., Kirk, K. I., Svirsky, M. A., Ertmer, D. J. and Osberger, M. J. (1998). Imitative consonant feature production by children with multichannel sensory aids. *Ear and Hearing* 19: 72–84.

Selkirk, E. O. (1982). The syllable. In H. van der Hulst and N. Smith (eds) *The Structure of Phonological Representations*. 337–83. Dordrecht, Netherlands, Foris.

Serry, T. A. and Blamey, P. J. (1999). A 4-year investigation into phonetic inventory development in young cochlear implant users. *Journal of Speech, Language, and Hearing Research* 42: 141–54.

Serry, T. A., Blamey, P. J. and Grogan, M. (1997). Phoneme acquisition in the first 4 years of implant use. *The American Journal of Otology* 18(Suppl.): S122-S4.

Sheldon, A. and Strange, W. (1982). The acquisition of /r/ and /l/ by Japanese learners of English: Evidence that speech production can precede speech perception. *Applied Psycholinguistics* 3: 243–61.

Shepard, R. N. (1972). Psychological representation of speech sounds. In E. E. David and P. B. Denes (eds) *Human Communication: A Unified View*. 67–113. New York, McGraw-Hill.

Shriberg, L. D., Aram, D. and Kwiatkowski, J. (1997a). Developmental apraxia of speech: I. Descriptive and theoretical perspectives. *Journal of Speech, Language, and Hearing Research* 40: 273–85.

Shriberg, L. D., Aram, D. and Kwiatkowski, J. (1997b). Developmental apraxia of speech: II. Toward a diagnostic marker. *Journal of Speech, Language, and Hearing Research* 40: 286–312.

Shriberg, L. D., Aram, D. and Kwiatkowski, J. (1997c). Developmental apraxia of speech: III. A subtype marked by inappropriate stress. *Journal of Speech, Language, and Hearing Research* 40: 313–37.

Shriberg, L. D., Austin, D., Lewis, B. A., McSweeny, J. L. and Wilson, D. (1997). The percentage of consonants correct (PCC) metric: Extensions and reliability data. *Journal of Speech, Language, and Hearing Research* 40: 708–22.

Shriberg, L. D., Gruber, F. A. and Kwiatkowski, J. (1994). Developmental phonological disorders III: Long-term speech-sound normalization. *Journal of Speech and Hearing Research* 37: 1151–77.

Shriberg, L. D. and Kwiatkowski, J. (1982). Phonological disorders I: A diagnostic classification system. *Journal of Speech and Hearing Disorders* 47: 226–41.

Shriberg, L. D. and Kwiatkowski, J. (1994). Developmental phonological disorders I: A clinical profile. *Journal of Speech and Hearing Research* 37: 1100–26.

Shriberg, L. D., Kwiatkowski, J., Best, S., Hengst, J. and Terselic-Weber, B. (1986). Characteristics of children with phonological disorders of unknown origin. *Journal of Speech and Hearing Disorders* 51: 140–61.

Shriberg, L. D. and Lof, G. L. (1991). Reliability studies in broad and narrow transcription. *Clinical Linguistics & Phonetics* 5: 225–79.

Siegel, S. (1956). *Nonparametric Statistics*. New York, McGraw-Hill.

Sievers, E. (1881). *Grundzüge der Phonetik*. Leipzig, Germany, Breitkopf & Hartel.

Singh, S., Woods, D. R. and Becker, G. M. (1972). Perceptual structure of 22 prevocalic English consonants. *The Journal of the Acoustical Society of America* 52: 1698–713.

Slobin, D. (1973). Cognitive prerequisites for the development of grammar. In C. Ferguson and D. Slobin (eds) *Studies of Child Language Development*. 175–208. New York, Holt, Reinhart and Winston.

Slobin, D. I. (1971). Data for the symposium. In D. I. Slobin (ed.) *The Ontogenesis of Grammar*. 3–14. New York, Academic Press.

Slowiaczek, L. M. and Dinnsen, D. A. (1985). On the neutralizing status of Polish word-final devoicing. *Journal of Phonetics* 13: 325–41.

Smit, A. B. (1986). Ages of speech sound acquisition: Comparisons and critiques of several normative studies. *Language, Speech and Hearing Services in Schools* 17: 175–86.

Smit, A. B. (1993a). Phonologic error distributions in the Iowa-Nebraska Articulation Norms Project: Consonant singletons. *Journal of Speech and Hearing Research* 36: 533–47.

Smit, A. B. (1993b). Phonological error distributions in the Iowa-Nebraska Articulation Norms Project: Word-initial consonant clusters. *Journal of Speech and Hearing Research* 36: 931–47.

Smit, A. B., Hand, L., Freilinger, J. J., Bernthal, J. E. and Bird, A. (1990). The Iowa Articulation Norms Project and its Nebraska replication. *Journal of Speech and Hearing Disorders* 55: 779–98.

Smith, J. (2002). Phonological augmentation in prominent positions. Unpublished doctoral dissertation. University of Massachusetts, Amherst.

Smith, J. E. K. (1976). The assuming-will-make-it-so fallacy. *Journal of Verbal Learning and Verbal Behavior* 15: 262–3.

Smith, L. B. and Kemler, D. (1977). Developmental trends in free classification: Evidence for a new conceptualization of perceptual development. *Journal of Experimental Child Psychology* 24: 279–98.

Smith, L. B. and Thelen, E. (1993). *A Dynamic Systems Approach to Development: Applications*. Cambridge, MA, MIT Press.

Smith, N. V. (1973). *The Acquisition of Phonology: A Case Study*. Cambridge, UK, Cambridge University Press.

Smith, N. V. and Tsimpli, I.-M. (1995). *The Mind of a Savant: Language Learning and Modularity*. Oxford, Blackwell.

Smolensky, P. (1995). On the structure of the constraint component Con of UG. Unpublished manuscript, University of California at Los Angeles. [Available on Rutgers Optimality Archive].

Smolensky, P. (1996a). *The Initial State and 'Richness of the Base' in Optimality Theory (Tech. Rep. No. JHU-CogSci-96–4)*. Baltimore, MD, Department of Cognitive Science, Johns Hopkins University.

Smolensky, P. (1996b). On the comprehension/production dilemma in child language. *Linguistic Inquiry* 27: 720–31.

Smolensky, P. (1997a). Constraint interaction in generative grammar II: Local conjunction, or random rules in Universal Grammar. Hopkins Optimality Theory Workshop/Maryland Mayfest '97, Baltimore, MD.

Smolensky, P. (1997b). Optimal sentence processing. The Johns Hopkins Optimality Theory Workshop, University of Maryland.

So, L. K. H. and Dodd, B. J. (1994). Phonologically disordered Cantonese-speaking children. *Clinical Linguistics & Phonetics* 8: 235–55.

So, L. K. H. and Dodd, B. J. (1995). The acquisition of phonology by Cantonese-speaking children. *Journal of Child Language* 22: 473–95.

Stager, C. and Werker, J. (1997). Infants listen for more phonetic detail in speech perception than in word-learning tasks. *Nature* 388: 381–2.

Stampe, D. (1969). The acquisition of phonetic representation. *Chicago Linguistic Society* 5: 433–44.

Stampe, D. (1973). A dissertation on natural phonology. Unpublished doctoral dissertation. University of Chicago.

Stemberger, J. P. (1993). Glottal transparency. *Phonology* 10: 107–38.

Stemberger, J. P. (1996). Syllable structure in English, with emphasis on codas. In B. Bernhardt, J. Gilbert and D. Ingram (eds) *Proceedings of the UBC International Conference on Phonological Acquisition*. 62–75. Somerville, MA, Cascadilla Press.

Stemberger, J. P. and MacWhinney, B. (1984). Extrasyllabic consonants in CV phonology: An experimental test. *Journal of Phonetics* 12: 355–66.

Stemberger, J. P. and Treiman, R. (1986). The internal structure of word-initial consonant clusters. *Journal of Memory and Language* 25: 163–80.

Steriade, D. (1982). Greek prosodies and the nature of syllabification. Doctoral dissertation, Massachusetts Institute of Technology. [Published by Garland Press, New York, 1990.].

Steriade, D. (1994). Complex onsets as single segments: The Mazateco pattern. In J. Cole and C. Kisseberth (eds) *Perspectives in Phonology*. 203–91. Stanford, CA, Center for the Study of Language and Information.

Steriade, D. (1995). Underspecification and markedness. In J. A. Goldsmith (ed.) *The Handbook of Phonological Theory*. 114–74. Cambridge, MA, Blackwell.

Steriade, D. (2001). Directional asymmetries in place assimilation: A perceptual account. In E. Hume and K. Johnson (eds) *The Role of Speech Perception in Phonology*. 219–50. San Diego, Academic Press.

Stevens, K. N. (1998). *Acoustic Phonetics*. Cambridge, MA, MIT Press.

Stoel-Gammon, C. (1985). Phonetic inventories, 15–24 months: A longitudinal study. *Journal of Speech and Hearing Research* 28: 505–12.

Stoel-Gammon, C. (1996). On the acquisition of velars in English. In B. Bernhardt, J. Gilbert and D. Ingram (eds) *Proceedings of the UBC International Conference on Phonological Acquisition*. 201–14. Somerville, MA, Cascadilla Press.

Stoel-Gammon, C. and Cooper, J. A. (1984). Patterns of early lexical and phonological development. *Journal of Child Language* 11: 247–71.

Stoel-Gammon, C. and Dunn, C. (1985). *Normal and Disordered Phonology in Children*. Austin, TX, Pro-Ed.

Stoel-Gammon, C. and Herrington, P. B. (1990). Vowel systems of normally developing and phonologically disordered children. *Clinical Linguistics & Phonetics* 4: 145–60.

Stoel-Gammon, C. and Stemberger, J. P. (1994). Consonant harmony and phonological underspecification in child speech. In M. Yavas (ed.) *First and Second Language Phonology*. 63–80. San Diego, CA, Singular.

Storkel, H. L. (2002). Restructuring of similarity neighborhoods in the developing mental lexicon. *Journal of Child Language* 29: 251–74.

Storkel, H. L. (2003). Learning new words II: Phonotactic probability in word learning. *Journal of Speech, Language, and Hearing Research* 46: 1312–23.

Storkel, H. L. (2004a). Do children acquire dense neighborhoods? An investigation of similarity neighborhoods in lexical acquisition. *Applied Psycholinguistics* 25: 201–21.

Storkel, H. L. (2004b). The emerging lexicon of children with phonological delays: Phonotactic constraints and probability in acquisition. *Journal of Speech, Language, and Hearing Research* 47: 1194–212.

Storkel, H. L. and Morrisette, M. L. (2002). The lexicon and phonology: Interactions in language acquisition. *Language, Speech and Hearing Services in Schools* 33: 24–37.

Straight, H. S. (1980). Auditory versus articulatory phonological processes and their development in children. In G. H. Yeni-Komshian, J. F. Kavanagh and C. A. Ferguson (eds) *Child Phonology, Vol. 1: Production*. 43–71. New York, Academic Press.

Svirsky, M. A., Sloan, R. B., Caldwell, M. and Miyamato, R. T. (2000). Speech intelligibility of prelingually deaf children with multichannel cochlear implants. *Annals of Otology, Rhinology & Laryngology* 109 (No. 12, Pt. 2).

Swets, F. (2004). *The Phonological Word in Tilburg Dutch*. Utrecht, Landelijke Onderzoekschool Taalwetenschap.

Swingley, D. and Aslin, R. N. (2000). Spoken word recognition and lexical representation in very young children. *Cognition* 76: 147–66.

Swingley, D. and Aslin, R. N. (2002). Lexical neighborhoods and the word-form representations of 14-month olds. *Psychological Science* 13: 480–4.

Swisher, W. E. (1973). An investigation of physiologically and acoustically facilitating phonetic environments on the production and perception of defective speech sounds. Unpublished doctoral dissertation, University of Wisconsin, Madison.

Templin, M. C. (1957). *Certain Language Skills in Children, Their Development and Interrelationships (Institute of Child Welfare, Monograph Series 26)*. Minneapolis, MN, University of Minnesota Press.

Tesar, B. and Smolensky, P. (1998). Learnability in optimality theory. *Linguistic Inquiry* 29: 229–68.

Thelen, E. and Smith, L. B. (1994). *A Dynamic Systems Approach to the Development of Cognition and Action*. Cambridge, MA, MIT Press.

Thomas, M. S. C. and Karmiloff-Smith, A. (2005). Can developmental disorders reveal the component parts of the human language faculty? *Language Learning and Development* 1: 65–92.

Thompson, S. and Newport, E. L. (2003). Statistical learning of syntax: The role of transitional probability. The Boston University Conference on Language Development, Boston, MA.

Tobey, E. A. and Hasenstab, S. (1991). Effects of a Nucleus multichannel cochlear implant upon speech in children. *Ear and Hearing* 12 (Suppl.): 48S-54S.

Tobey, E. A., Pancamo, S., Staller, S. J., Brimacombe, J. A. and Beiter, A. L. (1991). Consonant production in children receiving a multichannel cochlear implant. *Ear and Hearing* 12: 23–31.

Tomasello, M. and Akhtar, N. (2003). What paradox? A response to Naigles. *Cognition* 88: 207–14.

Tomes, L. and Shelton, R. L. (1989). Children's categorization of consonants by manner and place characteristics. *Journal of Speech and Hearing Research* 32: 432–8.

Travis, L. and Rasmus, B. (1931). The speech sound discrimination ability of cases with functional disorders of articulation. *Quarterly Journal of Speech* 17: 217–26.

Treiman, R. (1985). Onsets and rimes as units of spoken syllables: Evidence from children. *Journal of Experimental Child Psychology* 39: 161–81.

Treiman, R. and Baron, J. (1981). Segmental analysis ability: Development and relation to reading ability. In G. E. MacKinnon and T. G. Waller (eds) *Reading Research: Advances in Theory and Practice*. 159–97. New York, Academic Press.

Treiman, R. and Breaux, M. (1982). Common phoneme and overall similarity relations among spoken syllables: Their use by children and adults. *Journal of Psycholinguistic Research* 11: 569–98.

Treiman, R. and Zukowski, A. (1996). Children's sensitivity to syllables, onsets, rimes, and phonemes. *Journal of Experimental Child Psychology* 61: 193–215.

Tyler, A. A. (1996). Assessing stimulability in toddlers. *Journal of Communication Disorders* 29: 279–97.

Tyler, A. A., Edwards, M. L. and Saxman, J. H. (1987). Clinical application of two phonologically-based treatment procedures. *Journal of Speech and Hearing Disorders* 52: 393–409.

Tyler, A. A. and Figurski, G. R. (1994). Phonetic inventory changes after treating distinctions along an implicational hierarchy. *Clinical Linguistics & Phonetics* 8: 91–108.

United States Census Bureau. (2000). United States Census Supplementary Survey. Retrieved February 18, 2002, from http://www.stats.indiana.edu/.

Van Riper, C. (1963). *Speech Correction: Principles and Methods*. Englewood Cliffs, NJ, Prentice-Hall.

Vanvik, A. (1971). The phonetic-phonemic development of a Norwegian child. *Norsk Tidsskrift Sprogvienskap* 24: 269–325.

Velten, H. (1943). The growth of phonemic and lexical patterns in infant speech. *Language* 19: 281–92.

Vennemann, T. (1988). *Preference Laws for Syllable Structure and the Explanation of Sound Change: With Special Reference to German, Germanic, Italian and Latin*. New York, Mouton de Gruyter.

Vihman, M. M. (1978). Consonant harmony: Its scope and function in child language. In J. H. Greenberg (ed.) *Universals of human language 2: Phonology.* 281–334. Stanford, CA, Stanford University Press.

Vihman, M. M. (1996). *Phonological Development: The Origins of Language in the Child.* Cambridge, MA, Blackwell.

Vihman, M. M., Ferguson, C. A. and Elbert, M. (1986). Phonological development from babbling to speech: Common tendencies and individual differences. *Applied Psycholinguistics* 7: 3–40.

Vihman, M. M. and Greenlee, M. (1987). Individual differences in phonological development: Ages one and three years. *Journal of Speech and Hearing Research* 30: 503–21.

Vitevitch, M. S. (2003). The influence of sublexical and lexical representations on the processing of spoken words in English. *Clinical Linguistics & Phonetics* 17: 487–99.

Vitevitch, M. S. and Luce, P. A. (1998). When words compete: Levels of processing in perception of spoken words. *Psychological Science* 9: 325–9.

Vitevitch, M. S. and Luce, P. A. (1999). Probabilistic phonotactics and neighborhood activation in spoken word recognition. *Journal of Memory and Language* 40: 374–408.

Vitevitch, M. S. and Luce, P. A. (2004). A web-based interface to calculate phonotactic probability for words and nonwords in English. *Behavior Research Methods, Instruments, & Computers* 36: 481–7.

Vitevitch, M. S., Luce, P. A., Charles-Luce, J. and Kemmerer, D. (1997). Phonotactics and syllable stress: Implications for the processing of spoken nonsense words. *Language and Speech* 40: 47–62.

Vitz, P. C. and Winkler, B. S. (1973). Predicting the judged 'similarity of sound' of English words. *Journal of Verbal Learning and Verbal Behavior* 12: 373–88.

Walley, A. C. (1984). Developmental differences in spoken word identification. Unpublished doctoral dissertation, Indiana University, Bloomington.

Walley, A. C. (1987). Young children's detections of word-initial and -final mispronunciations in constrained and unconstrained contexts. *Cognitive Development* 2: 145–67.

Walley, A. C. (1993). The role of vocabulary development in children's spoken word recognition and segmentation ability. *Developmental Review* 13: 286–350.

Walley, A. C. and Metsala, J. L. (1990). The growth of lexical constraints on spoken word recognition. *Perception Psychophysics* 47: 267–80.

Walley, A. C., Metsala, J. L. and Garlock, V. M. (2003). Spoken vocabulary growth: Its role in the development of phoneme awareness and early reading ability. *Reading and Writing: An Interdisciplinary Journal* 16: 5–20.

Walley, A. C., Smith, L. B. and Jusczyk, P. W. (1986). The role of phonemes and syllables in the perceived similarity of speech sounds for children. *Memory & Cognition* 11: 220–9.

Walter, M. A. (2002). Final position, prominence, and licensing of contrast. 2nd International Conference on Contrast in Phonology, University of Toronto.

Weiner, F. F. (1981). Treatment of phonological disability using the method of meaningful minimal contrast: Two case studies. *Journal of Speech and Hearing Disorders* 46: 97–103.

Weismer, G. (1984). Acoustic analysis strategies for the refinement of phonological analysis. In M. Elbert, D. A. Dinnsen and G. Weismer (eds) *Phonological Theory and the Misarticulating Child (ASHA Monographs No. 22)*. 30–52. Rockville, MD, ASHA.

Weismer, G., Dinnsen, D. A. and Elbert, M. (1981). A study of the voicing distinction associated with omitted, word-final stops. *Journal of Speech and Hearing Disorders* 46: 320–8.

Werker, J. and Stager, C. (2000). Developmental changes in infant speech perception and early word learning: Is there a link? In J. B. Pierrehumbert and M. B. Broe (eds) *Papers in Laboratory Phonology V: Acquisition and the Lexicon*. Cambridge, UK, Cambridge University Press.

Wexler, K. (1982). A principle theory for language acquisition. In E. Wanner and L. R. Gleitman (eds) *Language Acquisition: The State of the Art*. 288–315. Cambridge, UK, Cambridge University Press.

Wexler, K. and Culicover, P. (1980). *Formal Principles of Language Acquisition*. Cambridge, MA, MIT Press.

Wiig, E. H., Secord, W. and Semel, E. (1992). *Clinical Evaluation of Language Fundamentals–Preschool*. San Antonio, TX, Harcourt Brace & Company.

Wiig, E. H., Secord, W. and Semel, E. (1995). *Clinical Evaluation of Language Fundamentals–Revised*. San Antonio, TX, Harcourt Brace & Company.

Wike, E. L. and Church, J. D. (1976). Comments on Clark's 'The language-as-fixed-effect-fallacy'. *Journal of Verbal Learning and Verbal Behavior* 15: 249–55.

Williams, A. L. and Dinnsen, D. A. (1987). A problem of allophonic variation in a speech disordered child. *Innovations in Linguistic Education* 5: 85–90.

Williams, K. T. (1997). *Expressive Vocabulary Test*. Circle Pines, MN, American Guidance Service, Inc.

Wilson, B. S. (2000). Strategies for representing speech information with cochlear implants. In J. K. Niparko, K. I. Kirk, N. K. Mellon, A. M. Robbins, D. L. Tucci and B. S. Wilson (eds) *Cochlear Implants: Principles and Practices*. 129–70. Philadelphia, Lippincott Williams & Wilkins.

Winitz, H. (1969). *Articulatory Acquisition and Behavior*. New York, Appleton-Century-Crofts.

Winitz, H. (1975). *From Syllable to Conversation*. Baltimore, University Park Press.

Yavaş, M. (1998). *Phonology: Development and Disorders*. San Diego, Singular.

Yeni-Komshian, G. H., Kavanagh, J. F. and Ferguson, C. A., Eds. (1980a). *Child Phonology, Vol. 1: Production*. New York, Academic Press.

Yeni-Komshian, G. H., Kavanagh, J. F. and Ferguson, C. A., Eds. (1980b). *Child Phonology, Vol. 2: Perception*. New York, Academic Press.

Žagar, L. and Locke, J. L. (1986). The psychological reality of phonetic features in children. *Language, Speech and Hearing Services in Schools* 17: 56–62.

Zamuner, T., Gerken, L. and Hammond, M. (2004). Phonotactic probabilities in young children's speech production. *Journal of Child Language* 31: 515–36.

Zec, D. (1995). Sonority constraints on syllable structure. *Phonology* 12: 85–129.

Zoll, C. (1998). Positional asymmetries and licensing. Unpublished manuscript, Massachusetts Institute of Technology, Cambridge. [Available on Rutgers Optimality Archive].

Zonneveld, W. and Nouveau, D. (2004). Child word stress competence: An experimental approach. In R. Kager, J. Pater and W. Zonneveld (eds) *Constraints in Phonological Acquisition.* 369–408. Cambridge, UK, Cambridge University Press.

Author Index

Index of constraints by chapter

Markedness constraints

Constraint	Definition	Chapter(s)
*θ (*see also* *Fʀɪᴄ)	Interdental fricatives are banned	1,4,5,6,8,9
*Aꜰꜰʀ (*see also* *CᴏᴍᴘʟᴇxSᴇɢᴍᴇɴᴛ)	Affricates are banned	
*#Aꜰꜰʀ	Word-initial affricates are banned	4
*Cᴏᴍᴘʟᴇx (*see also* *sl, *sn, *sw)	Branching structure is banned in syllable onset position	11,12,13,14
*CᴏᴍᴘʟᴇxOɴꜱᴇᴛ	Clusters are banned in syllable onset position	1,11
*CᴏᴍᴘʟᴇxSᴇɢᴍᴇɴᴛ (*see also* *Aꜰꜰʀ)	Affricates are banned in syllable onset position	11
*Dɪꜰꜰ[ꜱᴏɴ] < 3	No sonority differences between onset consonants less than 3	12
*dl	Alveolar stops are banned before liquid consonants	4
*f (*see also* *Fʀɪᴄ)	Labial fricatives are banned	1,4,5,6,8
*#f	Word-initial labial fricatives are banned	14
*Fᴇᴀᴛᴜʀᴇ	Voice, place or manner features are banned	9
*Fʀɪᴄ (*see also* *θ, *f, *s)	Fricatives are banned	1
*#Fʀɪᴄ	Word-initial fricatives are banned	4, 14
*Gᴇᴍ	Geminates are banned	4
*k	Dorsal consonants are banned	1,4,8,9,14
*#ᴋ	Word-initial dorsal consonants are banned	8
*l (*see also* *Lɪǫᴜɪᴅ)	Lateral consonants are banned	12,14
*Lᴀʀʏɴɢᴇᴀʟ	Laryngeal features are banned	9
*Lɪǫᴜɪᴅ (*see also* *l, *r)	Liquids are banned	11
*LɪǫᴜɪᴅPʜᴏɴᴇᴍᴇ	Contrastive use of /l r/ is banned	11
*LɪǫᴜɪᴅSᴇǫᴜᴇɴᴄᴇ	Consonant+Liquid clusters are banned	11
*M/α (*see also* *M/λ and *X-Oɴꜱ)	α may not occur in the syllable margin	13
*M₁/α	α may not occur in M₁ position	13
*M₂/α	α may not occur in M₂ position	13
*M/λ (*see also* *M/α and *X-Oɴꜱ)	λ must not be parsed as a syllable Margin (i.e., associated to Onset or Coda)	14
*P/α	α may not occur in the syllable peak	13
*r (*see also* *Lɪǫᴜɪᴅ)	Rhotic consonants are banned	14
*s (*see also* *Fʀɪᴄ)	Grooved coronal fricatives are banned	1,4,5,6,8
*sl (*see also* *Cᴏᴍᴘʟᴇx)	Initial s+liquid clusters are banned	12
*sn (*see also* *Cᴏᴍᴘʟᴇx)	Initial s+nasal clusters are banned	12
*sw (*see also* *Cᴏᴍᴘʟᴇx)	Initial s+glide clusters are banned	12
*t/[back]	Coronal consonants are banned before back vowels	1
*VdV	Intervocalic voiced stops are banned	4
*Vf (*see also* *f)	Postvocalic labial fricatives are banned	14
*VᴏɪᴄᴇᴅCᴏᴅᴀ	Voiced coda consonants are banned	9

504

*X-Ons (see also *M/α and *M/λ)	X is banned in a syllable onset	12
AGREE	Alveolar stops are banned when preceded or followed by a (nonadjacent) consonant with a different place feature	4
#-AGREE	Word-initial alveolar stops are banned when followed by a nonadjacent consonant with a different place feature	4
DISSIMILATION	Identical consonants are banned within a word	4
FINAL-C	Word-final vowels are banned	5
FINALPROM	The final constituent of a syllable, foot or prosodic word must be prominent	9,15
INITIALPROM	The initial constituent of a syllable, foot or prosodic word must be prominent	9,15
INTEGRATEDGEOM	Vowel place features must be licensed by a consonantal place node	9
LENGTHEN	Short vowels are banned before voiced consonants; long vowels are banned elsewhere	4
NOCODA	Coda consonants are banned	4,5,8,9,13,15
NC-f	Coda labial fricatives are banned	5
NC-p	Coda labial stops are banned	5
NC-s	Coda coronal fricatives are banned	5
NC-t	Coda coronal stops are banned	5
NOCODA-FRICS	Coda fricatives are banned	8
NOCODA-STOPS	Coda stops are banned	8
ONSET	Onsetless syllables are banned	13
SEGREGATEDGEOM	Consonant and vowel features must be fully segregated	9

Faithfulness constraints

Constraint	Definition	Chapter(s)
DEP	No insertion	4,12,14
FAITH	Inputs and outputs must be identical	1,4,5,11
FAITH[HighFreq]	Corresponding segments in high frequency words must be identical	1
P-FAITH	The perceived surface form and the lexical representation must be identical	1
IDENT	Corresponding segments must be identical	12,14
ID[continuant]	Corresponding segments must have identical [continuant] features	1
ID[feature]	Corresponding segments must have identical voice, place, or manner features	9
ID-PROM[feature]	Corresponding segments in prominent contexts must have identical voice, place, or manner features	9
ID[grooved]	Corresponding segments must have an identical [grooved] feature	4,5,6,8
ID[laryngeal]	Corresponding segments must have identical laryngeal features	9

ID-Coda[laryngeal]	Corresponding segments in coda position must have identical laryngeal features	9
ID-Onset[laryngeal]	Corresponding segments in onset position must have identical laryngeal features	9
ID[manner]	Corresponding segments must have identical manner features	4,5,8,9
ID-Prom[manner]	Corresponding segments in prominent contexts must have identical manner features	9
ID[place]	Corresponding segments must have identical place features	1,4,5,6,8
ID-Initial[place]	Corresponding segments in word-initial position must have identical place features	1
ID[sl]	Corresponding segments in an s+liquid cluster must be identical	12
ID[sn]	Corresponding segments in an s+nasal cluster must be identical	12
ID[sw]	Corresponding segments in an s+glide cluster must be identical	12
ID[weight]	Corresponding vowels must be identical in terms of length (or weight)	4
Max	No deletion	1,4,8,9,12,13,14
☞Sym	A candidate's faithfulness violations must be cumulative relative to the flower candidate	4
Uniformity	No coalescence	12

Other constraints

Constraint	Definition	Chapter(s)
Comparative markedness	Basic constraints for $_O$Markedness and $_N$Markedness are defined above	4,5
Locally conjoined	Individual conjuncts are defined above	4,6,8
Stringently formulated	Non-stringent versions are defined above	12

Subject index

Printed in the United Kingdom
by Lightning Source UK Ltd.
135541UK00001B/13-24/P

9 781845 531218